An Introduction to
POLITICAL SCIENCE

John A. Jacobsohn
West Virginia University

West/Wadsworth
I(T)P® An International Thomson Publishing Company

Belmont, CA • Albany, NY • Bonn • Boston • Cincinnati • Detroit • Johannesburg • London • Madrid •
Melbourne • Mexico City • New York • Paris • Singapore • Tokyo • Toronto • Washington

Political Science Editor	*Clark Baxter*
Assistant Editor	*Sharon Adams-Poore*
Production Editor	*John Lindley*
Marketing Manager	*Jay Hu*
Copyediting	*Joanne Engelking*
Text Design/Editing/Composition, Illustrations, Captions, Photoresearch, Appendix, and Index	*Pradyumna and Pradipta Upadrashta, Electronic Publishing Division, PRAD, Inc.*
Art Direction	*Radhika Upadrashta, PRAD, Inc.*
Cover Design	*Ross Carron*
Printing	*Courier Companies, Inc. (Kendallville)*

Printed in the United States of America
1 2 3 4 5 6 7 8 9 10

For more information, contact Wadsworth Publishing Company, 10 Davis Drive, Belmont, CA 94002, or electronically at `http://www.thomson.com/wadsworth.html`

International Thomson Publishing Europe
Berkshire House 168-173
High Holborn
London, WC1V 7AA, England

International Thomson Editores
Campos Eliseos 385, Piso 7
Col. Polanco
11560 México D.F. México

Thomas Nelson Australia
102 Dodds Street
South Melbourne 3205
Victoria, Australia

International Thomson Publishing Asia
221 Henderson Road
#05-10 Henderson Building
Singapore 0315

Nelson Canada
1120 Birchmount Road
Scarborough, Ontario
Canada M1K 5G4

International Thomson Publishing Japan
Hirakawacho Kyowa Building, 3F
2-2-1 Hirakawacho
Chiyoda-ku, Tokyo 102, Japan

International Thomson Publishing GmbH
Köningswinterer Strasse 418
53227 Bonn, Germany

International Thomson Publishing Southern Africa
Building 18, Constantia Park
240 Old Pretoria Road
Halfway House, 1685 South Africa

This book is printed on acid-free recycled paper.

LIBRARY OF CONGRESS CATALOGING-IN-PUBLICATION DATA
Jacobsohn, J.
   An Introduction to Political Science
/ J. Jacobsohn
      p. cm. -- (West/Wadsworth publication)
   Includes index.
   ISBN 0-314-20546-2
   1. Political Science I. Title. II. Series

A mi
'YAPITA'

Contents

PART THREE: POLITICAL BEHAVIOR AND PROCESSES

Part Four: LAW AND POLITICAL INSTITUTIONS

Preface

Textbooks in political science are often written as if they are encyclopedias, meant to contain all the available information on their subject. The main goal of books like these appears to involve making available a trackless ocean of data for the reader to navigate alone.

This book is different. While it does provide ample information and factual material, it does so in the service of discussing concepts and ideas designed to make readers think. Two of these concepts are worth mentioning here.

First, as the world's population grows — explosively in many places — and as societies grow larger, the power of these societies to dominate the life of any state tends to consolidate and grow, just as the power of individuals tends to diffuse and diminish. Therefore, this book emphasizes the relationship between the society and the state, rather than between the individual and the state as many other books do.

Second, the explosive birth rate in many societies mirrors the relatively recent explosion of separate governments. There are over 90,000 governments in the United States, and 512,000 elected officials. How much power can any individual or even an office exercise over such a patchwork? In the 17th-century France, King Louis XIV could control personally much of the day-to-day life of the state; today, an increasing number of decisions that bear directly on French citizens arise out of The European Union, a government beyond French control that was not even contemplated sixty years ago. So as the state itself diffuses, it is losing its central role as the glue that holds society together.

In addition, this book draws on as much cross-cultural and even historical information as possible. For example, the discussion on political leadership introduces students to Fidel Castro and Louis XIV among many other notable figures. As a scholar born and raised in Germany and who lived for many years in Bolivia, my approach is but natural, and seems the only sensible and realistic way to present a topic as universal as politics.

Finally, I freely and even hopefully acknowledge that not everything in this book will please everybody. There will be times when students and instructors alike may have the urge to hurl this book across the room because of what it says or a perspective it advances. Please feel free to do so. Without controversy and debate, learning can only become oppressive and tedious, and it cannot lead to the critical thinking and free exchange of ideas that it is intended to promote. If any controversies arising out of these pages leads a reader to further study or research, this book will have done its job, and I will be pleased.

Acknowledgments

Every work is a product of not only the author who writes it, but also of many individuals who directly or indirectly influence that work. This textbook is no exception. The whole Department of Political Science at West Virginia University helped either by giving advice, lending resources, or reading first drafts of chapters. I thank the following colleagues — Professors Neal Berch, Richard Brisbin, Jr., Robert DeClerico, Robert Dilger, Robert Duval, Joe Hagan, Allan Hammock, Paul Hoyt, Susan Hunter, John Kilwein, Hong Kim, Kevin Leyden, Christopher Mooney, Sophia Peterson, Donley Studlar, James Whisker, Jeffrey Worsham, and Rodger Yeager. I also thank Lee Ann Greathouse, the department administrative assistant, for all her help.

Two individuals deserve special recognition — Clark Baxter, editor/publisher of West/Wadsworth and John Lindley, production editor at West Group. Further, PRAD's team under the guidance of Kamesh Upadrashta have transformed a raw manuscript into this well illustrated, elegant text.

The most special thanks go to *mi yapita*, my wife Zulie, who had to endure many lonely evenings and nights while I was hacking away at the word processor. Her care for me during my illness goes beyond courage and devotion. She has my everlasting love. In their own way my children, Suzanne Couch, Michael, and Ely, helped, too, by encouraging me to go on when my words did not seem to flow as readily as I had wanted. Thanks kids!

Finally, I am grateful to the following professors for reviewing the manuscript and offering helpful suggestions:

Karen Beckwith
College of Wooster

Michael Bordelon
Houston Baptist University

Rod Briece
Mount Hood Community College

Michael Corbett
Ball State University

Brian W. Coyer
Henry Ford Community College

Richard Davis
Brigham Young University

Thomas Dickson
Auburn University

Larry Elowitz
Georgia College

Sheldon Goldman
University of Massachusetts, Amherst

Ceferina G. Hess
Lander University

Samuel B. Hoff
Delaware State University

U. Lynn Jones
Collin County Community College

William E. Kelly
Auburn University

Kay Knickrehm
James Madison University

Melvin A. Kulbicki
York College of Pennsylvania

Mark Landis
Hofstra University

Willie M. Legette
South Carolina State University

Wayne Parent
Louisiana State University

Gregory G. Rocha
University of Texas

Charles Strickwerda
Calvin College

John Travis
Humboldt State University

T.Y. Wang
Illinois State University

— *John A. Jacobsohn*

Photocredits

AFASD	Australian Foreign Affairs & State Department
AFL-CIO	American Federation of Labor - Congress of Industrial Organizations
AOC	Architect of the Capitol
AT	Austria Today
BIS	British Information Service
BPMP	Bush Presidential Materials Project
BSDA	Bi-State Development Agency
CQ	Congressional Quarterly
CT	Canada Today
DOJ	U.S. Department of Justice
DOS	U.S. Department of State
DOT	U.S. Department of Transportation
ES	Embassy of Spain
FE	French Embassy
FT	Florida Today
GAO	U.S. General Accounting Office
GIC	German Information Center
HUD	U.S. Dept. of Housing and Urban Development
IFC	International Finance Corporation
INSS	Institute for National Strategic Studies, U.S. Dept. of Defense
JCP	Joint Committee on Printing, U.S. Congress
JCPC	Jimmy Carter Presidential Center Library & Museum
JIC	Japan Information Center
LC	Library of Congress
LEB	FBI Law Enforcement Bulletin
MHR	Minnesota House of Representatives, Public Information Office
MMA	Metropolitan Museum of Art
NA	National Archives
NC	Nelson Canada
NGS	National Geographic Society
NPL	Novosti Photo Library
NPS	National Park Service, U.S. Dept. of the Interior
OMB	U.S. Office of Management & Budget
OPM	U.S. Office of Personnel Management
OSHP	Ohio State Highway Patrol
OSTP	U.S. Office of Science & Technology Policy
OTA	U.S. Office of Technology Assessment
OVP	Office of the Vice President, United States of America
PCT	Peace Corps Times
PJB	Providence Journal-Bulletin
R	Reuters
RBNP	Reuters/Bettmann News Photos
SCHSC	U.S. Supreme Court Historical Society Collection
SI	Smithsonian Institution
SMP	St. Martin's Press
SSA	U.S. Social Security Administration
UN	United Nations
UNDP	U.N. Development Programme
UNHCR	U.N. High Commissioner for Refugees
USAR	U.S. Army
USCS	U.S. Customs Service
USNWR	U.S. News & World Report
WB	World Bank
WP	The Washington Post

In the credits below, the location of pictures on each page is indicated by: t (top), b (bottom), l (left), and r (right).

3: LC (R. Baker); 12: LC (J. Higgins) 13: LC; 15: AOC (S. Eastman); 18: LC; 23, 24: UN; 26: LC; 37: MMA; 49: Raphael; 67: LC; 70: RBNP; 86: SI; 99: LC; 101t: LC; 102: LC; 123: AOC; 135: LC; 137: NPL: 141: HUD; 144t: INSS; 144b: USAR; 173: LC; 174, 175, 179, 180, 182tl, 182tr, 185, 187b: LC; 187t: ES; 195: MHR; 197: NPL; 198: GIC; 199: UN (J. Isaac); 201: UNDP (L. Kantrow); 202: UN (M. Grant); 209l: INSS (B. Sullivan); 209r: UN (M. Grant); 213: LC; 214: DOJ; 217: SMP; 219: LC; 221: LC, 222: CQ; 231: LC; 237: FT; 241: MHR; 243: DOT; 244: PJB (R. Thayer); 249: IFC; 250: MHR; 251: LC; 261: LC; 265: R. M. Jenkins; 267: NC; 273: LC; 274: UN; 277: LC; 278: AOC; 282t: DOJ; 282b: LC; 283t: NA; 283b: LC; 297: UN; 298: LC; 301: JCPC; 307: NA; 325: LC; 327: LEB (G. Weaver); 314: WB (K. Chernush); 315: LC; 316: UN (P.S. Sudhakaran); 325: LC; 330: AOC; 333: LC; 334t: LC; 334bl&br: LC; 336: LC; 337: UN; 339: NA; 345t: BIS; 345b: NGS; 348: LC; 349: JIC; 351: BIS; 352: JIC; 356: FE; 361: AOC; 364: R; 365: GIC; 366t: LC; 366b: JIC; 367t&b: AFASD; 368t: FE; 368b: LC; 371, 373t, 373m, 373b: JCP; 375: LC; 376: AOC; 377: LC; 380: BPMP; 381: LC; 383: NPS (C. Highsmith); 386l: UN (J. Isaac); 386r: DOT (P. Marston); 387: UNDP (I. Rajeswary); 388t: INSS (M. Libicki); 388b: DOT (J. Garvey); 389: OPM (L. Rothenberg); 391: OVP; 392: UNDP (C. Hart); 398: LC; 409t&b: JCP; 411: NPS (R. Lautman); 413t: LEB (J. Higginbotham); 413b: DOS; 414: AFL-CIO (E. Dotter); 416t&b: GAO; 417: DOJ; 419: LC; 421: OPM (P. Souza); 422: JCP; 423t: OMB; 423b: DOJ; 425, 426, 429: LC; 431: IFC; 433t: WAPDA, Pakistan; 433b: LC; 434: OMB; 435: HUD; 437t&b: SSA; 438: BSDA; 440: UNDP (S. Kendall); 441: OSTP; 442: DOJ; 445: NPS (R. Lautman); 448: OSHP (D. Lee); 450t: NA; 450b: CQ; 453: HUD (P. Blixt, Portland Community College); 454: LC; 455: LC; 456: WP; 457: SCHSC; 458: LC; 459, 463: LC; 464tl&tr, 464b, 465t: DOJ; 465b: AT (ORF); 466, 467tl: DOJ; 467tr: USNWR (C. Archambault); 467b: USCS (G. Corcoran, Jr.); 469: LEB (D. Schatz); 475: UN (Y. Nagata); 478: LC; 484: NA; 486: UN; 488: NA; 490, 491: LC; 495: UNDP (W. Raiford); 496: PCT; 499, 501: UN (H. Arvidson); 502: OTA; 505: UN (M. Grant); 506: CT (W. McCarthy); 507: UN (H. Vassal); 508: UN (J. Isaac); 509: AT; 511: UN (J. Isaac); 517: UN (M. Tzovaras); 518: UN (M. Grant); 519: INSS (S. Johnson); 521t: UNHCR (P. Mountzis); 521b: UN (S. Whitehouse); 524t: UNDP (L. Gubb); 524b: UN (M. Grant); 526, 527: UN; 528: UN (L. Stone).

Introduction

PART ONE

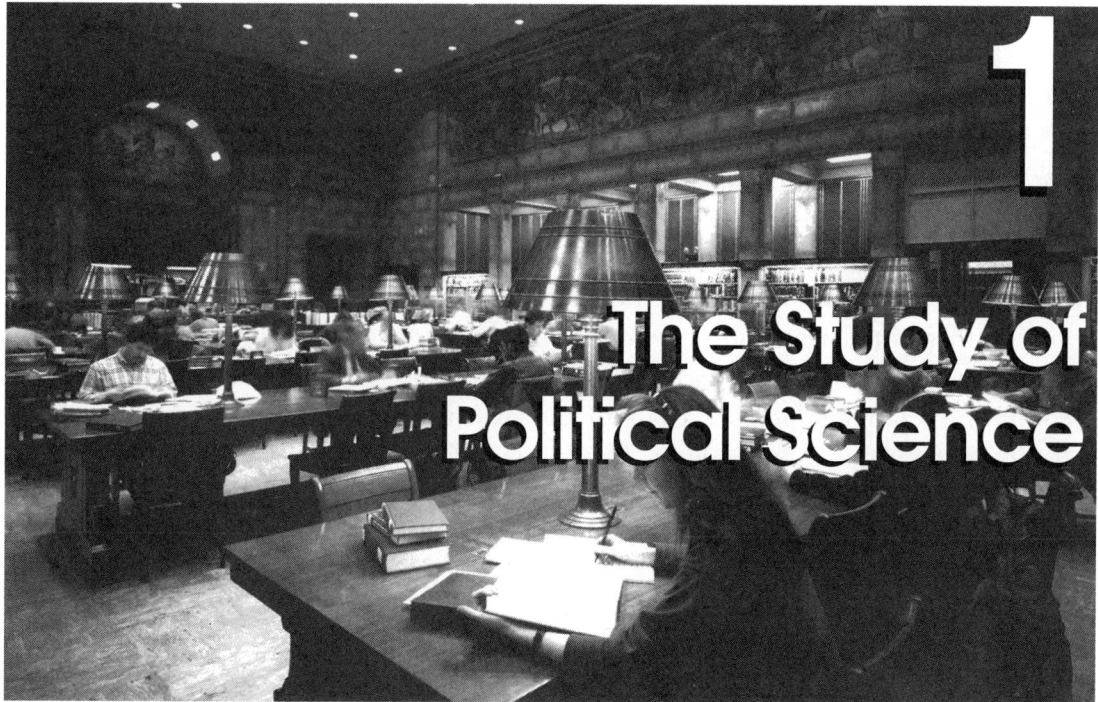

The Study of Political Science

⬤ Outline
- What is Political Science?
- The Subfields of Political Science
- How Political Phenomena are Studied
- Our Theme: The Importance of Society
- How to Study Political Science

Politics is something we discuss daily. Whether it is criticizing an actual legislator or administrator, or a nominee who covets these positions, or complaining about a policy contemplated or in practice we talk about political concerns with others. We may even mumble about these to ourselves. We also discuss the weather. Complaining about it being too hot, too cold, too wet, too dry, or too something else we appear to make the weather a subject that is very important to us. However, when discussing or complaining about the weather we are not engaged in meteorology, the science that deals with atmospheric conditions, including weather and climate. Similarly, when discussing politics we are not engaged in political science. Most of the time, most of us, even those who make political science their profession, when discussing politics are not political scientists just as most of us are not meteorologists when complaining about the weather.

What is Political Science?

Political science is the analysis of the state and the relations people have with government. These relations could be as mundane as paying traffic tickets or as esoteric as running for the elected position of dog catcher in a community. **Government** consists of the institutions through which a society makes and carries out laws. These institutions usually are divided into the executive, legislative, and judicial branches. Each branch also is divided: the executive into ministries or departments, the legislature into chambers, and the judiciary into levels. The government and the laws government makes compose a **state**.

Unlike most other people who usually use data to back up their biases and prejudices, political scientists *study* data regarding the state and the relations people have with government. For example: "2,000 peacefully assembled civilians were shot and killed by government troops" is data of possible interest to a political scientist studying human rights violations. On the other hand, if the 2,000 civilians had died in a natural disaster instead, despite it being of human interest, political scientists would not be interested in this data, unless government responded to it.

Data are not necessarily facts; data also can be opinions, values, and beliefs. Your evaluation of the candidate for the local school board is an opinion, not a fact. That evaluation as other data may be wrong. Data, to be of value for the political scientist, are analyzed to determine whether they are facts. Facts, however, no matter how interesting by themselves, have little value in advancing our understanding unless they are compared to other facts and placed within a context. This context is usually a model or a theory, which are creations of the mind.

Models order axioms, assumptions, and facts to imitate an aspect of reality. Axioms are self-evident truths. The United States government is based on the familiar axiom that "all men are created equal, that they are endowed by their Creator with certain inalienable Rights, that among these are Life, Liberty, and the pursuit of Happiness." Assumptions *probably* are true; but, unlike axioms, they are not necessarily true. For example, "most adults vote" is an assumption. Axioms may be considered facts in themselves; assumptions seldom would be considered facts.

Political theories, which are often composed of models, are an attempt to explain more of reality than models do. Indeed, models frequently are developed to make theory less abstract. A political scientist studying a theory that states political participation within a society is directly correlated with the size of the gap between the rich and the poor must first study several representative models of communities with varying levels of political participation and gaps in income. What complicates this process is that most analyses of facts, which involve comparing facts and placing them in some order according to a model, are used to disprove theories or parts of theories.

Furthermore, political science has not yet produced an all encompassing theory that incorporates most, if not all, of its models as those that exist among the natural sciences, such as the theory of relativity in physics or evolution in biology. In political science many existing models cannot be applied to any theory or become part of different theories that conflict with each other. It may precisely because there is no unifying theory in political science that makes it so exciting. Everyone can develop his or her own theories and models and claim to have discovered the TRUTH, until someone else comes around to disprove them.

Neither can political scientists pinpoint the exact cause of an important event, as physical scientists can. A chemist in a laboratory can isolate a single variable and watch how it changes — and changes in — its physical environment. A political scientist studying an important event cannot definitively determine that a single variable among thousands involved was the major cause of the event. For example, Ernesto Samper Pizzano won the presidential election in Colombia in 1994. Did he win because his party had more money to spend on the campaign than his opponents? Did the allegation that some of the money came from drug lords hurt or help him in securing votes? Was he perhaps considered the most capable candidate? Or did he win because the party that nominated him had been in control of the government for the past decade? All these factors as well as many others may have led to Samper's election.

Yet, because these variables can never be duplicated, none can be *proved* to have led to his victory. The event itself cannot be replicated. This is different for a chemist who in the laboratory can not only control the variables that lead to an event, but can duplicate the events that others have produced. For this reason the chemist can state that by combining such and such variables that the particular event will take place. By combining many such events and placing them within the framework of a theory, the chemist can predict what can happen should there be a mix of variables whose interactions have been studied. Political scientists have difficulty doing this with the variables they study because they cannot most of the time separate the variables that produce an event from those that do not. Nor can they control the environment so that only the desired variables can make something happen. Neither can they duplicate the variables that led to an event.

Yet, political scientists do study political phenomena. They study the past and present not so much to influence the future, as physical scientists mostly do, but to make the present more understandable. In this world of so much complexity, the political scientist attempts not to change the world but to explain it, to give him or herself and others the anchors by which to relate to the political world, a world that has become for many the pivot around which their lives revolve.

Subfields of Political Science

What exactly do political scientists study? Since political science covers a broad spectrum of relations and institutions, it is broken down into several subfields. These subfields are political theory, public opinion and behavior, public policy, public administration, public law, state and local government, comparative government, and international relations.

Political theory

Theorists study the political philosophies of such classic masters as Plato, Aristotle and their successors. Chapters 3 through 6 cover some major political philosophers of the past. Some theorists also use statistical and algebraic models to examine political phenomena. Among the new theories expounded in political science is rational choice, which is a method heavily emphasizing mathematics and deductive reasoning that can be applied to the analysis of most political facts.

Public opinion and behavior

Public opinion and behavior is the study of individual and group behaviors as they affect government, such as voting behavior, activities of individuals, pressure groups and political parties, and electoral systems. Attitude surveys and opinion polls are also included in this subfield. Chapters 7 through 13 investigate this area.

Public policy

How are policies made by governments? Who makes them? How are they carried out? Who gains and who loses by them? How are they evaluated, and how are they changed? This subfield focuses on the making and implementing of policies. Chapters 14, 15, and 16 of this text deal with public policy.

Public administration

The organization of governmental institutions is studied in this subfield. Issues such as budgeting and finances, personnel administration, administrative law and ethics, and decision making are considered. This area overlaps with public policy. Public administration is discussed in Chapters 15 through 18.

Public law

The making and interpreting of laws are the focus of this subfield. A major part of this area is the study of constitutions and their interpretation by legal and scholarly authorities. The judicial branch of government and agencies involved in the making and interpreting of laws and other acts of government are investigated. Also in this subfield is the criminal justice system, including the police and the penal system. Chapter 14 discusses this area.

State and local government

This subfield, which exists mainly in the United States, covers any topic that deals with municipal, county, regional, and state governments. In other countries this field involves municipal, prefectural, provincial, and departmental governments.

Comparative government

The study of any type of political phenomenon in a society, area, or state outside the one in which the investigator lives is comparative government. When a Canadian political scientist studies French, Australian, or American political data, he or she is engaged in comparative government. Examples from the study of comparative government appear throughout the text.

International relations

The interactions of societies, especially states, are analyzed in this sub-field. Also studied are international law and international organizations, and the making and implementing of foreign policy. Chapters 20 and 21 focus on the relations of societies.

As you can see, these subfields often overlap each other. For instance, the making and implementing of foreign policy can be studied from the viewpoint of public policy, public administration, comparative government, or international relations. Each of these subfields may provide its own perspective to what is being studied, sometimes making it difficult to integrate all that is known about a subject. This can become even more frustrating as each subfield develops its own jargon and concepts, thus making it more difficult for outsiders to communicate with those in the subfield.

How Political Phenomena are Studied

Political scientists study their data in the following ways. The *case study method* involves intensive examination of data from one area of political activity (e.g., the influence of local clergy in policy making regarding adoption of newborns in Jamaica in 1978). The *comparative method* examines several sets of data from many different societies (e.g., the role of village elders of several different Indian groups in Latin America in resolving domestic disputes). The *statistical method* compares data statistically and determines any significant variations (e.g., the turnout of university graduates in municipal elections in several different societies).

Our Theme: The Importance of Society

As we will see, Western political philosophers since the end of the Renaissance emphasized that the individual is the primary object of concern in the study of government and politics. Accordingly, governments have tended to serve the individual rather than society. This notion was preserved in the 1930s by the idea that political science is the study of "who gets what, when, and how." Later this idea was extended to cover groups within a society that make demands on government.

The idea of "who gets what, when, and how" involves conflict. It suggests that life is made up of winners and losers, advantages and disadvantages, rich and poor. One person gets the sale, the competitors do not.

A factory closes in Ontario, Canada and moves to Mexico. Students in Mexico City now can afford to go to college; students in Toronto suddenly cannot. If someone gets something, someone else does not; if someone gets something now, it may be taken away later. The danger is ever present that something I possess now may be taken away by force. From this perspective, government is usually the entity that will either protect what I have or take it away and give it to someone else.

Another aspect of this idea is that a finite quantity of "what" (i.e., goods, services, benefits, advantages, or whatever) exists and for the government to dispense and that this quantity is not sufficient to serve everyone. If a sufficient amount of "what" exists for everyone, then getting it becomes irrelevant. Nevertheless, the idea of "who gets what, when, and how" has permeated not only the profession but also the public at large as government is viewed as a dispenser of "what" to some and not to others. But does the state really exist to serve the individual? In this book a different viewpoint will be examined.

Too often political scientists tend to look at the trees and miss the forest. A forest is more than just the aggregation of trees. If I were to plant a thousand trees on a fifty-acre plot, I would not have a forest. I would have a thousand trees on a fifty-acre plot. A forest is a total ecology; a forest is not only the trees that grow there, but also the relationship the trees have with all the other living things that inhabit the area. Even the trees themselves relate to each other in pollination, space, and competition for sunshine, nutrients, and air. A lone Douglas fir in an open field and another growing in the forest are different in the way they look and the way they grow.

So, too, with humans in society. Society is not an aggregation of hermits. A human being living alone is different from a human being in society. The ancient Greeks were right in saying that unless a person actively participates in the affairs of the community he or she is either a beast or a god, but certainly not human. It is precisely the relations we establish with others that fulfill our need to be social creatures.

People with common values, goals, beliefs, norms, and patterns of behavior who live in a certain place and time form a **society**. Although individuals can easily survive without the state, as indeed they have done so until quite recently, they cannot do so without society.

Although society can be divided into several parts — haves and have nots, producers and consumers, old and young, officials and nonofficials, etc. — it is nevertheless a closed unit, a whole. If one part does not get what it needs to contribute to the welfare of society, then the whole society may suffer. The wealth generated by a society may not need to be distributed equally to everyone if everyone has enough to be a productive member of the society.

Sometimes, however, an individual or a group within a society will increase its wealth by preventing others from getting sufficient resources or causing loss of resources for everyone. For example, leaders of a community who refuse to equip its fire department properly because they do not want to pay more taxes may cause the whole society to lose when part of it goes up in flames. Societies cannot endure when members do not spend their resources for necessary measures that benefit all members.

Society created the state to enhance its ability to survive and, therefore, to allow its members to survive. As we will learn in Chapters 2 and 7, the state is the means by which a society organizes its members. Yet, to endure in the future society may need to downgrade the state in its importance. New processes and structures require society to either bypass the state or make it merely an administrative component. For example, economic relations among societies take place today outside the control of the state as do many person-to-person interactions.

Further, unlike the state of the recent past in which the monarch was the principal authority and policy implementors were few, the state today has become boundless. Monarchs used to make policy that dozens of underlings carried out. Today in any industrial society millions of persons and thousands of governments composed of many thousand institutions are involved in making and implementing policies, none of which can be understood or controlled by one individual or group of individuals. Harry Truman is said to be the last U.S. president who understood and could knowingly talk about the entire federal budget. In the almost half-century since he left the White House, the workings of the U.S. Federal government have become too enormous for any one person to understand or describe in detail. Add to that the workings of fifty state governments; the thousands of municipal, county, special district, and regional governments; and innumerable agencies and school boards, and the shear complexity of the governmental web boggles the mind.

Today millions of people closely associated with their respective societies work in the many different government entities. Around the world billions of people receive services from government officials. Almost every family on this planet has a member working for a government or receiving services from it. We are governments and governments are us.

Paradoxically, of course, this complexity and pervasiveness of government has diluted the influence one individual or group of individuals can have on policy or the political process. One person or a small group of persons cannot govern a modern society, even one with a small population. Nevertheless, for society, the way in which policies are made or by whom is less important than that they are made and the means are available to modify and add to them as circumstances change.

The fragmentation of policy making is actually beneficial for society because no single policy can become so crucial that its absence will cause major disruptions. For decades Germany had no speed limits on its major highways. Nevertheless, the number of accidents on them was not appreciably higher than in other industrial countries. Even when a major change in public policy causes significant disruptions in one area of social relations, as Prohibition did in the U.S. in the 1920s, its long-range effects on society may not last long. By the 1950s, only twenty years after its repeal, Prohibition's effects were no longer discernable in American society. In some instances policy debates of thirty or more years ago that caused violent confrontations are no longer remembered today. Generally, over time, societies can smooth over the rough edges that periodically appear in their strategy to survive. Within a beehive or an ant-hill, violence may erupt and some bees or ants may even be driven out, yet the colony endures.

This does not imply that bee or ant colonies or human societies remain viable forever once they form. Societies have disappeared. They either were forcibly taken over or absorbed by others, as ancient Rome eventually succumbed to nomadic tribes and to Christianity, or they were incapable, as a society, of overcoming the challenges facing them and simply died out, as did many Native American societies in North America. Many contemporary societies are struggling to stay alive, some with the help of outsiders. Bangladesh, Rwanda, and Haiti are considered ripe for takeovers by others or incapable of surviving; likewise the society that once was Yugoslavia is struggling to keep its identity. Nevertheless, the international political community has been trying not only to keep these societies going but also to help them build new institutions and processes to improve their capacity to overcome further challenges to their viability.

By taking society as the focal point in this book, we will not only get a better understanding of the relationship between politics, government, and state and society, but also of the relationship that exists between you and me and these entities that are never that far from our minds.

How to Study Political Science

Many concepts and facts are presented in a book like this. They can be studied as abstractions, memorized, and regurgitated in quizzes and tests. This is the wrong way to study political science.

Just as in chemistry or physics, the best way to study political science is through the laboratory. In chemistry laboratories students apply what they have learned in lectures and from the text by conducting experiments. This is also the case with political science. But there is no laboratory, you may say. Of course there is. The laboratory is the world outside the classroom as seen in newspapers, magazines, news programs, documentaries, political speeches, campaigns, and lobbying efforts. Today political data is easy to acquire from radio and television news programs, city hall or court events, or student government activities. With the arrival of the Internet and the World Wide Web, political news from all over the globe is never more than a few mouse clicks away.

Examine data from these sources and apply them to the concepts you will hear in lectures and read in this book. By doing this, you will find that not only the data, but also the concepts themselves make more sense. Most importantly, determine whether data presented is factual.

Another way to make the material in this book more understandable is to discuss it with others. Discussions jog the memory and put data and concepts into a clearer perspective that makes them more meaningful. Discussion and debate make ideas clearer so they can become a part of your general understanding of the world.

While studying from this text,

This Ukrainian political scientist helped organize her country's new Parliament using the computer search facilities at the U.S. Library of Congress.

Home page of the Library of Congress, Washington D.C.

make it a point to look for what seem like inconsistent or even wrong models or theories as well as for ideas with which you do not agree. When you think you have found one, do not be afraid to say so to your instructor, classmates, or friends. Quite possibly they will agree with you.

Finally, integrate the knowledge of political science you learn from this text with the knowledge you have acquired from other sources, be they courses, books, instructors, or colleagues. Does it all fit together? Or are there inconsistencies? Make political science part of your "philosophy." Above all, take your time in reading this book. There is much material here and, just like a good meal, it will take time to digest it.

TERMS TO REMEMBER

government
state
society

SUGGESTED READINGS

Finifter, Ada W., Ed. *Political Science: The State of the Discipline II*. Washington, D.C.: The American Political Science Association, 1993. A compendium of articles written by different scholars in political science describing research methods used in the field.

Frankfort-Nachmias, Chava, and David Nachmias. *Research Methods in the Social Sciences*. 4th ed. New York: St. Martin's Press, 1992. To understand this text, the reader should have some background in calculus and statistics.

2

The Organization of Society

⊕ Outline
- Development of the State
- When is a State a State?
- Whither the State?

Suppose you wanted to take someone to see a movie with you tonight. More than likely you would ask him or her either in person or over the telephone and arrange it all in a matter of minutes. Suppose you wanted to take ten people to see a movie. You would have to express this desire to them, but the arrangements would take much longer to complete, perhaps a few hours.

Now suppose you wanted fifty people to go to a movie with you. The arrangements become complicated and take even longer to complete. In fact, you might not be able to make them by yourself; you might have to hire a secretary or bring everyone together in a meeting to decide which movie to see, when to see it, and how you will get to the theater. To accomplish this, you would need to create some organization. This might take weeks, the chances of all fifty attending together would be much less likely than if you went with fewer persons.

The more people involved in an activity, the greater the need for coordination. The more coordination involved, the more organization that results. A smaller number of people requires less and different kinds of organization. Therefore, in any endeavor the number of people involved (and their proximity to each other) determines the type of organization needed for a successful outcome.

Development of the State

Human societies, like those of other animals, developed opportunistically; they developed best in places where their members could overcome environmental challenges. A swarm of bees, for example, may choose to nest in an area in which the plants are eventually killed by drought, making viability of the hive very precarious. Another swarm may choose to nest in an area in which the lush flowers not only maintain the hive but also increase the number of bees so much that some of them leave to form another hive.

So, too, with human societies: Some settled in areas in which the environment posed so many challenges that survival was always near the precipice; other societies settled in areas in which prosperity came easy. Societies flourished when their members successfully met challenges that they were capable of surmounting. Each society adapted to its own ecological niche and developed its particular manners, norms, and customs.

For hundreds of thousands, if not millions, of years humans lived in groups numbering no more than a hundred. Within these groups, individuals attaining maturity had to provide food, clothing, and shelter for themselves and for those who could not. Although all family members would help each other, adult individuals were on their own. The family and society were one and the same. The family provided the individual with adequate nutrition to survive the first years of life, knowledge and skill to remain alive and propagate when mature, and protection against threats and forces that an individual alone could not overcome.

Survival or viability of society soon emerged as the most important objective for humans. Without the aid of society the individual could not survive or, more importantly, leave progeny. The family, or society, was self-sufficient and its organization was simple: one or a few individuals, usually older males, gave direction to the group, enforced the rules, and mediated violent conflict. All members were organized in a simple **hierarchy**, which is a ranking of individuals or groups based on dominance, influence, or status.

When families grew in size (because of either internal growth or merger with other families), specialization of tasks became necessary for efficient use of resources and provision of security. Individuals increasingly occupied socioeconomic niches based on competence and ascription. As the nuclear family became the focus of identification for the individual, and society, a loose grouping of these family units, appeared. Besides providing security from outsiders, society's main function was to prevent violence in interfamily conflicts. Within the family, violence was used primarily by those at the top of the family hierarchy to resolve conflict. Society developed other techniques, however, to control bloodshed and destruction between family units.

Law and the Institutionalized Use of Force

Laws were first developed in response to interfamily violence. The use of force was slowly abolished in interactions between members of different families, except in specially approved circumstances. In time, only society itself was allowed to use force against a recalcitrant member, but it could do so only in certain situations according to the **norms**. A norm is a do or don't. Therefore, norms that stipulated conditions in which force must be used in society became the kernels for development of future laws.

A **law** is an "if . . . then" statement. For example, one law may state that if anyone steals then he or she shall be given a jail term of up to ten years. The "if" part is the behavior that is not wanted; the "then" part is the punishment or **sanction**. Laws are the only norms that can be sanctioned by force. At first, enforcement of these norms was left to each member of society. Each individual was the judge of infractions of the customary law and the executor of punishments to the delinquents. Evidence that customary norms became laws is shown by the fact that society did not punish those who did punish or sanction violators of legal norms.

A new level of societal organization was reached when a few select individuals were given the prerogative of judging whether laws had been disobeyed and then determining what sanction or punishment would be carried out. As these select individuals began to interpret norms, some of their decisions may have seemed to contradict customary norms. These

In many countries, such as China, caning has been a traditionally accepted form of legal punishment for various minor offenses. The severity of caning depends on the degree of the offense.

leaders, of course, used custom to justify their interpretations, but there were always those in society who disagreed and insisted that their interpretation of custom be followed.

The interpretation of proper custom, and therefore law, created friction within the ever growing societies. To prevent further disagreement over interpretation, the authority to make, implement, and interpret legal norms was removed from individuals and given to institutions. **Institutionalization** means that a function is attached to an office, not to an individual. An individual can perform that function only if he or she is allowed to occupy the office. Before, an individual became a leader because of some perceived superior ability, age, or parentage; he or she then was given the added role of judge or interpreter of the system. Later, one became a leader by appointment, selection, or birthright to a given office. Whereas the leader once made the office, now the office made the leader. When the making, implementing, and interpretation of legal norms became institutionalized, violators often received their punishment from the same persons who established the norms.

Once institutions to make and implement legal norms became necessary, governments were formed. In time, governments completely controlled the use of force. Individuals were forbidden to use force even when sanctioning delinquents. Under the law, force could only be used in a prescribed form within the family and in self-defense against strangers.

As the use of force became more centralized within governments, they became more important in the determination of law. By creating and implementing laws within institutions, the leaders of society assured its continuation through the propagation of its members.

As populations grew, the number and complexity of institutions and, therefore, governments increased. Not only did more people need to be controlled but also the relationships between them became more varied. In part, this was caused by the greater dependence individuals had on each other because of ever increasing specialization and improvements in materials and tools used to augment the individual's well-being. Greater dependence by individuals on society for providing more of their needs resulted in the need for more coordination. Also, communication through the written word and rudimentary transportation (camel, horse, boat) brought people together who once were distant and otherwise unknown to each other. Laws were made not only to prevent violent conflict among the population but also to regulate the multiplicity of interactions among the members of society. Soon different institutions were each charged with separate types of lawmaking and implementation.

Another relationship, the interactions of societies, also became institutionalized. Societies began to relate to each other because they were either situated nearby, were interdependent, or possessed coveted resources. Neighboring societies learned each others' customs, norms, and laws. Soon norms regulating intersocietal relations appeared. Violence among societies in conflict with each other lessened as more of these norms were applied and institutionalized. Later, the institutions that dealt with intersocietal matters were differentiated from those that dealt with intrasocietal needs and conflicts. The greater the number of societies any one society had to relate to and the greater the number of the interactions by that society with them, the greater the number and complexity of the institutions it needed.

Even when societies were interacting with each other on a large scale, each society still tried to maintain its self-sufficiency. Until the end of the Middle Ages, interdependence among European societies was averted through conquest or internal development. Famine and disease kept population growth low in the 1300s and 1400s. Once these "evils" were overcome, however, populations began to increase rapidly. With more people to coordinate, the influence of governmental institutions increased.

Another change that occurred after the Middle Ages was the dependence families had on each other. Family life, especially in the rural areas, centered on self-sufficiency until the end of the 1400s. The family provided for the needs of its members: security, food, shelter, and clothing. Although each member of the family had a specialized task to perform in society, the family as a whole acquired the resources to provide for its members' needs by bartering or receiving wages. After the Middle Ages, society increasingly began to provide for these needs, especially security — security not only for the person but, very importantly, also for property.

Law to Protect Property and Capital

Coping with the issue of property has always been a central societal problem. From the definition of what is property to the determination of its ownership, societies have attempted to resolve the problem, for the most part unsuccessfully, through laws and institutions.

When the family and society were one and the same, the property of the family and the property of society were indistinguishable. Individuals had no property. The boundaries of family property changed as the family grew, diminished, or moved; the leaders, or elders, decided who was to work what parcel of land. Personal belongings were often considered extensions of the person. The spear and the person were one while the person carried it. When the spear was laid down and its user was not nearby, it might be taken by another who then considered it his.

Societies probably appeared at the same time large families began to break up because of internal rivalry and conflict over landed property. Property cannot be defined except through law. The land that a particular nuclear family uses cannot be allowed to be sequestered by another that may want it. The owning family can feel secure in its ownership if another will be punished for taking it away; otherwise there is no reason for working it. This punishment can only succeed if society guarantees it. Otherwise, the owning family will constantly be subjected to threats from others and eventually the strongest will possess all the land. While this may work in the short run, eventually the strongest themselves will separate or the weaker may join together to oppose them. When society guarantees ownership of property, it establishes a right. Since a right cannot exist without a corresponding obligation to observe it, law is thereby created.

With the institutionalization of lawmaking and enforcement, property law was determined by those who occupied office in the institutions or governments.   Claiming to represent society, these leaders redefined property law, claiming that all property that belonged to society and individual ownership was but a trust or lease.   Thus, when society was seen as the ultimate owner of property, the leaders could then manipulate individual owners to the point where they lost rights to that property. Therefore, by the Middle Ages all property in Europe was either owned directly by the aristocracy or entrusted to individuals with the understanding that if they were not using that property for socially useful purposes, as interpreted by the aristocracy, the trust could be taken away.

After the Middle Ages, the issue regarding property centered on capital accumulation.   Land was not only a sign of wealth but, more importantly, also a sign of status.   Unless the land was worked, it did not represent wealth at all.   Capital, however, was plainly a sign of wealth. Since status determined power in the Middle Ages, those with wealth, in order to acquire power, had to obtain status.   Status could frequently be bought by becoming the aristocracy's financier, by marrying into the nobility, or by becoming so wealthy that one controlled a good part of the government.   The revolutionary changes of the late 1700s and early 1800s replaced the landed aristocracy in the seat of power with the newer wealthy dwellers of the city.

The purpose of law and government, therefore, expanded from insuring safety from outsiders, peaceful resolution of conflict, and protection of landed property rights to protection of capital.

The Modern State

Further changes occurred in the seventeenth and eighteenth centuries. Some of those who accumulated capital, the industrialists, attracted thousands of former peasants and land workers to the cities to operate machines.   As health care improved, infant mortality and death rates decreased, and the modern population explosion began. With the attempt to create more efficient use of capital and resources, specialization through education increased, making the individual even more reliant for his livelihood on the production and distribution of goods through society. All these changes caused greater understanding and self-awareness among the population, and increased its demands for government to alleviate poor conditions created by the wealthy.   Laws became more numerous, institutions of government became more complex.   The concept of the state, as a governmental body that bound together the laws, institutions, and people in a given region, appeared.

Until the 1800s the state provided for the welfare of groups within society, be it the family; the economic, social, religious, or national group to which one belonged; or any other group such as the military, clergy, or aristocracy. From the mid-1800s, however, the state began to provide for the welfare of the individual, bypassing any group affiliation. By making the individual the focus of all its programs and policies, the state loosened the ties that bound people together, thereby fragmenting the members of society. Even the family, in some places like the United States, began to disappear. Since it no longer could provide the social security and services the individual needed to survive, the family was replaced by the state in many of its functions.

By the middle of the twentieth century, the state's concerns centered on providing an adequate standard of living for what was now a huge society. To do that, the state had to insure not only employment, education, and welfare to all members of society but also the production and distribution of required goods and services. The state is now seen not only as the defender of society, the enforcer of rules, and the protector of property (landed and capital), but also as the provider of goods and services, without which neither individuals nor society itself could survive.

The state, then, is modern society's means of organizing its members. It is a construct that developed over time to satisfy the changing organizational needs of an ever growing society. The form of its particular institutions today, however, is strictly European, imbedded in Western civilization. The way governments are organized, how and when positions are filled, who is allowed to participate in the making of policy are all products of a European legacy. The physical and social environment of Europe was such that developing societies could disseminate, through the state, sometimes by brutal force, their organizational norms to the rest of the globe.

When Is a State a State?

When is a state a state? A state is an entity comprised of legal norms enforced by a government on a people living in a given space or territory. However, not all entities that possess these characteristics were or are considered states. Also, some states do not possess these traits. The questions "When is a state a state?" and "What really is a state?" cannot be looked at from the perspective of the political organization of society as we have done thus far. Rather, we must search elsewhere.

The state is a creation of law, just like a corporation. We cannot see a corporation or a state. What we see are parts or aspects of a corporation, such as employees, products, buildings, organizational chart, and liabilities and assets. We may make checks to or get checks from the corporation. None of these by themselves or even together make a corporation a corporation.

What makes an entity a corporation is a charter. A charter is a piece of paper outlining the organization and purposes of an entity that is approved by a governmental institution. By approving the charter, the government creates a "person." Law regulates persons only; it does not regulate objects, animals, or plants (although it may regulate how persons deal with objects, animals, and plants). By approving or granting an entity its charter, the government creates by law a person. The corporation then has all the rights and obligations (except those that are political) of a person. The corporation is a **legal fiction,** a creation of law.

A state, too, is a legal fiction. Although we can see the people, territory, or organizational chart of the government and its laws, these either by themselves or together do not make a state a state. To be a state, an entity must be recognized as such by other states; this act of recognition, therefore, is what makes a state. Once a state comes into existence, it gains the same rights and obligations of existing states. One of these rights is

Raising the flag at the United Nations is a momentous occasion for a new nation.

that no other state can formulate, interpret, or enforce laws on the people under its jurisdiction. The act of recognition and the resulting rights and obligations are determined by international law. Today, a state's admission to membership in the United Nations is equivalent to government approval of a corporate charter.

States have no obligation to societies that are not recognized as states. The Ottoman Empire, the Aztec and Inca Empires, and the Cherokee Confederation consisted of people living in a territory under an independent and effective government that enforced law. Yet, because they were not Christian, they were not considered states by the European monarchies, which could colonize, exploit, and attack them at will. A state has the obligation to respect the territory and independence of another state; it cannot attack or intervene in another state, unless the other state is an illegal aggressor. (For example, the takeover of Kuwait by Iraq was considered an illegal act that had to be punished. It was the only attempted conquest of a state by another state since World War II.)

Some members of the United Nations may not be states. How independent and effective are the governments of some Third World states that are manipulated by large industrial states for the latter's own interests? Were Grenada or Panama "states" when the U.S. armed forces

The discovery of vast oil fields in the Middle East has greatly changed the political and economic relationship between the western world and the Arab countries.

controlled their governments? What about Nicaragua, Honduras, Cuba, and other countries in which U.S. Marines were stationed against the will of the governments and the people in the early 1900s? What about the Eastern European countries that the Soviet government controlled through their economies, politics, and defense? Is Taiwan a state? Is Bosnia-Herzegovina one?

Besides being the legal organization of a society the state is also, especially in its interactions with other states, a creation of law with obligations and rights.

Whither the State?

Our European ancestors legally defined what a state is while simultaneously discovering the means by which large societies could be managed and organized. The treaty of Westphaliea of 1648 which put a formal end to the religious wars in Europe spelled out the nature, rights, and obligations of the modern state. To the extent that all societies seek to maintain or achieve their political independence through government institutions that are all rather similar and want to be recognized as states, they have become westernized. The governmental structures of states in Africa, Asia, the Americas, and Europe differ little, although cultural values and beliefs may be very different.

Societies, however, will continue to develop, merge, consolidate, and break up. Institutions and processes will arise to meet new challenges. Globalization of Western political institutions could be the reason that the state may be supplanted in importance by other organizational structures. As societies' self-sufficiency has disappeared in the modern period, new interactions among societies have been generated. Though France is still France and Belgium is still Belgium for the citizen of each, the state is no longer as important as it once was because of the increasing influence of the institutions of the European Union. In the spring of 1992, for example, the Court of the European Union forced the municipal government of the city of Berlin to increase the price of a parcel of land it was selling to a private corporation.

The Belgian-educated Spanish surgeon may set up his practice in London today without having to go through any governmental red tape. Complete freedom of movement among the citizens of the European Union, whether for pleasure or work, is now possible. The same is true of capital and services. In the near future, one monetary unit may circulate

A pictorial representation of the creation of the first French constitution in 1791 depicting Jean-Jacques Rousseau, Benjamin Franklin, Montesquieu, Voltaire, Cicero, Demosthenes, and others. The leader of the French Assembly, Honoré Mirabeau, is at the center.

throughout Europe; there may also be one foreign policy. In short, Europe may become one economic unit with one foreign policy. Perhaps the result of this development will not be unlike that of the United States after its Constitution was ratified in 1791, although the institutions would be much different from those that prevailed then.

Global institutions have proliferated so much in this century that listing them requires a book. Since states are beginning to lose control over their actions, the need increases to find some mechanism to coordinate them. What this mechanism will be and how and by whom it will be controlled is a question that begs an answer. One thing is certain: in the year 2050 the political organization that you will live under will be as different as the current organization is from what prevailed in the last century.

What follows is a summary of the thinking of some of the most important Western political theorists in the last two thousand five hundred years. Though the state was a result of a natural development, its form and shape were determined, at least to a small extent, by the values and aspirations of these men. They gave their own answer to a question for which we to this day have not found a definitive solution. The question is: What is the relationship among the individual, the society, and the state?

TERMS TO REMEMBER

hierarchy
norms
law
sanction
institutionalization
legal fiction

SUGGESTED READINGS

Claude, Inis L. *States and the Global System: Politics, Law and Organization.* New York: St. Martin's Press, 1988. The role of the state within the evolving new international political order by the author of a leading text on international organizations.

Cohen, Ronald and Elman R. Service, eds. *Origins of the State: The Anthropology of Political Evolution.* Philadelphia: Institute for the Study of Human Issues, 1978. Several excellent articles by anthropologists on where, why, and how government began.

Fried, Morton H. *The Evolution of Political Society: An Essay in Political Anthropology.* New York: Random House, 1967. Emphasizing ancient Middle East kingdoms such as those of Babylonia, Fried develops ideas on how governmental institutions originated.

Kelsen, Hans. *General Theory of Law and State.* Translated by Anders Wedberg. Cambridge, MA: Harvard University Press, 1945. A classic study of the role of law in society written by one of the foremost scholars in international law.

Mair, Lucy. *Primitive Government.* Baltimore: Penguin Books, 1970. How governments originated in various parts of the globe according to the anthropological perspective.

Political Theory

PART TWO

3
The Greeks

About twenty-five hundred years ago, in a place called Hellas, a handful of thinkers originated political philosophies that are the basis for modern political beliefs and thoughts.

Polis

The people who inhabited the area now called Greece dwelled in communities, each of which was called a **polis**. A polis was not just a geographic place, what some authorities have called a city-state. Polis was an idea of a total community not segmented into social, political, or economic parts, and conscious of its past and united toward its future.

Each polis was completely independent of the others. The largest had about thirty thousand free inhabitants and ninety thousand slaves. Each polis determined its domestic and foreign affairs and had its own army that it frequently organized to fight other poleis. What unified the people of all these poleis was a common language (ancient Greek), belief in common transcendental beings (Greek mythology), and, mostly, a common way of life.

The people were so strongly attached to the polis that they could not imagine permanently living outside it. Of course, some occasionally left the polis for trading or warfare, but they seldom left forever. Many considered banishment from the polis a punishment worse than death.

Hellenics believed that all people were not born equal; some were born slaves. A function of government then was to lessen the effects of this inequality, making it possible for each individual to contribute to the general welfare. This was accomplished, for example, by providing services, such as pasture owned by the community, to everyone regardless of wealth or status, and by making laws protecting slaves from abuse by their masters.

Notice that this idea is just the opposite of what the founding fathers of modern states thought. They believed in the inherent equality of all people by birth. If nature, which is perfect, makes everyone equal, then imperfect humans cause inequality through social and, especially, political institutions. Nature's perfect equality is destroyed by imperfect man's government. Therefore, to the founding fathers, government at best was an evil that must be kept out of people's affairs. On the other hand, the ancient Greeks believed that government should be very active in correcting nature's imperfection in making humans unequal.

Today we agree with both the Greeks and the founding fathers in an eclectic sort of way. On the one hand, we believe that the accident of our birth should not prejudice a person's full participation in the economic, social, political, and cultural opportunities offered within society. Consequently, we favor public policies that prevent discrimination against persons who are disabled and are physically different from us, that is, are not equal to us. On the other hand, we believe that everyone is born equal but that society instills within many of us biases and prejudices against others. To that end we use the political process to prevent our societally engendered biases and prejudices from influencing our public interactions and policies. Accordingly, we believe that nature makes us unequal and equal and that society not only causes unwanted discrimination but also brings about equality through its political processes and institutions.

Universality and the Four Cardinal Virtues

One of the most important legacies of the Hellenics was the idea of universality of knowledge. Before this era many people believed that knowledge was particular for a time and space. According to this notion, truth was true to a given place at a specific time; tomorrow or in another place, today's truth may be false. To the Hellenic, Truth was real here and everywhere, today and always. Hellenics introduced philosophy to European civilization. Philosophy, the study of life, or better yet, the contemplation of life, uses logic and reason (as opposed to belief or faith) in the determination of Truth.

The ancient Greeks believed in four cardinal virtues that every one should strive for to be considered a good person. The first virtue, wisdom, was considered a composite of knowledge, logic, and what is known today as common sense. Since common sense is gained through the trials and errors of experience, the Greeks assumed that only older persons could be wise.

The second virtue was courage. Courage meant to be true to oneself, to stand up for one's beliefs, and to defend one's beliefs honorably. It did not mean to sacrifice one's principles for money or to risk one's life to get a medal or a story in a newspaper.

The third of the cardinal virtues was temperance. Temperance meant moderation not only in one's beliefs but also in what one did publicly and privately. The Greeks had little use for fanatics or for those whose ideas went beyond the limits of what was considered respectable. The Greeks would not have looked favorably upon the excessive drinking and eating, and sexual and other habits prevalent among some modern populations.

The fourth virtue was justice. Justice meant . . . well, that is the problem. The Greeks had a problem defining justice, just as we have today. They knew that of the four virtues, justice was the only one that demanded interaction with others. A person could be wise, courageous, and temperate alone in his or her living room. But to be just he or she had to have someone else around. One could not be just to oneself, but only in relation to others. So then what is justice?

Justice is the theme of what is probably the most important book (Plato's *The Republic*) that was written during this period in man's history. Before we get to that, however, let us look again at the polis.

Athens

There were many poleis in Hellas. Two of the most famous were Sparta and Athens. Sparta was renowned for the physical prowess of its citizens and especially for its discipline. Today we call someone's existence "spartan" when that person leads a very disciplined life without any luxuries, with just enough food, clothing, and shelter to maintain the body in good shape. Ancient Sparta was a dual monarchy; it had two kings, one for foreign affairs and one for domestic affairs.

Athens was a different polis. At various times it had tried every form of government imaginable. It had a tyranny, a benevolent dictatorship, an oligarchy, and, more importantly for us, a **direct democracy**. In this direct democracy, all citizens of Athens participated not only in the creation of public policy, but also in its implementation.

Every so often all Athenians would get together in a stadium to discuss and vote on various issues. Every month some Athenian citizens would be randomly chosen to serve as government officials. Offices usually were held for one month (a few, like generals of the army, were held for up to one year), and office holders usually could not succeed themselves. When called upon, however, they had to serve. (Today's jury system operates this way.)

From a citizen's participation viewpoint this was paradise because everyone makes and carries out policy. But from a pragmatic perspective it never could have worked for long. And it did not. By the time of Socrates, Athenian democracy had degenerated into a factional fight among oligarchies; two generations later it was replaced by a despot, Alexander the Great. Why did it degenerate and why is that important for us?

One area that advocates of democracy frequently have ignored is time. It takes time to study the needs of society, to gather the information necessary to make rational decisions among alternative policies. It takes time to reflect, contemplate about priorities and develop one's values. The thirty thousand or so Athenian citizens, even with the ninety thousand slaves who worked for them, just did not have the time to be pure democrats. It was easier for Athenians to follow the opinions and rhetoric of others than to develop their own. The few who did found it expedient to use those who did not for their personal advantage. Soon, you had those who *sounded* wise becoming more popular than those who *were* wise, and the personality of one turned against that of the other. Eventually rational decision making became impossible.

We have the same problem today. Everyone cherishes the notion that our government is a democracy because everyone can participate in the process. Yet, very few do participate. For example, in a recent excess school levy referendum in your author's county, less than 20 percent of the voters (85 of 475 registered) turned out. Generally, less than one percent of people participate in the political process beyond voting. It is easy to blame the apathetic, alienated, or ignorant voter (we will have more to say about them later), but more serious problems may exist.

When a person comes home from work (or school), he or she usually is too exhausted to bother with decisions regarding society. An issue must be very important for that person to get involved. In addition, the issues are more complicated today and the choice among candidates is difficult. It is much more relaxing to watch TV, play tennis, or engage in other recreational activities. Let us not forget that there are other commitments that people, especially parents, have today, such as taking a child to music lessons or to sport practices and games, attending parties, and socializing with neighbors and friends. And they have to do the dirty work themselves — clean the apartment or house, cook, do some gardening, etc. Most people do not have the time to involve themselves with politics. Therefore, is it possible to have a democracy when people cannot be democrats?

Back to Athens. While Athens was degenerating into an oligarchy, its citizens were preoccupied with the education of their children. How was this done? Children were educated at home up to about the age of fourteen. Either a family member or a hired tutor would teach the basics necessary for life. If affordable, the family would hire a live-in tutor. When the tutoring ended, a young boy would be apprenticed to a craftsman until he was ready to work on his own.

Some parents wanted their sons to be further educated. In the streets of Athens a group of loquacious characters hung around the corners surrounded by young people. These "characters" are the equivalent of today's professors.

Ancient Greece did not have universities or colleges, or even buildings, where one could go to obtain an education; however, poets, mathematicians, and philosophers sat or stood in the streets lecturing. If a young man found the lecture interesting, he would remain until it was finished. Then he would toss the "professor" a few coins and be on his merry way. Imagine yourself at a university city and, instead of buildings with classrooms, you find hundreds of professors standing or sitting on sidewalks all over town giving lectures. All you have to do is walk by, listen to some and, if you like what you hear, throw a few bills.

Some of these "professors" in Athens who were considered better than others had a devoted following of students, who probably paid them by the month or year. Sometimes these "professors" let the students stay all day.

Socrates and Plato

One of these curbside professors was a man named **Socrates** (4697-399 B.C.E.). He was a big, obnoxious, loudmouthed person who liked to get into a fight and was frequently drunk. Nevertheless, he knew how to think and especially philosophize. If not for Socrates, we might not have philosophy today.

Before Socrates, individuals' mental capabilities were judged on how well they could recite stories handed from one generation to the next. Usually these stories were recited in verse (so they could be remembered easily). Socrates believed that recitation, *per se* had no meaning. He believed it was more important to apply logic to a given set of facts (including historical stories); that is, to deduce or induce consequences from these facts that may be useful in explaining phenomena or in resolving problems.

Socrates was an excellent teacher. He taught by making students active participants in the learning process, posing questions that they had to answer. These were what we now call "loaded questions" in that they could be answered in only one way: the teacher's way. This way of teaching is called the Socratic Method.

Socrates taught this way because he, like others at the time, believed in an all-knowing world soul of which each person had a part. He believed that the trauma of childbirth made one forget everything learned before birth; therefore, teaching would bring back the knowledge once forgot. This method is similar to that of asking questions about someone's whereabouts to jog his or her memory about where missing keys were left.

Since Socrates never wrote anything of consequence, how do we know what he said? Well, he had some good students who took notes, almost like students do in lectures today. Many throw away these notes at the end of the semester or at the end of their college career. Most of Socrates' students did that too, but a few did not. One of those who did not was **Plato** (427-347 B.C.E.). Long after Socrates' death, Plato went back to his notes, put them in order, rewrote some, edited some, and then "published" them. Later others reorganized them again and divided them into sections.

The notes that Plato published of Socrates's lectures are known as *The Dialogues*. There are fifteen dialogues; they are so called because Socrates taught by engaging the student in a dialogue, a conversation. Plato just wrote down the questions and the answers.

The death of Socrates.

Socrates was convicted by his fellow Athenians and condemned to death for corrupting the youth of Athens by teaching them ideas that the populace did not approve. He had the chance of fleeing from jail, but he believed that running away would imply that he was not true to his teachings. It also meant leaving Athens forever. He could live with neither, so he committed suicide in jail by drinking the juice of a poisonous hemlock.

The Republic

The most famous and longest of *Plato's dialogues* is **The Republic.** It begins with Socrates coming back to Athens with his students after paying his devotions at a new shrine. He is invited to celebrate the birthday of an older man, Cephalos. Socrates accepts this invitation to the party that begins in the evening and more than likely lasts till the morning . . . a week later. The entire contents of *The Republic*, all three-hundred pages, takes place at that party, so it must have been a long one.

Age and Wealth

After exchanging how-do-you-dos with Cephalos, Socrates converses with him, asking him how it feels to be getting old. Cephalos answers:

> Well, my dear Socrates, I will tell you how I feel. . . . Most of us when we meet are full of lamentations; we miss the pleasures of youth, we talk of our old love affairs, and drinking and feasting, and other such things; and we regret them as if we had been robbed of great things, as if that were real life, and we were hardly alive now. . . . But in fact I have met others who don't feel like that about it, Sophocles the poet, for instance. I was with him once, when somebody asked him, 'What about love now, Sophocles? Are you still able to serve a woman?' 'Hush, man,' he said, 'I've escaped from all that, thank goodness. I feel as if I had escaped from a mad, cruel slave driver.' . . . Indeed, there is a great and perfect peace from such things in old age. When desires go slack and no longer tighten the strings, it is exactly what Sophocles said; perfect riddance of frantic slave drivers, a whole horde of them. No, Socrates, both here and in family life there is only one reason for what happens; not old age, but the man's character. For if they are decent, even-tempered people, old age is only moderately troublesome; if not, then youth is no less difficult than age is for such people. [1]

Well now, we have a little discourse on the differences between the young and the old. Socrates does not believe all this for he says, "You bear old age easily, . . . not because of character, but because you have a large fortune; rich people have many consolations." Cephalos partially agrees with him when he says, "Even a reasonable man would not bear old age quite easily in poverty, but the unreasonable man, if he were rich, would not be at peace with himself." The conversation now turns to money.

Socrates asks Cephalos whether he made his fortune or inherited it. The latter answers that his grandfather inherited wealth and increased it manyfold but his father squandered most of it. Cephalos built the family fortune back up to where it was when his grandfather inherited it.

Socrates then says that it seemed to him that Cephalos must have been born into wealth because, he tells Cephalos:

> . . . You seemed to me not to care much for money. Those who don't are generally those who have not earned it; those who have [earned it] welcome money twice as much as the others. . . . Those who have earned money take it seriously as their own work, not only for its use as the rest do. So they are difficult people to deal with, because they will praise nothing but money.

Socrates is saying that a difference exists between people who are born wealthy and those who earn it. The former respect money for what it will buy; the latter respect money for its own sake and therefore think of nothing else. Cephalos agrees. And now Socrates asks Cephalos what is the "greatest good you have gained from getting great wealth?" Cephalos answers:

> Something which I could perhaps not make most people believe. Know well, Socrates, that when a man faces the thought that he must die, he feels fear and anxiety about what did not trouble him before. Think of the tales they tell of the next world, how one that has done wrong here must have justice done him there — you may have laughed at them before, but then they begin to rack your soul. What if they are true! And the man himself, whether from the weakness of old age, or because he is nearer, death has a better sight of them. Suspicion and fear fill him then, and he runs up his account, and looks to see whether he has wronged anyone. If he finds many wrongs in his life, he often starts up out of his sleep like a child in terror, and lives with evil expectations; but one who has no wrong on his conscience has always Hope beside him, lovely and good, the old man's nurse. . . . I put down possession of wealth as worth a great deal, not to every man, but to the decent man. Never to deceive anyone even unconsciously, never to be dishonest, nor to be debtor to any god for sacrifices or any man for money, and so go to that world in fear — to possess money contributes a great share in avoiding all this. It has other uses, many indeed; but setting one thing against another, I would put this as the chief thing for which wealth is most useful to a sensible man.

Let us stop for a moment to understand what is happening. Two basic themes run through this dialogue. The first involves aging. What is said here is that we are not the same person when we are old as when we are young. We have different preoccupations when we are young than we do when we are old. While in college, we are mostly interested in becoming proficient in a subject and finding a mate. As we mature, we become concerned with securing the right job and starting a family. When we are in the thirties and forties, our priorities become education for our children and moving ahead in our profession. Once we reach the fifties, the higher education of our children and retirement preoccupies us. Once we retire, death becomes a more constant preoccupation.

In each of these phases, our political orientations are different. While in college, why should we care about funds for public schools, old-age pensions, and safe neighborhoods? Of greater importance are questions relating to the military draft, abortion (especially for women), and the availability of funds for college education. When we are old, these issues recede and the major political questions hinge around social security, health benefits, garbage removal and other city services, and safety in the home, on the streets, and while traveling. Our political perspectives change as our priorities change; and our priorities change as we get older. We are captives of our biology.

The second theme that runs through this conversation involves money. Money makes us immune from some of the evils that plague the poor. For example, it immunizes a person from being corrupted. A politician who barely ekes out his or her existence is more susceptible to corruption when offered a bribe of a few thousand dollars for political favors. On the other hand, a wealthy politician would not be likely to take such a bribe.

The other advantage of money is that it does seem to buy happiness. A person who has money and does not abuse it does not have to worry about whether all the bills or other debts have been paid. He also contributes to charity and in doing so makes peace with society and the gods. Therefore, he can go to his grave knowing that he has not wronged anyone.

What Is Justice?

The conversation then proceeds to what becomes the main theme of the rest of *The Republic*. What is justice? Who is a just man? Socrates begins:

> But this very thing justice — are we to say that it is just simply to pay what one has received from anyone? Or is it true that this may be sometimes just and sometimes unjust? For example: Suppose you have received weapons from a friend when in his right mind, everyone would say that you should not give such thing back if he were mad when he asked for them. Then it would not be right and just to give them back, or always to tell him the whole truth in such a condition.

Justice, obviously, does not mean to give every one his or her due. You do not give back a gun to its owner when he or she is in a state of rage.

Nor does justice mean to tell the truth all the time, because truth can be quite harmful to some people at times (as when someone prone to heart attacks is brusquely told that a dear relative or friend has died). Justice is not only a deed by itself but also the consequences of that deed. A just act, then, is a deed that has just results.

Another person at the party states that justice is obedience to the laws but laws are always made by rulers to strengthen their already strong position. Therefore, a just person, invariably, is a loser. Socrates argues against this in the following manner. Ruling is an art, like medicine or shepherding. Though they may make mistakes, doctors and shepherds use their art for the benefit of their subjects, patients or sheep. The same is true of rulers. Rulers use the art of ruling for the good of their subjects, the citizens. A ruler who does not do so is a bad ruler, as there are bad doctors and bad shepherds.

Then the dialogue turns to the issue of whether it is better to be just or unjust. Frequently the unjust are better situated than the just. "In public affairs," says one of the discussants, "when there are taxes and contributions, the just man pays more and the unjust less from an equal estate; when there are distributions the one gains nothing and the other much." Socrates stated that this may be true but it does not mean that justice, by itself, is either useless or without virtue.

Another participant gives the following example. Suppose you had two persons. The first was renown in the community for being extremely just, but was in actuality a crook. The other was renown for being a very unjust person, but in reality was very just. Who would be better off? Socrates agrees that the first person would have greater material wellbeing than the second. However, the second, would have much greater mental well being; he or she can sleep nights soundly without a troubled conscience or worry about being discovered. For Socrates, injustice is a mental disease.

FOCUS — ANALOGIES

Socrates is comparing a society to a living being, in this case a person. To look at something as if it were something else is an **analogy**. To see a table in terms of a chair is an analogy. By describing the table as something to sit on, a new perspective of the table has been developed, a perspective that is usually not associated with table. Analogies are models that show aspects of what is being looked at in perspectives and relationships with which they are not usually associated. Care, however, must be taken not to confuse the analogy with the real nature of what is being examined. Even though a table may be used as a chair, the table is not a chair.

Two types of analogies have been used to explain society — the organic analogy and the mechanistic analogy. The **organic analogy** looks at something that is not alive as if it were a living thing, an organism. The **mechanistic analogy** looks at something as if it were a machine.

An organism is born, matures or develops, and dies. The question of why it is born is irrelevant. A society is frequently seen as going through these stages of developing or maturing, then becoming more developed or mature, and sometimes degenerating or dying. Third World countries are developing societies. The United States is a developed country. The American Indian societies are said to be dying. An organism has organs that are not of equal importance but are all interrelated, making the whole organism capable of being alive. When one organ is infected or diseased, all can become so. Society also has its "organs." The government, universities, and the press have been called the brains of a society, the religious institutions its heart, and the military its muscle. Blood keeps the organs alive as it circulates throughout the body. Money maintains the vitality of institutions as it "circulates" throughout society. Organs and the body become diseased and need to be cured, sometimes by operations. Institutions, groups of people, and society need to be cured too. Inflation is cured by the "bitter medicine" of unemployment. Groups are "quaran-tined," put in camps and re-educated, for example, so they can be made healthy; heads of labor unions are "surgically removed" to get rid of the union's "infection." And certain groups or institutions are labeled the "cancer" of society (e.g., drug pushers).

According to the mechanistic analogy, it is important to understand why the machine (or society) was created. What is its purpose? A machine also needs a creator. Who created society and for what purpose? An American would say that his or her society was created by God to bring freedom and democracy to the world. In the past the clock was the typical machine; today it is the computer. A machine is made of parts, each as important as the others but each apart from the others. It is a system. These parts all interact to make the machine, or system, do what it is supposed to do in the most efficient manner possible. Each part is evaluated in terms of how much energy it consumes in relation to how much it produces. Social institutions, according to this analogy, would be measured in terms of their efficiency. Just like parts could be taken out and altered to increase their output, so could institutions. A new part could be devised to replace several others; so, too, institutions can be created or revamped and old ones destroyed.

Analogies are useful because they explain relationships that otherwise might not be noticed. However, it is important to note that society is not a machine or system; nor is it an organism. Society is society, a unique entity that developed to promote the welfare of the individuals that compose it.

None of this, however, defines justice or the just person. Socrates states that, since the just person may be too small an entity to investigate, perhaps justice can be found in something that is like a person but much larger — the republic. This is precisely what Socrates commences to do, build the just republic.

The Just Republic

Socrates asks what is necessary to build a just society. He says that shoemakers are necessary. Everybody agrees that, yes, shoemakers are needed to make and fix shoes. He then says that dentists are needed. Of course, everybody agrees that dentists are needed to fix teeth. He then asks why would you not want the dentist to fix shoes and the shoemaker to fix teeth. The obvious answer is that the one does not know the art of the other. What do we mean by "know"? The shoemaker has **expertise,** which is the knowledge of leather (what can and cannot be done with it) and the skill to apply that knowledge. The same holds true for the dentist and knowledge of teeth.

The relationship between the shoemaker and shoes and between the dentist and teeth is referred to today as an "objective" relationship, one governed by man's rational capabilities. No emotion or irrationality is involved when one applies one's expertise to a given task. The shoemaker does not say to the piece of leather he is cutting up, "You poor thing, how it must hurt when I cut you. It really hurts me more than it does you." The dentist also shows no emotion regarding the teeth that are drilled or pulled.

Besides shoemakers and dentists, other workers in the crafts and trades and in farming will people society. These **citizens** are all hard-working people doing the best they can to satisfy their desires. According to the conversationalists at the party, a polis needs more. It needs road builders, garbage collectors, artists, musicians, poets, philosophers, writers, scientists, teachers, etc. A polis, then, is more than just many persons each earning a living by exercising his or her craft or trade. A polis is a community that uses and generates culture in its broadest sense; a community whose members establish and maintain relations that will provide for the community's continuance and their enrichment. A polis also must have a government to make laws.

If shoemakers fix shoes and dentists fix teeth, who will make the laws? Is not lawmaking an art like shoe making and dentistry, but ever more important for the welfare of society? If so, then there must be individuals who possess the expertise to make laws. If the shoemaker's relationship to shoes is one of objectivity, then the lawmaker's relationship to laws must be objective also. Whereas shoemakers or dentists need not be objective when dealing with things other than shoes or teeth, lawmakers must be objective in all matters because they make laws for everyone and may be called upon to make them at any time.

Objectivity means being knowledgeable and rational. Therefore, the republic needs a group of people who are always completely rational. They are called the **guardians.** These guardians are in charge of the laws.

Remember the notion of universality? In this situation it implies that one guardian's law must coincide with another guardian's law regarding the same subject. Therefore, this republic needs only one lawmaker, called the **philosopher-king**. He is the 100% rational lawmaker in this just society.

Notice, despite this being written about 2,400 years ago, we are discussing virtually the same issue: Do we want government by computer? Computers are "100% rational" and they do make decisions for us. They are not swayed by our appeals for mercy, or forgiveness, or love or any other "irrational" input. A University's or the Internal Revenue Service's computers are emotionless. But, do they know us! (Better than we do ourselves.)

Besides the lawmaker and the citizens, Socrates says two more groups are needed for the republic. Lawmakers make laws, but they do not necessarily **implement,** or carry out the laws or defend the city. Those who become the policy implementors and those who defend the city are not supposed to be rational. In fact, they are not to ask how or why but to do and die. They are the loyal, trusting, and spirited individuals who carry out their missions without complaints. Socrates calls these people the **auxiliaries**.

Since the guardians, including the philosopher-king, and the auxiliaries are "on-call" all the time, they cannot become distracted from remaining completely rational or spirited. Since most distractions emanate from problems caused by property or family, both are abolished in the republic. All property is held in common and, in true communal fashion, each person contributes according to his or her ability and each receives according to his or her needs.

Men and women live in segregated housing and are allowed to conjugate only during special holidays. Babies stay with their mothers until they are weaned and then are taken to institutions and raised there. (This actually happened in the early period of the kibbutz in Israel. Several reliable studies were conducted on the life styles, personality, and interrelationships of the people raised there.) At a very young age children are tested and placed into one of three tracks: rational, spirited, or desirous (citizens belong to the latter group). Special education for those in each track is provided, with continuous testing. Men and women are treated and educated equally.

Actually this tracking is not unlike what occurs today in many countries. In Japan, for example, toddlers who do not test well do not get into the right nursery school or kindergarten. If they do not get into the right kindergarten, they cannot go to the right primary school. If they do not get into the right primary school they cannot get into the right secondary school. If they do not get into the right secondary school, they cannot go to the right university. And if they do not go to the right university, they cannot get the right executive job that they need to become "somebody" in their society. To a lesser extent this also occurs in the United Kingdom and other European countries. In the United States tracking usually takes place at the ninth grade, when students decide whether to pursue the general, vocational, or college track. In some large cities they can attend magnet schools that specialize in preparing students for particular careers.

Thus, Socrates planned for a communal society composed of three classes — rational guardians, spirited auxiliaries, and desirous citizens. This is the just republic.

Someone asked Socrates how this republic can be brought into existence, and Socrates answered, "The philosophers must become kings in our cities, or those who are now called kings and potentates must learn to seek wisdom like true and genuine philosophers, and so political power and intellectual wisdom will be joined in one." This imaginary republic becomes reality only when kings become philosophers or philosophers become kings.

Another problem is apparent. How do you keep this republic from changing? The "justness" of this republic depends on the existence of three classes, each doing its appointed tasks. How do you prevent change and maintain stability? Socrates invents what has been called the **Socratic white lie**. He says that the following is what you must teach your children and their descendants as if it were the truth:

One day the gods on Olympus decided that the earth needed to be populated. So they placed seeds into the ground. On the first day they allowed the seeds to sprout and out came **children of gold** who possessed the ability to reason. On the second day the seeds again were allowed to sprout and out came **children of silver** who were spirited. On the third day the seeds sprouted and out came **children of brass or bronze** who were the desirous ones. After the latter sprouted, there were no more seeds. The children of these children possess one, and only one, of these characteristics. Therefore, everyone is either a child of gold, of silver, or of brass or bronze. There is no escaping what the gods have decided, so we must all act like and be satisfied with our nature.

Today we might think that this is a crude and perhaps silly myth that no one would believe. True enough; we do not believe in these old myths. But we do believe in some myths. No state could exist today if the myths underpinning its institutions and processes were not believed. We believe in consent of the governed — that our government is by and of the people. Yet in the United States, the governed have seldom consented to anything: not to the Constitution (a few men in Philadelphia and a few others in each state capital brought that about), not to the governors (less than 30 percent of the voters elect them), not to the laws (a few hundred legislators and judges are involved in the process of making and interpreting them). We believe our societies to be the home of the free, yet hundreds of thousands are forced to live in the streets and many more do not know how to exercise any freedom because they cannot read or write. We believe that anyone can run for office, yet we know that campaigning has become so expensive that for the most part only the rich can undertake it. Nevertheless, we maintain these beliefs if for no other reason than their alternatives are worse.

Of course, there is no rational reason I should obey laws made hundreds of years ago by people whose values and aspirations were much different from mine. However, I cannot make laws, not because I am not able, but because I do not have the time. I have to earn my keep and take care of my family. So instead of my arguing with others about what the laws ought to be, I just go along with the ones already made. This is easier and much less time consuming. Also, this attitude prevents society from falling apart as groups begin to bicker and even fight among themselves.

How else does one explain the case of the United Kingdom where there are two distinct classes in society — the nobility and the commoners? Each knows where it belongs and does not try to involve itself in the business of the other. Yet the only reason this division exists is that it has continued for hundreds of years. Originally, the British may have believed that God created this division; today, they believe that what time has created no one shall put asunder. So they continue with their quaint but unified society composed of two classes determined by birth.

One difference, however, between the British republic and Socrates' republic is that in the latter a person's class is determined by competence or ability (children born of the citizens, for example, may be placed in any of the three categories), whereas in Great Britain class is determined by birth (children of commoners never can become nobility).

Socrates believed that the republic is a whole that exists irrespective of the members that compose it. The individuals are unimportant. The republic is just; and it being so is not based on whether the individuals in it are just.

Justice and the Just Man

This then is *The Republic.* You may ask, "Oh! What happened to justice and the just man?" Well, this is what Socrates had to say about justice:

> Justice is that very thing, I think, or some form of it which we laid down at first when we were founding the city, as necessary conduct in everything from beginning to end. And what we did lay down and often repeated, if you remember, was that each one must practice that one thing, of all in the city, for which his nature was best fitted. . . . Further, that to do one's business and not to meddle with many businesses is justice. . . .

This brings us back to the shoemaker and the dentist and how one could not do the other's work. This is justice; each person does his or her appointed task. The republic is just because the rational guardians make the law, the spirited auxiliaries carry it out, and the desirous citizens maintain society's well-being by making and trading goods.

Then who is the just person? If society is but a larger form of man, then man must be a small duplicate of the just republic. Therefore, the just person is one who uses reason to make decisions, is spirited in carrying them out, and keeps his or her desires under control.

> He must not have allowed any part of himself to do the business of other parts, nor the parts in his soul to meddle in many businesses with each other; but he must have managed his own will, and himself have ruled himself, and set all in order, and become a friend to himself. He must have put all three parts in tune within him, highest and lowest and middle, exactly like the three chief notes of a scale, and any other intervals between that there may be; he must have bound all these together and made himself completely one out of many, temperate and con-

cordant; and then only do whatever he does, getting of wealth, or care of the body, or even matters of state or private contract.

The three qualities of the just person — reason, spirit, and desire — each have a specific task within a person. One quality does not do what the others do. When each is allowed to do its proper task, all are in *harmony* with each other and the person is at peace with himself or herself. Therefore, the Socratic notion of justice has been called the "harmonious" theory of justice.

Critique

Now that we have examined the just republic contained in *The Republic* and explained what Socrates had meant by all this, we can see that some of his notions may be wrong.

First, should what is rational to me always be rational to you? Two plus two equals four to me, you, and everybody else. We can agree with this because we base mathematics on a specific theory of numbers predicated on ten. A theory based on twelve or two, for example, would not produce the same result. Reason, however, is method more dependent on premises, which may not be shared by everyone. Two computers may not produce the same output when given the same input. Each computer's output is not only dependent on the hardware but also on the software, the programs. The same can be said about rational decisions. Rational decisions are decisions based on known values, knowledge, and logic. Even if we all shared the same knowledge and forms of logic, we still may not agree on values. It is our values which make each of us unique.

Second, Plato's student Aristotle made a profound comment regarding the republic, "Only the wearer of the shoe knows if it pinches." What he meant by this was that the shoemaker may apply expertise in making a pair of shoes for me and consider them the epitome of perfection. Yet when I put them on, they pinch. He says that this is impossible; yet I insist that they do pinch. Maybe I do not like them and I am only making an excuse, or maybe I am a hypochondriac. To me it makes no difference, they pinch. The philosopher-king can make the best or most perfect laws; yet I may not like them and think that they are wrong. After all, being a citizen in the king's republic, I am governed by desire. How can I communicate my desires to a person who only understands reason? And how can I understand the rationality of the philosopher-king?

Third, a devastating argument was made by the Roman Cicero. He asked, "Who guards the guardians?" How does one know for certain that the guardians, including the philosopher-king, do not overstep their boundaries and start making policies based on their own desires? This is a problem that has been with us since the beginning of government. How does one keep the governors, or guardians, honest and rational? What happens if the philosopher-king falls on his head and becomes irrational? Who can know?

Finally, is the republic really a human community? Can we exist without family ties? Is not the family the most important social unit in our lives, at least until we leave home?

Socrates' republic is a model for us of a good and perhaps just government. Rational decision makers and spirited policy implementors would make any society very efficient. But at what risks? And at what price?

Aristotle

So much for Socrates. Plato, after Socrates's death, started something new. Instead of gathering students at a street corner, as Socrates and others had done, Plato took them to a building on one of the hills in Athens and sat them on benches. This was the beginning of our modern school system. The hill on which the building stood was Mount Academicus. Plato wrote two works, *The Laws* and *The Statesman*.

Aristotle (384-322 B.C.E.) attended Plato's academy and, when older, was the tutor for Alexander the Great. At the time he lived, Athenian democracy had ended. When he died, the poleis were gone because they had all become part of the Greek Empire under Alexander.

Aristotle and Plato walk together at the School of Athens discussing philosophy as a group of students look on. Painting by Raphael, 1483-1520.

Development of the Polis

In *The Politics*, one of Aristotle's major works, the relationship between politics and ethics is examined. It begins by tracing the development of the polis. Aristotle says that the family came first.

> First of all, there must necessarily be a union or pairing of those who cannot exist without one another. Male and female must unite for the reproduction of the species — not from deliberate intention, but from the natural impulse, which exists in animals generally as it also exists in plants, to leave behind them something of the same nature as themselves. . . . The first form of association naturally instituted for the satisfaction of daily recurrent needs is thus the family.[2]

Notice that Aristotle contemplates a natural development; a development as it may have truly been as opposed to one as it should have been. Socrates, as you remember, creates his republic from his imagination. After the family, writes Aristotle, comes the village.

> The next form of association — which is also the first to be formed from more households than one, and for the satisfaction of something more than daily recurrent needs — is the village. The most natural form of the village appears to be that of a colony or offshoot from a family; and some have thus called the members of the village by the name of 'sucklings of the same milk', or again, of 'sons and the sons of sons'. . . . This, it may be noted, is the reason why each Greek polis was originally ruled — as the peoples of the barbarian world still are by kings. They were formed of persons who were already monarchically governed [i.e., they were formed from households and villages, and] households are always monarchically governed by the eldest of the kin, just as villages, when they are offshoots from the household, are similarly governed in virtue of the kinship between their members.

The village is a conglomeration of households whose heads are related to each other. It is a large extended family, where the oldest male member, or patriarch, decides the family's affairs.

Just as the village naturally developed from the family, so the polis grew from the village.

> When we come to the final and perfect association, formed from a number of villages, we have already reached the polis — an association which may be said to have reached the height of full self-sufficiency; or rather [to speak more exactly] we may say that while it *grows* for the sake of mere life [and is so far, and at that stage, still short of full self-sufficiency], it *exists* [when once it is fully grown] for the sake of good life [and is therefore fully self-sufficient].

Ethics

The polis is a confederation of extended families. There relations are no longer based on "blood", (i.e., on relatedness) but on something that only humans are capable of — **ethics**. Aristotle defines ethics as the proper and customary behavior that can be rationally determined, and says "it is the peculiarity of man, in comparison with the rest of the animal world, that he alone possesses a perception of good and evil, of the just and the unjust." Ethics does not play a role among friends and relatives; consequently, it does not apply in the family or village. But in the polis, where relations are principally among strangers and are impersonal in nature, ethics becomes the determining factor in those relations.

Many persons today come from towns or villages that do not number more than a few thousand inhabitants. Everybody knew everybody else and many were related. When something happened to one of them, everyone else knew about it within a few minutes. Relations were all personal. The dos and don'ts of the community were well known by everyone. When someone did something he or she should not have, family, friends, or minister were brought in to straighten out the matter. Usually, the police or sheriff were used only when all the others failed. The town or village was indeed a "family."

The polis, however, was a different way of organizing society. Although the village developed first chronologically, "the polis is prior in the order of nature to the family and individual" because only within the polis do humans become truly human. According to Aristotle, humans share friendship and relatedness with other animals. And friendship and relatedness determined the relations in the village and family.

But only in the polis do humans' "perception of good and evil, of the just and the unjust" direct their relations; only in the polis do persons use their ability to reason to develop norms of behavior. Ethics concerns behavior, not values or ideals.

Political Animals

Furthermore, Aristotle says, humans have an obligation to be active participants in the formulation of ethics in a polis. It is their participation in this endeavor through rational discussions that makes humans political. Unless they do so, they are not human.

> It is evident that the polis belongs to the class of things that exist by nature, and that man is by nature an animal intended to live in a polis. He who is without a polis, by reason of his own nature and not of some accident, is either a poor sort of being, or a being higher than man. . . . The man who is isolated — who is unable to share in the benefits of political association, or has no need to share because he is already self-sufficient — is no part of the polis, and must therefore be either a beast

or a god. . . . Man, when perfected, is the best of animals; but if he be isolated from law and justice he is the worst of all. . . . Justice belongs to the polis; for justice, which is the determination of what is just, is an ordering of the political association.

Humans are by nature political animals. Political activity, such as formulation of ethics, differentiates humans from all other beings. And, according to Aristotle, the study of politics, or how ethics in a community are derived, is the "master science."

When people rationally determine the ethics of a polis, the result has been called the **golden mean.** Aristotle never used the term, but others have attributed it to him and defined it as the ethics reached by consensus in a political community. This implies that ethics in each polis or community differs.

Note that Aristotle is writing about ethics and society, not about the ethics or morality of the individual. As long as an individual participates in the politics of the community and follows its ethics, his or her actions are unimportant.

FOCUS   ABSOLUTE AND RELATIVE MORALITY

Aristotle says that each polis forms its own ethics. Socrates, on the other hand, developed one model, the just republic, and meant to apply it everywhere, anytime. The difference is that Aristotle is advocating **relative morality,** whereas Socrates is **advocating absolute morality.**

Relative morality, sometimes called situational or conditional morality, differs from place to place and in time. Models are based on certain standards derived from reality and then are applied to reality. If the model does not match the reality, *the model is changed.* Thus, no model is applicable to all situations at all times. The people in each polis, according to Aristotle, develop their own model of ethical behavior.

Absolute morality, or universal morality, is true everywhere at all times. Models also are based on certain standards, which usually are derived from deductions of certain premises that may or may not be based on reality (e.g., the word of God). The model is applied to reality. If the model does not fit reality, *reality is changed.* The just republic will be instituted, said Socrates, when philosophers become kings or kings philosophers — in other words, when reality is changed.

Some contemporary morality issues that are argued from both relative and absolute viewpoints are abortion and capital punishment. Some say that abortion is wrong in all circumstances, whereas others argue that each situation is different and that no one, including the state, can determine when abortion is wrong. In addition, some say that capital punishment is wrong no matter what the crime, while others say that it is appropriate for certain crimes.

Critique

It appears that Aristotle was more of a realist than Socrates. After all, Aristotle was an anthropologist, biologist, medical doctor, and philosopher all rolled into one. However, some authorities argue that he placed too much emphasis on rationality consciously determining the ethics of a community. Are ethics, as he defines them, consciously created by members of a polis or do they become established without people being truly aware they are creating them?

Moreover, by defining politics as the conscious participation by a person in the formulation of ethics in the community, Aristotle divorces politics from most of the people. Most people then (as now) had a hard time finding time and resource to acquire knowledge to develop ideas on what is right, as well as argue and debate them with others. Politics, became the pursuit of the leisure class (i.e., of the rich).

> You gentlemen, who teach us how to live correctly
> And how to prevent sinning and wrongful deeds,
> First you must give some grub to us,
> Then you can make speeches: that is how it all begins.
> You, who love your paunches and our courage
> Know this for once and always:
> No matter how you ever turn it or you ever twist it
> First comes the grub, then comes the ethics.
> First it must be also possible for poor people
> To cut their share from the great supply of bread.[3]

Greek Typology of Governments

Before we leave the ancient Greeks, one more idea needs to be presented. Socrates, Plato, Aristotle, and others of their time developed a categorization of governments, they systematized the various types of government of which they were acquainted into one typology, now known as the **Greek Typology of Governments.** The whole typology and each of the six governments listed were models by which to measure existing governments.

Under this system are two forms of government. The *pure form of government* is rational and exists for the good of the polis. The *impure form of government* is irrational and exists for the good of those who govern. Bearing in mind that for the ancient Greeks a good law was a rational law and a rational law was for the good of the community, the types of government were ranked according to how close they came to this ideal. The more rational the lawmaker, the higher the rank of the type of government. Each form consists of three types of government according to the number of persons who govern: one, few, or many.

The best type of government is the appointed **monarchy**: one completely rational person governing for the good of the polis (e.g., the philosopher-king).

The second best type of government is the appointed **aristocracy**: a few superior rational individuals governing for the good of the polis. The idea here is that the irrationality of one will be cancelled by the rationality of the others. However, unlike the rational monarch, an aristocracy may not completely be able to overcome the irrationality its members occasionally manifest. (In modern societies this is called the committee system. If you have served on a committee, you know that committees can spend countless hours making a decision that you alone could have made in only minutes. Committees are formed because group decisions provide rationality and objectivity that may not occur when one person making decisions acts out of self-interest.)

The worst in the pure form of government is **democracy**: which means many persons governing. But for whose best interest do the many govern? In the pure form of government the many are usually rational and govern for the good of the polis. When the many make public policy based on information, logic, and proper values, then they will also consider the customs and traditions of their community as well as its future. This is the pure form of government.

When the many, however, are irrational and govern for the good of themselves, democracy becomes the best in the *impure* form of government. In this situation the many make policies based on their passions and desires and implement them strictly for their own momentary self-interest. This is the distinction between a deliberating legislative assembly, like a town meeting or a public hearing, and a mob. The persons in one may belong to the other. As a deliberating assembly the persons create laws for the common good; as a mob the same persons act only in their impassioned self-interest and thus make decisions that result in rampage and destruction.

As you recall, the polis is defined as an idea of a total community aware of its past and striving toward a common future. This consciousness of the past and future distinguishes the pure democratic polis from the impure democratic city of the here and now. In a pure democratic polis the people are foresighted, community-oriented, and philanthropic.

In an impure democratic city of the here and now the people are more interested in themselves as individuals than in the community and are short sighted, and uncharitable. Democracy, therefore, can be rational or irrational, for the good of the polis or for the good of each of the many (here and now).

Although we do not have a democracy where everyone directly participates in the making of public policy, we do have representative legislatures. We, the people, vote for the legislators. When we vote for them, is our vote bought, that is do we vote for a candidate on the expectation that we as individuals will profit if he or she wins? Do we vote because of what we think is best for the community or what is best for ourselves? Do we vote truly knowing who or what we are voting for? In short, are we pure form democrats, in the sense of being rational and doing good for the community, when we vote? The same questions can be posed about those we elect. Do the legislators have the time, energy, resources and volition (will) to make rational decisions about issues that concern the community? Or do they fall more into the category of irrational lawmakers?

This leads to the fifth type of government, the second worst, **oligarchy** which is government by the irrational few for the good of the few. There are few governments today that are not oligarchies. A small group of people control most of the world governments. In Latin America, for example, in countries like El Salvador, Guatemala, Colombia, Honduras, Paraguay, and Peru a few families decide who will be nominated for office (and frequently who will win the office), who will be appointed to head departments, who will be promoted, and what policies will be approved. Invariably these groups profit tremendously, while the masses barely eke out a living.

In the United States, some cities and states had been dominated by political party machines controlled by a few persons. The most notorious of these was Tammany Hall of New York City where a dozen or so party leaders controlled the Democratic party and therefore the politics of that city. Other political party machines were labeled according to the person who controlled it, such as the Daly machine in Chicago or the Long machine in Louisiana. Also in the U.S. groups, called by President Eisenhower the military-industrial complex, less openly shaped many public policies by influencing Congress and certain executive departments, such as Defense, State, Commerce, and Agriculture. Virtually every president of the U.S. in the last fifty years complained about his lack of freedom in making policy because of the undue influence of pressure groups or political action committees representing the self-interest of a small segment of society.

In the worst impure form of government, **tyranny,** power is vested in a single, irrational ruler for his or her own benefit. Tyrants of the past include Nero and Caligula of Rome, Hannibal of Carthage, Ivan the Terrible of Russia, Hitler of Germany, Stalin of the Soviet Union, Duvalier of Haiti, Idi Amin of Uganda, and Ceausescu of Rumania. Today tyranny is considered a type of government that is no longer possible. The complexity of modern society prevents a single individual from controlling a government. When a powerful individual wants to run government, he or she invariably needs help from others and forms an oligarchy instead of a tyranny.

These, then, were the six types of government that the ancient Greeks systematized into their typology and ranked from best to worst: monarchy, aristocracy, pure democracy, impure democracy, oligarchy, and tyranny.

THE GREEK TYPOLOGY OF GOVERNMENTS

Government	Pure Form	Impure Form
of One	Monarchy	Tyranny
of the Few	Aristocracy	Oligarchy
of the Many	Democracy (Pure)	Democracy (Impure)

Best   Worst

These ancient Greeks also perceived that government can change from good to bad. Monarchy can easily turn into tyranny when the monarch suddenly becomes irrational. Aristocracy becomes oligarchy when the rulers decide to look after their own welfare instead of the community's. Pure democracy can become impure democracy when the people, the many, begin to act selfishly or irrationally and no longer pay attention to the polis.

Another aspect about the dynamics of this typology relates to the quality of the rulers. If a community cannot find an all rational ruler, it may turn to a few almost completely rational ones. If these cannot be found, the people may rely on their own rationality and try to govern themselves. However, rational assemblies can turn into mobs that can be quickly taken over by a few who use the many for their own advantages (this was the stage of the Greek government at the time Socrates and Plato lived). Eventually, one person emerges from the few to take over the government for his or her own profit.

The ancient Greeks did not believe that government could make a natural progression from bad to good. They believed that only violence could end tyranny so that a pure form of government could be established.

To prevent movement from good to bad government, the ancient Greeks believed that citizens needed to control their societies through the use of reason. As we have learned, reason, or rationality, is what makes societies truly human. The impure form of government, after all, is seen in other animal societies. The basic difference between a society of pigs and a society of humans is that the latter uses reason to control its welfare and future.

Therefore the ancient Greeks were concerned with the maintenance and welfare of society. These goals could be attained rationally through government and politics. Paramount to the achievement of these goals was the welfare of the polis. The individual, although recognized, was considered irrelevant. Neither Socrates, Plato, nor Aristotle would have thought of basing his theory on the welfare of the individual. Community, polis, and society made the individual a human being; without them the individual was either a beast or a god.

TERMS TO REMEMBER

polis
direct democracy
Socrates
Plato
The Dialogues
The Republic
analogy
organic analogy
mechanistic analogy
expertise
citizens
guardians
philosopher-king

auxiliaries
Socratic white lie
children of gold
children of silver
children of brass or bronze
Aristotle
The Politics
ethics
golden mean
relative morality
absolute morality
Greek typology of governments
pure form of government
impure form of government
monarchy

aristocracy
democracy
oligarchy
tyranny

📖 SUGGESTED READINGS

Aristotle. *The Politics of Aristotle.* Translated by Ernest Barker, with introduction, notes, and appendixes. Oxford: Clarendon Press, 1968.

Aristotle. *The Politics.* Translated by Carnes Lord, with introduction, notes and glossary. Chicago: University of Chicago Press, 1984.

Aristotle. *The Nicomachean Ethics.* Translated by J. E. C. Welldon. Buffalo, NY: Prometheus Books, 1987.

Jaeger, Werner. *Paideia: The Ideals of Greek Culture.* Vol. 1. Translated by Gilbert Highet. New York: Oxford University Press, 1965. A scholarly and detailed description and analysis of Hellenic society and culture, emphasizing daily life and political organization.

Plato. *Great Dialogues of Plato.* Translated by W. H. D. Rouse; edited by Eric H. Warmington and Philip G. Rouse. New York: The New American Library of World Literature, Inc., 1956.

Plato. *The Laws of Plato.* Translated by Thomas L. Pangle, with notes and interpretive essay. Chicago: University of Chicago Press, 1988.

Plato. *The Republic.* Translated by Allan D. Bloom, with notes and interpretive essay. New York: Basic Books, 1968.

Plato. *Statesman.* Translated by Joseph B. Skemp, with notes and interpretive essay. New Haven, CT: Yale University Press, 1952.

Sinclair, R. K. *Democracy and Participation in Athens.* New York: Cambridge University Press, 1988. An analysis of life and politics in Athens.

Spiro, Melford E. *Kibbutz: Venture in Utopia.* New York: Schocken Books, 1971. One of the classical studies on life within the communal farm communities established in Israel.

Stauss, Leo. *The City and Man.* Chicago: Rand McNally & Co., 1964. Three essays on Aristotle, Plato, and the Athenians by the foremost interpreter of Aristotelian political philosophy from the University of Chicago.

✒ NOTES

1. All quotes from *The Republic* are from the W.H.D. Rouse translation. (New York: Mentor Books, The New American Library of World Literature, Inc., 1956).
2. All quotes from *The Politics* are from the Ernest Barker translation. (New York and London: Oxford University Press, 1958).
3. Bertold Brecht, *Die Dreigroschenoper* (*The Three Penny Opera*), translated by J. Jacobsohn (New York: Columbia Records, 1958).

4

The Romans and the Middle Ages

W e now turn to the Romans. Actually there is not much to write about them. They were known more as doers than thinkers. Most of their artistic endeavors and writings were adaptations of Hellenic art and thought. What the Romans did contribute was a system of law, which we will discuss later, and the history of an empire.

Romans and After

Despite Romans creating an empire that lasted almost one thousand years, they did not substantially add to the Old Greek perceptions of the relationship among the individual, society, and the state. Following the later works of Plato, *The Laws* and *The Statesman,* Romans perceived the state to be not only a creation of law, but law itself. Law and state seemed equivalent.

Law, to the Romans, was a product of reason that in turn was part of human nature. Of course, they realized that some laws were bad, unjust, arbitrary. However, laws that were such were considered unnatural and irrational.

Because all men share human nature equally, law is based on the equality of men, according to the Roman view. In this the Romans were different from the Old Greeks who believed that nature created inequality and that it is through government that this inequality is overcome for the social good. Romans, on the other hand, believed law did not make everyone equal, but more so that law has had to protect and continue the equality that nature had created. In this respect, our ideas about equality before the law stem from our Roman heritage.[1]

Despite the importance given to law by the Romans, their politics were anything but orderly processes. Throughout its long history, Rome's leaders infrequently assumed office by legal means. Consuls, emperors, caesars killed their predecessors or banished them. At times the people rebelled; but even their successes were short lived. Insofar as equality,

FOCUS   WHO HAS THE RIGHT TO RULE?

The problem rulers in the Middle Ages faced is a recurrent one in the relationship between ruler and ruled. Who has the right to rule?

One answer is the person or group with the most strength. This is the "might makes right" argument. Strength, or might, may not involve only physical strength; it may include the ability to form alliances, cunning, ability to manipulate others, and other factors. No matter what the factors are, the ruler is perceived as stronger than the ruled.

Another answer is the person or group is appointed by some superior entity, usually God. In this case the ruled have no choice but to accept what has been decided for them. This is acceptable as long as the ruled believe that the superior entity

exists and has a right to do the appointing.

The third answer is whomever the ruled choose. This is usually accomplished through voting, or sometimes by choosing others to make the selection. In this scenario no one can rule unless the ruled have chosen the ruler.

These are the only possible ways for someone to become a ruler. After the fall of the Roman Empire rulership by strength of position ("might makes right") was modified to include use of divine intervention as justification for the right to rule. The ruled did not gain the right to directly choose the ruler until the middle of the nineteenth Century. Today, elections are the accepted form of determining who rules.

Rome was divided into the rich and the poor. The poor had little influence in governing, while the rich manipulated the high offices of government for their advantage. Rome and its empire was never a model of a well-governed state, although in its treatment of conquered peoples it was often humane.

Before the Roman era, societies vanquishing another population either assimilated or enslaved it. The Egyptians, Babylonians, and Greeks all forced the people they conquered to assimilate. The Romans, on the other hand, allowed defeated populations to practice their customs and keep their values, but forced them to pay tribute. Tribute was either money, tangibles (e.g., food, cloth, stone, salt), or services (e.g., road building, military, housekeeping). Consequently each province in the Roman Empire was allowed to develop its own culture.

When the Roman Empire began to disintegrate after the fourth century, two major developments occurred. First, in each of the former Roman provinces power struggles ensued about who would rule. This stage in the formation of new political societies, generally known as the **consolidation of power,** involves a conflict among the individuals or groups who want to occupy the position of policy maker and implementor. Usually the conflict was determined by those with the most military strength. Not only did a struggle for power within a society occur, but also a struggle among the societies for supremacy. Those who were governing or leading one society wanted to take over other societies as well. Thus, the potential enemies of a governor were contenders from both inside and outside the society.

Second, by the end of the sixth century the Catholic Church had become institutionalized as part of society in many former Roman provinces and was a contender for the power of policy making. The church, through its spokesman, the Pope, believed it was the deputy, or representative of God on earth. As the deputy of God, it believed it knew better than anyone God's will for the people in any given society. Since very little falls outside the purview of divine will, the Church concluded that it had a right to participate in policy making.

The Church's beliefs represented a direct challenge to the authority of the aspiring princes and kings. They had a major problem of **legitimacy** to contend. Legitimacy is the acceptance of standards by which one acquires the **authority** to rule. Authority is the rightful use of power over others. Since the people believed that God's will directed the course of all events and, thus, sought divine signs to direct their behavior, the princes and kings began to use the notion of divine intervention to justify their actions even though they used force to acquire their authority to rule. For example, if a king won a battle, he would say that God must have been smiling on him because otherwise he would not have been victorious or, if he escaped an assassination, of which there were many, God must have protected him. Soon the princes and kings believed that they also were selected by God to do his bidding on earth. Further, the princes and kings hired genealogists to trace their family ancestry back to biblical figures, especially David. In this way, too, they could claim divine lineage.

This situation had two major effects. First, it created a conflict between the Church and the state. Second, it separated the state from society.

The Two Swords Conflict

In the Middle Ages the conflict between the Church and the state was known as the **two swords conflict.** The Pope was depicted as holding two swords. In one hand he held the **spiritual sword** that represented matters relating to the soul of the individual and to matters eternal. In the other hand he supposedly held the **secular** or **temporal sword**. This sword represented the everyday affairs of individuals and the concerns of the body, such as food, clothing, shelter, and safety. The conflict involved who was to control these swords.

Princes and kings wanted to control both of them. The Pope also wanted control of both. Each of these former Roman provinces, soon to be states, resolved the matter in its own fashion. In France, for example, the king got complete possession of the secular sword and part of the spiritual sword. To this day in France, the head of state has to approve the appointment of all bishops by the Church. In Germany, the state collected the dues that all inhabitants, unless excused, had to pay to the churches. During the Reformation some states made the monarchs head of the Protestant churches. For example, in the United Kingdom the monarch is the formal head of the Anglican church (the Archbishop of Canterbury is the actual head, but the monarch appoints him). Other states, especially those that have been under Spanish or French domination, have established an official state religion in their constitutions. Other religions are tolerated, but the clergy of the established religion invoke all official functions.

In the United States the conflict of church and state was handled differently. Some writers of the Bill of Rights wanted complete liberty of religion in the union and did not want the state to be involved in anything dealing with organized religion. Others wanted the state to establish an official religion, but could not agree on which one. Both contributed to what actually was written in the First Amendment, namely, "Congress shall make no law respecting an establishment of religion, or prohibiting the free exercise thereof . . ." This principle, of course, is known to us as the separation of church and state.

This issue is still on the social agenda of the United States today is manifested by the many attempts to return prayer to public schools and the attempt to give tax relief to parents who enroll their children in parochial schools.

The State Is Not Society

During the Middle Age the rulers of Europe thought that they, in addition to the Pope, had the divine spark. In the early 1600s, James I of England coined the phrase "**the divine rights of kings**". The belief that princes and kings also had a "hotline" to God brought about the view that they were different from the rest of people in society. Therefore, they had rights that others did not possess. They were **sovereign**; they could read, speak, or write anything, whereas other members of society could do only what the state or church allowed.

Another right these monarchs possessed was that they did not have to obey the laws they made for the rest of society. A king or queen who does not have to obey his or her own law is said to have **absolute power**. There is no greater power than to have the authority to make others do what you do not have to do.

The "absolute" monarchs, therefore, separated the state from society. Government institutions and the people were divorced from one another. The people became the *subjects* of the monarchs; citizens ceased to exist. "*L'etat c'est moi*" I am the state, Louis XIV of France supposedly said. With this separation came the preeminence of the state as the organizational mechanism for an ever growing society.

Since absolute monarchs were needed to govern society, everyone believed that society could not govern itself. In fact, the idea of a self-governing society became inconceivable. Societies needed an "outside" government to ensure their viability. Societies were thought to be imperfect, needing the state to make up for their shortcomings. People believed that the harsher the government, the more imperfect the society under it.

The framers of the new government of the United States, believed that government should be weak because God chose American society to lead the world in liberty. (Remember the mechanistic analogy?) The more perfect American society was, the less government it needed. "That government is best, which governs the least," Thomas Paine supposedly stated. He also wrote, "Society in every state is a blessing, but government, even in its best state, is but a necessary evil; in its worst state, an intolerable one" (*Common Sense*, 1776).

The idea that government can be "evil" could not be harmonized with the notion that government and society are basically two faces of the same coin; if government is evil, then society also must be evil. Government could be considered evil and society good only when government and society were not the same. Like Paine, the Founding Fathers did not accept the idea that society and the state were one. They believed that American society was good and, consequently, needed only a weak ("evil") government.

Power and Corruption

Another legacy of absolute monarchy is the idea that "power tends to corrupt and absolute power corrupts absolutely." This quotation (from Lord John Acton of England) expresses a belief that has become almost enshrined in Western political thought. Most persons do not want to give power to any individual, fearing that the power will be abused. Abuse of power, indeed, has happened occasionally, but there are thousands of powerful authorities who do not abuse their power.

Power is a means, a tool, with which its possessor can do good or bad. The ancient Greeks believed that a person of reason, who knew what was good, would never abuse power and that the irrational person should never be given power.

An effect of this fear of power is that many people have become afraid to allot power to those institutions or individuals that need to carry out the task of providing for the general welfare of society. In the U.S., for example, the federal system, the system of separation of powers and checks and balances, and suspicion of politicians all prevent the rapid and efficient formulation and implementation of policies. Because of this diffusion of power, responsibility for misguided or simply bad policies cannot be pinpointed. Who is to blame for the savings and loan associations and bank scandals and those of the department or ministry of housing and/or urban development?

Absolute monarchs, however, were no more corrupt (or unethical) than those whose powers were more limited. On the contrary, a case can be made that those who view their power as too limited for their goals may, through corruption, try to increase it. The individuals who are sufficiently powerful to accomplish their tasks do not need to be unethical. Those whose power is sufficient to accomplish their goals may attempt to apply even more stringent ethical constraints upon themselves. ". . . [T]he Action assertion that 'power tends to corrupt . . .' is a gross oversimplification of the facts, since power also ennobles; and powerlessness also corrupts and ennobles . . ."[2]

Absolute power did not guarantee a ruler's safety. Many monarchs and princes in the Middle Ages died prematurely of unnatural causes. The deadly political struggles of the British nobility are well chronicled in Shakespeare's plays. The rivalry and conflicts among them were life-and-death encounters, not just game playing. (In Canada, the United States, and most European states today, politics is not a life or death matter. No politician in these states has been assassinated by someone who wanted to take his or her position. One reason for this is that elections determine the winner.) Furthermore, more than a thousand independent political entities existed in Europe during the late Middle Ages. Most cities of 30,000 to 75,000 inhabitants and countries, like France and England had the beginnings of modern states, but smaller entities, such as Liechtenstein, Andorra, and Monaco, were constantly engaged in making and breaking alliances and confederations. Rulers had to be constantly on guard to prevent their "kingdoms" from being gobbled up or their own lives from being cut short.

Niccolo Machiavelli

Machiavelli

The relationship between power and politics changed significantly during the Renaissance with the writings of **Niccolo Machiavelli** (1469-1527). The son of a lawyer whose family had long lived in Florence, Italy, Machiavelli received a liberal arts education reflecting the intellectual fervor typical of the Renaissance.

One important characteristic of this period was the discovery of *man*. During the Middle Ages the whole (i.e., society, the church, or the group to which one belonged as worker or professional) was emphasized and the individual was but a mere part. During the Renaissance the focus was on the individual, who became the center of the universe. Although considered the equivalent of an atom when compared to society, man became the subject of art and intellectual activity. Thus, the Renaissance is said to have atomized the universe.

Leonardo da Vinci, the archetypical "Renaissance man" and a contemporary of Machiavelli also from Florence, sought to define the ideal prototype of the universal man through science, engineering, art, philosophy, and literature. Michelangelo, another Florentine, did the same through artistic endeavors, of which his statue of David remains the model of "perfect" man.

This emphasis on man began with lessening influence of the Church. Between the end of the fourteenth century and the middle of the fifteenth century, the Church was beset with so much internal turmoil and corruption that people no longer viewed it as the sole proponent of values and beliefs for society. After the 1400s, the Church would never again fulfill the central role within European society.

The Church also lost its virtual monopoly on the discovery and distribution of knowledge. Until the Renaissance much of the available knowledge was recorded in writing by monks or by clergy in their free time. Those who wanted that knowledge had no choice but to depend on the Church for it. That changed dramatically with the invention of the printing press by Johannes Gutenberg in the mid-1400s. Written material was not only more available and less expensive but also could no longer be censored by the Church. This made it possible for anyone who had something to say to have the material printed and circulated to a wide audience.

For fourteen years Machiavelli was employed by the city of Florence in a midlevel management position that allowed him to travel as a diplomat and negotiate agreements with other Italian city-states and states such as France and Prussia. At this time Florence was a republic. In 1512 he lost his job when an absolute ruler, Lorenzo de Medici, took over the city government. Machiavelli was imprisoned, tortured, and banished to a farm outside Florence.

In the sixteenth century, the Italian peninsula was divided into several

Johannes Gutenberg's invention of the printing press in the mid-1400s led to the mass production of written material and the spread of democratic ideas.

distinct republics, kingdoms, duchies, and papal states. They frequently fought among themselves, sometimes influenced to do so by the Austrians, English, French, Spanish, or the Church. Machiavelli began looking for a job and, to make a good impression on a possible employer, a prince, he wrote a long letter outlining his thoughts on the desirability of uniting the Italians and how this might be accomplished. In that letter, which is now called *The Prince*, he also wrote about the relationship between ruler and ruled and gave a new definition of politics.

There is a difference between what is and what ought to be, Machiavelli asserts. And a ruler must always remember this difference.

> . . . for how we live is so far removed from how we ought to live, that he who abandons what is done for what ought to be done, will rather learn to bring about his own ruin than his preservation. A man who wishes to make a profession of

goodness in everything must necessarily come to grief among so many who are not good. Therefore it is necessary for a prince, who wishes to maintain himself, to learn how not to be good, and use this knowledge and not use it, according to the necessity of the case.[3]

Man, Machiavelli seems to say, is basically evil. Although some are good, most men are not. Since a ruler must deal with the many, he or she must be able to use the means that these many use, namely evil. He continues, ". . . for if one considers well, it will be found that some things which seem virtues would, if followed, lead to one's ruin, and some others which appear vices result in one's greater security and wellbeing."

Politics, Machiavelli wrote, is the pursuit of power. Power is the goal of all political activity. For its acquisition and maintenance everything is but an expedient. Morality, ethics, good deeds, and mercy are all means to the end, which is power. If a ruler has to rob or kill to stay in power, that is acceptable. If he or she has to be nice and kiss babies, that is all right too. A ruler can pardon a murderer or hang the thief who stole a loaf of bread if that will maintain his power. To acquire and maintain power, a person can use what is today called selective terror. By causing pain and death to randomly chosen members of society, a ruler instills fear among them. A fearful population is a docile or passive one that can be easily ruled.

> A prince, therefore, must not mind incurring the charge of cruelty for the purpose of keeping his subjects united and faithful; for, with a very few examples, he will be more merciful than those who, from excess of tenderness, allow disorders to arise, from whence spring bloodshed and rapine, for these as a rule injure the whole community, while the executions carried out by the prince injure only individuals.

When forced to decide whether being feared is better than being loved, Machiavelli suggests that the prince choose the former.

> . . . [I]t is much safer to be feared than loved. . . . For it may be said of men in general that they are ungrateful, voluble, dissemblers, anxious to avoid danger, and covetous of gain; as long as you benefit them, they are entirely yours; they offer you their blood, their goods, their life, and their children, as I have before said, when the necessity is remote; but when it approaches, they revolt. And the prince who has relied solely on their words, without making other preparations, is ruined; for the friendship which is gained by purchase and not through grandeur and nobility of spirit is bought but not secured, and at a pinch is not expended in your service. And men have less scruple in offending one who

makes himself loved than one who makes himself feared; for love is held by a chain of obligations which, men being selfish, is broken whenever it serves their purpose; but fear is maintained by a dread of punishment which never fails.

Furthermore, Machiavelli had an appreciation for public relations. He states that the image that the ruler portrays is more important than what he does.

> . . . men are so simple and so ready to obey present necessities, that one who deceives will always find those who allow themselves to be deceived. . . . Thus it is well to seem merciful, faithful, humane, sincere, religious, and also be so; but you must have the mind so disposed that when it is needful to be otherwise you may be able to change to the opposite qualities. . . . A prince must take care that nothing goes out of his mouth which is not full of the above-named five qualities, and, to see and hear him, he should seem to be all mercy, faith, integrity, humanity, and religion. And nothing is more necessary than to seem to have this last quality, for men in general judge more by the eyes than by the hands, for every one can see, but very few have to feel. Everybody sees what you appear to be, few feel what you are, . . . and in the actions of men, and especially of princes from which there is no appeal, the end justifies the means.

Machiavelli was one of the first to posit the notion that man by nature is evil. He did not base this idea on a religious axiom but on experiences and history. His experiences and reading of history, however, have been criticized for being too one sided. He did not take into account the millions of persons who, even in his time, had done acts of kindness and the many rulers who were genuinely sincere in doing good for others and did not use ruthless and deceptive methods to acquire and maintain power.

Numerous persons who suffered much more than Machiavelli did not condemn humanity for its evilness. A fifteen-year-old girl, Anne Frank, hiding in an attic in Amsterdam in 1945 and terrified of what would happen to her if she were found by the Nazis, wrote in her diary:

> It's really a wonder that I haven't dropped all my ideals, because they seem so absurd and impossible to carry out. Yet I keep them, because in spite of everything I still believe that people are really good at heart. I simply can't build up my hopes on a foundation consisting of confusion, misery, and death. I see the world gradually being turned into a wilderness, I hear the ever approaching thunder, which will destroy us too, I can feel the sufferings of millions and yet, if I look up into the heavens, I think that it will all come right, that this cruelty too will end, and that peace and tranquility will return again.[4]

There may be more truth about human nature in this short statement than in what *The Prince* has to offer.

Machiavelli's measure of politics is the individual. There is little in his writings that deals with what is good for society. The prince, the ruler, the welfare of the individual is the standard by which everything is judged. He implies that the individual who can manipulate, cheat, and oppress others for his or her own benefit is a better individual than the rest. Also, the rest exist for the welfare of that individual. Society becomes the means for personal aggrandizement.

The idea that anything is acceptable in securing and holding political office is as disturbing today as it must have been during Machiavelli's time. In the summer of 1989 we looked with horror at the Chinese government mowing down hundreds of protesters in Tiananmen Square. On May 21, 1990, the *Pittsburgh Post-Gazette* carried a story about the execution in 1965 by the government of Indonesia of hundreds of thousands of opponents (mostly members of the Communist Party), many on lists supplied by the Central Intelligence Agency of the United States.

Recent history is full of names of rulers who have used their power to terrorize their societies for the purpose of increasing their own wealth. Saddam Hussein of Iraq, Ayatollah Khomeini of Iran, Idi Amin of Uganda,

Students from Peking's Nationalities Institute mourn the death of communist party leader Hu Yaobang. Thousands of people participated in the demonstration in Tiananmen Square seeking democracy and freedom.

the Duvaliers of Haiti, and the Somozas of Nicaragua are just a few of this type of ruler who fostered the image of a "good" man while actually impoverishing their societies. Yet, an overwhelming number of rulers have abided by the norms defining their offices. They have not abused their powers, nor enriched themselves through them.

During the last few years, negative campaigning, criticizing an opponent through innuendo and half-truths, has become commonplace. In addition, some candidates receive from special interest groups large donations that are illegal and therefore not reported. Frequently politicians who are convicted for illegal activities are criticized for being caught rather than for engaging in the illegal act.

Machiavelli's philosophy also influenced the business, or economic, sector. Wealth became an end for which everything else became a means. Today insider stock trading, embezzlement in savings and loan banks, and kickbacks on the sale of goods and services are in the news because people have tried to get rich by any means. Avarice, greed, dishonesty have become inshrined in the temple of economic success at any costs. For those within the temple, society can be damned.

An attempt is being made in colleges and universities to ameliorate the Machiavellian pursuit of power or wealth by increasing the level of "social consciousness" among those who will be engaged in politics or business. The argument is that unless our society remains viable, their power or wealth will become useless or irrelevant. According to this theory power and wealth cannot be end pursuits but the means of enriching the lives of all members of the community, unless we all gain, no one, no matter how powerful or wealthy, will gain.

TERMS TO REMEMBER

consolidation of power
legitimacy
authority
two swords conflict
spiritual sword
secular or temporal sword
divine right of kings
sovereign
absolute power
Niccolo Machiavelli
The Prince

SUGGESTED READINGS

Brucker, Gene A. *Renaissance Florence.* 1969 ed. Berkeley: University of California Press, 1983. An introduction to the social life, religion, politics, and commerce of Florence in the late 1300s and early 1400s.

Elias, Norbert. *The History of Manners* (The Civilizing Process: Vol. 1). New York: Pantheon Books, 1978. Customs and patterns of behavior in every day life during the feudal epoch. Written in the 1930s.

Elias, Norbert. *Power and Civility* (The Civilizing Process: Vol. 2). New York: Pantheon Books, 1982. Feudalization was a process and has remained imbedded in Western Civilization.

Frank, Anne. *Anne Frank: The Diary of a Young Girl.* Translated by B.M. Mooyart — Doubleday. New York: Pocket Books, Inc., 1958.

Hale, John R., J.R.L. Highgield and B. Smalley, eds. *Europe in the Late Middle Ages.* Evanston, IL: Northwestern University Press, 1965. Essays which primarily deal with the politics in France, Germany, Italy, Netherlands, and Spain in the XIII through XVI centuries.

Huizinga, Johan. *The Waning of the Middle Ages: A Study of the Forms of Life, Thought and Art in France and the Netherlands in the Fourteenth and Fifteenth Centuries.* 1924 ed. F. Hopman, trans. New York: St. Martin's, 1985. A classical analysis of chivalry and religious thought.

Machiavelli, Niccolo. *Chief Works, and Others.* Translated by Allan Gilbert. Durham, NC: Duke University Press, 1965.

Machiavelli, Niccolo. *Machiavelli: The Prince.* Edited by Quentin Skinner and Russell Price. Cambridge; New York: Cambridge University Press, 1988.

Machiavelli, Niccolo. *The Prince.* Translated by Luigi Ricci. New York: New American Library, 1952.

Morrall, John B. *Political Thought in Midieval Times.* 1958 ed. Toronto: University of Toronto Press, 1980. Good general introduction to the philosophies of several prominent midieval thinkers.

Morris, Colin. *The Papal Monarchy: The Western Church from 1050 to 1250.* New York: Oxford University Press, 1989. History of the Western church covering many topics including growth of the papal monarchy and church-state relations.

Ridolfi, Rokberto. *The Life of Niccolo Machiavelli.* Cecel Grayson, trans. Chicago: University of Chicago Press, 1963. Machiavelli is depicted as a likeable human being in sharp contrast to the philosophy he advocated.

Rogow, Arnold and Harold D. Lasswell. *Power, Corruption, and Rectitude.* Englewood Cliffs, NJ: Prentice Hall, 1963. An examination of power and corruption in the administration of several U.S. leaders.

Schmitt, Charles B., et al., eds. *The Cambridge History of Renaissance Philosophy.* 1988 ed. Cambridge: Cambridge University Press, 1990. Unique compendium of essays by noted authorities on historical and philosophical topics covering the period between 1350 and 1600.

Tuchman, Barbara. *A Distant Mirror: The Calamitous 14th Century.* New York: Knopf, 1978. A best seller describing French life in the 1300s.

NOTES

1. A source for the Roman concept of law is Cicero. *De re publica, De legibus.* (translated by Clinton Walker.) Cambridge: Harvard University Press, 1928.

2. Rogow, Arnold A. and Harold Laswell. *Power, Corruption, and Rectitude,* (Englewood Cliffs, NJ: Prentice-Hall, 1963). pp. 130-31.

3. All quotations from *The Prince* are from the Luigi Ricci translation. (New York: Mentor Books, The New American Library of World Literature, Inc., 1952).

4. Frank, Anne. *Anne Frank: The Diary of a Young Girl,* translated from the Dutch by B.M. Mooyart-Doubleday (New York: Pocket Books, Inc., 1958). p233.

5

The Social Contract Theorists

⊕ Outline
- The State of Nature and the Social Contract
- Thomas Hobbes (1588-1679)
- John Locke (1632-1704)
- Jean-Jacques Rousseau (1712-1778)
- Differences Among the Three Theorists

The emphasis on the individual, as opposed to society, continued in the political writings of the social contract theorists. Up to the early 1500s, the world view of thinkers focused on the family or the group. They viewed society itself as a confederation of families or groups, leaving individuals to the margin. Groups were either the professional guilds; the social-economic segments such as serfs, peasants, burghers, nobility, and clergy; or the ethnic and religious subgroups.

The State of Nature and the Social Contract

Social contract theorists structured their political philosophies on an imaginary **state of nature**; a stage in the development of man that preceded the formation of society, in which the individual was supposedly *sovereign*. The individual, unrestricted by social norms, did whatever he wanted, which was similar to what monarchs were perceived as doing. Although a law derived intuitively from nature or through reason or experience was meant to curtail some of the more vicious predispositions in men, this did not happen. According to Thomas Hobbes, for example, men behaved worse than wild animals. Even in Jean-Jacques Rousseau's version of the state of nature, which was almost like the Biblical Garden of Eden, men in developing their passions became uncontrollable. According to the state of nature theory, the individual bonded with no one; he was an isolate, an atom whose primary mission was his own survival.

Since each man was king in the state of nature, all men were equal. Each man had not only his strong points but also weak points that cancelled the strong ones.

> Nature has made men so equall, in the faculties of body, and mind; as that though there bee found one man sometimes manifestly stronger in body, or of quicker mind than another; yet when all is reckoned together, the difference between man, and man, is not so considerable, as that one man can thereupon claim to himselfe any benefit, to which another may not pretend, as well as he. For as to the strength in body, the weakest has strength enough to kill the strongest, either by secret machination, or by confederacy with others, that are in the same danger with himselfe.[1]

One day, according to these thinkers, men in the state of nature had an inspiration and formed government and/or society. This occurred through an agreement they made with each other, or a **social contract**. Society, therefore, was composed of individuals who consciously had chosen to become part of it. It is important to note that it was the individuals who agreed, not families or groups of individuals. Since it was the individual who consented to their formation, government and society had to respond to his needs and wants. As inventions of man, society, and government were artificial (i.e., not natural) and could not exist by themselves.

Nevertheless, those who advocated the state of nature recognized that within society all men were not equal. The cause of inequality, they said, was either the individual's own misfortune or someone else's actions that prevented the individual from achieving equality. If the latter was the reason for inequality, then artificially created society was not functioning like "perfect" nature.

The state of nature theory is flawed. First, the state of nature never existed, humans as a species, no matter how far back their origins are presumed, never lived as isolates, nor could they have. Society is no less "natural" to human beings than is the idea of the individual. There is little more natural than the mother-infant bond, the base for most other bonds, and one that cannot be denied or avoided if normal individuals are to be created. Because of this bond, humans are never alone or sovereign. The mother-infant bond also produces many, perhaps most, social norms by which an individual lives. From this mother-child relationship other relationships develop, such as the individual with his or her father, siblings, aunts, uncles, or grandparents. These family relations, once they grew beyond a certain size and complexity, required organization, the kernel around which societies and governments developed.

Second, the social contract theorists (except for Rousseau) spoke only of man in the state of nature and defiantly omitted any reference to women. If they had included women, they would have had to deal with the mother-infant relationship. These theorists also did not pay much attention to children and the care they must have received from adults in this supposed presocietal stage.

Third, the presumption that one day nonsocialized individuals created government and society becomes even more preposterous when one considers that for these men to agree, they obviously needed a way of communicating with each other. Any form of communication, such as language, was developed from human relations that had to have had a long history. Consequently, groups would have existed before or at least at the time language developed.

Regardless of whether the state of nature ever existed, the notion that there is a direct link between individuals and government or society has become embedded in modern political thought. By emphasizing the individual's relation to government, these theorists ignored the development of society and governments' role in it. Since governments cannot cater to every individual in a large society, individuals become grouped together according to their economic or demographic status. Since individuals often do not think of themselves as part of such a group, they often feel separated from government and society.

This feeling of separation is inconsistent with the idea, derived from the social contract, of consent of the governed. If government needs my consent, then it ought to be concerned with me. Unfortunately, my consent is not needed for government to exist; and society and government have become too big and complex for government to be concerned with my individual predilections.

Nevertheless, thanks to the social contract thinkers, those in government, whether elected or appointed, do not derive any more benefits from government than the lowliest citizen. The social contract theory elevated the individual, making him or her equal to a monarch or ruler. Everyone is now considered equal and has the same rights, and the rulers have to obtain the approbation of the people.

Thomas Hobbes

Thomas Hobbes (1588-1679) lived through the reign of Charles I, the English civil wars, the Commonwealth and Protectorate, and the Stuart Restoration. In short, he witnessed tremendous political turmoil in England. In addition, while a young man, he was employed by a duke who was financially insecure and who had rivals for his title. Thus, security became the priority for Hobbes.

Thomas Hobbes

In the state of nature that Hobbes postulates, men are equal and can manage to live on a subsistence level. However, they are in a perpetual state of war with one another because of their need for power so they can "live well." He discusses this need for power in *Leviathan*.

> So that in the first place, I put for a generall inclination of all mankind, a perpetuall and restlesse desire of Power after power, that ceaseth onely in Death. And the cause of this, is not always that a man hopes for a more intensive delight, than he has already attained to; of that he cannot be content with a moderate power: but because he cannot assure the power and means to live well, which he hath present, without the acquisition of more.

Power is needed for security. In Hobbes' state of nature, humans cannot "live well" because it is in their nature to make war upon each other.

> Hereby it is manifest, that during the time men live without a common Power to keep them all in awe, they are in that condition which is called Warre; and such warre, as is of every man, against every man . . . So the nature of War, consisteth not in actuall fighting; but in the known disposition thereto, during all the time there is no assurance to the contrary.

What, then, is life like in this state of nature? Hobbes gives what has become a classic description of humans without government.

> Whatsoever therefore is consequent to a time of Warre, where every man is Enemy to every man; the same is consequent to the time, wherein men live without other security, than what their own strength, and their own invention shall furnish them withall. In such condition, there is no place for Industry; because the fruit thereof is uncertain: and consequently no Culture of the Earth; no Navigation, nor use of the commodities that may be imported by Sea; no commodious Building; no Instruments of moving, and removing such things as require much force; no Knowledge of the face of the Earth; no account of Time; no Arts; no Letters; no Society; and which is worst of all, continuall feare, and danger of violent death; And the life of man, solitary, poore, nasty, brutish, and short.

This is what humans are like without norms that force them into certain behavior. Life would be "solitary, poore, nasty, brutish, and short." Hobbes imagined humans to be worse than animals! Lions, tigers, and hyenas kill gazelles for "lunch," humans kill each other to "live well." This perpetual state of war is not duplicated anywhere in the real world of animals. And, though there may be individuals whose lives today are "solitary, poor, nasty, brutish, and short" (the homeless of the United States, the hungry of the Third World), the causes are not the actions of individual persons, but rather the mistaken policies of governments or the prejudices and ignorance engendered by society.

Yet we do have to recognize that there are individuals in most modern societies who live in disregard of the rules. We call these individuals criminals. Among criminals, the greatest fear is other criminals, not the police; many more criminals die at the hands of other criminals than at the hands of law enforcers. Such criminals may be said to live in the Hobbesian state of nature.

According to Hobbes, humans had to find a way out of their miserable lives. So they made a social contract, a covenant to empower "one Man, or Assembly of men" to make policies that provide security for them.

This is more than Consent, or Concord; it is a reall Unitie of them all, in one and the same Person, made Covenant of every man, in such manner, as if every man should say to every man, *I Authorise and give up my Right of Governing my selfe, to this Man, or to this Assembly of men, on this condition, that thou give up thy Right to him, and Authorise all his Actions in like manner.* This done, the multitude so united in One person, is called a COMMON-WEALTH, in latine CIVITAS. This is the generation of that great LEVIATHAN, or rather (to speak more reverently) of that *Mortall God,* to which wee owe under the *Immortall God,* our peace and defence. For by this Authoritie, given him by every particular man in the Common-Wealth, he hath the use of so much Power and Strength conferred on him, that by terror thereof, he is inabled to forme the wills of them all, to Peace at home, and mutuall ayd against their enemies abroad. And in him consisteth the Essence of the Common-Wealth; which (to define it,) is *One person, of whose Acts a great Multitude, by mutuall Covenants one with another, have made themselves every one the Author, to the end he may use the strength and means of them all, as he shall think expedient, for their Peace and Common Defence.* And he that carryeth this Person, is called Soveraigne, and said to have *Soveraigne* Power; and every one besides, his SUBJECT.

Humans transfer or renounce their individual sovereignty to a person who is *not* part of the agreement and, by doing so, lose their sovereignty to that person forever. In short, they lose their ability to participate in the making of decisions that affect them. Thus, they create a political society (i.e., Leviathan, Mortal God, or Common-Wealth). This is not a compact between government and people, but one among individuals appointing one person to be the government. The resulting government creates society, exists separately from it, and is not accountable to the people but rather only to itself.

By totally giving up their sovereignty, the people lose all capacity for self-government and have become subjects instead. They have created an absolute government to gain security, because a harsh rule (no matter how intolerable) is still much more pleasant than the state of nature. (Criminals in jail often feel more secure than they would out of jail because they know the warden and prison staff will protect them.)

Although Hobbes' theory may not be considered revolutionary today, it is in the sense that it took God out of the relationship among humans, government, and society. Hobbes is considered the "Father of Modern Political Thought" because he re-secularized political philosophy. His state of nature, his social contract, and his resulting absolutist government may seem preposterous to us; yet they form the basis for the whole notion of government by and of the people. According to Hobbes, we freely consented to have an individual or group govern us. It does not really matter how or on what basis we gave that consent; it suffices that we gave it. The "we" in "we consented" implies a continuum from our ancestors to us, as if time did not separate us from them.

For almost a thousand years, rulership was based on divine intervention. In *Leviathan*, Hobbes replaced God with the people — a revolutionary thought for people who believed so strongly in divine will. From that point in time the people themselves became the foundation on which government (and, hence, the state) is established.

John Locke

John Locke (1632-1704) practiced medicine and became close to those who wielded or wanted to wield political power in London. He did most of his writing while exiled in Holland for five years because he antagonized the then British government and returned in 1688 as part of the entourage of Prince William and Queen Mary of Orange, whom he befriended.

Locke's works are significant because they influenced the framers of the U.S. Constitution. Locke believed that all our knowledge (indeed, all our being) is a consequence of experience. Who we are and what we know results from our sensations or our mind's organization of these sensations. Our mind is a *tabula rasa*, a blank slate on which the social and physical environment leave their inscriptions.

All ideas come from sensation or reflection — Let us then suppose the mind to be, as we say, white paper, void of all characters, without any ideas: — How comes it to be furnished? . . . To this I answer, in one word, from EXPERIENCE. In that all our knowledge is founded; and from that it ultimately derives itself.[2]

Locke's notion that each human being is a product of environmental influences is the basis of the modern ideas of conditioning, behavior modification, and socialization. He believes that every person is infinitely malleable and, therefore, can be molded from birth into anything

John Locke

by those in charge of his up bringing (e.g., family or government).

But nature also has its laws. They are based on reason and common equity and are deduced from experience by every person. These laws of nature supposedly can be overcome only by people organized into a society. However, in the state of nature, where although man is completely free, they must be adhered to. For example, in the state of nature no one can destroy himself or others: In his *Second Treatise of Civil Government* Locke writes,

> But though this be a *State of Liberty,* yet it is *not a State of Licence,* though Man in that State has an uncontroleable Liberty, to dispose of his Person or Possessions, yet he has not Liberty to destroy himself, or so much as any Creature in his Possession, but where some nobler use, than its bare Preservation calls for it. The *State of Nature* has a law of nature to govern it, which obliges every one: And Reason, which is that Law, teaches all Mankind, who will but consult it, that being all equal and independent, no one ought to harm another in his Life, Health, Liberty, or Possessions. For Men being all the Workmanship of one Omnipotent, and infinitely wise Maker . . . they are his Property . . . made to last during his, not one anothers' Pleasure . . . Every one as he is *bound to preserve* . . . by the like reason when his own Preservation comes not in competition, ought he, as much as he can, *to preserve the rest of Mankind.*[3]

Individuals cannot destroy themselves nor be coerced by others to do so, according to Locke. The law of nature stipulates that everyone has the responsibility not to cause injury to anyone else so as to "preserve the rest of Mankind." Moreover, those who commit breach of this law can be punished by others. Every individual has *"a Right to punish the Offender, and be Executioner of the Law of Nature."* This right of every person to carry out laws and to mete out punishment to those who do not follow them is known as **self-help**. In our modern society the remnant of this right is **self-defense**, that is, the right, by force, to prevent an injury or loss of property to oneself. Locke's state of nature, therefore, is not completely lawless; nor are offenders not punished.

One aspect of the law of nature that many writers of the fifteenth through eighteenth centuries had difficulty explaining was that of property. If God gave the earth to Adam and *all* his descendants, then why do some people have more of it than others? How can one justify property when everything was held in common? If, indeed, the state of nature was true, then would not the consent of everyone be required to establish property?

Man in the state of nature so far had his life and liberty guaranteed. Locke attempts to also explain man's right to property. Suppose you were a person in the state of nature looking for something to eat. You see a juicy apple on a tree. You climb it, pick the apple, go down, sit in the shade and, as you are opening your mouth to take the first bite, a person comes along and says to you, "Don't eat that apple; it is mine." You answer that it is not, the apple is yours. How do you justify this? According to Locke, you would say it is yours because you picked it; you spent your energy, or labor, to remove it from the commons and made it your property.

> Though the Earth, and all inferior Creatures be common to all Men, yet every Man has a Property in his own Person. This no Body has any Right to but himself. The Labour of his Body, and the Work of his Hands, we may say, are properly his. Whatsoever then he removes out of the State that Nature has provided, and left it in, he hath mixed his Labour with, and joyned to it something that is his own, and thereby makes it his Property. It being by him removed from the common state Nature placed it in, hath by his labour something annexed to it, that excludes the common right of other Men. For this Labour being the unquestionable Property of the Labourer, no Man but he can have a right to what is once joyned to, at least where there is enough, and as good left in common for others.

This idea that something is yours because you worked for it and that an item's worth is determined by how much labor was spent in extracting or making it is called the **labor theory of value**. This has nothing to do with how many items there are, nor how scarce they are. The labor theory of value states simply that costs equal labor, period. Locke made this the pivot on which his conception of property is built.

There is, however, a limit to how many apples you can gather. You cannot accumulate so many that they rot, and then prevent someone else from having any.

> . . . As much as any one can make use of to any advantage of life before it spoils; so much he may by his labour fix a Property in. Whatever is beyond this, is more than his share, and belongs to others. Nothing was made by God for Man to spoil and destroy.

Just as the apples are yours when you expend labor on them, so is land. "As much Land as a Man Tills, Plants, Improves, Cultivates, and can use the Product of, so much is his *Property*. He by his Labour does, as it were, inclose it from the Common." Locke then argues that by adding labor to commonly held land, you add to its worth, and, since there is so much of it, you do not deprive others of it by making it your property.

In the state of nature, however, confusion may set in regarding what is yours and what is mine. Suppose I was the person who contested your ownership of the apple in the last example. And I said to myself, "Fine, the apple is yours because you worked for it. I am going to make the tree my property by caring for it." Now, when you come along and pick an apple from *my* tree, even though you labored for that apple, it is not yours because the tree is mine. Who owns the apples if a third person comes along and tills the land around the tree?

Another problem appears. The apples from my tree are more than I can consume. I am not allowed to let them rot. I can, however, exchange them for something else I need. At first I barter the apples, say, for oranges and these I can then barter for still something else and so on. Eventually, I short-circuit this whole process by exchanging the apples for "money." Somehow, money makes its appearance in Locke's state of nature.

"And thus *came in the use of Money*, some lasting thing that Men might keep without spoiling, and that by mutual consent Men would take in exchange for the truly useful, but perishable Supports of Life."

What happens if someone uses force to take something I believe belongs to me. Although I could probably protect myself and my property against another, I could not do so if I am attacked by many others. Therefore, I make a compact with my fellow humans and form a community whose laws govern everyone's life, liberty, and property.

> For when any number of Men have, by the consent of every individual, made a Community, they have thereby made that Community one Body, with a Power to Act as one Body, which is only by the will and determination of the majority. . . . If a man in the State of Nature be so free, as has been said; If he be absolute Lord of his own Person and Possessions, equal to the greatest, and subject to no Body, why will he part with his Freedom? . . . To which 'tis obvious to Answer, that though in the state of Nature ha hath such a right, yet the Enjoyment of it is very uncertain, and constantly exposed to the Invasion of others. For all being Kings as much as he, every Man his Equal, and the greater part no strict Observers of Equity and Justice, the enjoyment of the property he has in this state is very unsafe, very unsecure. This makes him willing to quit a Condition, which however free, is full of fears and continual dangers: And 'tis not without reason, that he seeks out, and is willing to joyn in Society with others who are already united, or have a mind to unite for the mutual *Preservation* of their Lives, Liberties and Estates, which I call by the general Name, *Property*.

So, humans in Locke's state of nature willingly decide to unite to form communities or societies to preserve their life, liberty, and property. (In the Declaration of Independence the last word of that phrase was changed to "pursuit of happiness" which to Jefferson meant the acquisition and enjoyment of property.) When communities are formed, the most important element of the three is the protection of property. "The great and *chief end* therefore, of Mens uniting into Commonwealths, and putting themselves under Government, is *the Preservation of their Property.*" This social contract then legitimizes the inequality of property among individuals in the state of nature.

Once they join society, individuals give up their right to self-help; society, through its laws and their implementation, protects individuals against those who do not abide by its laws. Society, however, needs government. Therefore, a compact among those in society is made by which they *delegate* to that government their right to make, implement, and judge laws. A government makes the laws *for* the people.

The relationship between government and society is similar to that of an attorney and a client. The former acts on behalf of the individual as long as he or she grants the power of attorney. If the client perceives that the attorney is no longer working for his or her best interests, he or she can take that power away and transfer it to another attorney. Likewise, consent given to a government can be taken away. The majority, acting for the whole of society, can alter or change the government when it no longer provides for the preservation of life, liberty, and property of the people. (Locke is not concerned with the minority or its rights when they are trampled on by the majority.)

Nevertheless, Locke's government is not one *by* the people. People, even when in majority, do not make laws (just as they do not represent themselves in court); they are merely approving or disapproving umpires of policies made for them by those in the government.

Those in government are themselves members of society and, hence, are subject to the same laws as everyone else. Locke emphatically stated, *"No man in Civil Society can be exempted from the Laws of it."* If rulers have to abide by their own laws, then the law is superior to them. It is the law that governs, not the ruler.

Government that consists of rulers who have to abide by their own laws and that is compelled by these laws to provide for the welfare of the people, is known as **limited government**. Limited government is constrained in its use of power, it cannot do whatever it pleases to whomever it wants. This is the opposite of absolute government. Limited government is also referred to as **constitutional government**.

Thus Locke developed the rationale for modern constitutional, or limited, governments. Both the U.S. Declaration of Independence and the Constitution are based on Locke's notion that rulers are obligated to protect their subjects from losses to life, liberty, and property as interpreted by the majority and, if they fail to do so, they can be replaced. The idea that "no one can be deprived of life, liberty, or property without due process," which is strictly Lockean, is the foundation of American government.

The issue of property raised by Locke needs further elaboration. Is what is mine, really mine? There is not much controversy over whether the apples nurtured and harvested from a tree on my land are really mine. They are. What happens if, instead of growing apples, I were to grow an illegal crop such as marijuana plants? Are they mine? Can I do on my property whatever I wish?

Property rights are regarded from two viewpoints. First, Locke's view that I have complete liberty to do with my property whatever I want, as long as it is not harmful to others is called the **absolute right to property**. It allows few, if any, restrictions on my use of my property. This view, until recently, was the basis for many legislative, executive, and judicial decisions in the U.S. Until this century laws regarding child labor, income taxes, zoning practices, and antitrust regulations were ruled unconstitutional by U.S. courts on the basis that they infringed on property rights.

The most serious challenge to absolute property rights came in the 1950s and '60s when leaders of the U.S. civil rights movement insisted that white property owners be forced to rent to qualified minorities. Property rights advocates claimed that homeowners do not have to rent to anyone they do not like because they own the property and can do with it whatever they want. The courts ruled that sometimes discrimination against minorities is a greater evil than the protection of property rights and, therefore, equal rights outweigh property rights.

The second view regarding property, known as **restrictive right to property**, states that my ownership of property is a trust given to me by society and that ultimately society owns it. Although I "own" my property, I can only do with it what society through its government deems useful. In owning my property, I am society's agent. Clearly, under this view government can legislate what I can do with my property. In most countries, except the United States, this is the accepted view regarding property rights and is usually incorporated in their constitutions. The United States, however, does appear to be moving closer to this view, as all types of legislation and regulations have been adopted telling its citizens what they can and cannot do with their property.

Both Hobbes and Locke viewed government as something separate from society, although the latter thought that government is part of it. The people of society were considered subjects of the rulers or governments until Rousseau, the next social philosopher of significance, converted the "subjects" into "citizens."

Jean-Jacques Rousseau

Jean-Jacques Rousseau (1712-1778) was born in Geneva at a time when that city was a direct democracy — its Calvinist citizens actively participated in policy making. After he lost his mother when he was ten months old, he lived with his father, who was a watchmaker and later a dance instructor. From about ages six to fifteen, he lived with aunts and uncles in the countryside. He was then apprenticed to an engraver in Geneva, but could not stand the discipline the latter imposed and so left that city.

After traveling through Italy and France, Rousseau settled down for a while in the northern part of what is now Italy at the home of Madame de Warens, a 28-year-old divorced woman. They became lovers. He converted to Catholicism (which he renounced later in life). After staying with Madame de Warens for about eight years he journeyed to Paris, where he took up residence and was employed at a variety of jobs, such as engraver, secretary to an ambassador, tutor, copier of music, and composer.

Rousseau hired a maid, Therese le Vasseur, who remained with him until his death. She had five children with him, each of whom he gave up for adoption. He eventually contracted a venereal disease that made him the subject of jokes.

While in Paris Rousseau became quite renown as a conversationalist in the *salons*, which were gatherings of members of the French intelligentsia in the homes of either the rich or the nobility to discuss current issues. Among those who attended these *salons* were Voltaire, Diderot, D'Alembert, and other important figures of the **Enlightenment**. The Enlightenment was a movement in the mid-eighteenth century in France that attempted to provide rational solutions to all of humanity's problems, especially those relating to man's role in society and government. Man was viewed in need to be released of the shackles imposed on him by religion, society, and the state. The ancient Greeks and Romans were taken out of the dust bins of history and restudied. Socrates, Plato, Aristotle, and many Greek and Roman playrights, historians, and thinkers were translated into French and discussed. Their myths inspired artists. Artworks were created of eighteenth century personages in the clothing styles of ancient Greece and Rome (e.g., the statue of Washington in a toga that is displayed at the Smithsonian Museum of American History). Writers of the Enlightenment criticized many religious practices as superstitious and barbaric. They also thought that all knowledge should be written down and made available to everyone, so they compiled the first encyclopedias. In short, the Enlightenment, in that it emphasized the application of reason, as opposed to faith or tradition, in the analysis of data, was the precursor to the scientific movements that would dominate western thought over the next two centuries.

Statue of George Washington in a toga (marble, Horatio Greenough). Located at the Smithsonian Institution.

Although Rousseau lived during the Enlightenment and was friendly with its spokespersons, he was not a part of the movement. His ideas, however, which frequently were opposite of those espoused by the movement's adherents, brought him fame.

Rousseau's ideas led to many historical trends and events. He laid the foundation for the modern romantic movement in literature and other arts. He developed the principles upon which our school system is based. He was the first modern environmentalist. He turned the "subjects" of a society into "citizens" and a society under a government into a "nation."

The French Revolution started with the storming of the Royal prison, Bastille, on July 14, 1789. The failure of the government to prevent the release of the political prisoners marked the end of its authority. The revolution of 1830 did not result in a republic, but in a more liberal monarchy under a junior member of the Bourbon dynasty, Louis Philippe. Later in 1848, following a major economic recession, the political opposition forced Louis Philippe to relinquish the throne and a republic was established ending the monarchy.

He also is credited with influencing the start of the French Revolution, which was the most important revolution in Europe.

An important concept in Rousseau's thought was that emotions govern the behavior of humans and that reason is but a handmaiden to emotions. According to Rousseau, when emotions are allowed pure expression, unencumbered by reason, they inevitably allow their expresser to do good. This of course is the basis of romanticism. Humans ruled by their emotions do not cause harm or injury to anyone or anything. Thus, the Don Juans in Spanish literature, the American cowboy in Westerns, and the television city detective or police officer all have a good heart, are at the right place at the right time, and do not think too much. Their enemies, the bad guys, are usually the conniving, scheming, and plotting characters who obviously use their brains.

Children, according to Rousseau, are not miniature adults (as they were frequently depicted in literature and in paintings such as Gainsborough's *Blue Boy*). They are beings who grow and develop into adults through a natural process that cannot be hurried. He believed that the best way to raise children is to allow them to explore their own environment at their own speed, not to force them into a confined, disciplined atmosphere where they have to follow the teachings of adults. Memorization is to be shunned and understanding encouraged. The best teacher for the first six years is the mother and afterwards the father, since both have only the interest of the child in mind and do not teach for the sake of money or glory. Rousseau expresses these notions in his novel, *Emile*. *Emile* contained statements which neither the Church nor the State approved of. After the book was published Rousseau felt compelled to leave France and moved to England to live with the philosopher Hume for a while. He eventually became a recluse during the last few years of his life.

Rousseau also wrote about the state of nature and the social contract in the essay "Discourse on the Origin and Foundations of Inequality." Unlike Hobbes and Locke who believed that humans were in the state of nature at one moment and in society in the next because of the social contract, Rousseau thought that the change from the state of nature to society occurred gradually over time.

From Rousseau's viewpoint, humans initially were only interested in maintaining themselves; they did not interact with each other and lived very much as part of nature. They were true to their original emotions. Rousseau's state of nature was like the Garden of Eden before the expulsion. Although there were differences among the inhabitants of that original state of nature, none were so severe that they created any rankings. Not only did these humans not hurt one another, but they also helped each other. The reason for this was pity.

> . . . I shall not surely be contradicted, in granting to man the only natural virtue, which the most passionate detractor of human virtues could not deny him, I mean that of pity, a disposition suitable to creatures weak as we are, and liable to so many evils; a virtue so much the more universal, and withal useful to man, as it takes place in him before all manner of reflection; and so natural, that the beasts themselves sometimes give evident signs of it.[4]

Pity, or commiseration, is a sentiment that evokes sympathy for the sufferer and is far more prevalent in the state of nature than in civilized society, which is a creation of reason that causes humans to become self-absorbed.

. . . It is reason that engenders self~love, and reflection that strengthens it; it is reason that makes man shrink into himself; it is reason that makes him keep aloof from everything that can trouble or afflict him; it is philosophy that destroys his connections with other men; it is in consequence of her dictates that he mutters to himself at the sight of another in distress, You may perish for aught I care, I am safe . . .

. . . It is this pity which hurries us without reflection to the assistance of those we see in distress; it is this pity which, in a state of nature, takes the place of laws, manners, virtue, with this advantage, that no one is tempted to disobey her gentle voice: it is this pity which will always hinder a robust savage from plundering a feeble child, or infirm old man, of the subsistence they have acquired with pain and difficulty if he has but the least prospect of providing for himself by any other means: it is this pity which, instead of that sublime maxim of rational justice, Do to others as you would have others do to you, inspires all men with that other maxim of natural goodness a great deal less perfect, but perhaps more useful, Do good to yourself with as little prejudice as you can to others. It is in a word, in this natural sentiment, rather than in finespun arguments, that we must look for the cause of that reluctance which every man would experience to do evil, even independently of the maxims of education. Though it may be the peculiar happiness of Socrates and other geniuses of his stamp to reason themselves into virtue, the human species would long ago have ceased to exist, had it depended entirely for its preservation on the reasonings of the individuals that compose it.

Initially man in Rousseau's state of nature is the **noble savage**. He is considered noble precisely because of the emotions and compassion that make him respect the life and possessions of others. He is considered savage because he has not yet learned to use the ability to reason and, therefore, has not developed "laws, manners, and virtue" but lives in harmony with nature. Note the difference between the following Rousseaunian description of paradise and the hellish Hobbesian state of nature in which life is "solitary, poor, nasty, brutish, and short."

Let us conclude that savage man, wandering about in the forests, without industry, without speech, without any fixed residence, an equal stranger to war and every social tie, without any need of his fellows, as well as without any desire of hurting them, and perhaps even without ever distinguishing them individually one from the other, subject to few passions, and finding in himself all he wants, let us, I say, conclude that savage man had no knowledge or feelings but such as were proper to that situation; that he felt only his real necessities, took notice of nothing but what it was his interest to see, and that his understanding made as little progress as his vanity. If he happened to make any discovery, he could the less communicate it as he did not even know his children. The art perished with the inventor; there was neither education nor improvement; generations succeeded generations to no benefit; and as all constantly set out from the same point, whole centuries rolled on in the rudeness and barbarity of the first age; the race was grown old, and man still remained a child.

But men, and women, do not remain children forever; inevitably, they do grow up. And so it happened with the noble savage. According to Rousseau several factors made humans evolve. One of the factors was that their wants increased as nature made things more difficult by producing cataclysms, such as earthquakes, floods, and fires, that had to be overcome. To overcome these, the savage had to be inventive; once the inventions were made, they could then be applied to noncataclysmic needs and wants. For example, to overcome the cold, the savage invented clothing by covering himself with cloth woven from leaves; later he used the same technique to weave, let us say, a hammock or a blanket. Then he would find that, although he got along perfectly well without one before, he "needed" that hammock or blanket. Consequently, his desires increased in intensity to a point at which they became passions and he wanted more and more. Eventually the passions became uncontrollable and, when he could no longer satisfy them completely, he became abusive.

While some of their emotions turn into passions, men and women bond to each other and begin families. Husbands and wives, who until then had led the same type of life, began to differentiate their roles. Husbands provided, wives nurtured. As families increased in size, specialization also increased. Sons and daughters would take care of different tasks needed to maintain the household. Cooperation among individuals also became necessary because the size of the game required to feed more people was larger and, therefore, more difficult for one person to hunt alone.

Another cause of human evolution was the ability to name things. At first grunts had no meaning, but in time these sounds became definitive and began to stand for things such as "this oak tree," "this river," etc. The need to communicate increased as the number of humans increased. Speech developed as words were needed to denote not just a particular object (e.g., "this tree"), but also generic things (e.g., "trees"). Knowledge was not only transmitted among individuals but, most importantly, among generations, so as it accumulated each generation knew more than the preceding one.

With the development of speech came the development of the ability to reason. Speech developed into language as words were put together in a certain order. Humans became rational beings as they learned to use language to formulate ideas.

Once this step in their evolution occurred, humans, without realizing it, formed society. These societies were governed like families, with one or perhaps several older persons in authority who created laws, institutions, ideologies, etc., to keep the other members of society compliant. It was at this point, according to Rousseau, that the inequalities among humans were created.

This then is the irreversible evolution of humans from noble savages to a society, according to Rousseau in "Discourse on Inequality." This was a construct, something that Rousseau invented to prove that humans were originally all equal. He admitted that his scenario was not necessarily the way it happened (although it is closer anthropologically to the truth than the theories of Hobbes and Locke). Inequalities, he said, were a result of **convention**, or human rational creativity (i.e., customs, traditions, laws, mores, institutions). Inequality among humans therefore, was artificial, not natural.

Rousseau then probably thought, "If only this movement toward greater and greater inequality could somehow be stopped, or even reversed! If humans could only regain the freedom they had in the original state of nature! If only each human was the political equal of the other!"

In his *The Social Contract*, Rousseau sets down once and for all the idea of human political equality. He reiterates that the family is the model of governance in primitive societies. He also notes that, at times, the strongest rule. However, when humans perceive that their preservation is endangered by the oppression of fellow humans or when the individual alone cannot surmount obstacles imposed by the organized few, then humans will combine their forces and unite to reclaim their freedom through a social contract. To Rousseau the state of nature lasts as long as there is no social contract, although society and government may exist in the state of nature. Through the social contract,

> . . . the whole strength of the community will be enlisted for the protection of the person and property of each constituent member, in such a way that each, when united to his fellows, renders obedience to his own will, and remains as free as he was before.
> . . . [w]hoso gives himself to all gives himself to none. And, since there is no member of the social group over whom we do not acquire precisely the same rights as those over ourselves which we have surrendered to him, it follows that we gain the exact equivalent of what we lose, as well as an added power to conserve what we already have.[5]

Rousseau's social contract is an act of rebellion by society against its oppressors. An analogy to the Rousseaunian development of society is the development of the person. As an infant a person is good, pure, and innocent. Within his or her limitations an infant is free. As the child grows, he or she becomes more knowledgeable, wiser, and aware of roles within the family. The father is the ruler who makes decisions; the child obeys out of love, loyalty, or fear. One day, however, the child rebels and makes a conscious decision that from then on he or she will make the decisions and assume responsibility for them. The child has become an adult and he or she has regained freedom.

By its act of rebellion society, too, becomes mature. Its members regain their lost freedom. Society takes control of government and the state and never transfers or delegates the power to govern to another entity. Society is sovereign. Society is the state. And society is each and every person within it.

> . . . Each individual comprising the [body politic] contracts, so to speak, with himself and has a twofold function. As a member of the sovereign people he owes a duty to each of his neighbours, and, as a Citizen, to the sovereign people as a whole. . . .
> But the body politic, or Sovereign, in that it derives its being simply and solely from the sanctity of the said Contract, can never bind itself, even in its relations with a foreign Power, by any decision which might derogate from the validity of the original act. It may not, for instance, alienate any portion of itself, nor make submission to any other sovereign. To violate the act by reason of which it exists would be tantamount to destroying itself, and that which is nothing can produce nothing. . . .
> Now, the Sovereign people, having no existence outside that of individuals who compose it, has, and can have, no interest at variance with theirs.

Just like Hobbes and Locke, Rousseau states that humans lose the individual sovereignty they possessed. However, Rousseau's humans acquire "civil liberty," the right to participate in the governing of their society. This right can never be taken away. How is this governing occur?

Rousseau notes that monarchy has one advantage over other forms of government. That one advantage is that the monarch is both chief policy maker and chief policy implementor. The monarch is one, one individual who does not disagree with himself nor one who has to convince others of the correctness of his policy in order to get it implemented. To maintain this advantage, Rousseau creates a theory of wills. Each individual or group of individuals expresses demands and wants, what he calls **individual wills**. If you were to add together these individual wills, the sum

FOCUS — HOBBES, LOCKE, AND ROUSSEAU — A MODERN DAY STORY

Hobbes, Locke, and Rousseau found themselves looking down at the street from the twenty-fifth floor of a skyscraper in New York City. Since it was rush hour, a police officer at an intersection was directing traffic, yelling and flagging his arms to get everyone moving.

"Ah," says Hobbes pointing at the police officer, "that sovereign has complete control of a situation that without him would turn into complete chaos and mayhem."

"Nonsense," says Locke, "although the man has the situation under control, many people are not happy with what he is doing. Hear the way they are blowing their horns. The man should be more attuned to what the people down there want."

Rousseau, looking at the whole length of the street, notices that at another intersection no one was directing traffic, yet it was moving along thanks to a traffic light. "See that," he says to the others pointing to the light, "that is the general will that is giving directions."

would be the **will of all**. The common element of all these wills — their common denominator — is the **general will,** which is the most important. Society is governed by the general will, and every citizen contributes equally and constantly to it. The people, through the general will, are the lawmakers and the law implementors since they supposedly will carry out their will. Therefore the advantage of the monarchs is also present when society governs itself through the general will. Although kings and queens may have titles to rule, they can do so only in the name of the general will.

Each society has one, and only one, general will. Rousseau states, "It is essential that there be no subsidiary groups within the State, and that each citizen voice his own opinion and nothing but his own opinion." Every person must obey the general will or be compelled to do so or leave.

Through the general will the people exercise their sovereignty and become a nation. For Rousseau a nation is a society that either governs itself or aspires to govern itself; therefore, the social contract transforms a society into a nation. The evolutionary process within the state of nature stops once nationhood is achieved. However, any nation that allows itself to be governed by another reverts to a state of nature. Unless conscious decisions by members of society are continuously made, nationhood can be lost.

> Man is born free, and everywhere he is in chains. Many a man believes himself to be the master of others who is, no less than they, a slave. How did this

change take place? I do not know. What can make it legitimate? To this question I hope to be able to furnish an answer.

Were I considering only force and effects of force, I should say: "so long as a People is constrained to obey, and does, in fact, obey, it does well. So soon as it can shake off its yoke, and succeeds in doing so, it does better. The fact that it has recovered its liberty by virtue of that same right by which it was stolen, means either that it is entitled to resume it, or that its theft by others, was, in the first place without justification." But the social order is a sacred right which serves as a foundation for all other rights. This right, however, since it comes not by nature, must have been built upon conventions.

The social contract then is not a natural product. It is a creation of humans, rational humans, which allows each of them to recapture the freedom they once had in the state of nature. The state, then, is the product of conscious decisions by individuals.

Rousseau, like Aristotle, made it essential that every person have the right to be a political activist, to participate in the making of decisions for his community. He made every person the political equal of another — in short he made every person a citizen. Thus kings and queens, princes and princesses, dukes and duchesses, and others could not claim to be superior political "animals." From then on every citizen is a monarch, and every monarch a citizen.

Each person's equality emanates not only from the early stages of the state of nature, but also from every person's subscribing to the social contract. The few persons with more political powers than the others in each society enjoy this privilege, not because they are inherently superior, but because they have been elected or appointed to a position of power by the rest. Stripped from their position, they have no more power than all the others. (Note how quickly "heads" of state — presidents, prime ministers, governors, etc. — become innocuous members of their respective societies once they leave office.)

It is easy to see how the French Revolution, which began in 1789, was an outgrowth of Rousseaunian thought. The motto "Liberty, Equality, and Fraternity," the Declaration of the Rights of Man written by the revolutionary National Assembly, and most of that period's writings, official or not, were inspired by the state of nature and the social contract as interpreted by the watchmaker's son of Geneva.

Further, many artistic and literary creations of the late 1700s and the 1800s were influenced by Rousseau's philosophy. His theories about man's interactions with nature are represented in the music extolling nature (e.g., Beethoven's Sixth, Mahler's First, for example), and, of course, romantic poetry and prose. Marie Antoinette, wife of Louis XVI, had shepherd huts built at the Palace of Versailles where she, dressed like a shepherdess, would frolic around with sheep, in an effort to reclaim Rousseau's state of nature. (If you visit that palace today you will find a patch of land overgrown with weeds next to the main building and manicured lawns and gardens. When your author first saw it, he asked the tour guide whether the funds to mow the grass had run out. The reply was, "But, sir, this is a Rousseaunian garden.")

Rousseau may have provided us with the foundations for our environmental, educational, artistic, literary, and political perspectives, but he also, unintentionally, highlighted a problem for which we have yet to find a solution. Who decides what is the general will? Tyrants such as Hitler, Stalin, Somoza, Amin, and Pinochet said they "knew" what the people wanted. Yet all ordered the slaughter of thousands to millions of innocent victims. There are few leaders in any society today who do not claim to know what the people want. But do they really? Every one of us contributes in one way or another to the general will; however, none of us knows what it is.

VIEWS OF THREE SOCIAL CONTRACT THEORISTS

	Description of State of Nature	Reasons for Leaving State of Nature	Type of Government Established
Thomas Hobbes	Man lives in a perpetual state of war.	Man yearns for security.	Absolute, with a sovereign ruler for all time.
John Locke	Man lives by experience and common sense; follows laws of nature.	Man wants to preserve life, liberty, and property.	Delegated, that could be abolished if it does not preserve life, liberty, and property.
Jean-J. Rousseau	Man Initially lives in paradise and is good; population growth and ability to reason force interactions among people who select a "father" to govern primitive society.	Man wants to regain freedom and ability to make decisions.	Society is government; the "general will" rules.

In conclusion, the idea that each person within a society is politically equal has become an integral part of our beliefs. None of the hundreds of political thinkers since Rousseau has added substantially to the social contract theory regarding the relationship among man, citizen, and state. Since Rousseau, no political theorist has seriously questioned the "inherent" political equality of humans. By accepting the idea that before society and government were established all men and women were equal, modern thinkers have made it possible to speak of human rights that are conferred to us simply because we are human (as opposed to rights granted to us because we belong to a racial, sexual, ethnic, religious, or national group or because we hold a certain position such as ruler, administrator, or professional athlete). If the social contract theorists had related equal rights to some social norms, then equality would have to change as these norms change; however, by postulating that the state of nature preceded the development of society, they have tied human rights with supposed immutable natural laws.

Throughout recent history, however, some racial and religious groups, such as black Africans and Jews, have not been accepted as equal by others. These viewpoints are not taken seriously from a philosophical or political theory perspective. Even the Afrikaners (i.e., white majority of South Africa) had to realize that their notions of the differences among the races were built on philosophical quicksand.

Although some of us might call those who are in government positions "them," deep down we know that "them" is really us. We are the government and the government is us. The king is not sovereign, the state is not sovereign, but the people are sovereign. The people govern.

This then is what Rousseau and the other social contract theorists have contributed to our understanding of man and state. This is their legacy to us. Unfortunately, by accepting it we have also accepted the erroneous foundations of their theories and conclusions. The state of nature and the social contract never existed; individuals never consciously decided to form society and the state.

As you shall read in the next section, Karl Marx, almost a hundred years later, attempted to do with economic man what Rousseau had done with political man. He tried, not too successfully, to make us believe that economic equality is even more important than political equality; that to have the latter, you must also have the former.

📖 TERMS TO REMEMBER

state of nature
social contract
Thomas Hobbes
John Locke
self help
self defense
labor theory of value
limited government
constitutional government
absolute right to property
restrictive right to property
Jean-Jacques Rousseau
Enlightenment
noble savage
convention
individual will
will of all
general will

📚 SUGGESTED READINGS

Gildin, Hilail. *Rousseau's Social Contract: The Design of the Argument.* Chicago: University of Chicago Press, 1983. Rousseau's ideas on government, sovereignty and the general will, and the sovereign people and government are examined.

Hampton, Jean. *Hobbes and the Social Contract Tradition.* New York: Cambridge University Press, 1986. Scholarly analysis and evaluation of Hobbes' state of nature and social contract as expressed in Leviathan. Not for the casual reader.

Hobbes, Thomas. *Leviathan.* Edited by C. B. Macpherson. Middlesex, England: Pelican Books, 1968

Hobbes, Thomas. *Leviathan.* Edited by Richard Tuck. New York: Cambridge University Press, 1991.

Jones, W.T. *Hobbes to Hume: A History of Western Philosophy.* New York: Harcourt Brace Jovanovich, Inc., 1969. Description and analysis of the writings of seven of the major thinkers of the seventeenth and eighteenth centuries. (does not include Rousseau).

Locke, John. *An Essay Concerning Human Understanding.* Edited with a foreword by Peter H. Nidditch. Oxford: Clarendon Press; New York: Oxford University Press, 1979.

Locke, John. *Two Treatises of Government: A Critical Edition with an Introduction and Apparatus Criticus.* Edited by Peter Laslett. 2nd ed. London: Cambridge Univerisity Press, 1967.

Rousseau, Jean-Jacques. *Emile.* Translated by Barbara Foxley. Introduction by P.D. Jimack. London: Dent; New York: Dutton, 1974.

Rousseau, Jean-Jacques. *On the Social Contract; Discourse on the Origin of Inequality; Discourse on Political Economy.* Translated and edited by Donald A. Cress. Introduction by Peter Gay. Indianapolis: Hackett Publishing Co., 1983.

Rousseau, Jean-Jacques. *The Confessions.* New York: Random House, The Modern Library, nd.

Rousseau, Jean-Jacques. *The Social Contract and Discourse on the Origin of Inequality.* Edited by Lester G. Crocker. New York: Washington Square Press, Pocket Books, 1967.

Rousseau, Jean-Jacques. *The Social Contract.* Edited by Sir Ernest Barker. New York: Oxford University Press, 1962.

Schama, Simon. *Citizens: A Chronicle of the French Revolution.* New York: Knopf, 1989. A lengthy but interestingly written history of the antecedents and events of the French Revolution.

Tully, James. *A Discourse on Property: John Locke and His Adversaries.* New York: Cambridge University Press, 1980. A detailed analysis of Locke's and his contemporaries' ideas about property.

NOTES

1. All quotations from *Leviathan* are from the C.B. Macpherson edition. (Middlesex, England: Pelican Books, 1968).

2. Locke, John. "An Essay Concerning Human Understanding" in *Hobbes to Hume: A History of Western Philosophy*, by W.T. Jones. (San Diego, Harcourt Brace Jovanovich, Inc., 1969), pp245-46.

3. All quotations from "The Second Treatise of Government: An Essay Concerning the True Original, Extent, and End of Civil Government" are from *John Locke: Two Treatises of Government*, ed. Peter Laslett. (New York: Cambridge University Press, 1960).

4. All quotations from the "Discourse on the Origin and Foundations of Inequality" are from *The Social Contract and Discourse on the Origin of Inequality*, ed. Lester G. Crocker. (New York: Washington Square Press, Pocket Books, 1967).

5. All quotations from *The Social Contract* are from *Social Contract*, ed. Sir Ernest Barker. (New York: Oxford University Press, 1962).

6

Karl Marx

🌐 Outline

The recent demise of Marxism has been broadcast from one corner of the world to the next. The events in the Soviet Union since 1985 when Mikhail Gorbachev assumed control and in Eastern Europe since 1989 supposedly have shown that communism is dead and the free market system reigns supreme everywhere. In certain respects Marxism has died, but not just recently; rather, it died a long time ago, perhaps even with **Karl Marx** in 1883. In other respects, Marxism is alive and well in every one of us because of what we believe and how we perceive the social world around us. As for the free market system, it indeed died with Adam

Smith in 1790. No one can seriously claim its continued existence when large business corporations have driven out the nation's "small shop-keepers" from their most vital economic activities. (The latter were the mainstay of Smith's economic system.)

Perhaps it is fortunate that the Soviet Union's economy has collapsed. Since Marx was so much identified with it and Marxism loathed by so many because of it, its demise may now give us the opportunity to restudy Marx's writings with more objectivity. After all, Marx was a titanic thinker of the nineteenth century alongside Darwin, Huxley, Pasteur, Comte, Durkheimt Kant, Hegel, and Nietzsche.

The basic thesis found in Marx's works is that economic relations determine all other societal relations and their concomitant institutions. This idea, novel in the latter part of the nineteenth century, has become the cornerstone of late twentieth century social thought. There is hardly a problem discussed today — drugs, crime, homelessness, abortion, government corruption and reorganization — that is not seen in economic terms or for which economic solutions are not offered.

Nor is this all. One major goal of every government today is the redistribution of wealth within society. The goal is that the rich through taxation or other forms of governmental regulation will transfer some of their wealth to the poor in order for them to have an adequate quality of life. Most students, for example, receive governmental aid in the form of subsidization of their education (costs to educate them are greater than the tuition and fees they pay). Most students also receive state scholarships or grants, or government guaranteed loans. These are examples of redistribution of the wealth in a society. Other examples are worker's compensation, unemployment compensation, subsidized housing, food stamps, welfare payments, and progressive taxation. All these result from Marx's idea that a society whose members are healthy economically will be healthy in every way.

Now let us turn to Marx's life which is complicated, to better understand how his economic and political philosophies arose.

Marx's Life

Marx's father, Herschel Levi, was the son and grandson of rabbis (the educated spiritual leaders of a Jewish community). He grew up in a sheltered environment (Trier, in the German Rhineland) that offered little interaction with the hostile Christian surroundings. However, Herschel received a secular edu-

Karl Marx

cation and was influenced by the writers of the Enlightenment. He studied law, changed his name to Heinrich Marx, began to practice his profession, and married.

As a Jew, Marx could practice law because Napoleon, who brought the ideas underlying the French Revolution to various German provinces, forced the German rulers to accept Jews as citizens. Followers of Rousseau had argued that Jews should be allowed to become citizens like everyone else.

However, in 1816, after Napoleon was defeated, Prussian rulers enacted anti-Jewish laws that abolished Jews' rights as citizens. Marx could no longer practice law. Cut off from his family because of his freethinking ways, he had to find a way to make a living. After he and his wife converted to Lutheranism in 1817, he was allowed to practice his profession. (Many Jews in the nineteenth and even in the twentieth Century converted to Christianity to become accepted in

Napoleon Bonaparte

society, among them Heine, Disraeli, Mahler, and Mendelssohn.) In 1818, Karl was born, the second of eight children.

As a child and adolescent, Karl Marx was guided intellectually by his father and a neighbor who were rather current in the educated and liberal thought of that time. When he was seventeen, he enrolled at the University of Bonn to study law. A year later he enrolled at the University of Berlin.

His move to Berlin was momentous. Berlin was a bustling city with all the good and bad things with which big cities are identified.

Trier and Bonn were, in comparison, small towns where nothing of consequence ever happened. Life in these towns was pastoral — easy going, friendly, not rushed (being caught in rush-hour traffic for five minutes was considered a horrific calamity). Marx suffered culture shock; he was disoriented, confused. The reality of Berlin and the reality of Trier and Bonn were so different that no common element seemed to tie them together.

Influence of Hegel

Also important to the intellectual development of Marx at the University of Berlin was his introduction to the philosophy of **Georg Wilhelm Friedrich Hegel** (1770-1831) who had recently passed away while teaching there and who had a very large following among students and faculty.

Georg Wilhelm Friedrich Hegel

Hegel's philosophy is very difficult to understand, yet very important because of his impact on philosophy in general. Here we are going to content ourselves with just two basic concepts that he developed.

The first is *Volksgeist*. *Geist* means soul or spirit and *Volk* means people (consider folk as in folklore, folk music). To the Germans *Volk* means more than just people here and now. To them it has a somewhat mystical meaning by which a timeless people are merged with the land upon which they live and with a transcendental being who watches over them and protects them. Consequently, *Volksgeist* is the spirit or abstract essence of such a community.

The second concept is the **dialectic**. The dialectic is a method of reasoning by which a proposition is stated followed by its opposite premise from which an amalgam emerges. The proposition is called a **thesis**, the opposition is its **antithesis**, and the amalgam of both is the **synthesis**. The synthesis then becomes the thesis for a new antithesis that brings forth a new synthesis and so on. For example, one thesis is that all abortions are immoral; the antithesis is that all abortions are moral. The synthesis then is that some abortions are immoral, others moral. If this synthesis becomes the thesis, the antithesis would be that the abortions that are said to be immoral are moral, those said to be moral are immoral. The new synthesis then would be that some abortions considered immoral are now moral and some others considered moral are now immoral. The effect is that abortions that are considered moral will constantly change.

For Hegel, history was a progression of the *Volksgeist* according to the dialectic. Within this *Volksgeist* a constant conflict occurs among societies' ideals, values, and beliefs, which at the same time determine our relations among ourselves and our institutions. The *Volksgeist* is what makes us do what we do.

Further, to be free, we have to internalize the *Volksgeist*, make it part of our essence. It is almost like the difference between a professional basketball player and an amateur. As amateurs, when we play, we give much attention to the rules, otherwise the game breaks apart; since we concentrate on the rules, we do not pay much attention to the ball. The professional knows the rules so well that he does not even think of them when playing and, consequently, is free to concentrate on the ball and how to get it through the hoop. These rules do not change. But the *Volksgeist*, thanks to the dialectic, constantly changes. This means that at any one point in time we really do not know what the total *Volksgeist* is and therefore cannot internalize it completely, unlike the rules of basketball. Regarding the *Volksgeist* we are like amateurs, concentrating more on the rules than on making the rules work for us. Because of our inability to internalize the whole essence of our community, Hegel says, we can never truly be free in our relations with that community.

Hegel was also popular because of his desire for the unification of all the German provinces under one state. The dozen or so German provinces were independent of each other with very few formal ties to each other. Using language as the main unifying force, many intellectuals, especially students felt the time had come for greater Germany to come into existence. These scholars organized themselves into small groups and called themselves the Young Hegelians. In time, Marx became an active and respected member.

The Making of a Communist

The Prussian minister of education clamped down on these young "revolutionaries," expelling most from the faculty of the university. Marx, who was studying law, switched to philosophy. He met Moses Hess, a publisher from Cologne, who believed in the abolition of private property and who invited him to write for his radical newspaper, the *Rheinische Zeitung*. Within a few months, Marx became its editor. A year later, in 1843, the government closed the newspaper operations. Meanwhile, Marx finished his work for the doctorate at the University of Jena and married the daughter of his father's neighbor.

That same year he left Germany and went to Paris to edit a radical German-French journal. He joined with other exiles from Austria, Russia, Italy, Hungary, and other European states in organizations espousing socialism. Marx, unlike many others, joined a group composed mostly of workers and craftsmen, not intellectuals. They called themselves communists. He met another German expatriate, the well-to-do son of a cotton manufacturer named Friedrich Engels. The two became lifelong friends, and their collaboration extended even beyond Marx's death as Engels edited and rewrote unpublished manuscripts left by Marx. Engels, receiving money from home, also supported Marx when the latter was destitute, which was often.

From among the little band of communists, Marx rose to prominence because of his oratorical skills and brilliant intellect. After he was expelled from France in 1845 because of his revolutionary activities, he settled in Brussels, continued to edit his journal, and traveled to other countries to associate his group of communists with others. In 1847, the London center of the Communist League asked him to write a statement outlining the goals and beliefs of the movement. In early 1848, the League published that statement as *The Manifesto of the Communist Party* or *Communist Manifesto*. Few publications have ever risen to such historical significance. Eighteen forty-eight was the culminating year for the decade-long ferment for political change in Europe as the continent was ravaged with unsuccessful revolutions. The *Communist Manifesto* may have had little to do with the political upheavals of that year (despite Marx's claims), but it certainly captured its ardor. It begins:

> A spectre is haunting Europe — the spectre of Communism. All the powers of old Europe have entered into a holy alliance to exorcise the spectre; Pope and Czar, Metternich and Guizot (the Austrian and French prime ministers, respectively), French radicals and German police-spies.
>
> Where is the party in opposition that has not been decried as communistic by its opponents in power? Where the opposition that has not hurled back the branding reproach of Communism, against the more advanced opposition parties, as well as against its reactionary adversaries? Two things result from this fact.

I. Communism is already acknowledged by all European Powers to be itself a Power.

II. It is high time that Communists should openly, in the face of the whole world, publish their views, their aims, their tendencies, and meet this nursery tale of the Spectre of Communism with a Manifesto of the party itself.

To this end, Communists of various nationalities have assembled in London, and sketched the following manifesto, to be published in the English, French, German, Italian, Flemish and Danish Languages.

I

Bourgeois and Proletarians

The history of all hitherto existing society is the history of class struggles . . .

And ends, about 30 pages later:

The Communists disdain to conceal their views and aims. They openly declare that their ends can be attained only by the forcible overthrow of all existing social conditions. Let the ruling classes tremble at a Communist revolution. The proletarians have nothing to lose but their chains. They have a world to win.

Working Men of All Countries, Unite![1]

In actuality, the Communists did not make anybody tremble then. The ruling classes did tremble but not for the reasons Marx gave. A revolutionary fervor fueled by demands for more political freedoms swept through several western and central European states. Metternich and Guizot were axed from their positions in 1848. Marx returned to Paris, but the revolutionary governments could not hold on to power and the old groups returned. Marx again left Paris. This time he settled in London, where he remained until his death in 1883. He earned his living as a writer and as the London correspondent of the radical *New York Tribune,* the largest circulation newspaper in the United States in the 1860s and '70s.

So much for Marx's life. Now what did he say that was so controversial? Let us start by describing the conditions that prevailed in the big cities of Europe, especially London.

Why the Poor Are Poor

Works of the British author Charles Dickens, such as *Oliver Twist* or *A Christmas Carol,* give a flavor of life in London. On the one hand, the very rich, who lived in beautiful mansions on exclusive streets, paid more attention to the form of their lives (e.g., proper manners, formal relations) than to the content. On the other hand, the poor who could not make ends meet, wore rags, lived in the streets, carried diseases, and had no families. A small but growing middle class did exist, but the poor were the largest class.

French authors Alexandre Dumas and Victor Hugo wrote about similar conditions in Paris and other large cities. Although characters in their novels were fictitious, the conditions that these authors depicted were real. Life was harsh for everyone except the wealthy.

Some people questioned why these large gaps existed between the rich and the poor. Many answered that the poor were God's favorite children because there were so many of them; therefore, it was God's will that there be rich and poor people. Others said that the poor were poor because they were lazy good-for-nothings, more interested in getting drunk than doing constructive work. It was Marx, and others like him, who said that the poor were poor because society made them that way. He believed that poverty was neither divinely ordained nor self-inflicted; it was a result of a malfunctioning economic process in society.

How did this happen? One way was the result of the manner in which employers compensated workers. According to Locke's labor theory of value, cost equals labor. For example, if you and I pick fruit at the same time, my oranges are worth the same as your apples. Fine. This theory, however, does not place a value on the labor a mother applied in nurturing and caring for a child. What was that worth? What could she exchange to get something else? Also, what about the disabled, the ill, the elderly, and children? Were they all to die because they did not have sufficient energy to pick oranges, apples, or whatever?

Consider the problem inherent in Locke's theory in the following example. Two coal miners of the same age each produced the same amount of coal, worked the same hours, and received the same compensation, such as $1,000 a month. The first miner was married and had three children; the second was a bachelor. The first miner with a family of four obviously had many more expenses than the second. In fact, with a salary of $1,000 the first miner could barely make ends meet, while the second could live in comfort. But from a societal perspective, who contributed more? The first miner did, because he produced new productive members of society. The second miner did not. This is not all. Who would pay the social security for the second coal miner? The children of the first miner would, which means that the first miner subsidized the second. Fortunately for society, the first miner probably did not make his decisions on getting married and having children strictly out of economic considerations.

What if one of the miners had an illness that required constant care and medication that was expensive. Was it his fault that he had an illness? Who should have compensated him for it? Or, what if one of the miners accidentally hurt himself on the job. Who should pay the medical costs then? Suppose that because of the accident he became crippled and could no longer work. Who should support him and his family? During Marx's time, the worker was on his own. There was no unemployment compensation, health insurance, or social security for workers.

Another problem with Locke's theory is that of inheritance. The fruits of my labor are mine, true enough; but should my children profit from them when I die? They, after all, have not labored for what I have. Should they, like Cephalos' father (in *The Republic*) be allowed to squander it while not laboring at anything?

In addition to the problems described in the coal miner's story and that of inheritance, other situations make the theory of cost-equals-labor less appealing. What about the notion that your labor is worth what the free market determines? The problem with this is that there never was and is not now a free market of labor. Today your salary is determined not only by how much your labor is worth to society but also by who your parents are, how rich they are, what schools you attended, who your friends are, who you married, how you dress and what manners you possess, and who your press agents are (if you have any). Expertise is only one factor among many that determines the value of a person's labor in the so-called free market, which explains why one person's labor is worth more than $500,000,000 a year while many others worth is less than $8,000.

Marx, of course, analyzed all this and did not like it. He wanted to investigate how the economic process itself was injurious to the worker in addition to the problems caused by the cost-equals-labor and free market theories.

The Means of Production

One reason Marx believes the free market does not provide an equitable distribution of income among members of a society is that workers are easily exploited. The cause of this exploitation is not the actions of evil people or a nefarious plot; rather, the cause lies in the ownership of the **means of production**. Means of production are the tools, machinery, and raw materials used to make something out of something else or to extract something from the earth. Whoever owns the means of production controls the laborer who needs to use them to earn his or her living. The worker's contribution to what is produced, that is the labor itself, becomes reduced to being a commodity. Let's see how this works through some examples.

I have a clogged drain that I cannot fix. I call two plumbers for estimates. Both state they will charge $35 for the job. The first has been in business for some time and owns all the necessary tools. The second is just starting out and has to rent wrenches and a plumber's snake. If I hire the first plumber, he deducts $3 for depreciation of his tools and earns $32. If I hire the second plumber, he deducts $10 for tool rental and earns only $25. Since he relies on rented tools, the second plumber is at the mercy of those who own the tools because the rental price can increase at any time. Whoever controls the tools, controls the plumber. Thus, whoever controls the means of production, controls the worker.

Let us take another example. A Scottish husband, wife and children of the 1850s live in a cottage and work on their farm. They produce just enough to get by and perhaps, have a little left over to buy something they take a fancy to but do not really need. The wife decides she needs a new dress for a wedding she and her husband must attend. She spends 3 MUs (monetary units) on cloth and another MU for needles, thread, and buttons. In total, she spends 4 MUs.

She attends the wedding in her new dress. A man sees her and says, "My, what a beautiful dress you have." She beams and answers, "Thank you, I made it myself." He then asks her, "Won't you make dresses for me?" At first she is taken aback and does not know what to make of this offer. The man, then, goes on to explain that he sells dresses and that he will supply her with everything she needs to make them; all she has to do is sew. After consulting with her husband, she agrees to do so.

Now let's examine what happens to the cost of a dress when it is made for someone else. The man buys the materials at a reduced price because he is purchasing a large quantity. He pays 2 MUs for cloth, and 0.50 MUs for thread, buttons, and needles. The total cost for materials is 2.50 MUs per dress. The man, however, has other costs. He has to take the cloth to the dressmaker, pick it up from her, and deliver it to the buyer. These transportation costs of his horse and carriage are worth about 1 MU per dress. He then has to add labor costs for himself and the dressmaker: he gets 1.50 MUs and she gets 1. So far the expenditures for the dress amount to 5 MUs. Now he says, "If I had put the money I am spending for each dress into a savings account and collected interest, I would have received at least 0.50 MU." So he has to add the 0.50 MU to the cost of each dress. Since the dress now costs 5.50 MUs, the man will not make any profit. So he adds 3.50 MUs as profit (he is not greedy). The cost to a customer is 9 MUs. (The customer may pay less if the dress does not sell immediately, the customer may pay more if many people want to buy it.)

So how many dresses does the dressmaker have to make before she can afford one that she made? If she gets 1 MU per dress, then she has to make nine. Assuming she has 4 MUs in savings (which is the amount she spent for the dress she wore at the wedding), she still has to make five more. The dress she made for 4 MUs, and the dress for which she now has to make nine dresses, might very well be the same dress. The difference between their costs is described by the *theory of surplus value*. This theory states that other costs besides labor determine the price of an item. These other costs do not change the item that was produced by those who provided the labor, but only increase its price to the consumer. The increase may be due to costs in administration and distribution, interest, or profit. The greater the number of intermediaries between the laborer and the consumer, the greater the administrative and distribution costs; and the greater the number of people who make a profit on a product, and the higher the price.

Marx believed that labor is the basis of profit, because without labor no profit can be made by anyone involved in production of goods. He borrowed this idea from English economic philosopher David Ricardo. Labor is a commodity just like goods, according to Marx. The capitalist, a person who has accumulated money, can spend it on goods that give pleasure or on workers' labor to produce objects which can be sold for profit. Thus, goods alone may not produce profit, but labor power may.

> The capitalist buys this labor power for a day, a week, a month, etc. And after he has bought it, he uses it by having the workers work for the stipulated time. For the same sum with which the capitalist has bought their labor, for example, two marks [the German monetary unit], he could have bought two pounds of sugar or a definite amount of any other commodity. The two marks, with which he bought two pounds of sugar, are the price of the two pounds of sugar. The two marks, with which he bought twelve hours' use of labor power, are the price of twelve hours' labor. Labor power, therefore, is a commodity, neither more nor less than sugar. The former is measured by the clock, the latter by the scales.

The capitalist uses the profit from workers' labor to make more money. Marx asked, "Does a worker in a cotton factory produce merely cotton textiles? No, he produces capital. He produces values which serve afresh to command his labor and by means of it to create new values." Since the worker does not have any spare money, wages earned are spent on living expenses. So the capitalist gets richer while the worker continues to live barely at the edge of subsistence. The gap between those who have and those who do not have increases.

Let's go back to the example of the dressmaker to consider another phenomenon of labor known as alienation. By entering a money economy to make dresses the wife no longer is able to help her husband in the fields; therefore, farm production drops. Money, which had not been used as a means of exchange, now becomes important. The children are neglected because the wife is too busy to take care of them. Family ties are weakened; individuals become isolated from each other. in time, the sewing machine is introduced in the home and the wife is paid not by the dress but by the hour. She is forced to work more quickly; therefore, quality deteriorates. Then she is placed in a factory, where she specializes in making parts of the dress instead of the whole dress. Soon she will not even know what the total dress looks like.

Thus, the wife becomes separated from her family and society by feeling exhausted and from the product of her craft by specializing in production of only a part of it. She is aware of what is happening and does not like it. However, she feels trapped and powerless to change her condition. According to Marx, she has become alienated. **Alienation** is the feeling of helplessness to improve one's condition or to resolve the surrounding problems. It is a significant problem for workers because they feel estranged from life itself.

According to Marx, the problem is exacerbated when those who control the means of production use societal institutions, especially those of the state, to keep others in their place and to exploit them. From this viewpoint, governments are the oppressors of the workers; and are utilized to make the rich richer and the poor poorer. The same is said of organized religion. These institutions are believed to take more from the poor than they give back. Marx claimed that without the state or churches, the owners of the means of production could not maintain their position of supremacy.

Consciousness and Classes

This, in simplified form, is what Marx thought caused of the social problems of the nineteenth century. Next, he placed these problems within an historical context. Remember, Hegel said that the *Volksgeist* determines behavior, that is, the essence or spirit of a community determines the relations among its members. Marx said the reverse, that it is the relations among its members that determines this essence or spirit. He stated that one's relation to the means by which one makes a living determines one's values, beliefs, and ideals — in short, one's *consciousness.* With this viewpoint Marx, according to some, stands Hegel on his head. It is the real, the material, which determines the ideal, according to Marx; not the ideal that determines the real, as in Hegel. Furthermore, Marx said that this relationship to the means of production also changes through the dialectic. The way by which one earns a living has changed according to the dialectic from hunting and gathering of our distant ancestors to the earning of salaries by modern workers for tasks whose purpose is not always clear. Therefore, Marxism is called *dialectic materialism.*

In the preface to *A Contribution to the Critique of Political Economy,* Marx writes:

> In the social production of their life, men enter into definite relations that are indispensable and independent of their will, relations of production which correspond to a definite state of development of their material productive forces. The sum total of these relations of production constitutes the economic structure of society, the real foundation, on which rises a legal and political superstructure and to which correspond definite forms of social consciousness. The mode of production of material life conditions the social, political and intellectual life process in general. It is not the consciousness of men that determines their being, but, on the contrary, the social being that determines their consciousness.

This notion, that history is made according to how people behave rather than how people think, is not far removed from the modern view of history. We frequently talk about "women's consciousness" as if sexuality determines how and what a person thinks. The same holds true when we speak of "black consciousness," implying that the color of a person's skin gives that person an identity. We go as far as to state that men cannot represent women in political or other gatherings and that blacks cannot represent whites. If this is true, then why not say that a person who owns the means of production cannot speak on behalf of a person who does not? Where does one draw the line in differentiating among human groups?

From Marx's viewpoint, our relations to the means of production determine not only our personal consciousness but also our institutional and societal values. The state, for example, can use its coercive power to maintain one group's power over another. According to Marxism,

Democracy in a country where the majority is composed of illiterate, destitute workers who cannot differentiate among the alternatives offered, is a sham, a cover-up for the maintenance of control by those who manage the economy. (Consider the political situation in most countries in the early and mid 1800s. Because of the disenfranchisement of women, property ownership qualifications, poll taxes, and literacy requirements less than 10 percent of the population participated in elections. Is this true democracy?) Marx believed that those who own the means of production use every way possible to maintain their power and to prevent those who are powerless from obtaining any.

According to Marx, this conflict, the dialectic among different ways of controlling the means of production, has gone on for millennia, but will soon end. In the past, the dialectic has gone on among many different groups in each society, but now the dialectic is between only two groups: those who own the means of production, **the bourgeoisie**, and those who do not, **the proletariat**. Because each possesses its own consciousness, each is a **class** by itself. A class is a sub-group of a society that is defined by how it earns a living and which in turn develops its own consciousness. Once the conflict between the bourgeoisie and the proletariat is resolved, through a proletarian revolution, the dialectic will end and a communist society will come into being.

The Communist Utopia

What will this communist society, this utopia, look like? The means of production will be owned by society as a whole, not by individuals or groups. Hence, this society will be classless. No one will own property. Everyone will be expected to give according to his or her ability and receive according to his or her needs. As Marx wrote, "from each according to ability, to each according to need." Everyone will be economic equals. The state will "wither away" since there no longer will be a need to oppress any groups. This does not mean that there would not be a need for police officers, people who put up stop signs, health inspectors, etc. These people will be needed to perform routine tasks. (It appears that Marx, like many Germans of his time, believed that the state is outside society, not coincidental with it.) If social conflict is a result of the dialectic between those who own the means of production and those who do not, then in a communistic society, where there is no such dialectic, peace will prevail.

This utopia, in which there is economic and consequently political egalitarianism, is not unlike the early stages of Rousseau's state of nature, Locke's without the use of money, or, for that matter, the Garden of Eden. In fact, a few million years ago that was probably the way our ancestors lived. They had no property, there was no state, and everyone did what he or she could to help and shared whatever the group had. In this sense, Marx was a true revolutionary because he wanted society to go back to the good old days (the word *revolution* actually means to go back to a former time, like the dials of a clock). In modern times monasteries and convents usually operate this way, and in Israel the kibbutz is a form of communal or communistic agricultural cooperative.

How to Get from Here to There

This, then, is reality and utopia. If Marx had stopped here, he would have been considered a great economic philosopher and would, by now, have been largely forgotten. However, he was also a political activist, not content with analyzing reality and envisioning a utopia. He had to find a way just as Socrates did) to get from here to there. Therefore, he wrote and spoke about how his egalitarian "republic" could be actualized.

Since the bourgeoisie would not give up its power without a fight, the proletariat needed to organize itself and wrest this power away by force. The clever bourgeoisie, however, brainwashed society into accepting things the way they were, convincing people that they had never had it so good. Therefore, those who were true to the proletarian consciousness had to take control of the proletariat. Marx referred to these supporters as the **vanguard of the proletariat**, and believed that they could be organized into the **Communist Party**. Since there is only one proletarian consciousness, there can be only one vanguard, one Communist Party.

In Marxism, there also can be only one bourgeois consciousness. When the bourgeoisie took control of the state from the aristocracy (as in the French Revolution), it used the terminology of democracy to receive the support of the peasants and workers. As we have seen, the bourgeoisie never had any intentions of sharing power, so it only used the form or trappings of democracy to win support. It offered alternate solutions and candidates, but all were bourgeois. After all, Marx asked, what was the difference between Liberal and Conservative candidates in Great Britain or Democratic and Republican candidates in the United States? He believed all candidates said basically the same things, with the only difference being details on issues or how they expressed themselves. Bourgeois democracy was a sham, a farce, he thought.

Socialism

Consequently, according to Marx, the Communist Party must do all it could to deprogram the proletariat. It must also do whatever it can to weaken the bourgeois state and destroy it. Then the party, on behalf of the proletarians can take over the institutions of the state and run them in the interests of the proletariat. Marx called this the **dictatorship of the proletariat**. Government will be placed in the hands of the representatives of the workers, the class in society that was formerly exploited by those who owned the means of production, the bourgeoisie.

The means of production and all property will be taken from their owners; the state will administer them as a trust for society. Except for one's homestead and bare necessities, private property will no longer exist. Neither will anyone be allowed to own machinery or other major tools by which to manufacture products. They, too, will be managed by a government composed of members of the Communist Party. All vestiges of bourgeois consciousness will be eliminated. Workers will get many of their needs supplied for, but will also get compensated on what and how much they produced. Total economic equality will not yet exist. This stage in the development between capitalism and communism is what Marx called **socialism**.

Socialism was to be an interim or preparatory stage toward the achievement of a communist society. During this stage, as the threat of bourgeois consciousness disappeared, the state would be dismantled. The Union of Soviet Socialist Republics was in this stage from 1917 to its demise in 1991.

Whereas the transition from the feudalist state to the capitalist state and from the capitalist state to the socialist state required the use of force, the transition from a socialist state to a communist self-governing society would be peaceful. After the achievement of this communist society no more transition would occur. These successive transitions are what history is all about. For Marx then, history is an inevitable succession of events culminating in the different relations individuals have with the means by which to earn their living; it is based on economic relationships. History moves forward according to the daily physical or material struggle to survive among members of a society, not according to the clash of values, ideals, or other norms. This theory is known as **historical materialism**.

FOCUS   MARXISM AND SOCIAL DARWINISM

Social Darwinism is a philosophy that developed at the end of the nineteenth century partially as a response to Marxism. The defining phrase of Social Darwinism, "the survival of the fittest," was applied to the interactions of individuals within a society. According to this notion, only those who are the most aggressive in their pursuit of success (however defined) would be respected in their society. Those not aggressive enough would deservedly lose and would not merit the "hard earned" charity of those who are successful. Since this supposedly natural process reflects what occurs throughout nature, men and women should not interfere with it.

The phrase "survival of the fittest" was coined not by Darwin but by peace loving Herbert Spencer in 1852. Spencer applied the phrase to the struggle among individuals within a species to find greater resources to overcome population pressures, which eventually would lead to a more cohesive society. Those who obtain the greatest resources, according to Spencer, pass this ability to their descendants. He based this idea on the theory made famous by Jean-Baptiste Lamarck at the end of the eighteenth century that acquired characteristics are inherited. Lamarck's followers opposed Darwin's theory of natural selection.

When Spencer's theory of survival of the fittest was combined in the late nineteenth century with Adam Smith's philosophy of capitalism, the free market became the arena where survival of the fittest occurred and economic forces determined the outcome of the struggle to survive. Economic success determined a person's worth to society. Since nature did not allow every person to be equally successful and economic resources were limited, those who were successful had no "natural" responsibility to share resources with those who were not successful. Consequently, the welfare of society was determined by economically successful individuals.

Marx viewed society not as a struggle for survival among individuals but as a struggle between those who have control of wealth and those who do not. After this struggle was overcome, Marx and his successors believed that a society of peace and tranquility would prevail. On the other hand, Social Darwinians believed that the struggle for survival continues forever.

Another issue on which Marxists and Social Darwinians disagreed was compensation for one's labor. Social Darwinians believed the free market would determine labor's worth. Marxists, of course, had no such notions, believing instead that society had an obligation to provide for the needs of everyone.

This discourse led to differing views on why a person works at all. Marxists, who believed that one's labor need not be rewarded, said individuals work for the sake of working, be it for the satisfaction they find in the work or for the sense of doing good for society or for something else. Social Darwinians, on the other hand, felt that the only reason people work is for the material rewards it brings them and that without these material rewards people would not work at all. In other words, to a Social Darwinian it would not have made sense for the richest person in the world to spend ten or more hours a day working hard at something simply for enjoyment if he or she made no financial gain.

Critique

Just like most of the authors we have studied, Marx did not, perhaps could not, envision future changes that societies undergo. Societies are not static entities; they have their own internal processes propelling them in directions that we cannot predict. The *Communist Manifesto* was out of date six months after its publication. Marx's thought was outdated within a few years of his death.

Most of the welfare programs that states have adopted were responses to the needs of the people. If these needs were not satisfied they would have caused societies to fall apart or lag behind economically and socially. A healthy, well-educated labor force is a precondition for a modern technological society. Since many third world countries as those in Africa and Latin America (and some states in the United States — e.g., West Virginia, Nebraska) do not have the resources to build such a labor force, they have been relegated to underdeveloped status.

All this does not mean that Marx and his ideas are more outdated than those of others we have studied. One significant contribution is his influence on our values. Not only do we expect governments to provide us with services (e.g., welfare, loans, education, social security, roads) as a right, but we also no longer tolerate the despicable conditions that our ancestors allowed. Today we are concerned about the homeless, the starving Africans, the prisoners of conscience, and those experiencing discrimination in South Africa and elsewhere. We make financial contributions to Live-Aid, Farm-Aid, Oxfam, Amnesty International, the Red Cross, and many other organizations. A hundred years ago thousands of people were homeless, starving, imprisoned unjustly, discriminated against, or murdered by government forces, and yet hardly anybody complained or did anything else about it. Certainly governments were not pushed to do anything about alleviating these conditions. Today if someone starves to death in an industrial society, this tragedy becomes a major media event, hearings are held, and policymakers and imple-mentors scurry around trying to make sure it does not happen again.

To a great extent we have become Marxists. We do believe that everyone's labor should be rewarded by wages or a salary that will provide him or her with a decent standard of living; that it is society's responsibility to provide for those who cannot provide for themselves; that excessive profit at the expense of others is wrong; that in a society in which there is economic well-being, conflict will be minimal and progress great; and that government is the societal entity which must bring about and regulate economic well-being.

This does not mean that all is well. The gap between the rich and the poor is widening in almost every society. In most societies too many people are still living in dreadful conditions. However, because of our values, we are not only aware of these conditions but are trying to force governments to do something about them.

Is economic equality a prerequisite for political equality? This question makes us feel uneasy. It seems almost as if our minds say "yes," while our hearts say "no." (All of us would like to be richer and have more than others.) We do know that the typical citizen of any country, for example, cannot afford to run for public office. Even if the citizen received contri-butions from others, he or she still would have to invest much of personal funds for the campaign. Assuming a coal miner received some contribu-tions, could he or she afford to take time off from work to campaign? Could this person afford to take off from work for two or three months every year to serve in a state or provincial legislature? Would the employer allow him or her to do so?

How open is the "democratic" process to the poor? How typical of the American voters, is the membership of the U.S. Senate, where more than half its members are millionaires, or the U.S. House of Representatives, where more than two-fifths are so? What about the notion that money buys political influence? Every week we hear or read about a pressure group achieving a legislative approval for a project, a corporation winning a lucrative government contract by making political donations, a team of corporate lawyers beating a charge or a lawsuit brought against them by an individual or public interest group, a pressure group or corpo-ration using extensive advertising to manipulate voters into doing its will.

The issue that Marx raised is still there. We sometimes like to sweep it under the rug and try to ignore it. Occasionally, however, it appears and highlights the major weakness in our concept of democracy.

Another legacy that Marx and some of his contemporary economic theorists left us is the view that economic relationships determine all other relations, including political ones. As we saw in our discussions of the Greeks, they viewed the polis, or society, as an entirety, a whole. The social-contract theorists had a similar view. However, the proponents of Marxism and their rivals, the Social Darwinians, validated the view that society is segmented into abstract economic, social, cultural, and political divisions of which they believed the economic is the most important.

This segmentation is artificial. Members of society do not state they are economic members, social members, cultural members or political members. Nor do they state that one moment they belong to one segment and the next to another. The economic members cannot be separated from the others, even in the abstract. (Where does economics begin and end?) Those who compose society, no matter how they earn their living, are bound together as a unit precisely because they share their society's norms, values, beliefs, and patterns of behavior.

Of course, members of society in their relations with each other develop patterns of behavior and norms that are of an economic nature. Some of these economic relations may even determine certain organizational aspects of a society. But so do many other non-economic relations. To point to the economic ones and state they are the most important is too simplistic. A society's composure and other features are the result of the totality of the relations its members have with each other.

On the other hand, since modern society cannot be organized but through political institutions, the political aspects of society become the most important in determining that society's viability and future. Politics determines economics (not the other way around, as Marx and some modern economists would have it). Societal policies are not made by individuals or groups of individuals solely on the basis of economics, but on the basis of many other variables some of which are never known. That policy makers' decisions have economic consequences as well as social and cultural consequences is obvious. However, the decisions themselves are made within a political context, within institutions created and legitimized through the political process. The role politics plays in the maintenance and viability of society is the focus of the next three parts of this book.

📖 TERMS TO REMEMBER

Karl Marx
Georg Wilhelm Friedrich Hegel
Volksgeist
dialectic
thesis
antithesis
synthesis
Communist Manifesto
theory of surplus value
alienation
means of production
dialectic materialism
bourgeoisie
proletariat
class
vanguard of the proletariat
Communist Party
dictatorship of the proletariat
socialism
historical materialism

📖 SUGGESTED READINGS

Deutcher, Isaac. *Marxism in Our Time.* Edited by Tamara Deutscher. Berkeley, CA: Ramparts Press, 1971. Highlights from works of the foremost biographer of Marx.

Lichtheim, George. *Marxism: An Historical and Critical Study.* New York: Praeger, 1962. An older but still enlightening analysis of Marxism.

Marx, Karl. *Karl Marx: A Reader.* Edited by Jon Elster. New York: Press Syndicate of the University of Cambridge, 1986. Selections from the work of Marx with some introductory comments from the editor.

Marx, Karl and Frederick Engels. *Selected Works in One Volume.* New York: International Publishers, 1977. A collection of pamphlets and articles written by the two proponents of communism by the Soviet publishing house.

Peel, J.D.Y. *Herbert Spencer: The Evolution of a Sociologist.* New York: Basic Books, Inc. 1971. An analytical biography of Spencer.

NOTES

1. All quotations from Marx are from *Karl Marx and Frederick Engels: Selected Works in Two Volumes.* (Moscow: Foreign Languages Publishing House, 1955).

Political Behavior & Processes

PART THREE

7

Society and Politics

The idea that all humans are politically and, perhaps, economically equal has influenced the modern belief that the individual is the principal player in society who must be catered to by all human invention, including institutions. By elevating the individual to the level of monarchs, social philosophers have relegated society to the dustbin of human endeavors.

Let us look a little closer at the role society plays in human lives.

Society and the Individual

What is society in relation to the individual? We know that society is composed of you and I and everyone else exhibiting the same behavior, speaking a similar language, and believing in similar ideals, values, and

123

norms. Without us society would not exist. But is society the sum of the individuals that compose it? Or is society more than the sum of its parts?

Hermits and Gurus

You and I would be much different if were we hermits, living divorced from society. An individual without family or society is terribly lonely and may exhibit pathological symptoms. He or she may manifest symptoms of extreme alienation, or have problems of depression or authoritarian symptoms. (The latter may occur when an individual "blindly" follows a supposed leader, who actually is a tyrant, as a substitute for a father.) Alone in the voyage through life, such an individual would have slim chances of survival. If this is the situation today, then in the supposed state of nature could man alone have survived predators? Could men and women alone, by themselves as individuals have overcome the challenges the environment constantly hurled against them?

While young, we not only needed others for our physical well being, we needed them for our psychic well-being. People, especially infants, need to be physically touched by others. Infants and toddlers who are deprived of human touch and are not caressed, handled, and played with do not grow up to become normal persons. They become extremely shy, aggressive, very fearful of anything strange, and incapable of forming social bonds. These psychological problems often lead to mental or physical illness. Our mental and physical health is established and maintained through interactions with others.

Adults who have problems forming social bonds often become mentally ill. They keep to themselves, while believing that others (even those assigned to help and protect them) are out to destroy them or take away what they hold dear. Frequently, material objects become more important to them than people. Mistrust of others causes them not to read or to listen to anybody, except perhaps a small group of like-minded individuals. Since they are not able to bond with others, these individuals have difficulty interacting with persons of the opposite sex, family members, and professional colleagues; often they cannot keep a job. They blame everyone else for their misfortune, and their anger may lead them to violence, including terrorism.

The bonds we develop with others over the years make us what we are. Society, in other words, allows each of us to bring forth something that makes our humanity realizable. Yes, each of us can live as hermits in a forest or as gurus on top of a mountain, but while living as such we are not truly human. Our needs, as determined by our genes, are unfulfilled. Note that in the criminal justice system one of the most extreme punishments is isolated confinement. Aristotle was right: Without society we are either beasts or gods but not humans.

Locke said that we are the product of our experiences. Most of these experiences emanate from the social environment, from society itself. According to Locke, and many contemporary social psychologists, we are largely the product of society. Our individuality, which makes each of us unique and is largely the result of our thinking processes, is formed unconsciously by our social experiences. Since, society shapes us, without it we would be less "human" than what we are.

Society also allows each of us to develop our own identity. We define ourself in terms of the society in which we live. When we say I am a German, or Nigerian, or Australian, or Cuban, we are implying that German, Nigerian, Australian or Cuban society determines who we are, that somehow without this social identity we cannot really define ourselves.

Society then must be something more than the sum of its parts because it allows individuals within it to become human beings, to become themselves.

Societies Are Not Alike

Not all societies are alike. Not only is the physical environment different (i.e., availability of natural resources, climate, topography), but the internal composition is as well. Some societies, for example, are large and spread out (e.g., U.S., Canada, and Russia) while others are small and compact (e.g., Singapore). Some, like the Netherlands, have a disproportionate number of older persons over age fifty, others, like Yemen, have many young persons under age eighteen. Small, dense societies containing many youngsters will invariably have different processes, institutions, norms, and behavioral patterns than large, sparsely populated ones with more working-age persons.

Societies, in adapting to ever-changing environments, drag their members with them. The desire to succeed or even just to remain alive makes, individuals do what others within their society are doing. Potato farming is the main occupation among the Aymara Indians in the high plateau of Bolivia. Ethics, religion, dress, and daily life revolve around the planting, caring, and harvesting of potatoes. Stealing a bag of seed potatoes is a worse offense than stealing a bicycle, even though the latter may cost more. The importance of religious holidays is determined not only by their intrinsic value but also by how closely they fall into the various cycles of potato cultivation. A person who makes a living mining cannot appreciate the meaning and symbolism of the customs, traditions, beliefs, and norms of the potato farmers. If the miner lives among these farmers for awhile, he or she will eventually participate in the culture to avoid being different. Societies shape the individuals within them.

As for a person's humanity, however, it may make little difference to what type of society he or she belongs. Any society can provide the social environment required to satisfy each individual's need to bond.

Why Do We Do the Things We Do?

If society influences our behavior, to what extent are we, rational homo sapiens, in control of ourselves? To what extent are our lives under our rational control? To what extent then are government institutions and the state the result of our conscious and deliberate efforts?

To answer these questions we need to look at humans from a somewhat different perspective. Have you ever wondered why in a setting that does not have a fixed seating arrangement most persons continually sit in the same seat? Why do our routines hardly ever change? In many ways our behaviors are predictable because we do things without thinking. We have observed that all animals (e.g., dogs, cats, horses, cattle, and birds) do things repetitively. We attribute their behaviors to nonrational capacities, sometimes calling them instinct or, as with my dog that barks for no reason, stupidity. When judging the cause of human behavior, however, we seldom use the word *instinct*. (At times we do use the word *stupid*, but only in assessing the consequences of that behavior.) Yet, are not the causes of human behavior similar to those of animals?

Of Ants and Humans

It may be undignified to compare humans with ants (not sure whose dignity would be more affected), but look at the characteristics ants possess.

Age-grading, antennal rites, body licking, calendar, cannibalism, caste determination, caste laws, colony-foundation rules, colony organization, cleanliness training, communal nurseries, cooperative labor, cosmology, courtship, division of labor, drone control, education, eschatology, ethics, etiquette, euthanasia, fire making, food taboos, gift giving, government, greetings, grooming rituals, hospitality, housing, hygiene, incest taboos, language, larval care, law, medicine, metaphorphosis rites, mutual regurgitation, nursing castes, nuptial flights, nutrient eggs, population policy, queen obeisance, residence rules, sex determination, soldier castes, sisterhoods, status differentiation, sterile workers, surgery, symbiont care, tool making, trade, visiting, weather control.[1]

Many of these characteristics could also be attributed to humans. In fact, a similar list for humans contains the following.

Age grading, athletic sports, bodily adornment, calendar, cleanliness training, community organization, cooking, cooperative labor, cosmology, courtship, dancing, decorative art, divination, division of labor, dream interpretation, education, eschatology, ethics, ethnobotany, etiquette, faith healing, family feasting, fire making, folklore, food taboos, funeral rites, games, gestures, gift giving, government, greetings, hair styles, hospitality, housing, hygiene, incest taboos, inheritance rules, joking, kin groups, kinship nomenclature, language, law, luck, superstitions, magic, marriage, mealtimes, medicine, obstetrics, penal sanctions, personal names, population policy, postnatal care, pregnancy usages, property rights, propitiation of supernatural beings, puberty customs, religious ritual, residence rules, sexual restrictions, surgery, tool making, trade, visiting, weaving, and weather control.[2]

These are characteristics that human societies supposedly share whether they are in cities, such as Toronto or Paris, or deep in the Amazonian rain forest. But there is more. We have all at one time or another been fascinated by a column of ants moving to or from its colony. So assume a giant ant in a spaceship is hovering above one of our large cities. It might say something like, "Our traffic patterns going to or from work appear to be very similar to those of humans."

Indeed, the behavior and patterns created by movements of large numbers of individuals appear very similar, whether they are ants, antelope, elephants, or humans driving in cars on the interstate or in tanks in the Arabian Desert. Such patterns are influenced by the type of terrain, the number of individuals, the climate, and other factors. Individuals, however, within a given movement are not necessarily aware of the pattern they contribute to and may not even be aware of the influences exerted on them. For example, when walking to and from classes or work, few, if any, individuals are aware of the hundreds or thousands of others doing the same thing.

Genes and the Environment

Behavior is the result of many variables, particularly genes and the environment. The genetic variables, of which we are only now beginning to understand, were inherited from our ancestors and consequently live on in future generations. They sustain our physical characteristics and many of our social and psychological ones, too. The environmental variables, ranging from the society and landscape in which we grow up to the climate we adjust to influence us permanently. The influence of other variables may be as temporary or transitory as the words you read on this page. Some variables we could probably list, others will remain unknown. Some may be more influential than others.

Why is sugar sweet and desirable to us? Chemists have identified the compounds of sugar and their molecular structures, which do not cause sweetness. Our taste buds determine sweetness. But, why do we find the taste of sugar so pleasant? More than likely our ancestors millions of years ago discovered that ripe fruit gave them energy. The natural sugar content in ripe fruit is high. So, over the millennia a gene for sweet taste developed that makes us content when we consume something sweet.

On the other hand, environmental factors often influence us in subtle ways. In our industrial and service-oriented society, where everyone has to be at a given place at a given time, punctuality is so ingrained in us that it has become an automatic response. When we have an appointment at a given time, we arrive within a few minutes of that time. If we are late, we feel guilty. Today time is counted in minutes (sometimes even seconds), but centuries ago time was counted in periods of the day (i.e., before noon, after noon, evening, night), and before then in seasons. Seasons were important to our ancestors who planted crops and hunted prey; but today seasons are no longer important because we labor in lighted, air-conditioned offices, doing tasks for which the weather or time of day is irrelevant. In those past times, a family did not disown a member for being late; today, however, an employer may dismiss an employee for tardiness.

Hierarchies

Our genetic makeup and the environment in which we live often determine our status within society. For example, the fact that we need others to survive is part of our genetic makeup; we really cannot help but be social animals. However, group membership forces upon us a ranking within that group, especially if the group is very large. We may be ranked according to age, sex, physical strength or appearance, abilities and capacities in certain endeavors, and other characteristics.

Basically, two types of hierarchies exist. In the traditional nuclear family a straight-line hierarchy exists in which the father is at the top followed by the mother, and then the children in birth order. Everyone knows where he or she stands in relation to the other members of the family.

The second type, the pyramidical hierarchy, operates among groups of unrelated persons, such as gangs. A few members are at the top, somewhat more persons in the second rank, more in the third, and still more in the bottom ranks. The lower in rank a member is, the less influence he or she has on what the group does and the more demands he or she receives from those in the higher ranks. An army is organized in a pyramidical hierarchy.

Today individuals are members of many hierarchies. Students may find themselves near the bottom of the college community hierarchy while also near the top of their hometown community hierarchy. A student may be the newest member of a sorority or fraternity, and at the same time be the captain of a sport team. Each of us is a member of many hierarchies and it is sometimes difficult to realize that we cannot transfer our 'exalted' status in one hierarchy to another.

Besides belonging to several hierarchies simultaneously, humans have yet another unique feature regarding their organization. While relationships in animal species can only be one-on-one (i.e., the dominant male can force acquiescence from a lower ranked animal, but he cannot force the second animal to make a third do something), relationships among humans can be interactive (i.e., an individual can interact with several others in various levels of the hierarchy). One person may tell a second person to tell a third what to do. For example, the general in an army gives a command to the colonels; the colonels command the lieutenants; the lieutenants the sergeants; and the sergeants the privates. What the general wanted, the privates carried out; but the general was not in contact with the privates, nor did he give commands to them directly. Individuals in each hierarchial level can become active participants in the chains of command from the top to the bottom. This no other animal can do.

Among animals, the top animals command each individual of the group directly; there are no intermediaries. Since the top animal can only control a few animals in such manner, animal groups tend to be small. Human groups can be almost limitless in size because more levels can always be added between the top and the bottom. Lost under this system, however, is the control that the top level has over of the bottom. Each level in the hierarchy, by interpreting and filtering the commands from the top level, lessens the importance of the top. Furthermore, each level needs the support of the lower levels to get anything done, resulting not in a hierarchy in which dominance is the main feature but in one in which each level cooperates with those above and below it. This cooperation is not among equals, but among individuals ranked differently.

To what extent do we as individuals control our rank in most of these hierarchies? Not one of us chose the womb from which we were born or the environment that nurtured us. When we were young we did not have the capacity or ability to choose. As we mature the decisions we make that place us at a given rank in the hierarchies are invariably influenced by what we experienced and learned when young.

How Significant is Human Thought?

A few decades ago meteorologist Edward Lorenz watched his computer generate a line graph from calculations based on a dozen or so variables that influence the weather. At one point he stopped the computer and got some coffee. When he returned, he entered the figures again but rounded them to three decimal points. He noticed that the waves of the new graph were somewhat different from those on the previous one. He let that computer continue to generate the lines while starting a second graph with the figures rounded to six decimal points.

When he compared the output at the same number of calculations, Lorenz found that the waves began to diverge to the point where they were no longer the same. His explanation for this was that by rounding off, even to the third decimal point, he had changed the values slightly and the computer, by making millions of calculations based on these changed values, had magnified the differences. It was then that he stated a phrase that has since become a reference for workers with quantifiable variables: "When a butterfly flaps its wings over Beijing, it affects the weather in Peoria. "

Minute changes in the values of its variables affect the weather. Weather, however, is but one variable that affects human behavior. Another variable, for example, is the small amount (usually measured in milligrams) of chemicals (i.e., medication) that make us feel better physically and psychically. Hundreds or thousands of different variables combined determine what we do at any moment. Included in this myriad of variables is one that we often presume is the most important — thought.

Of the countless variables that affect human behavior, how important is thought? Our ability to think, after all, determines everything we do and is the most distinctive feature we possess. Yet, in our daily travels, for example, we seldom take a different route. When we do make changes in our routines, we often feel uncomfortable. When writers have stated that we are captives of our destiny, they implied, that we are not in control, through our thought processes, of what happens to us.

Decisions we make are often based on impulse or emotion. We are like funnels through which undefinable variables propel us in one direction or another. How often have we done something, even something important, that later with some reflection we wish we had not done?

Our genetic make up, our physiology, the physical and social environment in which we live, the drinks we imbibe, the food we eat, the air we breathe, and many other variables influence our behavior. These variables even influence what we think, as anyone who has drunk too much alcohol or taken psychedelic drugs knows only too well.

Societal Policies

If countless variables affect what you and I do, then these variables must also affect what society does. Since government is part of society, it must also be affected by countless variables. If this is the case, then how significant were the thoughts of important writers to the development of political processes and institutions? Did they shape events, or did they only describe events that were happening or merely rationalize past events? To what extent do the members of society consciously determine its future? The organization and development of society proceeds regardless of who said what, when, where, or how.

This brings us to a terrible dilemma. If government is a result of variables, most of which lie beyond the control of members of society, how can it be judged? Given the demographic and territorial characteristics of the United States or Canada, could these two countries have had any different organizational structure than what they now possess? Can ethical evaluations be made of Hitler's Germany or Stalin's Soviet Union when an individual or small group of persons cannot be blamed for actions that they may not have completely controlled? If members of a society are not in control of their government, why should they be judged, and how?

Perhaps there is a way out of this dilemma. Policy makers, be they legislators or executives, may make decisions that are in harmony with the innumerable variables that determine societal development. When this happens, society develops efficiently and without disruptions. When these decisions, however, are not in harmony with the variables leading to societal development, inefficiency and social disruptions may occur and eventually the decisions are corrected. Since each society's development hinges on its own mix of variables, every society, including the state is different. Policy makers and their decisions can be judged on whether the consequences that occur helped or disrupted the development of the society.

An important point to remember is that policy decisions cannot be measured or evaluated in terms of months or even years because a society's life span exceeds by far those of the members that compose it. Societies exist for centuries, even for millennia; an individual lives less than ninety years. How important to a society today were the decisions made by its individual members a century or more ago? Obviously, legislators and executives debated among themselves the merits of their decisions. However, is societal development the accumulated decisions or policies individuals made over the years? Or do these decisions and policies have, at best, a weak influence on the complex mix of variables upon which societal development depends? How important are the societal (i.e., political, economic, social, cultural) decisions that any one individual makes?

Integration of the Individual to Society

To individuals, their decisions are very important. Decisions indicate how well individuals are integrated with society and its development. We should not be as concerned with how individuals mold society but rather with how well they adapt to society and the variables that determine its development. Unless individuals successfully relate to society, they cannot fully use what society provides nor be psychologically at peace with themselves.

Why should we bother with issues and problems today that have little direct bearing on our lives? We bother with them because we want to be an integral part of society. Unless we relate to them today (and have informed opinions of them), we cannot relate to others in our society. And it might just be possible that our perceived resolutions of issues and problems will help foster their societal resolution.

In fact, one of the most important burdens we have is showing how well integrated we are. We feel a constant need to prove we belong to a group, be it a social organization with its own patterns of behavior or even a make-believe group, such as followers of an athlete or of a fashion designer, with its own dress code, jargon, and attitudes, or to society in general. Usually the clothes we wear, the foods we eat, the politics we engage in shows others that we are similar to them and therefore part of society. We need this integration not only for psychic and physical well-being but also to avoid being treated as an outsider.

We show our integration in the community in different ways, such as volunteering in private or public organizations and participating in cultural events or sports. Political activity is just one way to show integration, but it is a very important way. After all, society is held together through the state and politics. Organizations and cultural events cannot exist without the state. We cannot escape its influence no matter what or where we are. Therefore, we are forced to deal with the issues and problems that affect the state. And, let us remember, whatever the state does affects the development of society.

We, as individuals, are the means through which societal development occurs. Our contribution to that development, individually or collectively, may be small, but we have to provide for the propagation of future generations by becoming closely associated with our fellow members of society.

The Selfishness of Political Participation

Seen in this perspective, political behavior is less a determinant of societal policy or organization and more of an adaptive strategy for survival within a society. Political participation then is a selfish act by the individual, done for his or her benefit. Hopefully, it will also benefit society, and by that be philanthropic. (It is not altruistic, as this implies sacrificing one's own welfare for that of others.)

But what is "selfishness?" Is it "selfish" to read a novel instead of attending a group's meeting? Selfishness is frequently defined in social terms (i.e., selfishness is posed as the opposite of philanthropy) despite the benefits to the individual. Yet, and this is the irony, being selfish also may mean to manifest societal values and norms. Reading a novel instead of attending a meeting may actually be more beneficial for society in the end if what is learned by reading is more relevant to that individual's current or future behavior than what would have been learned or contributed in a meeting.

Participating in politics for one's own benefit and deriving profit from it, can still be for the good of society, if such benefit or profit also carries over to society. My wish to integrate with society is not only good for me but also for society. By participating in politics, even for my own selfish purposes, I am applying and propagating the values, norms, and behavior of my society.

The individual is the tool that society uses to develop its future; society is the tool that the individual uses to develop his or her future. For the welfare or viability of the one or the other, the individual and society must be integrated.

Despite it being a mechanism by which survival is made easier, society can also be an obstacle to that survival. Society's norms, values, and beliefs can be impediments to the welfare of individuals, especially when they are near the bottom of the social or economic totem pole. Women and minorities have had to struggle against social norms to assert themselves and acquire independent standing socially and economically. The replacement of prevailing social norms is not easy. Often the political process is the only way this can be achieved, sometimes after long, arduous efforts.

Prevailing social norms harmful to one's welfare can also be overcome through subsocial groups that reject these norms. For example, political behavior or even better, "un-behavior," of the downtrodden and poor is shown in the high rate of crime committed and low voter turnout and participation in politics in general.

On the other hand, a society's well-to-do commit few crimes and participate in politics. They live in harmony with society's norms, values, and beliefs and make good use of them, frequently to exploit the poor. Whether through voting, nonvoting, or actual policy making, individuals use government processes and institutions for their own advantage. Some may indeed abuse them. However, this abuse does not last long. Some policies or structures may temporarily profit one group as opposed to another; but eventually society's corrective variables will even things out.

(For instance, two centuries ago the rich profited disproportionately from the resources of U.S. society. Their descendants in the U.S. are not listed among the Forbes 400 wealthiest Americans today.)

Political Acculturation and Socialization

How important is political participation for the individual? It is very important. The act of voting, for example, allows the individual to participate in a ritual that shows political integration in the society.

This integration emanates from two sources: political acculturation and political socialization. **Political acculturation** is the continuing process in which an individual learns and accepts the values, beliefs, and norms of government institutions and processes of society. We accept and have been accultured to many of the concepts and values of the political philosophers, especially of the social contract theorists, which laid the foundation for our own ideas on the relationships among the individual, society, and the state. **Political socialization is** the process in which an individual learns and accepts the prevalent behavioral patterns toward that same government and its processes. Political socialization is demonstrated by the way we express our opinions and attitudes toward government, interact with a police officer or a legislator, behave at public meetings, show respect for laws and their enforcers and interpreters, and utilize our voting rights.

These values, beliefs, norms, and behaviors are not inventions of yesterday, but rather cumulative results of generational development. Each of the authors we have studied had a special term for these values, beliefs, norms, and behaviors calling them golden mean, general will, *Volksgeist*, or class consciousness.

An example of political acculturation. School children in a California town parade with the scrap metal they have collected for the war effort, May 1942. School activities such as saluting the national flag and participation in scouting are vital in instilling patriotic values in children in many countries.

We become accultured and socialized in many ways. For centuries individuals interacted mainly with members of their families, seldom with strangers. Today individuals interact mostly with persons outside the family, and less with family members. This shift required a considerable change in normal behavior. In the family, behavioral patterns, such as manners, deference to elders, idioms, and habits, were largely determined by the family itself. As the family bonds loosened and individuals interacted more with strangers, the strangers determined the behavioral patterns. For greater cohesiveness among individual members (as opposed to the weakening families), society demanded greater acquiescence to the new behavioral norms.

Family, friends, peers, media, teachers, government all pressure us to accept the prevailing norms. Often we are not even aware that we are being conditioned to them. If we don't approve of something and complain about it, upon reflection we usually realize that it is an insignificant matter, hardly affecting development of society.

Today we have many more societal controls to inhibit our behavior than ever before, from placing our garbage in different containers according to recyclables to not jaywalking to wearing different clothing for different occasions to using proper etiquette when sending e-mail.

We are forced to adapt to these controls and to **internalize** them, making them part of our inner nature so that we abide by them unconsciously. For example, when we learn to drive an automobile, we are so conscious about the do's and don'ts in getting the car moving that we often do not pay attention to where we are driving. In time, usually without us being aware of it, the rules become so habitual that we are no longer conscious of them and can therefore pay more attention to where we are going. Many societal rules that we follow today developed without anyone being particularly aware that they were there.

Becoming accultured and socialized takes much effort. In industrialized countries today at least sixteen years of schooling is needed. A hundred years ago twelve years of schooling was necessary and a thousand years ago, six. Oddly, being educated means being controlled. Much of what we learn are the concepts and jargon of society's norms.

Saying No to Social Norms and Values

It is easier to go along with the current trend than to change. Change involves risktaking, which many people are not willing to do because they

An adult literacy class in inter-war Russia. People as they acquired education eventually built up a store of aspirations and grievances, that led to later democratic developments.

are comfortable with the way things are. Generally, people do not want to appear different from anyone else, even if they do not agree with existing conditions. In *The Revolt of the Masses*, Spanish writer José Ortega y Gasset states that even educated men and women succumb to pressures of conformity and become like cows in a herd, doing what others do for no other reason than that the others are doing it. In the United States the cliche, "keeping up with the Joneses," also implies this. Not many individuals are willing to sacrifice a lot to stand up and say "no" when others say "yes." Conforming to the prevailing norms, however, can be harmful for society because problems remain hidden and unaddressed.

Government officials frequently attempt to force conformity to their strongly held beliefs by using the full power of public institutions and law. Many times this approach fails, as it did in Nazi Germany and the pre-Gorbachev Soviet Union, because what the people are expected to believe and how they should behave are so different from how they have been socialized and acculturated or from what they have learned from books, peers, family, and friends.

On the other hand, sometimes segments of society try to force the government to impose their strongly held beliefs, especially on proper behavior, on the rest of society. Current controversial social issues such as abolishing a woman's right to abortion and censoring certain works of art, are examples of how a persistent and vocal group can gain government and society's attention.

Consensus

We label individuals who do not conform to the prevailing norms, beliefs, values, and behavior of a society as troublemakers, outsiders, radicals, etc. This implies that most other people consider the nonconformist's desires, demands, or behavior intolerable, unacceptable, and not consensual. Most decisions in a society are made by a consensus of its members. **Consensus** is what most everyone in society will tolerate; not necessarily what they agree with but rather what they can live with. When given a choice you might rank

A over B, B over C, and C over D. Others rankings may be B, C, D or C, A, D or A, D, B. But unlike A, B, or C no one opposes D to the point they won't even include it in the ranking. Since D may be the alternative that almost everyone can live with even though they might not agree with it, D becomes the consensual choice. Those who cannot live with D are troublemakers, radicals, etc.

In consensus making, an individual's values and desires are less important than his or her adjustment to the consensus. Who initiated the decision and how it came about is not of consequence; what is important is that society has incorporated new norms and behavior through which it continues to develop. Individuals who accept the change are considered integrated; those who do not, are considered outcasts. Remember that outcasts do not have popular support, and, therefore, seldom are successful effectuating the changes they advocate.

Humans, as other living beings, are captives of their genes and their environment. Society is part of the environment to which everyone has to adapt. Each society has its own composition and dynamics. Society outlives any one of its members; therefore, its members have only limited influence on its dynamics. To succeed within a society individuals must become integral members who exhibit behavior in accord with society's norms. The political process facilitates this integration.

TERMS TO REMEMBER

political acculturation
political socialization
internalize
consensus

SUGGESTED READINGS

Adorno, Theodor W. and others. *The Authoritarian Personality.* New York: Harper, 1950. The classic compendium of articles by scholars in various fields on the causes and effects of authoritarianism.

Bettelheim, Bruno. *The Informed Heart: Autonomy in a Mass Age.* Glencoe, IL: Free Press, 1960. A psychiatrist who spent time in a concentration camp before World War II evaluates his experience and projects it to society in general.

Degler, Carl N. *In Search of Human Nature: The Decline and Revival of Darwinism in American Social Thought.* New York: Oxford University Press, 1991. A history of the attempt to base social science thought on Darwinian ideas.

Des Pres, Terrence. *The Survivor: An Anatomy of Life in Death Camps.* New York: Oxford University Press, 1976. The nobility of humans even when forced to live in the most degrading conditions is explained and analyzed.

Gleick, James. *Chaos: Making a New Science.* New York: Viking, 1987. A popular account of chaos theory, fractals, and other new perspectives developing in the sciences.

Gould, Stephen Jay. *The Mismeasure of Man.* New York: Norton, 1981. Essays by a paleontologist on the adaptation of animals, including man, to their environments.

Kummer, Hans. *Primate Societies: Group Techniques of Ecological Adaptation.* Chicago: Aldine-Atherton, 1971. Field observation of baboons and what we can learn from their behavior.

Masters, Roger D. *The Nature of Politics.* New Haven: Yale University Press, 1989. Political behavior and institutions are linked to natural selection, evolution, and adaptation.

Ortega y Gasset, Jose. *The Revolt of the Masses.* Translated, annotated, and with an introduction by Anthony Kerrigan. Notre Dame, IN: University of Notre Dame Press, 1985. Observations by the foremost twentieth-century Spanish political philosopher on the results of population growth, industrialization, and mass political participation. First published in 1930.

Wiegele, Thomas C. *Biology and the Social Sciences: An Emerging Revolution.* Boulder, CO: Westview Press, 1982. Over twenty articles by scholars in all social science fields on how new studies in animal behavior are influencing their thinking and research.

Wilson, Edward Osborne. *On Human Nature.* New York: Harvard University Press, 1978. Modern concepts of sociobiology are applied to the human condition.

Wilson, Edward Osborne. *Sociobiology: The New Synthesis.* New York: Belknap Press of Harvard University Press, 1975. The classic work by which genetics, evolution, adaptation, and natural selection are used to explain and predict animal behavior.

Wilson, Richard W. *The Moral State: A Study of the Political Socialization of Chinese and American Children.* New York: Free Press, 1974. A comparison of how children are socialized in Chinatown (New York City), Hong Kong, Taiwan, and northern New Jersey.

Wolfe, Alam. *The Human Difference: Animals, Computers, and the Necessity of Social Science.* Berkeley, CA: University of California Press, 1993. Social science, inasmuch as it is the study of human behavior, interactions, and institutions, has very little use for models from the physical sciences or biology.

NOTES

1. Wilson, Edward O. *On Human Nature.* (New York: Bantam Books, 1978). p23.
2. Murdock, George P. in *On Human Nature,* by Edward O. Wilson. (New York: Bantam Books, 1978).

8

Public Opinion

Outline
- Attitudes and Opinions
- Opinions, Beliefs, and Ideologies
- Role of the Media
- Publics
- Public Opinion
- Accuracy of Polls

A s we have seen, we are not in full control of our political behavior because of certain constraints with which we have to live. These constraints are genetic determinants, environmental factors, learning and conditioning of which we are not conscious, and a small amount of learning of which we are. Change any of these variables, even by a small amount, and the consequences they produce would be different. All these factors predispose us to do and say certain things when stimulated. Often we are not even aware of these predispositions, because we have not experienced the stimuli that trigger them.

Attitudes and Opinions

When these predispositions are expressed, they are called **attitudes**. An attitude then is an expressed predisposition. For example, suppose I insulted you and you immediately punched me in the nose. Hitting me is an attitude, and in so doing you are expressing a predisposition. Sometimes we express our attitudes verbally (i.e., with words). A verbally expressed attitude is an **opinion**. If you cursed at me after I insulted you, you would be giving your opinion of me.

I could also encourage you to give me your opinion by just asking you a question, such as "What would you do if I were to say something insulting to you?" Your answer is an opinion that displays an attitude, which is based on one or more predispositions. In politics we are not interested in discovering how you react to an insult, but we are interested in your opinions regarding political phenomena, such as what candidates you prefer, what you think are the important issues, what policy alternatives should be undertaken, and how you evaluate the effectiveness of government procedures, institutions, and policies, etc. Answers to these types of questions guide students and actors of politics in their determinations of what governments should do and what the people under their jurisdiction will tolerate.

Opinions, Beliefs, and Ideologies

Although a person's opinions generally change over time, beliefs seldom change. Beliefs are formed from childhood learning (conscious and unconscious) and take a long time to crystallize; opinions stem from adulthood experiences and are voiced as soon as the opportunity to express them arises. Beliefs are an extremely important part of a person since they form the basis of one's character. (By my beliefs, you will know me.) Not everyone is fully conscious of his or her beliefs; often one's beliefs show themselves only under unusual circumstances (such as a disaster). For some persons beliefs are such important attributes that he or she might be willing to die for them.

No one ever really dies for their opinions. People sometimes get into fights over their opinions, but they do not willingly want to die for them. Opinions are usually more complex and ill-defined, because situation and time determine the mix of attitudes that prevail. Beliefs are simpler and succinct. Opinions may change because of logic or new information; logic and information will seldom, if ever, change beliefs.

Since an individual may have many beliefs, some inconsistencies and conflicts may result. This is especially true regarding political beliefs. Therefore, many people accommodate their beliefs by systematizing them into a hierarchy. A hierarchy of beliefs is an **ideology**. An ideology structures economic, social, and political beliefs into a unified order, ranking them according to a set of principles or a set of publicly accepted axioms. Anarchism, fascism, and communism are based on principles; American welfarism, democracy, and free enterprise are based on accepted axioms. Ideologies based on principles that are not generally accepted are viewed with disdain and considered disruptive; those based on premises generated and accepted by a society are, obviously, approved by that society.

Normally an individual's opinions are not ordered or ranked. They appear to float all over the place and indeed may be inconsistent and in conflict with each other. Since they change, there is no need to systematize them.

Role of the Media

More so than at any time in the past, opinions are formed on the basis of information from the mass media. Decades and centuries ago written information was too costly for the average person or simply unavailable, and the main source of information was word of mouth, either from family members, friends, neighbors, or government or church officials. Today, the individual is besieged with information, which is either free or very inexpensive, from the Internet, radio, television, newspapers, and magazines.

In the last few decades, computerized data storage and retrieval systems have collected and made available more information than in all of human history. New data, or *news,* is constantly being generated, collected, stored, and retrieved. It is not the quantity of data that determines what is known today, but rather the selection of which pieces of data are published or broadcasted.

The process of selecting data to publish or broadcast is made by anyone with access to it. Data is always managed. Data managed by government agencies to influence public opinion is usually labeled **propaganda**. During the Persian Gulf War in the winter of 1991, Iraq launched several Scud missiles against Israeli cities and some targets in Saudi Arabia. To keep Israel from retaliating, the United States placed modified Patriot anti-plane missiles in Israel and targeted the Scuds. Soon the news pro-

When Iraq attacked Israel with Scud missiles during the 1991 Gulf War, the U.S. deployed Patriot missiles to Israel.

grams were full of stories, based on information from government officials, about the number of Scuds shut down by the Patriots. President George Bush even went to the factory that made the Patriots and congratulated the designers and workers on their diligence in producing the missiles. Less than three years after the war, the media (from information supplied by other government officials and other sources) revealed that the Patriots were highly inaccurate and inefficient and actually shut down, at most, two of the dozens of Scuds launched. Did the U.S. military command know this at the time? Yes, but they released inaccurate data to the media to influence Israeli and American opinion. Much of what government agencies release as data is simply just that; therefore, reviewers of the data have to determine whether it was

NBC's Bryant Gumble interviewing soldiers deployed in operation Desert Shield. Instant global communication has a tremendous impact on combat operations. Knowing the enemy is watching can be turned to a commander's advantage. When the enemy sees well-trained, well-equipped, and well-confident soldiers, it goes a long way toward countering propaganda.

made public solely to influence opinion. Besides government agencies, other groups, such as corporate public relations departments, research institutes, and the media, determine what is important for the public to hear, see, or read. Although we categorize the purveyors of data as entities such as media, agencies, departments, or institutes, in actuality, individuals within these entities make the decisions about what data to release to the public.

The question then is: What expertise do these managers of data bring to their vocation? Too often, as in the media, expertise is limited to writing or reading a report. Editors also evaluate written or oral material and, very importantly, assess the public's reaction to that material. However, most editors and reporters do not have the competence to *understand* every issue or subject that they write or speak about.

Let me explain the difference between knowing and understanding with some examples. When I turn the light switch on, the lights go on; I know that, but I do not understand why or how. The U.S. government debt is more than five trillion dollars; that is much, much more than the eight dollars I have in my pocket; I know that, but I do not understand what effect that debt has on my standard of living or what consequences it will have on my children's way of life or on society overall. Much misery exists in the world and some of it is in our own society; I know that, but I do not understand its causes, its effects, and what I can do to relieve it.

I know these things because I experienced them or read about them. I do not understand them because I am not a physicist or an electrical engineer, an economist, or an expert in social problems. Even in my field of expertise, political science, I do not understand much of the political phenomena that I am aware of; I cannot even claim to know of all these phenomena. To understand something, one has to be able to put it in an historical, causal context and logically deduce or induce consequences over a wide spectrum of phenomena organized into models and theories. That requires much training and education.

Our ancestors more than likely 'understood' the world around them more than we do ours today, because data was very limited and easier to understand. Their understanding of the world may not have been the same as our understanding of their world. Nevertheless, our ancestors probably felt more at peace with their social and political environment than we do with ours. Since we do not understand our world, we are not at peace with it and demand more information (i.e., data), which befuddles us even more. Easy access to printed, audio, and visual materials, has allowed us to know more than any of our ancestors (e.g., a college graduate has read more than any eighteenth century person would have read in his or her lifetime), and yet we understand the world less.

Our opinions, therefore, are formed from what we know, not what we understand. Since our brain is like a data processing machine, with limitations, what we know today, we might not know tomorrow because we forget. Therefore, new information reshapes our opinions within the context of our beliefs, values, and ideology. Although our opinions might be constantly changing because of new information we learn from the media, our understanding of that information is not necessarily increased nor are our beliefs, values, or ideologies altered. This may be a cause of what is called the "generation gap." Since information changes, each generation grows up with different information than that of the previous generation, which explains how people acquire different perspectives of the world.

One group that claims to "understand" nearly all the new data disseminated today is media commentators and analysts. They have been criticized for selectively choosing data that conforms to their own biases, prejudices, beliefs, values, and ideologies to "educate" the public by interpreting current events and issues. One commentator tries to explain the Middle East crisis one week, U.S. health care problems the next, causes of a recession the week after that, and reasons for the demise of the Soviet Union the following week.

Actually these commentators do not explain or understand data any better than most other people; what they do provide are arguments to buttress our own biases, prejudices, beliefs, values, and ideologies and to influence our opinions. Only too often, consciously or not, we parrot these arguments in discussions with others. Then after a few days, perhaps weeks, we either forget them or, because new data becomes known to us, reject them and go back to not understanding what we once thought we understood. Since commentators propound social and political values, beliefs, and norms, they not only serve as venues for political acculturation but also provide us with a measurement of our level of social integration. Commentators and the media in general, willfully or not, shape our opinions to conform to the political culture of our society.

The media which tends to emphasize conflict, has been accused of giving the impression that public decisions and politics in general are a result of conflict. Elections are viewed as races, public hearings are reported as matches between protagonists and adversaries, and simple discussions are described as debates between a proponent and an opponent. Often differences are exaggerated, and similarities de-emphasized. This view of politics by the media which can be found in many societies has caused even those in government to regard issues and problems within a "black-or-white" framework. Therefore, the public tends to view issues and candidates this way, too.

This perspective of politics makes persons who do understand the issues appear wishy-washy or indecisive. To these trained experts the issues are often far too complex to explain in a announcement or commercial or to compose an attention-getting one-sentence statement. Unfortunately, such short statements repeated over and over may influence public opinion more than the articles or books written by these experts.

Publics

Governmental officials are seldom interested in *your* personal opinion. What they are interested in is public opinion. What is a **public**? A public is a collectivity of people with a common interest. Collectivity denotes a complete absence of organization; the only link among those in a collectivity is their common interest. They are *not* a group. They may not even perceive that they have an interest in common. The common interest may be attributed to the public by an outsider. For example, if I wanted to know the preference of toothbrushes among toothbrush buyers, I would attribute toothbrush buying as the common interest that forms my public. I have created a toothbrush-buying public. The people within this public do not consider themselves as constituting a public. A public, consequently, is an artificial creation.

Each of us is a part of hundreds, if not thousands, of publics. Some of these publics are huge, such as the American voting public, others are small, such as the public reading this book; some have been around for a long time, such as the French public, others are ephemeral, such as those watching a television documentary; some are composed of older people, such as the public of retirees, others of younger people, such as the Game Boy using public. Publics are as numerous and varied as the interests one can attribute to them.

Public Opinion

What then is **public opinion**? By putting together our definitions for *public* and *opinion*, we get: Public opinion is the verbally expressed attitude of a collectivity of people with a common interest.

Public opinion interests governments today. Remember Rousseau and his theory about the general will and what was stated about consensus? Public opinion, instead of the general will, is frequently used today to justify what governments do. Few government policies are advocated or implemented today that are not justified in terms of satisfying what the "public" wants or will tolerate, what the consensus is. Just as the general will was enthroned by Rousseau as the decider of societal policies, public opinion is enthroned today as such a decider.

When public opinion is unified and strong, policy makers have very little latitude in choosing what policies to make. If policy makers develop policy that a determined public does not want, they risk losing their positions regardless of how good their policy is. Only when the public is sharply divided or does not hold strong views about a given policy can decision makers acquire the latitude that allows them to choose among alternatives.

Public Opinion and Societal Integration

Public opinion can be used as an index of an individual's integration into society not only by society but also by the individual. Societies tend to dis-

---

FOCUS   HOW TO INFLUENCE THE VOICE OF THE PRIMITIVE

In the evening I had a long talk with my mother who, to me, always represents the voice of the people. She knows the sentiments of the people better than most experts who judge from the ivory tower of scientific inquiry, as in her case the voice of the people itself speaks. Again I learned a lot; especially that the rank and file are usually much more primitive than we imagine. Propaganda must therefore always be essentially simple and repetitious.

In the long run only he will achieve basic results in influencing public opinion who is able to reduce problems to the simplest terms and who has the courage to keep forever repeating them in this simplified form despite the objections of the intellectuals.

Dr. Joseph Goebbels, Head of the German Reich Ministry for Public Enlightenment and Propaganda, 1933-1945.
From *The Goebbel Diaries: 1942-1943*. Edited, translated and with an introduction by Louis P. Lochner. Garden City, NY: Doubleday & Co, Inc., 1948, p. 56.

approve of opinions shared by only a tiny percentage of its members. Frequently, the majority uses ridicule and humiliation to correct the opinions of that minority. Or by ignoring those opinions, the majority shunts them so they are not a main concern of the society.

As the strength of the family and the groups that people relied on for support eroded over time, individuals became more isolated and therefore felt a need to find a standard for measuring their integration into society. **Opinion polls** (sometimes called attitude surveys), which measure verbally expressed attitudes, quickly became this standard.

An important development that occurred at the time opinion polls began to become popular was the dispersement of their results through the mass media. Improved and less costly communication technology, increased use of newspapers, magazines, radio, and television, which bring poll results to the individual shortly after they are tabulated, provide an immediate mechanism for gauging the "correctness" of one's opinion.

Individuals measure their integration by the degree to which their opinions conform to society's current principal attitudes. When individuals give their opinions, they invariably are concerned about how others will accept these opinions. Very few of us enjoy being part of a small disapproved of minority. Most of us want to be with the majority or, at least, a significant minority. By expressing opinions of the majority or a large minority, we apply a standard by which we prove to society and ourselves that we are a legitimate part of society.

Of course, we also show our integration into society by the clothes we wear, the food we eat, the places we visit or dwell in, and the behavior we manifest in public. Some of these may not be in harmony for a particular place, time, or social setting (e.g., wearing sneakers to a formal dance). However, these "unsocial" types of behaviors may either be a conscious effort to rebel against the prevalent patterns or are in harmony with patterns of subgroups. For example, the dress, behavior, and opinions of the hippies, yippies, Black Panthers, and other radical groups of the 1960s and 1970s was first interpreted by the majority as rebellious reactions to prevalent patterns in the United States but quickly became a harmonious pattern of several subgroups.

Interestingly, those who express ideas and opinions that are not mainstream but want to be taken seriously (e.g., Lenin, Mao, Hitler, Castro) must dress and behave according to established patterns. A revolutionary has to appear quite "unrevolutionary" and in harmony with most of the society's behavioral norms.

Polls, Campaigning, and Societal Development

Opinion polls have become very important for anyone who runs for political office. Campaigns use them like a crutch; politicians are reticent to say anything that is not in harmony with the prevalent opinion trends. If the public's opinion on an issue is either divided, fluctuating, or too general to be useful (as it often is), candidates speak eloquently in generalities or, even worse, appeal to the dysfunctional prejudices and biases of their constituents.

This is not necessarily all bad. Revolutionaries (i.e., persons who want to change the direction society is moving or want it to move faster) are not always the pillars upon which true societal development depends. Implementation of their policies might very well throw societies off balance and cause disruptions that may take decades to correct. It will be interesting to see how Lenin (the leading founder of the Soviet state) and Gorbachev (the leading dismantler of that state) will be evaluated by future generations of Russians. The Russian people wanted change, therefore, change had to occur, but did either Lenin or Gorbachev move them in the right direction?

Reliance on polls may force candidates to support policies that are within tolerable limits of societal development and to vote against policies that cause disruptions. This, however, assumes that public opinion is in harmony with policies promoting the peaceful process of development, which may not always be the case. Polls may show that public opinion lags behind or even is opposed to policies that would further societal change. For example, in the 1920s public opinions largely supported the **status quo** (i.e., the existing state of affairs) at a time when the U.S. economic processes were obviously out of whack with the needs of society.

Today we may ask whether the prevalent opinions are serving American society's long-term needs. American society is as susceptible to collapse as the former Soviet union was, especially when considering the following prevalent opinions: opposition to increased government funding for social needs, scapegoating of various societies for the inability of millions of Americans to find employment, reticence in accepting or even thinking about new governmental organization (are the fifty states the best way to administer American society?).

In the 1920s, Walter Lippman, a highly respected journalist, warned public officials about the dangers of following public opinion too closely. He urged government leaders not to enthusiastically use public opinion as the foundation for their policies because that opinion could be wrong.

FOCUS   THE ERRORS OF PUBLIC OPINION

The rule to which there are few exceptions . . . is that at the critical junctures, when the stakes are high, the prevailing mass opinion will impose what amounts to a veto upon changing the course on which the government is at the time proceeding. Prepare for war in time of peace? No. It is bad to raise taxes, to un-balance the budget, to take men away from their schools or their jobs, to provoke the enemy. Intervene in a developing conflict? No. Avoid the risk of war. Withdraw from the area of conflict? No. The adversary must not be appeased. Reduce your claims on the area? No. Righteousness cannot be compromised. Negotiate a compromise peace as soon as the opportunity presents itself? No. The aggressor must be punished. Remain armed to enforce the dictated settlement? No. The war is over.

The unhappy truth is that the prevailing public opinion has been destructively wrong at the critical junctures. The people have imposed a veto upon the judgements of informed and responsible officials. They have compelled the governments, which usually knew what would have been wiser, or was necessary, or was more expedient, to be too late with too little, or too long with too much, too pacifist in peace and too bellicose in war, too neutralist or appeasing in negotiation or too intransigent. Mass opinion has acquired mounting power in this century. It has shown itself to be a dangerous master of decisions when the stakes are life and death.

The errors of public opinion in these matters have a common characteristic. The movement of opinion is slower than the movement of events. Because of that, the cycle of subjective sentiments on war and peace is usually out of gear with the cycle of objective developments. Just because they are mass opinions there is an inertia in them. It takes much longer to change many minds than to change a few. It takes time to inform and to persuade and to arouse large scattered varied multitudes of persons. So before the multitude have caught up with the old events there are likely to be new ones coming up over the horizon with which the government should be prepared to deal. But the majority will be more aware with what they have just caught up with near at hand than with what is still distant and in the future. For these reasons the propensity to say "no" to a change of course sets up a compulsion to make mistakes. The opinion deals with a situation which no longer exists.

From Lippman, Walter. *The Public Philosophy.* New York: The New American Library of World Literature, Inc., 1955, pp. 23-24.

Public opinion that is in harmony with policies that further societal development may indeed be the pillar upon which that development takes place peacefully. But, public opinion that is not in harmony with societal development, and is converted into policy can cause much suffering for future generations. Societies have changed and will continue to do so according to their own dynamics. Publics will be judged by how well their opinions led to policies that furthered useful change.

What Polls Do

Polls divide publics into subpublics and attempt to determine their relative size. For example, a poll of a public revealing that 60 percent prefer X and 40 percent prefer Y shows that for every three persons who favor X two favor Y. The X-preferring subpublic is, therefore, one-third larger than the Y-preferring one. Each of the subpublics is then considered as a public and again subdivided. The X-preferring public can be asked why they favor candidate (or policy) X. The subpublic favoring X because of his or her stand on the issues can be treated as a public and further subdivided according to what issue they consider the most important.

In a 1995 poll of Canadian adults conducted by the Gallup Organization from October 4 through 10, 53 percent supported the Liberal Party, 13 percent the Progressive Liberal Party, 13 percent the Bloc Quebecois, 12 percent the Reform Party, and 8 percent the New Democratic Party. More than half of the public can be included in the subpublic favoring the Liberal Party; little less than half were evenly divided among subpublics favoring each of the other four parties. The poll then treated the subpublic supporting the New Democratic Party as a public and asked them which one of four candidates they would support as their next leader. A third of this public favored Svend Robinson as their leader, another third was evenly split between two other candidates, and 5 percent favored the fourth candidate. The Gallup Organization could have treated the subpublic favoring Mr. Robinson as a public and asked it a question so that the public could be further divided into subpublics.

What polls usually do not measure is **intensity** of opinion, (i.e., how strongly individuals maintain the opinion they express). Some people express an opinion rather casually because they are momentarily affected by current trends, have a desire to impress, or to hide ignorance, or are influenced by any one or more of the hundreds of factors that lead to fleeting answers. In a different circumstance or at some other time the same person might answer the same question differently.

On the other hand, some people have such strong opinions that they might never change them. In this situation opinions are closer to beliefs.

For instance, some people who supported former President Nixon in 1952, 1960, and 1968, continued to support him in the '70s after his involvement in the Watergate affair and other unethical practices changed millions of voters' opinion of him.

Polls generally do not differentiate between the fleeting opinion and the enduring one, between a whimsical answer and a contemplative one. The relative size of subpublics, therefore, is ever changing.

Accuracy of Polls

No poll can have 100 percent accuracy. Pollsters aim to achieve results that are as close as possible to what is known as the "True Poll." This is an abstract model that is not achievable because polled populations are artificially created. In general, pollsters calculate a **margin of error** of 3 to 6 percent, which means that the results are within 3 to 6 percent of the "True Poll." A poll showing that 48 percent of voters favored candidate X and 52 percent favor candidate Y may actually reflect a "True Poll" in which X was favored by either 51 percent or 45 percent and Y by either 49 percent or 55 percent depending on whether the 6 percent margin of error is added or subtracted from the results. Therefore the gap between X and Y could be anywhere between two points favoring X and 10 points favoring Y, which is not an insignificant gap. The margin of error must be considered when interpreting poll results.

Table 1 shows the increasing accuracy of the Gallup Poll. Note the small percentage of the errors after the 1952 elections. Poll results may be inconsequential if ephemeral conditions (e.g., weather) or events (e.g., news stories) influenced the respondents (those who answer the poll questions). Accuracy of poll results can also be affected by the number of indecisive voters. For example, in Table 1 the large percentage of errors in the 1964 and 1980 elections was partially a result of many voters not deciding which candidate to vote for until the last moment. A series of polls in which the same questions are asked over a period of time may give more accurate results. **Trend analysis** is the evaluation of the results of polls given at different times. By using trend analysis pollsters may get more meaningful insights into the true state of public opinion. Table 2 shows the results of the same poll given several times during President Clinton's administration.

According to the poll results, President Clinton's support among American voters wavered between two-fifths and one-half, from a low of

Table 1. The Gallup Poll record in presidential elections after 1948

GALLUP POLLS VS. ACTUAL RESULTS					
Election Year	Sample Size	Winning Candidate	Gallup Poll Prediction (% of Vote)	Election Result (% of Vote)	Poll Error (%)
1952	5,385	Eisenhower	51.0	55.4	+4.4
1956	8,144	Eisenhower	59.5	57.8	-1.7
1960	8,015	Kennedy	51.0	50.1	+0.9 of 1
1964	6,625	Johnson	64.0	61.3	+2.7
1968	4,414	Nixon	43.0	43.5	+0.5 of 1
1972	3,689	Nixon	62.0	61.8	-0.2 of 1
1976	3,439	Carter	49.5	51.1	-1.6
1980	3,500	Reagan	55.3	51.6	-3.7
1984	3,456	Reagan	59.0	59.2	+0.2 of 1
1988	4,089	Bush	56.0	53.9	-2.1

Source: The Gallup Poll (American Institute of Public Opinion) as cited in Freedman, David et al., *Statistics*, 2nd ed. (New York: W.W. Norton & Co., Inc., 1991), p. 314.

38 percent to a high of 51 percent, during the fourteen months in which the poll was conducted. If you look at the results from 11/94, 12/94, or 4/95 you would assume that more voters disapproved of Clinton than approved of him. Yet if you evaluate the whole series of polls, Clinton was supported more often than not. This becomes even clearer when the "Don't Knows/NA" are eliminated. Then the results would be as shown in Table 3.

The average support of 51 percent for Clinton is within the 3 percent margin of error. Half of the above poll results (i.e., 12/94, 10/95, 12/95,

Table 2. New York Times / CBS News poll results on the question: "Do you approve or disapprove of the way Bill Clinton is handling his job as President?"

POLITICAL ATTITUDES									
Month/ Year	11/ 94	12/ 94	02/ 95	04/ 95	08/ 95	10/ 95	12/ 95	01/ 96	Avg
Approve (%)	43	38	45	42	45	48	51	47	45
Disapprove (%)	48	49	43	46	43	38	38	40	43
Don't Know /NA (%)	9	13	12	12	13	14	11	13	12

Source: New York Times / CBS News Poll, "Political Attitudes: Clinton and the Republicans." Latest survey: Jan 18-20, 1996. http://www.nytimes...cs/123tables.html.1/23/96.

Table 3. New York Times / CBS News poll results on the question: "Do you approve or disapprove of the way Bill Clinton is handling his job as President?" with "Don't

POLITICAL ATTITUDES									
Month/ Year	11/ 94	12/ 94	02/ 95	04/ 95	08/ 95	10/ 95	12/ 95	01/ 96	Avg
Approve (%)	47	44	51	48	52	56	57	54	51
Disapprove (%)	53	56	49	52	48	44	43	46	49

Adapted from: New York Times / CBS News Poll, "Political Attitudes: Clinton and the Republicans." Latest survey: Jan 18-20, 1996. http://www.nytimes...cs/123tables.html.1/23/96.

and 1/96) fall outside the margin. Therefore, each of the other poll results (i.e., 11/94, 2/95, 4/95, and 8/95) could have gone the other way without affecting the outcome. That is, if the 2/95 poll would have stated 49 "approve" and 51 percent "disapprove" the poll would still have been accurate. What this means is that despite what the polls actually show, the number of respondents who approved of Clinton between 2/95 and 8/95 was as large as those who disapproved of him and that after those months his approval ratings improve.

Also note that the results of all eight polls would change with just a small number of respondents taking the opposite stand. For example, the 1/96 poll is based on the responses of 1,076 persons. If twenty-five of the respondents who approved of Clinton had stated that they did not approve of him, and twenty-five of those who "did not know" said that they disapproved of him, the results would have shown that the number of those who disapproved was larger than that of those who approved. Despite a result with a difference that is outside the margin of error, the outcome could have been the opposite with only less than 5 percent of the respondents giving a different answer. Even though 38 percent of 1,076 respondents were firm in their approval of Clinton during the fourteen months the poll was conducted, less than 5 percent of them could have changed the poll's rating from approval to disapproval.

Representative Sample

A public, such as the Canadian or German voting public or the public attending a football game, is a whole. A public is a segment of the multitude of people on earth who are grouped together because of some perceived common interest. Another word that students of public opinion use instead of public is **universe**. The people in a universe have different characteristics. They may be short, tall, fat, skinny, rich, poor, young, old, male, female, short-haired, long-haired, liberal, conservative, socialist, etc. When a universe is polled about its attitudes, pollsters assume that some of these characteristics are more important than others in influencing individuals' attitudes. For example, in a poll to determine the best quarterback of a particular football team, length of the respondents' hair in this universe is not an important determinant; however, annual income or gender might be. On the other hand, in a poll regarding shampoo preference, length of hair of the shampoo-using public may be a very important determinant.

Therefore, each universe has its own important set of characteristics that determine its attitudes. These characteristics are not present in equal proportions within each universe. Young people may outnumber old ones, females outnumber males, or poor outnumber rich. Pollsters use census figures, demographic data, and other attitude studies to obtain the configuration and proportion of the determinants they think are important in a given universe.

Usually the universe is too large to ask everyone for his or her attitudes. For instance, the American voting public is composed of about 180 million people, a football public of about 100 thousand, the green hair public of several hundred. Since it is often impossible to poll everyone, then only part of the universe can be chosen. The problem is determining which part.

Suppose you wanted to find out about students' attitudes toward their university bookstore. You could stand in front of the bookstore on a certain day and poll everyone who either walked in or out. However, you would not only miss a large part of your universe because not every student uses that bookstore, but you would also include nonstudents in the poll since not everyone who uses the bookstore is a student. So your first step in conducting this poll is to ask only students. But you would also have to go elsewhere to ask students who don't use the bookstore. So you stand in front of the student union, but some people entering or leaving the building have used the bookstore but are not students. You do not want their answers. How typical of the university student universe are the students who use the student union? You may not know. Therefore, you need to ask your questions of students in other locations as well. Even after doing all this, you still have not gotten responses from the entire universe, only a part of it. Did those who responded reflect all the characteristics of the universe in the proportion in which they exist?

What are the important determinants of the university student public regarding its attitudes toward the university bookstore? We can list some of them: frequency of use of bookstore, grade point average, major, year in school, sex, age, size of home city or town, need to work while in school, marital status, number of dependents, amount of financial aid. But knowing these characteristics is not enough. You also have to know how each of these is broken down in terms of ratios. For example, how many females are there to males; what is the ratio of first-year, sophomore, junior, senior, masters, doctoral, special, and professional students; what is the proportion of single students to married and divorced students? Without specifically asking students to respond to questions about these characteristics, you will not know whether you have polled enough of each type. Determining the important characteristics in the universe and the proportion in which they are represented should always be accomplished before polling is undertaken.

Before the 1936 U.S. presidential election between Roosevelt and

Landon, the editors of a respected magazine, *The Literary Digest,* decided to conduct a telephone poll among the American voters about their preference for president. Based on the results of their poll, the editors predicted a landslide victory for Landon. A few months after the election, the magazine went out of business. The editors' error was that they inadvertently polled mostly Republicans because they owned more telephones than the less wealthy Democrats. Telephone owners in 1936 were not representative of the American voting public. (In the 1990s telephone owners still may not be representative. Many people — the poor, the homeless, and migrant laborers — do not have telephones. Also, many people have answering machines, so if they do not answer the telephone they are not polled.)

This brings us to the **representative sample**, which is part of a universe containing all its important characteristics in their proper proportions. Thus, if marital status is considered an important determinant of an attitude and a given universe of 1,000 persons includes 400 singles, 500 marrieds, and 100 divorced, then in the sample of this universe for every four singles there would have to be five marrieds and one divorced. These 10 persons reflect the proper proportion regarding marital status in this universe of 1,000. If the sample is larger, say 100 persons, the 4:5:1 ratio regarding marital status remains the same.

Since attitudes in a universe are never composed of one determinant, several must be considered in preparation for polling. The size of the sample in proportion to the universe is determined by the number of determinants involved; therefore, the more determinants included, the larger the sample. A universe of 100 persons in which 10 determinants have been selected might need a representative sample of 70 persons, over 66 percent of the universe. But a universe of 1,000 persons with 10 determinants may also require a sample of 70, less than 10 percent. Pollsters use a sample of about 1,000 persons to determine the opinions of the American voting public. Yet of the 900,000 West Virginian voting public, they poll 500 persons, for example. Note the difference in the proportion of the sample to the universe in both.

Pollsters often refer to **random samples**. These are polls of arbitrarily chosen respondents forming a representative part of a universe. Assume that I place 1,000 name tags into a hat (a very large hat) and ask you to pull out 100. I expect that these 100 respondents will have a proportional amount of the important characteristics of the universe of 1,000. Frequently, the random sample does not represent the universe. Even, if it does, I may not be sure which universe it is representing. For example, if I interview every tenth person listed on each white page of the local telephone directory, my universe, at best, is the telephone-white-pages-listed public. This public is unique. It is mostly males (among marrieds only the husband's name is usually listed), who have consented to have their name listed in the directory and live in an area defined by the telephone company and, of course, have a telephone number. There is very little else that I can know about this universe unless I ask the respondents questions about themselves.

To get at a more politically relevant universe by using the telephone book as a source, I can ask respondents questions in relation to the characteristics I had determined before the poll. Thus, I can shape my sample to conform to the characteristics of the universe. That means I cannot use answers of the respondents who do not possess the predetermined characteristics. (In fact, many reputable pollsters operate in this manner. For example, to achieve a representative sample of 1,000, they may poll 5,000 to 10,000 respondents.)

Two Types of Questions

Over the decades since World War II, pollsters have devised basically two types of questions that elicit most accurately the opinion of the respondent. As we will see, the type of question that is simple and easy to tabulate often is also the least accurate ones.

The **closed-ended** question is similar to a multiple-choice exam question in that the respondent can choose only one of the alternatives offered.

In a closed-ended question, the question is clearly stated so the respondent can easily pick an answer. Tabulating the results in a poll based on closed-ended questions is easy since it involves only counting the number of responses for each answer.

One disadvantage of closed-ended questions, however, is that they may not reveal the respondent's real opinion. First, a respondent in an election poll might not have voted for the candidate because of the candidate's stand on the issues, but she circled one of the answers simply because she felt compelled to make a choice. Second, she may have voted for the candidate because of his stand on several issues, each of which was very important to her, but the poll allows for only one answer. Third, she may have liked her candidate's stand on issues that were not listed, such as the environment or women's rights. If she circled "None of the above", her preferences would not appear in the results. Fourth, her interpretation of the

TYPES OF QUESTIONS IN AN OPINION POLL

▶ ## The Closed-Ended Question

Of the issues discussed in the last campaign, which one did your candidate best address? **CIRCLE ONE ONLY.**

a. Unemployment

b. Problems of the poor

c. The national economy

d. Health Care

e. Taxes

f. Federal budget deficit

g. Crime

h. National defense

i. Foreign affairs

j. None of the above

▶ ## The Open-Ended Question

What was it about the candidate you voted for that you liked?
USE AS MUCH SPACE AND TIME AS NEEDED.

answers may be different from that of others. She might think of battered women or rape when she reads crime, or nutrition when she reads health care or problems of the poor, which may not be what most others think.

Closed-ended questions are easy to tabulate; but they also are most inaccurate in revealing opinions. One way to ameliorate the inherent inaccuracy of this type of question is to use several questions. Follow-up questions can ask for more specific responses to the original question. Or the same question may be repeated with different choices. Or one question may be asked that allows for selection of only one answer, and then it is repeated in a format that allows as many answers as needed. The answers to one closed-ended question may not be accurate, but the composite answers to several questions might be. The problem with this approach is the length and complexity of the questionnaires. Giving too many choices or asking too many questions could make the survey difficult to administer.

The second type of question used in polls is the **open-ended question**, which allows the respondent to answer in his or her own words. It is similar to an essay question in an exam.

The answer to this question may be brief, a sentence or two, or long, several paragraphs or even pages. Analyzing the responses to this kind of question, however, is very complicated. The answer has to be interpreted and then broken down into categories. This takes much expertise, effort, and time, all of which costs money. The additional expense in adminis-tering and tabulating answers to open-ended questions does not enhance their popularity among pollsters.

One major problem with the open-ended question is that it assumes respondents can put their attitudes into words and that everyone within a given public also can do so. Obviously this is not true. Often those with less education have great difficulty in expressing themselves, while those with much education use many words, some of which they do not know the meaning. Answers to open-ended questions, therefore, may not accu-rately reveal the opinions of the respondents or the entire public.

Furthermore, open-ended questions are seldom used because many respondents are reluctant to spend the time and effort to answer them. Before this type of question can be answered, the respondent has to take time to think through attitudes and then put them into words, often in writing. Most people just do not want to be bothered with doing all this.

Other Ways of Determining Public Attitudes

A still more time-consuming and very expensive type of questioning is the **in-depth interview**. By this method the respondent is virtually locked up, sometimes for a few days, with a trained professional interviewer (usually a psychologist). The latter, through observation and questioning, attempts to ascertain a multitude of the respondent's attitudes. Analysis of the results of this type of interview takes a long time. Since political pollsters want quick results, they seldom use in-depth interviewing.

A variant of the in-depth interview is the **focus group**, which is a care-fully selected small group that evaluates at length issues, candidates, products, or services. The group may meet once or periodically under the supervision of trained interviewers; group members can interact among themselves. The interviewers write, tape-record, or videotape the discussion and then analyze the results, which is a costly and time-consuming but also reliable process.

Another way of ascertaining public opinion is by observation. When the public votes, it is revealing its preferences. Newspaper letters to the editor reveal the preoccupations of the writers. Other ways to show support for an individual or a particular cause is through demonstrations, contributions of money or time, petitions, and participation at public events. There is no need to ask for an opinion on abortion from an individual who is chained to the closed gates of an abortion clinic; the attitude is made perfectly clear by the actions. Observation of people in action reveals much about their attitudes.

The problem with observation is that the activity of one person, or even several persons, does not necessarily represent the entire public. In voting analysis, for example, one has to remember that those who voted were only part of those who could vote. Many voters, sometimes most voters, stay home. Not everyone who has opinions about something writes letters to the editor or calls radio talk shows. Nor does every individual who supports a cause participate in demonstrations or donate money or time. Opinion polling of a whole public, such as the voting public, gives only a partial clue to the attitudes of all voters because those who actually do vote may represent only a small part of the whole.

The Manipulation of Polls and Their Results

Polling is a science made possible by the technology developed for accumulating, categorizing, storing, correlating, and evaluating data. Most professional polling organizations perform admirably in determining the opinions of the public. They are also very much aware of their limitations. Unfortunately, they cannot control what is done with the data generated or prevent hucksters from using some methods and data to manipulate them for unsavory purposes.

One of the most common methods of manipulating polls to obtain desirable results is to manipulate the sample. Polling only students who enter a university bookstore about what they think of the bookstore, as we showed before, will skew the results because they do not include the views of those who will not enter it because they are very much upset with it. Asking only medical doctors about health care policy will obviously influence the results in a direction that may not be favored by other segments of the general public. If everybody is aware of the manipulation, there is no problem.

FOCUS THE GENERAL WILL IS ALWAYS RIGHT BUT THE PEOPLE MAY BE DECEIVED

... (T)he general will is always right and ever tends to the public advantage. But it does not follow that the deliberations of the People are always equally beyond question. It is ever the way of men to wish their own good, but they do not all times see where that good lies. The People are never corrupted though often deceived, and it is only when they are deceived that they appear to will what is evil.

From Rousseau, Jean-Jacques. "The Social Contract," book 2, chap. 3. *Social Contract*, edited by Ernest Baker. New York: Oxford University Press, 1962.

However, a problem arises when those who conduct such polls use the results to show that a fair sample of the universe was polled and the results accurately reflect attitudes of the public. If I am part of this public, I will react differently when I see that 85 percent supported X than if I had seen that only 35 percent supported it. On issues like the university bookstore or health care I might not like to be part of the 35 percent minority in opposition. (Remember, I am trying to evince my integration to society.) The skewed poll manipulates me to form opinions that it wanted to foster so that in a subsequent, more legitimate poll, I might answer that I support X.

In politics this is done all the time. Newspapers, TV, and radio announce the results of polls based on erroneous samples designed to sway me to an opposing viewpoint. One headline may state, "60% of Democrats polled support Dole." This may be true, but the Democrats polled were attending a bankers' convention, hardly a place where the typical Democrat would spend an evening. The purpose of that poll is to make Democrats think that it is perfectly all right to support Republican candidate Dole and that they should because so many Democrats already do. Thus, who is polled often determines the results.

Another way to manipulate the results is through the questions asked. Words can have positive, negative, or neutral connotations. If I were to ask you, "Who do you prefer, beautiful Miss Piggy or ugly Oscar?" The words *beautiful* and *ugly* would invariably influence your answer (you are already manipulated by the choices given because you really prefer Grover).

Words may also have different meanings to different people in different regions. The word *grass* may mean one thing to a person in the inner city, another thing to a suburbanite, and still something else to someone living in the Arizona desert. The same is true of the word *family* which people on the campaign trail banter around. *Family* may have different meanings for various ethnic groups and for persons with different marital backgrounds.

Not only must the questions contain words that are neutral and understood by all in the same way, but they also must not lead anyone in a preconceived direction. We are all well acquainted with loaded questions (i.e., questions which, unless answered in a prescribed fashion, make one look foolish, incompetent, or even a misfit.) Usually these begin with something like, "Do you agree . . . ?" Invariably the respondent is compelled to say "yes," otherwise he or she will feel uncomfortable. Frequently loaded questions are asked after several innocuous ones: "Do you think there are serious problems in this country today?" "Do you think health care is one of the serious problems?" "Do you think everyone deserves proper health care?" "Do you think candidate X's proposals are one way of resolving the health care mess?" "Do you think that with candidate X's proposals the health care problems will be resolved?" Normally every one of these questions will be answered "yes." Once a respondent answers "yes" to a few, he or she will not change the rhythm of the answers by saying "no." The only answer that will be recorded, however, is the last one. Consequently, the pollster will announce that most persons agree with his candidate's solution to the health care problem. Illegitimate polls try to get us on the bandwagon of a particular candidate or issue that we may normally oppose.

The appearance of the interviewer can also affect the respondent's answer. The Caucasian in a business suit will elicit different answers than the informally dressed African American when asking the same questions of persons in an African-American inner city ghetto, of Caucasian professionals in an advertising agency, or of unemployed farm workers in Georgia. Such ephemeral, subtle, and otherwise unnoticed factors can easily influence opinions.

Another factor is the mood of the respondent. Mood influences opinion. Therefore, whatever induces a certain mood in an individual will influence his or her opinion. To obtain negative answers from respondents about an incumbent politician or an existing policy, interviewers conduct polls on cloudy, rainy days, especially if they fall on a Monday. Generally people feel more depressed on these days and therefore are less inclined to be satisfied with the way things are.

Candidates are not the only persons in the political arena who use these manipulations; government officials, appointed or elected, use them frequently as well. Many incumbents parade favorable results from polls that were taken right after a speech (e.g., State of the Union), an event (e.g., opening ceremony of the Olympics), or aid given after a cataclysm (e.g., earthquake) to prove their popularity with the public. The manipulation of opinion by governments is certainly not new; it probably predates the Egyptian pharaohs.

To get support from the people, government leaders have often wrapped themselves in glories in which they took no part (e.g., good harvests, discoveries of new lands, inventions, demise of enemy states through internal conflict). These leaders have also used and abused beliefs and values of the public by professing to be their sole defenders and protectors. After gaining public support, the leaders often subverted these values and beliefs for their personal gain.

If publics were not so easily manipulated, candidates, governments, and other public and private institutions would not be spending billions of dollars each year to do so. Polling would not be such a large industry. (In business, polling comes under the rubric of market research.) But then you and I, as part of these publics, want to show how much we belong to our society, how well integrated we are. We are uncomfortable being misfits, out of the ordinary. Therefore, if 80 percent of people support X, you and I most likely will support X, too.

TERMS TO REMEMBER

attitudes
opinion
ideology
propaganda
public
public opinion
opinion polls
status quo
intensity (of opinion)
margin of error
trend analysis
universe
representative sample
random sample
closed-ended question

open-ended question
in-depth interview
focus group

SUGGESTED READINGS

Entman, Robert M. *Democracy Without Citizens: Media and the Decay of American Politics.* New York: Oxford University Press, 1989. Part I is a critique of mass media's interdependence with politicians and citizens. Part II concentrates on improving the media.

Glasser, Theodore L. and Charles T. Salmon, editors. *Public Opinion and the Communication of Consent.* New

York: Guilford, 1995. The history and theory of public opinion polls and the various approaches to their study is scholarly analyzed in the almost twenty essays of this book.

Graber, Doris. *Mass Media and American Politics*. 3rd Edition. Washington, DC: Congressional Quarterly Press, 1991. Textbook focusing on the role of the media in policy making and politics in general.

Key, V.O. *Public Opinion and American Democracy*. New York: Knopf, 1961. The classic analysis of the role public opinion plays in American politics and society.

Lippmann, Walter. *Public Opinion*. New York: Free Press, 1922 (reprinted 1965). One of the first studies on the importance of public opinion in the making of U.S. policy.

Miller, Thomas I. and Michele A. Miller. *Citizen Surveys: How To Do Them, How To Use Them, What They Mean*. Washington, DC: International City/County Management Association, 1991. Do's and don'ts in conducting a poll.

Packard, Vance O. *The Hidden Persuaders*. New York: D. McKay Co., 1957 (reprinted 1969). A very popular book when it came out showing how market research and polling has been used to influence Americans' shopping and voting patterns.

Pierce, Roy. *Choosing the Chief: Presidential Elections in France and the United States*. Ann Arbor: University of Michigan Press, 1995. An analysis of poll results for the 1988 French presidential election compared to the poll results for the 1984 and 1988 United States elections as gathered by the American National Election Study.

9

Leadership

The determination of who is to lead a society in making and implementing policies has always been a pivotal one. In ages long past, the individual most skilled in controlling small groups was considered a leader. Later, in somewhat larger societies, small groups of selected individuals chose leaders based on narrowly defined expertise. To become leaders, individuals had to show their qualifications by overcoming challenges, defeating enemies, or passing endurance tests.

When societies grew in size and complexity, the qualities of leadership changed and the old methods of selecting leaders no longer proved practical. Leaders had to possess a multiplicity of qualities they could not acquire by just being adept at overcoming everyday challenges. They had to be taught or trained. A notion developed, although never stated as such, that anyone could be a leader if given the proper training, education, and experience. This was the societal basis of hereditary monarchy. Those brought up in the royal household, who were from the biological perspective no different than anyone else within the society, were placed in an "enriched environment" and trained as leaders.

Furthermore, the need to have others carry out the monarchical orders counterbalanced any harm that bad leaders could do to a society. For a monarch to provide effective leadership he or she had to depend on many others for carrying out royal orders. When, in time, education became more widespread within society, those trained in royal households no longer retained the exclusive expertise to lead. Also, as societies grew larger, they demanded more leadership skills than those learned in the royal households. The education of the nobility became a hindrance to effective societal leadership because it did not teach them how to competently administer a government institution. (Note the negative influence the Russian czars had on that society because, like most of today's monarchs, they were not trained to be government administrators.)

As governments grew in size because of societal dependence on their ability to provide necessary services, individual leaders became less and less important.

Diffusion of Leadership

Since the 1800s, when democratization and bureaucratization of governments appeared, society has not needed leaders to lead. The organization of governments, the determination of who is to do what regarding societal functions and roles, the direction of armies to victory, the keeping of society itself together has not been done by any single individual or small group of individuals but by a multitude of policy makers and implementors. Each policy maker is responsible for only a fragment of all of a society's policies.

When we refer to policy making, we invariably refer to an individual segment of societal development. Each policy area, even when defined generally, is but only one field among thousands, which together define the direction of society's development. Policy makers, being so specialized, make only part of the entire societal policy, often without knowing what others are doing even in their own area. Society itself weaves all these different fragments of policy and other variables together and harmonizes them. How important then is each piece of policy? Not very.

The more pieces or segments of policy, the greater the number of policy makers; the more policy makers, the more specialized and particular each piece of policy becomes and the less important is any one policy maker or fragment of policy. So-called leaders today give only the appearance of makers and implementors of policy because those who actually do these tasks are bureaucrats and nongovernmental residents, those millions in the larger societies who provide for the needs of the populations by making and implementing small segments of the total policy.

This diffusion of leadership has made society's need for leaders questionable. Since World War II, Italy has had periods of up to six months without a prime minister because the parties controlling the legislature could not agree on one. Were there any negative effects? Hardly. Government services were still supplied, taxes were collected, and bills paid. In 1973 in Morgantown, West Virginia, for ten weeks the city council could not agree on a mayor and could not conduct any formal business. Nothing collapsed; services were rendered and everything continued as normal because city workers did their jobs and were paid as usual. As we have witnessed in times of crisis, such as earthquakes, floods, fires, and famines, citizens can organize themselves quite well to overcome the challenges.

The bureaucratization of government was both the cause and the effect of many developments. As stated previously, government became larger because of increased specialization among the population, reduction of self-sufficiency of the family unit, greater dependence on technology for coping with everyday problems, and increased stranger-to-stranger interactions requiring societal control and coordination. Government became a more tangible presence in the everyday life of society members, not only because it supplied necessary services but also because it employed many individuals who obviously had personal relations to those not in government. Government and citizenry became so intertwined that it was difficult to tell where one ended and the other began.

In addition, as more people were needed to fill government positions, the pool of educated persons who could become bureaucrats needed to be enlarged. Private enterprises also needed an enlarged educated labor pool to remain competitive and profitable. When educated individuals become concerned about their livelihood, they want to have input in decisions that affect them. Employees generally want a say in the environment of the workplace. Let's face it: For most of us government has become directly or indirectly our workplace, and we want a say in it. How else to give us that say than through elections? (This is a reason the government of South Africa has dismantled *apartheid*. Just like most governments, South Africa's government had increased in size, adding thousands of educated blacks as employees. Private enterprises, too, had been hiring millions of educated blacks. Consequently, the black South Africans demanded a say in the making of overall South African policy. Now they have it.)

Elections in few, if any, countries, however, determine general societal policies. Sometimes through initiative and referenda voters can influence a particular aspect of a policy; but, even this type of direct input can be offset by other policies or social variables over time. Changing beliefs, values, and norms have always been even more important influences on the policies of a society. Elections, however, decide a society's leaders at a given moment. At least they are supposed to. Is this always true?

A few years ago this author served as a city council member with thirteen other people, including the mayor. Council sessions were held in public, and persons in the audience could hear and see what was done during the sessions. The same half dozen persons would attend each session. One of these used the public comment part of the sessions to harangue individual council members or the city administration in general. In time, the vitriol this individual lashed out caused some council members to cease to speak at all, others spoke very little, and all felt at least somewhat intimidated. Also present was another individual who hardly ever spoke. She quietly sat through the sessions; occasionally she would say something to a council member after the meeting or call him or her by phone. During the sessions, however, when someone spoke, she would periodically nod her head. Those who did speak and had known her would more likely than not look toward her as they spoke. The more often she nodded, the calmer and more confident the speaker felt. Without perhaps being aware of it, she, too, controlled what was said during council sessions. By influencing what was being said, these nonelected individuals, each in his or her own manner, also influenced the council's votes.

Who made the policy that came out of council chambers: the council members and city administrators and others who had a direct interest in the particular subject or those two members of the audience who appeared to be influencing the council's debate? Were the latter two individuals leaders of the city? If so, what was this author? After all, he was elected.

Why Do We Need Leaders?

Why have we needed leaders? As stated before, societies need organization. Other than the most primitive, societies need to apportion roles, functions, and obligations, especially those relating to security and defense. Before the 1800s most members of society did not possess the qualities considered necessary for effective leadership, therefore, those few who did possess them became the leaders. These qualities included birth to the right parents, age, good health, general knowledge, ability to reason, organizational skills, ability to forecast, courage, sheer strength, cleverness, and lack of inhibition to do others harm. Whatever particular qualities these leaders had were endowed at birth or learned from tutors or through experience. Leaders, those who made and implemented policies, were different from other members of society. Today those we elect as leaders do not possess pertinent qualities that are different from those of a large segment of society's population.

Yet leaders are as necessary today as ever, but not as policy makers or implementors. Leaders today coordinate others to work together to provide needed services or tasks. By persuading, cajoling, and manipulating subordinates, leaders can get matters accomplished without contributing anything of substance to the results. While others make or carry out policy, leaders just make sure that everyone cooperates with everyone else in the project. In fact, leaders may not have any expertise in the area of a particular policy that is being developed. What these leaders may possess is the skill to get people to work together.

We need leaders for more personal reasons, just like our ancestors centuries ago needed them. Have you ever noticed when traveling on an interstate highway that there are two types of drivers: the followers and the leaders? Some drivers hardly ever pass another car in front of them, but others, no matter how fast the car in front is traveling, always pull ahead. Most of us are not confident in arranging our little world by ourselves and need help and encouragement from others. We feel uncomfortable when we are alone with no guides to direct us in proper behavior, opinions, beliefs, and values. Who better to personify all these qualities than the leaders of societies? As Rousseau pointed out, leaders may be looked upon as surrogate fathers. Then, as now, people may need a person to emulate as the idealized "father."

Leaders are also symbols of the culture of a society. Candidates for leadership in any country do not stray too far from their society's cultural mold. They use all types of contrivances and gimmicks to prove that they are typical of everyone else in that society. Who would not like to have his or her picture taken looking out of the turret of a tank, even if it looks ridiculous? No matter how wealthy the candidates, they still have to show that they can act like the neighbor next door. It does not make that much difference what the candidates or leaders state regarding the issue of the day. What is important is that they use the language, symbols, beliefs, and values of the people in what they say. Let us remember also that what they say is often written by someone else, who we usually do not know.

We need these leaders not because they actually lead, but because they focus our attention on who we are. Their appearance, behavior, and speeches reflect what the rest of society finds appealing. (How many elected government leaders are there who are short, bald, pudgy, and bearded? These individuals' appeal is confined to only the inmates of a university.) Unlike leaders of the past, today's leaders do not possess any qualities that are different from those of most others in their societies. Presidents, prime ministers, chancellors, and legislators are no more educated, skilled, or courageous than many of the citizenry that elected them. Thatcher and Major of the United Kingdom, Kohl of Germany, Mitterand and Chirac of France, Gonzalez of Spain, and the innumerable prime ministers of Italy look as if they escaped from the advertising pages of clothing magazines. Except for a few minor quirks, Clinton is Mr. American, the idealized version of Americans, as are Gore, Bush, Dole, Gingrich, and even Perot. In most circumstances each could be a stand-in for the others. And, precisely because of this, it does not really matter which of them becomes the leader. Besides, as we will learn later, only a small percentage of the population determines who will be elected.

Evaluating Leaders

How does one differentiate a good leader from a bad one? Fidel Castro has been governing the small island of Cuba for more than thirty-five years. Few would argue that, if free elections were held in Cuba today,

Fidel Castro led Cuba's communist revolution in 1959, and ruled first as prime minister and then continued as president.

Castro would be elected. Despite the economic downturn of the island and the failures of its foreign policy, the people support Fidel. But Cubans who have relocated to Miami, Montreal, New York, or Toronto think Castro is evil. Most U.S. federal leaders share this view. Is he a bad or a good leader? It depends on who you ask.

Certainly Castro is successful, is one of the two or three contemporary leaders who has held onto power the longest. Although he has used some nasty tactics at times to get rid of the opposition, he has been remarkably benevolent and outlived the more oppressive leaders elsewhere. In the first years of his regime he improved living conditions for the Cuban masses while badgering the rich and despoiling them of their wealth. The masses loved him; the rich detested him. But was he good for Cuba? By what objective criteria can one answer that question?

Economically Cuba is not doing too well; its economic indicators, such as growth of gross national product and per capita income, are down but improving. Since Cuba was so economically dependent on the former Soviet Union, the loss of this trading partner and benefactor has caused considerable dislocations in trade patterns. On the other hand, Cubans' level of educational attainment is one of the highest in the Western Hemisphere, and their health care programs are also among the best (1993 mortality rate for persons less than five years old was the lowest among Latin American and Caribbean countries[1]). Under Castro's leadership, Cuban society has overcome challenges that in other societies would have caused serious and long-term disruptions to economic development. But Castro's leadership also led to a strong dependence on the Soviet Union, which proved to be economically disadvantageous in the long run.

Castro, as any leader, is a child of his time and place. In the first decade of the nineteenth century, Napoleon was adulated by the French who viewed him as the person who kept French society together, but detested by other European leaders for attempting to diffuse French ideals to the

King Louis XVI

rest of the continent. In later years, even the French have questioned his proficiency as a statesman and military strategist. French King Louis XVI, who was beheaded in 1793 to the delight of most Frenchmen, is being reevaluated two hundred years later as not such a bad leader.[2] The major problem in evaluating leadership is that one cannot separate the leader from the society during the period of his or her leadership. Society, at any one time, is greater than any leader. The leader not only is the product of society but also is constricted in what he or she can and cannot do. At times potential leaders cannot lead because those who could follow do not want to be led. If there are no followers, can there be leaders? Leaders cannot influence followers who are not receptive to that influence. Society's receptivity is determined by innumerable variables. Leaders with great ideas cannot carry them out if members of society do not favor them. Is Socrates' all-rational philosopher-king a leader if the citizens in the republic cannot even understand him?

We may be hitting the crux of the problem here. Generally, we consider leaders as those who have a following. Yet those who make and implement societal policy may have only a few followers. The Minneapolis postal carrier who "invented" the red, yellow, and green traffic signal had a tremendous impact upon society, but he is not considered a leader. Individuals may have a great influence upon a society's development, yet remain unknown. Leaders who have a following are obviously known, yet may have little influence upon their societies. Often leaders of political parties who never win elections do not influence the making or implementing of policies. They are not really leaders even though their followers think otherwise. Is Castro a leader? Of course he is; he still has a very large following. Is he a good leader? He has made and carried out many policies that have improved the living standards of most

Cubans. Was Louis XVI a leader? To most Frenchmen at the time he was not. Did he make and implement policy? Of course he did, after all he was the king. Were his policies good? From today's perspective, many were quite good. Are Castro and Louis XVI good leaders? Yes.

What Makes a Leader a Leader?

One of the most perplexing questions has been "What makes a leader a leader?" Among dominant animals certain variables have been identified that distinguish the leader of the pack, such as age, appearance, physical well-being, strength, social rank of the mother, knowledge of the territory, sociability, and past fighting experiences. For humans, identification of determinant variables has been much more difficult. One reason is that individuals may evince certain traits that make them stand out in small groups but not in large ones or that may be very effective before mass audiences but inappropriate in smaller ones.

Effective verbal and nonverbal communication are usually two important variables. Oratorical skill has generally been considered a hallmark of leaders. When small groups of people selected leaders, effective communication was personal (i.e., the individual had to impress a few people by using succinct, appropriate language). Verbosity was frowned upon. Manners, etiquette, and facility in social interactions also were seen as important attributes.

When masses began to select leaders, the latter three attributes no longer could be judged and became irrelevant. What became important was speech making. In the recent past Lenin, Hitler, Churchill, Castro, Kennedy, and King became leaders partially because of their ability to communicate orally. To those who cheered them what they said may not have been as important as much as how they said it. The words used, their intonation, and the rhythm and cadence of phrases and sentences had a mesmerizing effect on audiences, not unlike the rap songs of some rap groups today.

John F. Kennedy

Some of these leaders also had something to say. Often their speeches contained ideas with which people identified. These ideas may not have been original, but they were stated in such a way that people remembered them and identified the speaker with them. Few people who were around in the 1960s have forgotten King's "I Have a Dream" speech or Kennedy's "... ask not what your country can do for you. Ask what you can do for your country. ... " from his inaugural address.

Unfortunately, in the last two decades technology has made it possible to virtually manufacture an individual's communications skill. First, modern audio technology can make persons with soft, high-pitched voices sound authoritative, voluminous, and deep. Second, speeches are written by several writers who specialize in an aspect of speech making, such as specific topics to cover, grammar, rhythm and cadence, and expressions. Third, other professionals prepare the speaker in proper delivery and body language. Finally, many individuals are placed in the audience to make appropriate reactions to the speech, encouraging others to do the same. Since communications professionals have established an image or model of the perfect speech and the perfect delivery and work with numerous speakers, many speeches sound alike. For example, President Bush's speeches, although delivered awkwardly, were very much like President Reagan's because Bush used most of the same team of writers.

Since many voters cannot differentiate among candidates based on what they say, votes may be cast on the basis of what the candidates do. Some voters find legislative records so complex that they might consider the private activities of the candidates instead. Although a candidate's past private life (including sexual relationships) is irrelevant criterion for political office, it nevertheless becomes an important factor in an election. The "ideal" private past life is still in the process of being defined, but it has become something candidates need to be elected. (Perhaps voters feel that, since everything else about a candidate is manufactured, his or her private life is the only genuinely unique and human aspect left.) In many societies, a famous family name makes it easier for candidates to become leaders (i.e., Churchill in the United Kingdom, Kennedy in the United States, and the same six families in Colombia produced most presidents in the twentieth century).

One attribute leaders supposedly need is **charisma**. What exactly this attribute is nobody really knows. It is the "X" factor that makes the candidate appealing and attracts others to him or her. It consists of a combination of verbal and nonverbal communication skills, with probably a greater emphasis on the latter. Charisma probably is not learned but hardwired into us at conception. The caudillo in Latin America and the local party boss in American cities became leaders precisely because they possessed this quality.

A person with charisma is immediately recognized in small groups and in mass audiences. But somehow charisma is lost in radio and television broadcasts and in movies. Since campaigning for national office today is done mostly through the audio and visual media, candidates no longer need to exude charisma; it is not as important as it was before the arrival of the video screen. However, in elections that require personal contact between candidates and voters, charisma is still important, despite its nebulous character.

Unfortunately, important characteristics, such as intelligence, knowledge, rationality, and expertise have been relegated to the bottom of the heap of criteria by which leaders are selected through the electoral process. Any candidate who tries to capitalize on these characteristics to garner votes will seldom win unless voters like some of his or her other attributes. The list of losers in national American politics is filled with names of individuals who supposedly possessed more of these intellectual attributes than their opponents: Dewey, R. Taft, Stevenson, Mondale, Dukakis.

On the other hand, level and place of education is important in most societies. Graduates from any distinguished school of higher education have opened doors, through contacts made at school, to leadership positions. Admittance to these schools, however, often depends on where one was born or is living. A young person from a rural area or small town or city who cannot afford to live in the metropolis where the major university is located, or the student who does not get admitted to that university because he or she lives on the other side of the country may not get the opportunity then to make contacts that eventually might lead to important positions in society. The top bureaucrats in the Mexican federal government are graduates from the National University of Mexico in Mexico City. Despite a student population of more than 100,000, the university does not enroll anyone who does not originate from one of the surrounding areas of the city.

Another drawback to admittance to one of the top schools is high cost. Parents or relatives who barely make a living cannot afford the expense or the loss of income that a young adult generates by working. Higher education often is a prerogative of the affluent.

Wealth is a prerequisite for obtaining a leadership position. Wealth is normally measured in terms of money, but it can be measured in other ways. The hunter who can bring down the biggest animals controls, because of his prowess, the food supply of his group. The meat that he brings to the table is his wealth. Aeons ago in some areas, the person who owned the society's scarce water supply invariably became a leader. Water was wealth. Anything that a society treasures or wants more of can be considered wealth. Intelligence, knowledge, courage, and other such attributes are unimportant unless they can be converted into wealth. Knowledge and intelligence become qualities in leadership, when they have benefitted the individual materially.

Society has always supported wealth regardless of whether it is potential or actual, imagined or real. Wealthy persons who gave to others some of what they had, no matter how unjustly acquired, built a following among them. Even the most ruthless leaders were supported. People gave support when they believed they might gain something, such as a piece of meat, a barrel of water, land, or a promise that something in their life would remain the same. Or the gain may have been status, position, or wealth. Leaders would, of course, manipulate the perception of gain to their best advantage, but could lose support if people perceived a greater gain from someone else.

Wealth is still an important attribute of leaders, because they virtually have to buy their position. More than two-fifths of the members of the U.S. House of Representatives and over half the U.S. Senators are millionaires, and since World War II over two-thirds of the candidates for the U.S. presidency have been millionaires. Even those who run in local elections have to spend quite a bit of money to campaign. The higher the office desired by the candidate, the greater the expenditures. Although contributions, large and small, are made to campaigns, candidates must use a considerable amount of personal funds to pay for advertising, travel, and campaign staff expenses and to make up the loss of income from leaving their job during the campaign. Leaders of a society neither in the past nor present have come from the poor.

Finally, another attribute of leadership that should be mentioned is luck. By being at the right place at the right time, otherwise ordinary individuals have been catapulted into positions of leadership. Individuals who were doing their "duty" to help alleviate the consequences of a dis-

Nelson Mandela, after thirty years of imprisonment by the apartheid government in his country, South Africa, was elected president in May 1994 in the nation's first truly democratic elections under a new constitution of which he was the principal architect.

aster, for example, suddenly find themselves interviewed by the media and the subject of conversations by a good portion of society. Others may have suffered a terrible tragedy such as the accidental loss of a dear one, and by using that experience to help others avoid the same tragedy, they become well known throughout society. In some societies innocent persons are arrested and imprisoned without a fair trial. When they leave prison and tell of their traumatic experiences, they become instant celebrities and often leaders of movements demanding changes in government policies. (In South Africa, leadership of the black community was granted only to those who were imprisoned or accused by an oppressive government of being a traitor. These are the leaders of the African National Congress.)

No matter how it is acquired, leadership can be no more than what artist Andy Warhol stated, fifteen minutes in the spotlight. Leadership is fleeting; today you are toasted and hailed as the great leader and five years from now very few will remember your name. Some leaders die in their prime and are remembered in books, poems, and songs; but most just fade away into history as a footnote in an article or book. Not many persons today know the names of legislative leaders of thirty years ago, and even historians have to dust off their tomes to find the names of political leaders who basked in the spotlight a hundred years ago. For society, time is a powerful leveler; it reduces the known powerful few to the position of the anonymous many.

Nonelected Leaders

So far we have been discussing leaders in government. However, some leaders outside of government also can influence government policies. Today these nongovernment leaders, from a societal perspective, may be more important than those in government.

FOCUS   MITTERRAND THE LEADER

PARIS (AP). Francois Mitterrand leaves office Wednesday as the longest serving president of France, taking with him a wealth of secrets and leaving a legacy rich in controversy.

Passing the mantle to conservative President elect Jacques Chirac, Mitterrand closes a 14 year period of Socialist rule that ultimately defied the party mold. It became the Mitterrand era, and he espoused a notion of French grandeur that even enemies admired.

A consummate strategist, Mitterrand did not shirk at Machiavellian tactics, but remained loyal to friends tainted by corruption scandals that plagued his administration.

Mitterrand outlived the scandals, outwitted rivals and persevered without apologies for a past that included service in the collaborationist Vichy government.

Waging a battle against prostate cancer, Mitterrand, 78, retires amid an outpouring of attempts to unlock his mystique.

He bid farewell Tuesday with a brief written statement, saying he preferred not to appear on television to make a "theatrical adieu."

"I hope (Chirac) leads France in peace and justice," said the statement, addressed to the French people. "I extend to you my gratitude for all that I owe you and send my wishes for happiness to each and every one of you."

The dark silhouette of Mitterrand's trademark fedora and overcoat came to epitomize his solitude and secrets. In the public eye for more than half a century, he eluded familiarity.

Mitterrand is "an immense and complex personality," National Assembly speaker Philippe Seguin, a Chirac loyalist, said this week. "One of the greats of the century is going."

Changes during Mitterrand's presidency include abolishing the death penalty, decentralizing government, a shorter work week and longer vacations. The numerous architectural projects he sponsored altered the face of Paris.

But Mitterrand considers his paramount bequest to be the vision of a united Europe that he and Chancellor Helmut Kohl of Germany polished and promoted.

True to form, Mitterrand ignited controversy in a last farewell to Europe during a speech in Berlin on

May 8 to celebrate the Allied victory in World War II.

Calling German soldiers courageous, he said they "loved their country" despite the "bad cause" they fought for.

Some denounced the speech. Others said it was Mitterrand's finest hour.

"I have rarely been so moved by a political discourse," Jean d'Ormesson, a member of the prestigious Academie Francaise and critic of Mitterrand's policies, wrote in Le Figaro newspaper. "He was France, he was Europe, he was the reconciliation... between France and Germany, he was the voice of peace, justice and truth."

So it seemed the day he dropped a bouquet of lilies into the Seine River at the spot where skinheads drowned a Moroccan immigrant during a far-right march May 1. It was precisely the gesture the nation needed.

The fact that it came from Mitterrand, who had been accused of giving the extreme right too much political clout in order to divide his conservative opponents, made it all the more notable.

Forced into two periods of "cohabitation" with the right when the conservatives took over Parliament and the Cabinet, Mitterrand was defiant. "They're not going to shut me up in a rat trap," the leftist president growled.

Contradictions feature in any description of Mitterrand: a Vichy-decorated Resistance leader, a pragmatic politician who almost became a writer, the man who said he was as moved watching a flight of geese as by the liberation of Nazi occupied Paris.

Few were indifferent to Mitterrand. Polls throughout his two terms placed him as the most or least popular president of modern France.

He was alternately idolized by the nation and spurned even by his own party. Now the tide has turned again. Recent polls show a solid majority of French people believe he will have a major place in French history.

It remains to be seen how history will compare Mitterrand with Gen. Charles de Gaulle, the rival against whom Mitterrand always measured himself.

But Mitterrand's legacy will endure.

"He remains an adversary," wrote d'Ormesson. "But an adversary who, all of a sudden, has entered into grandeur."

Before the 1800s, when monarchs were the principal policy makers, only those in government who were close to the monarchs could influence policy. Seldom was an outsider to the monarch's inner circle allowed to speak to the king or queen, much less to suggest policy. Later, when leaders were elected, they had to maintain an open line of communication with their constituents. To be elected or reelected leaders have to listen to the "people."

The "people" are those who speak on behalf of the voters. Generally the "people" are the leaders of groups. Mohandas Gandhi of India, Martin Luther King of the United States, and Bertrand Russell of the United Kingdom are some of the most renowned leaders of modern times because they influenced policies without being part of government. Less

Martin Luther King, Jr.

Bertrand Russell

renowned are the thousands of others who, in a lesser way, have done the same thing. Nongovernmental leaders are important to government because they articulate the needs and demands of the people who are needed to support government policies and processes. The leaders of government today cannot lead without the support of nongovernment leaders, which has led to further diffusion of society's leadership.

In societies in which government leaders are not elected, nongovernment leaders do not surface. Those who want government policy changed are persecuted and frequently eliminated by imprisonment, banishment, or murder. Others do not emerge because the futility of their efforts inhibits them or they fear being persecuted.

Of course, elected governments also have some leaders who are not elected, such as those who are appointed because they were leaders of other groups or, in some instances, have special abilities.

Interestingly, the attributes of nonelected government leaders and nongovernment leaders are different from those of elected government leaders. Wealth, although still an attribute, is less important. Intelligence, knowledge, rationality, expertise, ability to communicate effectively, courage, and charisma play a more significant role because leadership is gained through personal relations within groups.

Since elected government leaders are selected on the basis of attributes that are irrelevant in policy making, nonelected and nongovernment leaders often assume important policy making roles. They, after all, have become leaders because of their intelligence, expertise, and, most important, ability to communicate. Elected leaders, therefore, are often only as effective as their staff of professionals and the messages these professionals place in their mouth. Nevertheless, citizens still focus their attention on the elected leaders.

Elites

The word **elite** is often used to describe leaders in a society. Centuries ago it was a useful term; today, however, the word confuses more than it explains. Who is the elite of the United States? Is it Michael Jackson and Madonna? Michael Jordan and Joe Montana? Merryl Streep and Paul Newman? Robert Dole and Bill Clinton? Lee Iacocca and Ross Perot? Saul Bellow and Stephen King? They have all been called, at one time or another, part of the U.S. elite. Besides notoriety and, for some, prominence in their fields, what do these people share?

The term elite is so nebulous in the context of today's society that it makes little sense. People attribute elite status to others, sometimes without their knowledge. Persons who may be true leaders, but who operate away from the limelight of those they lead, may not be considered elite; whereas leaders who manipulate circumstances so they can be in the spotlight and be considered elite may not really be as good as the people think.

Sometimes the word *elite* is used more narrowly to denote trendsetters in a given profession or another functional aspect of society (e.g., bowling elite, show-business elite, sports elite, literary elite, academic elite, and political elite). Some individuals who belong to an elite group may indeed be leaders. However, the vast number of elite groups and subgroups within a society make it meaningless to speak of a societal elite. As in hierarchies, a person may be an elite in one group and be a nobody in another.

In addition, an individual can be considered elite from a global perspective. To achieve global eliteness, one must have already gained elite status in several societies. Global trendsetters, therefore, are leaders not only in a segment of their own society but also in similar segments in several societies.

However, a global leader could also be considered a nonleader in his or her own society. One example from recent politics is Mikhail Gorbachev.

FOCUS

DICTATORS

A leadership style that appeared in the last century and became prominent in this century, especially among states in the Southern Hemisphere, is the dictatorship. A dictator is an individual who occupies the highest level in a government and has control of the policy making processes. As the word itself suggests, a dictator dictates policy and does not allow dissension within the government and often within society. A legislature may be allowed, but only if it does not oppose the dictator's policies. When a dictator promulgates policies that are for the good of the masses, he or she is called benevolent.

Usually a dictatorship is established when the dictator forcibly overthrows either a previous dictator or the legitimate chief executive. Sometimes a dictator is able to win an election. Since dictators either achieve or maintain power by using force, which is usually supplied by the military, most dictators since World War II have come from the military forces.

Generally dictators do not stay in power long. Most are ousted by the same means they used to gain office. In Argentina, for example, the average dictatorship lasted two years. Some dictators have been in control of their country for twenty or more years, while others keep the office within the family (i.e., sons or brothers inherit the position). Jean-Claude "Baby Doc" Duvalier inherited the position of "President for Life" in Haiti from his father Francois "Papa Doc" Duvalier. Together they gov-

erned the island for more than thirty years. The Somoza family governed Nicaragua for more than forty years.

Although dictators appear to have complete control of their government, in reality they often do not. Just like absolute monarchs had to constantly look over their shoulders for someone anxious to depose them, modern dictators also have to do so. Pretenders to their position are always ready to make a grab for it. To prevent them from becoming a threat, dictators, either find a way to dispose of them physically, or bargain with them by offering a policy making position, thereby weakening their hold on the government.

Are dictators leaders in their societies? Some are, of course. Others think of themselves as such, but are often manipulated by individuals or groups to maintain or increase their share of a society's wealth. Sometimes these individuals and groups are from other societies. For example, U.S. corporations and U.S. government agencies have been involved in manipulation of government control by most of the dictators of Guatemala, Honduras, and other Latin American states and certainly the former Soviet Union controlled most of the dictators of Eastern Europe until recently.

Dictators are frequently "make-believe" leaders; they believe they are leaders. To the many who suffer through some of their worst policies and to outsiders, they may be just puppets on strings operated by others.

Gorbachev received respect and adulation from people in the many societies he visited. In the United States he was considered a world leader. Yet in the Soviet Union, especially at the end of his term, he was seen as an irrelevant participant in the politics of his country. Even today he is considered a leader by many more people in Europe, Canada and the United States than in Russia. Gorbachev is certainly part of the elite of world leaders but not of the political elite in the states that seceded from the Soviet Union.

Mikhail Gorbachev

In the United States, where government authority and leadership is so diffused, elite status is confusing. For example, Sonny Bono at one time was part of the show-business elite. Then he was elected mayor of Palm Springs. Once he was elected, his elite status in show business disappeared. In Palm Springs he was not considered part of the political elite at first because other politicians regarded him as a gate crasher. After a few years of hard work he did achieve Palm Springs political elite status. Yet on a state and national level Bono has not achieved the level of eliteness he had in show-business, even though he has served in the U.S. House of Representatives since 1994.

In most societies thousands of government leaders, elected or not, are not considered part of the political elite; yet these people make and implement policies that are far more important for the future of society than those of the few who are considered part of the political elite. Some want to be considered elite and think that an elected position will bring this status; however, very often this does not happen because of the great number of elected officials and the complexity of public institutions. The people grant elite status to only a few, sometimes the wrong few.

Choosing Political Leaders

One of the main political problems confronting any society is how to choose or replace its government leaders. This is frequently referred to as the **problem of succession**.

There are only four ways of filling government positions. First, a person is born to parents who already are government leaders by birth (i.e., monarchs). Second, he or she is appointed by a few, such as a legislature or a gathering of family heads, as in Saudi Arabia. Third, one takes over the government by force and claims the highest office for him or herself (i.e., dictator). Fourth, an individual is elected by voters, a system justified by Locke and Rousseau.

Except for a handful of monarchs, kings and queens today have little power. Most are primarily figureheads and are not considered government leaders. One of the few with some power is King Hussein of Jordan, who has governed for the last forty years. King Juan Carlos of Spain governed for a short period after the end of the Falangist government of General Franco and before the establishment of a democratic regime.

Legislatures or other institutions established to appoint policy makers and implementors, such as the U.S. electoral college, are rooted in the electoral process. In other words, those who do the appointing are themselves elected. Saudi Arabia and some other Arabian states select a king by convening a conference of the heads of various royal families, who choose one of their own to govern; however, this system is just another version of leadership by birth.

Some leaders are selected through violence. This has been a very common way of filling high government positions; in the 1970s over half the governments in Africa, Asia, and Latin America were run by persons who gained office by force. In many areas of the world the use of force to gain high political positions is considered part of the political process. Sometimes this method is even desired by the populace because it is usually a quick and efficient way of getting rid of incompetent or corrupt officials. The main problem with this method is that it does not necessarily ensure a long tenure for the officeholders; nor does it allow those who won their positions through violence to sleep soundly at night.

Elections are by far the most popular method of selecting government leaders; but they are hardly a perfect way of doing so, as we will soon see. However, elections do what they are supposed to, namely fill vacant positions in the highest levels of government.

King Juan Carlos' dedication to the principles of constitutionalism and democracy paved the way for Spain's adoption of a constitutional monarchy in 1978.

Certain constitutions specify that the president be elected by an electoral college instead of directly by the people. In the first African Gold Coast Colony elections in 1951, a farmer was nominated and elected unopposed to the electoral college.

Why Would Anyone Want to be Elected?

Persons aspiring to be elected leaders are not typical of others in a society. Few persons are willing to go through the drudgery and frustrations of a campaign. A candidate's average day begins very early in the morning (about 6:00 A.M.) with shaking hands and saying a few words to workers who need to start their job by 8:00 A.M. By 11:30 A.M. he or she has met with the staff to plan the activities for the following days and has made many telephone calls. Often this occurs on a plane or bus on the way to a location the candidate knows little about. At noon the candidate gives a speech appealing for votes, makes appearances at places that will provide good photo opportunities for the local and national media and, perhaps, appears as a guest at a talk show for radio or television. By late afternoon the candidate again takes a plane or bus to a place where another speech is given, an interview is conducted with reporters, or a panel discussion is planned. At 9:00 A.M. there is another meeting with more people. By midnight a plane or bus takes him or her to a motel for the night. Sometime during the day speeches are reviewed and policy positions discussed. The candidate may finally go to sleep at 1:00 A.M. only to get up again at 6:00 A.M.

While the candidate is actively campaigning, family life is virtually nonexistent. With very little time to keep up with anything but the tightly managed world of politics, the candidate is cut off not only from family, but also from friends, professional associates, and clients. Almost every minute of the day and night is scheduled and programmed, including food eaten, clothes worn, books and newspapers read, and people to meet — none of these may be the candidate's choice. This continues for about four months before the party nomination and two to three months before the election. Long before the nomination process occurs, the candidate spends a great amount of time fund-raising and planning campaign strategy.

Why would anyone want to go through all this? What does elected office offer that makes an individual willing to give up a part of his or her life?

Usually it is not money. The salaries of elected officials generally are less than what they earn in their profession. Elected officeholders often experience not only a salary cut but also higher living expenses if they have to live in the capital. However, in less industrialized countries or areas, especially those in which a shortage of employment opportunities for skilled and professional workers exist, winning an elected position does insure income. Even in the United States and Canada, the only local elected positions with a paid salary are sheriff, assessor, magistrate, and county clerk. In addition, the fringe benefits of elected office are not extraordinary when compared with those offered in the private sector.

Usually the higher the elected position sought (and the more expensive the campaign is), the less enticing the material rewards. Certainly wealthy individuals, such as U.S. Senator Jay Rockefeller, do not run for elected positions because of the salary and fringe benefits. Most candidates for prime minister, president, or national legislature in industrial states do not run for election for monetary reasons.

The rewards of elected office are ordinarily more subtle than material benefits and more difficult to pinpoint. Virtually every candidate for elected office wants to do good (i.e., participate in the promotion of good in society). Candidates feel strongly, like missionaries, that they can best lead society away from an actual or potential slide toward the bad. They generally are aware that they do not possess all the answers, but they are convinced that their intentions are stronger, if not nobler, than those of the rest of society. By winning an election, they affirm their superiority. (When they lose, candidates generally blame something other than the purity of their intentions for defeat.)

What better way to have one's good intentions recognized than by having a multitude of people vote in approval. Recognition through the ballot box is a tremendous ego inflator for anyone, even more than witnessing thousands cheering one on at a rally or convention. The cheers of thousands, the applause of the respected few, the adulation of many others, and the votes of majorities or pluralities all give some prospective leaders a good feeling. Candidates feel exuberant, very content with themselves, and capable of doing the greatest feats imaginable when they win an election. Obviously people who feel very uncomfortable speaking to even small groups, are fearful of large audiences, or dislike notoriety and their name in the media will seldom venture into the world of elected politics.

Once elected the candidate continues to feel recognized and important by occupying the office itself and being part of a small select group of people (i.e., the elite). The office physically does not have to be plush; it may be nothing more than a closet under a stairwell. What is important is what the office symbolizes: the facade of power.

No doubt some pursue power and want to possess it. But what is **power**? Power is a relationship in which a person or group believes that it can give orders to a second entity and the latter believes that it is obliged to follow the orders. The archetypal example of power is the master-slave relationship. The master gives orders and the slave carries them out. Physical strength of the individuals involved is not important. What is important is that the master considers him or herself a master and the slave believes that he or she is a slave. If either believed otherwise (i.e., the master no longer believed capable of giving orders or the slave no longer believed obligated to follow them), the master-slave relationship no longer exists.

Power is less a result of one's wanting to give orders and more a result of manipulating someone else into wanting to take orders. Those who take orders involuntarily may be intimidated by violence associated with the strength of whoever gives the orders. Or, more likely, those who take orders may be persuaded not necessarily by the strength of the order givers as much as by their communicative skills.

By being persuaded to vote for a certain candidate, the voter is also promising to follow any "orders" given by the candidate after gaining office. If I vote for you to be my policy maker, I am not only relinquishing my ability to make policy but also stating that I will follow your policy decisions. In theory this gives you power over me.

Actually the power that elected officials strive for is only a facade. The individual legislator or executive whom I have elected cannot tell me to do anything, and I do not have to do what he or she wants me to do. An individual government official does not make policy alone.

Policy making requires the cooperative support of hundreds, maybe thousands, of others who not only agree with the policy but also can manipulate me to want to follow it. The totality, the government, has power over me; it can force me to do things I would rather not do. However, the elected official's part in getting me to do what he or she originally wanted is small, almost inconsequential. Furthermore, since I helped elect the official, I can un-elect him or her as well. In the next election (and there are always next elections) I may actively try to defeat the incumbent whose policy orientations or decisions I disagreed with. What then is the elected official's real power? Not much.

Often elected officials have a staff to help them. Some staff serve at the mercy of the official, who can dismiss them at will. Obviously this staff would try to do everything to remain in the official's good graces. The elected official has power over them. Sometimes this power is abused, as when the official demands sexual favors from employees. Yet, the power these elected officials have in this regard, is not different from that of any chief executive officer over nonprotected staff who depend on him or her for a job.

Ironically, the power of the elected legislator or executive emanates from his or her role as my servant; not my slave, but my servant. As a member of society, I want my elected official to resolve problems or issues that are important to me. The official, through his or her own expertise or that of staff, colleagues, and others, is in a better position than I to operate the processes and institutions of government. Invariably the issues and problems that concern me concern others too. The degree of power the legislator or executive possesses basically depends on his or her expertise of government operations and ability to manipulate others to do what I and other citizens want done. If we want the elected official to do and say nothing, he or she would not have any power. Whatever power elected officials have, therefore, is ultimately based on the demands citizens make of them.

The power that candidates seek is illusionary. They may wrap themselves in the symbols of power (which might very well be all that some seek), but do not possess any real power. However, symbols of power may be important in that they are considered rungs in the ladder of status within some elements in a society. Symbols of power might confer social status, just as the scepter conferred the status of royalty. To be addressed as "The Honorable So and So" or "His Excellency" implies having more status than everyone else, being a member in a very exclusive club.

Candidates and elected officers endure much to move up on the ladder of status. Higher status infers greater visibility. Status may engender respect and acknowledgment of some superiority; and, for young adults, it may attract potential mates and job offers.

Most candidates and officeholders are status seekers — people who, for professional advancement or psychological reasons, want to be distinguished from the herd. Unlike most of us, they are not satisfied with anonymity. And, unlike others who also seek status, candidates try to do it in a less demanding way. Most of us, at one point or another, will be professionals. As such we will compete with others in our fields, and depending on expertise, motivation, support, and luck some will rise to the top while most of us will remain as journeymen in our field, anonymous. We will be content with our lot as long we can earn a living. Candidates, however, are seldom satisfied with their lot, and consequently want to rise to the top in ways other than in the field for which they have been trained. Of the thousands of candidates who run for election, not many have achieved a high status based on their expertise within their own professions. Elections are a way in which otherwise common people can move up the ladder of status. Through the electoral process "nobodies" seek to become "somebodies."

Finally, another reason individuals run for public office is for the challenge that campaigning and officeholding present. Just as marathon joggers who know they will not finish among the top fifty keep on running until they cross the finish line, so, too, many candidates who know they will not win will enter the race just because they enjoy it. And, who knows, they might get lucky; or they may win because their previous defeats honed their campaigning abilities.

Once in office, elected officials may also enjoy the wheeling and dealing involved in policymaking. The bargaining and compromising with other elected officials and the seemingly unresolvable conflicts based on the most picayune and arcane ideas excite those who are elected. Even when they are aware of the futility, or insignificance of their efforts, these officials, nevertheless, derive contentment from knowing that they are affecting the development of their society.

The reasons people run for office are as complex as their attributes. Most likely, many attributes and reasons mix to determine the commitment and success of any one candidate. No one can state what that mix should be. As long as there are elections, there will be candidates trying to present to us, the voters, those attributes and reasons that they hope will garner the most votes.

TERMS TO REMEMBER

charisma
elites
dictator
problem of succession
power

SUGGESTED READINGS

Burns, James MacGregor. *Leadership.* New York: Harper & Row, 1978. Distinguishing between "political leadership and the arbitrary exercise of power" the author weaves personal anecdotes with scholarly research into an analysis of modern leadership.

Centeno, Migel Angel. *Democracy Within Reason: Technocratic Revolution in Mexico.* University Park: The Pennsylvania University Press, 1994. The emergence of the technocrat under the Salinas de Gortari's regime in Mexico in the early 1990s is examined in terms of institutions, elites, and ideology.

Hook, Sydney. *The Hero in History: A Study in Limitation and Possibility.* Boston: Beacon Press, 1955. Originally written in 1943, this book by the well known political philosopher analyzes whether men and women make history or history makes heroes.

Hunter, Floyd. *Community Power Structure: A Study of Decision Makers.* Chapel Hill: University of North Carolina Press, 1953. A pioneering study on the over 1,400 governments that regulate the lives of people in a metropolitan area.

Lindholm Charles. *Charisma.* Cambridge, MA: B. Blackwell, 1990. The influence Jim Jones, Charles Manson and Adolf Hitler had on their followers is analyzed through the anthropological perspective.

Mills, C. Wright. *The Power Elite.* New York: Oxford University Press, 1956. The major work of the radical sociologist who suggested that small groups of persons control most decisions made in even small communities.

Ober, Josiah. *Mass and Elite in Democratic Athens: Rhetoric, Ideology, and the Power of the People.* Princeton: Princeton University Press, 1989. The role of orators in ancient Athens in propagating democratic values on a society based on inequality is the theme of this book.

Pye, Lucian W. *The Mandarin and the Cadre: Chinese Political Culture.* Ann Arbor: Center of Chinese Studies, The University of Michigan, 1988. A classic study on the role of the leaders and bureaucrats in determining the policies of China.

Riordon, William L. Plunkitt of Tammany Hall: *A Series of Very Plain Talks on Very Practical Politics.* New York: E.P. Dutton & Co., 1963. How to become a political leader as stated by an early 20th century "statesman" of New York City politics.

NOTES

1. UNICEF, "National Performance Gaps: Under-five Mortality Rate," http://www.unicef...on95/statoo3.html, 5/9/96.

2. For a new perspective on Louis XVI see Vincent Cronin, *Louis and Antoinette* (New York: Morrow, 1975). Also Simon Schama, *Citizens: A Chronicle of the French Revolution* (New York: Vintage Books, 1989).

10
Voting

In the early 1990s in the United States about 511,039 elected officials[1] served in about 86,743 governments.[2] During the four-year period recently I cast my vote for: five members of the board of education, seven members of the city council (twice), three county commissioners (actually four because one died in office), one county prosecuting attorney, one tax assessor, one county clerk, one surveyor, one sheriff, one circuit court clerk, one circuit judge, five magistrates, four representatives to the state house of delegates (twice), one state senator, one commissioner of agriculture, one state auditor, one state treasurer, one secretary of state, one state attorney general, one state supreme court judge, one governor, one U.S. representative (twice), one U.S. senator, one president and vice president for a total of 55 officers. Almost all these offices were contested (some by candidates from four different parties); I had to choose among at least 110 persons. Since I also voted in the primaries, I had to choose from at least another 110 persons for the party's nominees. In sum I made 110 choices from among more than 220 alternatives.

Additionally, I voted on twelve **referenda** (i.e., policy decisions requiring approval by the electorate) dealing with constitutional amendments, tax levies, and school bonds. I also voted for a few dozen party officials and party representatives to the conventions. In metropolitan areas, where multiplicity of governments is greatest, voters may have twice as many choices.

Had I lived in a state that was not a federation, did not have a presidential system of government, or did not have primaries, I would have fewer opportunities to elect officials. In the United Kingdom, Germany, Spain, Japan, India, Israel, Ghana, and other countries I would have voted for no more than thirty officials in the same four-year period. The choices, however, would have been no less difficult. In France the number of elected officials is as large as that of the U.S., even though France's population is one-fourth that of the United States'. The choices are more difficult because France has three times as many political parties.

Taking the task of being a voter seriously is not easy, especially in the United States and France where so many choices need to be made. Although the total time to decide who or what to vote for may not be much (I estimate that I spent about fifty-five hours in four years, which is thirty minutes on each decision), disentangling the complexity of the offices and the issues takes much more effort. For example, What does the commissioner of agriculture do? What is the job description? What credentials should a candidate for that office possess? Or, are the credentials for state senator different from those of U.S. senator, for governor from those of U.S. president, or city councilor from those of county commissioner? Unless one considers elections strictly popularity contests, substantial time, resources, and effort must be invested to make an educated decision in the voting booth.

The Importance of Elections to Society

From the perspective of society the act of voting is more important than for whom or what one votes. Policy making and implementing have become so diffused and fragmented that individual elected officials and

plebiscites (any proposal voters are asked to vote for or against) make little difference. Elections are significant because the intellectual ferment and discussions that precede them allow for scrutiny of the values, beliefs, norms, and behavior of the state. Since the state keeps society together, it has to adjust to society's ever present changes.

The electoral process is the mechanism by which society maintains harmony with the state. Changes in the organization of the state and its relation to society and the individual are first perceived through elections. Candidates enunciate the needs, demands, and wishes of the populace that are different from those of candidates in previous elections. Today the campaign speeches of U.S. presidents Eisenhower, Kennedy, Johnson, Nixon, Carter, Reagan, and even Bush appear dated and out of synchrony with the times. As society changes, the language of politics changes; and the language of politics is never more pronounced than before elections. Elections are important even in states governed by one party or a dictator because they keep the political vocabulary current as citizens and campaigners are forced to respond to each others wishes, demands and questions face to face.

The electoral process is not always the best way to keep the state and society in harmony. The electoral process in Germany in the 1930s virtually caused the destruction of a society by a state. German society in 1932 did not want to destroy itself; yet by giving a plurality of votes to the Nazi Party, it did just that. Hitler and the Nazis capitalized on the divisiveness of German political opinion, which was caused by the sudden

Voting for the Russian Constituent Assembly of October, 1917 — dissolved by Lenin and the Bolsheviks after their *coup d'etat.*

loss of legitimate leadership after the demise of monarchical rule and by the inability of the Weimar Republic to establish commonly held values, beliefs, and norms regarding the state. In the absence of a consensus on the nature, function, and role of the state in German society at that time, any group that received support from the public could claim legitimate authority. A similar situation prevailed in France after the Revolution of 1789 and in Russia after the first revolution in 1917.

October 3, 1990 was declared *Tag der Deutschen Einheit* (Day of German Unity). Nearly one million citizens participated in the celebrations at the Brandenburg Gate.

When the force of the state bottles up divisions within a society, elections can cause the collapse of the state and society. In Poland, Hungary, Rumania, Albania, and Bulgaria in the mid 1980s, each state had to be replaced after elections showed an uncompromising majority opposed to it. A few years later in the German Democratic Republic, elections forced not only the disappearance of the state but also the reabsorption of East German society into its western counterpart. Recently in the Union of Soviet Socialist Republics and Yugoslavia both the state and the society disappeared after elections. In all these countries elections manifested a lack of a consensus among the population.

States need the consensus of those in society to remain in existence. The chief function of elections is to maintain this consensus. Since elections usually are held not more than six years apart, they mold and bring forth a gradual change in the consensus of a society. During an electoral process, voters fine-tune their beliefs, values, norms, attitudes, and opinions to those expressed by candidates, the media, and other shapers of opinion during a campaign. These, in turn, fine-tune their pronouncements to the leaders of society, who want feedback from voters. Thus, a

Czechoslovakia was split into Czech and Slovak as a result of voting by people in 1992. The two Republics joined the United Nations in 1993.

communications loop develops in which voters give feedback to candidates, and the media, who give voters' feedback to the leaders, who then respond to this feedback through the candidates and the media. Through the many candidates who get elected and the many voters who work for government, the state, which is the outcome of the consensus of a society, also helps mold that consensus.

Without elections and the hoopla that precede them, society has few, if any, means available to establish the consensus needed to maintain the state. Although part of its population gets its paycheck from the government, these bureaucrats are highly specialized in a small aspect of government and, therefore, are not aware of all the general concerns of society regarding government and its policies. They, too, need elections to identify, define, and resolve the issues outside their area of expertise and to help them to rethink their own role in formulating public policy. The electoral process brings to the foreground questions, issues, and criteria that even those in government do not have the time or opportunity to examine or on which to form an opinion.

For those in government elections are also important because their outcomes determine how long they keep their positions as policy makers and implementors. Although more than 90 percent of **incumbents** (elected officials who occupy an office) are reelected in most states, some do lose. For all candidates elections are a risk but for incumbents defeat usually means political death. The fear of losing political status keeps elected officials from making decisions that would not achieve consensus. Nonelected government officials also stay atuned to public consensus because they, too, can lose their job. Elections keep all government officials just insecure enough to stay alert to the voting public's dissatisfaction with their policies.

Low Voter Turnout: A Modern Dilemma

Since World War II fewer and fewer voters make the effort to go to the polls each year. In 1996, only 49 percent of the voting population cast a

AVERAGE PERCENTAGE OF NONVOTING POPULATION IN NINETEEN INDUSTRIAL STATES (1971-80)

State	Average % nonvoting
Italy	6.53
Belgium	12.17
Austria	12.24
Sweden	12.44
Denmark	13.23
Australia	15.52
Germany	15.78
New Zealand	16.39
Finland	17.82
Israel	17.85
Netherlands	18.46
Norway	18.68
France	23.16
Ireland	23.44
United Kingdom	25.01
Japan	27.09
Canada	32.85
United States	45.78
Switzerland	56.71

Adapted from Jackman, Robert W., "Political Institutions and Voter turnout in 19 industrial democracies." *American Political Science Review* '81, no. 2 (June 1987): p. 420.

ballot for president. The percentage of eligible voters who do not vote in presidential elections has increased from 37.2 percent in 1960 to 49.9 percent in 1988. In two states, Georgia and South Carolina, 61 percent of voters stayed home in 1988 (versus 34.5 percent in Minnesota).[3]

Voter turnout for primary and statewide elections is very low, about 15 to 30 percent; the turnout for referenda has been as low as 8 percent. This trend is evident not only in the United States (the 1992 elections were an exception) but also in other countries. In the German state of Hessen voter turnout in the 1995 elections was 66.6 percent, which was 4.2 percent less than in 1991.[4] In addition France, Japan, India, Mexico, Israel, and the

Forty percent of Niger's registered voters, including many women, turned out for the country's first multiparty elections in 1993. United Nations Development Programme played a pivotal role in the electoral process.

United Kingdom have experienced low voter turnout over the last three decades. Why?

Voters avoid the polls for many reasons, some more important than others in particular elections. One of the most important reasons is that voting has lost its exclusivity; at one time voting was viewed as a ritual for a specially favored group. Numerous voting restrictions, such as property qualifications, literacy and residency requirements, sexual discrimination, and poll taxes (i.e., fees for voting) eliminated many persons, thereby making voters a select public. Until the 1880s less than a third of the voting age population could vote, but about 80 percent of those eligible did vote. Participation in politics, was regarded as an endeavor of the privileged, of the elite perhaps as a legacy from the monarchial era. To be a somebody, one voted. In the United Kingdom some citizens were even allowed to cast two ballots.

Since World War II all voting restrictions have been eliminated universally; upon reaching a certain age, everyone can vote. Universal suffrage, however, has made voting commonplace, almost banal. Voting no longer differentiates one person from the next. Since everyone can vote, the relevance and status of the individual vote lessened significantly. My ability to vote no longer is an important manifestation of my political acumen. In fact, if I want to show others my political abilities I would need to be elected. (The number of candidates for elected office in the United States today is greater than the total number of votes cast for president in every election through the 1830s.)

Since my vote is diluted by the votes of so many others, it is no longer momentous to me; I also do not consider my vote as crucial to society. In 1992 more than 104,425,000 votes were cast for U.S. president besides mine; 683,100 of those votes came from my state. Would the outcome have been different if I had not voted? What would I have missed had I stayed home on election day?

What about the notion previously discussed that political participation shows integration into society? Since ballots are secret, no one, except those who saw me in the voting booth, knows if I vote. As a self-imposed test of integration into society, voting does not have much credibility. After all, I can walk into the voting booth and, with a mental flip of the coin choose candidates I do not know. This does not prove much about my integration into society. So why bother in the first place?

In addition, voting is inconvenient. In the United States elections are generally held on Tuesday which is a workday. People are too rushed before work to vote and too exhausted afterwards to make the effort. In most other countries elections are held on Sunday, which also is not ideal because many citizens choose to do other activities on their "day of rest." Polling places may be too far away from home to get to easily or too noisy, dirty, and crowded to feel comfortable. Persons not motivated to vote will find something unsuitable about the place or time of elections. In an attempt to increase the number of votes cast the state of Washington introduced voting by mail in 1995. It will be interesting to follow several elections to determine whether voting in the privacy of one's home increases the number of ballots cast. Another hurdle for the unmotivated voter to overcome is registration, which in many countries, such as the United States, must occur thirty or more days before the election. This process takes some time (usually you have to wait in line) and can be

In 1989, more than 700,000 Namibians registered to vote. The independence process was supervised by United Nations Transition Assistance Group (UNTAG) composed of 8000 members from 109 nations.

a hassle, with forms to fill out and questions answered. The process is usually repeated every time a new house or apartment is moved into. Since driver's licenses also need to be re-applied for every time one moves, especially across state lines, the Federal government recently passed a law that requires states to register voters at the time driver's licenses are issued. This should ease the process somewhat but does not remove it completely.

In addition to the diminishing significance of voting, what other factors cause low voter turnouts? Do the choices among candidates and the types of issues on the ballot make a difference? The choices offered do not bring in hoards of voters. For most people there is no choice of candidates. Mass marketing has made candidates' level of competence, stand on issues, personality, and other criteria so indistinguishable that is difficult to tell them apart. In their attempts to appeal to the greatest number of voters, candidates, simplify their stand on issues to the point where cliches and brief phrases on commercials predominate. Why vote for a candidate if he or she cannot be differentiated from the others?

Even those who profess to be ideological moderate their views when confronting the electorate. Ideologues such as La Pen of France, Buchanan of the United States, and Zhirinovsky of Russia sounded much different before they seriously entered the political arena. Their opponents often have to remind the electorate exactly what these individuals espoused before they became candidates.

It is quite possible that the differences among candidates diminish simply because of the sheer size of the electorate and the large number of candidates. Citizens are often expected to choose candidates for fifty different offices among two hundred or so entirely different personalities, with varying stands on issues, and past performances. It is too overwhelming for most voters. In the United States over half a million elected officials serving in 87,000 governments elected by, at most, 104,425,000 voters out of a possible 189,044,000 produces an amalgam in which differences are sublimated and sameness elevated.

In the United States there is one elect official for every 370 potential voters, in France one for about every 200. In other societies the proportion is much greater; in Canada there is approximately one elected official for every 1,500 voters, in developing countries one for every 150,000. The fact that those who want to be elected have to listen and respond to the needs, demands, and wishes of so many persons at the same time might also create a banal sameness in what they say and do. Originality, eloquence, and interest in the individual voter cannot be expected from candidates who give ten speeches a day for months before election day. Yet, if the candidate does not appeal to me as a voter, why vote?

Even voting along party lines rather than for individual candidates does not allow for pronounced choices as in the past. The platform of the Conservative Party of the United Kingdom has a platform that is no longer much different from that of the Labor Party or the Liberal Democratic Party. The same is true among the Liberal, New Democratic

FOCUS   WHY EGYPTIANS MAY NOT VOTE

CAIRO, Egypt (AP). Low turnout and claims of intimidation marred elections Wednesday for the upper house of Egypt's Parliament.

The elections came less than two weeks after the government made criticizing the regime a criminal act to try to stifle opposition. The opposition includes a 3-year-old campaign by Muslim militants to replace the regime with strict Islamic rule.

A few banners hanging outside polling stations in the crowded capital were the only outward sign of the elections. Final results are expected Thursday.

A third of the consultative council's 264 seats are to be filled. They are being contested by President Hosni Mubarak's ruling National Democratic Party, two opposition parties and independent candidates.

Mubarak's party is expected to maintain its majority on the council, which has only an advisory function.

The party also has a majority in the People's Assembly, Parliament's lower house, which has legislative power and is due for elections later this year.

The president's party has been criticized because none of its 87 candidates are women or Coptic Christians. Copts make up about 10 percent of Egypt's nearly 60 million population.

Low turnout is typical of Egyptian elections, mainly because of voter apathy and widespread claims of intimidation and fraud.

In Alexandria, a supporter of the Muslim Brotherhood running as an independent took the unusual step of sending faxes to news organizations asking help in stopping police from interfering in the polling.

"Help us. Security forces are killing us in front of the polling stations ... the results are tampered with in favor of the government candidate," said Medhat el-Hadad, who was detained at least three times by police during his campaign.

The moderate Muslim Brotherhood is, in effect, Egypt's largest opposition political party. Officially outlawed, its candidates run as independents or with other parties.

Election officials could not be reached for comment on the charges of vote tampering.

In the luxurious Cairo suburb of Heliopolis, where Mubarak cast his vote, polling stations were almost deserted. It was slightly more busy in downtown Cairo.

"Voter turnout is around 30 percent, but after the work day ends, we expect more people," said Abdel-Aziz Mohamed, an election official at a downtown voting station.

"And for people who claim fraud, I tell them to come and see for themselves," he said. "There is no fraud or intimidation."

About 10.6 million Egyptians are eligible to vote for 88 council members. More than 200 candidates are vying for the seats, about 30 of them unopposed.

Council members serve six-year terms. One-third are appointed by the president. Elections take place every three years for half the elected members.

Party, Reform, and Progressive Conservative parties of Canada. In Germany the Christian Democratic Union's policies are very similar to those of the Social Democrats, Free Democrats, and even the Greens. Certainly in the United States, where platforms have never been that important anyway, the Republican and Democratic platforms have few meaningful differences. (Recently I asked an active New Jersey Republican how his state party platform differed from the Democratic one. He told me he didn't know — and he was one of the writers of the Republican platform!)

The realization that one's vote, even when cast for the winner, does not significantly affect public policy also causes voter reluctance. As stated earlier, public policy is so fragmented among so many people, most of whom are not elected, that any one elected official cannot make a significant difference. People deal with many bureaucrats over whom elected officials have virtually no control. Whether it is garbage collection, street repair, payment or receipt of funds, and any other of the hundreds of daily interactions which citizens can have with government, elected officials control none.

Although these officials depend on voters for their position, they alone cannot effectuate change on behalf of the voters because they are too removed from the operations. To which elected official can I complain if my transcript is not granted to me? To which elected official can I complain if the highway on which I drive every day is inadequately maintained and repaired? To which elected official can I complain when my garbage is not picked up as it should be? City council members and state and national legislators have little or no influence in these areas. Elected government officials' ability to promote the welfare of the citizenry is limited not only by their own proliferation but also by the multiplicity of government workers. As a voter I am made aware of this when the person whom I have elected admits his or her inability to resolve my grievances. Why then should I bother voting?

In time I might turn my back on the whole electoral system because elections may not decide anything of consequence for me. I may feel that it does not do anything, except waste my time. Then I have become alienated. Many nonvoters are said to be alienated. They feel helpless in bringing about any meaningful change to their life through government actions. They are not less knowledgeable or concerned about government and its policies than voters, but they no longer perceive the value of the vote. Since government has been unresponsive to their plight, many among the poor have lost all interest in elections. Ironically some of the rich are also nonvoters, but only because they have found more effective ways to influence policy.

Another type of nonvoter is the apathetic voter. The apathetic nonvoter not only does not care about government but also does not care to know about it. Ignorant and misinformed, the apathetic voter sulks about his or her misery, blames government for it, and has no interest in getting out of it. Fortunately, only a small minority of nonvoters is apathetic.

Finally another reason for low voter turnout is that government or its opposition may not want people to vote. Voting may be discouraged by parties in control of government if they believe high voter turnout will cause them to lose control. On the other hand, opposition parties to a vulnerable government may not want people to vote in support of the government because a government with the increased strength of the electorate behind it will be able to intimidate or even prosecute its opposition. As "Why Egyptians May Not Vote" shows, in states in which intimidation of the voter is possible (and probable), the voter may decide that it is not worth the risk to vote.

Why Vote?

If there are so many reasons citizens do not vote, why then do so many others vote? Why did 104,425,000 U.S. citizens cast their ballot for president in 1992? Why did 1,967 citizens (out of 11,247) in Morgantown, West Virginia cast their ballots on March 7, 1995 to decide whether to continue a tax levy to help pay for improvements to parks, recreation facilities, and the city library?

Why do graduates participate in graduation ceremonies? Commencement neither augments nor subtracts anything from the transcript or diploma one receives upon finishing the degree requirements. Many graduates do not participate, but most do. Commencement is a ritual only for those who have completed certain requirements; it denotes completion, an end. After commencement there is a beginning. For those who take part in it, commencement symbolically shows that a period in one's life definitely has been transcended.

Elections also are rituals marking the end of periods, political and historical periods at both the societal and the personal level. Whereas in the past the assumption of power and the dethronement or death of monarchs were considered the dividing lines in history, today elections, in bringing forth different political personalities, fulfill that function. Each election signifies an end to a period and the start of a new one. Even when incumbents are reelected, there is the expectation that something new will occur after the officials are sworn in again. Those who vote want to be part of the transition from the old to the new.

For the individual voter, elections also mark an end. The end to discussions of the identification, definition, and resolution of issues; of the merits and drawbacks of candidates; of the positive and negative effects of the media's handling of the campaigns; and of the role of government in society and for the individual.

In the modern media-saturated society, individuals must make a tremendous effort to escape the impact of electoral politics. One is invariably sucked into the whirlwind of the campaigns. Voting is the culmination of a citizen's political activity for the preceding period. The ritual of casting one's vote is similar to reaching out and accepting the diploma at commencement. And, just as the graduate may continue with his or her studies, so may the voter continue political activity. Both commencement and elections are a seal of satisfactory compliance with the requirements before one takes the next step. (Participation in commencement after completing easy courses with low passing grades is possible as is voting without having done any political "homework." In either case, the ritual is far less rewarding for the individual and continuation to the next step will be much more difficult.)

By voting the citizen manifests concern for the well-being of society. Individuals have little opportunity to show that they not only are integrated into society but also want to influence its future well-being. Participating in charitable work, preparing new community programs and policies, brainstorming at meetings, or attending public forums takes more time than most people have. Political discussions with neighbors, friends, and colleagues do not take time away from other demands on an individual's time, especially since these discussions occur in social settings that are part of daily life. Elections, therefore, offer the opportunity to focus discussions on political problems, especially for people who have a need to show their concern for society. Additionally, the act of voting itself ratifies a citizen's preoccupation with society's well-being.

Voting can be viewed as an adaptive strategy to maintain one's viability among others with whom one interacts. If my colleagues or neighbors or friends vote, I should also do so because that is what is expected of me. I might lose the association with any or all of them if I were not to vote and they found out about it. Polls are manned by poll-workers who often keep an eye out for friends and neighbors and are critical of those who do not show up to vote. These workers also tell their friends who voted and who did not. (In smaller towns and villages throughout the globe this is one of the strongest pressures exercised on citizens to vote.) In addition, trying to justify not voting is difficult. By not voting am I showing that I think I am better than everyone else or that I do not care about the issues or candidates everyone else talks about? Regardless of the reason, by not voting I am separating myself from those who do vote, which will not endear me to them.

Many citizens vote because they truly believe that their one vote will make a difference; casting that one vote means candidate X will win or proposition Y will pass. The fact that X loses by many votes and Y passes by many more does not necessarily discourage that voter; there is always the next time.

By voting, however, the citizen can also show displeasure with what is going on in society. Voting against incumbents and in favor of referenda is stating "no" to the status quo. Citizens have few opportunities to express dissatisfaction with the way things are going. Voting, therefore, becomes an outlet for frustrations, anxieties for the future, and even a feeling of helplessness.

Voting is not only considered a right but also an obligation in some societies. By law citizens are required to vote; if they do not, they can be fined and jailed, as in most Latin American states and in Australia. In

Voting in South Africa's first non-racial and democ-ratic election, April 1994, in which Nelson Mandela was elected President and 46 years of apartheid ended. The voter turnout was estimated at 86 percent of the 23 million eligible voters.

Angolans calmly awaited their turn to vote in the country's first multiparty elections in September, 1992. The two major parties secured 49.57 percent and 40.07 percent votes, the remainder being divided among nine other parties.

other societies citizens experience social pressures to vote. And in all societies those who are acculturated feel guilty if they do not go to the polling booth on election day. How much guilt a person feels for not voting depends on the degree to which voting norms have been internalized.

A Profile of Voters

Generally the more educated and wealthier one is, the greater the likelihood of voting. Older persons are more likely to vote than younger ones, and women vote slightly more frequently than men. The higher the percentage of voters, the less difference between voters and nonvoters. In Canada, for example, which has a 75 percent voter turnout,[5] age, gender, ethnicity, and religion do not appreciably affect who will vote; however, the poor and less educated do seem to avoid the polls somewhat more so than the rich and educated. In Australia, on the other hand, where voter turnout since the 1980s hovers around 95 percent,[6] no differences can be found between those who vote and those who do not.

Only in the United States, which has the lowest voter turnout of any industrial country except Switzerland, do significant socioeconomic differences appear between voters and nonvoters. Hispanics vote less frequently than African Americans, the latter vote less often than Caucasians. Jews are more apt to vote than Catholics, and Catholics more than Protestants. Those recipients of the lowest 20 percent of aggregate income vote less often than those in the upper 20 percent. Citizens between the ages of forty-five and sixty-five are most likely to vote, while eighteen to twenty-five year olds are the least likely. College graduates go to the polls more often than high-school dropouts. Suburbanites vote more frequently than city folk, and the latter vote more often than their country kin.

In states in which elections are not compulsory, those who vote tend to find the campaign interesting or perceive that the outcome may affect them personally. Therefore, either as a referee or a profiteer, the citizen will be enticed to vote. To the less educated the campaign may seem boring; to the poor the outcome may not alter their condition. Is it any wonder then that the less educated and poor do not vote? Since Hispanics and African Americans in the United States are among the less educated and poor, they are less likely to vote; however, their participation improves when Hispanics or African Americans run for office. Unfortunately, in the United States, as almost anywhere else, the uneducated or poor do not run for office, nor are they encouraged to do so.

TERMS TO REMEMBER

referenda
plebiscites
incumbents

SUGGESTED READINGS

Davidson, Chandler and Bernard Grofman, editors. *Quiet revolution in the South: The Impact of the Voting Rights Act 1965-1990.* Princeton: Princeton University Press, 1994. Using rigorous empirical analysis the authors of these essays demonstrate that the Voting Rights Act was the principal reason for the increase in minority voting in the Southern states.

Hamilton, Richard F. *Who Voted for Hitler?* Princeton, NJ: Princeton University Press, 1982. The thesis of this work is that Hitler was given support from all levels of German society.

Levin, Murray Burton. *The Alienated Voter: Politics in Boston.* New York: Holt, Rinehart and Winston, 1960. One of the first works focusing on alienation as the cause for non-voting.

Niemi, Richard G. and Herbert F. Weisberg, editors. *Controversies in Voting Behavior..* Washington, D.C.: Congressional Quarterly Press, 1984. Who votes, who does not and why are examined in a series of essays.

Piven, Frances Fox and Richard A. Cloward. *Why Americans Don't Vote.* New York: Pantheon Books, 1988. The authors blame voter registration procedures for most non-voting in the United States.

Tullock, Gordon. *Wealth, Poverty and Politics.* New York: B. Blackwell, 1988. Twelve essays using public choice theory in analyzing the relationship among wealth, poverty, and politics.

NOTES

1. U.S. Bureau of the Census, 1992 Census of Governments (http://gopher.census.gov:70/0/bureau/pr/subject/gov/cb95-18.txt. 10/27/95).

2. U.S. Bureau of the Census, *Statistical Abstract of the United States: 1994,* 114th ed. (Washington, D.C., 1994), p. 295.

3. All U.S. electoral statistics cited in U.S. Bureau of the Census, *Statistical Abstract of the United States: 1994,* 114th ed. (Washington, D.C., 1994), pp. 288-89.

4. German Information Center, *The Week in Germany,* New York, February 24, 1995.

5. Ronald G. Landes, *The Canadian Polity: A Comparative Introduction* (Scarborough, Ontario: Prentice-Hall Canada, Inc., 1991), pp. 372-73.

6. Ian McAllister, et al., *Australian Political Facts* (Melbourne: Longman Cheshire, 1990), p. 64.

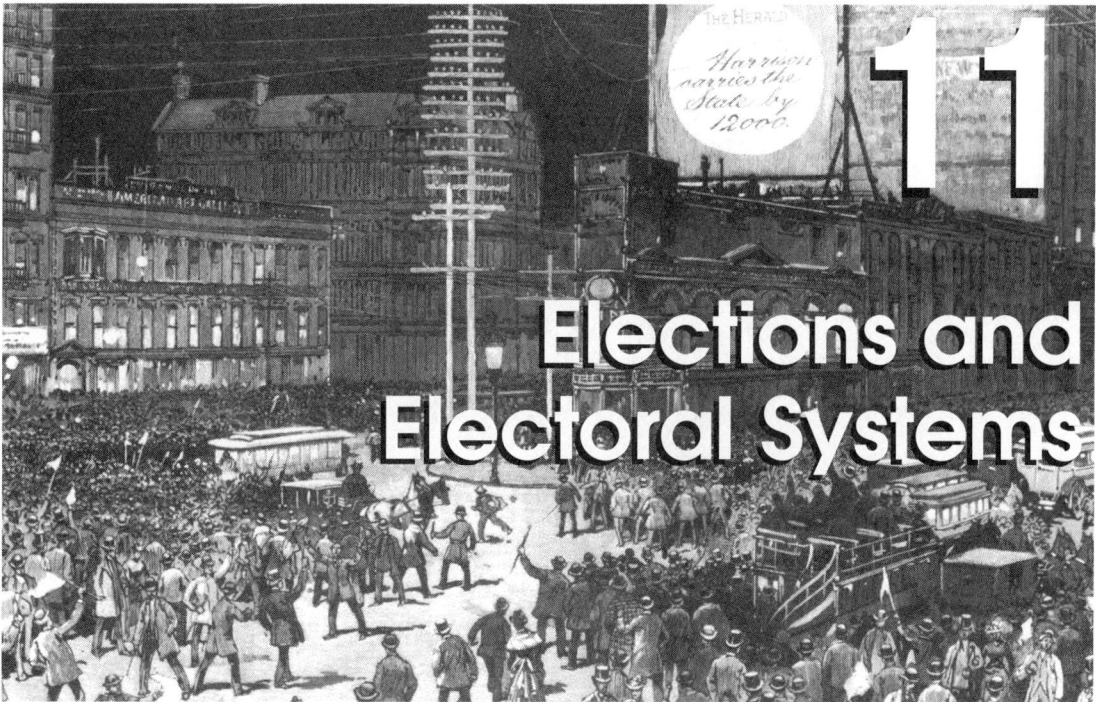

11

Elections and Electoral Systems

🌐 Outline
- Who Can Participate in Elections?
- The Political Function of Elections
- Direct and Indirect Elections
- Primaries
- Electoral Systems
- The Effects of Electoral Systems

Elections are very much intertwined with the number and organization of political parties and with the legislative process. The function and role of legislators depend on how they are elected and how the parties compete; party competition depends on how nominees are selected and elected. How nominees are elected depends on the number of major parties and the functions of the legislature. If the function of the legislature changes, then the electoral process and the parties' organization change; if the electoral process changes, then the parties and the legislature change; and if the parties change, then the legislature and the electoral process change.

A naturalization ceremony held on Ellis Island, New York, in which a United States District Judge addressed 100 new American citizens in April, 1991 in observance of the 100th anniversary of the establishment of the Immigration and Naturalization Service.

Who Can Participate in Elections?

Societies allow only certain individuals to participate in elections. Candidates for election and voters must be citizens. A **citizen** is an adult recognized by the state as possessing all the political rights (and obligations) society grants. Adults who legally reside within a society but are citizens of another state do not possess political rights and are called **aliens**. Aliens usually enjoy most, if not all, of the economic, social, and cultural rights within the society, but they cannot vote or be elected to office.

To participate in elections voters, and candidates, have to be citizens of a state and registered to vote with a government agency. In some countries citizens carry an identification card issued by the state and, upon presentation of that card at the polls, can vote either wherever they want or, in other cases, only in the area from which the card was issued, usually the place of birth. In other countries, such as the United States, citizens have to formally apply to a government agency (usually the county clerk's office), which issues a voter registration card and includes their name in the voters' registration records of the area in which they live. If voters move from that area, they have to register again in their new place of residence. In some countries registration is permanent if the citizen votes regularly. In others it has to be renewed every so often, in some cases before every election and in others perhaps every five years.

To run for office candidates usually have to file an application with a government agency. The state sets deadlines for filing since it not only oversees the elections, but also administers them. The state prints the ballots, delivers them to the proper locations, hires the personnel required to oversee the voting procedures and to tabulate the results, and announces the results. Usually the candidate pays a fee at the time of filing.

The Political Function of Elections

Besides their societal functions that we discussed in the Chapter on voting, elections also have the political function to fill government offices for which constitutional provisions demand elections. If this constitutional provision does not exist, the government position may be filled in other ways.

In every election, the winner fills the vacant elected office. The winning candidate occupies that office until a successor is elected. In some states officeholders serve only for a set number of years or terms. Most Latin American presidents, for example, are restricted to serving one term; in the United States the president can serve for no more than two full terms. Generally restrictions on length of time for elected offices apply to executives or policy implementors in the presidential system of government.

Few legislators anywhere have limitations on the length of time they can serve. An exception is Mexico, where by law legislators cannot be reelected for consecutive terms. In most countries legislators serve two-, four-, or six-year terms and can run for reelection as often as they wish. However, in most states with a parliamentary system of government, members of parliament serve for an indefinite period because elections may not be held at regular intervals. The British, Canadian, and most other Commonwealth constitutions stipulate that elections must be held within a five-year period. They can be held anytime before the five years are over, and in case of a national emergency they need not be held at all, as occurred in Great Britain during World War II.

Once in office the elected official faces a quandary: On what basis do I make decisions? The way I was elected will determine in large part how that question is answered. If I was elected on behalf of a political party, my party will make my decisions. If voters could decide only which party to vote for, then those elected must follow the dictates of the party. In Italy, Japan, France, Germany, Spain, and Israel the ballot contains only names of the political parties. If names of persons appear on the ballot, they are of no consequence in tabulation of votes, because only votes for parties are counted. (Names may be used on ballots to influence citizens to vote for the party whose candidates they prefer.) The individual who wins office represents the party in the legislature and therefore has an obligation to follow the decisions it makes.

On the other hand, if the electoral system allows voters to choose among candidates regardless of their party affiliation, the winner can then make his or her own decisions rather than strictly follow party positions on issues. Basically this is the case in the United States, where winners to elected office make decisions based on what is going to give them the greatest benefit. They can make decisions based on what their constituents want, which may help them be reelected; what they personally perceive is the best choice; or what the party wants. The officeholder is a free agent in regard to what influences his or her decisions.

An exception to this situation occurs in the United Kingdom where voters choose among candidates, each belonging to a different party. Yet after the election the winners invariably succumb to the wishes of their political party when making decisions. Why? Each political party's leadership determines who the nominee is and the area in which the nominee will run. Since the party leadership decides who can run for office, it controls the individuals who win office. For example, if the party decides that Jean Smith from London would be a good candidate from the electoral area of Manchester, then it sets up an office in Manchester from which she campaigns. If she wins the election, she will represent Manchester in Parliament for her party and will vote on issues as the party wishes rather than as the citizens of Manchester prefer.

In the United States candidates who run for office have to be, by law, a resident of the area they will represent. If they establish residence in an area just to win an elected office, they are called **carpetbaggers**. Since the word *carpetbagger* is an epithet that can cost a candidate many votes, candidates either run for election from their home district or become a resident of a particular area years before they actually intend to run.

Direct and Indirect Elections

We tend to look at elections as the act of voting for a candidate to fill a vacant elected office. Most elections indeed are **direct elections** in which the voters' choice fills the office. Another type of election in which voters elect others to select an individual for office is called an **indirect election**. At one time the president of France was chosen by most of the country's

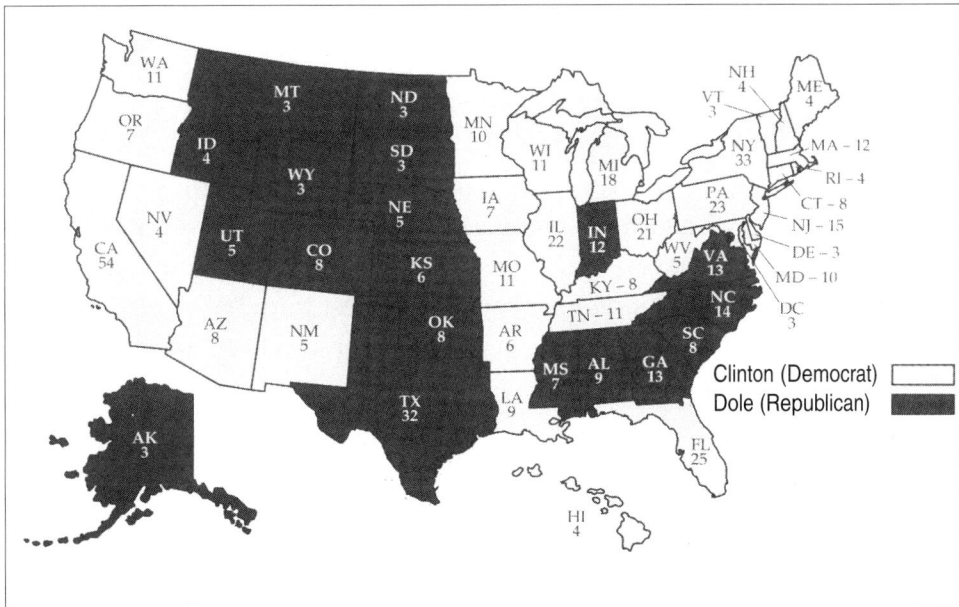

1996 Electoral Vote Distribution in the United States — Clinton 379, Dole 159.

elected officials (about forty thousand). The U.S. president also is chosen indirectly. Although voters seem to elect the president, they actually are voting for a set of electors (i.e., the Electoral College) who by a majority select one of the candidates for the presidency based, theoretically, on the voters' choice. The number of a state's presidential electors is equal to its number of Congressional legislators, and all of the electors go to the candidate receiving the most votes in that state. Therefore it is possible that the candidate who receives the majority of the Electoral College's votes may not have received the highest number of total votes from voters in all states.

Primaries

A type of election that has become important in determining which candidates' names will be placed on the ballot for elected government offices is the direct primary. A **primary** is an election by the adherents of a party to choose that party's nominees for office. In the United States the primary has become the way in which more than 90 percent of the nominees for the two major parties are selected. (The leadership of the minor parties selects nominees for elected positions.) The primary gained popularity after the era of political bossism in which decisions were made in smoke-filled rooms by a few powerful individuals. This was an important step in the democratization of American politics.

There are two basic types of primaries. The **closed primary** allows only registered party member to choose among candidates for that party's nomination. Only registered Democrats can vote in the Democratic primary; only registered Republicans in the Republican primary. In an **open primary** registered voters can ask for the ballot of either party and vote for that party's candidates for nomination, regardless of their party registration. A few states even allow voters to choose different parties for different offices. In the open primary, the request for a ballot from one of the two parties means that for this particular election, the voter has become an adherent of that party.

Electoral Systems

All states use one of three electoral systems — plurality/majority, proportional representation, or preferential list. Each has positive and negative consequences, and each affects the party structure and the legislative process in a different way.

Plurality/Majority

The plurality/majority system used in the United States is the easiest system for tabulating ballots. **Plurality** means the most votes; **majority** means one more than half. (Whereas all majorities are pluralities, not all pluralities are majorities.) In some elections a *weighted* majority is needed. This means that to win, a set figure above 50 percent + 1 is needed, such as 60 percent, two-thirds, or three-fourths. Plebiscites and referenda often require weighted majorities for passage.

The difference in the number of votes among candidates is irrelevant in determining who wins. One candidate may have one more vote than the nearest rival; another may have 90 percent more votes. Statistically no significant difference may exist between the votes two or more competitors receive. What is important is that *by law* the winner is the candidate with the most votes.

Plurality elections are easy to tabulate, especially in electoral areas in which only one candidate is elected. These areas are called **single-member districts**. To determine a winner, the votes for each candidate are counted and the one with the most wins. Everyone else loses. If a majority is required but no one receives it, a subsequent election, or **run-off election**, is held between the two candidates with the most votes.

To resolve the hotly disputed Hayes-Tilden presidential election in 1876, the U.S. Congress established an electoral commission (shown here deliberating by candle light) composed of five senators, five members of the House of Representatives, and five Supreme Court Justices. Voting strictly along party lines, the commission voted 8-7 giving Republican candidate Hayes the disputed electoral votes.

Since the winner gets everything and the loser nothing in plurality elections, citizens who expect their candidates or party to lose may decide to stay home on election day. To them there is no point in voting because they have nothing to gain. To a lesser extent this is also true of those citizens who believe their candidates or party will win; they may decide not to vote because they believe their candidate will win anyway. Therefore, plurality elections do not encourage high voter turnout.

With their emphasis on the highest number of votes, plurality elections tend to promote two-party systems, thus discriminating against minor parties. Minor parties on the left or the right of the political spectrum cannot compete with the popularity of the major parties. Minor parties can, however, become major ones when a significant shift in public attitude toward them occurs or when formerly disenfranchised citizens, such as the nonpropertied, are given the right to vote.

In the early part of twentieth century the British government enlarged the electorate by allowing all adult males to vote. At the same time a part of the existing electorate that had supported the Liberal Party began to demand greater services from the government. The result was that the Labor Party, which was supported by many of the new voters and the disgruntled Liberal Party members, pulled in more votes than the Liberal Party and became one of the two major parties in the United Kingdom.

The emphasis on obtaining the most votes also gives candidates in plurality elections little incentive to voice positions favored by those who are not part of the mainstream. Therefore, those at the extremes of an opinion continuum are not included in political discussions and are not catered to in campaigns. Since they have nothing to vote for, these neglected citizens also stay home on election day.

In addition, candidates hesitate to say anything controversial that might upset their supporters. This results in boring campaigns which force citizens to make decisions based on irrelevant factors, such as candidates' character, physical appearance, or sound of name. Therefore, the outcome of elections are decided by citizens who make their choice based on trivial factors, rather than on issues. Even in states in which votes are cast for political parties, as in Great Britain and France, party differences have lessened over time.

In plurality elections candidates usually win by no more than a few percentage points over their opponents. When a candidate or party receives 54 percent or more of the votes, it is considered a landslide. Often the difference between the winner and the loser is less than five points, which means that the outcome would be different with only 3 percent of citizens voting differently. Often elections are determined by such a small percentage of votes from citizens who make their choice at the last minute (with little intensity) based on irrelevant factors. Consequently, plurality elections are the least meaningful type of elections because they do not provide voters a choice of candidates or parties with perceived real differences or allow strong support to build for candidates or parties.

Besides determining who wins an elected office, plurality elections do little else for the political process. Since candidates and parties are reluctant to suggest controversial policy alternatives, take clear ideological positions, or propose long-term programs, plurality elections seldom show what the electorate wants the government to do. And those elected who did not enunciate any definite or clear proposals because they did not want to lose supporters, will not be among the vanguard of political leaders. Consequently, nonelected political leaders provide more guidance to society than elected leaders.

Plurality elections also tend to encourage voting for candidates rather than for political parties. No matter how they are nominated, the candidates become the focus for the electorate. Their representation of the party lessens as the media concentrates more on personal characteristics of candidates than on issues. Since there are so many electoral districts, each with candidates from at least the major parties, candidates are forced to campaign on local issues on which the parties stands are only very general. Thus, the local media finds nothing substantive to report and focuses instead on candidates' personal attributes. The same situation occurs at the national level, where party differences have become trivial and irrelevant, forcing the national media also to emphasize candidates' personal attributes. This type of media coverage results in contests between two candidates rather than in debates on party differences on major issues.

When a voter casts ballots for all the candidates of a given party, this is called **straight-ticket voting**. Ballots show a space to fill in next to the party symbol to indicate that the voter chooses all the candidates for that party. This method of voting is popular when parties are strong, that is when parties command fervent allegiance among their followers. To get the most benefit from straight-ticket voting, a party in control of the legislature would **gerrymander** electoral districts, which means it would draw the boundaries of electoral districts to give itself the greatest advantage. Often this results in neighborhoods with nothing in common joined together or other neighborhoods split apart because one party has stronger support in part of the area. Gerrymandering is no longer commonplace because courts have frowned upon the practice, and straight-ticket voting has become less popular.

The Gerrymander

In the past citizens who had established a reputation for leadership within their communities were given the "honor" of being elected to public office. Being elected was akin to receiving a medal for the good deeds one had done. This was especially true in early U.S. history, when most elected political leaders had become renown before they were elected.

Today a reputation for leadership, if ever found at all, comes after the election, and then only through legislative or administrative deeds.

Gerrymandering. North Carolina's First and Twelfth Districts were drawn to give the state its first black representatives in 93 years. Source: *Congressional Districts in the 1990s: A Portrait of America* (Washington, D.C.: Congressional Quarterly, 1993), p548.

Plurality elections appear to bestow honor upon those who deserve it. In actuality those who deserve to be honored seldom submit to the travails of the electoral process. Those who do submit and move from one elected position to another become professional politicians, having acquired an expertise in campaigning. This expertise may contribute little to successful policy making and implementation. In fact, since most elected officials have few leadership qualities, the role of nonelected leaders becomes

TOTAL NUMBER OF VOTES FOR LEGISLATIVE CANDIDATES

Candidate	Party	Total Votes
Francis	Democrat	7,452
Samuel	Democrat	7,152
Greg	Democrat	6,632
Pete	Democrat	6,343
Robert	Republican	6,110
Nancy	Republican	5,800
Joan	Republican	5,450
David	Republican	4,846
Norman	Socialist	3,325
Beth	Socialist	2,532

FOCUS — THE FRENCH VOTE BY MAJORITY FOR THE PARTY

PARIS (AP). The governing conservatives took a halting lead over the left on Sunday in the first round of French municipal elections. The far right, with some strong showings, threatened to be the spoiler in the runoff.

With results still incomplete, the extreme-right National Front placed among the top three candidates in at least 27 cities of more than 30,000 residents. The anti-immigration party will be present in runoffs next Sunday in more than 50 such towns.

"Tonight, the movement I have the honor of presiding over appears like a victor," National Front President Jean-Marie Le Pen said on French television. The political mainstream considers his party a pariah.

Le Pen, who scored a record 15 percent in presidential elections five weeks ago, vowed to make his party count in the local elections, hoping to establish an enduring foothold in the French heartland.

Still, extreme-right candidates got just 6.6 percent of the total vote, according to a projection by the CSA polling firm.

The conservatives scored about 45.4 percent and Socialists and Communists about 43 percent in an election with the lowest turnout since 1947 — about 65 percent.

With Jacques Chirac's victory in the presidential elections, the conservative majority controls the presidency, prime minister's office, National Assembly, Senate and regional councils. It hopes to lock up France's five biggest cities by taking Marseille in next Sunday's runoff.

Interior Minister Jean-Louis Debre said he felt the right could take about 10 additional towns with more than 30,000 residents in the runoff.

Paris power brokers often field status candidates — even those who hold other major offices in cities to assure victory. Such was the case with Bordeaux, where Premier Alain Juppe, gaining a majority, was elected as mayor in the first round.

The Socialists, who led in municipal elections six years ago, took feifdoms like Strasbourg and the lead in two of Paris' 20 districts, all held by the right since 1983.

But another Socialist bastion, the northern city of Lille, run by former Premier Pierre Mauroy, was forced into a runoff with the conservatives.

The National Front did well in several cities: an estimated 30 percent in Mulhouse in the east, 22 percent in the southern port city of Marseille and 32.5 percent in Tourcoing in the north.

Bruno Megret, the party's No. 2 man, got an estimated 43 percent of the vote in the industrial town of Vitrolles.

Such scores mean the party could help decide next Sunday's runoff in numerous towns and cities. A score of at least 10 percent is needed to advance to the runoffs.

The National Front put up 25,000 candidates in 477 towns to implant itself locally.

> The voting is unique in Europe: no other country chooses so many representatives — more than a half- million municipal councilors — in so many villages, towns and cities: 36,772.

ever more important. The extent to which these professional politicians can be considered leaders of society depends on the number and significance of the nonelected leaders.

In the United States both primary elections and the plurality system of voting discourage state and national party leaders to run for elected office because of their low public profile; they are seldom heard from or known. Each party has state and national officers and executive committees; yet the role they play in the formulation of policies remains a mystery because their influence on nominees and elected officials depends on many variables, only one of which is how well they are able to get them to heed their counsel.

The plurality election system, therefore, tends to discourage voting, creates two-party systems, reduces party differences to a minimum, encourages voting for candidates rather than for parties, and does not necessarily result in the election of gifted leaders to government positions. The latter aspect has an important bearing on the policy making role of legislatures and even executives because, as we will discuss later, elected officials do not formulate policy as much as react to it. Nevertheless, the plurality election system does determine winners.

Proportional Representation

Proportional representation is a voting system that awards seats in the legislature according to the ratio of votes parties receive in an election. For example, ten elected offices must be filled and 1,000 votes are cast in the following manner: party A receives 400, party B 300, party C 200, and party D 100. The ratio is 4:3:2:1. Therefore, the ten elected offices would be divided as follows: party A would receive four seats, party B three seats, party C two seats, and party D one seat.

Since a real electoral outcome is seldom clear and definitive like this example, a formula is used to tabulate results. The first half of the formula is equation 1:

$$\frac{\textit{Number of votes cast}}{\textit{Number of offices need be elected}} + 1 = \textit{Electoral Quotient}$$

This establishes the **electoral quotient** (EQ), which is the number of votes a party needs to have one of its nominees elected. The " + 1 " is a tiebreaker. Then to determine how many nominees from a given party are elected, the second half of the formula, equation 2, is applied:

$$\frac{Number\ of\ votes\ for\ party}{Electoral\ Quotient} = Number\ of\ party\ nominees\ elected$$

Proportional representation works only in **multimember districts,** which means that two or more persons (usually about five) are elected from an electoral district. In this electoral system votes are cast for the party, not the candidate.

The following table gives the results of an election to a state legislature from a district that elects four representatives. Ten nominees of three parties run for those four positions: four Democrats, four Republicans, and two Socialists.

In a plurality election all four Democrats would have won because they had the four highest vote totals; all the Republicans and Socialists would have lost. If Robert, a Republican, had received 235 more votes, he would have been elected over Pete, a Democrat. The Democrats together received 27,669 votes, (for which the average is 6,917 votes, 27,669/4). The Republicans together received 22,206 votes, averaging 5,552 votes. The Socialists together received 5,857 votes, averaging 2,929 votes. Although the Republicans received only 1,365 (10 percent) fewer votes on the average than the Democrats out of a total of 12,469 average votes for both parties, all the Republicans lost while the Democrats received 100 percent representation.

Now let us assume that these electoral results are tabulated on the basis of a proportional representation system. The Democrats received 6,917 votes, the Republicans 5,552 votes, and the Socialists 2,929 votes. If we add these together, we get 15,398 votes cast for all these parties. Using equation 1, we get the following electoral quotient, EQ:

(15,398 / 4) + 1 = 3,851

This means that for every 3,851 votes cast for one of the parties, that party gets one nominee elected. To determine how many nominees from each party have been elected, we use equation 2 and divide the number of votes each party received by the EQ and get the following:

$$6{,}917 \:/\: 3{,}851 = 1.\,796 \;\; Democrats$$

$$5{,}552 \:/\: 3{,}851 = 1.442 \;\; Republicans$$

$$2{,}929 \:/\: 3{,}851 = 0.761 \;\; Socialists$$

The Democrats had 1 plus 0.796 nominees elected, the Republicans 1 plus 0.442, and the Socialists 0 plus 0.761. Since positions are awarded in whole numbers (i.e., we cannot have a 0.796, 0.442, and 0.761 nominee), the two remaining positions are apportioned based on the largest number to the right of the decimal point. The numbers 0.796 and 0.761 are larger than 0.442; therefore the Democrats win a second position and the Socialists one. Under the proportional representation system the result of the election is the Democrats receive two positions, the Republicans one position, and the Socialists one position. The ratio 2:1:1 in the proportional representation system is far more reflective of the ratio 6,917:5,552:2,929 of total votes cast for each than is the ratio 4:0:0 in a plurality election.

The parties determine which individual candidates are elected. Some parties allow their leadership to choose among the candidates either before or after the election. Sometimes parties hold a convention of delegates selected by the rank and file to choose the nominees. Often the party is allowed to place the names of the nominees on the ballot so that voters know who will be seated. This may be done in order of preference so that the first person listed on the ballot is elected if the party wins one seat, the first two persons if the party wins two seats, the first three persons if the party wins three seats, and so forth. Sometimes party leaders choose among candidates regardless of the number of votes they receive or the order their name appears on the ballot. Those chosen are beholden to the party and will be pressured to vote according to party wishes. In some countries the party forces a prospective nominee to sign an undated letter of resignation from the elected seat that is dated if that nominee wins but does not vote the way the party wishes.

Since proportional representation requires choice among parties rather than individual candidates and attempts to have legislatures composed of representatives that reflect the diversity within the voting public, not only are more parties encouraged to participate in the electoral process but also, and more importantly, citizens are encouraged to vote. Their vote does count, although only in proportion to the votes of others.

While in this example the Republicans appear to have been cheated of about 2,000 votes and the Socialists given about 500, in a plurality system the Republicans would have been cheated of their total of 5,552 votes and the Socialists of their total of 2,929 — a complete loss for both parties. In the plurality system the Democrats would have been the only winners, but not so under the proportional representation system. Under the latter system Republicans and Socialists also would have won seats, thereby preventing the Democrats from passing programs or policies that they alone favor.

Since parties have a better chance of gaining elected office under the proportional representation system than under the plurality system, a larger number of them compete and win. A significant problem with many parties serving in a legislature is that it becomes more difficult to pass legislation. So in countries in which this electoral system prevails, **coalition governments** usually are formed. These are governments run by two or more parties working together. In the previous example, if the Democrats and the Socialists work together to enact a legislative program, they have formed a coalition government. When the two largest parties decide to work together in a legislature, the resulting government is called a **grand coalition**.

In Austria the two largest parties, the Socialist Party and the People's Party, usually agree to cooperate with each other in the new legislature before the elections. Germany's legislature and government are coalitions composed of the Christian Democratic Union (CDU), Christian Social Union (CSU) which is the Bavarian branch of the CDU, and the Free Democrats, a party that frequently gets less than 10 percent of the vote.

In Israel the small ultrareligious parties receiving 2 to 10 percent of the vote exercise enormous influence upon a government dominated by one of the two major secular parties (each receiving 30 to 40 percent of the vote). Since the entire country is one electoral district with 120 representatives, Israel's electoral quotient is so small that a party receiving forty thousand votes out of 2.5 million will get a seat in the Knesset, Israel's legislature.

These three examples point out the shortcomings of the proportional representation electoral system. In Austria a citizen's vote is meaningless because, no matter what the electoral results, the two major parties form a grand coalition and together govern the country. Despite the difference in

FOCUS   THAILAND GOVERNMENT DISSOLVED

BANGKOK, Thailand (AP). The prime minister dissolved the lower house of parliament Friday rather than face a no confidence vote he was sure to lose, and called new elections.

Chuan Leekpai, who was swept into power after pro-democracy demonstrations toppled the military junta in 1992, had hoped to become the first elected prime minister to finish his term of office.

But his ruling coalition collapsed after its third largest partner, the Palang Dharma Party, announced this morning it would not support the government in a no-confidence vote scheduled for later in the day.

A Palang Dharma spokesman said Chuan's party, the Democrats, had failed to clear up suspicions over a land-reform scandal that accused them of giving land meant for poor farmers to wealthy individuals.

Without Palang Dharma's 46 votes, the coalition could not have survived. Chuan told a news conference he and his remaining coalition partners could find no acceptable way to retain power.

"Therefore the best way is to return power to the people and let them consider what is best," Chuan said. He set elections for July 2.

He was Thailand's longest serving elected prime minister, having completed 32 months of his four year term.

The last elected prime minister, Chatichai Choonhavan, was ousted by a military coup in 1991 — one of more than a dozen such coups in Thailand since the end of World War II.

Daily life and business continued normally in Bangkok, with no sign of military activity. The stock market also reacted calmly.

"In the past people would have expected a military takeover," said Suchit Bunbongkarn, dean of the political science faculty at Chulalongkorn University. "Nobody is talking about that at all this time. Our democracy is unstable, but it is gradually developing."

Despite continual problems holding his coalition together, Chuan recently expressed confidence that he could survive the political onslaught of his opponents.

"Many people are not accustomed to a coalition government lasting more than 2 1/2 years," he told a meeting of the Foreign Correspondents Club. "They better get used to it."

their names, the Socialist Party and the People's Party have similar policy objectives since both compete for the large number of politically centrist votes. The smaller Austrian parties have little impact on policy making because they are left out of the legislative process.

On the other hand in Israel the smaller parties, of which there may be twelve, hold the larger ones hostage, as the latter cannot govern without the support of the former. The smaller parties play one large party against the other, forcing the larger ones to make concessions to them in order to effectively govern. Although the two largest parties have formed a coalition, the differences between them make this cooperation only temporary.

Germany to some extent has controlled the number of small parties that can be represented in the Bundestag, the lower house of the German legislature. By law no party that receives less than 5 percent of the total vote in the country can have representation in the Bundestag. This has eliminated all but about five parties from that house. The large parties, the CDU/CSU and the Social Democratic Party (SDP), normally form a coalition with the Free Democrats or the new Greens because they rarely receive majority representation in the Bundestag. Russia also requires that a party needs a minimum of 5 percent of votes to get representation in its legislature, the Duma. However, so far no party (among more than forty that contest elections) has garnered more than 23 percent of the total vote.[1] Israel requires a party to receive at least 1.5 percent of the vote before it can be represented in the Knesset.

Proportional representation, which emphasizes the different perceptions and opinions prevalent in a society, forces legislators to reconcile these differences at least to the degree that the legislature can enact laws. However, these differences cannot be ignored or relegated to the sidelines; but if they are so severe that they cannot be reconciled sufficiently to bring about a working coalition government, the parties involved must accept the consequences. In time uncompromising parties either lose support or, if they persuade voters of the correctness of their positions, become even more popular.

For a party to successfully pass its legislative agenda under this electoral system, it has to wheel and deal with the other parties, thereby losing the purity and efficacy of its programs and policies. By doing so parties lose their separate identity and become ever more alike. The alternatives enunciated during the electoral campaign, even by parties with a clear victory, soon become emaciated by the negotiating that occurs in the legislative process. As the legislative session goes on voters find fewer differences among the parties. (Remember that in a plurality system each elected official, not the party, is the policy maker. Each official has to wheel and deal with his or her colleagues to get a bill enacted.)

Under this electoral system parties are constantly placed under pressure either to remain true to their policy objectives or to compromise them. If they do the former, voters may consider them obstructive and stop supporting them; if they do the latter, they lose their identity and their voters' support. To remain viable the parties over time have to adjust to the ever changing political environment, especially to public opinion. However, since the candidates as individuals have little importance, opinion centers on regional and national, not local, issues and policies. Concerns about individual nominees' character are not as important; the focus is on the issues.

Concentration on issues has both positive and negative features. On the one hand the public discusses problems in society and their possible resolutions. However, since the public can be easily swayed by the simplistic and facile solutions enunciated by demagogues, highly disruptive and destructive societal policies can be formulated and implemented when such demagogues assume power. The most notorious example of this in recent times is the power of Hitler over German citizens. In modern France, Russia, Italy, Belgium, Germany, and other states the presence of demagogues, usually leaders of small parties, raises caution about the political efficacy of the proportional representation system. Although demagogues rise to power in the plurality system as well, unless they and their supporting nominees clearly win, they cannot do much damage because other officials are elected by their local constituencies and can keep a demagogue's power in check.

Another negative consequence of emphasizing issues in an election is that needless societal divisions may be created. Some issues are best resolved without the spotlight focused on them. The more an issue is discussed, the greater the tendency to create irreconcilable differences among the population. Since issues often become moralized or infused with religious undertones, deep social resentments surface that can create havoc in maintaining unity within the society.

A more positive result of emphasizing issues in an election is that the public becomes better informed about the problems, controversies, and public policy directions of the society. Much of how well this is done depends on the competence of the media to translate the various proposals, solutions, and agendas of the parties effectively and serenely. It also depends on whether the public wants the media to do this. Unfortunately, in times of crisis the public often prefers the media to simplify the complicated, sensationalize the obvious and plain, and sweeten the bitter. The public is also impatient with proposals that take a long time to achieve. Nevertheless, publics not in crisis spend considerable time, resources, and efforts to learn, through the media, about the issues parties address and to make reasoned decisions when voting. An issue-oriented public is usually a politically informed public.

Examples of recent issue-oriented campaigns occurred in 1992 during the election in Great Britain for a new House of Commons in which the merits of continuation of "Thatcherism," the conservative policies of the former Thatcher government, were discussed and during an Israeli election of a new Knesset in which the major issues were whether to allow new settlements in the West Bank and Gaza and whether to transfer these areas to an autonomous Palestinian entity. Meanwhile in the United States elections for President and the House of Representatives focused on whether marital infidelity, draft dodging, and check bouncing were criteria that affect a candidate's character and ability to carry out the functions of elected office.

Supreme Court's "pro-slavery" decision of 1857 in Dred Scott v. Sandford had a significant impact on the 1860 presidential race. The four presidential candidates adversely affected by the decision were forced to dance to Scott's tune. Clockwise from upper right: Republican Abraham Lincoln, Constitutional party candidate John Bell, Democrat Stephen A. Douglas, and southern Democrat John C. Breckinridge.

In elections based on proportional representation, it is highly probable that party leaders will be elected. Generally the party leaders are also the leaders of the legislative and executive branches of government. Therefore, identification of policy makers is easy. In Austria, Italy, Finland, Germany, India, Russia, and Spain the individuals who are most influential in determining party policy are the majority and minority party leaders in the legislature.

Since parties are hierarchically organized, not everyone who is elected is at the top of the hierarchy; most are in a subservient position to those at the top. These backbenchers, who do what the leadership tells them (or else), may have less influence in the party's affairs than nonelected leaders. Just because one is a member of Parliament does not signify that one is a party leader. A member of Parliament may have less power than a member of Congress, because the latter is elected because of who he or she is and the former because the party nominated him or her.

Proportional representation de-emphasizes the individual candidate while focusing on the political party and subsequently on issues affecting society. The voter has a greater and more meaningful choice of alternatives because there are more parties and therefore more policy alternatives from which to choose. This may encourage more people to vote; but it may also spur divisiveness in society. Legislative leaders are the party leaders.

Preferential List

An even more complicated system of voting is one that allows the voter to rank preference of candidates. Most elections, just as most opinion polls, do not measure *intensity* of choices. An individual may decide on a candidate on the basis of a flip of the coin or the considerable amount of time and effort spent studying the choices.

The **preferential list** system of voting compels voters to spend some time deciding who to vote for because they have to rank all candidates for all offices. Fewer than a handful of countries use this system. As in proportional representation, multimember districts are the norm. If a district elects four representatives, for example, voters choose four of the candidates and rank them from first to fourth choice.

Tabulation of votes is, even with use of computers, complex and time consuming. One way of determining the number of votes candidates receive is to weigh each preference vote on a graded basis so that a first-place vote is equal to four votes, a second-place vote three votes, a third-place vote two votes, and a fourth-place vote one vote. Winners have the highest total of weighted votes.

Another way of tabulating the results is to determine the electoral quotient for each office, as in proportional representation, and then to decide which candidate in each race reaches the quotient on first-choice votes alone. Those that do are the winners. If all four offices cannot be filled based on first-choice votes, second-choice votes are added to the first-choice votes. If some offices are still vacant, the third-choice votes are added to the other two. After the fourth-choice votes are counted, all offices should be filled. Australia uses this system.

Although candidates in the preferential list system are ranked, citizens tend to vote along party lines, choosing candidates of the same party as their top choices. Therefore the voter's choice shows not only who, as an individual, he or she prefers but also what issues the voter wants resolved and how that should be accomplished, as noted by the political parties.

This places quite a burden on the voter, who not only must be familiar with the distinct policy orientations of each party but also must judge and compare the positive and negative qualities of the candidates. In this way serious voters using the preferential list system are forced to be better informed in politics than their counterparts using the plurality or proportional systems.

The major problem with the preferential list system is that it requires highly sophisticated technology to tabulate results quickly. In Australia which is a large country, tabulation of national elections takes about a week.

Combined Systems

These three electoral systems are used in all states that depend on elections for the succession of legislators and executives; some states, however, use combinations of these systems. In the German Bundestag half of the members are elected by proportional representation and half by plurality. In 1994 New Zealand and Russia adopted the same combination of systems to elect legislative members. In Mexico three-hundred deputies are elected by plurality and two-hundred by proportional representation. In Italy, although voters choose a party in a proportional representation system, they also can choose which party candidate listed on the ballot they want to be seated. In some countries delegates to the national legislature are chosen by proportional representation but local officials are chosen by plurality.

In 1996 Israel changed its electoral system so that Knesset members are elected by proportional representation but the prime minister is elected by majority vote. If the prime minister is a member of a party that is part of the ruling coalition, not much will change from current practice. However, what will happen if the prime minister is a member of a party that is not in the coalition? That situation, which is similar to French elections in which the president may be of one party and the legislature is controlled by an opposing party, can lead to some interesting politics.

The Effects of Electoral Systems

Electoral systems can be a means to control party structures and the composition of legislatures. They shape the role political parties play in determining the manner in which legislatures influence the making and implementing of public policy. In the nineteenth century elections were regarded as the principal method of forcing government officials to respect the wishes of the people; however, as they were incorporated into government processes, their consequences for party and legislative functions and structures were not discerned.

Since electoral systems have become a tradition in most societies, they are virtually impossible to change. In newer states change is possible; Japan changed from a plurality to a proportional representation system in the 1980s. In states that have had an electoral system for over a century, such as the United Kingdom, the United States, and most countries in Latin America, electoral reform is nearly impossible. In these countries reform of the party system and of the legislature have been discussed; however, reform movements invariably die stillborn due to lack of widespread interest.

By forcing voters to focus on either the candidates or the parties, electoral systems frame the political discussions that government officials, elected and nonelected, use as guides for their behavior as well as their policies. In candidate-focused discussions questions about the character and qualities of the nominees prevail, making government officials cautious about crossing the line of acceptable policy alternatives and standards of behavior. In party-focused discussions questions about which issues are important and how they ought to be resolved prevail, making government officials cautious of dealing with issues that society has not expressed an interest in or of resolving accepted issues in unique or novel ways.

Electoral systems link governments to the citizenry. They prevent government officials from isolating themselves from those whose life, liberty, and personal security need to be serviced, coordinated, and defended. Through elections citizens hold government in place, preventing it from losing its anchor in society.

📖 TERMS TO REMEMBER

citizen
alien
carpetbagger
direct elections
indirect election
primary
closed primary
open primary
plurality
majority
single-member districts
run-off election
straight-ticket voting
gerrymander
proportional representation
electoral quotient
multimember districts
coalition governments
grand coalition
preferential list

📖 SUGGESTED READINGS

Alexander, Herbert E. and Anthony Corrado. *Financing the 1992 Election.* Armonk, NY: M.E. Sharpe, 1995. The ninth volume in a series begun in 1960, this work contains a wealth of data on contributions to presidential, congressional, state, and local candidates running for office in 1992 and on how the funds were spent.

Amy, Douglas. *Real Choices, New Voices: The Case for Proportional Representation Elections in the United States.* New York: Columbia University Press, 1993. Would proportional representation destroy the United States political processes and its institutions?

Butler, David and Martin Westlake. *British Politics and European Elections 1994.* New York: St. Martin's, 1995. How British parties and electorate perceived and participated in the elections for selecting members to the European Parliament is the subject of this work.

Carstairs, Andrew McLaren. *A Short History of Electoral Systems in Western Europe.* London: Allen and Unwen, 1980. An older book but still useful in describing the development of electoral systems in Europe including the Scandinavian states.

Cole, Alistair. *French Electoral Systems and Elections Since 1789.* Aldershot, Hants, England; Brookfield, VT: Gower, 1989. A book full of interesting data and insights into the French electoral systems.

Cronin, Thomas E. *Direct Democracy: The Politics of Initiative, Referendum, and Recall.* Cambridge, MA: Harvard University Press, 1989. The good and bad about citizen policy making in the United States.

Ernst, Harry W. *The Primary That Made a President: West Virginia 1960.* New York: McGraw-Hill, 1962. Winning West Virginia's primary was crucial to the candidacy of J.F. Kennedy. How this was done is analyzed in this study.

Fleming, Daniel B. *Kennedy vs. Humphrey, West Virginia, 1960: The Pivotal Battle for the Democratic Presidential Nomination.* Jefferson, NC: McFarland, 1992. A more recent study of the 1960 West Virginia primary.

Glennon, Michael J. *When No Majority Rules: The Electoral College and Presidential Succession.* Washington, D.C.: Congressional Quarterly, 1992. The role of the Electoral College in determining who the president of the United States will be is the theme of this work.

Guinier, Lani. *The Tyranny of the Majority: Fundamental Fairness in Representative Democracy.* New York: Free Press, 1994. A frequent theme, the tyranny of the majority, is given a new treatment in light of the social issues of the United States in the 1990s.

Leonard, Dick and Richard Natkiel. *World Atlas of Elections: Voting Patterns in 39 Democracies.* London: Economist Publications, 1986. Data on elections and their outcomes in mostly European and North American countries.

Lijphart, Arend. *Electoral Systems and Party Systems: A Study of Twenty-Seven Democracies. 1945-1990.* Oxford; New York: Oxford University Press, 1994. The relation of electoral systems and party systems in democracies.

NOTES

1. Jack F. Matlock, Jr., "The Russian Prospect," *The New York Review of Books* vol. XLIII, no. 4 (February 29, 1996): p. 43

12

Pressure Groups

Democracy is generally defined, to paraphrase Lincoln, as government by, of, and for the people. Who are the "people" who are supposed to govern and be governed? Except in direct democracies in which all individuals in a community made public policy (e.g., ancient Athens and New England town meetings), the term *people* has been used in the collective sense. The *people* is not the summation of all the individuals living

237

in one place at the same time but rather all individuals in an abstract, composite sense akin to Rousseaus's general will. Consequently, *people* is more than the sum of its parts, the individuals, as well as separate from its parts. It is a body usually used in the singular, not the plural, as in the people *is*, rather than the people *are*. Policy makers inevitably refer to "the people" in the singular. However, this image of the *people* as a singular entity, includes not only the individuals that compose it but also the individuals organized into groups.

As it is impossible for every individual in a modern society to take part in the making of policy, groups have become the venue through which "the people" expresses its demands, wishes, and needs. This organizational pattern devolved from patterns established in the Middle Ages that used a model from biblical times.

History of Pressure Groups

When Jacob settled in ancient Egypt he brought his sons and their families with him. Over generations the families of these sons evolved into twelve tribes. While in Egypt, and throughout the exodus to Israel, each of these tribes specialized in a particular economic or religious activity. A man was known by the tribe he belonged to or by the activity in which he was involved.

Government, led by either Moses or the Israelite kings, coordinated, defended, and serviced the tribes, not the individuals. Each tribe parceled out to its members the resources, rights, and obligations that government decided it could have. Each tribe also petitioned the government for more resources and rights, thus competing with other tribes. Since the individual had all needs provided by the tribe, his or her relationship with the government was indirect. To petition government, the individual had to go through the tribe. If the tribal leaders thought the petition was worthy, they would report the matter to the governors.

Centuries later in northern Europe, after the collapse of the Roman Empire, the process of feudalization began, which resulted in the establishment of relations between the individual and the government that were similar to those of ancient Israel.

An important feature of this process was determination of the ownership of land. Individuals and their families fought against others to determine who would own the land. Eventually only a few families owned much of the land.

To maintain control of their land, owners needed help from others to protect it. Since those who protected the land wanted something in return for their efforts, the landowners, who had nothing else of value, gave them land. However, the owners kept the authority to control what was done on it. An individual may have had a title or ownership to some land, but had to comply with the dictates of those who had authority over it. The new titleholders then found others to work the land.

The individual who controlled the largest area of land became the monarch. At first the monarch, who was usually a male and therefore a king, was an equal among equals. However, by the thirteenth century kings who had the greatest number of land protectors could force others with authority over land to abide by royal edicts. When kings were victorious in battle and acquired more land, they either gave more land to those with authority over existing parcels or gave more people authority to govern the newly acquired land. Therefore, society became organized in the following hierarchy: the monarch and his aides, those with authority over parcels of land, those who owned the land, and those who worked the land.

Those with authority over parcels of land, often called dukes, competed among themselves to get the most benefits from the monarchs while supplying them with the least support, mostly financial. The dukes controlled the landowners, and the landowners controlled the peasants who worked the land. A peasant could petition the landowner but seldom anyone above that level; a landowner could petition the duke but not the king.

As trade and mercantilism became increasingly important in the Middle Ages, an additional player in the feudal organization appeared — the bourgeois, a city-dwelling tradesman, merchant, independent craftsman, or money lender. Towns that developed into cities were also ruled by an authority, sometimes the king himself. As the trades of the bourgeois became more specialized, standards were established for measuring the quality of their work. In time organizations devoted to individual trades appeared. These were called corporations, royally chartered groups of individuals licensed to perform a given task for the good of society. Organizations centered on a craft were called guilds.

In time, guilds became an economic-social-functional group. Each guild was centered on an economic activity, such as masonry, gold smithing, or tailoring. Guild members were ranked in a hierarchy according to their mastery of the craft. Apprentices were students learning the craft; journeymen had completed their formal education and could work for others; craftsmen no longer needed supervision and could establish an independent business; and master craftsmen were those who set standards for the whole guild. The progression from apprentice to master craftsman was directed and managed by the guild leaders. Most members never ranked higher than journeyman. Guilds played an important function in society by providing crafts that city dwellers needed and establishing regulations for those crafts.

The guild also provided for the well-being of its members. Each guild was like an extended family that cared for every member and his family. What we now know as unemployment insurance, workers' compensation, social security, and personal security were all provided by the guild. Frequently, all guild members and their families lived in the same area of the city.

A guild member could not petition government directly but rather indirectly through the guild. In the late Middle Ages, the affairs of the city, which were subject to the authority of the king's appointee, were determined by a council composed of the guild leaders and other bourgeois corporations. Therefore, both in the countryside and in the city the individual's welfare was determined by groups and corporations competing among themselves for resources and rights from the rulers.

In both ancient Israel and northern Europe of the Middle Ages, society was composed of a confederation of groups. In Israel, ancestry of individuals determined a group's configuration; in Europe the economic, social, and functional activities of individuals did so. This organizational pattern differed significantly from Aristotelian version of society. Aristotle said society was a confederation of households, which was probably true in his time. Today many would like this to be true. Unfortunately, during the Middle Ages a layer, inherited from biblical times, was imposed between the household and society. The group or corporation, which was often permanent and highly structured, caused the dissipation of rulers' policy decisions for individuals and of individuals' grievances with government policies. Yet the groups and corporations were more efficient and organized than a collectivity of individuals or even families; therefore, they were better able to mobilize resources for the welfare of society and to petition the government for services on behalf of individuals.

The competition among these European corporations for the services and rights that governments dispensed has become embedded in modern political processes. In some societies the competition is principally among pressure groups; in others it is among political parties. Today the individual's influence on public policy is filtered through these groups just as it was ages ago.

Although today governments can provide most services to individuals directly due to technological advances, and individuals can directly petition governments to resolve grievances, groups have the most influence on policies that provide services and grant individual rights. Without these groups, efforts by individuals to affect government policy making would be impossible. On the other hand, governments could not function without the support of at least some pressure groups.

Interest Groups, Pressure Groups — What's the difference?

In Chapter 8 we stated that a public is a collectivity of people with a common interest. An **interest group** is an organized public. To be more precise, an interest group is an organized collectivity of people with a common interest. The organization can be highly structured, such as a fraternity or sorority or the Rotary club with its coterie of officers and regularly scheduled meetings, or unstructured, such as a neighborhood book club or choir whose members come together occasionally to have a good time. Whatever their structures, interest groups are organized and their interests are varied. Although interest groups are important in a society because they allow individuals with similar interests to interact, most interest groups are politically irrelevant.

Pressure groups, however, are politically important. A **pressure group** is a type of interest group; it is an organized collectivity of people with a common interest that uses the political process to achieve its aims. The important difference between an interest group and a pressure group is the latter's emphasis on gov-

Jocelyn Hoffarth, a member of Minnesota Citizens Acting Together (COACT), lost the front half of the cow (Pete Ranum) as it moved to center stage at the State Capitol in April, 1989. The pair supported a bill that would prohibit farmers from using bGH, a genetically-engineered hormone, to increase dairy cow's milk production. This is an example of an interest group.

ernment policies to actualize its interests. Public policy is that which a pressure group tries to affect. To that extent, every pressure group is a component among the many variables that determine general societal policy.

Pressure groups may do more than lobby government officials. Many groups undertake education projects, disseminate information, or sponsor charity events — all to influence citizens to support their quest to maintain or change some government policy. Although pressure groups do many worthwhile tasks, they do them not for the sake of the tasks themselves but for the influence their work will have in achieving their policy goals. Interest groups, on the other hand, do such tasks for their own sake; they are not interested in affecting public policy unless that policy endangers their activities. In that situation they can quickly become pressure groups.

The basic purpose of some interest groups, such as labor unions, is to provide for the welfare of its members. To achieve this goal, however, interest groups need public policies that support it. Therefore, interest groups are ever vigilant about changes in government policies that might endanger or aid their activities. Although they were not formed to influence public policy, interest groups nevertheless depend on that policy for their well-being and therefore want a say in what it will be. Consequently, the line dividing interest groups and pressure groups is often very fuzzy.

An advantage of being labeled an interest group is that nonprofit organizations do not pay taxes. In many societies, the state taxes organizations that exist primarily for influencing government policy; therefore, pressure groups usually pay taxes on income no matter how it is obtained. It is to the advantage of a group to be labeled an interest group.

Today, especially in the United States, the terms pressure group and interest group are used interchangeably. This is unfortunate. The community choir, garden club, bowling team, and social club are interest groups that do not influence government, and they are significantly different from groups that want to affect public policies such as gun control, abortion, tobacco use, and farm subsidies. We will consider any group that spends a considerable amount of its resources on influencing government policies as a pressure group.

Goals and Types of Pressure Groups

Though the general goals of pressure groups are quite simple, to change governmental policy or keep it the way it is, the classification of the types

At a 1983 press conference transportation secretary Elizabeth Dole announced her support of Mothers Against Drunk Driving (MADD), a pressure group, and of congressional legilslation to raise the minimum drinking age in the U.S.

of pressure groups is a little more complex. Domestic groups are those that exist within a society; foreign groups are headquartered outside. Among domestic and foreign groups are private and public ones. Also, religious groups get in the fray of policy making.

Although there are many types of pressure groups, their goals are the same. They attempt either to maintain the status quo (i.e., the existing state of affairs) by discouraging governments from adopting new policies or to promote change by encouraging governments to make and implement new policies. Theoretically, for every group that favors a change, there should be one opposing it. In reality this is not always true. Pressure groups are more likely to advocate change than to support the status quo. Groups challenging change, however, are usually more effective than those advocating change; the latter groups have to fight not only the government and others opposed to change but also those groups that want change in a different way.

Domestic Groups

Domestic groups can be a whole society. For example, Lithuania was a pressure group within the Soviet Union. Although we would normally not perceive a nation to be a pressure group, nevertheless it was such since Lithuania attempted to change the Soviet Union's policies for its own benefit, not unlike the fraternal order of police that tries to influence municipal policies to its favor. The Palestinians, who are trying to change Israeli policies that affect them, are another pressure group that encompasses a whole society.

Private Pressure Groups

Most pressure groups, however, represent segments of society. They are private in the sense that they are governed by their own internal struc-

Protestors form a Ring of Humanity as they press for ethics reform at the Rhode Island Capitol in 1992. The achievements of the pressure group include tightened limits on state election campaign contributions, revamped state's ethics commission, broadened anti-nepotism law, and a ban on elected and appointed state officials from taking most state jobs for a year after leaving office.

tures or institutions and raise their own funds. Private pressure groups may have millions of members, such as the American Association of Retired Persons; others may be very small, such as many neighborhood associations. The Mexican Council of Businessmen (Consejo Mexicano de Hombres de Negocio), which has no more than one hundred members, has more direct access to top Mexican administrators than any other Mexican pressure group. Some members of pressure groups are individuals, others are organized groups, such as PACs (political action committees), which are confederations of organizations or corporations. The Japan Federation of Economic Organizations (Keidanren) consists of 800 major corporations and 120 trade associations.

Some pressure groups appear to be a part of an interest group, yet they may be independent organizations, such as COPE (Committee on Political Education), which is nominally part of the AFL-CIO (American Federation of Labor - Congress of Industrial Organizations), the largest organized union in the United States. A corporation often organizes and funds its own pressure group, also called a PAC, through its public relations department or allows that department to actually take on the role of a pressure group.

PAC CONTRIBUTIONS TO GINGRICH CAMPAIGN

**CONTRIBUTIONS TO CONGRESSMAN
NEWT GINGRICH**
NOVEMBER 1992 TO JUNE 1994
AS REPORTED BY THE FEDERAL ELECTION COMMITTEE
October 1994
(Dates Contributed Omitted)

Georgia Republicans	$450
Nat'l Republican Congressional Committee	$75
Action Cmte. for Rural Electrification (ACRE)	$500
Action Fund of Lehman Brothers Inc.	$500
Aetna Life and Casualty Company PAC	$500
Aflac Inc. PAC	$3,500
Air Line Pilots Assoc. PAC	$3,500
Aircraft Owners and Pilots Assoc. PAC	$11,000
Akin, Gump, Strauss, Hauer & Feld LLP Civic Action	$500
Alabama Power Co. Employees Federal PAC	$1,000
Allied Pilots Assoc. PAC	$1,000
Allied-Signal PAC	$1,500
Allstate Insurance Company PAC	$500
Alltel Corporation PAC	$2,000
American Airlines PAC	$1,000
American Assoc. of Clinical Urologists PAC	$1,000
American Assoc. of Nurse Anesthetists	$500
American Bakers Assoc. Bread PAC	$500
American Bankers Assoc. Bank PAC	$3,000
Am. Chiropractic Assoc. PAC	$3,000
Am. Comml. Lines Inc. Effective Gov't.	$500
Am. Council of Life Insurance	$3,000
Am. Crystal Sugar PAC	$2,500
Am. Dental PAC	$2,700
Am. Express Company PAC	$500
Am. Financial Services Ass'n PAC	$500
Am. Furniture Manfrs. Assoc. PAC	$3,500
Am. Health Care Assoc. PAC	$1,500
Am. Hotel Motel PAC	$500
Am. Inst. of Certified Public Accountants	$6,000
Am. International Group Inc Employee PAC	$1,000
Am. Maritime Officers, AFL-CIO Retirees Assoc.	$2,000
Am. Maritime Officers, AFL-CIO Voluntary PAC	$6,000
Am. Medical Assoc. PAC	$5,000
Am. Occupational Therapy Assoc. Inc. PAC	$500
Am. Optometric Assoc. PAC	$500
Am. Physical Therapy Congressional AC	$500
Am. Society of Anesthesiologists PAC	$4,000
Am. Society of Travel Agents PAC	$1,150
Am. Sugar Cane League PAC	$500
Am. Sugarbeet Growers Assoc. PAC	$500
Am. Telephone & Telegraph Co. Inc. PAC	$1,640
Am. Textile Mnfrs Institute, Inc. Committee	$4,500
Am. Veterinary Medical Assoc. PAC	$1,000
Am. Wood Preservers Institute PAC	$750
Am. Yarn Spinners Assoc. PAC	$500
Americans for Free Internat'l Trade PAC	$5,000
Amoco PAC	$1,500
Amway PAC	$500
Anheuser-Busch Companies Inc PAC	$2,000
Arthur Andersen / Andersen Consulting PAC	$1,000
Associated Builders & Contractors PAC	$1,000
Associated Credit Bureaus PAC	$500
Associated General Contractors PAC	$1,500
Atlanta Gas Light Co. for Good Gov't. Cmmttee	$450
Baker & Hostetler PAC	$500
Bank South Corp. Committee on Public Affairs	$750
Barnett People for Better Gov't Inc.	$2,500

Beef PAC of Texas	$500
Bellsouth Telecommns Inc. Fed. PAC	$4,000
Bluebonnet Fund (Baker & Botts)	$1,750
Boeing Co. PAC (BPAC)	$1,000
Bowling Proprietors Assoc. of Am. PAC	$500
Bracewell & Patterson PAC	$1,000
Brentwood / Westside PAC	$200
Brown & Williamson Tobacco Corp. Employee PAC	$4,000
Brown-Forman Corp. Non-Partisan Cmmttee	$1,000
Browning-Ferris Industries PAC	$500
Build PAC	$4,000
Burlington Industries Good Gov't Cmmttee	$3,000
Career College PAC	$1,000
Carepac, The Blue Cross & Blue Shield Assoc.	$2,695
CH2M Hill Companies Ltd. PAC	$1,500
Chemical Bank Fund for Good Gov't.	$1,000
Chemical Manufacturers Assoc. PAC	$1,000
Chevron Employees PAC	$1,000
Chrysler Corp. Political Support Cmmttee	$3,000
CIBA Employee Good Gov't Fund,	$1,763
Cigna Corp. PAC,	$1,000
Citicorp Voluntary Political Fund,	$1,000
Citizens Organized PAC	$5,000
Civic Involvement Program / General Motors Corp.	$1,000
Coal PAC	$1,000
Coca-Cola Co. Nonpartisan Committee	$3,500
Coca-Cola Enterprises Inc. Employee Nonpartisan Commitee	$1,000
ColPAC	$500
Committee for Responsible Gov't.	$500
Connaught Laboratories, Inc. PAC	$500
Consolidated Rail Corp. Good Gov't Fund	$1,000
Coopers & Lybrand PAC	$2,000
Corp. for the Advancement of Psychiatry PAC	$500
Council of Insurance Agents & Brokers PAC	$1,000
Cracker Barrel Old Country Store Inc.	$3,000
Credit Union Legislative Action Council	$4,000
CSX Transportation Inc. PAC	$1,500
Dairymen Inc. Georgia PAC	$3,500
Dealers Election Action Committee	$1,500
Dean Witter, Discover & Co. PAC	$1,000
Delaware Valley PAC	$1,500
Delta Airlines Inc. PAC	$5,000
Detroit Edison PAC-EDPAC	$1,000
Dickstein, Shapiro & Morin PAC	$1,000
Distilled Spirits Council PAC	$2,500
Dow Corning Management PAC	$500
DSC Communications Corp. PAC	$500
Dupont Good Gov't Fund	$1,000
Ela Lease-PAC FKA AAEL Lease-PAC	$1,000
Eli Lilly & Co. PAC	$1,000
Employees' PAC Southeast R	$1,000
English Language PAC	$500
Ernst & Young PAC	$2,000
ESOP PAC	$500
Exxon Corp. PAC	$1,000
Federation of Am. Health Systems PAC	$500
First Financial Management Corp. PAC	$1,000
Florida Congressional Committee,	$2,000
Fluor Corp. Public Affairs Committee,	$4,500
FMC Corp. Good Gov't Program,	$500
Food Distributors Voice in Politics Cmmtee	$499
Food Marketing Institute PAC	$3,500

PAC CONTRIBUTIONS TO GINGRICH CAMPAIGN (continued)

Ford Motor Co. Civic Action Fund,	$3,300	Nat'l Assoc. of Broadcasters Television	$3,000
Gen. Agents and Mgrs Assoc. of the Mut...	$1,500	Nat'l Assoc. of Convenience Stores	$2,500
General Aviation Mfrs Assoc. PAC	$1,000	Nat'l Assoc. of Fed. Credit Unions PAC	$1,000
General Electric Co. PAC	$3,500	Nat'l Assoc. of Independent Insurers PAC	$1,000
Georgia Power Co. Fed. PAC Inc.	$2,500	Nat'l Assoc. of Life Under Writers PAC	$5,000
Georgia US Corp. PAC	$500	Nat'l Assoc. of Medical Eqpt Suppliers	$500
Glaxo Inc. PAC	$1,500	Nat'l Assoc. of Mutual Insurance Cos.	$500
Gold Kist Political Action for Farmers Inc.,	$100	Nat'l Assoc. of Psychiatric Health Systems	$500
Goldman Sachs Partners PAC	$1,000	Nat'l Assoc. of Retired Fed. Employees,	$100
Groery Mfrs of America Inc PAC	$1,500	Nat'l Beer Wholesalers' Assoc. PAC	$8,000
Grumman PAC	$500	Nat'l Broiler Council PAC	$2,000
GTE Corp. Political Action Club (GTE PAC)	$2,000	Nat'l Cable Television Assoc.'s PAC	$10,000
H & R Block PAC	$1,000	Nat'l Cattlemen's Assoc. PAC	$1,000
Halliburton PAC	$1,000	Nat'l Concrete Masonry Assoc. PAC.	$500
Harris Corp.-Fed. PAC	$1,000	Nat'l Cotton Council Committee	$2,000
Health Industry Distributors PAC	$1,000	Nat'l Data Corp. PAC	$1,000
Health Insurance PAC	$500	Nat'l Emergency Medicine PAC	$2,500
Heathcare Compare Corp. PAC	$500	Nat'l Federation of Independent Businesses	$1,000
Heartland PAC FKA: Youngstown PAC	$2,000	Nat'l League of Postmasters PAC	$500
Holiday Inns Inc PAC	$1,000	Nat'l Multihousing Council PAC	$500
Hoechst Celanese Corp. PAC	$1,000	Nat'l Restaurant Assoc. PAC	$5,000
Houston Industries PAC	$500	Nat'l Retail Federation Store PAC	$500
Hudson Valley PAC	$1,000	Nat'l Right to Life PAC	$1,875
Hughes Aircraft Co. Active Citizenship Fund	$1,000	Nat'l Society of Professional Engineers PAC	$1,000
Ice Cream, Milk & Cheese PAC	$1,000	Nat'l Solid Wastes Management Assoc.	$500
IDS PAC	$500	Nat'l Tooling & Machining Assoc. (NTMA)	$2,000
Independent Ins. Agents of America Inc.	$4,716	Nationsbank Corp. PAC	$2,500
Inn/PAC Int'l Assn of Holiday Inns Inc. PAC	$500	Norfolk Southern Corp. Good Gov't Fund	$1,000
Internat'l Assoc. of Amusement Parks	$1,000	Northern Telecom Inc. PAC	$1,000
Internat'l Council of Shopping Centers Inc.	$3,000	Northwest Airlines PAC	$500
Internat'l Mass Retail Assoc. PAC FKA IMRA	$500	NRA Political Victory Fund	$4,950
JC Penney Co. Inc. PAC	$2,500	Nynex Employees' Federal PAC	$2,000
Joseph E Seagram & Sons, Inc. PAC	$1,500	Occidental Petroleum Corp. PAC	$1,000
Kemper Corp. Political Action Fund	$500	Ogden Corp. Political Action Fund	$500
King & Spalding Nonpartisan Committee		Outback Steakhouse Inc. PAC	$500
for Good Gov't,	$2,000	Owens-Illinois Inc. Employees	
Kraft General Foods Inc. PAC	$1,000	Good Citizenship Fund	$1,500
Liberty Mutual Insurance Co. PAC	$1,000	Pacific Telesis Group PAC	$2,000
Lincoln Club of Orange Count,	$1,000	Pepsico Concerned Citizens Fund	$5,000
Lockheed Employees' PAC	$5,000	Petroleum Marketers Assoc. of America	$500
Loews Corp. / Lorillard Public Affairs Cmte	$1,000	Philip Morris Cos. Inc. PAC	$2,000
Long John Silver's Restaurants, Inc.		Philips Electronics North America Corp.	$1,500
FKA Jerrico PAC	$250	PAC of the American Hospitals	$3,500
Loose Group, The	$4,000	PAC of the American Osteopaths	$1,000
Louisiana Land and Exploration Co. PAC	$500	Price Waterhouse Partners' PAC	$1,000
Manville Corp. Employee Action Program	$1,000	Principal Mutual Life Insurance Co.	$500
Mapco Employees PAC	$1,000	Printing Industries of America	$2,000
Marathon Oil company Employees PAC	$1,500	Procter & Gamble Co. Good Gov't Cmte.	$2,000
Marion Merrell Dow Inc. PAC	$1,000	Prudential Insurance Co. of America Fedl.PAC	$1,000
Martin Marietta Corp. PAC	$2,500	Prudential Securities PAC	$1,000
Massachusetts Congressional Victory Fund	$800	Realtors PAC	$4,000
McDonald's Corp. PAC	$1,000	Responsible Gov't Cmte of Gulf Employees	$250
MCI Telecommunications PAC	$500	Rhone-Poulenc Inc. PAC	$1,000
Merrill Lynch & Co. Inc. PAC	$1,500	RJR PAC / RJR Nabisco Inc.	$3,000
Mid-America Dairymen Inc.		Rockwell Internat'l Corp. Good Gov't,	$1,000
Agricultural & Dairy Educ.	$1,000	S & A Restaurant Corp. Employees PAC	$1,000
Minn-Dak Farmers Cooperative PAC	$250	Salomon Brothers Inc. PAC	$3,000
Mississippi Power Co. State PAC	$250	San Diego Community PAC Inc.	$1,000
Mobil Corp. PAC	$750	Sears PAC	$500
Morgan Companies PAC	$3,500	Securities Industry PAC	$1,000
Mortgage Bankers Assoc. of America PAC	$500	Sheet Metal and Air Conditioning	
Motorola Employees Good Gov't Cmte	$1,000	Contractors' PAC	$2,500
Mutual of Omaha Co.'s PAC (IMPAC),	$1,500	Shoney's PAC	$500
Nalco Chemical Co. PAC	$500	Sirote & Permutt PC Lawyers for Good Gov't.	$1,000
Nat'l Action Committee - NACPAC	$2,000	Southeastern Lumber Mfrs. Assoc. PAC	$250
Nat'l Air Traffic Controllers Assoc. PAC	$3,000	Southern Co. Services PAC	$1,250

PAC CONTRIBUTIONS TO GINGRICH CAMPAIGN (continued)			
Southern Minnesota Sugar Coop. PAC	$850	Warner-Lambert PAC	$1,500
Southern Nuclear Operating Co. Inc.		Watkins Associated Industries Inc.	
Employees PAC	$750	Employees for Good Gov't.	$1,500
Southwestern Bell Corp. Employee Fedl. PAC	$3,500	Wholesaler-Distributor PAC	$500
Springs Industries Inc. PAC	$2,000	Williams & Jensen PC PAC	$400
Sunbelt Good Gov't Cmte. of Winn-Dixie	$1,000	Wine and Spirits Wholesalers of America PAC	$2,000
T2 Medical Inc. PAC	$2,500	WMX Technologies Inc.	
Team Ameritech PAC	$2,000	Employees' Better Gov't.	$2,500
Tenneco Inc. Employees Good Gov't Fund	$500	Women's Alliance for Israel	$2,500
Texaco Political Involvement Committee	$2,000	Women's Pro-Israel Nat'l PAC	$3,000
Time Warner Inc. PAC	$2,000	Yellow Corp. PAC	$1,000
Title Industry PAC	$500	Zeneca Inc.	$1,000
Tobacco Institute PAC	$1,000		
Torchmark Corp. PAC	$1,000		
Transportation Political Edu. League	$25	***Note: Congressman Gingrich at the	
Travelers Insurance Group Inc. PAC	$2,500	time of this report was House Minority	
Trucking PAC of the America	$1,000	Leader, elections were four months away.	
Turner Broadcasting System PAC Inc.	$2,500		
US West Inc. PAC	$1,000	**SUBTOTAL CANDIDATE: Gingrich, Newt**	
US Tobacco Executives, Administrators		**CONTRIBUTIONS: $459,013**	
and Managers	$2,000	**FOR: 3,275**	
Union Pacific Fund for Effective Gov't.	$3,500	**AGAINST: 0**	
United Parcel Service PAC	$5,500		
United Services Automobile Assoc. Grp. PAC	$500	FEDERAL ELECTION COMMISSION	
United States Telephone Assoc. PAC	$1,000	QUARTERLY SUMMARY DATABASE	
Voluntary Contributors for Better Gov't.	$1,000	1993-94 THROUGH 6/30/94	
Voluntary Hospitals of America Inc. PAC	$500	10/13/1994	
Vulcan Materials Co. PAC	$500	COMMITTEE CONTRIBUTION AND	
Wachovia Bank of Georgia NA		EXPENDITURES FOR CANDIDATES	
Fund for Better Gov't,	$300		

Public Pressure Groups

An array of organizations that are seldom considered as pressure groups are government institutions themselves, usually referred to as public pressure groups. One of the most powerful pressure groups in all societies, especially in developing countries is the military. If the military is opposed to a government program or policy, implementation becomes difficult, if not impossible. Not only does the military control the government's physical forces, but it also has many followers throughout society, such as businesses with which it contracts for services and products, former members of the military, and friends and relatives of current members. The military however is not always an homogeneous entity. Rivalries between the army, navy, and air force are legendary in most societies. Usually "the military" refers only to the commissioned officers' corps, which comprises one-tenth to one-sixth of those belonging to all the military units.

Other public pressure groups are government departments or ministries, each of which lobbies and competes for more jurisdiction, prestige, and funds. In Japan, the Ministry of International Trade and Industry, the

Ministry of Foreign Affairs, the Ministry of Finance, and the Economic Planning Agency have attempted to outflank and outmaneuver each other in an attempt to industrialize their society.[1]

Provincial or state governments also act as pressure groups. Legislators or professional lobbyists hired by the province or state government lobby the national government for funds, services, and goods. Municipalities, too, hire lobbyists to represent them to provincial or state and national governments. Lobbyists who represent government units earn their keep by not only rendering the interests of those who pay their salaries but also channeling information from higher government levels quickly to them.

Foreign Groups

Similarly, foreign governments also can be pressure groups, although they are not usually regarded as such. In Latin American states, as in most other states of developing societies, the U.S. Embassy and embassies of other industrial states have greater influence on the national government than home-grown pressure groups. The line between diplomatic negotiations and influence as a pressure group is thin and murky, if it exists at all. In the spring of 1995 the U.S. government via its embassy in La Paz, Bolivia, pressured the Bolivian government to eradicate more than four thousand acres of coca plants, an action opposed by most Bolivian unions, national legislators, and peasant organizations. The opposition was so strong that it, in part, contributed to the government's declaration of martial law (i.e., temporary abrogation of most civil rights and use of the military to patrol streets to maintain order).

International government organizations also act as pressure groups. For example, the International Monetary Fund has compelled governments to promulgate austerity plans that most other organizations or institutions of their societies have opposed.

Foreign governments and international government organizations are not the only foreign pressure groups with which a government has to contend. International nongovernment organizations, associations representing peoples in foreign societies, and foreign private enterprises also attempt to influence public policy. Amnesty International is an international nongovernment organization that tries to get governments to strengthen their commitment and implementation of human rights legislation. The China Lobby, a strong pressure group in the United States in the middle half of the twentieth century, was composed of Chinese residing in the United States, their supporters, and representatives of the Chinese Kuomintang Government (i.e., the government ousted by Communists under Mao Zedong). Its mission was to get policies enacted favoring the former Kuomintang Government that settled in Taiwan after 1948. International corporations, too, whether they are involved in harvesting and transporting bananas, manufacturing of automobiles or appliances, or providing services such as banking and insurance are notorious for the influence they wield on foreign governments.

In many developing societies foreign pressure groups often control the policy making process. Since these groups have resources, such as information and money, that the domestic groups and often the governments do not possess or cannot withstand, they become the makers and implementors of policy rather than legislators and administrators. Those who work for the government are beholden to these foreign groups and therefore do their bidding, even if it means acting against their own society's interests. Honduras and Guatemala have been called "banana republics" because the United Fruit Company, the main producer and exporter of bananas, and the U.S. Embassies had virtually dictated policy to their governments.

Philips Lighting Poland, a joint venture formed when Poland's largest producer of lighting products was privatized, received a loan from International Finance Corporation (IFC) to help modernize its operations and products, and improve environmental cleanup activities.

Religious Groups

Religious groups can become pressure groups when they try to either impose their beliefs on public policy or prevent government from enacting policy. The Catholic Church and some other organized religious groups have been in the forefront of the attempt to de-legalize abortion and divorce. On the other hand these same religious groups also pressure governments to stop human rights violations and to improve the living conditions of the destitute.

Roles of Individuals in Public Policy Making

Society and the state are intertwined. The state, being the organization of society, must act in concert with the ever changing needs and demands of the people who compose society. However, the modern state cannot possibly respond to the wishes of millions of people on an individual basis.

For example, the General Assembly of the United Nations had fifty four members when it was first formed in 1945 . The ambassador of each member state freely interacted with colleagues and together they made policies. Each ambassador's opinions were heard by all. Today the assembly has more than 190 members. No ambassador wants to hear the opinions of all the others. No longer can everyone discuss suggested policies at the same session. Policies are discussed within "blocs,"

Six-year old Mingda Liu wore a "Free Speech" headband at the Minnesota State Capitol in May, 1989. His father, a University of Minnesota graduate student, and mother, both from China, and twenty five Chinese students showed their support for Chinese students and others who demonstrated for democracy in Beijing's Tiananmen square.

with each bloc usually representing a geographic area, such as the Latin American bloc, the Arab bloc, the African bloc, and the NATO (North Atlantic Treaty Organization) bloc. Each bloc becomes a pressure group and, with its staff and leaders, attempts to bring about policies it wants.

For recommended policies to become actualized, discussions need to be conducted in an organized manner. Government officials simply do not have the time or resources to consider every suggestion and demand that comes to their desk. Demands to be considered by public officials, must be streamlined, vocalized, and presented in an orderly fashion. Individuals are frequently inept or incapable of doing that. Nor can most individuals approach government officials: some do not know how, others may not be able to because of distance, time, etc. But besides the shortcomings of individuals, no matter how competent they are, their suggested policies lack one very important attribute before a government official can seriously consider them: credibility.

Millions of people think they have the answers to all the problems. Some teeter on the verge of lunacy. I am sure you have met some. Since these resolvers-of-all-problems act by themselves, no government official takes them seriously, nor should he or she. A group, however lends credibility to an idea or act, and the larger or more influential the group, the more plausible its suggestions. For this reason General Assembly blocs are predominant in the U.N. (They are effective in filtering out insipid suggestions from a foreign minister or ambassador.)

The United States is a "pluralistic democracy." Thousands of pressure groups operate throughout the country; more than twenty thousand have offices in Washington, D.C. Policy is influenced through these groups, and for that reason they become the principal political actors rather than individuals or even political parties. Individuals with the brightest solutions to problems will not get beyond a friendly smile in a policy maker's office unless they can show that they have the support of a group; individuals representing a large group of constituents receive far more consideration even if their ideas are half-baked.

NATO was established in 1949 for the collective security of its member countries. Seen here is the then U.S. General Dwight D. Eisenhower (center) in a meeting with his counterparts from France and the United Kingdom.

Pressure groups mobilize individuals to maintain the link between the state and society. In every society there are those who are satisfied with the way the state is performing. They may want changes here and there, but by and large they do not seek major alterations. In industrialized countries those who are generally satisfied are the majority. These individuals are quickly mobilized to support the state should there be a major challenge to it. Whenever a group with some strength appears to oppose the general structure of the state, the satisfied majority, usually with the support of the state, will outshout, outvote, and sometimes outfight the challengers.

In many countries in Latin America, Africa, and Asia, government officials prevent very unsatisfied individuals from organizing. For many of them, policy changes in their favor cannot be accomplished without restructuring government institutions and procedures or even society itself. Since government officials' positions would be endangered in any restructured government, they not only prevent the dissatisfied (who are often the majority) from organizing but mobilize the satisfied (who are often the minority) to support the prevalent structure of the state.

The state in such countries depends on these supportive minority pressure groups. Without them, the structure of the state might be radically transformed if the dissatisfied challengers overcome those satisfied. In these countries, because of the chasm between the supporters and the challengers, pressure group politics either is confined to a small portion of the population (because a large part of the majority is challengers) or is a recurrently violent conflict between groups that support the state and those that oppose it.

As a modern industrial society, the United States has a great many persons who are generally satisfied with the way the state is structured and performs. Its large, mobile, and educated population inhabits a vast land mass and possesses a highly technological culture. Despite their political and cultural homogeneity, or perhaps because of it, Americans make varied demands upon their governments and suggestions to change various structures. Besides social issues and what services governments ought to provide, Americans differ on who should control public schools, proper length of terms for public officeholders, amount of government regulation on manufacturers, etc. Thus this multitude of individual viewpoints has resulted in creation of various organized pressure groups. Despite the array of pressure groups, none of those who have gained respect advocate major changes in the government's institutional and procedural structures.

Despite their variety of interests, pressure groups in most industrialized societies do not advocate wholesale change in the political structure of the state. In fact, the overwhelming number of pressure groups do not advocate any such change because, if such changes occurred, the groups would have to readapt their strategies for influencing policy making. Not only would this require much time, resources, and effort, but also the result could be less rewarding than the current situation. Since each pressure group is only interested in affecting a small fragment of the policy making process, it uses many other fragments to advance its cause. Therefore, it would not want these other fragments to change. For example, many pressure groups support incumbent legislators, even those who were not totally supportive of their causes, because these legislators are known quantities that have been adapted to.

The Institutionalization of Pressure Groups

When an individual desires a change in a given public policy (either because of a grievance or an idea), he or she foments interest in it by talking to others. If others show support, then either a group may form to pursue and further that policy change or an already existing group may take it on as an additional cause. If that policy change becomes the focus for the group's existence and it acquires a formal structure, then the interest in the policy change has become **institutionalized**.This means that the interest's future is no longer dependent on the individual that originated it; it is now dependent on the group that has developed around it. The group, in fact, exists independent of the members that compose it.

For example, suppose that I believe that a constitutional amendment should be passed forbidding anyone over sixty-years-old from being eligible to run for the position of governor general of Canada. After talking it over with colleagues, friends, and acquaintances, a group called "Youngsters for Governor General" is formed with several officers; I am elected honorary chair. Time passes, the group attracts more members, and Chapters are formed in many provinces. However, after some meditation and rereading of Socrates I change my viewpoint and believe that we need a constitutional amendment that raises the age limit for governor general to at least sixty-years-old. Youngsters for Governor General throw me out of the group and continue to lobby for their amendment. Some of the group leave (they may move, die, grow older), but the group persists nonetheless as long as there are people willing to maintain it.

Those who begin and maintain pressure groups need to possess three components — education, money, and time. Obviously, knowledge about the processes of the government operations one wishes to influence is important. Which government officials to approach and how to do so are matters that one has to learn. There is no sense in dissipating energy on attempts to influence a municipal, state, or provincial official when a federal official makes the policy decisions. The ability to communicate is also crucial. Not only is the proper form (i.e., grammar, intonation, syntax, spelling, punctuation) important, but also the content of the message. A hastily composed note is usually not effective. A document evincing serious research and written in understandable language is effective. Of course, to do the latter, one has to understand the problem one wishes to correct. To express support for health care reform, for example, is not enough to influence policy. One needs specific proposals that government can enact and that address questions and concerns of policy makers. Which policies should be changed? What new policies should be adopted? What will be their short- and long-term costs and consequences? Who will be affected, when, and for how long? What alternatives exist? What are the shortcomings of other proposals? Answers to these questions imply thorough understanding of the problem and of the government's ability to resolve it.

Money is also necessary because both the acquisition of knowledge and the propagation of information to those who influence policy are expensive. Group meetings involve costs for telephone calls, transportation, room rental, public address systems, photocopying, mailings, etc. Raising money also costs money. Without money, pressure groups cannot exist. If members are unable to meet the group's financial needs, outsiders may be asked to donate. If outsiders do not make contributions, the group disappears.

When education and money are not available, pressure groups cannot function. Lack of education and money is the main reason governments do not address the needs and interests of the poor. The poor in every society have neither the expertise nor the resources to approach government officials, present their views, and influence policy. In some societies other groups, such as organized religions or political parties, may mobilize the poor and represent their interests to governments. Unfortunately, these groups often are more interested in their own causes and only use the poor to advance their interests.

Lack of institutionalization of interests may also be a factor in the poor's inability to influence public policy making. This is nothing new. The serfs, landless peasants, gypsies, and migrant workers, have never had any influence on those who make public policy. In the Middle Ages they were never part of a corporation. The poor depended on the benevolence of government leaders or on those who, like Moses or Marx, spoke for them.

Because the political processes have ignored them, the poor have devised an apolitical subculture complete with their own language and norms. Street jargon or argot, rich in descriptions of the behavior and fashions of the affluent, is a type of code by which the poor, especially in the cities, communicate among themselves. The norms of the poor subculture exclude political participation because integration into their society is evinced through other means, such as language and a common behavior toward the affluent. From a social perspective, integration of the poor is really not very important because society can exist without them.

While the poor lack education and money, the affluent often lack the third component, time; therefore they pay others to represent their interests. Most pressure groups have paid staff members. Even neighborhood groups hire lawyers and other professionals to write proposals and present them to policy makers. The community pressure group in which volunteers do all the work is disappearing, not because for lack of expertise in these groups, but for lack of time to devote to the interest.

The obligation of work, family, and social activities do not leave enough time for people to participate in matters that they perceive as important. Therefore pressure groups hire professionals, sometimes from within their groups to write proposals and advocate on their behalf on such issues as preventing government agencies from enlarging an airport or from giving licenses to build incinerators, power plants, or highways .

The days are long gone when two or more citizens could gather and assign a group member to approach a policy maker to affect a certain policy. Interests involve so many complex issues and are so difficult to resolve that a pressure group member cannot focus on more than one issue at a time. Stopping a power plant from being built, for example, requires so much time (for meetings, research, proposal development, fund-raising, communications, public education, and lobbying) that the typical citizen devoted to that cause would not have time to participate in another cause. That citizen, who becomes a semiprofessional power-plant stopper through the experience, still has to rely on engineers, scientists, and lawyers to wade through the data needed to justify a position. In addition, more pressure groups have evolved as issues have become very complex and policy making has become professionalized.

The professionalization of policy making and pressure group activity has significantly lessened the individual citizen's influence in public policy making. Like the corporation of ages ago, the pressure group has become an aide in the determination of societal policy. Government policy makers use the pressure groups to supply them with information on issues and concerns from the important segments of society (which do not include the poor). These officials respond by making policy. Over the years, or perhaps even generations, a particular policy can be altered or revoked because of influence from pressure groups. The individual, even if a "leader," cannot overcome the influence of pressure groups and complicated policy making processes to get his or her way with a specific policy. The only way an individual can affect policy is by becoming active in a pressure group.

From the government's perspective, only institutionalized interests are worthy of consideration. If no group exists to support an interest, it is unimportant. Yet if the interest becomes institutionalized, it also becomes depersonalized. Individual support of an interest no matter how fervent, is insignificant compared to the group's ability to the whole policy making process when its interests are not satisfied.

Government officials do not have to listen to the demands of a pressure group; they can completely ignore them. However, if this happens and the pressure group is well mobilized, it can threaten to bring down the government officials who ignored it. Individuals who pose this threat could never have as much impact as a group. For example, the school board that ignores the demands of a teachers' union or parents' association may not be reelected or, occasionally, have its functions taken over by another state institution. In countries where coups occur, pressure groups can cause the government itself to be toppled and a new one installed. Consequently, government officials usually pay attention to pressure groups, even if they do not present viable policy options.

The Iron Law of Oligarchy

What do pressure groups do for the individual? Why would individuals bother with them? Besides wanting to do something to better the community or the world, individuals can have a selfish reason for joining a pressure group — maintaining or improving their standard of living no matter what harm this causes others. For example, they may request that government officials not issue a permit for a power plant to be built in their neighborhood or they may ask for more health, education, and welfare benefits for themselves. Results of effective pressure group activity often mean that individual situations improve materially and, as we will see later, psychologically.

At the turn of the twentieth century Swiss-Italian writer Robert Michels coined the phrase "iron law of oligarchy," which has become a hallmark for those involved in pressure groups (eventhough Michels applied it only to political parties and trade unions). "Iron law of oligarchy" means that in every mass organization leaders emerge who inevitably try to subvert the interests of the group for their own selfish purposes. Writing about socialist parties and their attachment to the working class, Michels said:

> . . . The party, regarded as an entity, as a piece of mechanism, is not necessarily identifiable with the totality of its members, and still less so with the class to which these belong. The party is created as a means to secure an end. Having, however, become an end in itself, endowed with aims and interests of its own, it undergoes detachment, from the teleological point of view, from the class which it represents. In a party, it is far from obvious that the interest of the masses which have combined to form the party will coincide with the interests of the bureaucracy in which the party becomes personified. The interests of the body of employees are always conservative, and in a given political situation these interests may dictate a defensive and even a reactionary policy when the interests of the working class demand a bold and aggressive policy; in other cases, although these are very rare, the roles may be reversed. By a universally applicable social law, every organ of the collectivity, brought into existence through the need for the division of labor, creates for itself, as soon as it becomes consolidated, interests peculiar to itself. The existence of these special interests involves a necessary conflict with the interests of the collectivity. Nay, more, social strata fulfilling peculiar functions tend to become isolated, to produce organs fitted for the defense of their own peculiar interests. In the long run they tend to undergo transformation into distinct classes.[2]

Michels means that a large group by requiring organization creates a body of leaders and staff (i.e., bureaucracy) that in time loses touch with the people the group is representing and with the members of the group itself. The leaders and staff become more interested in securing their positions and welfare then in securing the goals and interests of the organization.

In a less abstract manner, let me illustrate with the following example. Ten families living on the same block get upset when they discover that an oak tree, a landmark for the community, is scheduled to be removed as part of city plans for street improvements that will make driving easier for hundreds. Representatives of the families come together to discuss what they could do to prevent removal of the tree. They discuss several strategies, such as getting signatures on petitions, picketing city hall, and hiring attorneys. All the strategies have pros and cons. After hours of discussions the group agrees on a strategy. Regardless of the strategy, people are needed to make it work. Who will do this work?

As stated previously, one component that these workers must have to pursue a given strategy is time — time to attend meetings, time to carry around petitions, time to make telephone calls, etc. The persons who work to preserve the tree will have time; however, they may not necessarily have the greatest expertise in dealing with the issue.

What is the person who devotes time to this cause getting from this experience? It may be anything from escaping the routine of the day to an excuse for getting out of the house to seeing his or her name in print in the media. The reward (which the person might not consciously perceive) motivates that person to undertake the task. Suppose this person knows that by making one telephone call the tree will not be removed. Would he or she make that call? Most likely not. Why? Because when the issue is resolved, the rewards stop. The greater the rewards if the issue remains unresolved, the less likely those who are receiving the rewards will want it resolved. The issue becomes secondary to the rewards engendered by the issue. Often, these rewards become so highly prized that workers ward off anyone who may challenge their position. Rule of the few for their own benefit frequently becomes the hallmark of pressure group organization. This is partially what Michels meant by "iron law of oligarchy."

Here is another twist to the example of the tree removal. Suppose that no one in the group has time and, being a wealthy community, it decides to hire an attorney at a monthly or hourly rate to fight the removal. Will the attorney hurry to have the issue resolved? The quicker it is resolved, the less he or she can collect in fees. The attorney, too, will try to drag out the issue. A similar situation occurs if the group decides to hire a staff (e.g., clerks, researchers, public relations personnel) because these persons derive their livelihood from the interests of the group. Certainly they would not want the group to disappear.

Now suppose that after months, or maybe even years, the issue is resolved. Members of the group, especially those that actively worked on the issue, have invested a lot of time, resources, and effort in the resolution. Will they return to their everyday lives? Not likely. Since they have an organization and some expertise in the political process, group members will look for other causes so they can make use of what they invested in the first cause. So the group that originally wanted to save one tree in their own neighborhood may now expand their efforts to save trees in the community. Many national and state pressure groups began in this innocuous fashion. The point to remember is that unless there are rewards, perceived or not, individuals will not go out of their way to labor for the betterment of community or society.

Another aspect to the "iron law of oligarchy" is that many persons join a group only for the reward of being associated with it, which means that they may not really be interested in what the group does or how it is organized. They want to be part of the group because it brings prestige and renown and may lead to a job. (Many persons join fraternities, sororities, and professional organizations with this in mind.) Since the leaders of the group know this happens, they can then manipulate the group to satisfy their own goals. Many members do not care to know for what purpose the group's leaders and staff are using the political process. In fact some members do not know that leaders and staff are using the political process at all. For example, many union members do not know that their leadership often finances political campaigns or pressures legislators to oppose programs that they favor, such as decriminalizing the use of some narcotic drugs.

But what about the person who selflessly devotes energy to a cause without thinking about or getting any rewards? Yes, there are still a few of these people around. As any spectator of pressure group politics will tell you, however, they are a dying breed — they are outnumbered, outspent, and out-manipulated. The surviving consumer and environmental groups that began with many volunteers on a shoestring budget in the 1960s and 1970s have nearly all been transformed into professional lobbying organizations with staff, headquarters, and publications. The selfless volunteer can still be found among them, but he or she most likely is doing menial tasks while the "professionals" do the policy making.

These professionals, who are usually paid, do not necessarily believe in the causes for which they are working. They are paid for their performance, not for their beliefs. Their performance is measured in terms of amount of funds raised and number of government leaders approached, people educated and, most important, favorable public policies adopted. Often these professionals move from one group to another, even to an opposing group, as in the situation of the professional lobbyist for a consumer group taking a similar position with a manufacturer that the consumer group opposed. Centuries ago battles were led by mercenaries, professional soldiers who sold their services to the king that paid the highest salary. Today much of public policy making is influenced by another type of mercenary, leaders of pressure groups.

"The iron law of oligarchy," stated almost a century ago in another context, has become descriptive of a developmental process by which a new societal layer is added to the diffusion of policy making. The pressure group "oligarchy," which is always based upon a group, generates its own priorities, not always in harmony with those of the rest of the group, much less of society overall.

Tactics of Pressure Groups

Nevertheless, these professionals of pressure groups, usually called lobbyists, are as necessary to the policy making process as government officials themselves, as long as they have access to the latter. Access to policy makers and administrators is crucial to the success of pressure groups.

How do pressure groups get the government to do what they want? If government officials shut their doors to representatives of a pressure group and will not listen to them, the pressure group may take actions to persuade others to listen to their cause and to help influence the government. They can rally hundreds and thousands of supporters to march noisily through the main streets of the capital to show their strength and commitment. Government officials not secure in their position may feel intimidated when throngs of disgruntled citizens parade through the city. The throngs may get out of control and begin to destroy property, causing even more anxiety to the property owners, who, may also join in and demand that government listen to the malcontents. Unless the police and the military conduct a blood bath (which will cause the world media and human rights groups to react negatively toward the government), government officials will not only listen to the leaders of the demonstrators but also negotiate with them.

Another way to get the attention of government officials is to call for a strike against a private or a public enterprise that will disrupt the economy. Labor strikes can paralyze the whole society. For example, if bank employees do not show up for work, no financial transactions can be conducted. When employees of a public transport system stay home, many other workers cannot travel to and from work. If the truckers do not show up to work, food products cannot reach cities. If teachers go on strike, students stay home, often without supervision. Any one of these situations can cause considerable hardship to a lot people who will look toward government for relief.

In some societies several groups strike at the same time; this is called a **general strike**. If the strike is successful, the financial loss to society and the suffering of the people is staggering. Few governments can overcome the effects of a general strike and, therefore, may never allow the situation to reach that point. They will either attempt to prevent the labor unions from mobilizing their members or negotiate with their leaders.

If, however, a government forbids demonstrations and strikes and threatens to arrest leaders who advocate these tactics, group members may believe that violence is the only other way of getting their demands heard. Often the severe risks involved in unlawfully destroying property or in maiming or killing people are consciously taken to force the government to open the public policy making process.

A 1936 sit-in strike by employees of a General Motors plant in Flint, Michigan. The then Governor Frank Murphy negotiated an end to the strike that forced the corporation to recognize the workers' new union, the United Auto Workers. The Supreme Court in 1939 declared such sit-in strikes illegal as they prevented corporations from continuing operations by hiring strikebreakers.

If that process is already open, persuasion is the main tactic pressure groups use to influence public policy makers and implementors. If corruption is rampant among government officials, bribes may be used to pressure them. A more secure tactic is to mobilize supporters to vote for an endorsed candidate. This is especially effective for groups with large memberships. In many societies a labor union's strength depended on how many endorsed candidates could be elected by its supporters. The National Rifle Association of the United States has been credited with mobilizing its supporters to defeat incumbents who voted against policies it supported. Groups with small memberships might try to use publicity to convert nonmembers to its cause of defeating candidates it does not want elected.

The most popular way of influencing policy, although not always the most effective, is lobbying. **Lobbying** involves talking to legislators and administrators to persuade them of the correctness of one's position. To accomplish this one must be able to confront people, and communicate what one wants. Therefore, a lobbyist is knowledgeable not only about government and its officials but also about the pressure group's issues and their implications if put into effect. Those who are thus knowledgeable are often former legislators, close relatives of legislators or former members of legislators' staffs. Having been so close to the legislative process, these persons have the advantage of knowing not only how the process works but also the people within that process.

As Birnbaum and Murray point out many former members of Congress and former Congressional staff members became lobbyists for groups they may have supported through legislation while they were still working in Congress. Relatives of members of Congress also are lobbyists.

Roles of Lobbyists

Lobbyists try to affect public policy in favor of the group they represent. To do so lobbyists not only develop close contacts with policy makers, they also perform several roles important to the well functioning of the policy making process itself. These roles are dispensers of information, influencers of values and beliefs, and provisioners of job security to the makers of policy.

Lobbyists choose pertinent information from the myriad of facts and data available on a given issue to present to government policy makers. Obviously, this information is selected and systematized by the leaders

FOCUS — LOBBYING AGAINST THE TAX REFORM BILL OF 1986

...With billions of dollars of tax breaks on the line, major corporations, trade associations, and pressure groups hired the biggest names in Washington to protect themselves. ...

Many of the lobbyists were former members of Congress and former aides, whose stock-in-trade was their expertise in the system and their access to old colleagues and bosses. The lucrative allure of tax reform caused ever more of these people to join the lobbyists' ranks. Congressional and administration officials were transformed, almost overnight, from being the people sought out for tax favors to the people who were doing the seeking. They traded power for money. Two of Rostenkowski's (Richard Rostenkowski, former chair of the House Ways and Means Committee) former top aides—John Salmon and James Healey—were included among their ranks; both had left the Hill after many years to earn the big bucks of lobbying. Salmon represented a liquor company and one of the nation's largest tax-shelter syndicators; Healey worked for Allied Signal, Exxon, Johnson & Johnson, Chrysler-Mitsubishi, Union Pacific, Bethlehem Steel, and the investment banking house of Salomon Brothers. Buck Chapoton, the former Treasury tax official, also used his expertise to secure a highly paid lobbying position for commercial banks. Roderick DeArment, formerly Dole's (Robert Dole, the Senate Majority Leader) staff director on the Finance Committee, lobbied for a group of chief executive

officers who favored reductions in corporate tax rates, as well as for the Solar Energy Industries Association and for a trade association of cellular-telephone companies.

Tax lobbyists were a virtual who's who of the once-powerful in Washington. There were mini-alumni associations that comprised lobbyists who had once worked in the Senate for Russell Long (from Louisiana), Bob Dole, or Lloyd Bentsen of Texas. Their world was a kind of inbred village, in which everybody knew everybody else, and in which information swirled like gossip. It was a tightly knit network of tax insiders and former insiders. Everyone talked the same language and sought the same facts. "All of us have just come off the Hill. We worked with the people we lobby. They're our friends," explained lobbyist Denise Bode, a former aide to Senator David Boren, Democrat of Oklahoma.

There was plenty of work for everyone — U.S. Steel hired Kip O'Neill, the son of House Speaker Tip O'Neill; Senator Dole's daughter worked as a lobbyist for the real estate sales firm Century 21. Companies were tripping over each other to get their point across. The law firm of Patton Boggs & Blow, which was run by Tommy Boggs, the son of late House Majority Leader Hale Boggs, housed two hostile, corporate coalitions — the Coalition to Reduce High Effective Tax Rates, which favored reform's goal of abolishing tax breaks to pay for lower rates, and the Basic Industries Coalition, which favored retaining corporate tax breaks, even if it meant higher rates. ...

Lobbyists—or often their young, lower-paid legal assistants—lined up early each morning to get seats at the tax-writing markups (committee meetings where only members and their staffs participated). At Ways and Means, before the sessions were closed to the public, some eager committee-watchers would arrive as early as 5:30 A.M. to get at the head of the queue and have a chance for a front-row seat. The line sometimes stretched the entire length of the hallway, a city block long, and then wrapped around the corner. There were so many people that it looked like the committee was giving something away—which, at times, it was.

The lines were immense each day, no matter what subject the committee was discussing. Representative Pete Stark, Democrat of California, devised a formula to explain the phenomenon, which was equally pronounced in both the Senate and the House: "The fewer the number of taxpayers affected, and the more dull and arcane the subject, the longer the line of lobbyists." Some of those standing in the hall or sitting in the Senate's wired-for-sound auditorium two floors below billed their clients upward of $400 an hour for their loitering. Others charged as much as $10,000 a month per client. ...

During the eighteen months that ended June 30, 1986—the period that encompassed most of the congressional tax-reform debate—PACs contributed the staggering sum of $66.8 million to House and Senate candidates, according to a *Wall Street Journal* tabulation. ...

So much money was floating around Washington that even law-makers themselves began to look askance. ...GOP Senator Barry Goldwater of Arizona, who was always one to speak his mind, agreed: "It is not 'We, the people,' but political action committees and moneyed interests who are setting the nation's agenda and are influencing the position of candidates on the important issues of the day."

When normal channels for this lucre were tapped out, members and contributors resorted to more creative—and more questionable—routes. Federal election laws that limited contributions were routinely circumvented to channel even more money into the coffers of politicians. New terms were invented to describe the different routes. There was hard money: straight contributions subject to federal limitations; and soft money: indirect gifts of services, such as telephone banks and studio time, which were not subject to any legal restraint and which aided candidates without going directly into their treasuries. In addition to campaign funds, members also received "honoraria" for giving speeches, or in some cases just for showing up at meetings with well-heeled pleaders—that money went directly into the lawmakers' pockets. Tax writers regularly jetted all over the nation to address groups that wanted favors done in the tax-reform bill, charging two thousand dollars a pop.

Source: Birnbaum, Jeffrey H. and Alan S. Murray. *Showdown at Gucci Gulch: Lawmakers, Lobbyists, and the Unlikely Triumph of Tax Reform.* New York: Vintage Books, 1988, pp. 177-81.

and staff of pressure groups to reflect the group's interests. Yet without this prioritized information, policy makers could very well be at a loss in culling facts and data from a supply that is too large for any individual or group of individuals to know, much less understand.

Thus, determining the outcome of a certain policy becomes very difficult and time consuming for policy makers. Lobbyists attempt to make the task easier by saying, "This is the policy you should adopt and carry out and here are the facts and data to justify it." By providing information for government officials to make policy decisions lobbyists can be very influential in the development of public policy.

In this 1991 picture, lobbyists line up to get into a Senate Banking Committee meeting. The right to lobby the Congress is guaranteed by the U.S. Constitution.

When two groups compete for a policy outcome and present two different sets of data and information, one group's set is not incorrect or wrong. Each group's set is used to justify a different objective. The policy maker then has to decide which objective to adopt or, as is usually done, how best to reconcile the different objectives. Seldom is the veracity of the facts and data questioned. Despite this advantage in influencing decisionmakers through the provision of information, pressure groups and their lobbyists generally do not lie or invent data. If they are caught doing so, they would lose their credibility and therefore could no longer be effective.

Lobbyists also influence the values and beliefs that underpin public policies. By establishing close personal relationships with policy makers, lobbyists attempt to uncover weaknesses in their value and belief structures so that they can shape them to their image. The tactics used to achieve this range from becoming a "friend" to being a counselor or financial advisor to the policy maker. A good lobbyist not only knows about government institutions and processes but also acts as a psychiatrist, social worker, minister, and teacher.

Not the least of the ways of influencing the policy maker is to make assurances that he or she will stay in office. If the policy maker is an elected official he or she will receive money from the pressure group for the reelection campaign. If the policy maker was appointed, his or her superior will be reminded by the lobbyist of the official's merits. Hundreds of millions of dollars in the United States are spent each electoral period by pressure groups to support candidates for electoral office. Sometimes a pressure group will also support opponents to be assured that no matter who wins, the person elected will look favorably upon the pressure group's lobbyists.

How does a lobbyist become successful? Today's answer is networking. **Networking** is a process by which one becomes a part of or continues to be a part of an interconnected conglomeration of individuals, or network, involved in or concerned about a policy area. In computer terminology a network is several computers linked to each other. In policy making a network is individuals who frequently consult with each other to decide policy.

An example of a legislative network is a group of state legislators who stay at the same hotel when the legislature is in session. Since they work together and live together, these legislators develop personal relationships and inevitably discuss bills that are being considered. A lobbyist attempts to become part of this network. He or she will stay at the same hotel and eat at the same restaurants as the legislators, hoping to break into discussions with pertinent information when the legislators are together. In time the lobbyist may become an integral part of the network and thus can influence decisions through information he or she provides or by manipulating the opinions of a few of the network members.

Networks can become complex configurations, consisting of those who have an interest in policy decisions, policy makers and their respective staffs, and often officials from different agencies, branches, or levels of government. Networks may exist within networks, such as the higher education network that focuses on the subcommittee on higher education of a state education committee for the broader education network.

Policy makers receive help from various sources. The telephone and the fax machine make communications and exhange of data within a network easy. Since they often have to justify their policies to the public, policy makers may relegate research and scrutiny of policy options to their staff. This is as true for the U.S. Supreme Court as it is for a state's public utility commission. The staffs then form their own subnetworks, which often determine the policies that are eventually adopted. In these situations lobbyists do not need to have direct contact with the policy makers if they can influence the individual staff members responsible for making decisions.

The individual citizen with a policy suggestion cannot possibly influence the network unless she has lots of time and resources to do so. Individual policy makers may listen to her, but never with the same seriousness they listen to those in the network. When one considers the large number of governmental levels and agencies, each with their coterie of staffs and networks that are often watched and infiltrated by pressure groups, how can one expect the individual citizen to have any significant input with the policy maker? Whether through their influence with policy makers or staff, lobbyists and the staff of pressure groups are another example of the diffusion of policy making, and of the limited influence the individual has in the policy making process. Although governments of today are very much different from those of Ancient Israel and Middle Ages Europe, the individual's relation to the policy making process has remained restrained by the group.

Pro-choice activists of the National Action Committee on the Status of Women (Canada) celebrate the defeat of abortion bill in Ottawa, January

How Pressure Groups Influence Political Parties

The amount of influence pressure groups wield within a society depends on the strengths of the political parties. Usually the stronger political parties are, the more difficult the task for lobbyists to gain access to policy makers. In societies in which leaders of political parties choose the candidates for elected offices or in which party leaders occupy policy making positions within governments, lobbyists encounter difficulty in influencing government policy. Political parties in these societies filter out pressure group interests not in harmony with party programs or platforms. To gain influence in government policy making, pressure groups first have to influence the political parties.

In Great Britain pressure groups attempt to influence party members. Some pressure groups have developed a long history of cooperation with political parties. The Confederation of British Industries, for example, not only underwrites the campaign costs of Conservative Party candidates and members of Parliament but also provides funds for the party. In addition, the Trades Union Congress, a national federation of labor unions, has had a close partnership with the Labor Party. When a party becomes closely identified with a pressure group, the policy making role of legislators is diminished as party leaders give more attention to lobbyists than to legislators. The historical association of certain pressure groups with certain parties in Great Britain makes it unthinkable for those pressure groups to donate funds or otherwise support a different political party.

In Canada pressure groups focus more attention on executive officials than on the legislature. In the legislature political parties determine policy; however, the Canadian Prime Minister and the bureaucracy that he or she heads are open to influences of pressure groups. Unlike British pressure groups, Canadian pressure groups are not identified with a major political party and therefore can switch their support or even support two or more parties simultaneously. The Canadian government funds public pressure groups that represent the interests of a large segment of the population. For example, the federal government gave more than $250,000 to the Consumers Association of Canada in 1988 when it needed funds to survive. The federal government also subsidizes the National Action Committee on the Status of Women with $500,000 a year.[3]

In societies in which political parties are strong and the electoral system encourages the formation of parties, pressure groups may convert into parties. In Israel, for example, a group of emigres from the former Soviet Union and from modern Russia organized as a party, Israel for Immigration, for the 1996 elections. In Switzerland the Swiss Car Party, which is an offshoot of an automobile club, captured eight seats in the lower house of the legislature in 1991. The most ubiquitous examples of a pressure group forming a party are parties generated by labor movements and unions. Nearly all parties with the word worker or labor in their title were begun by and continue to be associated with those interests representing workers, such as Britain's Labour Party, Cote D'Ivoire's Ivorian Worker's Party, and Bolivia's Revolutionary Workers' Party.

Groups pushing for the interests of regions or provinces may organize themselves into parties, hoping by that to make their interests heard in national legislatures. Spain has more than forty parties representing regional interests (sometimes two or more parties representing the same region's interests).[4] Canada's Reform Party launched in 1988 in Alberta to represent its interests has since acquired a broad following among the voters of western provinces. An even older Canadian provincial party is the Quebec Party, which is devoted to the creation of an independent Quebec state.

No where are pressure groups more influential in policy making than in the United States, which has weak political parties. Pressure groups can directly influence legislators and administrators because the political parties have become ineffective in the public decision making process. The **iron triangle** of U.S. politics is composed of agencies that make policy, legislative committees that oversee the workings of these agencies, and pressure groups that attempt to influence the policy decisions of the agencies and legislative committees. Lobbyists work with the staff of the executive departments and agencies and with legislators and their staffs. Except for groups such as those for or against abortion, the death penalty, or gun control, most pressure groups do not spend many resources influencing party platforms or leaders. In the United States, therefore, political parties do not shield bureaucrats and legislators from pressure groups.

In the United Kingdom the equivalent of the iron triangle is composed of only two sides, administrators and political parties; and in Canada it has four sides composed of administrators, legislators, political parties, and lobbyists.

Whether they operate through political parties or directly with policy makers, pressure groups have become indispensable to the functioning of the modern state. Not only do they dispense information necessary for decision making but they also suggest alternative policies. As policies have become more complex and comprehensive, spokespersons and lobbyists for pressure groups have become more professional, thereby leaving the individual out of the decision making process.

TERMS TO REMEMBER

interest group
pressure group
institutionalized

iron law of oligarchy
general strike
lobbying
networking
iron triangle

SUGGESTED READINGS

Ball, Alan R. and Frances Millard. *Pressure Politics in Industrial Societies: A Comparative Introduction.* Atlantic Highlands, NJ: Humanities Press International, 1987. Pressure groups in several European and North American countries are examined and their influence noted.

Birnbaum, Jeffrey H. and Alan S. Murray. *Showdown at Gucci Gulch: Lawmakers, Lobbyists, and the Unlikely Triumph of Tax Reform.* New York: Vintage Books, 1988. Two journalists write about the politicking that culminated in the tax reform act of 1986.

Browne, William Paul. *Cultivating Congress: Constituents, Issues, and Interests in Agriculture Policymaking.* Lawrence, KS: University Press of Kansas, 1995. The author maintains that the iron triangle is not the appropriate model in analyzing Congress's role in the formulation of agricultural policy.

Dilger, Robert Jay. *The Sunbelt/Snowbelt Controversy: The War Over Federal Funds.* New York: New York University Press, 1982. This book follows the efforts of the Northeast-Midwest Congressional Coalition as it attempted to alter public policies benefitting the Snowbelt states and how Congressional delegations from the Sunbelt responded.

Drezon-Tepler, Marcia. *Interest Groups and Political Change in Israel.* Albany: State University of New York, 1990. Pressure groups' influence in the determination of politics in Israel is the topic of this book.

Hall, Melvin F. *Poor People's Social Movement Organizations: The Goal Is to Win.* Westport, CT: Praeger, 1995. The importance of organization in empowering social movement organizations is the theme of this work.

Hofrenning, Daniel J.B. *In Washington but Not of It: The Prophetic Politics of Religious Lobbyists.* Philadelphia: Temple University Press, 1995. Religious groups are not only interested in changing fragments of policy as other pressure groups do, but desire transformation of societal structures and values.

Michels, Robert. *Political Parties: A Sociological Study of the Oligarchical Tendencies of Modern Democracy.* Translated by Eden and Cedar Paul. Introduction by Seymour Martin Lipset. New York: Collier Books, 1962. The iron law of oligarchy and how it manifests itself in modern mass parties and organizations. Originally published in 1915.

Middlebrook, Kevin J. *The Paradox of Revolution: Labor, the State, and Authoritarianism in Mexico.* Baltimore: The Johns Hopkins University Press, 1995. A historical study on the role of labor in Mexican politics and how it has been coopted into the policy making processes and institutions.

Payne, Leigh A. *Brazilian Industrialists and Democratic Change.* Baltimore: The Johns Hopkins University Press, 1994. The basic premise of this work is that Brazilian industrialists are more concerned with maintaining political stability than the type of government under which they operate.

Pierce, John C., Mary Ann E. Steger, Brent S. Steel, and Nicholas P. Lovrich. *Citizens, Political Communication, and Interest Groups: Environmental Organizations in Canada and the United States.* Westport, CT: Praeger, 1992. This work is an analysis and comparison of the activities and successes of environmental groups in Canada and the United States.

Rosenthal, Alan. *The Third house: Lobbyists and Lobbying in the States.* Washington, DC: CQ Press, 1993. This is a basic text on those who carry the message of pressure groups to the United States Congress.

✒ NOTES

1. Jon Woronoff, *Politics the Japanese Way* (Tokyo: Lotus Press, 1986), pp. 128-31, 222-31.

2. Robert Michels, *Political Parties: A Sociological Study of the Oligarchical Tendencies of Modern Democracy,* transl. Eden and Cedar Paul (New York: Dover Publications, Inc., 1959 (English original, 1915)), p. 389.

3. Ronald G. Landes, *The Canadian Polity: A Comparative Introduction,* 3d ed. (Scarborough, Ontario: Prentice-Hall Canada, Inc., 1991), pp. 394-96.

4. Arthur S. Banks, ed., *Political Handbook of the World: 1992* (Binghamton, NY: State University of New York, CSA Publications, 1992), pp. 714-16.

13 Political Parties

"HOW HAPPY I COULD BE WITH EITHER IF THEY'D LET ME RUN THINGS!"

⊕ Outline
- Mass Parties and Elite Parties
- Conservativism and Liberalism
- Party Systems
- The Importance of Parties
- The Internationalization of Political Parties

Political parties are a form of pressure group. Whereas a pressure group is an interest group that uses the political process to achieve its aims, the **political party** is an interest group that uses the political process to achieve its aims *by filling vacant elected government offices with its members.* The primary function of any political party is to win elections. Therefore, if no elections are held, no political parties can exist. In countries like Saudi Arabia in which succession to political office is determined by birth and in those with dictators, so-called political parties are not much more than pressure groups because no one can get elected.

273

To win elections political parties conduct many different activities, such as educating the citizenry, sponsoring sports teams, giving to charity, disseminating information, raising issues, and popularizing ideologies. These are all means to an end, which is to secure the citizen's vote.

Political parties are new to the political process. They have been around only since the beginning of the last century when elections became the method for choosing government leaders. Although organizations attempted to influence public policy in ancient Israel, Greece, and Rome and during the Middle Ages, they were not political parties because their leaders were selected through birth to royal families or through wheeling and dealing among individuals representing various groups.

Political parties today are nothing like the original parties. In the early and mid-nineteenth century political parties were like exclusive clubs because membership was restricted to male property owners who were literate (i.e., able to read and write) and of voting age, which in some societies was less than 3 percent of the population. Political parties, therefore, had very few members. Only since the beginning of this century have political parties become the mass organizations with which we are familiar; at that time many voting requirements were dropped and later females were allowed to vote.

A 1964 picture of a grass-roots political party meeting in Camaroon, West Africa. Such assemblies form the basis for strong democracies. The Whigs and the Tories were the first political parties founded this way in England in the eighteenth century.

Mass Parties and Elite Parties

Most political parties attempt to gather the largest number of supporters possible. Whether it is the British Conservative or Labour parties; the French Radical, Socialist, or Gaullist parties; the Canadian Progressive Conservative, Liberal, or New Democratic parties; the Italian Christian Democratic or Socialist Unity parties; or the Mexican Institutional Revolutionary Party — all are busy recruiting and trying to keep voters. Becoming a party member is easy; one enrolls in their membership list or registers in that party as a voter. Often one does not have to contribute any funds or services or even vote for the party's candidates. Party revenues come from a few donors who make large contributions and from government subsidies. Members do not choose party leaders or decide how candidates are chosen. (The United States Republican and Democratic parties are exceptions; their candidates are selected in primary elections.) Activists who have high positions within the party hierarchy choose officers and determine. This type of party is a mass political party.

Although mass parties are in almost all societies, their number of supporters compared to the voting age population is small, less than 10 percent. In Mexico party membership is 2 percent;[1] in Japan less than 2,000,000;[2] in Australia the largest party, the Liberal Party, has less than 100,000 members.[3]

The U.S. Republican and Democratic parties also are mass parties. An unusual characteristic of membership in these parties is that inscription into a party list is not necessary. Through the electoral registration procedure, each state allows citizens to claim membership in one of the two parties. A citizen does not have to do anything for the party besides register to vote and claim membership. This custom is so pervasive that 85 percent of all American voters consider themselves either a Republican or a Democrat; nationally there are four Republicans for every five Democrats.[4]

The elite party was popular in the 1930s but has since virtually disappeared. Examples are Germany's National Socialist Workers Party (i.e., the Nazis) and the ever present Communist Party. Membership involved being invited to join, going through an indoctrination and probationary period, contributing sizable amounts of money and time, and publicly supporting party candidates. Membership was purposely kept small because leaders were more interested in the "quality" of members, not the quantity. The membership of the Communist Party of the former Soviet

Union seldom was more than 5 percent of the voting population. The party was organized in small units, usually called cells, and the membership chose leaders and established policies. Generally the elite party became a very important part of the member's life.

A third type of party seeks large membership but at the same time restricts it by charging high dues. In Japan the Liberal Democratic Party's dues make it impossible for low income citizens to join. The same holds true for many parties in Asia, Africa, and Latin America. Steep dues are necessary in these parties because most of their revenue comes from members rather than government subsidies and large private contributions, as in the United States and Europe.

Ideological Parties

Elite parties tend to be more ideologically based than mass parties. Members of an ideological party have to subscribe to its belief system and rigorously defend the correctness of the party's position. Party candidates espouse ideology when campaigning, interpreting reality to match that ideology. Persons not in complete agreement with this interpretation of reality frequently are looked upon as misguided fools or even inferior beings.

Communists, fascists, conservatives, and libertarians do not focus on particular problems or issues as much as on general, nonspecific value structures of citizens. Religious groups, such as the popular fundamentalist religious parties in North Africa and the Middle East and found in virtually every society today, are a variant of an ideological party in that they, too, shape reality to their image (supposedly derived from God).

Although ideological parties are very much concerned with shaping society in their image, their principal goal is to fill vacant political offices because they perceive the use of political institutions and processes as the most efficient means to bring about their desired reality. However, the major problem with a party based on ideology is that it always seems a little, and sometimes very much, out of date. Ideologies develop out of experiences and perceptions. (Sometimes these experiences and perceptions are borrowed from other societies, such as the Russian Bolsheviks borrowing from German-Anglos Marx and Engels.) Today's world is speedily changing. By attempting to mold that change into old, simplistic values and belief structures, ideologists not only misunderstand the implications and significance of change but also may not even see it. The institutions and processes they build and protect may be out of tune with

Lenin, Engels, and Marx

the present needs of their society. Ruling communist parties in both China and Cuba were forced to change much of their ideology, especially with respect to private enterprise and foreign investments, in order to adapt their societies to the modern world market economy.

That does not mean that members of an ideological party do not possess a visage of the future. They do indeed. However, their future is based upon a past that never was or upon a past that could not possibly be resurrected. The "good old days" are gone forever. Fascists and communists both attempted to go back to a simpler, more orderly lifestyle. Both also were incapable of incorporating citizens' newer changes in their lifestyle and values into the ideologies' own value and belief structures. Both collapsed under the weight of societal change.

Ideological parties tend to be uncompromising with others, making it difficult for a coalition government to function with them. Policy making involves a lot of compromise among policy makers, be they groups or individuals. Pursuit of ideological goals makes this compromise impossible. If ideological parties do compromise, they are accused of deviating from their belief structure; if they do not, they make governance impossible and are blamed for it. Therefore, ideological parties have difficulty cooperating with others to bring about policy changes and are prone to use intimidation, indoctrinations, and even violence to achieve their aims.

On the other hand, ideological parties have offered a systematic way of reforming society. They have led, often forcefully, recalcitrant majorities into a reformed and better society. The Communist Party of the former Soviet Union tore apart the old Russian feudal order and created the institutions and processes of an industrial society. Its ideology could not come to terms with the changes for which it laid the basis; this, however, does not diminish the party's original successes.

Except for religious fundamentalist parties, ideological parties are waning. Parties following strict belief structures, such as the fascists, socialists, and communists, are no longer serious contenders for elected offices. Some parties that began as ideological parties, such as the

European socialists, have given up adherence to rigid belief structures and become more pragmatic in seeking resolutions to their societies' problems and conflicts.

Pragmatic Parties

The pragmatic party has become the most prevalent type today. Parties of this type have programs and platforms, are more representative of one group within society than another, and deal with societal problems and issues on a case-by-case basis. They do whatever will bring them the greatest support at election time despite the beliefs professed by the bulk of the membership. Since these pragmatic parties are usually mass parties, they are composed of, or at least represent, a large segment of voters. Within these parties candidates have the greatest latitude to express their own viewpoints without looking over their shoulders to determine whether party officials approve of what they say.

This freedom, however, often causes pragmatic parties to split into **factions**, which are organized parts of a whole group that frequently fight for dominance within the group or campaign to win elections as a sub-group of the whole party. Usually prominent party activists or candidates for elected office lead factions. In the U.S. Republican Party, for example,

George Washington (center) was the only U.S. president who was not a member of any political party. He disliked the very idea of parties and distrusted factions that were primarily concerned with their own interests.

the conservative faction led by Ronald Reagan in 1980 took over control of the party from the more moderate faction led by former President Richard Nixon and supporters of former New York Governor Nelson Rockefeller. Following the return to moderate conservatism of the Bush presidency, a new crop of conservatives began to vie for the Republican leadership including former Senate Majority Leader Robert Dole, House Speaker Newt Gingrich, Texas Senator Phil Gramm, former Tennessee Senator Lamar Alexander, and news commentator Patrick Buchanan.

Personalist Parties

A personalist party is controlled by the one person who founded it with the sole purpose of getting elected to the highest executive position in the society. Juan Peron of Argentina in the early 1940s formed the personalist party to get himself elected as president. The party outlived him and adopted a loose ideology favoring state-sponsored social change with an emphasis on the worker, which was supposedly advocated by Peron. In Peru in the early 1960s General Manuel A. Odria formed a party to put himself into the presidency. After he died, the party continued for a decade before disappearing. Once the individual who formed the party is no longer able to control it, his/her closest associates take over that role. Since they often fight among themselves for control of the party, these associates end up destroying it.

Political Movement Parties

The final type of political party has been around only since the 1970s. It is formed from political movement, such as the environmental movement. In Europe the Greens, an environmental party, has established itself in virtually every state of the European Union. Its organization is very loose but maintains a very strong commitment to self-government and democratic processes. This loose organization, however, causes factionalism; small groups centered around an individual or small group of individuals break away from the party while remaining true to the movement. In Israel the peace movement became factionalized and has spawned splinter parties. In Iceland the women's movement produced the Women's Alliance, a party that in 1991 captured five seats in Parliament. By the mid-1990s, however, many of these parties appeared to be declining in importance as their support from the electorate waned.

Conservativism and Liberalism

The ideological, pragmatic, personalist, and movement-spawned parties are often divided into two groups: conservative and liberal. Conservative and liberal philosophies originated in Great Britain in the nineteenth century. The height of their importance came at the end of that century when conservative and liberal parties of those names competed for elected office in many countries.

Conservativism

Conservativism originated with Edmund Burke, a British political thinker who was appalled by the removal of the French king by the people during the French Revolution. Burke upheld the legitimacy of government, even a despotic government, against any insurrection. Political institutions, he felt, developed slowly from traditions and customs that the people, in their ignorance and passion, could not understand. Those in government, therefore, must act responsibly on the alternatives available with due deliberation, never in haste, and always adapting tradition to meet new challenges.

The importance of tradition in policy making has been a main pillar in conservatism. Another has been the notion that government is the entity that protects tradition and must instill reverence for it among the people. Traditional social beliefs, values, norms, and institutions must not be allowed to be corrupted by new ones. People cannot be trusted to remain uncorrupted because, left on their own, they cannot overcome the persuasion of those attempting to subvert what is traditional. Therefore, the state must act as the moral agent of society; the state, usually with the cooperation of the religious institutions, has to ensure that the proper, beliefs, values, and norms are maintained.

Moreover, conservatives believe that the individual, not the state, is responsible for personal economic and social well-being. Neither society nor the state is responsible for the misfortunes of the individual. Whether one is starving, homeless, ill, disabled, or uneducated, one must rely on his or her own efforts (or that of the family) to remedy the condition. Although the individual can appeal to others for help, no law obligates one to help others. Conversely, if one is rich and powerful, one is free to dispense what he or she has in any way. Society, much less the state, should never take away wealth from a law abiding individual. In other words, the state should not intervene in the economic relations among the members of a society.

The one action that the state can take to help the individual is to establish and maintain order in society. Conservatives view the lack of order as one of the main ways tradition is destroyed and nontraditional beliefs, values, and norms are brought into society. Disorder also causes disruptions in the normal course of economic relations, upon which a society's prosperity depends.

Liberalism

At the end of the eighteenth century Adam Smith, an early liberal, wrote *An Inquiry into the Nature and Causes of the Wealth of Nations.* He believed that in a world of free competition, gross economic inequalities among members of a society would not appear. He envisioned Great Britain as a nation of small shopkeepers who would be the mainstays of that country's economic power. Smith was among the first of a long line of liberals who, like Thomas Jefferson, Abraham Lincoln, and Theodore Roosevelt in the United States, had confidence in the typical individual to make the right choices to further society's development. Liberals looked upon the individual, not society, as the repository of what was good.

Since they believed in the primacy of the individual, liberals have been suspicious of the interference of the state in the determination of a society's beliefs, values, and norms. Liberals have claimed that individuals develop to their full potential only when allowed the greatest freedom possible. As long as one does not cause physical injury to others or to oneself, there is no need to shackle him or her with laws. Most importantly for the liberal, the individual should have unbridled freedom to self-expression and to savor any creative endeavor offered. In his essay "Liberty"(1859), John Stuart Mill wrote:

> If all mankind minus one, were of one opinion, and only one person were of the contrary opinion, mankind would be no more justified in silencing that one person, than he, if he had the power, would be justified in silencing mankind . . . We can never be sure that the opinion we are endeavoring to stifle is a false opinion; and if we were sure, stifling it would be an evil still.[5]

Until the beginning of this century, liberals generally did not want government to interfere with the legal actions of an individual. Two new notions were added, however, which changed the liberal's concept of the role of the state. The first was that the individual needed protection from the rich and greedy. By the end of the last century, large corporations had

The staff of the Antitrust Division of the U.S. Department of Justice investigate highway construction bid rigging conspiracies, and related areas including utility, water, and sewer lines.   Also investigation of price fixing on the sale of hot mix asphalt, sand, gravel, and stone forms part of a bid rigging case.

made their appearance and with this came the possible exploitation of the consumer and the worker. To protect the latter two, liberals began to demand that the state restrict the power of the corporation through regu-

A jobless father holds tight to his child as police lead him from the demonstration scene in Washington, D.C. Hundreds of out-of-work protestors demanding government relief participated in this Unemployment Riot of 1933. Provisions of the Social Security Act, like unemployment insurance, directly addressed the concerns of these workers.

lations. This resulted in antitrust legislation (i.e., laws preventing corporations from making agreements among themselves to control production, prices, wages, etc.). In the U.S., Federal officials began enforcing these laws, or trust-busting during the administration of Republican President Theodore Roosevelt. Protection of the worker through recognition of the strike was legislated during Democratic President Franklin D. Roosevelt's administration.

Another notion that entered liberal thinking at the same time

President Franklin Delano Roosevelt signing the Social Security Act into law on August 14, 1935. Besides the retirement program, the act also included unemployment and welfare programs to assist workers and children in need.

President Lyndon Baines Johnson signing the Medicare Act on July 30, 1965, as former President Harry Truman and Vice President Hubert Humphrey help him note the hour. The venue was Independence, Missouri, the hometown of Truman who was the first President to approve a health insurance plan to be financed by raising the Social Security tax. There were heavy objections to the concept in 1949 which lightened over the years as healthcare costs escalated, and by 1965 the time was right that Johnson recommend Medicare.

was the need to create a more egalitarian society. The redistribution of wealth from the rich to the poor became embedded in liberal thought due to the tremendous economic inequality that had existed since the 1870s and was exacerbated by the depression of the 1930s. The state was viewed as the only entity that could facilitate this redistribution by increasing both taxation and the welfare of individuals in need.

From both these notions — protection from the rich and transfer of wealth from the rich to the poor — came the liberal idea that the state must intervene in the economy of society for the welfare of that society. Aggressive taxation in the form of an income tax and welfare measures, such as unemployment compensation and workman compensation, medical care, and social security were instituted in the early part of the twentieth century.

The Irrelevance of Both

Like much of what the last century produced, ideologies such as conservatism and liberalism lost most of their meaning. The distinction between conservatives and liberals, perhaps meaningful a hundred years ago, no longer existed. In a documentary of the 1992 presidential campaign, a member of the conservative wing of the Republican Party discussed the importance of the traditional American family. The interviewer asked this conservative to define the "traditional American family," but she was not able to do so. As most sociologists state, the American family has undergone tremendous changes since the 1890s, to the point where it disappears once the children leave home for college or work. In half of American marriages today, one member has been divorced. One-third of American families have a member who is homosexual. One-fifth of American children live with only one parent. Very few of us regularly see our parents, siblings, or other relatives. Where is the "traditional American family" today?

Not only is the family drastically changing in the United States and elsewhere but also our way of life. How we live, where we live, how we prepare for employment, what we do to earn a living, and what we eat, drink, and wear are all much different from the conditions of our grandparents when they were young. Most of this is a result of the ubiquitous technology in our society that forces us to incorporate new products and processes into our life style. Our beliefs, values, and norms are not those of our ancestors a hundred or more years ago because we, in some conscious form, decided to change them. They are different because our society forced these changes on us. Our society's fast tempo of change makes beliefs, values, and norms obsolete in a short period. To adapt to this changing society, as we must to survive, we change our perceptions and therefore our values, beliefs, and norms.

Government's intrusion into our lives is not something about which we had a choice. Yet today we demand even greater and better services from the government than our ancestors did. Whether it is child or elderly care, consumer or environmental protection, up-to-date education, or guaranteed pensions, we want the government to provide it. Does anyone seriously believe we can do without public service or utility commissions, public universities, agencies that determine what is poisonous or unsafe, and government subsidies to those in need? Today's large populations with increasingly complex relationships need services that were not needed in previous times. For instance, in the past 40 percent of the population did not need to have a college degree to find a job; yet today we want even more people to obtain such a degree. With so many more services needed, the concern centers on where the funds are to come from and where they should go, not on whether they are needed. And discussions on these topics require expertise that most of us really do not possess. Discussions on government services have gone way beyond the armchair diatribes of dissatisfied spectators who are basically interested in bringing back "the good old days."

Yes, we long for traditions. Often we would welcome the anchors that tradition offers to our ever-fluctuating lives. We want stability. Conservatives and liberals are both subjected to the same societal forces that shape our lives. Tradition, order, liberty, and equality are all concepts from an age when change was slow and individuals thought they could

FOCUS — ISRAEL'S AND SWITZERLAND'S MULTI-PARTY SYSTEMS

Israel's party structure composed of several party blocs and independent parties. The 1996 elections produced the following results: the Israel Labor Party, received 34 seats in the Knesset; the Unity-National Liberal Party (Likud) composed of the Herut-Liberal Bloc, Integral Land of Israel movement, Peace to Zion, Crossroads (Tsomet), and Gesher received 32 seats; the Sephardi Torah Guardians (Shas), 10; the National Religious Party, 6; the Power-Democratic Israel (Meretz) bloc composed of the Civil Rights and Peace Movement, the United Workers' Party, and Change, 9; Israel for Immigration, 7; Hadash, 5; United Torah Judaism composed of Union of Israel and Torah Flag, together 4; The Third Way, 4; United Arab List, 4; and Homeland (Moledet), 2 seats. Because the Prime Minister was elected by the voters from the Likud bloc and several right of center parties, such as Shas, National Religious Party, Hadash and United Torah Judaism supported him, he was able to lead a coalition government. The minimum number of votes required to gain one seat in the Knesset was 45,774.

Source: Information Division, Israel Foreign Ministry. URL:http://www.israel-mfa.gov.il. December 23, 1996.

Switzerland's has only independent parties, some of which do join together after elections to form coalition governments. In the 1991 elections the following parties gained representation in the 200 member National Council, the lower house of the legislature: the Radical Democratic Party, 44 seats; the Social Democratic Party, 41; the Christian Democratic People's Party, 37; (the above three parties formed a coalition government, actually a grand coalition government;) the Swiss People's Party, 25; the Green Party, 14; the Liberal Party, 10; the Swiss Car Party, 8; the Independents' Alliance, 6; the Swiss Democrats, 5; the Evangelical People's Party, 3; Swiss Party of Labor, 3; the Ticino League, 2 seats. Two seats were filled by independents.

Adapted from Banks, Arthur S., ed. *Political Handbook of the World: 1992.* Binghamton, New York: State University of New York, CSA Publications, 1992. pp. 377-79, 744-46.

control events. They adapted to the changes of their society by simplifying them to their level of understanding.

The conservative tried to hold on to a stable and orderly world when the momentum of societal change began to speed up. Conservativism cannot exist without change. The Enlightenment and the French Revolution released a torrent of pent up dissatisfactions with the way things were; the reaction to them was conservativism. Is it not ironic that the British conservative, the upholder of traditional values, was also the one who, in the privacy of his Victorian bedroom, broke most of the morals he was advocating in public? In the United States, the epitome of the American conservative was the white slave-holder of the South, the Democrat, who produced many offspring in the shack with his African slaves. The liberal, the "destroyer of tradition", was the Republican abolitionist!

Liberalism, which stood for individualism, liberty, and later economic equality, has also lost its relevance. Individualism ceased the moment societies emphasized uniformity in education, ways of life, and work habits. How much of an individual can you be when you have to work from eight hours and up at tasks that hundreds, if not millions, of people perform; eat the same food that others eat; dress as the others; live like others; and communicate like the others? A primary goal of any modern society is to create a sameness among its members so they can be controlled.

Liberty has meaning only when you have the time to be free and when those who could prevent you from doing "your thing" are not constrained from doing so. Since most states have adopted complex administrative processes, laws, and the human or civil rights regimes, curtailment of liberties is no longer an important issue. Many arguments on liberty in post-industrial societies center not on government-citizen relations but on citizen-citizen relations, such as relations among members of a family, a corporation, or an association. Of course, injustices are still committed, and liberties curtailed, however, they are minor problems to the society in general (although not to those directly affected). A major reason for the fall of the Soviet state is that the citizens could no longer be restrained. With modern communication technology (e.g., the computer, satellite dish, fax machines) the state cannot prevent citizens from acquiring and distributing information that could undermine its efficacy if it does not perform well.

Unfortunately for liberals, redistribution of wealth has become a goal of conservatives, too. The issue is not whether it should be done, but how.

Here the answers are as varied as the pressure groups who want to benefit from it and as the theories of economic specialists. The issue is complex, containing many subissues, from health care to capital gains tax to fighting homelessness to labor-management relations. Making the issue a liberal-conservative debate does not resolve any part of it.

The liberal notion of encouraging societal change also has become irrelevant. Change occurs whether or not the liberal favors it. Even when a liberal sees his or her aspirations for society transformed into policies, the tendency is to protect and conserve what he or she worked and sacrificed for, which means no further changes are desired. Thus, the liberal becomes a conservative.

A few decades ago, this author met the perennial socialist candidate for U. S. president, Norman Thomas. The latter complained about how difficult it was to remain a liberal. Many programs he advocated had become policy, and the consequences of some of these he could not understand. Being already quite old, he had run out of new ideas.

In short, unless we turn the conservative-liberal dichotomy into a theory of developmental psychology, neither conservativism nor liberalism will provide any meaningful understanding for the political and social reality around us. We are almost in the twenty first century, but our political perceptions are still the same as those of our ancestors of the 1700s and 1800s.

Party Systems

States are frequently known by the number of viable parties that participate in elections. **One-party systems** are those in which one party dominates the electoral process. In Mexico, for example, the Institutional Revolutionary Party has won all presidential elections since 1923, some by as much as 80 percent of the vote. Other parties are allowed to operate, but they have not achieved a large following among Mexican voters. (Since the mid-1990s economic and social problems have worsened, and the major party is losing support to minor parties.) Another example of a one-party state is the state of West Virginia. Although Republicans do win office at times, more than 80 percent of the candidates elected are Democrats.

In **two-party systems** two parties have an almost equal chance of winning office and tend to alternate in dominance. The United States has a two-party system in which both Republicans and Democrats have strong capacities of winning elected offices, especially the presidency.

Besides the United States few states have a strictly two-party system. Some states have two parties that dominate elections, but other parties also gain representation in the legislature and may occasionally win the presidency. Another strictly two-party state is Jamaica, where the People's National Party and the Jamaica Labour Party alternate in controlling that state's Parliament.

Multi-party systems are those in which three or more parties vie for electoral power, with each capable of becoming the dominant one. None of them may actually dominate the others, but the potential is there. France has a multi-party system in which the Gaullist, Communist, Socialist, Nationalist, and Radical parties compete for elected office. New York City also has several strong political parties; besides the Republican and Democratic parties, the Liberal Party and the Conservative Party also win elected offices.

Usually in multi-party states, parties combine into fronts, blocs, or unions. **Political party fronts, blocs, or unions** are temporary arrangements among several parties formed before elections to win the greatest amount of support from voters. If a bloc or union wins the elections and gains control of the legislature, these arrangements spawn coalition governments composed of the same parties. In France the Union for France is composed of the Rally of the Republic, a party whose roots can be traced back to former President Charles DeGaulle, and the Union for French Democracy, a bloc composed of the Republican Party, the Radical Party, and the Social Democratic Party.[6]

Like party structures, party systems also are a consequence of the electoral system. As mentioned in the chapter on electoral systems, proportional representation leads to multi-party systems whereas plurality/majority systems tend to result in one-party and two-party systems.

The Importance of Parties

Political parties have been one of the most important institutions by which the individual is integrated into modern society. Relations between the individual citizen and the state are made possible by political parties, which in turn benefit by gaining supporters. Parties have given the appearance of including individuals in the decision making process, while using them to propagate the values, beliefs, and norms upon which the state is based. Political parties, then, are the political link between the individual and the society.

Like any successful pressure group, successful political parties do not foster major political change. They operate within the prevalent processes and institutions to affect changes in fragments of the whole societal policy. And as with any pressure group, the "iron law of oligarchy" is the operating principle around which political parties are organized.

However, in some societies since World War II political parties have lost their significance in the political integration of the individual. The degree to which political parties still predominate depends largely on the electoral system used, the secondary functions that parties perform within a society, the technology and financing of political campaigns, and the loyalty of party followers.

The Party and Electoral Systems

Political parties are strong in countries where elected public officials are selected by the proportional representation system. An exception is the United Kingdom, which uses the plurality system. Voters choose a party rather than an individual candidate because the candidate may be unknown in the district in which he or she is running (the party chooses the candidates for each elected office). When only parties appear on the ballot, they must be clearly identifiable to voters; when many parties are involved, the voter must be able to differentiate one from another. Fully aware of this, the parties distinguish themselves by carefully choosing spokespersons who follow the party's platform or program. Since the goal is to develop a platform or program that will maximize the vote, dissension among party members, especially during electoral campaigns, is not tolerated. Therefore, through their platform or program the political parties present public policy alternatives to the citizenry.

Political parties usually are not strong in countries that choose candidates by the plurality/majority electoral system. Candidates, even if they carry a party label, can advocate policies that either are not in their party platform or are in opposition to the party's position. For example, in the United States many Republican candidates have publicly supported the pro-choice position on abortion even though the Republican platform is clearly pro-life. The Republican Party can do little to prevent their candidates from taking a stand on an issue that does not adhere to the party platform. Often state and local candidates will not want national party leaders or candidates to campaign for them because close association with them may alienate supporters enough to vote for an opponent.

This situation in the United States has been aggravated by candidates who are selected through primary elections and do not feel compelled to follow the party line. To most of them, the party is just a label under which to campaign.

Another aspect of the electoral system's influence on party strength depends on who controls and makes decisions about the system. In most countries, especially those that use proportional representation, the electoral system is determined on the national level. Unlike most countries, the United States allows each of the fifty states to determine when elections are held, who can run for elected office, and how votes are counted and by whom. Except for listing the qualifications of those running for president and Congress, setting the date for presidential elections, setting financial contribution limits for national candidates, and ensuring fair campaign practices for national office, the federal Constitution and laws are silent about other elections. The states largely control the electoral process. Therefore, many differences exist among the states about which offices are to be elected (e.g., some states elect lieutenant governors, others do not), who can run in primaries and when they take place, when state government officials are elected (e.g., some states hold elections at the same time as presidential elections, others hold them in off years), how campaigns are financed, and what supervisory role parties have in elections. Parties, consequently, have to conform to state electoral regulations and constituencies more so than to national ones.

Since the United States has such a multiplicity of elected state and local officials, the state governments, by controlling the electoral process (i.e., who, when, how, and for what positions), also determine the contour of the parties. Each state has its own Republican and Democratic parties, organized independently from other state parties and from the national party. In fact, at least 102 political parties can be counted; two for each state plus the two major national parties that emerge every four years. The Democratic Party of one state may have more in common with the Republican Party in another distant state than with its counterpart in neighboring states. All this creates tremendous confusion among American voters and weakens the parties themselves. Even in other federal countries that have elected state and local officials (e.g., Germany, Mexico, and Brazil), this confusion is much lessened by the fact that national law determines the electoral process.

The role of political parties within any society depends very much on the electoral process. As stated earlier, without elections parties cannot

exist. Once elections are allowed to take place, the process of electing candidates determines how the parties organize themselves, what they can
do to win, and how important they are in that process.

Secondary Functions of Parties

To win elections, political parties assume other tasks such as education.
Political party activists taught most Americans' ancestors about U.S. government institutions and processes. In most countries, party functionaries
regularly visit schools to teach citizenship. However, parties educate
beyond the classroom; they also educate the voting public by raising
issues, proposing alternative solutions to problems, criticizing their opponents in power and defending their members in power, and constantly
generating data to support their positions and candidates.

Most importantly, political parties serve as the go-between for the
citizen and the public administration. In the modern, highly complex and
organized societies, the citizen is often incapable of moving through the
maze of regulations, processes, and institutions in order to have a
grievance heard and resolved. In such situations parties frequently
become adjunct interpreters and implementors of public policy. They do
not resolve the grievances; rather they bring together those who have
grievances and those who can resolve them.

Through their contacts in the administration, party officials readily
find out who can solve a citizen's issue. In many societies local party
leaders are the most important political officials to citizens because of their
political expertise, availability, and often, compassion.

Parties also function as charities. When disasters such as fires, floods,
or the death of a family breadwinner strikes families, parties organize
relief efforts from among their membership and donate funds to those
who need them. Party officials have also been known to go to local magistrates and jails to either pay bail or fines for constituents.

In the United States the role of go-between for citizens and administrators and of philanthropists are no longer filled by the parties, perhaps
because local party leaders are no better informed about the administration of society than the citizen and government agencies have been
established to provide charity and relief. Few U.S. citizens even know the
names of their party leaders, much less where to find them.

Parties also, very importantly, give members the opportunity to get
together with like-minded citizens. Parties give support to citizens who

are unsure about the correctness of their beliefs and opinions. Whether it is through meetings, newsletters, newspapers, sports teams, or even theater productions, political parties attempt to anchor citizens in the political process not only because they need to associate with others like them but also because society needs an organization for citizens' political integration. Citizens need not be political loners. Parties guide citizens to think in politically relevant terms and give approval to their beliefs and opinions.

Ultimately, parties define what is politically correct. By defining the problems and determining the possible resolutions, parties fulfill an important societal function. They organize citizens with opinions into acceptable groups by acting as a filter for the innumerable problems and issues that citizens bring. If a citizen's problem is not on the agenda of any party, then it is not important. If a party does not pursue a citizen's solution to a problem, then it is irrelevant.

Another task of political parties is to provide jobs for supporters if their candidates win office. In many societies government positions are awarded to those who took an active role in campaigning for the winning candidate. Selfishness to some extent prompts party activists to work for a candidate since a payoff in the form of a government job is a possibility. In fact, some choose parties based on the likelihood of getting a job through the party. This has been especially true in countries in which charismatic leaders suddenly appear and, by creating a personalist party, have a good chance of winning office.

Although today some look with disfavor on this function of a political party, we have to bear in mind that in the last century, when governments began to grow in size, the task of finding and filling new positions was made much easier by the parties. Party activists were known quantities; winning candidates knew their strengths and weaknesses and therefore were in the best position to match them with available government positions. Rarely have incompetent party activists been placed in high government positions. We also have to remember that testing for jobs was not known then nor is it infallible today.

In some societies with an abundance of qualified personnel for only a few government openings, hiring party activists can be beneficial for two reasons. First, if two or more individuals are qualified for the position, the party activist could be the best choice because his or her support of party policies is assured and he or she also will get along well with other like-minded officeholders. Second, if two or more major parties are contending for elected offices, a change in government leadership forces turnover in government positions and, with those positions filled by the winning party's supporters, brings in fresh ideas on the making and implementing of policies.

Generally in postindustrial societies political parties no longer give jobs to party activists. Bureaucracy has become too professionalized and qualified persons too few to allow parties to fill vacant positions. Unless one has the credentials for the job or passes a proficiency test, party support will not get one the job. And, once one has the job, one can be assured that the job is secure regardless of what party is in control of the government.

A similar task that parties perform is that of an employment agency. Parties try to bring employers and prospective employees together. Occasionally parties have even charged a fee for that service. Since party officials know their constituencies well, they can be rather adept at knowing where and when employment opportunities are available. Therefore, they attempt to have the positions filled with party activists.

Through these secondary functions parties gather many citizens to support and maintain the existing political processes and institutions and to foster change at a developmental pace rather than a revolutionary one. Parties that often win seldom make whole-scale changes because they do not want drastic change. These secondary functions tie the parties to citizens by voicing their demands, wishes, and grievances to the government while at the same time inculcating in them the value of the prevailing processes and institutions. When a party's candidates are elected, the citizens' wants are translated into policies. A party's capacity to effectuate policy determines its strength.

The Technology and Financing of Political Campaigns
When this author ran for city council a few decades ago, the party leaders of the ward he was to represent looked him over, held a meeting of all party members (to which about twenty-five persons showed up), and unanimously nominated him. For the following four weeks he rang the doorbell at every house and apartment in the ward, introduced himself, and left a one-page leaflet describing his credentials and priorities. He also made posters that he banged into the ground at selected places. He received 158 votes in the election, and his opponent who did not campaign as much received fewer than a hundred. This author spent a total of $18.50, to which the party contributed $10.00.

This author still lives in the same house in the same ward. Were he to run for city council today he would have to collect seventy-five signatures of fellow ward residents on a petition to have his name placed on the ballot, and citizens city-wide, not just in his ward, would vote in the election. He would have to hire individuals to hand out well-prepared brochures of his credentials and priorities and put up printed posters, buy radio and newspaper advertisements, and spend much time on the telephone talking to not only potential voters but, more importantly, potential financial contributors to his campaign. The campaign would cost at least $2,500. He would also spend a considerable amount of time with his staff, individuals who would help him develop campaign strategy and prepare advertising and speeches.

Campaigning for public office has changed drastically in the last few decades; not only is it expensive but it also has generated a large industry. In the past parties nominated individuals who were already well known to the electorate, used volunteers to campaign for them, distributed pamphlets containing credentials and speeches of the nominees, and made sure their supporters went to the polls. The nominee usually did not have to worry about campaign finances and strategies, just campaigned where the party leaders wanted him or her to do. In most countries this is still the case today.

However, in all countries campaigning has become extremely expensive because of technological improvements. First, getting around today is easier. One day in September 1992 President Bush campaigned in eight different states by plane. Although it has certainly shortened distances, the airplane also has increased the costs of transporting candidates. The horse and buggy may not have reached many different citizens' groups, but it was a lot less expensive.

Second, radio and television advertising, which is a means of communication that no candidate for almost any position can ignore, gets the candidate's message to large audiences but at a high price. A 30-second spot on a local radio station in a small city can cost up to $1,500; local television $5,000; a television network, up to $500,000. With production costs of up to $500,000, advertising is often the largest portion of a campaign budget. Ads in newspapers, magazines, and trade publications also are not cheap. A quarter-page ad in a small city's newspaper can cost $1,500; a newsweekly $5,000. No wonder candidates try to get as much free media publicity as possible.

FOCUS GERMANY: THE LAW ON POLITICAL PARTIES (SELECTIONS)

24 JULY 1967; AMENDED 31 JANUARY 1994

Section IV: Public Financing.

Article 18. Principles and Extent of Public Financing

(1) The State shall grant the parties funds to partly finance their general activities pursuant to the Basic Law. The criteria for the distribution of public funds shall be the parties' performance in European, Bundestag, and Landtag elections, the sum of its membership contributions and the amount of donations received.

(2) The maximum annual amount of public funds which may be granted to all parties together shall be DM 230 million (absolute limit)(about 160 million 1995 dollars) at the time of entry into force of this provision.

(3) The parties shall receive each year

   1.   DM 1.00 for each valid vote cast for the party list or

   2.   DM 1.00 for each vote cast for the party in a constituency where in the state concerned a list for that party was not permissible, and

   3.   DM 0.50 for each DM received from other sources (members' subscriptions or lawful donations); only amounts up to DM 6,000 per person are taken into account.

In derogation of numbers 1 and 2 above, the parties shall receive DM 1.30 per vote up to five million valid votes.

(4) Parties who according to the final result of the most recent European or Bundestag election have polled at least 0.5% or, in a state election, 1% of the valid votes cast for party lists shall be entitled to public funds in accordance with Para. 3, Nos. I and 3; in order to qualify for payments under Para. 3, Nos. I and 2, a party must meet these requirements in the election concerned. Parties who according to the final election result have obtained 10% of the valid votes cast in a constituency have a right to public funds under Para. 3, No. 2. The first and second sentences do not apply to parties of national minorities.

(5) The amount of public funds may not exceed the party's own annual income. The amount of funds made available to all parties together may not exceed the absolute limit.

(6) Upon the entry into force of this Law the Federal President shall appoint a committee of independent experts. This committee shall initially draw up a "basket" of goods and services that represent typical party expenditures. Using this as a basis the committee shall each year, beginning in 1995 and relating to 1991, determine the increase in the prices of party-relevant items. The committee shall submit the results to the President of the German

Bundestag. The committee shall be appointed for the duration of the term of office of the Federal President.

(7) Before making any changes in the structure and amount of public financing in excess of the price increases established in accordance with Para. 6, the committee referred to in Para. 6 shall submit recommendations

to the German Bundestag. This applies especially to the assessment whether conditions have changed considerably and whether, therefore, an adjustment of the total volume or a change in the structure of public financing is called for.

(8) If a party is dissolved or banned it shall from then on receive no public funds.

Other parts of communication expenses are the telephone and the satellite hookup. Even candidates for local offices easily make one hundred telephone calls a day, most of them not in their free dialing area. Candidates for national office can have one hundred telephone lines in their headquarters. Use of satellite hookups to give a speech or conduct a conference, which is becoming quite popular for candidates whose constituents are spread over a large geographic area, can cost $300,000 per hour.

Printing and distribution costs of pamphlets and other printed messages, which have been the staples of candidates' advertising campaigns, have increased substantially. A small mailing to 10,000 addresses costs about $5,000 including almost $2,500 in postage.

The third area of increased campaign cost is employment of a professional staff. Gone are the days when the candidate and a few friends and party functionaries sat around a kitchen table to devise the campaign strategy and party volunteers distributed the literature. Today poll takers, campaign strategists, campaign organizers, speech writers, advertising agencies, and even the individuals who hand out campaign literature on the street corners are paid professionals. This large staff of people makes a living from the campaign; they are hired (and fired) because of their expertise and competence. Some are part of agencies that do nothing but supply candidates with qualified people to run a campaign.

These professionals are not necessarily home grown or inexpensive. Campaign management has become an international enterprise. Recently winning candidates for president in Argentina, Bolivia and Colombia hired professionals from the United States and Europe. British campaign managers have been hired by American presidential candidates and Canadian parties.

Often these professionals do not care whose campaign they run. They do it for the money and get lots of it. Some top campaign strategists' salaries are more than $250,000 a year. Lucky is the candidate in a small city who does not have to pay someone to run the campaign. In the United States any candidate who needs more than 15,000 votes to win an office has a paid staff.

Political parties no longer can produce all the experts needed to run a successful campaign for their nominees. No matter what country one studies, its winning parties inevitably have used either career campaign professionals who conduct or study polls or electoral results or specialists in public relations or advertising. These professionals are recruited from universities, advertising agencies, the media, or public relations departments of corporations. The problem for these experts is to determine whether they work for the candidates themselves or for the party. Often they prefer to work for a candidate rather than the party because there will be fewer people looking over their shoulders.

Another reason parties rely on paid staffs is that few people have time to volunteer. Stuffing envelopes, making routine phone calls to potential voters, and distributing leaflets are not activities in which people who work all day find relaxing. In decades past women did many of these tasks, if for no other reason than to get out of their house. Today many women work outside or in the home and do not have the energy to perform these menial political tasks. Young persons, 18- to 25-years of age, also do not have time to volunteer because they are either in college or working.

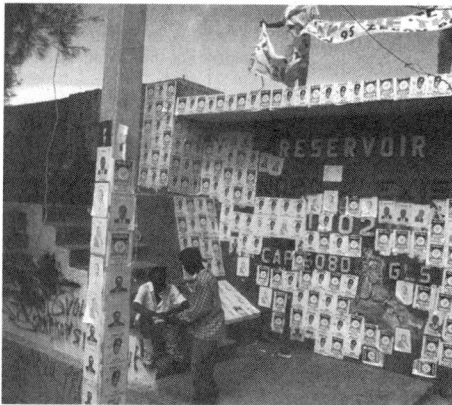
Workers setting up a campaign rally for legislative and local elections in the Caribbean nation of Haiti, in 1995. The electoral process was overseen by U.N.

In the United States a presidential campaign costs more than $110 million; governor $14 million; member of the House of Representatives $1 million; member of the Senate $2.5 million; and member of a state house, $25,000. These averages do not include the cost of primaries. In recent elections some candidates have spent $15 for every vote received. (Total reported campaign disbursements of candidates for U.S. Congress in the years 1991-92 were almost $700 million[7] and in 1996 may have been as high as $1,600 million).

Since neither political parties nor candidates themselves have the funds to pay for campaigns, where do they get the money? From any source possible. In many countries governments subsidize political campaigns of parties that have reached a certain minimum number of votes in a previous election. In postindustrial countries in which the electorate votes for parties rather than candidates government subsidies are the main source of party funding. Part of Germany's law on campaign financing is given as an example. Even in the United States presidential campaigns are subsidized by funds collected through a check on the federal income tax.

The largest source of funds, however, is from private sources — individuals, pressure groups, and corporations. Individuals donate money to candidates and parties, but these contributions are not significant. Although a small donation of less than $25 may show a voter's commitment to a given candidate or party, such a small contribution can cost the party more than it is worth. The expenses of accounting, and reporting it as well as sending an acknowledgement are almost as great as the money received. Therefore, parties and candidates like to conduct fundraisers with a minimum donation of $100. Many countries set contribution limits. In the United States the maximum an individual can legally contribute to a candidate is $1,000 per primary or election. However, voters in all countries have found ways to circumvent these limits by contributing on behalf of children, distant, or even dead relatives and friends and by providing services or goods to the campaign that either are not reported, underreported, or incompletely reported.

In the 1904 presidential campaign, Democratic nominee Alton Parker accused President Roosevelt's campaign manager of pressurizing big businesses for large campaign contributions. Though the charges had basis, Roosevelt strongly refuted them, and won the election with a wide margin.

Contributions of pressure groups and corporations also are limited by law, but just like individuals, they find ways to bypass these limits. Both pressure groups and corporations can actively campaign for a candidate or party without reporting their expenditures; therefore, they may work in conjunction with campaign committees and parties. In 1991 and 1992 political action committees (PACs) alone contributed more than $350 million to U.S. presidential and congressional candidates.[8]

In countries in which candidates rather than parties are elected, contributions can be made to an individual candidate and to a party. Consequently, a contributor can make the maximum donation to several candidates and parties. In addition, a candidate can establish several different accounts to which contributions can be made.

Almost every country requires that candidates keep campaign contributions separate from employment income; however, laws forbidding use of campaign contributions for personal matters often are not scrupulously obeyed. Candidates can encounter legal problems, such as the impeachment of the president of Brazil in September, 1992.

Since contributions from individuals, pressure groups, and corporations are usually larger than funds from a political party, candidates can act more independent of the party organization and the platform (including ignoring any campaign advice) than candidates that are not allowed to receive contributions directly from a nonparty source.

Some candidates attempt to get donations from individuals affiliated with another party. In the United States, for example, Democratic candidates may try to get contributions from Republicans. Since a Republican may not want to give support to the Democratic party but is willing to support a given Democratic candidate, the Democratic candidate, can keep his or her campaign committee (or committees) completely separate from the party's. To this extent, establishment of an independent campaign committee by a candidate is similar to establishment of a personalist party.

In countries in which plurality/majority elections for candidates predominate, campaign committees perform tasks that political parties did in the past. Therefore, the professionalization and expense of campaigning and the ability of candidates to raise their own funds has made the political party a mere appendage in the election process. Unlike parties, however, a campaign committee is temporary, existing only as long as the candidate has the funds to finance it.

Party Loyalty

Lenin, the leader of the Soviet Bolsheviks, coined the phrase **democratic centralism**, which is very descriptive of how party discipline or loyalty can be translated into party unity. What this phrase means is that when an issue or problem arises within a party, everybody participates in the discussion on how to resolve it. In the party hierarchy, each level transmits its perspective or a resolution to the next higher level. Once a perspective or resolution reaches the highest level, that level makes a decision (based on what the levels under it reported) and everyone in the party carries out that decision without question. This implies that everyone in the party helps in the formulation of policy and then carries it out, even if the result is not to one's liking. The question, of course, is why should anyone implement something with which one does not agree? In other words, what is the payoff?

Here we have to deal with two different party members in two different electoral systems — a system in which voters choose among parties and a system in which voters choose among candidates.

When voters choose a party rather than a candidate, those who are elected are beholden to the party for their position and often must follow the party line. Members of a parliamentary party, which consists of those who have a seat in the legislature because they were nominated by the party (e.g., in the United Kingdom), participate in formulation of legislation (not always in harmony with the party's wishes) and then vote as a party. Democratic centralism works predictably in the United Kingdom, Germany, Spain, France, Israel, and in most other parliamentary systems because members who do not vote the way the party wants will be expelled from the party.

However, regular members are not subjected to the demands of the party and cannot be thrown out of it. The party cannot compel someone to advocate something with which he or she does not agree. However, the individual may decide not to support a party with which he or she disagrees and leave the party voluntarily. Party leaders, who must be careful not to advocate policies that might alienate members, are therefore disciplined by those below them, the rank and file.

One way parties in Italy and Japan satisfy their regular members is by organizing as a confederation of smaller parties or factions. Very little general party policy is enunciated; but faction members may be compelled to follow faction policies. If, however, they do not like that faction's policies, they can simply become members of another faction within the same party. In Israel one of the two major parties, the Likud, is actually a confederation of several small parties, each of which campaigns under the Likud label.

Democratic centralism does not apply when voters choose candidates instead of parties. Members of the United States Congress are not compelled to follow any party line; therefore, their voting records may not strictly follow party lines on every issue. Much to the lament of those who would like to see more party-line voting in Congress, party platforms or policies cannot control how legislators vote. Since members of Congress have their own campaign committees they depend on party support much less than their counterparts decades ago. Some party discipline may still prevail in Congress and state legislatures, but

Jimmy Carter, with his wife Rosalyn, after taking the oath of office as the U.S. President, ignored the norms and walked through Pennsylvania Avenue like a common man. He won the 1976 election by directly appealing to the public rather than coming up through party ranks.

often this is due to expectations of receiving a reward in the form of better committee assignments or a leadership position in the Senate or House. Party loyalty disappears when party commendation becomes a liability in the next election. Except for their financial contributions, parties have become dispensable for the average candidate.

For rank-and-file members of parties in plurality systems, democratic centralism approaches the absurd. If you tell me you are a Republican, I would not know anything about your political views. Party labels are a means of identification, not a means of manifesting opinions or beliefs regarding politics or government. Most Americans are Democrats or Republicans because their parents were; most do not know, or even want to know, what their party platform states or what policies it advocates. They vote because of party identification, but without knowing or caring to know for what the party stands. In the United States policies are known for the person or persons who advocated them, not for the party under which these persons won office.

In many other countries, particularly in Latin America, party affiliation is unimportant in elections and regular members do not care for what the party stands. Usually members support parties because of the possible payoff in jobs, contracts, and services they award when they win. The higher the payoff, the more appealing the party is to voters; therefore, party loyalty goes only as far as one's material interests may be satisfied.

The Internationalization of Political Parties

One important aspect of political parties frequently ignored today is their international links to each other. Few parties do not participate within an international network.

The most infamous network of parties was the Communist International, which until the 1950s encompassed communist parties in every country and was completely dominated by the Communist Party of the Soviet Union. After the break between the Soviet Union and China the network split apart, with some parties joining the Soviet Union and the rest joining China.

The Socialist International network dates from the beginning of this century. Virtually every socialist party is a member of this loose confederation, which exchanges information and technical expertise among its members. The Christian Democrats and the Christian Socialists have similar organizations and receive help from Catholic Church organizations and Opus Dei, an international Catholic lay organization devoted to influencing public policy Conservatives are organized into the International Democratic Union, which consists of parties from fifty states including the Conservative Party of the United Kingdom, the Republican Party of the United States, Christian-Democratic parties of Germany and of the Czech Republic, the Liberal-Democratic Party of Japan, Rally for the Republic of France, and the Choice Party of Russia.

Among the Islamic states, several "pseudo-party" organizations link political groups of various countries (so called because many states do not allow elections). Two of the most famous Islamic parties with chapters in most Arab states are the Hizbullah, a fundamentalist group originating in Iran, and Hamas, or the Islamic Brotherhood, which originated in Syria but has been outlawed there. If these states allow open and free elections someday, the various parties will fight each other for dominance.

Both the U.S. Republican and Democratic parties have their own organizations devoted to providing information and expertise to parties in other states. These "institutes," as they are often called, are subsidized with both party and government funds. Some of these institutes have facilitated creation of political parties in Asia, Africa, and Latin America.

Although political parties are identified with the country in which they operate, they ever so slowly are being linked internationally. The parties in the member states of the European Union, which send representatives to the European Parliament, are becoming homogenized. In that parliament the Green parties sit on one side of the socialists who sit next to the Christian Democrats, which includes not only the Christian Socialists but also the Conservatives of the United Kingdom. As these parties work together on European issues they are losing their exclusive attachment to their states and becoming "Europeanized." The extent to which this European model is expanded or copied in other regions, such as the Arab or Latin American states depends on the degree to which the parties can find cooperative links.

How important are political parties today to the functioning of a society? The answer depends on the party's role in the electoral system, the type of secondary functions it performs, the importance of its role in candidate selection and the campaign process, and the level of voter loyalty. The individual's political integration into society is as necessary today as ever. However, the role of political parties in facilitating that integration may have been lessened by the influences of the modern media, pressure groups, and individual campaign committees.

TERMS TO REMEMBER

political party
factions
one-party systems
two-party systems
multi-party systems
political party fronts
blocs
unions
democratic centralism

SUGGESTED READINGS

Burke, Edmund. *Reflections on the Revolution in France and on the Proceedings of Certain Societies in London Relative to That Event.* Edited by William B. Todd. New York: Rinehart, 1959. Re-issue of a classic exposition of the conservative perspective on government and politics.

Garner, Robert and Richard Kelly. *British Political Parties Today.* Manchester, England; New York: Manchester University Press, 1993. Analysis of the modern British political parties and their role in government.

Lijphart, Arend. *Electoral Systems and Party Systems: A Study of Twenty-Seven Democracies, 1945-1990.* Oxford, England;

New York: Oxford University Press, 1994. A good analysis of mostly European political parties and the electoral processes they operate in.

McHale, Vincent E., ed. *Political Parties of Europe*. 2 Vols. Westport, CT: Greenwood Press, 1983. A good description of European political parties.

McPaul, Michael. *The Troubled Birth of Russian Democracy: Parties, Personalities, and Programs*. Stanford, CA: Hoover Institution Press, Stanford University, 1993. An early and speculative study on post-Soviet Union's emerging political actors.

Mill, John Stuart. *On Liberty and Other Essays*. Edited with an introduction by John Gray. Oxford, England; New York: Oxford University Press, 1991. A classic exposition of Liberal thought in the middle of the 19th century.

Remmer, Karen L. *Party Competition in Argentina and Chile: Political Recruitment and Public Policy, 1890-1930*. Lincoln: University of Nebraska Press, 1984. A historical study of the birth and early development of political parties in these two countries.

Riordon, William L. *Plunkitt of Tammany Hall*. New York: E. P. Dutton & Co., 1963. Originally published in 1905, this small book contains the wisdom of a New York City successful politician and advise on how to succeed in politics.

Smith, Adam. *An Inquiry Into the Nature and Causes of the Wealth of Nations*. Edited by Edwin Cannan. Chicago: University of Chicago Press, 1976. Reissue of the classic work on capitalism.

NOTES

1. Roderic A. Camp, *Politics in Mexico* (New York; Oxford: Oxford University Press, 1993), p. 64.

2. Jon Woronoff, *Politics the Japanese Way* (Tokyo: Lotus Press, 1986), pp. 39-76.

3. Jan McAllister, et al., *Australian Political Facts* (Melbourne: Longman Cheshire, 1990), p. 35.

4. U.S. Bureau of the Census, *Statistical Abstract of the United States: 1994*, 114th ed. (Washington, D.C., 1994), p. 286, table 446.

5. John Stewart Mill, *On Liberty and Other Essays*, ed. John Gray. (Oxford; New York: Oxford University Press, 1991).

6. Arthur S. Banks, ed. *Political Handbook of the World: 1992* (Binghamton, New York: State University of New York, CSA Publications, 1992), p. 265.

7. U.S. Bureau of the Census, *Statistical Abstract of the United States: 1994*, 114th ed. (Washington, D.C., 1994), p. 292, table 458.

8. U.S. Bureau of the Census, *Statistical Abstract of the United States: 1994*, 114th ed. (Washington, D.C., 1994), pp. 291-292, tables 455, 459.

Law & Political Institutions

PART FOUR

14
Law and Policy

Few persons in our time have not felt the crushing weight of law on their shoulders. From driving cars to building houses to throwing away garbage, we are made aware of the imperviousness of the rules and regulations that we have to abide. No humans have been subject to more laws than we are today. The law is here, there, everywhere. As hard as we sometimes try, we cannot escape it.

Law and What It Does

Law regulates our behavior. It forbids or forces us to do certain acts. Laws say that if such-and-such is done or not done, punishment will be meted out to the perpetrator. Although the action is punished, the intention behind the action also can be considered in determining the severity of the wrongdoing.

Law is present in all societies, even in the most primitive. Laws often seem like customs. Much of the law is derived from customs; however, the penalty for violating a custom is much different from that for violating a law. If a custom is broken the violator is ostracized but if a law is broken the wrongdoer can be forcibly deprived of life, liberty, or property. If one does something that is against customs, such as wearing the wrong clothes for an event, the group generally avoids that person by not inviting him or her to participate in future activities or ridicules him or her. If one does something that is against the law, however, he or she is fined, jailed, or, if a very serious wrong was committed, executed. All these can be forcibly done to the delinquent, who, of course, would rather not suffer any of these penalties. Of the many norms that we are supposed to obey, only laws can force us to do something that we would rather not do.

Law also is used to resolve conflict among individuals or among groups of individuals. Individuals or groups can resolve conflicts by making agreements or contracts that they promise to obey. Agreements create rights and obligations. A simple agreement is made when I buy a book of stamps from the post office. By taking on the obligation to pay $10 to the clerk, I acquire the right to own the stamps. The post office has the right to receive $10 from me and has the obligation to give me the stamps.

Within a society many types of agreements are made among groups and individuals. Some relationships involving agreements based on custom, words, or written contracts exist between employer-employee, landlord-tenant, husband-wife, parent-child, school-student, seller-buyer, and doctor-patient. Societies developed legal norms for the protection of its citizens; one of these stated that agreements within societies and among societies must be obeyed and that the rights and obligations contained in agreements must be honored. If the two sides have a different interpretation of the agreement, then society decides how to interpret the agreements.

Use of force is illegal except as a **sanction** or punishment for wrongdoing. (If the general use of force was legal, society could not enforce its laws.) In primitive societies punishment for legal wrongdoing is accomplished through self-help (remember Locke?). Everyone in society is prosecutor, judge, and executor of the law. Thus, when someone sanctions a wrongdoer, no one punishes the one who has meted out the punishment. In more advanced societies the making, prosecuting, judging, and executing of the law is centralized into one or several institutions. In the past all functions were under the control of monarchs; today law is under the jurisdiction of three branches of government — legislative, executive, and judicial. Except in cases of self-defense (which is narrowly defined) no one can use force against someone else. Even law enforcement personnel have many restrictions to follow in the performance of their duty.

Laws apply either to everyone in a society or to a specific part of it. If a law applies to a segment, such as the wealthy, the elderly, or automobile drivers, everyone in that segment has to obey it. Law forces us to conform to a uniform pattern of behavior that it establishes. By regulating behavior, law standardizes our actions. Since our interactions today are mostly with strangers and we cannot be expected to voluntarily comply with necessary social conduct, law obligates us to behave in a standard fashion regardless of our values, beliefs, family ties, or where we live within a society. Often in large societies in which people are segmented into many different religious, ethnic, economic, political, professional, and geographic groups, each with its own values, beliefs, and ethics, commonality of behavior in interrelationships is even more important than in the past when societies were smaller. Today law gives society a homogeneous appearance while allowing heterogeneous groupings. The United States, Canada, Russia, Germany and France, for example, have large minorities of Muslims, Hindus, Buddhists, and Jews besides the many Christian denominations. Despite their religious and cultural differences, these people all behave in the same way in public.

When societies were smaller and more homogeneous, law was not as prevalent because common beliefs and values provided the norms for common behavior. Infractions of the behavioral code or of value and belief codes were punished by either the family or close associates. Since common behavior was thought to be a result of shared common values and beliefs, many of these values and beliefs became the law. This notion was strongly advocated by those who preached ethics and morality or religion. However, today values and beliefs are not legislated and society relies instead on behavior modification to keep functioning smoothly and to allow individuals to become integrated.

A thousand years ago the Church established society's norms as they were set down by God and interpreted by the clergy. Infractions were considered sins, and sinners had to seek forgiveness from the Church. Since almost everyone sinned, the Church was considered the most important institution in society. Sinners were made to feel guilty for their infractions and, to avoid eternal damnation, they asked the Church to act as an intermediary between them and God.

Today few of us are not "criminals." Almost everyone has broken a law, such as a traffic law, antilittering law, tax law, antipollution law, or antiharassment law. When we hear police whistles or sirens our first thought is usually, "What did I do now?" We are immediately considered guilty by the law enforcers (e.g., tax auditors, police officers, inspectors).

We usually are guilty, but we just do not want our "criminality" discovered or our offenses punished. We do not ask forgiveness from the maker of these laws, the state, but rather we want to be ignored. (During the Holocaust inmates in concentration camps made tremendous efforts not to be noticed by the guards because they knew that if the guards noticed them they would be abused or even executed.) Those who do not want to be noticed can be inhibited in challenging the authority or even the legitimacy of the state and the actions of its law enforcers. This gives the state and its law enforcers more power over society.

Law, Government, and the State

By regulating behavior, law also confers rights and obligations to persons. **Rights** are norms forbidding certain behavior by others toward the people said to possess these rights. For example, I have a right to speak and government officials are forbidden to prevent me from speaking. A right is a constraint on another person or persons. Rights are derived from a variety of sources (i.e., moral, rational, and religious); however, legal rights, because they are enforced, are the basis for establishing behavior patterns within a society. Some rights are granted to everyone in a society; these are called **civil rights**. But some rights are granted only to certain individuals in a society.

In Chapter 2, law was stated as an "if ... then" statement. The "if" part is the behavior that must not be performed; the "then" part is the punishment or sanction that is applied when the undesired behavior is performed. This implies that someone has the right to carry out the sanction; some laws also identify the office or official charged with this duty.

Everyone does not necessarily possess the same rights. A police officer has the right to stop me from driving my car on a road. I have the obligation to do what he or she tells me to do. However, I have no such obligation if another person (even a tax collector, legislator, or chief of state) requires me to stop. The police officer has the authority, a right given by law, to force me to stop driving.

Society needs many persons to perform the great variety of tasks required to control the behavior of its members. Each person is given distinct authority (rights) to accomplish a particular task. The organization of these many distinct authorities is government. **Government** is the legal institutionalization of rights conferred on persons whose task is to make, enforce, and adjudicate legal social norms. Through law society determines the rights constituting government (rights that those who make, apply, and adjudicate law have). These rights are granted to individuals only for the duration of the particular task of determining or applying these norms. Once the official no longer performs the task, his or her authority ends. Government, then, is a systematic collection of norms determined by society that gives specific legal rights to certain individuals for the accomplishment of particular tasks.

Besides control of citizens' behavior, government officials also have authority to provide services and maintain government operations. For example, a personnel manager has the right to make, interpret, and implement rules regarding the hiring and firing of government employees which has little, if anything, to do with controlling citizens' behavior. Such a responsibility as well as every duty, responsibility, or power within a government is exercised through a right as defined by law.

All the laws of a modern society compose the **state**. However, the state is not only the legal do's and don'ts of a society but also the rights that make up the government. In societies in which no discernible institutions of government exist and all members make, apply, and adjudicate laws, there is no state, although there may be law. The state is the legal order of a society that provides separate institutions for rights dealing with making law, applying law, and adjudicating law. Few persons possess these rights.

Sometimes the same legal order or state may govern several different societies. Until recently Bosnians, Croatians, Macedonians, Montenegrins, Serbians, and Slovenians were governed by the legal order called Yugoslavia. The laws of Yugoslavia applied equally to members of these six societies. When the Bosnians, Croatians, Slovenians, and Macedonians felt that these laws should no longer apply to them and began to develop their own legal orders, Yugoslavia disintegrated as a state. A similar situation developed within Czechoslovakia and the former Soviet Union.

People in different societies can have valid reasons for wanting to break away from an overall state but, regardless of the reasons, the laws of that state become invalid for each society. In developing its own legal order, each society creates its own state.

Organization of State

Members of several societies can decide to cooperatively develop a legal order for extraneous matters that everyone in these societies must obey. The legal order created by such an agreement is minimal because it leaves the creation and enforcement of most of the legal norms to each society. This is a **confederation**. In a confederation each society is autonomous, developing its own legal order; the central government is basically a clear-inghouse of information of and to each society and is responsible for developing the common law regarding those outside the confederation. The resulting state is composed of the laws and governments of each component society and the central government. No confederations exist at this time, although the European Union could become one especially if it adopts a common foreign policy.

In a **federation** each distinct society or geographic area is given juris-diction over certain matters, such as education, transportation, family relations, and housing. Each region can make and enforce its own laws on these matters and can elect the proper authorities, such as governors, leg-islators, and judges. The government and the laws of each part, however, must be compatible with those of the central government. Canada, Germany, Mexico, and the United States are federal states.

In a **unitary** state all laws emanate from the central government. Their enforcement is left to state, provincial, and local officials whom the national government usually appoints, although elected councils and even legislatures may aid in appointment. Although several distinct soci-eties or regions are subject to these laws, the societies do not have a formal role in their formulation. In the past, states with monarchs were unitary states. Today France, the United Kingdom, Colombia, and Saudi Arabia are unitary states.

Whether in a confederation, federation, or unitary state, members of societies have to abide by laws. The difference among these three types is the level at which laws are made and the level at which laws are declared invalid. Laws of a confederation are made at the local and central level and can be invalidated only at the level at which they were made; laws of a federation are made at the local and central level, but the central level can invalidate some laws made at the local level; laws of a unitary state are made and invalidated at the central level. Both locally made law and centrally made law can force behavior upon individuals that they would rather not do. What real difference does it make to you and me what government level made the law we have to abide?

Cities or municipalities make laws, usually called ordinances, that can determine, for example, the type and location of housing built. A city's zoning ordinance, however, can be declared null and void by the state or provincial government. A city's relation to a state or provincial government is always of the unitary type; the latter government validates the former's laws. Yet, in countries that have unitary governments, the national government can invalidate the state or provincial laws. Therefore, cities in these countries may appeal the decision of a state or provincial authority to the national government to have it overturned.

This is not so in federal states, in which national governments cannot invalidate laws made by state or provincial authorities if the laws are within the latter's jurisdiction. If an Ottawa zoning ordinance, for example, does not conform to Ontario's laws, authorities in Ontario will invalidate that ordinance. However, the national government of Canada, whose seat is in Ottawa, cannot overturn decisions of Ontario's provincial authorities. If I build a house in London, I have to abide by London's ordinances. If I build a house in Ottawa, I have to abide by Ottawa's ordinances. At what level these ordinances or laws have been validated is of lesser importance to me than the fact that they exist.

Decentralization of Government

A state in which the national government makes laws that lower levels of government (i.e., provincial or state, regional, county, and municipal) have to follow is said to have **centralized** government. Lower and local units carry out national laws or policies under the scrutiny of national authorities. All local governments, therefore have the same laws. In addition, the national government acts as an arbitrator, if not police officer, for local governments by quickly resolving local problems and disputes.

A disadvantage of centralized government is that national authorities seldom take into account differences in local environments when making laws. These differences may have to be addressed to make the entire society capable of functioning. Furthermore, lower and local units may have to deal with complex issues and problems that the national government is incapable of handling.

Consequently, in the early 1980s a movement to encourage decentralization began among states and international organizations. In a **decentralized** government lower and local levels of government have authority to make and implement laws as long as they are within general guidelines of the national government. Decentralization not only increases the authority of lower and local officials but also prevents them from being able to blame the national government when results of their decisions are not what was expected. Some local officials do not want to accept this responsibility. On the other hand, some national authorities do not want to give up some of their power to determine local matters.

International organizations such as the European Union, the World Bank, and the Inter-American Development Bank, have been encouraging decentralization by making policies for and loans to local governments, bypassing national governments. These organizations have found that national governments are often unnecessary impediments to the development and implementation of policies that directly affect people. Often national governments are too far removed from the problems people experience, which impedes their ability to make a viable society.

Cooperative mechanical harvesting in rural Egypt — promoted by the World Bank as part of its program to gradually dismantle the role of the state through decentralization and privatization. An increase in the role of local officials and involvement of elected village councils encourages democracy and pluralism.

International Law

Although the state is the principal source of legal norms, lawmakers and law enforcers also are obligated to obey international law. **International**

law involves two separate bodies of legal norms. Customary law develops through the customary interactions of societies. Examples of customary law are the respect to the white flag of surrender during a battle and the twenty-one gun salute which is given when one head of state visits another. Conventional law is created by gatherings of individuals or groups of individuals authorized to represent a state to make treaties, agreements, and protocols.

A traditional concern of international law has been the regulation of war. Such treaties establish war protocol, including the protection of victims of war and the treatment of prisoners of war. Although many norms regulating war have originated from treaties, most are the product of custom. People have been fighting each other a long time and have developed certain rules about how to go about it.

Conventional international law is expanding in three areas as societies increasingly interact with each other. (Since not enough time has passed to develop customs in these areas, laws invariably are the conventional type.) First, standardization of regulations involving societal interactions, such as trade, travel and communication, has begun to be addressed through agreements such as the General Agreement on Tariffs and Trade and the North American Free Trade Agreement and by members of the European Union. Second, heightened concern for those who are exploited, oppressed, or terrorized has led to the enactment of human rights legis-

The International Court of Justice at the Hague, the Netherlands, resolves disputes among nations by applying the provisions of the international law.

lation. Codes of behavior for those with authority either to make or enforce laws require adherence to norms meant to protect every person's life, liberty, and personal security. Third, concern with the environment has produced new rules that oblige state officials to retard its degradation. Treaties dealing with environmental issues establish norms that were not even thought of forty years ago.

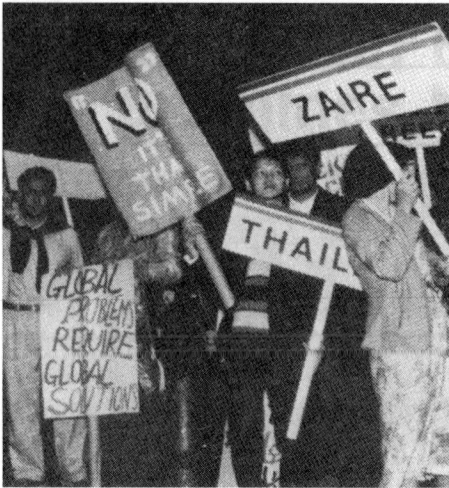

An anti-drug demonstration, Geneva, 1989. U.N. figures indicate the monetary value of traffic in illicit drugs throughout the world to be second only to that of trade in armaments.

International legal norms must be abided by authorities who make and enforce legal norms in a society even though the norms did not originate in that society. Just as the laws of one state are valid for individuals belonging to several different societies, international law is very much part of the law that all members of modern societies have to observe. Sanctions can be levied on individuals or an entire society if norms made by intersocietal or international conglomerates of states are disobeyed.

For example, the 1936 Convention for the Suppression of the Illicit Traffic in Dangerous Drugs requires state officials to charge anyone involved with narcotic drugs with a crime. Article 2 stipulates that those states that have ratified the treaty

make the necessary legislative provisions for severely punishing, particularly by imprisonment or other penalties of deprivation of liberty, the following acts — namely:

(a) The manufacture, conversion, extradition, preparation, possession, offering, offering for sale, distribution, purchase, sale, delivery on any terms whatsoever, brokerage, dispatch, dispatch in transit, transport, importation and exportation of narcotic drugs, contrary to the provisions of the said Convention;

(b) Intentional participation in the offenses specified in this Article;

(c) Conspiracy to commit any of the above-mentioned offenses;

(d) Attempts and, subject to the conditions prescribed by national law, preparatory acts.

This treaty forces lawmakers and law implementors to punish anyone committing these offenses even though their society tolerates use of narcotic drugs. Should these officials not do so, they and their society could receive sanctions, such as breaking of diplomatic relations, and suspension in international organizations.

Law and Policy

Despite its overbearing influence on our lives, law is just one element of policy. **Public policy**, the sum of all practiced norms by which members of a society live, is composed of many elements besides law, such as customs, religious canons (i.e., rules made by religious authorities), accepted behavioral patterns, and rules made by organizations from corporations to social clubs. Each of these components influences the others as well as the law. At different periods of societal development, some sources of norms are predominate. For example, customs and accepted behavioral patterns have been the most important norms in primitive societies, whereas religious canons were the dominate norms in societies in which belief in God was the unifying factor. The rising importance of law today is due to the declining influence of customs and religious canons. Their decline in turn is due to the increase of large, dense populations disbursed over large territories and to technological innovations that make old practices and beliefs obsolete.

The Purpose of Policy

Public policy's ultimate purpose is to hold society together and enhance its viability. Whether this is done through customs, law, or another means is not the primary concern. What is important is that the society's survival and growth in the face of challenges from other societies or the environment is accomplished with the least loss and the most gain over the long run. The purpose of public policy, therefore, is to ensure society's survival.

Of course, it is the capability of each society to surmount internal and external obstacles that ultimately determines whether it will endure. Public policy not only keeps a society's own members functioning together in relative contentment but also affects its interactions with other societies. Consequently, public policy is seen as the "glue" that holds a society together and as the catalyst determining the global environment in which it exists.

FOCUS U.S. HEALTH POLICY: WHAT IS IT?

Health policy includes not only all the laws, rules, and regulations that the national government makes, but also those of the state or provincial and local governments. These are in addition to the policies of medical organizations, insurance companies, hospitals, and pharmaceutical and medical equipment suppliers. To these we have to add the practices and values and beliefs of those in health care professions and the behavior, beliefs, and expectations of those receiving care.

As a whole, health policy cannot be understood by anybody. At most only some fragments of this policy can be understood by a few specialists. When referring to health policy today, we usually only think of the national government's role in paying for the cost of basic health care, but this aspect is but a small fragment of national health policy, not to mention of society's. Much attention has been given to this very specific problem. Yet, is this the main concern of the ill hospital patient, his or her doctor or family and friends concerned about the patient being well again?

To whom is the question about the national government's role in paying for the costs of health care an important question? Probably to you and me as taxpayers. But, to be very honest, I am not sure that you think it is so important. People who do not have much income and therefore cannot pay much more in taxes are not that concerned. Neither are those whose incomes are so high that they can afford almost any tax levied on them.

Groups that think it is important are those that do not get medical attention now but think they will once the national government pays for it, and those that will get paid for either the medical care they are currently giving and not getting paid for now or for the additional patients they will treat. Another concerned group is composed of individuals who will financially gain by it. I belong to this group, too, because I want to pay less for insurance and less for medical treatments my family and I receive. Others belonging to this group are insurance companies and equipment suppliers who want to sell more of their services or products, a considerable segment of the population.

However, government payment of health care is a crucial issue only for those who might get treatment that they are not getting now. For others, issues about funding for research, preventive health measures, education, drug use, and marketing of experimental drugs are of greater concern. All these are part of health policy that is seldom discussed.

All these issues of health policy will be resolved eventually. Society has a way of focusing on some issues while allowing others to develop their own solutions. And even those issues upon which the spotlight is focused will ultimately be resolved one way or another. If a society is going to remain viable, it has to possess a healthy population. Somehow this will be achieved.

The question is whether laws are going to impede or support this goal. Wrong laws can be made ineffective by other components of health policy; right laws can correct some components of health policy that may be out of tune with the times. In either case, the fragment of health policy dealing with the national government's role in paying for health care costs is a very small part of a much larger and more complex issue.

Since the viability of society is the principal task of public policy, the viability of individuals within that society is of lesser concern. Individuals have always been sacrificed for the welfare of the whole. Soldiers die for the good of their societies; some men and women were enslaved for the same purpose. Still others, such as the homeless, the destitute, and the illiterate, are often left to fend for themselves without help from society because they are dispensable and use resources that could be used for more efficacious purposes, such as strengthening the industrial and service sector to make the economy stronger. Although individuals within society show great concern for the plight of the downtrodden and many make sacrifices to help them, few societies' public policies do so. In those societies in which public policy does offer aid to the destitute, the motivating factor is that the society either needs them for work, does not want other segments of its population to become "infected" with the same problems, or does not want to be sanctioned by members of other societies.

As stated before, the poor often act outside the norms of society because they have little, if anything, to gain by conforming to them. When those who live in misery threaten the functioning of society, authorities use public policy, usually in the form of law, to curb their activities and behavior. For example, little attention is paid to drug pushers in rural areas because they do not affect society much; however, in cities these criminals are the focus of lawmaking and enforcement because they disrupt city life and cause various problems from property destruction to homicides.

The Complexity of Law and Policy

Because law is so ubiquitous today, especially in industrial societies, *public policy* and *law* are terms used interchangeably. Nevertheless, law's nomenclature is not so simple. Rules, statutes, regulations, edicts, decrees, orders, rulings, directives, ordinances, stipulations — all these, in as far as they are derived from laws and are made by agencies of a state, are themselves considered part of law, and therefore public policy. Just as law is composed of so many segments that no one can know it wholly, public policy, which is composed of many more components than law, is even less understandable as a whole. Consequently, *public policy* is an abstraction, a shorthand term for an inherently unknowable and vast aspect of society. At best we can refer to a specific law or policy dealing with a certain subject. Even then we need to be cautious because a policy or law on one subject, such as health care, can involve numerous complex issues.

Should Law and Policy Be Moral and Just?

Frequently attributes are attached to law and policy that in themselves are praiseworthy but in actuality are not necessarily related. I am referring to terms such as moral, just, equal, rational, decent, and correct and proper. Most of us want moral, just, equal, rational, decent, correct and proper laws and policies. Unfortunately, the test of a good law or policy is whether it has furthered development of a society, not whether it is just or moral. A just law or a moral law that caused a society's death is a bad law. So, too, is a rational and decent law that causes chronic disruptions in the long-term functioning of a society.

Many U.S. citizens believe abortion is immoral. If the morality of one group of people had been translated into law, would they have wanted to pay the social or economic costs for the maintenance and development of the more than forty million unwanted children who would be alive today if they had not been aborted in the years since *Roe v. Wade*? Since forty million U.S. citizens currently have no health insurance coverage,[1] what would the state of health care be today if forty million more were added to the list? Could the U.S. educational system have handled forty million more students without increasing budget deficits? Abortion for U.S. society, as for other societies, is a means of population control which must be endured for society to remain viable. If abortion was made illegal, it would continue to be performed if for no other reason than persons wanting one would find a way to have it. Large segments of society would support persons seeking illegal abortions because abortions fill a need for society.

Although today we consider slavery repulsive to our values, it nevertheless was an important means by which past societies persevered. It ended when the social costs of its maintenance were too excessive for the good it provided. Slaves by the middle of the last century were demanding education, health care, and property that the slaveholders could not afford. To keep the slaves, slaveholders had to increase repressive measures, which made the slaves even more reluctant to cooperate. Furthermore, introduction of industrialization required cheap labor, which freed slaves could provide. Maintaining slaves was more costly for the slaveholder than paying wages to freed slaves was for the factory or plant manager.

Slavery was eventually abolished through law. However, another important social institution went by the wayside without passage of law. The family farm or homestead has not been outlawed, yet it is almost gone. For an industrial or postindustrial society food production on small farms that use methods and tools of a bygone era is inefficient and no longer cost effective. In the United States and Canada the appearance of the large industrial-agricultural combine hastened the end of the small farm. In addition, higher wages in factories and city life enticed workers from the farm to the factory. With a dwindling supply of farm workers, the family farm could not increase production or expand to compete with the industrial farm.

Ironically, in France, Japan, and even to an extent in the United States, law artificially maintains the family farm through subsidies to farmers and trade barriers; these are the means by which states legally attempt to keep an obsolete social institution in harmony with the values of society. However, these values are changing as more citizens in these countries want cheaper food from other countries and question the costs involved in maintaining a traditional way of life for a part of society. In addition, the world trade industry is pressuring states to stop inefficient food production. Legal attempts to protect the family farm may not be sufficient because these other components of public policy are more dominant.

Abortion, slavery, and family farming are examples of relationships between law and public policy. Values are involved in all three. The value of maintaining the family farm is no longer consistent with the value of supplying cheap, efficient, and healthy food. In time demand for cheaper food will force the state to stop giving support to the small farm. Abortion, which is not a simple issue to analyze from a moral or ethical standpoint (and which few people are willing to do), became part of public policy after examination from a legal rather than a moral perspective. Slavery also was outlawed not because of its moral implications but because it became economically difficult to maintain. It was destined to disappear in all industrial societies, even without a civil war, and has in every one.

Policies develop according to the dynamics and momentum of a society. Given the innumerable variables affecting and determining policies, it is egotistical and irrational to assume that a policy must be moral, ethical, or rational. Why should a moral variable override all the others? Public policy is not personal policy. If an individual can determine his or her own policy, then society also must be able to determine its own, which may not contain the same variables that determine an individual's actions.

We make decisions without being aware that we made them, but even the decisions that we consciously make are influenced by variables of which we are not aware. These variables reside unconsciously within our mind yet affect what we do, think, and believe. We do not even remember most of the conscious decisions we have made in the past; yet these decisions also influence our present and future choices. Who we are and what we will become are invariably linked to the decisions we make consciously and unconsciously and to the many variables that influenced them.

Decisions made in the past consciously and unconsciously affect decisions we make today and in the future. Through interactions with others, variables in decision making become prioritized, as in a hierarchy. The importance of the variables also changes as the challenges individuals face within their society changes and the environment in which these challenges have to be surmounted changes. The accumulated and prioritized decisions made by individuals throughout the history of a society determine its present public policy.

A society develops incrementally and sequentially through the decisions diffused by its members; these decisions become part of its policy. Whether through law or other norms, society discards needless fragments of past policies and brings to the fore new ones to keep in tune with present challenges. Societies incapable of recognizing or surmounting new challenges disappear.

Since coercion is used in their enforcement, law and custom may be two sets of norms that, if too rigidly applied, may cause a society's end. Members of a society who cannot adapt their laws and customs to changing challenges and environment and who allow norms from other sources to surface prevent their society from developing policies that would enable it to survive. The Ottoman Empire collapsed in part because its laws and customs could not adapt to the European technology of the time. Iran, Saudi Arabia, and Libya today face a similar future. Their laws and customs discriminate to the point of abusing virtually half their population, namely women, and relegate them to economic inactivity. Saudi Arabia, in fact, imports workers from other societies rather than allowing women to become active participants in its economy, which is now demanded by the international economy. Societies that do not adapt their laws and customs to this demand cannot compete with other societies that have adapted.

When Is a Law a Law?

A very difficult question for any individual to answer is, When do I follow the law? When is a law a "law"? This problem is often subsumed under the heading "the legitimacy of law." If a lawmaking authority makes a law, does it mean that I have to obey it?

Positive Law and Natural Law

One school of thought, **positive law**, unequivocally answers "yes" to these questions. As long as the law was made by a duly authorized law making agency I have to follow it, regardless of how absurd I think the law (or policy) is, unless another has replaced it. Law enforcement personnel (i.e., police officers, auditors, and inspectors) are hired to enforce the law regardless of whether they agree with it. For them the law is a set of norms that has validity on its own. Other types of norms in public policy must conform to legal norms.

Another school of thought, **natural law**, states that other norms must validate law. Since lawmakers are fallible beings, the laws they make can be wrong or bad. Law is an aspect of public policy that is legitimatized by other norms, such as morality or ethics, reason, function, "nature," word of God, and custom and tradition. Followers of natural law believe that law alone is at best only a guide for behavior. I have to obey the law only if it conforms to a "higher law." In societies with a population of homogeneous values and beliefs, the school of natural law predominates; these values and beliefs validate the law. In other societies in which the government is determined to institute a particular set of values and beliefs, such as fascism or communism, those values and beliefs give legitimacy to the law. Today some societies are controlled by officials imbued with a religious fervor, such as in Iran, where only laws in harmony with the interpretation of the Koran must be followed.

Law as a guide to behavior also is found in societies in which customs are followed without the need for enforcement. In Latin America, for example, the saying *se obedece, pero no se cumple* (one obeys but does not comply with) means that laws are acknowledged but often are ignored because social pressures make established behavioral patterns the norm to follow. On highways in most countries drivers seldom comply with low speed limits because hardly anybody ever does. Those that do comply are honked at and made to go faster, especially when traffic is congested. Great chaos would occur if every driver on a highway followed a different speed, or traveled according to the speed limit in congested traffic. (Speeding tickets are most often given as a way to collect revenue for the state. Officers who give tickets do not care whether the "criminal" went five or twenty miles above the limit.) Most members of a society must conform to established behavioral patterns for that society's long-term viability. How this is achieved is of lesser importance.

In the United States arguments between followers of positive law and the followers of natural law are seldom heard mainly because of the unique method by which American society resolved this problem. The U.S. lawmaking agencies make policy that is enforced and obeyed. Individuals are compelled to comply with the law regardless of the norms they value. This is by-and-large the positivist perspective.

However, two institutions, which are in the judicial branch of government validate the law in the United States: the supreme courts and the juries. The supreme courts have the power of **judicial review** (i.e., the power to declare any law or act of government unconstitutional and therefore null and void [as if it never existed]). Using constitutions as a frame of reference, the supreme courts interpret these laws or acts in light of prevailing norms and decide whether they are valid. Most U.S. laws are never brought before a court for review and are obviously valid. However, if the courts decide a law is not legitimate it is simply not a law.

Juries may also invalidate law simply by not convicting the defendant of a crime for which the evidence clearly indicates guilt. This is called **jury nullification**. For example, many local governments passed antipornography ordinances, but many juries did not convict those who sold or distributed material banned by these laws; therefore, the laws are not valid. Juries also may not convict a defendant if they believe the sentence that will be imposed is too harsh for the alleged crime. In deciding guilt or innocence juries apply many sets of values and norms. Therefore, the supreme courts and juries validate law by judging it according to the other sets of norms that influence and compose public policy. Under this process the law that one is compelled to obey conforms to the "higher law" as interpreted by courts and juries.

Nevertheless, U.S. courts and juries have validated laws that were clearly not in the long term-interests of American society — slavery, "sep-

National Association for Advancement of Colored People (NAACP) under the leadership of Professors Charles Houston and William Hastie formerly of the Howard University Law School vigorously challenged the segregation in the United States. In 1936 the two professors hired their outstanding student Thurgood Marshall (Supreme Court justice 1967-91) as NAACP's counsel, and the team achieved numerous victories before the Supreme Court that outlawed racial discrimination in areas such as education, housing, transportation, electoral politics, and criminal justice.

arate but equal" legislation, and the disenfranchisement of minorities. In time the validity of these issues was reversed, sometimes by the courts themselves; but many people suffered grievously because of the original laws.

When Should the Law Be Obeyed?

Courts and juries can take too much time to make a decision which may be wrong. So, when do I follow the law? An easy answer is: always. By automatically following law, I do not need to decide how I should behave. I, in effect, let the lawmaker decide, even if I do not like the decision. Most of the time this works fine because the risks of being sanctioned for disobeying a law are not worth performing the forbidden behavior. That is why I stop at stoplights and usually obey traffic signs.

Sometimes, however, I disobey a law that I think is bad or wrong. In these cases I do not allow the lawmaker or law enforcer to set my behavior. Obviously, I take the risk of being apprehended and sanctioned for a crime that I have committed. If the risk of being apprehended is low and the sanction small (e.g., a low fine), then I might gain by disobeying the law.

But if the risk of being apprehended is high and the sanction is high also, then I think twice before breaking the law. I might still do it, perhaps to bring the law's shortcomings to the attention of others or to force those responsible for the law to realize its consequences. If enough persons pay attention to my plight and sympathize with my disobedience, then the law may be repealed. In this situation my norms and those of my supporters become the "higher law" with which the "bad" law did not conform.

Individuals who have said "no" to prevailing laws have caused much social legislation, ranging from labor unions' ability to strike to civil rights. These "criminals," who exist in virtually every society, bring forth other norms to negate laws. These other norms, if accepted by a significant part of society, become the determinants of that part of public policy that formerly was made through law.

Ineffective Law

If a law is not enforced, it loses its effectiveness. An **ineffective law** is a law that is not enforced and therefore is equivalent to no law. As societies change and new norms develop among its populace, those with the authority to enforce the law (who are part of that populace) can decide that it is not worth their effort to enforce certain laws. In this situation norms other than law determine public policy.

In fact, nonenforcement of law is one of the main methods by which makers of public policy keep obsolete laws from endangering the viability of society. Law, which does not change as quickly as other components of public policy, may become a hindrance to effective functioning of society. Therefore, law enforcers must become enlightened to which laws to enforce and which not to enforce.

Abuse of Law

Since law is the only normative order that people can be forced to comply with, it can be used to serve the illegitimate purposes of the few. In both the making of law and the enforcement of law individuals can discriminate against large segments of the population and can prevent whole societies from moving in the direction in which other components of public policy propel them.

Discrimination

We are all aware that those who make laws carry the prejudices, biases, and stereotypes of the society from which they come. Invariably, the laws they make will reflect these weaknesses. Since racial minorities and women often have been considered disadvantaged and are therefore underrepresented in lawmaking positions, laws have discriminated against them. Despite a growing awareness of the rights of racial minorities and women, men who impart antiminority and antiwomen biases are still the lawmakers in most societies.

The law enforcers also carry biases against minorities and women. Frequently it is they, more so than the lawmakers, who cause unfair discrimination. By either selecting the laws they want to enforce or interpreting

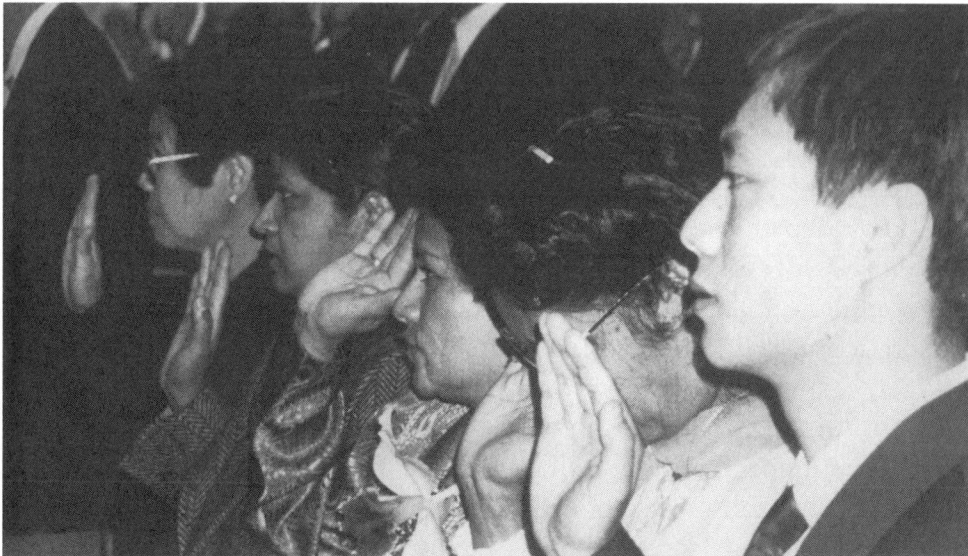

The citizenry of the United States and other developed nations is characterized by a diversity of religions, cultures, and races. Today law gives society a homogeneous appearance while allowing heterogeneous groupings.

laws according to their biases, law enforcement personnel choose not to prosecute many crimes committed against minorities and women and to prosecute many more crimes committed by members of these groups than those committed by others and to request more severe punishment. For example, an African woman shouting rape in a white neighborhood of a European or North American country will encounter difficulty in getting any law enforcer to listen to her. A white woman shouting rape in an African section of a European or North American country will have many law enforcers listening to her and will be presented quickly with several possible perpetrators to accuse.

Personal Gain and Imposition of New Ideology

A far more pernicious misuse of law occurs when laws are made either for the material benefit of those who make them or for an attempted transformation of the values of the members of a society. Many lawmakers, from legislators to bureaucrats to judges, use their authority to make policy (law) to enrich themselves and their allies (e.g., relatives, friends, business partners, and political followers). The practice of writing rules, especially concerning taxation, and making judicial decisions that hurt one's enemies and aid one's associates has occurred for a long time despite constant severe criticism and is still very much entrenched in virtually every society. Certainly not all, or even most, persons who make law do so to enrich themselves. Yet this phenomenon occurs in every society, in some more openly than in others.

Compared with other abuses of law, the use of law to enrich oneself and one's associates may not be very harmful to society as a whole if it does not deplete society's resources. The budget and gross national product (GNP) of industrial societies are so huge that the legal pilfering of a few million dollars would not affect the welfare of these societies. A billion dollars, which is less than a tenth of a percent of the U.S. federal budget, seems like a tremendously large amount of money to you and me, but American society as a whole would hardly miss it. On the other hand, one hundred million dollars may be the entire GNP of some societies, and the legal misuse of even a few hundred thousand dollars may have severe social consequences. Lawmakers and implementors can easily make that amount of money disappear into personal bank accounts; however, the resiliency of a society to such abuses will decide whether it survives.

The resiliency of a society is tested even more strongly when its policy makers pass laws that attempt to remake society entirely. Often policy makers attempt to impose a value system upon a society whose members either are not ready for it or were opposed to it because of prevailing values. Communists and fascists in the twentieth century attempted to use law to change their societies. Both failed miserably, causing the needless death of millions and pain and suffering to virtually every member of their respective societies. Germany is still recovering from the effects of the Nazi regime's laws; and the length of Russia's recovery from communism is difficult to estimate.

Religious fundamentalists are also guilty of attempting to legislate a value system that is out of sync with the beliefs of most other members of their society. When these fundamentalists cannot get others in society to agree with their beliefs, they attempt to force acceptance through law. Although religious fundamentalists are particularly well known in the Middle Eastern countries, they have made themselves heard in virtually every society, including the United States.

Unlike communists and fascists who tried to bring about a new order, religious fundamentalists attempt to prevent further changes in society, specifically changes that endanger their practices and beliefs. They view the changes in social relations caused by technology as inventions of a nefarious entity such as the devil. Their laws would prevent change in social interactions and to exclude technologies that cause these changes. Among the latter, for example, are contraceptive devices which have resulted in profound changes in relations between men and women. (One type of technology fundamentalists are generally not opposed to is that which they could use to clobber their opponents.)

Those who want to legislate their beliefs and values on the rest of society invariably will attempt to prevent any dissent from being heard by using laws to circumscribe what will be published or seen or heard over the air waves. Opposing political activity is made illegal. Through selected enforcement of the law, troublemakers and opponents are jailed, executed, or banished. The atrocities committed in the 1930s and 1940s by Germany and the Soviet Union were, with very few exceptions, in accordance with the law. The torture and execution of thousands of dissidents in the 1960s through 1980s in China, Indonesia, Argentina, Brazil, Chile, Mozambique, and other countries were also protected by law.

Maintenance of Power

Law is also used to silence, jail, execute, or banish political opponents of government leaders who want to keep their positions. Such leaders, who adamantly believe that they are indispensable for the growth of society, use law to maintain their power, especially when a large portion of society believes that they should retire. Papa Doc Duvalier of Haiti made a law proclaiming himself president for life. Alfredo Stroessner of Paraguay did the same. Mobutu of Zaire used all types of legal devices to prevent elections from being held because he knew that he would lose. Most of the world's dictators use law to keep themselves in power. In addition, dominant political parties often use their lawmaking and law enforcement powers to keep opposition parties from threatening them. The Institutional Revolutionary Party of Mexico, for example, has legally manipulated the political process to its own advantage.

Constitutions

One way abuses of lawmaking power have been curtailed is with development of a constitution. Since the end of the eighteenth century states, to be considered modern or advanced, have had to show that none of the laws made or implemented were arbitrary. The primary reason for establishing constitutions was to guarantee equal protection under the law to everyone, which meant imposing limits on the power of government officials.

Functions of Constitutions

As a part of societal policy, constitutions are important because they detail the organization of the state. All constitutions limit the power of government by prohibiting, or **proscribing**, certain acts. They also spell out, or **prescribe**, the procedures government must follow in the areas it can act. For example, some constitutions curtail government power by stipulating that an accused person must be charged with a crime within a short period after arrest, which is called a writ of **habeas corpus**, or that an accused person is considered innocent until proven guilty. Other constitutional provisions establish the areas in which laws can be made, and specifically exclude other areas from government jurisdiction. Some constitutions require government to provide education or give other types of support to the elderly, unemployed, poor, or disabled. Some constitutions also restrict government's authority in such matters as the rights society's members possess. "Congress shall make no law ..." begins the First Amendment of the U.S. Constitution that enumerates some of the basic rights of Americans which cannot be changed by law,

Signing of the U.S. Constitution, Philadelphia, 1787. The fifty-five delegates to the Constitution Convention presided over by George Washington endorsed the document that has become a blueprint for freedom and justice throughout the world.

such as the right to speak freely, the right of the free press, and the right to worship.

By specifying the procedures that government officials must follow, constitutions also limit their power. For example, a provision may state that due process of law must be followed when a person is brought to trial. This implies that passions, biases, and other influences that might sway the decision of the court should be eliminated or at least kept under control through rules that outline the many steps involved in achieving a just verdict. For some who have witnessed a crime the sometimes lengthy process is viewed as a waste of time or resources; however, unless this process is always followed, the innocent could be unjustly convicted and punished or the guilty could be allowed to go free.

Constitutional procedures also determine who has the authority to do what. Generally the function of legislatures, executives, and judiciaries are explicitly stated to avoid conflicts over jurisdiction. Furthermore, by detailing how these institutions are to be organized, constitutions provide voters insight into the governmental process and consequently give them some control of who determines their laws.

Although all the laws of a state are normally in harmony with its constitution, the constitution itself is not law. As we stated in Chapter 2, a law is an "if...then" statement. In constitutions no "then" phrase is added to the "if" part (i.e., no punishment or sanction is stipulated). The U.S. Constitution's Fourteenth Amendment, for example, states that no one can be deprived of "life, liberty, and property, without due process of law." Yet in 1942 the federal legislative, executive, and judicial branches all supported the forceful removal of some American citizens to "resettlement areas" (i.e., concentration camps) with complete disregard for the law. These Japanese Americans, were not compensated for property loss incurred or given indemnity for their inability to continue to earn a living. No sanction was ever levied against any government official involved in this obvious violation of constitutional rights.

In addition, when an illegal seizure of government, a **coup d'etat**, occurs, constitutional provisions cannot be followed because leaders of the coup forcibly remove the constitutional functionaries from their offices. Unfortunately, these leaders are seldom punished because they control the means by which force is used. Invariably coup makers claim that their new laws follow the rules or norms of the constitution. Constitutions do not specify sanctions in such cases.

How important a constitution is to a society depends in part on how its citizens view it. First, a constitution can be seen as providing legitimacy to government. Although seldom approved by the citizenry, a constitution implies consent by those governed of those who govern. Since the right to rule emanates from the constitutions, it gives the appearance of popular approval to government.

Second, a constitution can be viewed as a blueprint of government. Just as the blueprint of a building tells the location of various components, a constitution tells what the government of a state looks like. By reading the U.S. Constitution, one receives a clear impression of the various institutions of the federal government, their functions, and member selection.

Third, for many societies or groups of societies with unstable organization, a constitution often is perceived as an ideal to be reached as opposed to a blueprint of the here and now. Since such a constitution is not based on the political reality of its society, it contains provisions impossible to implement. Often such a constitution is written by well meaning idealists who do not understand the political reality of those who will govern.

Components of Constitutions

Modern constitutions have many different components. The United Kingdom and Israel, for example, do not have a written constitution, which means that they do not have a document called a **Constitution** (with a capital *c*). Most other states have a written document called a Constitution or a Basic or Fundamental Law, which can be viewed in a government building, is often quoted, and used to determine any conflict involving constitutional questions.

Other components of **constitution** (with a lower case *c*) are customs and traditions, laws, court decisions, and writings of famous persons. Most limitations of government power and most procedural determination have been established through customs. Most do's and don'ts affecting political parties, for example, have developed through traditions. The two-party system of the United States, which has become part of the political reality of that society, is a result of patterns of behavior that have become so entrenched in American society that its members cannot perceive alternatives to them.

An important component of a constitution is law. Some laws become so important over time that they are deemed part of the constitution. The

A picture of King John signing the Magna Carta, illustrative of the nineteenth century view of the historical progress of democracy.

United Kingdom's Magna Carta is often referred to as the oldest constitutional document; however, it is a law promulgated during the reign of King John. Although most of its provisions are very outdated, some are still considered part of the British constitution. Civil rights legislation in the United States became the basis for many of the rules by which discrimination, especially in voting, was abolished. Laws that created programs such as unemployment insurance and social security are now perceived as constitutional rights. In many states legislative law can change the constitution; consequently, the legislature can decide to make a law part of the constitution.

Judicial rulings often become part of constitutions. This is true more so in states in which courts, such as the U.S. Supreme Court are authorized to interpret the constitution. Since the U.S. Constitution is so brief and its provisions general, the federal Supreme Court's interpretation of that document largely determines the authority and powers of government institutions.

Ideas of famous writers, government officials, and politicians are often incorporated into state constitutions. Many ideas contained in the *Federalist Papers*, for example, helped define the role of government in American society. Jefferson's emphasis on an agrarian lifestyle greatly

John Kennedy's successor to U.S. Presidency, Lyndon Johnson signed the landmark Civil Rights Act of 1964, that outlawed segregation and discrimination. Other major legislations during Johnson's tenure include: Medicare, Medicaid, aid to education and urban America, and the historic Voting Rights Act of 1965. Standing on the extreme right was Thurgood Marshall, nicknamed 'Mr Civil Rights'.

influenced Americans' perception of their relations with public institutions. Sir William Blackstone, a noted British jurist of the early nineteenth century, wrote manuals and digests of law containing principles that eventually became embedded in Anglo-Saxon based legal systems.

Finally, an important component of a state's constitution is the political ideology, or **constitutionalism**, of the people under its jurisdiction. When the political beliefs of a large number of people are not in harmony with the prevailing constitution, it must be changed or rebellion

Thomas Jefferson

Sir William Blackstone

will occur. The people's belief of what the relationship between government and citizen should be ultimately defines a state's constitution. A paper document called the Constitution may be of little value in determining the proper power of government if it is not supported by the people's constitutionalism.

People's changing constitutionalism will indeed change a constitution. If this does not happen, oppression and lack of faith in government results. Constitutions that do not have at least the tacit approval of a society do not exist for long. Often these constitutions are forced upon a people who would otherwise rebel against them. This does not mean that constitutions have to be universally accepted by a society. (The U.S. Constitution barely received enough support to be approved.) To be effective constitutions must have the support of a significantly large group of people.

Amendments

Changes to a constitution are called **amendments**. In most states amendments are made through the legislative process, just as changes are made in law. In a few states, such as the United States, amendments require federal legislative approval as well as state or provincial legislative approval. Seldom are the people brought into the amendment process. In states of the United States referenda are held to approve amendments to state constitutions that have received legislative approval.

Preventing Abuse of Law

Although constitutions are important elements of public policy, they do not prevent some officials from abusing the law to maintain discriminatory policies, impose their own values and belief systems, or keep a regime in power. Fortunately, developments in two areas that intertwine have resulted in a lessening of abuses — international human rights law and advancements in communication technology.

International laws in human rights compel policy makers and enforcers to abide by certain common standards such as those established by the International Covenant of Civil and Political Rights. These rights, or laws, supersede those made by individual governments; therefore, an international human rights law has precedence over any state laws that protect or deny human rights. Every government, regardless of type (e.g., fascist, communist, fundamentalist, or personalist) is bound to follow these laws.

Since human rights are determined by representatives from countries throughout the world and then become diffused to most persons in most societies, they have become standards by which persons of one society judge government actions of other societies. For example, the actions of the government of Syria are judged by the same standards by citizens of Sweden, Japan, and Lesotho. The international media disseminates reports about alleged human rights violations in Syria, and any Syrian official who visits another country will be asked about these violations and the Syrian government's actions in this regard. The Syrian official, who may have been unaware of the violations, can investigate the situation upon return to Syria.

Since human rights laws are so prevalent, any citizen or state official will have difficulty justifying violations to outsiders, and more than likely the situation will cause sufficient embarrassment that the violations will not be repeated. Americans still find it uncomfortable to discuss slavery or the incarceration of Japanese Americans during World War II. Serbians get all flustered when the subject turns to "ethnic cleansing." To justify actions violating international norms has become a very discomfiting intellectual exercise.

A 1963 demonstration march in support of the enactment of legislation guaranteeing civil rights for all Americans. The Civil Rights Act was passed by the U.S. Congress and signed into law by President Lyndon Johnson in 1964.

Use of video cameras, tape recorders, computers, and other electronic gadgets have made it almost impossible to keep abuses of law secret. People who disappear leave traces. Bad laws cannot be kept secret. Even jails cannot be insulated from the rest of society so that those outside do not know what is going on inside. Magazine articles, books, television and radio programs, movies, and e-mail diffuse this information globally. Those who commit the abuses are eventually discovered and then ...

And then if those who committed the abuse are not sanctioned, their descendants inevitably will be. Today being the child of a human rights violator is extremely difficult. The child grows up and through association with others learns what his or her parents or grandparents did. Since human rights have become so pervasive, children judge their parents on these standards. Most children of former Nazi SS officers in Germany have psychological problems. The same is true of the descendants of those who carried out the purges and executions under Stalin's regime.

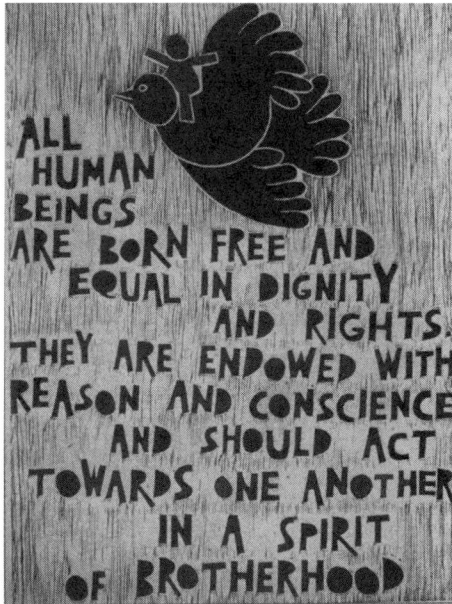

A United Nations poster for promoting the concept of human dignity along with individual freedom and rights as the basis for harmonious relationships.

International human rights laws, as a means to force government officials to use law properly, do not need to be enforced like domestic laws are. Because they are not enforced in this manner, some persons do not consider these laws as true laws. However, the sanctions imposed on human rights violators often are far more severe than any sanctions of domestic law. Jail is for the criminal only; shame and ostracism fall upon generations of relatives.

To maintain peace and order within a society law must be in harmony with the other components of public policy. This harmony is achieved through constitutions, human rights laws, and technological advancements in communications.

📖 TERMS TO REMEMBER

sanction
rights
civil rights
government
state
confederation
federation
unitary
centralized
decentralized
international law
policy
positive law
natural law
judicial review
jury nullification
ineffective law
proscribe
prescribe
habeas corpus
coup d'etat
Constitution
constitution
constitutionalism
amendments

📖 SUGGESTED READINGS

Hart, H.L.A. *The Concept of Law.* Oxford: Oxford University Press, 1961. An analysis of law and its role in society.

Heidenheimer, Arnold J., Hugh Heclo, and Carolyn Teich Adams. *Comparative Public Policy: The Politics of Social Change in Europe and America.* New York: St. Martin's Press, 1983. How select European governments and the United States government cope with issues that profoundly affect society.

Jacobsohn, Gary Jeffrey. *Apple of Gold:*
Constitutionalism in Israel and the United States. Princeton: Princeton University Press, 1993. Comparison of Israeli and American perspectives on constitutions.

Kelsen, Hans. *Principles of International Law.* Revised and Edited by Robert W. Tucker. New York: Holt, Rinehart and Winston, Inc., 1966. A classic textbook on international law from the positivist perspective.

Landy, Marc K. and Martin Levin, eds. *The New Politics of Public Policy.* Baltimore: The Johns Hopkins University Press, 1995. Essays on the new politics of public policy emphasizing the importance of deliberation and open discourse in the making of policy.

Nardulli, Peter F., ed. *The Constitution and American Political Development: An Institutional Perspective.* Champaign: University of Illinois Press, 1992. An analysis of the Constitution's influence on the development of American political institutions.

Palumbo, Dennis J. *Public Policy in America.* New York: Harcourt Brace College Publishers, 1994. The making, implementing, and evaluating of policy in the United States is described in this text.

Smith, Christopher E. *Courts and Public Policy.* Chicago: Nelson Hall Publishers, 1993. The role courts have in determining societal policy in the United States.

✒ NOTES

1. Public Information Office, U.S. Bureau of Census. "Census Bureau Releases Information on Income, Poverty, and Health Insurance Coverage in 1994." (Washington, D.C., October 5, 1995).

15

Presidential and Parliamentary Systems of Government

Almost all governments in the world are either a presidential system or a parliamentary system. The few that do not fit into one of these systems are variations of monarchical governments such as those of Saudi Arabia, Bhutan, Nepal, and Kuwait. The presidential system is found predominantly in Latin America and in the Arab Middle East; the parliamentary, everywhere else.

Some governments, such as dictatorships, do not conform to the pattern of either a presidential or a parliamentary system. Since they are usually nonconstitutional governments (i.e., their organization does not conform to what their constitutions stipulate), they can be regarded as temporary anomalies (even though some dictatorships have lasted for almost half a century).

Both systems depend upon elections for the selection of members to at least one chamber of the legislature and usually hold elections for local positions as well. In both systems the innumerable tasks involved in policy making and implementation are carried out by appointed functionaries. Government services are the same in both systems, and a citizen would not perceive any differences between them.

The major differences between these two systems are the number of people performing the duties of chief executive, their selection process, and the persons to whom they are responsible.

Functions of the Chief Executive

A chief executive performs four basic functions — chief of state, chief policy implementor, chief policy maker, and chief of the party in power. Because of the complex nature of each of these roles, however, the position of chief executive includes not only the person or persons elected or selected but also the many appointed adjutants needed to fulfill all the responsibilities that the job entails. A chief executive is more than just an individual; the office, such as the presidency, has become an institution composed of many persons, with the president as the principal leader.

As **chief of state** the chief executive symbolizes the unity of the people under the state's jurisdiction. He or she participates in ceremonial functions, such as greeting foreign dignitaries, proclaiming national holidays, visiting other countries, issuing pardons, and throwing the first baseball in a new season. The chief of state usually signs all laws passed by the legislature.

As **chief policy implementor**, the chief executive oversees the entire national bureaucracy. This bureaucracy, of course, carries out the laws of the state. When legislation is vague or general, the chief policy implementor can issue a **decree**, which is an executive-made order that has the force of law, to make the law operational. The chief policy implementor appoints the heads of departments or ministries, but the legislature must approve the appointees before they can take office. In the United States these individuals usually have the title of "secretary;" in other countries their title is "minister." The entire military is obligated to obey the chief executive, who serves as commander and chief of the armed forces. As chief policy implementor, the chief executive is ultimately responsible for what every government employee, civilian or military, does or does not do. In this capacity, the chief executive becomes the focus of attention for all the good and the bad that can be attributed to government.

As **chief policy maker** the chief executive is the originator of most of the important legislation that will become law. The national budget, which outlines the government's revenues and expenditures, is one of the most important documents for which the chief executive is responsible. Through the budget a chief executive can force the redistribution of wealth in a society and institute programs and projects he or she believes are important. In addition, as chief policy maker, the chief executive can "legislate" pet projects, such as criminalizing certain types of behavior, regulating commerce and industry, and changing the processes and institutions of government itself.

As **chief of party** in power the chief executive is the titular head of the party. Although he or she may not regard this position seriously and allow others to manage party affairs, the chief executive is viewed as the personification of that party. Often the chief executive is asked to support fellow party members by making a personal appearance and giving a speech on their behalf.

The Chief Executive in the Presidential System

In the presidential system the president fulfills all four functions of chief executive. Since it is virtually impossible for one person to stay informed about all these functions, the president may emphasize one or two functions over the others. If the president is more concerned about policy making than policy implementation, he or she can choose career administrators to oversee the various executive departments, allowing them to make decisions without interference. If the president does not like the functions of chief of state, the vice president or First Lady can perform the ceremonial duties. Presidents often let others oversee party matters because they usually do not like to engage in partisan politics.

A paradox occurs in the role of chief executive in the presidential system. Since the president is elected, he or she represents every citizen as chief of state; yet as chief of party in power he or she also speaks for party members and often rails against members of other parties. Do citizens of the United States view their president as the ideal American or as a Democratic or Republican leader? The president's effectiveness as policy maker and implementor is affected by the public's perception of him or her. The public's perception is influenced by the way the president views himself or herself. The more partisan he or she is, the less likely constituents will view the president as a national figure able to unite the

PRESIDENTIAL SYSTEM OF GOVERNMENT
— ELECTION AND LEGISLATIVE PROCESSES

LEGISLATURE

ELECTORAL DISTRICTS

PRESIDENT

CHIEF OF STATE

CHIEF LEGISLATOR

CHIEF ADMINISTRATOR

CHIEF OF PARTY

LAWS

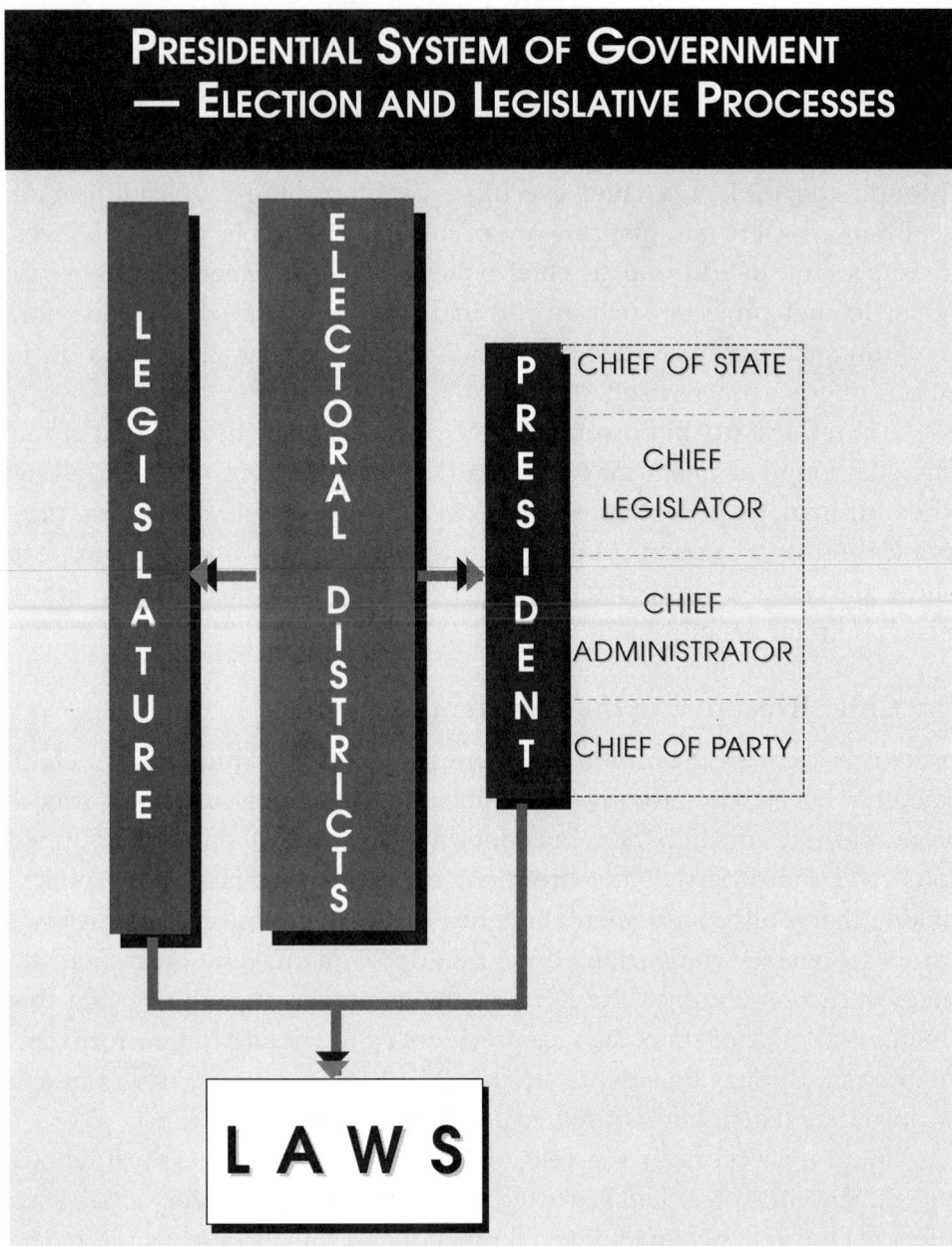

country. However, the president may have been elected precisely for his or her partisan policy objectives; voters may have wanted Democratic or Republican policy alternatives implemented. In the presidential system the lone chief executive wears many hats, but they may not all fit.

The president is elected either indirectly, as through the U.S. Electoral College, or directly by voters, as in Mexico. Since the president is elected, he or she is accountable to all citizens in the state. Every citizen may claim to have had a voice in choosing the president; and the president feels responsible to every citizen. A president serves for a fixed term, usually four to six years, and cannot be removed from office except through **impeachment**, a rare process used by a legislature to remove a government official accused of criminal activity. The president, therefore, knows when the term begins and when it ends. In some countries the president is limited to one term but can run for election again if he or she waits for one term. In others, the president can serve only one or two terms or a given number of years in a lifetime.

The shortness of the presidential term can be viewed as a curse or a blessing. Any individual, no matter how acquainted he is with the office of the presidency, needs a considerable amount of time to become familiar with all the duties of that office. After all, there are many do's and don'ts to learn about the job itself and about dealing with the legislature, media, public, and pressure groups. The limitations of the office as well as its power must be understood. After mastering these roles the president, unfortunately, becomes a **lame duck** (i.e., an officeholder who no longer can rely on the allegiance of former supporters because they are committed to a successor). Consequently, a president, whose term is limited to four to six years just does not have time to accomplish much because some of the term is spent learning how to be president and during some of the later years he or she becomes less effective as a leader after partisan support has dissipated.

On the other hand, the shortness of the presidential term allows voters an opportunity to replace an incompetent leader. Fortunately, presidents who attempt to abuse their power, or are corrupt, or do not care to resolve their society's problems cannot do too much harm in such a short period of time. Time limitations, therefore, prevent a president from causing the collapse of the government or the society.

The Chief Executive in the Parliamentary System

Two or more persons and their corresponding institutions perform the functions of chief executive in the parliamentary system.

In the parliamentary system a monarch often performs the functions of the chief of state. The queen or king, who obtains that title from birthright, conducts all ceremonial functions but rarely has any policy making or implementation powers. Occasionally, the monarch is chief of state of several states, such as in the United Kingdom where the monarch is chief of state of Great Britain and many member states of the British

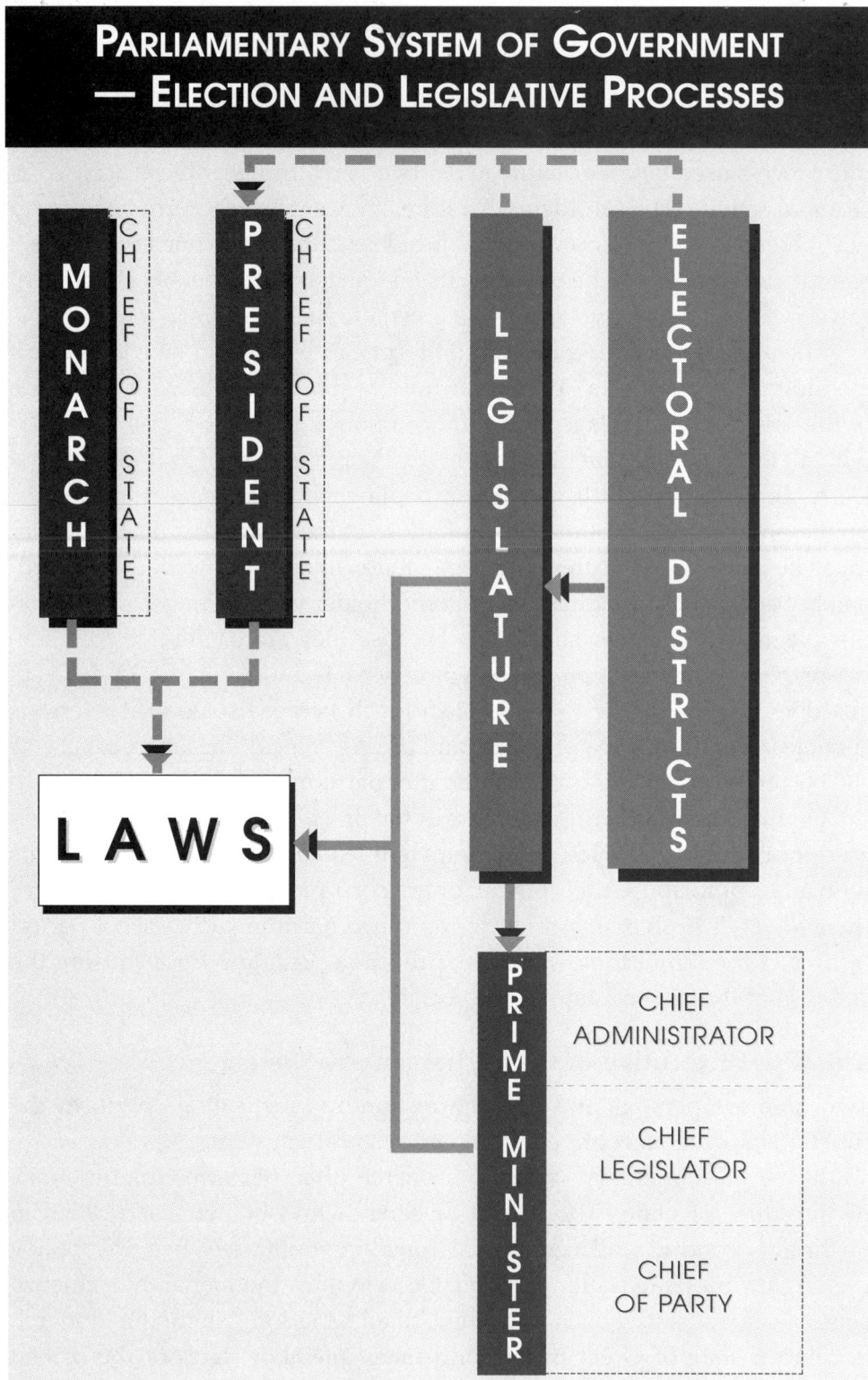

PARLIAMENTARY SYSTEM OF GOVERNMENT — ELECTION AND LEGISLATIVE PROCESSES

MONARCH — CHIEF OF STATE

PRESIDENT — CHIEF OF STATE

LEGISLATURE

ELECTORAL DISTRICTS

LAWS

PRIME MINISTER

CHIEF ADMINISTRATOR

CHIEF LEGISLATOR

CHIEF OF PARTY

Elizabeth II succeeded her late father George VI to the British throne in 1952. In the constitutional monarchy the King or the Queen completely abstains from political involvement, keeping the monarchy above political controversy. The monarchy personalizes the State, embodies national unity, and links the present with a glorious past.

Commonwealth of Nations (i.e., Canada, New Zealand, Australia, and all the Commonwealth states of the Caribbean). The monarch of the United Kingdom appoints personal representatives, known as governors, to act on his or her behalf in states outside Great Britain.

The powers of the monarchs or other chiefs of state usually are manifested only when a crisis occurs that prevents policy making or implementing agencies from performing their tasks. For example, a monarch may take control of the government when the leadership cannot agree on a successor to the chief policy maker or implementor or when transition occurs from one system of government to another. In the 1970s King Juan Carlos of Spain became the chief policy maker and imple-

King Jigme Singye Wangchuck of Bhutan, in traditional attire, travels to districts to meet elected representatives. Bhutanese have an ancient code of conduct approved by their national assembly. Church and state entwine in Bhutan, and the king consults with Buddhist leaders on matters of public policy.

mentor, as the government of Generalissimo Franco was dismantled and a parliamentary government replaced it.

In states that do not have monarchs, the chief of state is elected or appointed by the legislature. The chief of state of Germany is the president, who is selected for a seven-year term by the lower house of the legislature called the Bundestag. In Austria the president is chosen in a general election for a five-year term. Although the chief of state of a parliamentary system is called a president, he or she does not possess any power.

Regardless of how a chief of state is chosen, he or she is expected to refrain from activities involving political parties. If affiliated with a party, the chief of state must remain nonpartisan in public (and sometimes in private gatherings). A chief of state is supposedly above any type of partisan politics and therefore must refrain from criticizing anyone's political views, even if they are reprehensible to him or her.

In the parliamentary system the chief policy implementor is appointed by the legislature, usually the lower house in a two-chamber legislature, and is an elected member of that house. The chief policy implementor is a prime minister, premier, or chancellor. (In 1996 Israel changed its procedure of selecting the prime minister by conducting elections for the first time.) This position has no fixed term because the person selected serves as long as he or she is supported by a majority of the legislature. Terms have been as short as a few hours as in the fourth republic of France and as long as 11 years, such as Margaret Thatcher of the United Kingdom. The lower house of the legislature can remove the prime minister with a **vote of no confidence**. If a resolution expressing no confidence in the chief policy implementor is approved, he or she either has to resign or call for new elections within a short time, usually sixty days. If elections were recently held, he or she has to resign.

A vote of no confidence allows the legislature to easily remove an unpopular prime minister; however, it may have a difficult time agreeing on a successor. If this happens, there may be a period of time in which no one holds the office of prime minister. This situation is not as serious as it may seem because modern bureaucracies can function effectively without the presence of a high level official.

To prevent rapid turnover of chief policy implementors, as occurred in the Fourth French Republic and in modern day Italy, the German government instituted a **constructive vote of no confidence**, which involves introduction in the Bundestag of a resolution expressing no confidence in the chancellor and naming a successor. After a three-day waiting period, the legislature votes on the resolution. If it passes, the chancellor has to resign and the successor is sworn into office. This procedure apparently has worked well; it has never been fully used and just the threat of its use has caused several chancellors to resign.

Resignation also can be forced when the chief policy implementor's party or coalition members vote against his or her policy suggestions. In the United Kingdom this is tantamount to a vote of no confidence and the prime minister is forced to resign. Usually prime ministers are informed of such a vote in advance so they can resign before the voting begins. This situation has occurred several times in Great Britain, most recently in 1990 when Margaret Thatcher was prime minister.

Since the majority parties in the legislature's lower house choose the chief policy implementor, that person invariably will reflect the interests and perspectives of those in the majority. Usually the chief policy implementor has served as a policy implementor and member of the cabinet. In Italy, for example, where some prime ministers are removed after serving for only a few days, these leaders return to their former position as an agency or department head. In this manner leadership remains consistent despite the constant turnover of prime ministers. Thus, in Italy policy has not dramatically changed over the last five decades.

Effective governance by a chief policy implementor in the parliamentary system depends on the strength of the relationship between the legislature's lower house and the office of the executive. This relationship usually is not manifested in public but rather behind closed doors. Personality, whims, likes and dislikes, and simple political maneuvering are involved, making it difficult to detect who manipulates whom. In theory the legislature controls the executive; in practice a few legislators and members of the executive staff decide who is in charge of what.

Usually chief policy implementors are also chief policy makers. While implementing policies they become aware of the shortcomings and are likely to offer workable resolutions. Implementors also have continuous contact with the citizenry and therefore know its wishes, needs, and demands. Since the problems policies address are very complex and ever changing, implementors constantly rewrite, or at least reinterpret, existing policies. Sometimes they can do this without legislative input; but when this input is required, the chief policy implementor's staff is asked to frame new legislation and labor for its approval.

In 1979, Ayatollah Khomeini drafted the constitution for his newly proclaimed Islamic Republic of Iran, that created the position of supreme leader for which only a *faqih* (expert in Shi'a religious jurisprudence) would be eligible. He met the specifications precisely and occupied the position until his death in 1989.

Infrequently the chief policy maker has not had experience in policy implementation; in these situations policies usually are determined by the leader's ideology or beliefs. For example, in the former Soviet Union the general secretary of the Communist Party was the chief policy maker. In Iran in the 1980s religious leader Ayatollah Khomeini, who had never held a government position, was the principal policy maker. In societies organized around values and beliefs, the most outspoken advocates become the chief policy makers.

Most often the chief of the party controlling the legislature is chosen chief policy implementor and maker. In the United Kingdom, Canada, Israel, and Spain the head of the party that garnered the most votes in the most recent general election and that constitutes the majority (or part of the majority) in the legislature's lower house is selected as chief policy implementor and maker. For example, in the United Kingdom Margaret Thatcher, who was head of the Conservative Party, was selected by the House of Commons to serve as prime minister. When she resigned from that position in 1990, she also resigned as leader of the Conservative Party. Before her successor John Major could be chosen as prime minister, he first had to be selected as party head. For years Shimon Peres served as head of Israel's Labor Party. Then in 1991 the party chose Yitzchak Rabin as its head. Since the party won the most seats in the Knesset (Israel's one-house legislature), Rabin was appointed prime minister. Peres was appointed minister of foreign affairs, a position he occupied until he became prime minister in 1995 after the assassination of Rabin.

On the other hand, in Japan and Germany the chief policy implementor is not necessarily the chief of the party. The arrangements among

Emperor Akihito of Japan, as the "symbol of the State and of the unity of the people," performs such honorary functions as receiving foreign dignitaries. The emperor derives his position from the will of the people with whom resides sovereign power. His political tasks are symbolic acts like formally appointing the prime minister who is elected by the Diet or appointing the chief judge of the Supreme Court who has been designated by the government.

the factions of the Japanese Liberal Party allow for a formal head of the party from one faction, an informal head from another, and a prime minister from still another. Willy Brandt, head of the Social Democratic Party, was chancellor of Germany in the 1960s until a scandal involving a staff official forced him to resign. The Bundestag elected Helmut Schmidt as chancellor but allowed Brandt to remain as the head of his party.

Since state officials are so closely aligned to their political party, their government is labeled according to their party affiliation, such as the Conservative government of the United Kingdom, the Christian Democratic government of Germany, and the Liberal government of Japan. This designation also refers to the party that controls the legislature because top state officials are selected by the majority party in the legislature. Thus, when referring to Israel's Labor government, we are stating not only the party to which the prime minister belongs but also the party that controls the legislature.

This does not occur in a presidential system. When referring to the United States Democratic government we are not inferring that the Democratic Party controls Congress as well as the administration. When we label the administration as Democratic or Republican, we are not also labeling the party in control of the legislature.

The Majority of One *vs.* the Anonymity of the Cabinet

In the presidential system of government the president is responsible for all activities of employees in the executive branch. Although hundreds, if not thousands, of persons directly aid in policy making and implementation, he or she alone must answer for the derelictions, mistakes, and wrongdoings that they commit. This responsibility cannot be delegated to others. Additionally, the president is viewed as the source of power in policy making and implementation and as such should do no wrong.

In this respect the president can be compared with the monarchs of the Middle Ages. Both occupy the apex of the political hierarchy. Both are accountable for what their underlings do and don't do. Both can overrule what other officials recommend or promulgate. Each rules as a "majority of one" and is accountable to an ultimate source of all power — one to God, the other to the people.

Monarchs, however, could not be easily removed, while presidents serve for only a set time period after which they must be reelected to retain the office. Monarchs also could dismiss any officer they did not like; presidents are often stuck with officials they did not hire and cannot fire. Although presidents appear to have the powers of monarchs of ages long gone, in actuality they cannot affect policy that much because they have little control over most of the people involved in it.

Since chief executives must resolve problems that often are beyond their expertise or comprehension, they choose and then rely on advisors and assistants to actually formulate and implement policies. In many Latin American states, for example, any policy that the president wants to implement has to have prior approval of the minister under whose jurisdiction that policy lies.

Presidents have become coordinators of these advisors and assistants, allowing them the freedom to do their job as long as they do not cause unnecessary problems for each other. To this extent the president is like the conductor of an orchestra. Musicians play their part, in harmony with each other as directed by the conductor. Although the orchestra produces the music, the conductor, who ironically does not produce a single note, has the audience's attention. The president performs a similar role. He or she may not formulate or implement a single policy but is the focus of attention of the citizenry. And, like a conductor, not only does the president make sure that everyone performs according to expectations but he or she also tries to sell the products of those being conducted.

The president is, after all, the number one salesperson of the policies generated by the administration, traveling around the country making speeches to encourage citizens to support the work aides have produced. Invariably the president converts what the aides have produced to something he or she has produced. The policies of advisors and assistants become the president's policies; the president's political fortunes fall or raise depending on how these policies are sustained.

The heads of the departments or ministries form the **cabinet**, which is an advisory body to the president. The president is not a member of the cabinet because he or she can overrule any decision it makes. Some presidents choose to ignore the cabinet and, except for having its picture taken, not meet with it by not calling it into session.

In a parliamentary system **collective responsibility** is the governing process, which means cabinet members work together to make policy. No policy suggestion of the chief policy implementor is ever translated into policy without approval of the cabinet. In fact, unlike the president in a presidential system, a prime minister refers to policy as "our" or "the government's" policy.

In the parliamentary system one is never sure who introduced a policy and which cabinet members favor it because the cabinet, which includes the prime minister, acts as a united body. Divisions and conflicts within the cabinet are seldom, if ever, publicly mentioned. In New Zealand in 1993, the dissent of cabinet minister Winston Peters became widely publicized and he was forced to leave the cabinet and the National Party to form his own party.

Although the prime minister chooses the cabinet members, he or she is an equal among them, presiding over their meetings and serving as the official spokesperson but unable to impose policy on them. The prime minister's power in the cabinet is determined by many personal, political, and societal variables, but at best he or she can only persuade cabinet members to accept policy ideas.

The British Cabinet headed by Prime Minister John Major (sitting, center), 1990. The Cabinet is a collective decision-making body.

Prime Minister Tsutomu Hata (front, third from right) of the Japan Renewal Party with his coalition cabinet, April 1994. With only a minority of Diet seats their government faced problems from the very start.

Since prime ministers rise to their positions by making alliances and deals with politicians in their own party and other parties, they become beholden to them and in return give them or their associates cabinet positions. (In some countries, except the United States, the president also is obligated to reward those who have helped him or her.) Since the prime minister may not be able to remove these cabinet members if they become recalcitrant, he or she may have to accede to policies that he or she does not favor. Often a prime minister, instead of controlling the cabinet, becomes its captive instead. This has occurred in almost every state with a parliamentary system. In Germany the foreign minister often conducts foreign policy against the wishes of the chancellor. In the former Soviet Union the premier was a puppet of the Communist Party leadership, which occupied important cabinet positions. In Japan leaders of the Liberal Party's factions control ministries. In Israel leaders of the minority parties in the coalition government decide policy even against the wishes of those representing the largest party in the coalition.

Even when the prime minister cannot control the cabinet and has to publicly support policies he or she does not like, he or she is held responsible for whatever occurs in government. As cabinet spokesperson, the prime minister is the one held accountable. Thus, the prime minister is an easy target for legislators to vent their frustrations and opposition to cabinet decisions. (This is especially true in Italy.) The media also focuses on the prime minister, who is the official most often available for speech making and interviews. (Cabinet members usually are forbidden to say anything in public that has not been cleared first with the prime minister's office. On the other hand, they do give unofficial interviews, especially if they are unhappy with their leader.)

If the prime minister is a strong leader and can control the cabinet, he or she is not an equal among its members and has influence in policy making that approaches that of the president in the presidential system. Such a leader can make the cabinet acquiesce to most policy suggestions and can use it as a foil, blaming the cabinet for personal miscalculations and mistakes and then forcing the resignation of ministers for these mistakes. Nevertheless, this situation rarely occurs today. Even in the few instances in which a strong prime minister controlled the cabinet (e.g., Thatcher in the United Kingdom and Adenauer in Germany), forces within or outside the cabinet eventually began to use their influence to cause the fall of these dominant politicians.

Both presidents or prime ministers lend their names to a group of persons working in a complex set of processes, agencies, and institutions that together is called the administration. These persons, along with countless others in and out of government, make and implement policy.

A president or a prime minister may want to bask in the public's spotlight; neither one, however, can prevent that spotlight from moving toward a power seeking competitor. The durability of those in the pinnacle of political power is short lived; presidents have term limitations and prime ministers share power with the cabinet.

The Presidential-Parliamentary System of France

And then there is France. The French have been experimenting with different forms of government ever since King Louis XVI had his head chopped off. They have had parliamentary systems, presidential systems, emperorships, monarchies, and variations of them all. Since 1958 France has had a presidential-parliamentary system (which served as a model for the current Russian government).

The French elect a president every seven years by majority vote. Their two-house parliament is composed of the Senate, whose members serve a nine-year term, and the National Assembly, whose members serve

PRESIDENTIAL-PARLIAMENTARY SYSTEM OF GOVT. — ELECTION AND LEGISLATIVE PROCESSES (FRANCE'S)

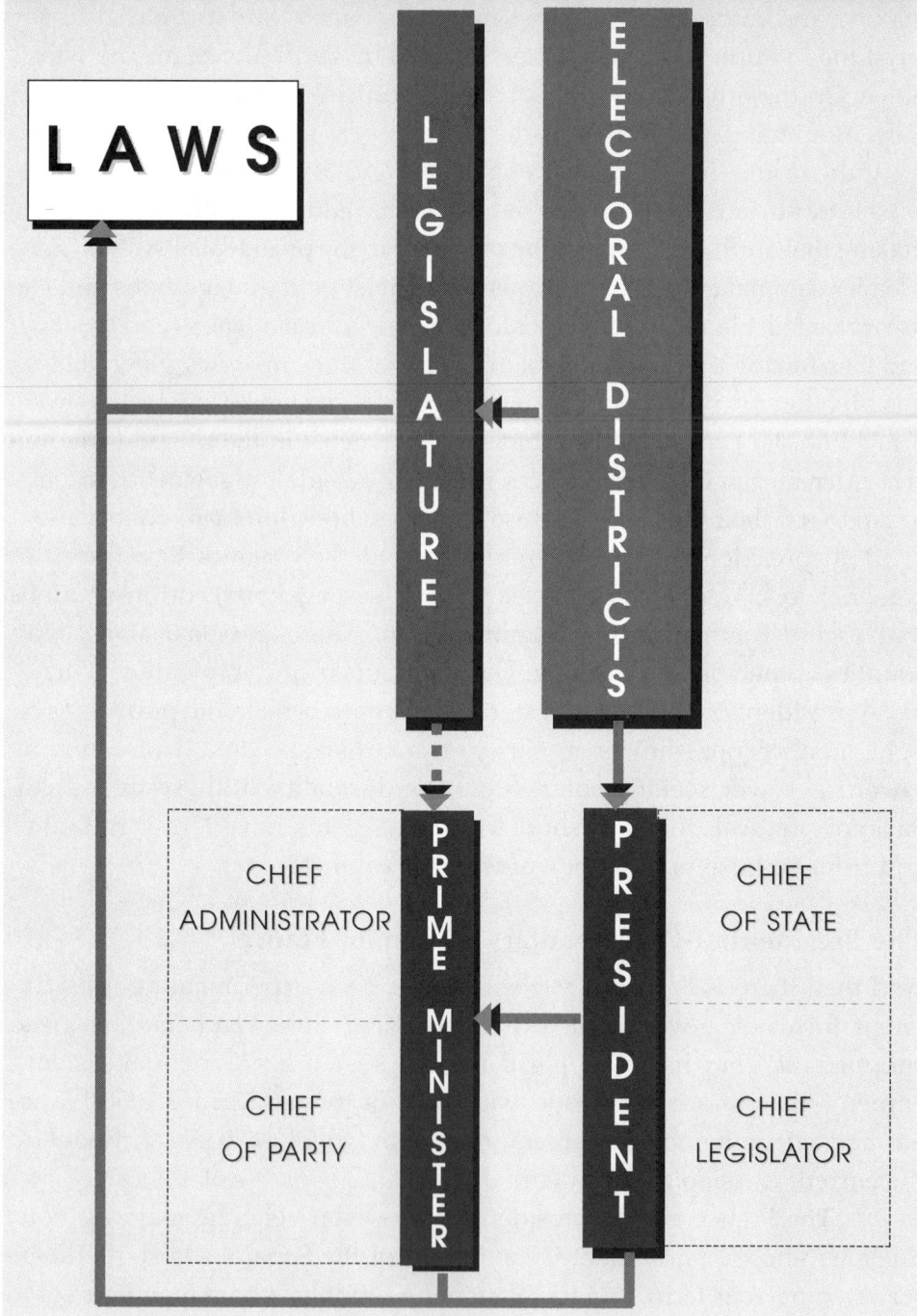

LAWS

LEGISLATURE

ELECTORAL DISTRICTS

CHIEF ADMINISTRATOR

PRIME MINISTER

CHIEF OF STATE

PRESIDENT

CHIEF OF PARTY

CHIEF LEGISLATOR

up to five years. The president appoints a premier, with the approval of the National Assembly. The premier recommends to the president legislators to serve as the other members of the cabinet, called the Council of Ministers; these legislators give up their seat while they assume a ministerial position. The president presides over council meetings.

Policy making and implementation are conducted by the Council of Ministers; each minister, including the premier, can be dismissed by the president or the National Assembly through a vote of no confidence. Since the premier works with parliament and needs approval of the National Assembly to assume that position, he or she usually is the leader of the political party with a majority in the National Assembly. The president, however, can be a member of another party. Therefore, regardless of their political affiliations, the president and the premier must cooperate with each other to work effectively. When push comes to shove, the president prevails because he or she can remove any official, even the entire National Assembly, by calling for new elections. Assemblypersons and ministers, therefore, try not to antagonize the president too much.

Another weapon the French president, like most other presidents, can use when matters do not run as smoothly as they should is emergency power. When the president declares a **state of emergency**, or **martial law,** many constitutional provisions are suspended and the president makes and implements policy alone. This is as close to having the power of an absolute monarch that modern presidents can get. The state of emergency usually does not last longer than six months, but during this time most civil rights are not enforced and the military are given police powers. Article 16 of the French Constitution states:

> When the institutions of the Republic, the independence of the nation, the integrity of its territory or the fulfillments of its international commitments are threatened in a grave and immediate manner and when the regular functioning of the constitutional governmental authorities is interrupted, the President of the Republic shall take the measures commanded by these circumstances, after official consultation with the Premier, the Presidents of the Assemblies and the Constitutional Council.
>
> He shall inform the nation of these measures in a message.
>
> These measures must be prompted by the desire to ensure to the constitutional governmental authorities, in the shortest possible time, the means of fulfilling their assigned functions. The Constitutional Council shall be consulted with regard to such measures.
>
> Parliament shall meet by right.
>
> The National Assembly may not be dissolved during the exercise of emergency powers [by the President].

French President Francois Mitterrand at a press conference in Paris. The content and tone are set by the President, with little or no opportunity for any probing or embarrassing questions.

Although parliament is not dissolved, it cannot prevent the president from doing what he or she thinks is necessary. Often recalcitrant legislators are intimidated and will not oppose the president's decrees. If the president censors the media and prohibits political gatherings, any opposition is silenced. Although Article 16 has been invoked less than half a dozen times since 1958, similar constitutional provisions in other presidential states, especially in those that are not very industrialized, are used more frequently.

Use of emergency powers are less common in parliamentary states. Prime ministers and their cabinets not only have the constant support of their adherents in parliament (unless they have antagonized their own supporters, the legislature gives them what they want within reason) but they also can be very quickly removed because their constituency is the parliament. In effect, a prime minister's relation with parliament is similar to a president's relation with the legislature in a state of emergency.

Sovereignty

In a parliamentary system of government the parliament is "sovereign." Although members of parliament are not sovereign, the institution as a whole is deemed such. The implication is that all authority, rights and obligations, and norms emanate from parliament. Just as the king in the Middle Ages could do no wrong, the parliament of the modern constitutional democratic era can do no wrong.

The parliamentary system is basically an evolved monarchical system in which the sovereignty of the monarch devolved on the parliament. Instead of one person as monarch, an institution now, in theory fulfills that role. In a monarchy the chief executive was the king, whereas in the parliamentary system the chief executive is actually the parliament. The absoluteness of the monarch was taken away by parliament, which eventually awarded itself the authority of absolute sovereignty.

Locke's theory of limited government involved lawmakers

(i.e., parliament) placing restrictions on monarchs' powers on behalf of the people. Limits on government powers have always been made by the representatives of the people. These restrictions resulted in removal of one of the most important powers of monarchs, appointment of government officials. In time, appointment of the chief of state, prime minister, cabinet, judges, and other functionaries involved in policy making and implementation became the responsibility of parliament. All these officials were responsible to parliament, which became the final arbiter of conflicts within government.

The role of the people in the parliamentary system is tangential. They are not sovereign, but they choose those who are sovereign. *People* and *sovereign* are terms that define unreal ideas. At best some citizens (who are part of the people) in a district choose one or a few candidates to serve as members of the institution considered sovereign. Actually all voters become sovereign in that instant when there is no parliament and they select the individuals to fill the vacancies. Only at that one instant can it be said that all authority springs from the people. At all other times parliament is the source of all authority.

Bearing in mind what was stated in Chapter 13 about control of parliament by political parties, one can infer that the members of political parties in control of parliament exercise sovereignty. Parliamentary government is indeed party government. However, if you add to this the iron law of oligarchy, you find that the leaders and staff of the political parties in control of parliament actually are the sovereign.

This brings us to another aspect about who or what is the source of all legal norms, rights, and obligations in a parliamentary system of government. The fact that the people are not sovereign is not of major consequence; basically the people view themselves not as participants in the government but as recipients and, therefore, judges of services. They demand a voice in the type, quality, and quantity of these services and will attempt to influence those responsible for their delivery. (In this sense the people are customers of the provider of goods and services.) The level of satisfaction about government's procedures and institutions depends on how well the provider communicates with the recipients.

The presidential system of government is also a derivative of the monarchical system. A president is like an elected king. The president has, in theory, far more power than a prime minister. After all, he or she is the sole chief executive and is not answerable to the legislature. A president's role in implementing policy is virtually unchallengeable. The only way the legislature can try to force the president to do something is by proposing a law; however with few exceptions, the president must approve it before it can become law. Therefore, the president's interpretation of that law is the one that will be implemented.

The president, however, is not sovereign; and most presidential powers are limited by the legislature. Not only is the term limited to a set amount of time but any executive function, such as determining the budget and making appointments to office, must be approved by the legislature.

The legislature in the presidential system certainly is not sovereign; it must share its lawmaking function with the president, who can use the veto power (i.e., the right of presidents to strike down bills approved by the legislature) to prevent legislation from being enacted. (In the parliamentary system prime ministers generally do not have veto power.)

If neither the president nor the legislature is sovereign, who or what is? By default the people are. Of course, the people elect the legislators (as they do in the parliamentary system) and the president (which they do not in the parliamentary system). Thus, the fact that the people elect the president, even if indirectly, changes the configuration of who or what is sovereign within a society. But this is a very tenuous reason for claiming sovereignty for the people. Since a president usually serves for only one or two terms, once he or she cannot be reelected, he or she is not responsible to anyone, not even the sovereign people.

The issue of who or what in a society is sovereign is irrelevant; it is residue of an age when justifications needed to be made for the imposition of control on executive power. In modern societies monarchs, parliaments, and people are not sovereign. The diffusion of leadership and of policy making and implementation, the reluctance of voters to vote on important issues, the intricacy of governmental institutions and processes, and the complexity of the problems modern societies face have made the explication for deciding who or what is sovereign too convoluted to be of any use or importance.

Societies have developed institutions and processes to overcome challenges to their viability. The parliamentary and presidential systems of government devolved from the European monarchical system, and almost all politically independent societies have adopted one system or the other. Western culture has become so pervasive that every state constitution organizes its government according to one of these systems. Although these documents either imply or refer to the sovereignty of parliament or of the people, they do not add or take away anything from the relationship between the people and government by doing so.

📖 TERMS TO REMEMBER

chief of state
chief policy implementor
decrees
chief policy maker
chief of party
impeachment
lame duck
vote of no confidence
constructive vote of no confidence
cabinet
collective responsibility
state of emergency
martial law

📚 SUGGESTED READINGS

Burns, James MacGregor. *Presidential Government: The Crucible of Leadership.* Boston: Houghton Mifflin, 1965. Classic work on the many ramifications of the presidency of the U.S.

Blondel, Jean and Ferdinand Muller-Rommel, eds. *Cabinets in Western Europe.* New York: St. Martin's Press, 1988. Several Western European countries' cabinets are analyzed and compared.

DiClerico, Robert E. *The American President.* Englewood Cliffs, NJ: Prentice-Hall, 1995. Standard text on the U.S. presidency with several case studies.

Jennings, Ivor, Sir. *Cabinet Government.* Cambridge: Cambridge University Press, 1951. A classic work on the British cabinet.

Linz, Juan J., and Arturo Valenzuela, eds. *The Failure of Presidential Democracy.* Baltimore, MD: Johns Hopkins University Press, 1994. Latin American presidential systems of government tend to lead to instability is the thesis of this collection of essays.

Lijpart, Arend, ed. *Parliamentary versus Presidential Government.* New York: Oxford University Press, 1993. A collection of essays comparing the two systems from both the historical and current perspective.

Lynn, Jonathan and Antony Jay, eds. *The Complete Yes Minister: The Diaries of a Cabinet Minister by the Right Hon. James Hacker MP.* New York: Harper & Row, 1984. Fictional and amusing accounts, based on a TV series, of the roles of a British minister and his administrative assistants.

Neustadt, Richard E. *Presidential Power and the Modern Presidents: The Politics of Leadership from Roosevelt to Reagan.* New York: Free Press, 1990. A leading scholar on the U.S. presidency examines the presidents from the 1930s to the 1980s.

Schlesinger, Arthur Meier. *The Imperial Presidency.* Boston: Houghton Mifflin, 1989. The noted historian takes a look at the increasing powers granted the U.S. president.

Wilson, Harold, Sir. *The Governance of Britain.* New York: Harper & Row, 1976. A former British prime minister muses over the manner government works in Britain.

16

The Legislature

Outline

- Functions of the Legislature
- Is the Legislature the Voice of the People?
- Organization of the Legislature
- Legislators as Human Beings
- Importance of the Legislature

In many countries the legislature is not considered part of government. It is viewed as a public institution that keeps the government in check by watching out for abuses committed by the executive branch. And this, despite all the discussions and debate regarding the functions of the legislature, is still its basic task.

Functions of the Legislature

Besides scrutinizing the executive branches' actions and ensuring the integrity of its own members, the legislature also checks that policies are made and implemented for the welfare of their constituents. Legislators seem to enjoy quizzing administrators to find any shortcomings of their initiatives. Legislators also try to change policies by reporting their constituents' grievances to the administrators. In the United Kingdom each week that the House of Commons meets, a session is set aside for members to ask questions of the ministers regarding their office. In the United States Congress' hearings on executive activities serve a similar purpose. The legislature prevents abuse of authority and trust by forcing the executive to justify policies and decisions publicly.

Legislators facilitate the relationship between the citizen and the executive. Activities of the executive branch of government intricately affect a citizen's everyday life. Whether fixing pot holes; supplying sanitation, water, and sewage facilities; regulating the safety of goods; or providing income, the executive branch is the focus for policy making and implementation. However, individual citizens often are not happy with the government because they did not receive what was due or are expected to give more than they believe they should. The citizen wants resolution of the grievance. Unfortunately, the executive branch is too extensive and complex to locate the appropriate official to resolve the problem. So the legislator is asked to find that official and then act as the citizen's agent to the official. In this capacity the legislator is as an intermediary between the citizen and the executive, a role that was performed in past decades by party leaders and is currently performed in Sweden by an official called **ombudsman**. Nevertheless, legislators in most states, regardless of level, execute this task.

Legislators also inform constituents about activities of the executive. Much of what citizens know about the activities and policies of government is first brought to their attention by legislators. Frequently they also report issues to the media, thereby diffusing the concerns and demands of the legislature throughout society. The role of disseminating information is most important in countries that do not have an active and independent media. In these countries the legislator might be the only source of information on executive policies. Major executive policy initiatives are first announced to the legislature, which interprets and reports them to the citizenry. For example, President Rafael Calderon of Costa Rica appeared before that country's legislative assembly in 1990 to announce his Structural Adjustment Program, an austerity measure designed to decrease the government deficit.

On the other hand, the legislator often is the only source of feedback from the population to the executive. Administrators depend on legislators to tell them about the populace's wishes, demands, needs, and aspirations. Administrators also learn the citizenry's evaluation of their policies and the processes by which they are implemented. In their policy deliberations legislators verbalize the attitudes of their constituents. The actual policy makers and administrators then fine tune their activities to ensure greatest acceptance. Consequently, legislatures are a necessary link between the executive and the citizens.

An often overlooked role of the legislature is that it serves as a training ground for future government administrators. Many department secretaries and ministers learned the in's and out's of government as a legislator. Some acquire expertise in an area that a future chief executive may find valuable. Others use their legislative experience to run for the office of chief executive.

A legislature legitimizes issues that need to be discussed within society. Public discussions may not focus on any single issue or on a topic that has gained acceptance by a particular part of the citizenry. Although homosexuality was discussed for decades, it did not become an important issue until legislatures began to hold hearings in the 1960s. Through these hearings that many stereotypes, biases, and misconceptions were finally aired and corrected and homosexuality became a valid topic for discussion for everyone. Similarly discussions on divorce, abortion, AIDS, addictive drugs, spousal and child abuse, and other issues became acceptable after legislatures gave their seal of approval.

We naturally perceive legislatures as policy making bodies. After all, their product is called legislation and legislation is equated with policy. Yet their role in making legislation is perfunctory, as most of the important policy that the legislature considers has been formulated by either the executive branch or groups outside government (i.e., pressure groups and political parties). Even the much flaunted "Contract With America," which Republican members of the U.S. House of Representatives aimed to convert into policy during the 1994-1996 session of Congress, did not get approval of either the Senate or the president (or the public) and therefore suffered an ignominious death.

In both the parliamentary and the presidential system of government, what the executive proposes, the legislature disposes. In the parliamentary system the legislature seldom rejects what the executive proposes.

The legislature in a parliamentary system appoints the chief policy maker and implementor, a role that is indispensable within the governing

On September 27, 1994, on the steps of the U.S. Capitol, 367 Republican House candidates led by the then-minority whip Newt Gingrich and Rep. Dick Armey signed the "Contract with America." Their pledge. "If we break this Contract, throw us out."

process. A parliamentary chief executive cannot make a policy unless it is first approved by parliament. However, policies proposed by the chief executive receive virtually no resistance from the legislature that appointed him or her.

In most parliamentary systems the legislature is limited to approving or rejecting legislation formulated by the executive. This is as true in the United Kingdom, Germany, and Spain as it is in Jamaica, Israel, and Japan. As discussed in the previous chapter, the legislature is reluctant to reject the executive's policies because such actions force the executive to resign or hold new elections — neither of which the legislature may want. Additionally, cabinet members often have served as legislators. As leaders of the largest legislative party, these cabinet members influence their former colleagues in the legislature to go along with what the executive wants. Consequently, in the parliamentary system, a legislature, acts as an institution for debate of executive legislation.

In a presidential system the legislature may be less reluctant to reject executive formulated policies (since rejection will not cause the executive to resign), yet seldom formulates its own policies. Since legislation policy must be approved by the president, legislatures tend to leave policy formulation to the president (or in provincial and state governments, to the governor). Despite all the fuss about the U.S. Congress' control of the purse, it only once has changed the president's budget by more than 3 percent in the last fifty years. (In 1980 Congress changed the 1981 budget by 8 percent, granting more funds to the Defense Department, but only after President Carter asked for the increase.)

A hundred or more years ago the legislature indeed may have formulated policies in some newer states, such as the United States, which was the intent of the founding fathers. Since modern problems are complex and legislators often lack expertise to deal with these issues, executives are better suited to devise policies because they have an accessible supply of experts to suggest policy alternatives and are better able to pull together the various suggestions offered. A legislature is generally too unwieldy to resolve issues or problems rapidly and it does not possess a staff that can provide information needed to understand these issues or problems. A president or prime minister acting alone can more readily catalyze decisions than a legislature.

Legislatures tend to be large. The Bundestag has 662 members, and the British House of Commons contains 651. The Italian Chamber of Deputies has 630 members; the French National Assembly 577, the Chinese National People's Congress, 2,987; and North Korea's Supreme People's Assembly, 687. Other countries with comparatively large parliaments are Cuba with 589; India, 545; Japan, 512; Brazil, 503; Indonesia, 500; Mexico, 500; and the U.S. House of Representatives, 435. Membership in most other parliaments range between 200 and 300; small countries have a membership of less than 100. Even with 100 members, parliaments have difficulty in quickly and decisively taking action in crises.

Deutscher Bundestag (German Parliament), assembly hall.

Despite its limited role in policy making, a legislature can have power over the executive if it is able to say "no" to policy suggestions or to embarrass the executive. In the presidential system a legislature's influence is enhanced by its potential capacity to say "no" to the executive budget, thereby preventing the implementation of policies and bringing government operations to a halt, as the U.S. Congress did in the winter of

The House of Commons of the British Parliament, the "Mother of all Parliaments." Members of the majority party and the "loyal opposition party" sit facing each other.

1995-1996. The fact that legislators seldom say "no" is of no consequence; just the potential capacity to do so makes administrators wary of alienating them. This gives legislators the ability to effectively act as intermediary between citizens and executives.

The National Diet Building in Tokyo houses the two national legislature bodies of Japan — the House of Representatives and the House of Councillors.

Is the Legislature the Voice of the People?

We tend to look at legislatures today as if they were the successors to the direct democracies of ancient Athens, Swiss cantons, or New England town meetings, in which the entire adult male population periodically assembled and made policy for the community. Legislatures then were viewed as the *vox populi* (i.e., voice of the people). However, most of the

The Australian Senate (upper house of the parliament) has seventy-six members, twelve elected from each state and two each from the capital territory and the northern territory.

The Australian House of Representatives consists of 148 members each representing a single-member constituency for a three-year term.

people seldom have been represented in legislatures.

The ancestors to the modern legislature are the European parliaments, specifically the British House of Lords and the House of Commons. Both these institutions developed to keep a check on the monarch's power to tax and to make policies that maintained the interests of the nobility and the bourgeoisie. During the late Middle Ages legislatures were concerned with protecting the wealth of the groups of society that inevitably paid the bill for government expenses. This has not changed. U.S. legislatures, as well as European and Asian parliaments, have seldom included representatives from the poor of society. These institutions that supposedly possess the power of the purse have consistently been protective of the purses of those who foot the government's bills. In addition, the average income of most legislators is higher than the average income of his or her constituents.

Legislators usually do not want government to provide more services. A legislature representing the upper classes can remove services that a prior government had given to the lower classes. Often the type of service reduced or eliminated is in the area of education. Such cuts invariably raise the consciousness of some citizens, who mobilize into action and make demands of government. Another area threatened with reduction or elimination of government subsidization is public broadcasting, which is often critical of society's lack of concern for the problems of the lower classes (e.g., homelessness, abuse, exploitation, unemployment, illness, and illiteracy). Public subsidized media not only holds up an ugly

Ministers at Palais de l'Elysée, Paris.

The Chamber of Deputies, Paris. The deputies (representatives) to the national assembly are elected by direct suffrage.

mirror image of government officials, especially of those who are elected, but also arouses sympathy for problems requiring further government expenditures.

Legislators are not unconcerned with the plight of the poor or the exploited. However, the concern for the poor by legislatures is always the effect of how the groups that these institutions do represent view the conditions of this underclass. When the poor are viewed either as a threat to the stability of the social fabric or as a resource for the benefit of the upper classes, legislatures will consider their problems. To this extent, the legislature does not act on behalf of an entire society, but on behalf of those who finance the executive's activities. In countries in which the executive wants to decrease the great disparity between the rich and the poor, legislatures that oppose this goal are disbanded. This has happened often in the last fifty years in countries such as Haiti, Peru, Argentina, Algeria, Zaire, Somalia, Ethiopia, Pakistan, Iran, Philippines, and Indonesia.

In addition, legislators' professional background does not reflect the professional divisions within society. The field that is dominate among members of legislatures is the legal profession. On the other hand, blue-collar workers, who mostly work with their hands and receive an hourly wage, and are the largest single group of taxpayers often are not represented at all. In countries in the southern part of the globe a smattering of blue-collar workers serve as legislators; in the northern part of the globe their presence even in provincial or state legislatures is an anomaly.

Besides law, other professions represented are those connected with real estate, such as sellers, appraisers, developers, brokers, insurance salespersons, and those involved in the financial aspects of selling and buying property. Journalists, medical doctors, architects, engineers, and educators also are found in legislatures, but only rarely in a state legislature or Congress.

As we learned in Chapters 9 through 13, many persons are excluded from running for an elected office because they cannot leave their job to campaign, some for financial reasons, others for inability to find a replacement. If the legislative position is part-time, many cannot leave their job for a few months and then return to resume their normal activities. In many countries in Africa, Asia, and Latin America in which most people are unable to read or write or a certain amount of property or wealth is needed to run for office, the legislatures are composed of individuals representing wealthy minorities. Therefore, many factors contribute to the unrepresentative nature of legislatures today.

Organization of the Legislature

An overwhelming number of legislatures are **bicameral**, which means they are composed of two houses. A one-house legislature, such as the Nebraska state legislature, the Israeli Knesset, and New Zealand's parliament, are called **unicameral**.

In a bicameral legislature the house or chamber with the most members and the shorter term of office, is called the lower house; the other house is called the upper house. In the United States the lower house is usually called the House of Representatives or House of Delegates; the upper house is universally called the Senate. In the United Kingdom the upper house is the House of Lords, which is composed of members of the nobility and of the Anglican Church, judges, and those who received life peerage, or titles, from the monarch — about one thousand persons in all. The British lower house is the House of Commons, whose members are elected. In Germany the upper house, or Bundesrat, is composed of members whom the *laender* or state governors appoint for the duration of discussion of particular issues. For example, when the agenda contains items dealing with transportation, the governors appoint transportation experts to serve while that topic is discussed. When the agenda changes, so do those who serve in that chamber. Members of the lower house, or Bundestag, are elected. In most other countries members of both houses of the legislature are elected.

Generally the lower house has more power than the upper house. The lower house in a parliamentary system selects the prime minister, approves the appointment of other officials, and ratifies treaties. In both systems nearly all legislation must be approved by the lower house; the upper house has jurisdiction over only some of that legislation. The German Bundesrat, for example, deals only with legislation that is enacted by the *laender* or states. The British House of Lords can deliberate any legislation, but its only power is the ability to delay implementation of a law by one year.

Since the upper house usually has fewer members than the lower house and are elected less frequently, the legislature gives greater prominence to individual senate members. Although the senate does not have as much power as the lower house, senators are viewed as speaking more eloquently, profoundly, and with less passion than members of the lower house. A United States senator is respected more than a member of the House. A member of the Bundesrat or of the French or Italian Senate has greater stature than an M.P. (i.e., member of parliament, a general title given to members of the lower house of a parliament, similar to the title of Congressman or Congresswoman in the U.S. House of Representatives). In fact, in many countries lower house members are considered by the upper class to be part of the rabble, the uneducated, noisy, and vulgar persons who are only out for their own self-interest at the expense of the aristocratic element of society.

The U.S. senates are unique in that most possess more power than the lower houses. Although any legislation involving appropriations and taxes has to begin in the lower house before the senate can consider it, the senate has jurisdiction over more areas than the houses. Executive appointees need approval of senates. The U.S. Senate, through its constitutional power of advise and consent, approves not only presidential appointees to the executive cabinet but also all ambassadors, military commissioned officers, judges, and board members of independent commissions and public corporations. In addition, the U.S. Senate must ratify any treaty negotiated by the executive. Lower houses in the United States do not approve executive appointments, and the House of Representatives is not involved in the treaty ratification process.

Presiding Officers

The chairperson in the lower house of a legislature in countries of Anglo-Saxon heritage is called the speaker of the house. In other countries the title is president or chair. The presiding officer in the upper house is usually called the president, such as in the U.S. senates. In both the lower and the upper house this officer usually is elected by chamber members and belongs to the political party with the largest number of members. (The U.S. vice president serves as president of the U.S. Senate. In some U.S. states the lieutenant governor occupies that position.) This individual usually directs the traffic of **bills** (i.e., proposed laws), appoints members to committees, calls sessions to order, and generally oversees the house's operations.

Other officials of the legislature are the majority and the minority leaders. These individuals preside over and organize their party in each house by making sure that fellow party adherents follow party policies. They are assisted by other officials called party whips in Anglo-Saxon countries. Leaders and whips are elected by their respective party members in each house.

Some of the most powerful officers in the legislature are the committee chairpersons. Their role is similar to that of the prime minister at cabinet meetings; chairpersons who control the other members of a committee can control the flow and acceptance of proposed legislation, but those who do

President Ronald Reagan addressing a joint session of the U.S. Congress. Seated behind him are Vice President George Bush and Speaker Jim Wright.

not control the other members do nothing more than just preside over the meetings. In the parliamentary system and in many presidential systems, however, the party leadership usually appoints chairpersons, who do not have much control of the committee.

In some presidential systems the person who has been a committee member the longest (has the most seniority) and is a member of the controlling party in that house is appointed chair. In this situation a chairperson may not fully cooperate with the house's party leadership or the executive, causing delays and rejection of bills. This occurs more frequently in the presidential system than in the parliamentary system, and in the United States is most evident in state legislatures. Presidents and state governors often have to cajole and "bribe" chairs of legislative committees with favors such as approval of projects in their state or district to get them to cooperate in the passage of legislation. Despite all the attention that chairpersons get in the media for their antics, they nevertheless are mere impediments to the speedy passage of policies and their actions have rarely affected long-range policies of society.

Committees

Nearly every legislative house has the same type of committee structure. The following are the types of committees.

A **standing committee** is a permanent committee created either through law or through the bylaws of a particular house. This committee oversees a general topic area, such as agriculture, or a specific department or ministry, such as labor. Membership may change, but the committee continues; only a law or bylaw can force its demise. Most bills go through a standing committee for approval before they are sent to the full house for discussion and a vote.

Special, ad hoc, and select committees are created temporarily when the house leadership determines that an issue, problem, or agency needs exploration. Once the house accepts the committee's report, the committee ceases to exist.

A **committee of the whole** is composed of the entire membership of a house. Often members of the lower house want to discuss a subject without the formal rules and restrictions of parliamentary procedure; they become a committee of the whole to deliberate the subject. Any action taken must be repeated when the legislators return as the regular house. Upper houses, which are smaller and more open to debate, do not have

The two largest committees of the 100th U.S. Congress — the House Appropriations Committee (above) has 57 members and the Senate Appropriations Committee (below) has 29 members. Most House standing committees have from 34 to 45 members and most Senate ones have from 14 to 20. Traditionally party ratios on these committees correspond roughly to the party ratio in the full Chamber.

Senator John Melcher of Montana (Chair, Senate Select Committee on Aging, the U.S. 100th Congress) speaking on issues concerning senior citizens.

the need to form such a committee.

A **joint committee**, which is composed of members of both houses of a legislature, can be a standing committee or a special committee.

A **conference committee** is a special joint committee that eliminates discrepancies between versions of the same bill passed by each legislative chamber. Since a bill must be approved by both houses of a legislature and each house separately discusses and amends it, the conference committee studies both versions and prepares a final one for each house to approve without changing. If it passes in both houses, it is sent to the executive for signing.

A **subcommittee** is part of a committee that has primary responsibility for a particular issue. Committees often are too large to effectively study and then accept, amend, or reject a complicated bill. Major deliberation on a bill usually begins in a subcommittee. After the subcommittee accepts a bill, it is sent to the entire committee for approval; if the bill is approved by the entire committee, it is sent to the house for a final vote. Most legislative committees have several subcommittees.

How a Bill Becomes Law

For consideration by the legislature, a bill is introduced by one or more members of a house. In the parliamentary system the ministers and prime minister are members of the same chamber, so the executive can directly introduce bills. In a few presidential systems the executive can directly introduce proposed legislation. Most often the president has to have at least one supportive member of each house introduce the legislation.

After a bill is introduced the presiding officer of the house sends it to a committee; the chair of the committee sends the bill to the appropriate subcommittee to act on it. Recommendations of the subcommittee are reviewed by the entire committee, which makes necessary changes and then votes on it. If the committee rejects the bill, the bill is considered dead and has very little chance of being acted upon by the full legislature. If the committee does not take any action on the bill or does not report its action to the house, members of that house can file a discharge petition. If a substantial majority, usually above 60 percent, vote in favor of the petition, the bill is discussed and acted upon by the entire house.

When a committee reports favorably on a bill that involves either appropriations or revenues, it is sent to the committee that is responsible for those aspects of the budget. Once that committee approves the bill, one of two events occur. The bill can be sent to another committee to decide when it will be deliberated by the entire house, under what conditions such deliberation will be made (i.e., how many members will be allowed to speak in favor or against the bill and how long they can speak), whether amendments will be allowed, and what voting procedure will be used. Or the presiding officer schedules the bill for deliberation on a certain date. Which method is used depends on the rules governing the particular house.

The bill is placed on the calendar (i.e., a date is selected for discussion and a vote). Most bills are placed on a unanimous consent calendar, which means they have no opposition and will automatically be approved on the day assigned; a vote may not be taken. Controversial bills are placed on the regular calendar. When a bill is placed on a calendar, it must be discussed and voted on that day. If for some reason a vote does not occur then the bill must go through the entire process again. However, if debate is not limited and continues beyond the 24-hour day, the day can be extended by stopping the clock a few minutes before midnight. After the vote is taken, the clock is started again.

An unusual custom of the U.S. Senate and some U.S. state senates, not used in legislative bodies of other states, is the **filibuster**, which literally means to talk a bill to death. A minority group opposed to a particular bill can continue deliberations until most of its opponents are too busy or tired to show up in chambers; then the minority group makes a motion to adjourn. If that motion passes, that day's calendar is terminated and the bill is sent to committee again. Sometimes filibusters last weeks, which keeps the senate from doing any other business. Members of the senate can stop a filibuster with a motion of **cloture**, which stops all debate; however, the motion requires a three-fifths majority of the members.

Depending on the rules by which a bill is placed on the calendar, the bill is discussed, perhaps amended, and finally voted on. Most bills require a majority vote of those present to pass. Some require a majority vote of all the members of a house; others require a weighted majority (55 percent to 75 percent) to pass. In the United States most legislatures pass laws based on a majority of those present and voting. In some U.S. senates some legislation (e.g., appointments, constitutional amendments, treaties in the U.S. Senate) requires a two-thirds majority.

Filibuster (a rendering by Howard Bodie). Senators Jacob Javits and Leverett Saltonstall listening to Senator Richard Russell filibuster against the Civil Rights Act in 1964.

Since each house of a legislature has different procedures, memberships, and constituencies, the same bill passed by one house could be different from the version passed by the other. After both houses have approved their own versions of a bill, a conference committee composed of the main proponents of the bill from both houses is appointed to resolve any discrepancies between the two versions. The conference committee, consequently, writes a new version of the bill that is sent to each house for final approval without changes. After both houses approve the bill, it is sent to the chief of state for his or her signature.

Voting Procedures

Voting is conducted in several different ways. The most popular is the **voice vote** by which those in favor say "aye" and those opposed say "nay." The presiding officer then counts the "aye's" and "nay's" and announces the result. Another way of voting is by **show of hands**. The presiding officer asks those who are in favor to raise one hand while he or she counts them; then those against raise their hands and are counted. The presiding officer announces which side had the most hands raised. The **teller vote** is accomplished by every member of the chamber leaving and then filing back in one of two doors — one door for those in favor, the other for those opposed. At each door clerks count each person going in. Records on individual legislator's votes are not kept in any of these voting procedures. Unless a nonmember is present at the time of voting and notices how legislators vote, there is no way of determining who voted for or against a bill or who was absent. The **paper ballot** is even more anonymous because it is secret. Legislators mark on a piece of paper whether they favor or oppose a bill. These pieces of paper, or ballots, are counted and the presiding officer announces the results.

The procedure that allows the greatest accountability in voting is the **roll call vote**, which often takes a long time to conduct. The clerk or presiding officer calls each member's name, and that member states "aye" or "nay" (or abstains from voting). The vote is recorded on a tally sheet

Electronic voting in the U.S. House of Representatives. Members insert plastic cards in voting boxes at stations throughout the chamber and vote either "yea," "nay," or "present." Their votes are displayed on panels above the Speaker's chair while a vote is in progress in the House Chamber.

and the results are announced. The tally sheet becomes public record. Modern electronic gadgetry has made it possible to record roll call votes and determine the permanent voting record of each legislator speedily and without error. Consequently, legislatures that can afford these devices use roll call voting almost exclusively.

Connecticut federalist Roger Griswald (a future chairman of Ways and Means) and Vermont representative Matthew Lyon battled on the House floor. In January 1798, in a heated debate over French naval belligerency, Griswald made an insulting remark on Lyon. Lyon spat a stream of tobacco juice in Griswald's face. In February, denied legal remedy, frustrated Griswald walked behind Lyon and started to beat him with a stick. Lyon responded with fire-tongs. The fight created confusion and furore in the House, exposing the emotional pitch of factional feelings in the Congress in 1790s. After all, legislators are also human beings.

Legislators as Human Beings

Frequently we forget that legislators, as all elected officials, are as human as any of us. They have the same foibles, travail, and wants as you and me. To be elected they had to show us that they are one of us; that is why they kiss or pat babies, eat ethnic food, and mingle with voters when campaigning. Legislators are not angels, but they are not beasts either. They are not super-wise or super-dumb; they are not super-moral or super-immoral; they are not super-compassionate or super-callous. Nor are they super-powerful.

A few months ago this author became highly frustrated while traveling on an interstate highway that was under repair. Two sections of road each about two miles long were being prepared. Only one lane was open for traffic. Between these two sections, however, an eight-mile stretch of road also had one lane closed. Altogether twelve miles of the highway were restricted to one lane. He called the state legislator in that district and complained about the needless closing of the eight miles of road. The legislator not only sympathized with the author's frustration but also told him that he had been trying to get the state highway department to open that stretch for the last five weeks and was not able to get the personnel to act on it. He too uses the road daily and is a senior member of the "powerful" appropriations committee in the chamber of which his party is in the majority. So, what power does this legislator have if he can neither influence the implementation of policy nor bring about a change in that policy?

Everyone who runs for office for the first time believes that the office will give him or her power to make changes viewed as imperative. If that person wins the election, he or she will try to make those changes ... and run into a stone wall. Every legislature has established procedures, a system of do's and don'ts. Learning these rules takes much time and effort. Until they are learned one cannot make that system work. Furthermore, the cooperation of hundreds of other people (e.g., other legislators, staff members, administrators, lobbyists) is usually needed to make anything happen. These hundreds of people do not need that one legislator, for they have many other legislators to help them; but the one legislator needs them. Therefore, after a while each new legislator moderates his or her wants and desires and "plays ball" with the others, even though he or she detests the game that is being played.

Legislatures have little power in policy making. How much less power does the individual legislator have? In legislatures in which the party decides the individual member's vote, the legislator has no power. On some issues, such as "issues of conscience," legislators can vote against the party line and either suffer the consequences, such as expulsion, or plead their justifications and hope they are accepted. In legislatures in which the party does not decide how individuals should vote, as in the United States, the individual legislator makes decisions that will affect not only his or her standing within the legislature but also the chance for reelection.

That legislator has to decide whom he or she represents. All the people in his or her district? Only the people who voted for him or her? The people who supported the campaign most generously? The state or region in which he or she lives? The entire nation? The ethnic, racial, religious, economic, and/or sexual group with which he or she identifies? Representing all groups simultaneously is not feasible because each group's interest conflicts with the others. The way the legislator answers this question determines his or her own identity and the manner in which outsiders, such as the media, perceive him or her.

A legislator also must decide whether to vote the way the "folks back home" want or the way he or she thinks is best, regardless of what the constituency wants. Will public opinion determine his or her stand on issues or will personal knowledge, intelligence, values, and beliefs determine that stand? Occasionally the two will overlap; but frequently they do not.

Thus, the legislator must claim to be either a **delegate**, an agent of the people, or a **trustee**, someone chosen by the voters to make decisions for them. If the legislator chooses to be a delegate, he or she will be viewed as a populist without a mind of his or her own; if the legislator chooses to be a trustee, he or she will be considered arrogant and callous.

It is impossible for a legislator to stay informed on all legislation, which includes such topics as social security, health care, veteran affairs, logging, food and tobacco production and subsidies, new military technology, trade agreements, ethnic fighting within dozens of countries, the problems considered by the United Nations, and the effects and control of illicit drugs. Any one of these issues is sufficiently complex for even the most learned person to keep busy for a lifetime. A legislator may have a smattering of understanding of one or two issues; on others he or she relies on other legislators' lead or gives his or her vote to the highest bidder. The result of wheeling and dealing often determines how a legislator votes. Frequently the legislator does not understand what he or she is voting for or the consequences of that bill. He or she may not even care about the vote, only what is obtained from it. Most likely what is achieved is future support for either the reelection campaign, legislation he or she favors, or jobs, vacations, or home improvements for the legislator or his or her family. A legislator who is manipulated by others is perceived as possessing no real power. Most of his or her votes are cast for someone else. In this situation the decision whether to act as delegate or trustee is not important; a legislator cannot be a trustee if he or she does not understand what he or she is voting for.

The job of a legislator can be frustrating. Those outside the legislature think the legislator determines policy, makes administrators shake in their boots when he or she approaches, and humbly accepts the pomp and circumstance that surround the office. In reality the legislator knows he or she has very little influence in the policy making process and that administrators have many ways to shield themselves from any machinations he or she wants to impose or propose. Ultimately, the legislator is just another cog in the indeterminable fabric of government institutions and processes — a cog, by the way, that is dispensable.

Importance of the Legislature

The only important function that a legislature performs today is keeping administrators from becoming absolute rulers. Even in that aspect they have not always been successful. Innumerable situations have occurred in this century in which a legislature went along with whatever the executive wanted or was unable to stop an executive action if opposed.

In fascist Germany, the legislature gave the executive, Hitler, all the power he wanted. The same thing happened in fascist Italy and Spain. In the Union of Soviet Socialist Republics and in eastern Europe during the cold war legislatures did not curtail executives' powers and could not prevent them from gaining more power. No legislature in Latin America during the 1960s through the 1980s stopped the executive from doing what he or she wanted, even when the executive was responsible for the arrest, banishment, or execution without due process of thousands of persons who spoke against the government. Legislatures in every country in Africa, including the Republic of South Africa, were unable to stop executives from getting what they wanted. Despite many attempts, the U.S. Congress has been unable to prevent the president from accumulating more power. (Even the War Powers Resolution, which restricted the authority of the president to use armed forces abroad was a failure in this respect. Not only is its constitutionality still questioned but it also did not prevent President Bush from sending hundreds of thousands of soldiers to the Persian Gulf *before* Congress authorized it.)

President George Bush sharing a meal with soldiers in the Persian Gulf. The "Operation Desert Storm" that drove Iraqi forces out of Kuwait was ratified by the U.S. Congress in January 1991.

Most legislatures make laws very general and allow the executive to fill in details. In such cases the executive has wide decree-making powers. Other legislatures, like those in the United States, make specific laws that do not give the executive much leeway in interpreting and filling in details. These executives have narrow decree-making powers. Most legislatures that enact general laws grant the executive wide decree-making powers that may be used years, sometimes decades, after the legislation has been approved.

When legislatures are not in session, executives can rule by decree; therefore, many executives try to govern without the legislature. In this situation their decisions are legal because they are based on laws made when the legislature was in session. From 1973 to 1983 in Chile, for example, President Augusto Pinochet governed by decree; no legislature was in session. His decrees were based on laws approved by the legislature before 1973. Since most executives have wide decree-making powers, legislatures are not needed for policy making.

If legislatures cannot stop executives from usurping their powers, of what use are they? Legislatures are institutions. As with any institution, a legislature is only as good as the individuals that belong to it. If members feel that they are inept in checking the power of the executive or they do not want to do so for whatever reason, then the legislature will not try. In situations in which legislators are elected and the electorate does not want to prevent the executive from acquiring more power, voters will choose candidates who will not challenge that power.

In the United States citizens want a powerful president who can make quick decisions when necessary and fulfill a strong leadership role. Congress is viewed as a junior partner in the policy making process. Why then take it seriously? One occasion in recent times when Congress was taken seriously was during the Watergate crisis. Congress only reacted to the population's demands. It did not initiate the demand for a Watergate investigation; the media created an avid interest among the citizenry that began the ball rolling. Therefore, the public, not Congress, was the first to condemn President Nixon for overstepping his limits in attempting to cover up his involvement in the burglary of the democratic headquarters in 1972. The actions of Congress, like any legislature, are intertwined with the wishes and demands of the citizenry. The citizenry ultimately decides the importance of the legislature in policy making and implementation.

Democratic Party head quarters in the Watergate building was burglarized in 1972 by members of the "Committee to Re-elect the President." President Nixon was indicted for overstepping his limits in attempting to cover up his involvement in the event. To avoid impeachment, he resigned.

📖 TERMS TO REMEMBER

ombudsman
bicameral
unicameral
bills
standing committee
special, ad hoc, or select committee
committee of the whole
joint committee
conference committee
subcommittee
filibuster
cloture
voice vote
show of hands
teller vote
paper ballot
roll call vote
delegate
trustee

📖 SUGGESTED READINGS

Close, David, ed. *Legislatures and the New Democracies in Latin America*. Boulder, CO: Lynne Rienner, 1995. Legislatures of seven Latin American states are analyzed in terms of their contribution to the democratization process.

Copeland, Gary W. and Samuel C. Patterson, eds. *Parliaments in the Modern World: Changing Institutions*. Ann Arbor: The University of Michigan Press, 1993. Case studies of the development of six European parliaments.

Harris, Fred R. *Deadlock or Decision: The U.S. Senate and the Rise of National Politics*. New York: Oxford University Press, 1993. Can the U.S. Senate be democratic and efficient at the same time? This is the central question this book asks.

Koopman, Douglas L. *Hostile Takeover: The House Republican Party, 1980-1995*. New York: Oxford University Press, 1996. Describes the strategies used by the House Republicans to ready themselves for a majority status when the opportunity came, as it did in 1994.

Olson, David M. *Democratic Legislative Institutions: A Comparative View*. Armonk, NY: M.E. Sharpe, 1994. Introductory text to comparative legislatures.

Peters, Ronald M., ed. *The Speaker: Leadership in the U.S. House of Representatives*. Washington, DC: CQ Press, 1994. Several essays, including three by former Speakers, on the role of the leader of the House.

Pool, Keith T. and Howard Rosenthal. *Congress: A Political-Economic History of Roll Call Voting*. New York: Oxford University Press, 1996. Analyzing 16 million individual roll call votes cast in the U.S. Congress since 1789, the authors conclude that 80% of the decisions made were done so on an ideological basis ranging from ultraliberalism to ultraconservativism.

Woodhouse, Diane. *Ministers and Parliament: Accountability in Theory and Practice*. New York: Oxford University Press, 1994. The interactions between ministers and Parliament in Britain is analyzed in this book.

17

Bureaucracy

⊕ Outline
- Bureaucracy and Business
- Bureaucracy and Change
- Evaluating Bureaucracy
- Max Weber's Theory of Bureaucracy
- The Decision Making Process

Governments can well exist without legislatures, but they cannot exist without bureaucracies. Bureaucracies make governments. In every society, from the primitive to the advanced, government is the largest employer. One out of every six working Americans receives a government paycheck, and these government employees do every imaginable task. Most types of workers are represented in government bureaucracy — teachers, carpenters, masons, plumbers, ditch diggers, garbage collectors, firefighters, police officers, soldiers, accountants, mathematicians, chemists, physicists, biologists, barbers, dentists, physicians, artists, painters, musicians, actors, directors, ... and the list goes on and on. Not all government employees are considered part of the bureaucracy, though. Teachers and soldiers are generally not included as members of the bureaucracy. Police officers, firefighters, scientists who conduct research or treat patients, and blue-collar workers are also often not included. The stereotype of a bureaucrat as someone who works at an office desk and receives a government salary is generally correct, although the desk can be in a plane, car, boat or someone's home or is a portable computer instead. For the purposes of this book, **bureaucracy** is the collectivity of those who work for a government, except soldiers, teachers, blue-collar workers, police officers, and firefighters. A **bureaucrat** is a salaried government employee who, with few exceptions, works at a desk performing a function requiring the ability to read, write, and do arithmetic. Supposedly bureaucrats carry out policies made by others and are selfless individuals akin to Socrates' auxiliaries who "do not question why, but do and die." In this respect they are often compared with soldiers, although bureaucrats are believed to be much less disciplined and more lethargic.

Bureaucrats do carry out policies, but they usually are policies they made. Bureaucrats are not selfless; they work, some for money, some for glory, some for satisfaction, and some because they couldn't find a better position. Their motivation is the same as anyone who works in a non-government setting. Furthermore, they do ask why; and it is precisely because they do ask that policies change. Very often they generate new policies for which others (e.g., presidents, prime ministers, and legislators) eventually assume credit. Most of them are neither undisciplined nor lazy. Most work hard at their job and often take work home with them. Very few bureaucrats work only an eight-hour day.

By definition bureaucrats are paid a salary by government. For most this salary is the only source of income. Without a government job, they would not have any money to live on. To this extent they are no different from other workers in a society. Discounting entitlements, the largest part of any government budget today (sometimes as much as 80 per cent) goes to pay salaries.

Bureaucracy and Business

Bureaucracy and government's role in determining the economic future of society are closely intertwined. When elected officials or political appointees attempt to improve the economy by decreasing the role of government, they inevitably attempt to reduce the number of government workers. Reducing the number of government workers has two immediate effects. First, it increases the number of unemployed, creating a greater need for government social welfare services to the unemployed. Second, it reduces the level of government services in general.

When government employees are dismissed, they can look for jobs in the private sector, which often are lower paying. Hence, the standard of living of these workers goes down, while that of the taxpayer goes up (i.e., they pay less in taxes). However, the whole economy eventually suffers because these laid-off workers do not have as much money to spend as in the past. Same situation occurs in the private sector when a business lays off workers. That business may make greater profits, but former workers who now earn less have less to spend. When people spend less, the entire business community (and government through lower taxes) suffers. At the same time unemployed and underpaid workers make greater demands on government services, which is a major stress on the economy of a society that already has a considerably high level of unemployment but also does not tolerate starvation and misery among its members. Before a government layoff the government received some service from its employees for its expenditures, but after a layoff it receives nothing for the payments and services it must provide to these same individuals. And unlike private businesses, which do not provide for the needs of dismissed employees and look to government to do so, government cannot pass this responsibility to another entity.

Government is not business and business is not government. Government provides services; business provides income to its investors. To provide the highest possible income to investors, a business purchases or produces goods and services at the lowest cost and sells them at the highest price possible. Lower cost and higher price means efficiency; greater efficiency means higher profits. In the 1980s many corporations that lost sight of their mission (e.g., IBM, General Motors, Eastman Kodak, Westinghouse, American Airlines, and other blue-chip companies) encountered problems due to their mismanagement. In addition, each year in the United States tens of thousands of businesses declare bankruptcy because they have been operating inefficiently.

Government is not a profit-making institution. For example, a service that government provides is education. For many governments education is the largest item in their budget, employing the largest number of people.

Education at all levels is crucial to both social and economic development. For many governments it is the largest item in their budget.

According to the U.S. Federal Highway Administration the federal government and the states are spending more than $34 billion a year on highways and bridges. This amount doesn't seem to be enough to keep up with all the maintenance requirements.

Education is the most important determinant of a society's future, and no one would measure its effectiveness by its profitability. Another service that has mushroomed in most countries during the last half century is the construction and maintenance of roads. It takes years, even decades, to evaluate the benefits of a highway or road. How can its profitability be measured?

One question seldom asked when government is criticized for inefficiency is, If government did not provide services, who or what would? Who are the alternative providers of these necessary services? Modern societies need an educated workforce that can commute to work, move to where work is available, and transport goods and services to consumers. If government does not facilitate this, who or what will?

Some government services could be provided by private enterprises but are not because of their low profit margin. These services include the postal service, inexpensive mass transit, radio and television broadcasting and in some areas, health care and utilities such as gas, water, electricity, and telephone. Profit is low or nonexistent in these services because they are considered essential to the welfare of all members of society and thus cannot be denied to anyone because of cost.

Profitability also is not possible because government has become a charitable institution. From student loans and subsidies to social security, from unemployment compensation to health care, government today provides services that in the past were dispensed on a much smaller scale by charities, such as religious institutions, fraternal and social organizations, and associations founded for the sole purpose of providing charity.

Patients awaiting their turn to be seen by a physician at a community health center in Rwanda. Providing free health care to low income population is a major responsibility of most governments in the world.

Government redistributes the wealth of a society through its service function (as well as progressive taxation policies). The main users of government services are those who could not afford them if they were provided by profit-making organizations. Student grants and loans, for example, are awarded to those who cannot afford college tuition or the high interest rates that financial institutions charge for loans.

Some government services are intertwined with policing functions, such as inspecting meat and other foods to ensure that they are safe to eat, enforcing safety standards on manufactured goods and housing, ensuring the safety of the workplace, and providing a clean and safe environment. None of these services produce profits.

Over two-thirds of all government employees, excluding the military, are involved in some service function. Most of government's growth in the last century has been through the provision of services. This growth is principally due to the demand of citizens on government, and it continues as citizens demand even greater involvement of government in providing for their needs, such as the demand in the 1990s for universal health care and fewer pollutants.

Government also performs two other functions, defense and coordination of people through the provision of law and order. Defense is always

B2 Stealth Bomber. United States and other major powers maintain strong defense forces equipped with sophisticated weaponry and delivery systems in order to prevent war and overt aggression by making the consequences of such acts clearly unacceptable to rational leaders of other nations.

an expensive responsibility of government; the greater the threat to a society by others, the higher the cost of defense. A government maintains a large army in order to *not* use it. How can profits be calculated for this function?

Coordination of people through provision of law and order involves not only making and enforcing laws protecting life, liberty, and property, but also placing traffic signals on roadways, licensing radio and television stations, and maintaining standards of weights and measures, among others. All these tasks of modern times are taken for granted as essential functions. Yet what profit is there in any of them?

A portable reflective CMS (Changeable Message Sign) displaying real-time information to motorists is a typical traffic control device that helps improve roadway operations and safety of existing facilities.

Bureaucracy and Change

In Chapter 2 we saw how with more people living closer together and performing specialized tasks, a greater need arose to coordinate and regulate their behavior. The coordination and regulation of behavior are done through laws that need to be made, interpreted, and enforced. The enforcement of law involves police personnel, prosecutors, defense attorneys, judges, wardens, guards, parole officers, and a plethora of other personnel that keeps the records. Each of these different categories of officials itself needs to be regulated in order for them not to abuse their authority or deny the proper rights to those accused or convicted of a crime. In other words, more people lead to more coordination and regulation of their behavior that in turn leads to more personnel involved in the enforcement of the rules that in turn leads to greater regulation of the personnel who do the enforcing that leads to more personnel regulating the regulators.

Bureaucracy increases as the population increases and interactions become more complex. Bureaucracy also increases as populations demand and receive more services from government. Consider the example of public education. As the school population increases, not only are more teachers needed but also more administrators to supervise and coordinate the teachers. In addition, more school and office buildings are needed for the expanding number of students, teachers, and administrators, which

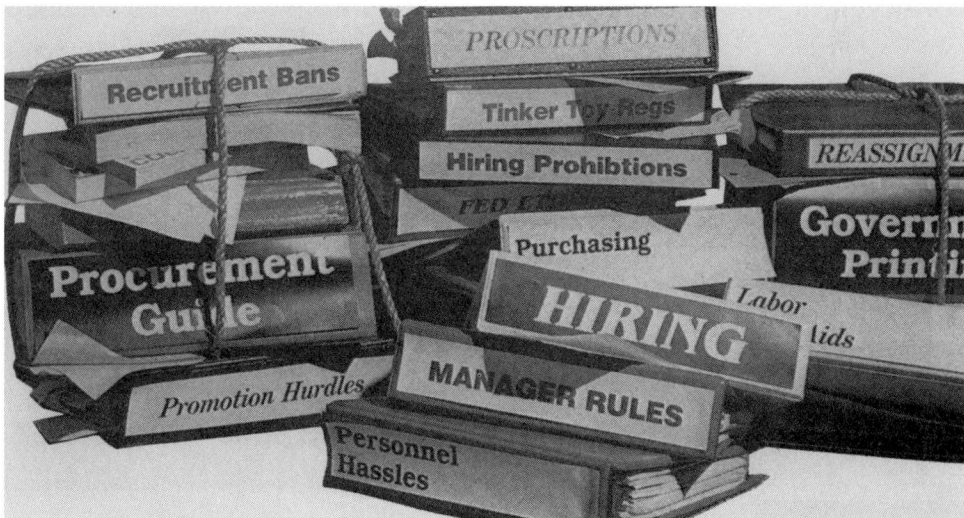

Technological advances are spawning comprehensive, integrated data systems which have a tremendous impact on improving the bureaucratic procedures in a variety of areas including payroll, personnel, accounting, budget, work reporting, procurement, and others.

leads to the need for more officials to examine architect plans and the construction of buildings. More supporting staff including maintenance personnel, secretaries, and kitchen personnel are needed. Increased number of school employees leads to increased number of accountants, auditors, bookkeepers, and, of course, payroll staff to write the checks. Since all these workers also need to be supervised and regulated, more regulations and regulators are needed.

A major problem of most bureaucracies is that their rapid increase in size during the twentieth century has caused an increase in the number of regulations under which they have to work. Overregulation was necessary because bureaucrats of the past were not as competent and educated as they are today, and therefore could not be trusted to do their job correctly. Everything they had to do was explained very precisely, leaving little room for interpretation or initiative. The result was creation of a whole regimen of bureaucratic regulations and regulators, which stifles employees' imagination and creativity.

Ethics

Not all bureaucrats are opposed to overregulation. The greater the number of regulations that a bureaucrat has to follow, the less need for him or her to make a decision. A traumatic moment for anyone is when a government official states, "Sorry, but I cannot help you because regulations prevent me from doing so." How often have individuals unjustly persecuted been told this by friends, neighbors, and even relatives, who were in government positions and could help, but did not. Regulations allow the government employee to avoid taking responsibility for his or her actions. People experience discrimination, and even persecution, by government officials because of their religion, race, sex, nationality, or sexual orientation; the officials claim they are just doing their job (even if they do not agree with the policies they are following).

If government officials would perform their functions according to their sense of ethics, most regulations would not be needed — also not much would be accomplished by these officials. Unfortunately, not every one has the same set of ethics. Bureaucrats cannot be allowed to disagree among themselves on what and how policies are to be implemented. For bureaucracy to work bureaucrats must be enmeshed with each other so well that if one leaves he or she can easily be replaced. Thus, every government official is a replaceable cog in a well-run bureaucracy.

Regulations encouraging justice and humanity, which are often based on human rights conventions, have been initiated to prevent bureaucrats from implementing bad or inhumane policies. In the United States these regulations tend to originate from supreme courts, which attempt to ensure the due process and rights contained in the Bill of Rights. The regimen of regulations and regulators has not been all bad.

Policy Changes

Bureaucracies are hierarchical organizations. In every one, ten to twenty levels of employment exist each containing several steps. The higher the position in the hierarchy, the greater the likelihood that the employee will have latitude in decision making and fewer restrictions on policy implementation. Policy, of course, emanates from these higher levels. In general, workers at the higher levels are older, more educated, and more experienced than those at lower levels. They also are knowledgeable about and comfortable with the prevalent norms of both society and, most importantly, the bureaucracy. Since high ranking bureaucrats are acculturated to these norms, they are less likely to make decisions that will cause major change. Consequently, these individuals maintain stability and place brakes on new policies, regardless of where they originated.

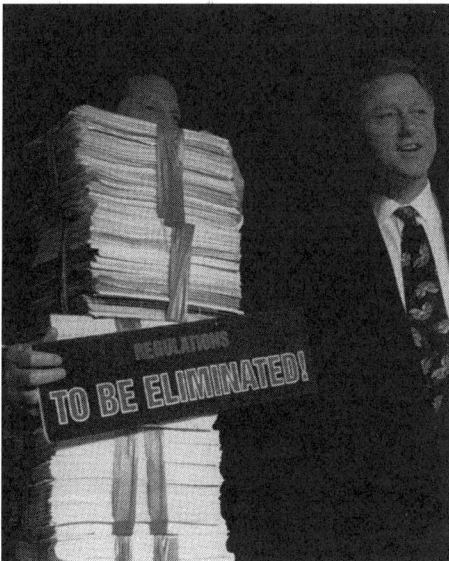

"Common Sense Government Works Better and Costs Less" — President Bill Clinton and Vice President Al Gore display federal regulations that were eliminated as part of the government's regulatory reform efforts, at the White House Conference on Small Business, June 12, 1995.

Therefore, outsiders to the bureaucracy, namely elected office-holders, try to create social changes. Occasionally, a new agency must be created and new, less experienced bureaucrats are hired to implement the new policies. Elected officials and political appointees who do not know the do's and don'ts of the bureaucracy often become stymied in their effort to get their policies implemented by long-time bureaucrats. In virtually every society, at one time or another, a struggle has been going on between those outside the bureaucracy who want change and those within the higher ranks of bureaucracy who oppose that change. In this struggle the same side does not always win. Usually, the more ideological and prone to use extralegal methods (including violence) the outsiders are, the greater the likelihood they will get their way. That is how revolutionaries can cause high ranking bureaucrats to abide by the new order.

Nevertheless, revolutionaries also do not always win. Sometimes their adherents are more interested in their own welfare than in the revolutionary causes which they supposedly are striving for. After getting a position in the new government, they try to maintain the office by ingratiating themselves with future political officeholders and those in lower level positions. Therefore they work to slow down the implementation of revolutionary policies.

Yet change can also emanate from a bureaucracy. After all, bureaucrats are part of society, and they have to overcome the same challenges as other members of society. Today, in times of rapid change, especially due to audio, visual, and computer technologies, bureaucrats often are forced to comply with regulations made before these technologies were even conceived. Most government workers today face the problem of adapting the bureaucracy to the computer age.

The old way — Customs clerks in Tanzania manually recorded all information as types, quantities, and origins of goods being imported. The high volume of paperwork piling up caused inspectors to fall nearly a year behind in record-keeping. The new way — Computers track the flow of imported goods, reducing paperwork and providing monthly accounts vital to long-term planning.

Evaluating Bureaucracy

If a government can be judged at all, it should be judged by citizens' level of satisfaction with its services. Despite some grumbling and complaining, members of societies generally are content with what they get from government. Major social and political upheavals caused by domestic clashes have been rare in the twentieth century. (Most major transformations in societies have been the result of international wars or influences or ethnic conflicts.) Of course, some people want from government more than it can provide. Governments have limited resources that are controlled to some extent by those who make great demands of government, such as middleclass taxpayers who vote against school levies but at the same time want better education for their children.

None of this is intended to imply that government cannot supply more services with its resources. In this respect government, like any institution, can operate more efficiently at times. If twenty bureaucrats provide a service to 100 citizens, they may be able to serve more people by making institutional or technological changes. Or fifteen bureaucrats could serve the 100 citizens and the remaining five can provide different other services.

Some societies, especially those in the Southern Hemisphere, have more government employees than are needed. However, government employment is considered a service in itself because some employees would not be able to find any other job. In these societies government jobs pay very little, but without the jobs these people could literally starve. Consequently, government provides jobs to avoid social, health, and economic problems. Government employment as a preventive health measure may seem strange, but in some very poor societies it is reality.

In other societies large bureaucracies have developed because the demand for traditional services from government has increased exponentially. Since high ranking bureaucrats distrust those below them, they developed a formal procedure to check the work of lower ranking bureaucrats. For example, suppose that you graduated from a Latin American high school and need an official transcript. Your high school administrator gives you the transcript, but in order for it to be official you need an official seal stamped on it. For this you go to the ministry of education, where a lower ranking official signs it. Then you must take it to his or her supervisor, who certifies that the low ranking official's signature is indeed legitimate. Next you go to the office manager, who certifies that the supervisor's signature is legitimate. You continue to go up the bureaucratic ladder to the ninth level for the signature of the minister of education. Only after this signature is added to all the others is an official seal placed on the transcript.

With only 100 high school graduates a year this procedure, despite its elaborateness, is not considered too time consuming for anyone involved. Many officials involved in the signing of the transcript did not have much else to do anyway. However, when the number of high school graduates each year reached one million, the problem of providing everyone with an official transcript became enormous. In their bureaucratic wisdom the Latin American officials have dropped the need for the minister's signature on high school transcripts, although many still require it for university diplomas.

Why are all these signatures needed? One reason is that it gives government employees who need a job and would not otherwise have one something to do. Another reason is that in the past Latin American bureaucrats were very cautious and meticulous in giving approval. During the colonial period Spain jailed bureaucrats who did not follow regulations to the letter. Still another reason, as previously indicated, is mistrust that stems from old beliefs of Spaniards and many Latin Americans who belonged to the upper classes and felt that others in society could not do anything as well as them. Therefore, they insisted that those of lower social standing be constantly checked and supervised.

Although the example of numerous Latin American bureaucrats performing unnecessary tasks is extreme, similar conditions exist in almost every society. Bureaucrats are often considered incompetent, in need of constant supervision, too cautious and meticulous, or untrustworthy.

Salaries

One way by which an institution or individual can be evaluated is by how much society allows them to earn. Government seldom pays bureaucrats what they could earn in comparable positions in private enterprise. Even the president of the United States earns only $200,000, which is about half of the salary of a football coach at a large university. Secretaries of U.S. departments make about $120,000 and U.S. Supreme Court judges earn less than $165,000, which is certainly less than the salary of a vice president of a small corporation or even of an established corporate lawyer. In other countries the president or prime minister, who is always the highest paid government employee, usually makes about $40,000. Is it any wonder then that those who earn more than these salaries look down upon bureaucrats?

Ironically, salaries of low ranking bureaucrats in industrial countries where there is a high demand for young, educated workers are relatively high. Starting salaries in the federal government for college graduates in the United States are between $25,000 and $30,000, which is commensurate with those in private enterprise. As these bureaucrats move up the hierarchy their salaries in comparison to that of those in comparable positions in the private sector are much lower. According to a long-standing tradition bureaucrats cannot earn more than a member of Congress (Congressmen's and Senators' salaries are $127,000 a year).

In countries with a surplus of workers government salaries are low; employees earn just enough to buy food for the family. Often their salaries are supplemented with income from other jobs, if available.

Corruption

Another way people supplement their salaries is through corrupt acts. However, what seems to be corruption by members of one society may not be viewed as such by those of another society. In pre-twentieth century China and Medieval Europe the position of tax collector typically was awarded to the highest bidders. Government ministers of emperors and monarchs promised the job to the person who offered to give the government not only a flat sum but also a certain percentage of taxes collected each year. Tax collectors were paid by commission, so the harder they worked, the more money they kept, the more the money government got, and the madder the taxpayers got. Tax collectors who operated in this manner, thereby exploiting the taxpayers, were more successful than those who were kind and sympathetic to the taxpayers' plight. (This painful experience of unfair tax collection caused anger and distrust of bureaucrats that became so embedded in our civilization that it may be the principal reason for citizens' distrust of bureaucrats today.)

Were the tax collectors corrupt? From today's perspective appointing persons to government service based on bids appears wrong. Not protecting taxpayers from possible abuses by tax collectors is also wrong. Yet, until a few years ago in many U.S. states, justices of the peace received a commission for every fine they charged. Collection agencies in some countries, including the United States, bid for the job of collecting overdue taxes, receiving commissions from the government on the funds received. Although these tax collectors have to abide by regulations their ancestors centuries ago did not, they nevertheless often harass those who do not pay.

Corruption is a relative wrong; wrongful exploitation of the naive or innocent for the benefit of society is often condoned, whereas exploitation of others for an individual's personal gain is not. Generally exploitation by highly paid bureaucrats is tolerated less than that of lower paid personnel. In some societies corruption is so much a part of the system that bureaucracy cannot operate without it.

As an example let's examine the case of an overworked, harried, and underpaid bureaucrat whose signature is needed on a document. The "customer" gives the bureaucrat the document, which she places it at the bottom of a heap of documents to be reviewed and signed. When asked how long it will take for that particular document to be reviewed, the bureaucrat answers, "A few months." The customer, who cannot wait that long, pulls out some money and gives it to the bureaucrat. The document then moves up the heap; the more money received, the higher the document moves. From the perspective of one who is not used to this type of bureaucratic performance this situation represents corruption, plain and simple.

Let us look at that type of incident in another way. The bureaucrat does not make a salary from which she can live in a manner society expects her to. After all, she has to dress well, and she has to maintain a healthy and clean home. Her regular salary is just not enough. So, she is forced to take money when it is offered to her. In return she does something extra, e.g., she reviews and signs documents faster. In a way, she works like most waitresses do. Waitresses cannot live off the salary they get; they need the tips we give them to make a living. Why should not the customer pay for the extra service? In this fashion, customers pay for the service directly to the person providing it. After all, why should the average taxpayer who does not need the services of the above bureaucrat pay for all her salary? Why should the taxpayer subsidize government employees whose services he will never use?

These questions are bothersome to those who demand equal treatment from every government employee. They expect documents of the poor to be signed with the same speed as those of the rich. Equal treatment, however, is a luxury not every society can afford because it is limited by the amount of resources available, which determines the number of bureaucrats employed and the level of their salary. Few societies can provide a sufficient number of bureaucrats and pay them enough to earn a respectable living.

Another activity that is considered a form of corruption in the Northern Hemisphere is **nepotism**, which involves a government employee giving government employment to a relative, regardless of his or her level of competence, over other qualified candidates. Citizens of industrial countries often do not approve of this type of favoritism. However, in societies in which the family is still an important institution, nepotism is an accepted practice. A person in a government position is expected to give preference to relatives when openings for other positions occur. If he or she does not, the family will consider him or her as an outcast and others will believe this individual does not honor his or her family. It is important to note that nepotism in private enterprise (in which the boss often arranges for a relative to be hired) is not an issue in any country.

Nepotism in government in advanced industrial societies occurs indirectly. A large portion of government jobs is filled in this fashion. In its simplest form it works in the following manner: A, who has a daughter looking for employment, works in agency X where there is a job opening. B, who has a nephew looking for a job, works in agency Y which also has an opening. A contacts B, and they arrange to have agency X hire the nephew and agency Y hire the daughter. Both the daughter and the nephew have the basic qualifications for their respective positions. Among the dozens of other applicants who also have these qualifications, some have even more but are turned down in favor of the two relatives. Since this manner of filling positions is virtually universal today, prospective job hunters are encouraged to use every possible friend or relative as a conduit to a job inside or outside government.

The practices of placing relatives in positions that should have gone to others and of accepting extra money for tasks that ought to be done anyway has its limits of acceptability even in the poorest societies. Although engaging in these corrupt practices to eke out one's existence is acceptable, doing so to get rich is not. Thus, a particular society may tolerate many corrupt bureaucrats and at the same time accuse others of a crime because they overstepped the limits.

A more serious type of corruption involves committing illegal acts for personal profit. For example, a bureaucrat accepts a bribe to sign and approve documents that will allow activities prohibited by law. This criminal act occurs in some societies more than others. Payment of the bribe can involve a job for the bureaucrat or relatives or friends, a vacation, or other benefits. Bureaucrats who do these things are no better than criminals who break the law because they are getting paid for it. A side aspect of these types of actions is that within a society, if these acts are not curtailed, two types of law begin to emerge — one for those who have wealth and another for those who do not. Establishment of these two types of law can be disastrous for a society because it creates a formal division between the rich and the poor. The poor, of course, are always more numerous. Fortunately, in all societies the overwhelming majority of bureaucrats do not sink to this level of criminality. However, the few who do give bureaucracy a bad name.

Max Weber's Theory of Bureaucracy

Apart from our basic mistrust of bureaucrats, the way we perceive bureaucracy today has been largely influenced by a German sociologist who lived at the turn of the twentieth century, **Max Weber**. In the late 1800s he studied the differences between Chinese and German bureaucracies; his publication created the mind-set for all future analysis of government employment practices.

Weber developed the now familiar organizational chart, which shows the hierarchical arrangement among persons or units in an organization. The higher one is on a chart, the greater the responsibility he or she has for the organization's operations. Those lower on the chart make decisions but for a much small segment of the organization.

A feature of bureaucracy that Weber found in Germany but not in China is each individual or unit in the organization is responsible to only one supervisory individual or entity. Two or more supervisors is not effective, according to Weber, because those being supervised can cause disorganization by manipulating one supervisor against the other. On the other hand, the number of individuals any supervisor can effectively supervise, called **span of control,** is limited and is typically between seven and fourteen. Under some circumstances this number could be increased (this occurs rarely). This means that if 100 workers are

Max Weber

needed to supply a service, 111 must be hired because for every ten persons one supervisor is needed and for every ten supervisors one higher ranking supervisor is needed.

The lower the level in the organization, according to Weber, the more specialized are the tasks. Conversely, the higher the level in an organization, the more general are the tasks. For example, a student union provides food services, meeting rooms, programs, and assorted services such as automatic bank teller machines and kiosks that sell sundries and other necessities. The food service personnel is organized so that cooks, dishwashers, servers, and the cleanup crew each performs its designated tasks well. Cooks prepare appetizing meals, dishwashers are proficient in washing dishes, food servers do a competent job in serving meals, and the cleanup crew work those brooms, mops, and vacuum cleaners with expertise. What happens when a food server is asked to wash the dishes, or when the dishwashers are asked to cook the meals? The tasks will no longer be done as well as before.

Their supervisor, who is a generalist, may not know how to cook a meal or how to operate the dishwashing equipment. More than likely this supervisor will have butterfingers when serving food or working the cleaning equipment. Yet he or she must know a little bit about all four of these tasks. The food service supervisor is a specialist in student union services, of which food is just one. The director of the union, however, will certainly not know as much about food as the food service supervisor, but he or she will know a little about it and about programming, scheduling meeting rooms, and the other services of which the food service personnel know nothing.

According to Weber, what generalists at the top know about the organization comes from the information sent to them from below. Information flows up the organization chart. When the dishwashing machine in the previous example breaks down, the first to know is usually the person who operates it. This person informs the supervisor who, if necessary, informs the director. Unless the dishwasher informs the supervisor, the latter will not know about the problem; and if the supervisor does not inform the director, he or she will not know. Therefore, one of the most important tasks of those at the top of an organizational hierarchy is to maintain open channels of communication with those below.

Weber wrote that in Germany, unlike China, people were hired for their competence, as evidenced by educational certificates or diplomas and passing grades on examinations, not because they were related to someone in the company, offered the highest fee for the position, or recently campaigned for the election of a government official. Since competence is the criterion for employment, bureaucracy is not the domain of families, clans, classes, or political parties. Also, every bureaucrat is replaceable by an equally or more competent one. Promotions are earned for competency, not because of seniority or other irrelevant factors. All this ensures that within the bureaucracy social status, family ties, or other social ranking mechanisms do not apply. The only ranking that does apply is the one engendered by the organizational hierarchy of the bureaucracy itself.

Individuals hired and promoted by government based on competence also possess tenure in their position; they cannot be dismissed because a supervisor does not like them or for any other reason not associated with their function within the organization.

According to Weber bureaucrats should not allow the public spotlight to shine on them; their actions should remain anonymous. They are to neither seek glory nor draw attention to themselves, which is acceptable only for their politically appointed supervisors.

Lastly, the bureaucrat's sole determinant for making decisions is reason based on existing regulations, according to Weber. Decisions based on political loyalty, pity, mercy, love, or personal relationships are strictly forbidden. Precedent is not a justification for decision making; past decisions are not reliable as they may not have considered present circumstances, were made based on different regulations, or simply were wrong. Rational decision making is the most important distinction between the bureaucrat and those who work for private enterprise. Workers in the private sector can regard clients with emotions such as, pity, mercy, and love and they are accountable only to their immediate supervisor. Bureaucrats, however, are accountable not only to their supervisors, but more importantly to the law from which all their authority originates. And law is passionless and in itself rational.

Max Weber's ideas have influenced not only how we perceive and study bureaucracy but also how bureaucracy is organized. Among Europeans and their kin in the Americas, the Weberian model of bureaucracy is the standard by which effectiveness and efficiency are measured. Every society, including China, has initiated a merit system for hiring, promoting, and guaranteeing job security for government employees. However, political appointees are not covered by the merit system in every society. Most employees in the U.S. Executive Office of the President, for example, are political appointees by design. In countries in the Southern Hemisphere where jobs are scarce for people with some education, political appointments still predominate, although the merit system covers an ever increasing number of government employees.

The emotionless, faceless, but competent and rational bureaucrat is still our ideal government worker. It is precisely because they do not measure up to that ideal that bureaucrats often are portrayed as villains or buffoons in plays, operas, novels, movies, and shows. Despite this ideal image, we frequently express reservations, if not fear, of the ideal becoming reality. Government by emotionless, faceless, competent, and rational bureaucrats is government by philosopher kings or computers.

If computers are allowed to govern, policy making and implementation are dehumanized. If bureaucrats allow themselves to be denied their humanity, they become rational decision-making machines. Fear of this type of policy maker has brought forth terms such as meritocracy, technocracy, and government-by-computer. All these terms mean that a professional group of policy makers, heedless of the desires, emotions, and passions of men and women and immune from the challenges of human frailty, is placed in the role of deciding the path of societal development. When dehumanized bureaucrats are formally organized into a hierarchy, the result is a dehumanized bureaucracy and therefore a dehumanized government. A dehumanized government is a government divorced from the people it is supposed to serve. If this occurs and people feel that the link between them and the government is too weak or broken, the situation is ripe for social change.

Max Weber's model bureaucracy, taken to its logical extension, is a pernicious destroyer of society in that it places the state above society. Since the people, being irrational, cannot possibly understand what the "rational" bureaucrats are doing for their benefit, they have to accept what government does in silence and with forbearance. Bureaucrats, of course, are people too; they know the do's and don'ts of their position and are aware of their own limitations. They know not to question supervisors or those who work in other agencies or departments. Since the people do not "know" all this, they cannot appreciate the intricate maneuvering involved in policy making and implementation. And because of this, they are irrelevant in the pursuit of governmental goals and objectives. Being irrelevant, they are also dispensable. Unless the people obey, bow down, and glorify the bureaucrats (i.e., the state), they may be purged. Fascism in the 1920s, 30s, and early 40s preached this viewpoint. A vestige of this type of thinking is still around, but it no longer is important.

Although Max Weber's model has its obvious weaknesses, it has been refined and amplified and remains the only viable one today. Fortunately, bureaucrats cannot meet the standards set by Weber, so they continue to be human and often act irrationally. Writers since World War II have attempted to qualify the Weberian model by regarding decision making as a process instead of just an act.

The Decision Making Process

The policy made by an individual who will be held responsible for it is a result of a lengthy and rather complex process that involves many variables. Decisions are made in time and are the culmination of many events. Decisions are made in space, that is, they are made in a particular environment and setting. Decisions are made in a social context; being social animals, individuals make decisions because of interactions with other humans. Decisions are made by an individual with physical, psychological characteristics that may, on the one hand, have created a uniqueness, while on the other, forced a sameness upon him or her.

Although decisions are made at a specific time and place, they are intricately linked to (1) past decisions; (2) characteristics of the decision maker, such as beliefs, values, norms, personality, character, and rationality; (3) the structure, environment, and objectives of the organization; and (4) the information available to the decision maker. Each factor is essential to the final decision.

Past Decisions

Any decision or policy is but a fragment of larger policy and becomes part of an already existing web of decisions made. Not only does this web of past decisions influence the current decision, but the current decision also will affect the web. To complicate things even more, not all past decisions equally affect the making of the new decision, nor does the new decision affect equally all the past decisions. As the web does not have definite boundaries or limits, decision makers are unaware of most previous decisions that affect the one they are making. Thus, decision makers have only partial knowledge of the decision or policy environment in which they act.

Furthermore, past decisions carry a momentum that considerably lessens the freedom to choose among alternatives. The time, resources, and efforts invested in the planning or implementation of a project or program are called **sunk costs**. Sunk costs give rise to what is called the gambler's syndrome. A gambler who has say $100.00 in quarters will have little inhibitions in walking away from a slot machine after placing one quarter into it; but probably will not leave that machine for another or stop gambling once he or she invested $50.00 in quarters. Once government agencies invest time, money, and resources into a program, they are inhibited from dropping it, for to do so means that the program was a mistake and what has been invested was wasted. The greater the sunk costs, the less likely that decision makers will change or cancel a program. Professionally and psychologically decision makers are unable to admit that they made a mistake. In addition, dozens, if not hundreds, of other bureaucrats (and their supporters outside the bureaucracy) may have a personal stake (their own sunk costs) in continuation of the program. Decision makers may want to avoid angry responses by these outsiders.

Characteristics of the Decision Maker

The policy maker's values, beliefs, and norms, which have been internalized through the acculturation process, will probably conform to those of society. A person raised in another society and confronted with the same situation would probably make a different decision. Since society must accept a bureaucrat's decision, it establishes the criteria for acceptance. Therefore the decision maker's values, beliefs, and norms are important only if they are consistent with those of society.

Personality and character are formed by values, beliefs, and norms as well as learned behavioral patterns and psychological attributes influenced by heredity and the environment. Although the policy maker is not conscious of these influences when making decisions, they do constitute a particular individuality that can leave an imprint on the decisions. However, the individuality must conform to societally established standards for the decision to be approved.

Rationality is one of the most perplexing factors affecting decision making. Although it has been a topic of discussion and debate for thousands of years, we still have problems finding an acceptable definition. The ancient Greeks called rationality a mix of intelligence, knowledge, common sense, wisdom, and pure consciousness. Today we are more inclined to view rationality as a process by which a desired end or objective is achieved with the least possible sunk costs. Individuals within an organization are faced with selecting from a set of alternatives the ones that will best bring about the desired results.

This view of rationality makes several assumptions. First, it assumes that decisions are related to objectives. Some decisions made by bureaucrats may have no objective. A motion to adjourn a meeting because fatigue has overcome those present does not resolve the issue being discussed, but does influence future decisions on that issue. In addition, a decision made when group members are physically or emotionally fatigued may not be the best decision, yet it resolves the issue. This is a rational decision even though not made with an objective in mind. Many labor-management disputes are resolved in this fashion, yet we would not label such decisions irrational or nonrational.

Furthermore, group decisions are the result of compromise. Several alternative solutions could each in its own way have the lowest sunk costs. Compromise means finding a solution that contains elements of all the alternatives; however, a compromise, although acceptable by most, is not necessarily the most cost effective or the best in any regard. During discussions about the best alternative to a particular objective, the objective not only can be redefined but also changed to the point where the new objective has little in common with the original one. For example, the acrimony among discussants can increase so much that they adopt a compromise solution, which is not the best way to resolve the problem but is the best way to keep the group from falling apart.

Second, rational decision making assumes that objectives are clear and known. Generally each decision must satisfy several objectives, some of which the decision makers may not even consciously acknowledge. Many decisions are made to satisfy egos, which often is vehemently and sincerely denied. Furthermore, imagined or unconscious objectives can veil real objectives; racist and sexist policies often are made by individuals who truly believe they are neither racist nor sexist.

Third, a problem exists with who determines the objectives. There are personal objectives, institutional objectives at different tiers, and finally societal objectives. Objectives at these different levels are perceived and ranked by the decision maker. However, the priorities can be used for meeting an objective while serving as a facade for the decision maker's real priorities. For example, a policy maker recommends creation of a health care program for the poor when he or she actually wants to increase the health care workforce.

Fourth, decisions invariably have unforeseen consequences. Some can be detrimental to the decision maker, the institution, and/or society, among others. Is a decision best when it achieves its stated objective but has disastrous unforeseeable consequences? For example, among several fish species that inhabit a lake one is undesirable because it has no predators and eats fish harvested and consumed by humans. A predator frog species is introduced, which eats the undesirable fish. The other fish flourish; however, when the frogs have no more undesirable fish to eat, they eat the desirable ones to the point where the frogs, which are not consumed by humans, become the sole inhabitant of the lake. With hindsight one can say that introduction of the frogs was not the best alternative; but at the time the decision was made it was the best. If the rationality of decisions can only be evaluated with hindsight, rationality cannot be part of the decision making process as a complete and infallible listing of possible consequences cannot be made and evaluated.

Fifth, another assumption is that every objective has a decision with the lowest sunk costs. How does one determine whether a particular decision is the one that possesses the lowest sunk costs? And is the lowest sunk cost necessarily the best solution to an objective? Concepts such as the least cost, although they might be quantifiable, contain elements that might be weighted differently by different persons, in different circumstances, or in different times. The values of time, resources, and effort are different in a capital-intensive environment than in a labor-intensive one. Each are perceived differently by a coal miner, a banker, an industrialist, a bureaucrat in the ministry of foreign affairs, and a bureaucrat in the ministry of transportation.

Another problem occurs in the determination of the lowest sunk cost. Time, resources, and effort can be evaluated in terms of society, government overall, a particular institution within government, or the individual. Whose sunk costs are involved? From an agency's objective, it can be highly cost effective to have bureaucrats work longer hours, for example, especially if they can be easily replaced. If these bureaucrats get sick to the point where they can no longer do their tasks, new bureaucrats replace them. But who will take care of the former bureaucrats? How are their families maintained? Who will pay for the old bureaucrats' or their families' maintenance and rehabilitation? What are the costs to society when sole bread winners are no longer able to earn any income? What are the effects on the former bureaucrats' family life, especially on their children?

Sixth, rationality as a process assumes that the person doing the rational thing has filtered out all nonrational influences. More than likely this is not the case since determining what nonrational influences affect a decision maker at any one time is impossible. The type of food consumed, quality of the air breathed, and temperature, barometric pressure, and humidity of the environment as well as many other physical factors influence human brain wave patterns and most certainly thought patterns. If a computer, which is an office machine fueled by electricity, is subject to variances in the fuel supply and its physical environment, then how much more is the human brain influenced by these and other variables?

Finally, does it make a difference for society if decisions are made rationally? Baboons, chimpanzees, gorillas, and virtually every other social species whose members live in groups make decisions that keep their societies viable. These social groups continue to exist for generations. Do these animals decide rationally? For human societies' viability and development, it makes little, if any, difference whether bureaucratic decisions are reached through the rational method or through another method. What is important is that wrong decisions, which are detrimental to societal development, are filtered out. This usually occurs when bureaucrats' values, norms, beliefs, and behavioral patterns cause them to prevent decisions from being implemented, regardless of how they originated.

Organizational Structure, Environment, and Objectives

The hierarchical structure of an organization (e.g., what offices report to which agencies, the number of different offices and agencies at a specific level, the number of bureaucrats that work in each office) determines what decisions will be made, by whom, and at which level. Obviously the Department of Agriculture will not make policies in areas in which the Department of the Interior has jurisdiction. However, when issues are placed under the jurisdiction of two or more departments, interagency conflicts result.

Each office, agency, and department has its own norms. These norms, whether written or customary, provide the basis for all policy making. In some agencies decisions are made by a group, and in others by an individual. In some offices decision makers get their information through memoranda and written reports, and in others information is gathered informally by word of mouth. Some agency heads hold weekly meetings with their assistants, others do so rarely, perhaps once every six months.

THE GOVERNMENT OF THE UNITED STATES

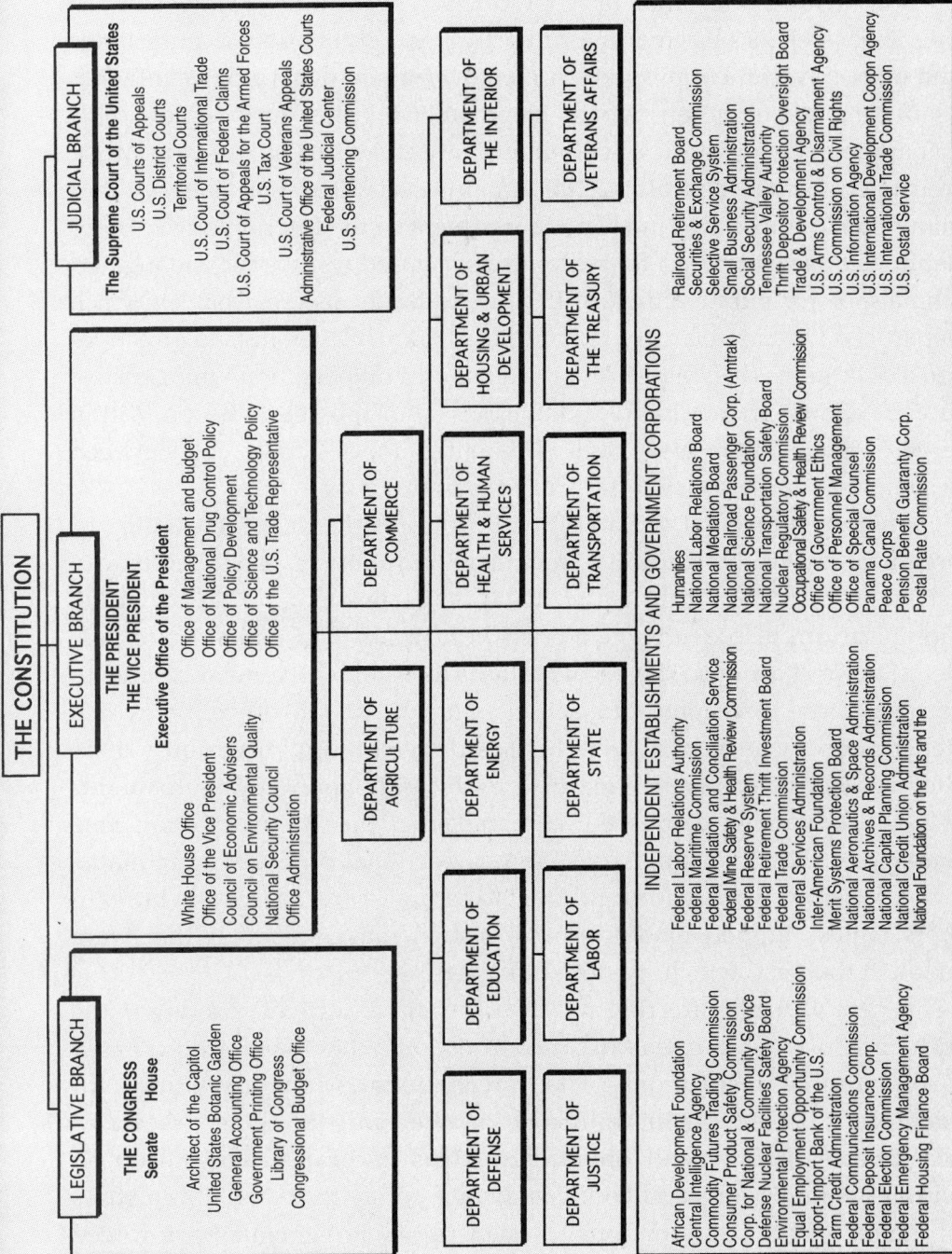

THE CONSTITUTION

LEGISLATIVE BRANCH

THE CONGRESS
Senate   House

Architect of the Capitol
United States Botanic Garden
General Accounting Office
Government Printing Office
Library of Congress
Congressional Budget Office

EXECUTIVE BRANCH

THE PRESIDENT
THE VICE PRESIDENT

Executive Office of the President

White House Office
Office of the Vice President
Council of Economic Advisers
Council on Environmental Quality
National Security Council
Office Administration

Office of Management and Budget
Office of National Drug Control Policy
Office of Policy Development
Office of Science and Technology Policy
Office of the U.S. Trade Representative

JUDICIAL BRANCH

The Supreme Court of the United States

U.S. Courts of Appeals
U.S. District Courts
Territorial Courts
U.S. Court of International Trade
U.S. Court of Federal Claims
U.S. Court of Appeals for the Armed Forces
U.S. Tax Court
U.S. Court of Veterans Appeals
Administrative Office of the United States Courts
Federal Judicial Center
U.S. Sentencing Commission

DEPARTMENT OF DEFENSE

DEPARTMENT OF JUSTICE

DEPARTMENT OF EDUCATION

DEPARTMENT OF LABOR

DEPARTMENT OF AGRICULTURE

DEPARTMENT OF ENERGY

DEPARTMENT OF STATE

DEPARTMENT OF COMMERCE

DEPARTMENT OF HEALTH & HUMAN SERVICES

DEPARTMENT OF TRANSPORTATION

DEPARTMENT OF HOUSING & URBAN DEVELOPMENT

DEPARTMENT OF THE TREASURY

DEPARTMENT OF THE INTERIOR

DEPARTMENT OF VETERANS AFFAIRS

INDEPENDENT ESTABLISHMENTS AND GOVERNMENT CORPORATIONS

African Development Foundation
Central Intelligence Agency
Commodity Futures Trading Commission
Consumer Product Safety Commission
Corp. for National & Community Service
Defense Nuclear Facilities Safety Board
Environmental Protection Agency
Equal Employment Opportunity Commission
Export-Import Bank of the U.S.
Farm Credit Administration
Federal Communications Commission
Federal Deposit Insurance Corp.
Federal Election Commission
Federal Emergency Management Agency
Federal Housing Finance Board

Federal Labor Relations Authority
Federal Maritime Commission
Federal Mediation and Conciliation Service
Federal Mine Safety & Health Review Commission
Federal Reserve System
Federal Retirement Thrift Investment Board
Federal Trade Commission
General Services Administration
Inter-American Foundation
Merit Systems Protection Board
National Aeronautics & Space Administration
National Archives & Records Administration
National Capital Planning Commission
National Credit Union Administration
National Foundation on the Arts and the

Humanities
National Labor Relations Board
National Mediation Board
National Railroad Passenger Corp. (Amtrak)
National Science Foundation
National Transportation Safety Board
Nuclear Regulatory Commission
Occupational Safety & Health Review Commission
Office of Government Ethics
Office of Personnel Management
Office of Special Counsel
Panama Canal Commission
Peace Corps
Pension Benefit Guaranty Corp.
Postal Rate Commission

Railroad Retirement Board
Securities & Exchange Commission
Selective Service System
Small Business Administration
Social Security Administration
Tennessee Valley Authority
Thrift Depositor Protection Oversight Board
Trade & Development Agency
U.S. Arms Control & Disarmament Agency
U.S. Commission on Civil Rights
U.S. Information Agency
U.S. International Development Coopn Agency
U.S. International Trade Commission
U.S. Postal Service

Different institutions have different objectives. The U.S. Department of Agriculture has as its objective the protection and promotion of the production of food and other farm products. The U.S. Department of the Interior has as its objective the protection and promotion of park lands and other government property. If the government owns a parcel of land, its future depends on which department gains jurisdiction. The Department of Agriculture will either lease it, sell it, or use it itself for research or actual food production. In any case, the department will not allow public use of the land. The Department of the Interior, on the other hand, will use that parcel for research, as a closed reserve for endangered animals, or for public activities. If you wanted to use that parcel, which department would you want to have jurisdiction? Differences in objectives can also be seen when ministries of defense are compared with ministries of foreign affairs. In addition, subdivisions and sub-subdivisions within larger organizations also have differences in objectives, as between accounting and personnel offices in the same agency.

Another important variable that influences the decision making of organizations is **institutional memory**. Individuals can overcome a crisis best if they can bring to it experiences and knowledge. Organizations also overcome a crisis best if they can make use of past decisions and actions. The organizations, consequently, must be able to retrieve these decisions and actions quickly and proficiently which depends on what records were kept and, even more important, where they were kept. An agency manned by recently appointed bureaucrats is at a disadvantage compared with an agency that has many long-time employees. The "old-timers" will remember what mistakes were made, what decisions were made, and how to locate the records. New bureaucrats, unless guided by "old-timers," often make mistakes that were made in the past, which wastes sunk costs.

A new variable affecting the decision making process today is the influence of international organizations on what have traditionally been national institutions. The International Monetary Fund, for example, has tremendous influence on the budgetmaking process in most states that depend on foreign loans or grants. The European Union's commissions and councils dictate policy to national ministries of member states. International human rights agreements have forced state agencies to adopt regulations and programs that they never would have adopted without these treaties.

The Congressional Research Service "hotline" (above) in the U.S. Capitol handles inquiries from Congressional offices. Specialist staff (below) prepare reports for members of Congress.

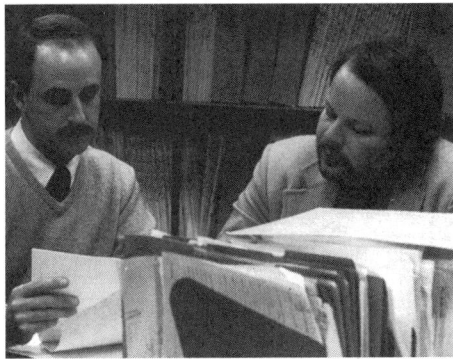

Information

Without information making decisions is difficult. Yet information is hardly ever neutral. The person preparing the information will often determine its content. Suppose you want to know how well the building you are in now is maintained. Information from the cleaning crew will be much different from that of building users, which also will be different from that of the owners. The information of an outside inspection agency also will be different from that of all three groups. Therefore, decision makers who want to make decisions that are not based on others' prejudgments need as many sources of information as they can gather.

More so than ever, today's decision makers depend on others to provide information, because they alone cannot possibly find all the information needed, or check on its accuracy and truthfulness. Good lines of communication therefore are crucial to good policy making. Those who provide information, however, also can control the decisions made by withholding information, which then skews decision makers' options. Total information is seldom available because information providers consciously or unconsciously filter out information they believe is unnecessary or is offensive to some of their internalized norms.

Nevertheless, the supply of information, due to the technological advancements of the twentieth century, has become limitless. A problem today is selecting data from the unlimited amount available. Consequently, decision makers increasingly rely on their staffs and others such as pressure groups, friends, suppliers, and consumers, to provide data. These people, who control the indispensable supply of information, become crucial partners in the decision making process, despite the perception that decision makers alone are responsible for policy development.

Decision making is not the act of one person but a process that inevitably begins with the collection of data from many different sources by many different individuals. Because this data is interpreted and reinterpreted as it moves up the hierarchy, each individual at each level becomes a part of the process. And, once a decision has been made at the top, its implementation is determined by the interpretation of that decision by those below. The "official" decision maker is but one individual within a process that involves many others.

TERMS TO REMEMBER

bureaucracy
bureaucrat
nepotism
Max Weber
span of control
sunk costs
institutional memory

SUGGESTED READINGS

Bendix, Reinhard. *MaxWeber: An Intellectual Portrait*. NewYork: Doubleday, 1960. A good analytical biography of the person who began the study of public administration.

Baldwin, Robert. *Rules and Government*. New York: Oxford University Press, 1995. The use of non-statutory rules, especially within the European Union, is the focus of this work.

Dowding, Keith and Desmond King, eds. *Preferences, Institutions, and Rational Choice*. New York: Oxford University Press, 1995. Collections of essays dealing with the use of rational choice in institutions and in setting priorities.

Gerth, H. H. and C. Wright Mills, eds. *From Max Weber: Essays in Sociology*. New York: Oxford University Press, 1958. A very popular compendium of Max Weber's writings.

Harris, Richard A. and Sidney M. Milkis. *The Politics of Regulatory Change: A Tale of Two Agencies*. 2nd ed. New York: Oxford University Press, 1996. The Federal Trade Commission and the Environmental Protection Agency have been subject to the attempts to curtail their activities by the Reagan Administration. This book deals at length with that issue and then takes it forward to the Bush and Clinton administrations.

Simon, Herbert A. *Administrative Behavior: A Study of Decision-Making Processes in Administration Organization*. New York: The Free Press, 1957. The first book that brought forth the idea of decision making as a process.

Thompson, Victor A. *Modern Organization*. New York: Knopf, 1961. A classic text on public administration.

Wallace, Helen and William Wallace, eds. *Policy Making in the European Union*. 3rd ed. New York: Oxford University Press, 1996. Fourteen case studies on how decisions are made within the various institutions of the European Union.

18

Administration

All executive branches of government are composed of ministries or departments with a chief administrator, either a president or a prime minister as the manager. Ministries and departments are hierarchically structured to perform tasks in a specific area, such as commerce, economic development, agriculture, education, defense, and foreign affairs. The state's constitution and laws determine the number of ministries. Some governments have few departments, such as the United States with fourteen, whereas others have as many as forty. This number changes as policy makers separate and consolidate tasks as the need arises. The trend in the twentieth century has been an increase in the number of ministries, which could continue as governments increasingly are called upon to provide more services.

The ministers or secretaries appointed to oversee a ministry or department are seldom supervised because the chief administrator often is too preoccupied in dealing with crises, real or imagined, which constantly crop up. Since much of what a chief administrator does relates to public relations (e.g., making speeches, holding news conferences, answering questions from legislators and the press, and making other types of public appearances), he or she cannot devote much time to managing appointees. Consequently, many departments enjoy free reign in their activities, until a department crisis gets the chief administrator's attention. In some countries in which political deals were made or the chief administrator is inattentive, department heads can virtually become lords over their bureaucratic fief. Under such circumstances corruption and other illegal activities can become widespread in these departments or policies are made and implemented without the chief administrator's knowledge or approval.

In Mexico, for example, the president appoints mostly cronies to ministerial positions. These associates in turn appoint their cronies to other positions within the ministry. The minister and the associates within the ministry are called a *camarilla*. When the president's term is over, he or she appoints someone from this network as successor. The new president continues the process. Each minister has considerable latitude in policy making and implementation and appointment of top administrators. In only a few states (usually those with few inhabitants) chief administrators can effectively supervise the appointees.

Usually departments or ministries are composed of many subdepartments or agencies, which makes it difficult for department heads to have total control of all of them. The many agencies in each department can be separated into divisions managed by an assistant secretary or vice minister. Again, like the departments, these subdivisions cannot be effectively controlled by head administrators. These agencies not only employ many workers but also are often in field offices located throughout the country, making it difficult for one person to oversee each operation. Of the approximately 2.8 million civilian employees of the U.S. federal government, fewer than 400,000 work in the Washington, D.C., area. If supervision at each of these departmental levels is so ineffectual, how are these institutions able to accomplish their goals and objectives? One factor that keeps institutions on the proper course is that all share the same social and cultural norms, among which is the notion that decisions are made by those with expertise. Also, each government worker knows in general the expectations regarding the tasks he or she was hired to perform. Both of these aspects keep government workers attuned to the demands of society.

The Americans with Disabilities Act (ADA) signed by President Bush in July 1990 provides protection against employment discrimination to individuals who are disabled but nonetheless able to work.

U.S. Foreign Service staff at the embassy at Minsk (the capital of Belarus, the former Soviet republic now on Russia's western border, north of Ukraine) with Secretary of State Warren Christopher (center), 1994.

Civil Service and Merit Systems

Virtually every society has adopted some variant of Max Weber's theory that bureaucrats should display competence in their work. Consequently every society has created an entity that establishes job qualifications and hires personnel accordingly. In the United States this entity, the Office of Personnel Management, is responsible not only for hiring qualified individuals but also for guaranteeing that employees are treated fairly and with respect, assuring them of deserved benefits and tenure.

Those who work as representatives of their state in other countries usually have to meet the qualifications initiated by a separate agency, a foreign service commission. This body operates similarly to a civil service commission, although qualifications for employment are much more stringent than those of a civil service commission.

These commissions fill government positions with qualified people. Since most of these positions involve skills that were unknown decades ago, the qualifications have become more demanding. In most societies being able to read, write, and do

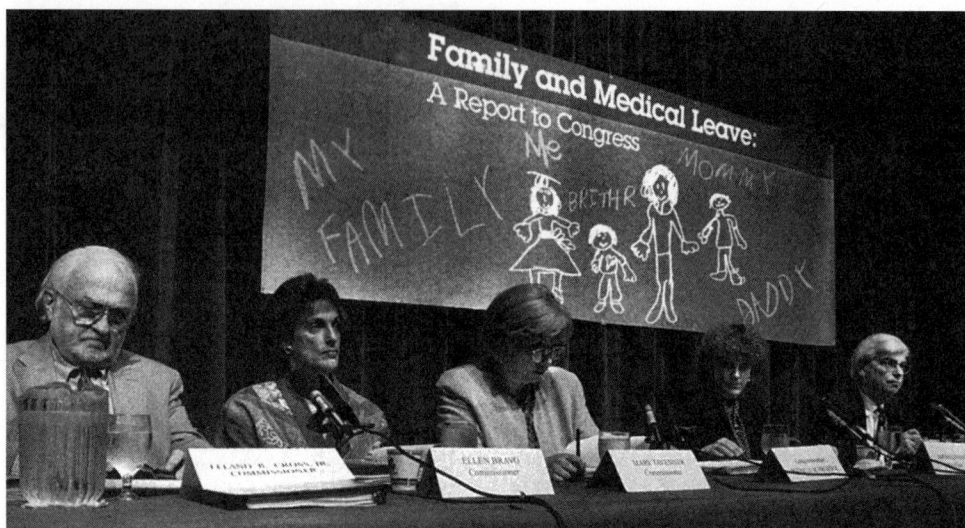

Members of the bipartisan Commission on Leave conducting a public hearing in Washington D.C., August 1995. Chair: Senator Christopher J. Dodd (right). The Family and Medical Leave Act (FMLA) of 1993 requires employers with 50 employees or more to provide up to 12 weeks of unpaid, job-protected leave to employees for the following reasons: care of a new-born, newly-adopted or foster child, spouse or parent with a serious health condition; or the serious health condition of the employee, including maternity-related disability. Employees are eligible to take leave if they have worked for a covered employer for at least one year, and for 1,250 hours over the previous 12 months, and if there are at least 50 employees working for their employer within a 75-mile radius.

basic arithmetic no longer is sufficient. Skills such as computer literacy, accounting, foreign languages, statistical analysis, and communications are becoming the norm. Government employees, therefore, must have a high school diploma, but also a degree from a college, university, or professional school or possess years of experience.

For many young persons in most societies military service provides a means to acquire the skills needed for government employment. In societies in which education is expensive to acquire the military is often the only source for obtaining an education and useful job skills. In addition, the military instills a healthy attitude toward work that is indispensable. Often military "graduates" are given incentives to work as civil servants.

One problem in the civil service is filling high level positions that require specialized skills. In France those who want a position in the higher echelons of civil service attend the National School of Administration, a professional school that teaches exclusively the skills necessary to obtain government supervisory positions. Societies that do not have special schools to train high level public administrators require a professional degree from a university in law, public administration, or policy analysis. Of course, promotions from within the civil service elevates bureaucrats who at least have the experience, if not the competence, for these offices.

The activities of these commissions are designed to maintain a professional bureaucracy, one that will do its job in the most efficient way with the least amount of notoriety. More than eighteen million people work for governments in the United States alone. In Australia one of every six workers is employed by a government. In many states government is by far the largest employer and provider of goods and services. What is surprising, despite all the negative comments about bureaucrats and bureaucracy, is that the process works. Scandals and shortcomings involving particular bureaucrats and agencies do not involve the overwhelming majority of government employees, who are committed to their work; maintain professional, social, moral, and ethical standards; and uphold their integrity and that of their government position.

Agencies That Oversee the Bureaucracy

To prevent bureaucrats from divorcing themselves too much from the needs, wishes, and demands of the citizenry and to hold them accountable to those who ultimately pay their salaries, institutions were established to supervise bureaucratic activity. In France, for example, two bodies ascertain whether agencies, regardless of hierarchical level, perform their functions according to law and expectation. One is the Council of State (*Conseil d'Etat*), which formulates and enforces clear and specific rules on how the bureaucracy relates with the citizenry. The second is the Court of Accounts (*Cour de Comptes*), which audits all government expenditures. Members of both these entities are chosen from the professional staffs of the bureaucracy.

The British do things somewhat differently. They have about two thousand quasi-autonomous nongovernmental organizations called **quangos**. These government-financed agencies, whose members are appointed by the ministers, oversee the operations of the bureaucracy. Although some members have executive powers, most have to be content with only advisory functions. Since they rely on bureaucrats to provide information, quangos can easily be manipulated by bureaucrats to their viewpoints.[1]

The U.S. General Accounting Office has functions similar to those of the French Court of Accounts. The GAO is a congressional agency, created by and responsible to Congress. Since almost everything that governments do involves the expenditure of funds, the GAO's staff has the

GAO's Headquarters Building is the base from which its staff conducts reviews of Federal programs worldwide. GAO was established by the Budget and Accounting Act of 1921, as an independent agency for the purpose of providing an independent audit of Government agencies. GAO is under the control and direction of the Comptroller General of the United States, who is appointed by the President with the advice and consent of the Senate for a term of 15 years.

A GAO team of fourteen members spent two weeks in Saudi Arabia during April 1991, assessing the military supply and distribution systems and the valuation of in-kind donations made by U.N. coalition members to support Operation Desert Shield and Operation Desert Storm.

authority to inspect any program or project undertaken by any federal agency. By reporting to Congress directly the GAO points out any wrongdoing to that branch of government that has at least nominal control of future appropriations and publicizes such misdeeds.

Independent Regulatory Agencies and Corporations

To insulate the professional bureaucrat from the deleterious effects of partisan politics in the United States, Congress and the presidency created of a set of offices called **independent regulatory agencies**. The agencies are called independent because the president appoints members to each of their governing boards, with the advice and consent of the Senate, for a fixed term, usually five to seven years. Unlike a department head, the president cannot dismiss these board members because he or she disagrees with the policies they make or enforce. As a result the wheeling and dealing of politics theoretically is not a factor in the consideration of policies by these agencies. Although Congress passes laws to establish and give authority to these agencies, it seldom would interfere with agency activities.

In many ways the independent regulatory agencies do tasks that are essential for effective functioning of society. They not only police and coordinate communications over the airwaves (i.e., radio, television, telephone) but also determine consumer fees for interstate transportation and communication and, among many other functions, decide the amount of money in circulation, which determines interest rates and other economic factors. These agencies are the last source of appeal in their area of jurisdiction unless a lawsuit is filed through the court system. Since these agencies seldom lose in court because of the vast amount of data they possess, they consequently are extremely influential in determining government policies in their respective areas.

A trial attorney in the Public Integrity Section of the Criminal Division in the Department of Justice reviews a case involving the corruption of an elected public official.

Because independent regulatory agencies effectively regulate so many relations between individuals and the providers of services and goods, they have **quasi-legislative** and **quasi-judicial** powers. Quasi-legislative power is the authority to make rules in harmony with duly made laws; quasi-judicial power is the authority to interpret rules according to norms established by the higher courts. These two powers and the power of enforcing rules, give these agencies total control in their narrow area of jurisdiction. They make the rules, interpret the rules, and enforce the rules. They can impose **civil penalties**, fines persons or corporations pay when they do not obey an agency's regulations. This is a lot of power. Although Congress and the president through law can override agency decisions, they seldom do so because neither has the expertise available to refute an agency's justifications for its policies or the power to overcome the interests that originally prompted the decisions. The control of these agencies thus restricts the executive's power to "rule," making policy making even more fragmented.

Most other countries do not have independent regulatory agencies. They would not exist in the parliamentary system because the legislature has total control of policy making, interpretation, and enforcement. In other presidential systems, such as in Latin America, presidential powers are heavily restricted already, so there is no point in adding more restrictions. Therefore, the independent regulatory agencies are a unique creation of the United States.

This does not mean that functions performed by the agencies are left undone in other countries. On the contrary, in other states these functions and many others are performed, often more effectively, by the ministries. Sometimes regulatory functions are given to a ministry that normally would not be identified with that task. For example, a ministry of housing might supervise the regulation of preventive health measures. Even in the United States some regulatory agencies in departments appear to have little to do with what is being regulated, such as the Coast Guard in the Department of Commerce. Usually, however, several regulatory functions are consolidated in one ministry, which explains why some countries have forty or more ministries. The goal in these countries is not to restrict the executive's power to "rule" because the prime minister or president can dismiss ministers without much fanfare. However, when so many ministries exist, the executive cannot supervise, much less control, everything that goes on in every ministry. Furthermore, as in the United States, these ministries or agencies have so much expertise in their area that inquiries and admonitions from the chief executive are at best an exercise in public relations and often an exercise in futility.

Neither the boards nor the ministers really operate these regulatory agencies or ministries. Each has a professional staff that makes the decisions. If the staff makes decisions based strictly on their expertise, everything is fine. However, sometimes decisions are made because groups being regulated offer rewards for a favorable decision. Regulation then becomes a facade for corruption, with consequences that cause distrust and even rebellion among the people. Fortunately, this situation occurs infrequently.

Public corporations operate in a similar manner as regulatory agencies or ministries. A public corporation is a government-owned enterprise that provides services or goods, usually for a fee. Besides the postal service, other public corporations in the United States include Amtrak and Conrail, rail services owned and operated by boards appointed to fixed terms by the president with the advice and consent of the Senate; the Tennessee Valley Authority, one of the largest electricity producing enterprises in the world; and the Public Broadcasting Corporation, producer of television programs. U.S. state, county, and municipal governments own and operate through public corporations water and sewage facilities, electric utilities, hospitals, and colleges and universities. The United States has the fewest public corporations of any industrialized country because it

Congress established the Tennessee Valley Authority that built dams and powerplants on the Tennessee River to prevent floods and produce cheap electricity for the farmers in the impoverished area.

prefers to regulate the services instead of owning them outright. Utilities in most countries of the world are public corporations. In the United Kingdom utilities, coal mines, some airlines, and trucking companies (and at one time the entire steel industry) are public corporations. Sidermex, the largest steel producer in Mexico, is owned and operated by the government. The French and Italian governments own and operate automobile factories. Public corporations own and operate most oil wells in the world.

Public corporations generally operate as efficiently as private ones. Since they operate under much greater public scrutiny and have many more regulations than private enterprises, public corporations generally provide services cheaper and better. Furthermore, they can make investments in a society's infrastructure, such as in power plants that do not have immediate payoffs or in manufacturing plants requiring much expensive machinery or labor, that go beyond the economic capacity of any group of private investors. Consequently government, through its ability to tax and borrow, can amass these investments, thereby upgrading the economic foundation of society. Sometimes government is forced to take over the control of an incompetently managed, privately owned industry, such as the railroads in the United States and coal mines in the United Kingdom, because of national security issues or an economy that cannot handle the high unemployment that would occur if the industry failed.

Policy Formulation *vs* Policy Implementation

Every bureaucrat who implements policy also makes policy. The bureaucrat who approves my application for a license makes a policy decision regarding the regulations affecting my application. He or she decides what regulations apply and if my application complies with them. Whether my application is approved may affect the regulations themselves in as much as it may set a precedent. However, those who determine the regulations and the application approval process may not be the same persons who implement them.

When bureaucracies are large and regulation making is a significant task in itself, sometimes an organizational distinction is made between those who formulate regulations and those who implement them. Functions geared toward relating to the public on a day-to-day basis (i.e., tasks that essentially involve policy implementation) are called **line functions**. Policy formulation functions, which rarely involve daily contact with the public, are called **staff functions**.

In most agencies the higher a bureaucrat is in a hierarchy, the more staff functions and the fewer line functions he or she performs. Most agencies, indeed all government departments or ministries, are mandated to implement policies that chief executives and their aides formulate and approve. However, as we have learned, chief executives cannot possibly formulate policies for all the agencies and therefore must rely on others to do so. Then where do government policies originate?

In most governments the cabinet, the ministers, and the individuals second in command of a ministry possess staff functions. Ministers and their closest assistants formulate policies that the chief executives tacitly or explicitly approve. In Great Britain these top professional administrators are collectively called the *mandarins* (a term formerly used for public officials in the Chinese Empire).

Since the 1930s in the United States several federal staff agencies have been created that only formulate policies. These agencies are collectively called the **Executive Office of the President**. The Executive Office of the President includes the Office of Management and Budget, the Council of Economic Advisers, the National Security Council, the Office of Science and Technology Policy, and the National Space Council, among others. Each council or office is headed by a director, who is appointed by the president, and a board composed of department heads, the vice president, and knowledgeable individuals within or outside government.

President Ronald Reagan, Vice President George Bush, and their advisory staff in the White House discussing administrative reforms, 1987.

Personnel at all levels in the Executive Office of the President serve at the discretion of the president, who can hire and fire workers at will. Although these bureaucrats receive the same fringe benefits as other bureaucrats, they have no job security. They are hired not necessarily because of competence but more so on the level of trustworthiness or confidence that the president has in them. Most of these six thousand to eight thousand bureaucrats pack their bags when the president leaves office.

The Executive Office of the President was meant to provide the president with his own set of advisors in as much as bureaucrats do not change when a new administration takes over (at least every eight years and often much sooner). Proposed department policies emanate from the mind-set of bureaucrats in that department; consequently, most policies are nonpartisan and void of any politics that brought the president into office. This was especially true during the administration of Franklin Delano Roosevelt, who desperately needed new policies to overcome the terrible economic and social conditions of American society. To get new ideas he met with his cronies in the kitchen of the White House, where they discussed and formulated polices. This "kitchen cabinet" has become institutionalized in the Executive Office of the President.

The Executive Office of the President contains the most important agency of the U.S. government, the Office of Management and Budget. Every request for funds and expenditures as well as for reorganization of agencies within a department must be approved by the OMB. The approximately eight hundred OMB employees prepare the federal budget and send Congress a condensed version to discuss and eventually approve.

Congressional Budget Office (CBO) was established by the Congressional Budget Act of 1974 to assist the Congress in reviewing the Federal budget (prepared by the President with the assistance of the OMB) and to make decisions on spending and taxing levels and the deficit or surplus these levels incur. As the Federal budget must be considered in the context of the current and projected state of the national economy, CBO provides periodic forecasts and analyses of economic trends and alternative fiscal policies. In the picture above: CBO staff reviewing computer reports on budget details (left), and reviewing a committee transcript on Federal appropriations (right).

The Budget

The budget is the most important law passed by a legislative body in a year or session. Since almost everything government does requires funds, the budget shows not only the hierarchy of programs, the increases and decreases in emphasis on programs over a period, and the programs created and ended but also the sources of funding.

As important as the budget is, however, one must consider that in societies today not one but many budgets exist. There are local community budgets, regional and provincial budgets, national budgets, and even international budgets. Dozens and sometimes hundreds or thousands of different budgets exist in any given society. A previous chapter stated that the United States has almost ninety thousand governments, each with a budget. The total U.S. government budget is the summation of all these budgets, which in 1992 was an estimated $2,262 billion.[2]

All budgets are divided into at least two parts. One part deals with **revenues**, the funds coming into government; the other part deals with **appropriations**, the funds government spends.

Revenues

The ultimate source of income for any government is the people. Both individuals and corporations, must send some of their material wealth to the government. In ages past they may have sent a cow or a chicken to the political leaders of their society; today payment is made in money.

PERCENT

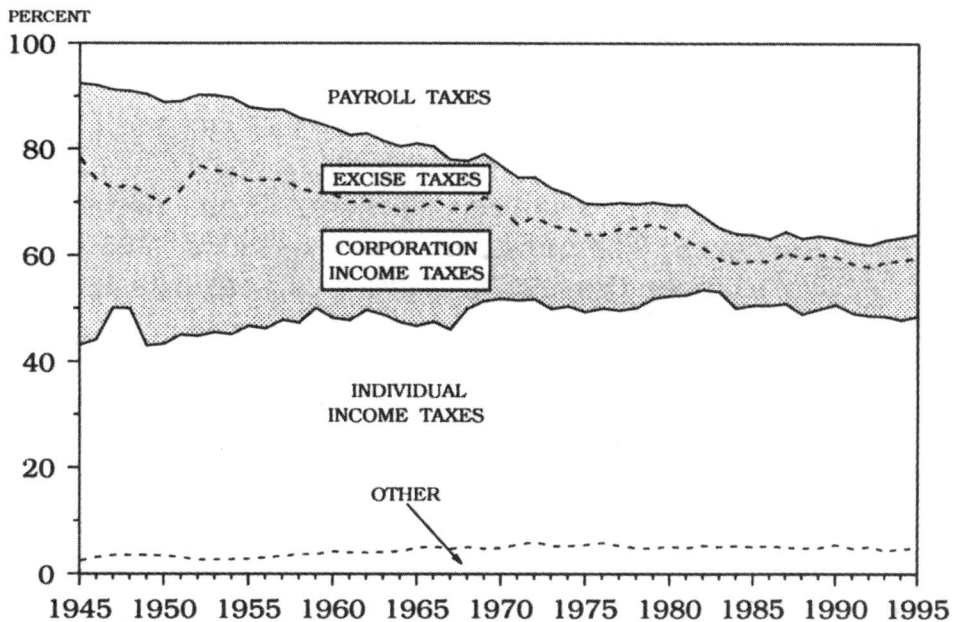

Sources of U.S. Federal receipts. The sources of Federal revenues have changed over the years. Before Congress established the individual income taxes early in the twentieth century, the Government received most of its revenues from excise taxes, customs duties, and sales of land. Gradually, income taxes accounted for a larger share of receipts.

Periodically government does not actually receive enough money to operate all of its programs; therefore it prints money (it owns or controls the printing presses). This works in an emergency or for a short term, but eventually the people pay for printing of extra money through inflation by having more money circulating the economy.

Revenue collection depends on the effectiveness of the technology used and the ability of bureaucrats to make collections with the least harm

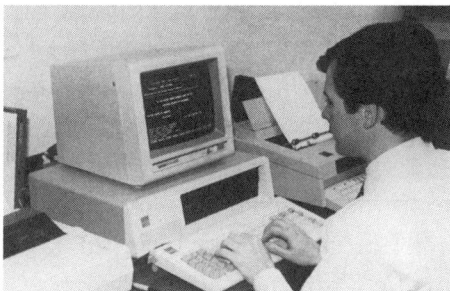

Use of a personal computer enables this trial attorney to keep track of volumes of data and documents to be used in trials involving abusive tax shelters.

to the authority and legitimacy of government. Modern technology has made it possible not only to create and retrieve large amounts of income and property data but also to rapidly calculate taxes based on that data. Computer technology has led to increased sources of revenue, enabling governments to provide new services. Large societies in particular depend on technology for effective use of the numerous resources for government revenue. For example, keeping track of the millions of payroll withholdings taken in by governments every week would be impossible without computers. Computers also make record-keeping of all sales and the amount of taxes collected much easier and efficient.

Property Taxes

Government uses a variety of ways to get money from the people. It can declare that the land and buildings a person or group owns have a certain value, part of which is owed to government as the *real estate property tax*, sometimes simply called *property tax.* This tax has nothing to do with the services, such as water or sewage, that the government may provide. It is a tax on land and buildings, which sometimes includes assets, such as machinery, vehicles, and tools that a private enterprise owns.

A similar tax is the *personal property tax*, which is a tax on the value of items owned, such as furniture, any means of transportation, jewelry, clothing, appliances, and machinery. In the United States personal property taxes are paid on automobiles, boats, and airplanes owned by individuals (but not corporations, because they are considered assets). In the United Kingdom and other states individuals pay a tax on televisions and radios; these revenues fund the British Broadcasting Corporation. In addition, individuals in some countries also pay a tax on any dog or cat owned; these are called *animal taxes.* Usually all these taxes are paid annually.

Sales Taxes

Another category of taxes, the *sales tax*, is based on items purchased. The most common way to collect a sales tax is by adding 1 percent to 12 percent on to the price paid at time of purchase. The seller becomes a tax collector by transferring this amount to the government. Occasionally, the buyer is not charged more than the price of the item; yet the seller has to transfer a certain portion of that price to the government. This is a *hidden sales tax,* often called an *excise tax.* Most gasoline is sold this way. Other excise taxes are levied on luxury goods, such as fine jewelry, furs, and expensive automobiles. Closely related to hidden sales taxes are *sin taxes,* which are levied on items that are legal but considered harmful to a person's well-being, such as tobacco products and alcoholic beverages. Often the price of this item is determined by the amount of taxes on it of which the buyer is not aware. The buyer may be paying an extra sales tax, of which he is aware, on an item whose price is basically determined by taxes. A $10.00 bottle of liquor may include $5.00 of hidden taxes. The customer has to pay, assuming a 6 percent sales tax, $10.60 for that bottle. This means the customer paid $0.30 on the $5.00 tax on that bottle.

Another hidden sales tax is the *severance tax,* which is either a fixed amount or part of the value of goods removed from their natural setting. Timber, coal, petroleum, and minerals extracted from the earth are subject to this tax, which is usually charged on a per-weight or volume basis.

The *tariff* is a hidden sales tax that was the main source of government revenue for more than two hundred years, until it was replaced by the income tax. A tariff, sometimes called an *import tax*, is a tax on an item manufactured in or extracted from another society. Generally, tariffs were levied as a way to generate income for the state and less as a way to limit imports. Of all taxes, tariffs are the easiest to administer. Goods produced by other societies come into another society only through certain roads,

Cartoon from a 1912 issue of Puck magazine. Two-faced protectionism — big business seeks high tariffs to protect the jobs and living standards of American workers; and then it employs cheap foreign labor. President Woodrow Wilson signed the Underwood Tariff of 1913, setting the stage for low tariffs. The purpose of the bill was to remove the special privileges protectionism had given to certain American businesses. The tariff remained moderately protectionist at twenty-nine percent (down from forty percent), but customs receipts decreased by 100 million dollars. To recover the lost revenue, the bill included an income tax provision, the first to be written under the recently ratified Sixteenth Amendment that authorized the federal government to tax incomes.

President John Kennedy signing the Trade Expansion Act of 1962. The Act provided the President with a five-year authority to negotiate tariff reductions of up to 50 percent, particularly with the European Common Market. Kennedy referred to the Act as "the most important international piece of legislation ... affecting economics since the passage of the Marshall plan." Wilbur Mills (third from left), Chairman, Ways & Means Committee was instrumental in pulling together the trade agreement.

harbors, rail lines, and airports. Tax collectors, called customs officials, inspect the goods being transported, decide whether they are allowed into the country, and then levy a percentage of the value of the goods as a tax. Importers pay the tax and then add it to the cost of the product.

In some less industrialized countries, especially those that do not possess the technology or competence to collect sales or income taxes, tariffs are still the predominant source of income, however, their use has been manipulated to favor some groups over others. For example, in the last century several Latin American states levied higher tariffs on machinery going to the industrial sector than on those going to the agricultural sector because the government was controlled by landowners of large farms. Many governments levied high tariffs on luxury goods and low tariffs on necessities. The tariff levied on a $30,000 Mercedes Benz imported into Argentina in the 1970s, for example, was $45,000; the customer paid $75,000 plus any overhead and the profit the importer and dealer added.

The *export tax,* which is a levy on goods leaving a society, is closely related to the tariffs but rarely used today. Until the 1800s it also was a very popular tax, but government dropped it when they realized that it harmed those attempting to further the economic well-being of society. Use of the export tax is forbidden by the U.S. Constitution. It is still used by a few governments, mostly in less industrialized societies.

A hidden sales tax that has become popular in many countries is the *value-added tax,* usually shortened to VAT. At each level in the manufacture, production, or extraction of a product a small portion, usually less than 2 percent, of the value of the cost at that level is added to the total price. The more stages in the production or extraction of a product, the higher the total VAT levied. Customers buy the product without awareness of the VAT. The seller, who knows the total VAT, sends it to the government. The European Union is financed through a VAT collected in all fifteen member states. Sophisticated bookkeeping technology is required to calculate and collect VATs.

Income Taxes

A third category of taxes is the income tax. Whereas sales taxes are levies on what one spends, income taxes are levies on the money or other wealth one acquires. Except for the inheritance tax, the income tax is relatively new. In the past goods and services usually were traded rather than paid for in cash, so determining an individual's income was very difficult. Furthermore, the technology required to keep records of transactions by which one acquired wealth has been available only since the last part of the nineteenth century.

Income taxes often are considered either *regressive* or *progressive*. An extremely regressive income tax levies the same amount on each person receiving income, regardless of whether the income is low or high. If the income tax is $400, both the person who makes $2,000 and the person who makes $30,000 pay this amount. Less regressive is the *flat tax*, which levies a specific percentage of income on everyone, regardless of their income level. If the income tax is 3 percent, the person who makes $2,000 pays $60 while the person who makes $30,000 pays $900. A progressive income tax increases the ratio of tax to income as the income increases. Therefore, a person whose income is $2,000 pays 3 percent, or $60, whereas the person making $30,000 pays 10 percent, or $3,000. The progressive income tax predominates in societies in which government is actively pursuing a redistribution of wealth. The regressive income tax is used in societies in which the government attempts to maintain or even create accumulation of wealth by those who already possess it.

One of the oldest taxes is the *inheritance tax*, which is a tax on all or part of wealth (i.e., an estate) that is given through a will from one person after death to another, usually a relative. The more valuable the items, the higher the taxes paid to the government by the recipient. An estate includes money (cash or bank accounts), stocks, bonds, loans, and property, both real estate and personal property such as jewelry, works of art, and antiques. Often parts of the estate are sold to pay the tax.

Another income tax is the *capital gains tax*, which is a tax on property that is sold for a higher price than it was acquired, such as a house. Suppose you bought a house for $60,000 and sold it for $90,000. The difference between the two prices is called capital gains; the government taxes part of this income but only once in a person's lifetime. Capital gains earned on other real estate or any item sold for a price that is higher than the original purchase price must be taxed at a portion of its value. If a house is inherited, the value of the house at the time of transfer of its title is considered the equivalent of a purchase.

A variant of the capital gains tax is a tax charged in some countries after the government makes improvements in a neighborhood or makes it more accessible to others. In Colombia, for example, when a road is built, the owners of the real estate located near the road are assessed a tax based on how close their property is to the new road. Neighborhood improvement projects frequently are financed from funds generated by taxes on the higher property values those projects are expected to generate.

Self-employed professionals and businesses pay a *business and occupation tax*. This tax is usually levied on the gross receipts of professionals, such as lawyers, piano tuners, and plumbers, and on all money paid to businesses, regardless of the amount of profit or loss. The tax, however, is usually very small, less than a tenth of a per cent.

The greatest single source of revenue for most governments today is the *personal and corporate income tax*. All funds, except loans, obtained by an individual over the course of a year and not otherwise taxed are subject to taxation as personal income, including wages, salaries, commissions, tips, dividends, and interest. Sometimes monetary gifts below a certain amount are excluded. Usually individuals can deduct particular expenses from their total income, thus distinguishing taxable income from gross income. For example, a person with $30,000 yearly income pays taxes on only $20,000 of that income, which is the taxable income.

In the past income taxes were paid at a certain time of the year. Usually the taxpayer could not pay the total amount owed and had to either borrow it or schedule payments with the government; some just simply forgot to file or refused to pay any amount. In the 1930s and 1940s the method of withholding income tax was initiated, which meant employees collected their employees' income taxes on wages, salary, or commissions earned in every pay period. Employees who paid too much in taxes received a refund at the end of the year; employees who paid too little owed the difference to the government.

Corporate income taxes are levied only on company profits. The corporation pay taxes on a monthly or quarterly basis that represent an estimate of its anticipated profits. At the end of the tax year company accountants tabulate the exact profits, and the company either gets a refund or pays the amount due.

Other Taxes

Until the middle of the twentieth century, some states in the United States, enforced a *poll tax*, which is a tax paid at the time of voting. The Twenty-fourth Amendment to the Constitution abolished this type of tax. Very few countries impose the poll tax; those that do use it to manipulate elections by making the tax so high so not to have the poor vote.

Another important tax in the past was the *stamp tax*. Official letters to a government agency had to be written on special paper and/or had to have a special stamp affixed to them. The paper and the stamp could be purchased only from the government, which was considered a tax on petitioning the government. The Stamp Act of 1765 passed by the British Parliament increased the price of these stamps to persons living in the thirteen colonies and was the cause of much resentment. Since they are easy to collect, many less industrialized countries still use stamp taxes.

American colonists protesting the Stamp Act. A riot led to the repeal of the Act, but colonial discontent remained and later exploded in the Revolutionary War.

Fees For Services

Governments charge fees for certain services. User fees are charges for using something owned by the government, such as pasture land, parks, museums, airports, and other facilities. Other fees include application fees for licenses or for certifications granted by government officials. Application fees are charged for drivers' permits and licenses, construction of or changes to buildings, admission to public colleges and universities, and passports. Government certification is provided to businesses to verify that an establishment is safe, healthy, and operates professionally or under government supervision. Tuition for public institutions of learning and charges for goods sold by governments, including electricity, postal services, and water and sewage services, also provide a considerable amount of revenue. During the last hundred years most national governments also have entered the insurance business, providing all types of insurance from medical insurance to pension plans for fees.

Finally, most governments also collect tolls for use of particular roads, rivers, harbors, airports and rail lines. Fees are easy to collect because they are charged at the time a government service or product is used.

Special Allocated Taxes

Usually funds collected through taxes are added to revenues generated by other means and are allocated to general appropriations in the budget. However, at times a special tax is designated to finance creation or maintenance of a special program or project. Income from special allocated taxes cannot be used to fund other government activities. For example, the gasoline tax and highway tolls have funded the maintenance of many U.S. interstate highways. In Bolivia a sales tax on coca leaves and alcohol partially funds its universities. A one-cent tax on a can or small bottle of soda pop sold in West Virginia is the main source of funds for the medical school of that state's main university.

TYPES OF GOVERNMENT TAXES

Property Taxes	Sales Taxes	Income Taxes	Other Taxes
Real estate tax	Excise or hidden sales tax	Business and occupation tax	Poll tax
Personal property tax	Export tax	Capital gains tax	Stamp tax
Animal tax	Sales tax	Flat tax	Special allocated tax
	Severance tax	Inheritance tax	
	Sin tax	Personal and corporate income tax	
	Tariff or import tax	Progressive income tax	
	Value-added tax	Regressive income tax	

Other Revenues

Few individuals in industrial societies have not paid a fine for some offense. For some local governments, especially those in areas used by transients (i.e., people traveling through an area) fines provide more than a third of the revenues. Many highways and police pension plans in the United States are maintained by fines levied on people who violate traffic laws. Usually courts assess fines; however, government agencies empowered to maintain standards or to collect taxes have the authority to levy fines, called civil penalties, on those who do not follow the standards or instructions. Restaurant owners who allow unhealthy conditions in their establishment are fined by health department officials. Taxpayers who violate federal tax laws are fined by the Internal Revenue Service. The power of independent regulatory agencies often stems from the ability to impose financial penalties on individuals and businesses for not complying with their rules.

One rather peculiar and increasingly popular source of government revenue is the lottery, which is based on the predilection of many persons to hope for miracles and an easy way to become rich. Most legally operated lotteries reward a few with wealth at the expense of the many who lose money spent on tickets. Lotteries, which take advantage of a wide-spread gambling syndrome generally considered bad by society, generate funds that often are used to maintain health clinics, schools, senior centers and other facilities for the elderly, young, or poor. Use of lotteries by government gives the appearance that it can encourage bad habits by citizens if it is for the good of society.

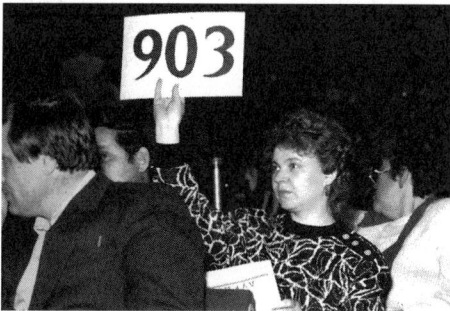

Russians bidding for businesses at an auction in 1992 by the City of Nizhny Novgorod, which was selling 2,000 small municipal enterprises. International Finance Corporation (IFC) helped in the design and implementation of the auction, that marked the beginning of Russia's privatization program.

Another nontax source of government revenue, which is almost as old as government itself, is called *privatization*. Governments own much property acquired through sale, conquest, confiscation, condemnation, inheritance, and development of services that private corporations would not provide, such as industries, utilities, and insurance and financial services. Occasionally governments sell some of these properties to private individuals or enterprises. In countries in the Southern Hemisphere many government-owned factories, mines, and utilities have been sold to private investors, usually at the request of international lending agencies that believe these facilities could be more efficiently run by the private sector.

In modern times privatization has been expanded to leasing properties or facilities to others to manage them. Public parks lease lodging and restaurant facilities to private businesses that pay either a flat fee or a percentage of the earnings to the government. Governments can use privatization to give the appearance of reducing the number of governmental workers while gaining more revenue. Users of these services encounter often an intermediate layer of business, which seeks to make a profit (remember Karl Marx's theory?), between them and those ultimately responsible for providing the service. For example, any bookstores in public universities in the United States are leased to privately owned companies, which reimburse a student only $8.00 for a $40.00 textbook that they will sell again for $32.00.

An important source of revenue for local and provincial governments is the national government. State or provincial governments, countries, special districts, and municipal governments receive funds from the national government. For some projects and programs state and local governments pay only a small part (as low as 10 percent) of the total cost and the national government provides the rest. Local governments get much of their revenue from state and national sources; however, the greater the amount of state or national government funding, the less autonomy governments have in setting the standards for the programs being funded.

Foreign aid is a source of revenue for national governments. Some national governments give grants, which do not have to be repaid, to other national governments to underwrite the expenses for specific programs or projects or to lessen budgetary shortfalls that are too great to make up. Most foreign aid, however, is given as loans from industrialized states to nonindustrial states to create the infrastructure required for industrialization to begin. Usually the government giving the aid sets the standards for spending it.

Finally a very important source of revenue for governments today is borrowing. Very few governments today anywhere are not in debt. The principal way governments borrow money is through bonds, which are loans made by a person or group. The government repays the bonds at their face value plus accumulated interest either within a specific time period (e.g., months, years, or decades) or in installments made on a daily, weekly, monthly, quarterly, or yearly basis. A bond is a loan agreement in which the borrower promises to repay the principal plus interest over a given time. Governments have in the last twenty-five years have borrowed more money than in all of history — a fact that worries many economists.

Construction of the Mangla Dam across the Jhelum River, Pakistan (1960s). Development of the Indus Basin was one of the largest projects of its kind ever to be undertaken. Funds were provided by World Bank loans, International Development Association (IDA) credits, and contributions from Australia, Canada, Germany, New Zealand, the United Kingdom, and the United States.

Liberty Bonds. In 1918, members of the U.S. Congress set an example for the nation by queuing up outside the Capitol to buy Liberty Bonds. Most citizens bought denominations of $50 to $10,000. War-savings certificates contained 20 war-savings stamps, each with a maturity value of $5. Thrift stamps were 25 cents each. About 21 billion dollars were raised in five bond-drives that provided two-thirds of the overall spending towards the nation's role in World War I.

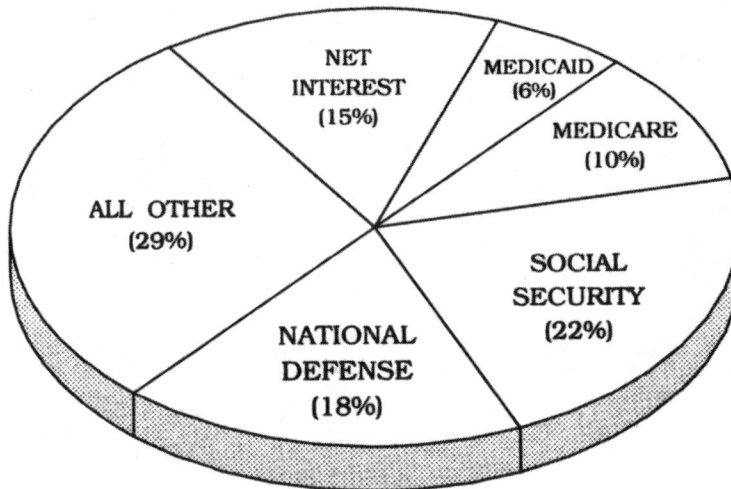

Over seventy percent of U.S. Federal spending is on a few major programs (1995). Foreign aid and welfare account for less than three percent of all Federal spending.

Utilization of Revenues

All these sources of revenue are often used simultaneously by governments within a society today. By spreading the sources of revenue, governments give the appearance that members of a society are not that heavily taxed. One percent of this, 2% of that, 3% here, 6% there, 20% still somewhere else, a few dollars for this, another few cents for that—all this adds up. In some societies 60% of an average person's income goes to governments. Local and regional governments may prefer one type of tax, national and federal governments another, and international governments still another.

In societies with many different levels of government, such as in a federal state, each level can have its own taxing authority. At each level different taxes can be levied; therefore, some states or provinces have income taxes and others do not; some have sales taxes and others do not; some have personal property taxes and others do not. Some local governments tax personal property and others do not; some have wage or salary taxes; and some have a tax on funerals. Additionally, the amount of taxation differs from state to state and even from community to community within a state.

With so many fragmented sources of revenue at all government levels, it becomes difficult, if not impossible, to determine a society's policy on taxation. Although people complain about a particular tax, they may not realize that many other sources of revenue exist, such as hidden taxes, that can be increased when another source is reduced or more income is needed.

When voters defeat a school levy, for example, the loss of revenues is made up by increasing charges for textbooks, raising admissions to games and other school events, requiring more participation by parents in school activities (the latter is also a tax since it takes away time from parents that could be spent by them on other pursuits) and by not providing the education necessary to their future taxpayers to get high-paying positions.

When government does not provide a service that is essential for the well-being of society, another entity will provide the service at a higher cost to those that need it or it will not be provided at all, causing some persons to incur significant losses. Suppose that a local government does not have $200 to place a stop sign at an intersection where at least one accident occurs each year. The average amount of damages to two cars is $3,000. Insurance companies pay $2,000 of the damages, and each driver pays a deductible of $500. Thus, the two drivers and those who pay the insurance companies' premiums pay for the damage. Although taxpayers saved $200 by not putting up that stop sign, some community members paid portions of $3,000 a year for that omission. The point is not to save taxpayers $200 but rather to prevent others from paying for losses incurred by government's inaction.

If a society is to remain viable, it must give its members the means for overcoming challenges the environment imposes. Thus, maintenance of roads, preventive health care programs, adequate housing, good vocational training, and good educational facilities are necessary for a society's survival. If government does not have the funds to provide these services, the society

A major goal of the U.S. Department of Housing and Urban Development (HUD) is to accomplish a racially stable and inclusive society through regulation of housing patterns and community facilities that foster interaction and eliminate prejudice.

will either languish and fall behind other societies or be taken over by more successful societies. Although no one wants to give more of their hard earned income to government, sometimes government has no other alternative than to generate needed revenues from that income in order to maintain a competitive standard of living for everyone.

Appropriations

Government spends the revenues it collects on programs for the welfare of society. The amount of revenue collected has never been higher; yet no government official will admit that the revenue allotted to his or her agency or department is sufficient to effectively provide for the welfare of those under that entity's jurisdiction. Government officials invariably believe that more funds will allow them to do more and to do it better. Often this is true; but if government collects so much revenue, how can anyone be in financial difficulty?

Times have changed. Government today provides more services than ever before and the costs of what government buys have increased tremendously due to technological innovations. A few decades ago the cost of a child's textbook and of a pair of socks was about the same. Today a textbook costs the equivalent of ten pairs of socks. (And the price of socks has increased, too.) In the past classrooms were equipped with a chalkboard, chalk, and an eraser. Today classrooms also must have expensive computers, telephones, intercoms, and other electronic gadgetry.

Is it really fair to compare the cost of a horse to that of a tank, a frigate to that of a nuclear-powered submarine, a musket and gunpowder to that of an Uzi, or a dirt road to a six-lane interstate? The total yearly appropriation of the U.S. federal government in the 1820s was about $15 million, which is less than the amount a city of 75,000 inhabitants spends today. On a per capita basis expenditures of the federal government amounted to about $2.00 during the administration of President James Monroe; during the administration of President Bill Clinton in the 1990s that amount was $6,000! Despite this huge growth in expenditures, policy makers have difficulty finding funds for programs and projects they believe are essential.

Budgets give policy makers very little leeway for cutting programs or beginning new ones. Some appropriations are fixed (i.e., they cannot be altered), such as debt repayment. Government must allocate funds to repay the principal and interest on loans and other borrowed money; otherwise it cannot borrow more. For some governments debt repayments represents

Social Security's first retirement beneficiary — Ida Fuller of Ludlow, Vermont. She received her first check numbered 000-00-001 dated January 31, 1940 for $22.54. Social Security Amendments of 1950 gave her the first-ever raise in monthly benefits. Shown here at age 76 in October 1950, with the check that reflected a raise by $18.75, she received benefits for 35 years in all, living to age 100.

President Reagan's Social Security Amendments Act of 1983 insured continued payment of benefits and set out a time frame for the gradual increase in retirement age among other financing provisions.

60 percent of total appropriations. (In the United States it is about 20 percent of the federal budget.) Other fixed appropriations are funds distributed to persons who have made contributions to government-sponsored benefits programs, such as social security pensions, health insurance, unemployment insurance, and workers' compensation. These expenditures cannot be altered below a base level because those who made contributions did so with the contractual agreement that some of their money will be returned when it is needed. In the United States these fixed appropriations are called **entitlements**.

Most government appropriations are not fixed; although the funds are for activities that must be performed, the level of funding can be increased or decreased as conditions change. Defense, for example, is an expenditure no state can do without. But how much should be spent on it? The answer depends on many variables, such as the number of current threats to national security, the cost of necessary technology, the personnel available, and the functions of the military when threats are minimal or nonexistent. In many societies the military is not principally involved in defense but, more importantly, in education. A good portion of the adult population acquires not only literacy skills through the military but also training in fields such as electronics, mechanics (especially of airplanes), and computer technology and programming. Cuts in a defense budget, consequently, reduce the level of educational programming, which will result in a shortage of technical personnel in the future. Government expenditures for defense are seldom more than 10 percent of total appropriations.

In many societies education is the largest government expense. Not only are more children being educated and over a longer time period than ever before, but also the costs for facilities, technology, and staff have risen enormously. Government can do little to curtail increased costs or to trim these expenditures. A similar situation occurs in criminal justice, in which all expenses must be covered because they involve salaries and other expenditures for the essential services of police departments, prosecutorial staffs, judicial staffs, and prison administration. None of these can be eliminated or cut below a particular amount without resulting in major social disruptions.

Defense, education, road building and maintenance, and criminal justice are all essential for a well functioning society, and their budgets cannot be cut below a certain base level. When these expenditures are totaled, little, if anything, is left over for new programs. Of all the limitations on government actions, budgetary constraints are the most effective since government cannot act without money. When money is not available but services must be provided, a government borrows. In the United States every president in the last forty years, representing different parties, ideologies, and interests, has tried to avoid borrowing money for programs. Yet when each left office, the amount borrowed was higher than before he assumed office, even when no new programs were initiated. And borrowing brings additional costs in interest owed on the loan.

To maintain current service levels in all the existing programs, U.S. Congress has to allow for $595 billion in spending in fiscal year 1998 budget. As the budget cap permits only $547 billion, significant cuts are needed in discretionary spending such as for infrastructure that includes mass transit.

Another way governments try to get around a tight budget is by mandating creation of services or programs without allotting any appropriations. This situation occurs frequently in less industrialized states in which governments, legally create programs but cannot implement them for lack of funds. Government officials hope that these programs will be funded somehow in the future. This also occurs in the United States but in a different way. The Federal government sometimes creates programs for states, counties, or municipalities to administer, but does not provide any funding for them. This shifts the financial burden to the state and local governments, which may be forced to cut necessary programs to fund those mandated by the federal government.

Revenues, Appropriations, and Policy Making

All executives are faced with a difficult problem. Should appropriations determine revenues or should revenues determine appropriations? At first glance the answer seems simple: If there are no revenues, there cannot be any appropriations. However, the revenue side of the budget can be flexible because of the many different ways to force people to part with more of their income or wealth. Obviously, people do not volunteer to be taxed, and often they complain vehemently about the amount of taxes they pay. Yet few have ever rebelled against being taxed. The number of people who refuse to pay taxes is so small in any society that they do not draw attention. (Many more people cheat on their income taxes, but that is another story.) In the United States about 20 percent of taxpayers actually pay more taxes than they should because they do not take the allowed deductions.

If people perceive that the taxes, tolls, or fees they pay give them something useful of or are helpful to them, they do not mind the expense. When parents see their child use his or her allowance to buy things of which they approve, they may think of increasing the allowance. But if the child spends the allowance on something the parents believe is wasteful, ugly, or unnecessary they will seriously think of cutting the allowance. If taxpayers perceive that their government does not spend their revenues properly, they will oppose a tax increase.

Consequently, taxpayers' perceptions of what government does with its revenues determine how much more revenue they are willing to contribute. Perceptions, of course, can be manipulated. To generate positive perceptions, government can build visible artifacts that glorify society's past (e.g., monuments, exhibits, and reconstructed landmarks), larger stadiums and parks, or more industrial plants and other buildings that society may lack the resources to operate. Thus, government shows that it is doing something worthwhile in order to raise more revenues to implement essential programs that do not receive widespread support, such as upgrading the prison system or sewage facilities.

Colombia brings government closer to people. Local authorities and communities are becoming responsible for building their own future. Power and resources are being decentralized from Bogota (the capital city) to underserved areas. A community leader explains new legislation in a Medellin barrio.

On the other hand, corruption and scandals create negative images of government. Generally, people hesitate to give more money to a government whose officials have used revenues for illegal or unethical purposes. Yet citizens also acknowledge that government, which is not the simple institution it was a hundred years ago, is so big and complex that their perception of the entire government is not tarnished by the wrongdoings of a few government officials. While the Watergate scandal was at its height in 1974 in the U.S., local and state governments and the federal government increased taxes without any unusual opposition.

Citizens' favorable perceptions of government make them more tolerant of tax increases. Yet this is only part of the answer to the question of revenues versus appropriations. No program or project of any government has ever been implemented without the support of at least some citizenry. Administrators can develop ideas for new services; however, unless some part of society supports these services, they will just remain ideas. To translate ideas into policy government officials need the support of some segments of society and little vehement opposition from other segments.

One way administrators make their ideas appealing and less controversial is by scaling them back. In the late 1950s universal health care as a U.S. government-sponsored program would have been considered politically irrelevant. Therefore, health care for the poor and elderly was as far as some

President Clinton and Vice President Gore believe that "all of us have a duty to ensure that every child has a chance to take part in the new information age." The President adds, "technological literacy must become the standard in our country. Computers can enrich the education of any child, but only if the child has access to a computer, good software, and a competent, good teacher who can help that child learn how to use it. Preparing children for a life time of computer use is just as essential today as teaching basic skills was a few years ago." The Department of Education's Goals 2000 provides grants for the development of state standards and the implementation of comprehensive reform in all 50 states. For example, the National Science Foundation has advanced mathematics and science education reform through programs such as the Statewide Systemic Initiatives and the more recent Urban Systemic Initiatives. These two NSF programs support 40 sites and serve over 25 million students.

policy makers at the time were willing to accede, at least in public. Today universal health care is becoming a reality in most societies. Innovative or new services and programs inevitably start small. In this way their efficacy is tested and taxpayers are given the opportunity to get accustomed to them and to accept them. As the service or program becomes larger, more encompassing, and more costly, taxpayers acquiesce to increased revenues needed to fund it.

Just as higher level governments can mandate lower level governments, members of a society can mandate that government does what it perceives is necessary or worthwhile. In the 1820s government-sponsored health insurance for carpenters was inconceivable. Today such a program is taken for granted. Two hundred years ago public education was considered a privilege; today it is considered a right not to be denied to anyone. Generally, through the interplay of prevalent, yet changing, values, beliefs, and norms, society forces government to adapt. We have to keep in mind that government is but a means by which society maintains its viability. Consequently, government policies, services, and programs are geared toward maintaining that viability. Therefore, the monetary cost involved accomplishing this may not be the determining factor. In fact, money may be the least important factor when a society's security is threatened.

Often segments of society demand that government institute new services or programs. For example, unemployed workers in the 1930s in the United States and other countries pressured government to create programs that ensure a "safety net" to all economically deprived members of society. The hundreds of programs and services related to environmental protection mainly emanated from various concerned groups throughout society demanding government action. In these situations funding is not the crucial factor in deciding whether to create services or programs considered essential by society. Despite lack of revenue, government is forced to act.

The per capita growth of U.S. federal appropriations from $2.00 in the 1820s to $6,000 in the 1990s did not occur because Americans were opposed to government programs and services. Nor can it be assumed that Americans were duped or manipulated into accepting these services by nefarious or power-hungry bureaucrats. On the contrary, most Americans demand better schools and services for their children, better and safer roads for travel, greater security on the street and in the home and workplace, cheaper health care, and a cleaner and healthier environment. And they are willing to pay for it as they have in the past.

The clean up of this sludge lagoon at a chemical plant site in Kansas City, Missouri, was accomplished by private parties upon the successful conclusion of litigation by the Land and Natural Resources Division of the Department of Justice. The Clean Water Act (CWA) and the Clean Air Act (CAA) are focal points of the Division's efforts to enhance the American environment.

On the other hand, adamant opposition by significant segments of society to a proposed government program, regardless of how important or necessary its formulators believe it is, will prevent its passage. For example, government officials, in an effort to obtain greater internal security, advocate programs that restrict privacy or limit rights, but public opposition is so high that the programs are usually shelved. Taxpayers are very much opposed to funding programs they perceive will take something away from them, especially rights.

The answer to the question of whether revenues dictate appropriations or appropriations dictate revenues (or, as stated in another way, whether finances dictate public policy or public policy dictates finances) is the availability of revenue and the level of public support for the public policies or programs receiving the appropriations. No society has been taxed to the point of its own destruction. Actually, no magic figure for a ceiling for taxation has ever been established; consequently, the availability of revenue is necessarily speculative. Therefore, the answer basically is that public support of policies and government dictates government's appropriations.

📖 TERMS TO REMEMBER

quangos
independent regulatory agencies
quasi-legislative
quasi-judicial
civil penalties
line functions
staff functions
Executive Office of the President
revenues
appropriations
entitlements

📖 SUGGESTED READINGS

Berman, Larry. *The Office of Management and Budget and the Presidency, 1921-1979.* Princeton: Princeton University Press, 1979. An historical examination of the OMB.

Collender, Stanley E. *The Guide to the Federal Budget: Fiscal 1998.* 16th ed. Lanham, MD: Rowman & Littlefield Publishers, Inc., 1997. After analyzing the Congressional debates on the 1997 budget, the author explains the new challenges to the 1998 budget such as the line item veto, entitlement spending, and the politics of divided government.

Dogan, Mattei, ed. *The Mandarins of Western Europe: The Political Role of Top Civil Servants.* New York: John Wiley and Sons, 1975. An analysis of the higher civil service in the United Kingdom and other European states.

Owen, Marguerite. *The Tennessee Valley Authority.* New York: Praeger Publishers, 1979. A history and description of the T.V.A. and how it fits into the institutions and politics of the federal government.

Rourke, Francis E. *Bureaucracy, Politics, and Public Policy.* 3rd ed. Boston: Little, Brown and Company, 1984. This work deals with two trends in the United States: repoliticalization of the executive branch and de-bureaucratization.

Studlar, Donley T. *Great Britain: Decline or Renewal?* Boulder, CO: Westview Press, 1996. Containing important insights into many of the controversies about British politics today, the book also describes the operations of its government.

Wildavsky, Aaron. *The Politics of the Budgetary Process.* 2nd ed. New York: Harper/Collins, 1992. An expert on the budget analyzes how it is made and implemented..

NOTES

1. Robert Presthus, "Mrs. Thatcher Stalks the Quango: A Note on Patronage and Justice in Britain," *Public Administration Review* vol. 41, no. 3 (May/June 1981): pp. 312-17.

2. U.S. Bureau of the Census, *Statistical Abstract of the United States: 1994* 114th ed. Washington, DC, 1994), p. 297.

19
The Judiciary

Outline
- Functions of the Judiciary
- Selection of Judges
- Organization of the Judiciary
- The Police
- The Penal System

A n old saying goes something like this, "If everybody would behave or act according to common accepted rules, no government would be necessary." This is nonsense. Government not only identifies future needs of society and coordinates tasks and individuals to surmount these but also interprets and decides rights and obligations that individuals make among themselves in the form of contracts.

Functions of the Judiciary

Judiciaries are essential institutions of states because they authoritatively determine what the rules are, and who did not obey them, who is right and who is wrong in a dispute. Judiciaries are necessary today more than ever before; few persons have not had to deal with a court matter.

Resolution of Disputes

Ages ago right and wrong were decided by group elders, parents, religious leaders, friends, and associates. In many societies disputes involving personal injury or interpretation of an agreement, the subject matter of **civil law**, seldom were taken to court for resolution because any other persons who could have resolved the dispute would feel insulted if the court system was used instead. A decision against the wronged party by an unjust, prejudiced family member or a member of the clergy was more socially acceptable than adjudication by a judge. Disputes were handled among the contending parties because people believed that the initial cause for the disagreement would become muddled if an outsider was brought in to help.

Another important reason for not using the judicial system was cost; in some societies both sides shared the costs, and in others the loser would pay all. In addition, judges were not always available. A complainant, who probably had to travel far, could go to court only at a certain time of the month or year. (Or, as in the early history of Canada and the United States, judges traveled a circuit and thus were available only when passing through a town.) A further cost involved hiring an attorney to represent the complainant in court. Thus, resolution of a dispute through the legal system was unaffordable for most persons, who chose instead to have someone else decide the dispute.

Many people in times gone by were afraid to have anything to do with government because they believed that once a government official knew of you, the government could cause problems by reviewing tax records or demanding enlistment in government service. The less officials knew about you, the better it would be for you. This notion is still very much alive in many societies in which government records are poorly kept and public officials learn of someone's existence only because that person used a government service for some purpose or another. Consequently, such beliefs inhibited individuals in the past from using the courts and sometimes have the same effect today.

In societies in which the government has extensive records of the members of society, people are less reticent to use the courts to resolve disputes. Since the influence of the family, religious institutions, and other social groups has weakened over time, individuals often have no choice but to use the court system. Also, the increase in the divorce rate and of the resulting family squabbles has resulted in creation of a new area of the law known as domestic relations.

Frequently those involved in disagreements today are large national or international institutions. Can one seriously think that a minister, priest, or rabbi can settle a dispute between one corporation and another, between or one government agency and another? Much of the litigation that occurs today involves enterprises and public agencies that do not mind spending much time and money on cases in which the court decision may become public policy.

Courts are readily available today. One does not have to travel far to see a judge or have one's case heard. Most courts are open year round. Advances in transportation and communication have made courts as accessible as the telephone or car. Court costs are no longer unaffordable to most, especially since magistrates, justices of the peace, and small claims courts have been established to reduce costs to complainants by eliminating the need for legal representation.

In one area of law, real-estate property conflicts courts are used less frequently today than in the past. Recordkeeping is improved and surveying techniques set boundaries more precisely. Property cases that end up in court usually involve disputes regarding inheritance, division of property after divorce, or liability issues.

Courts are essential today because they are the prevalent social institutions that resolve disputes between individuals or groups. Resolution of conflict, however, is but one of the four main functions of courts.

Determination of Guilt

Another function of courts is the determination of guilt or innocence of an accused. There are not only more people in every society but also more rules that govern behavior, as we saw in previous chapters. Persons engaged in manufacturing, trade, retail, transportation of goods, and other enterprises involving the exchange of goods or services are inundated with rules of which they have difficulty keeping track, despite weekly government newsletters and bulletins they often receive. Individuals today have so many rules to acknowledge that conscious or unconscious thoughts of not following some of them occur daily. (Many of these are traffic rules, which most drivers break a dozen times each day.)

Ohio Bureau of Motor Vehicles revoked 30,000 drivers' licenses in 1993 under the state's administrative license suspension laws. National Highway Traffic Safety Administration statistics indicate that 11,358 people died in drunk driving-related accidents in 1992, down 32 percent from a decade

Any time an individual or a group disobeys a rule made by a state institution a **crime** is committed. Crimes are distinguished according to the amount of force used in commission of the crime and the importance of the rule broken to society. Misdemeanors are crimes deemed of lesser importance to society in which little or no physical force was used; felonies are crimes considered grave violations of rules of greater importance to society or in which significant force was used. In general punishment is up to one year in jail for a misdemeanor and one year or longer for a felony. Most traffic violations are misdemeanors; assaults with a weapon are felonies.

Societies maintain order among their members through the determination of guilt for crimes and of the subsequent punishment. Order is necessary for members of society to feel secure. It makes almost no difference in determination of guilt and punishment if the accused person has never committed another wrong. The fact that an accused murderer killed only once is enough to make that person a danger to society. Similarly, a shoplifter is punished even if the value of the object stolen is not worth much. Courts are the only entities today that make the final determination of guilt or innocence and of appropriate punishment.

Courts in most states have convicted many times as many persons in the last few years as they did in the first decade of this century. This rise in criminal activity is not only due to the increase in population but also the greater amount of illegal activities conducted by people overall. The crime rate (expressed in numbers per 100,000 population) has doubled in the last fifty years in almost every state, although it is leveling off in some. Reasons for the drastic increase are attributed to changing demographics (a decrease in the mean age of the population), economic pressures due to the widening gap between the rich and the poor, increased alienation of young people and racial minorities, greater availability and variety of weapons, increased sale and use of illegal drugs, and other societal changes.

Some countries distinguish political crimes from other crimes, especially those with governors who are not well supported and are actively challenged. A political crime is a misdemeanor or a felony committed for a social cause. The perpetrators of such crimes claim that their social cause absolves them of any guilt. Prosecutors, to protect their own personal authorities, treat these criminals harshly and often convince courts to impose stiffer sentences than are usually given. In some countries trials of alleged political criminals are conducted by special courts, often military courts, from which no appeal is allowed. The United States does not make this distinction in any of its court systems.

Prevention of Wrongdoing

For about 500 years judiciaries in the British tradition have also assumed the responsibility of prevention of injustices, which is known as **equity**. Equity is preventive justice, that is, it is court-mandated actions that prevent injuries from being committed. These court mandates are called **writs**.

A **writ of injunction** stops an action from occurring. For example, my neighbor plans to close a ditch on his property that first runs through mine. If he did this, heavy rains would flood my land and ruin my garden. Therefore, I ask a judge to impose a writ of injunction against my neighbor to prevent him from closing the ditch; if he closes the ditch, the courts will punish him. In general these writs are simply referred to as injunctions and are given to employees who often fail to go to work because of a strike, causing their employers financial hardship.

The **writ of mandamus** forces someone to do something. Suppose my neighbor allows the ditch that runs through both properties to fill with debris, which causes flooding on my property. In this situation I ask the court to issue a writ of *mandamus* to force my neighbor to clean up his part of the ditch. These writs are issued most frequently when an individual refuses to release documents that another individual is entitled to receive.

When an individual who has received a writ does not comply with the court's request, he or she is in contempt of court, which is a punishable crime.

Policy Making

Another function of some courts is policy making, which is more likely to occur in societies that have inherited the British judicial system than in societies that have adopted the continental European system or any other juridical system.

A county clerk swears in a trial jury. The right to trial by a jury of one's peers has ancient roots in English law.

I'M RIGHT... AND YOU'RE WRONG!

SUPREME COURT OF YESTERDAY..

..AND TODAY

HISTORICAL REVERSALS

The principle of *stare decisis* binds the court to adhere to precedences. However, the court of the twentieth century feels free to depart from this principle in consideration of the changed circumstances that call for new interpretations of the Constitution.

Common Law

British jurisprudence is based on **common law**. Communities make common law through the jury system, which applies the values, standards, and norms of the community in its determination of a verdict. These standards and norms may not be written, but they supposedly reflect those of society. Since a record is kept of evidence presented and everything that is said in court, including verdicts, jury decisions become part of the written record.

A fundamental principle of common law is *stare decisis* (let the decision stand). According to this principle a court decision becomes a precedent for a subsequent similar case. Consequently, once a jury's decision is affirmed by a judge, other courts in the same jurisdiction must abide by that decision.

Jury decisions, however, can be appealed to a higher court. Judges in these courts do not reinterpret the facts of the case, instead they review the procedures followed and determine whether the proper laws were applied. Their decisions are explained in what are called the court's opinions. A judge's review of the facts, decision and opinion are called a case, which is cited as precedent for future decisions. The reasoning of appellant judges is considered **case law**. (In law school students study hundreds of cases to become familiar with case law.)

Decisions of lower courts, made by a jury must be affirmed by higher courts to become case law. Higher courts frequently overturn decisions of lower courts and in doing so they also make policy by establishing the precedent. However, until a higher court reviews a case and makes a decision, lower court rulings prevail.

Since a jury is not obligated to follow existing written law to determine its verdict (as stated in Chapter 14), any nonconforming decisions then are viewed as current public policy and can become law. For example, commissioners in the author's county passed an antipornography law. A video-rental store operator was accused of violating the law by renting pornographic videos to customers. Although the videos were deemed pornographic, the jury refused to convict the store operator because it did not consider pornography a punishable offense. Since then no other arrests have been made, although videorental stores still rent pornographic videos. Therefore, the jury decision prevails over the law and is considered public policy.

Juries also can make policy in situations in which there is no law to guide them. For instance, no law states that mowing a lawn at 6:00 A.M. on Sunday is forbidden. However, a jury can declare an accused guilty of a misdemeanor for this offense, thereby making policy.

Juries' interpretations of law and their determinations about which laws apply in which situations greatly influence business practices. A jury's interpretation of a law can differ from the original intent of the makers of that law, causing a change in the way a business is conducted. For example, the Mann Act passed by Congress in 1910 made illegal the transportation across state lines of "any woman or girl for the purpose of prostitution or debauchery." Juries have interpreted the law more broadly to include such activity within a state, thus making prostitution illegal everywhere even though the lawmakers intended to prevent only inter-state and international transportation of women.

Juries also decide which laws apply in situations in which several con-tradicting laws and regulations could apply. In *Tennessee Valley Authority v. Hill* a federal jury decided that a law made by Congress protecting endan-gered species did not apply in a project that was more than 50 percent com-pleted. (Appeals courts set aside the lower court's decision in this case.)

Jury decisions have been extremely important in determining public policy on the amount of damages in civil suits. In the last few decades American juries determined liability in malpractice and accident claims and awarded large amounts of money for damages to victims. In deciding who is liable for what to whom at what costs, juries have virtually deter-mined the relationship between professionals and their clients. Medical doctors, attorneys, plumbers, and auto mechanics have been found liable for damages and assessed high penalties, sometimes in the tens of mil-lions of dollars, for mistakes they made in conducting their practice. The result has been increased fees for professionals' services to cover the high cost of liability insurance and additional costs for more thorough testing and inspections and for salaries for witnesses present at all consultations and treatments. (This has also resulted in the loss of 'personal' relation-ships between professionals and their clients. For example, a medical doctor can no longer afford to become a friend to clients because even friends sue each other.) In May 1996 the U.S. Supreme Court decided that excessive damage awards by juries are unlawful.

Jury decisions in civil cases have also affected the relationship between a business and its customers and employees. The workplace environment has changed drastically in the last few decades. Changes in laws and government regulations have had some impact, but not as much as court decisions that hold producers or employers liable for injuries or damages incurred by employees or by consumers of their products or ser-vices. Whereas half a century ago the notion of *caveat emptor* (let the buyer beware) prevailed in customer and seller relations, today juries and judges are more likely to side with the buyer and find the business guilty of selling faulty or damaged goods.

The relationship between providers of services and goods and their customers, as determined by government either through legislative laws or court decisions, is not what our ancestors experienced. In the past this relationship was determined either by family or friends or by community

A staff attorney of Portland Legal Aid Service, addressing the local community on consumer fraud problems.

standards enforced through custom. As communities grew larger and conflicts became more frequent in the last hundred years, more formal processes (i.e., government controls) have shaped and changed this relationship. Therefore, the judicial system, which often is the most accessible and fast acting government institution, took over the role of determining proper relations between provider and recipient.

Under common law courts do indeed make policy. The jury system allows community values and norms to be translated into law. Consequently, law closely reflects the other elements that compose public policy.

Roman Law

Court decisions are less important in determining public policy in countries that do not follow common law. In these countries the executive has a significant role in lawmaking and law and public policy are more divergent than in countries that follow common law.

In most of these countries jurisprudence is based on Roman law and the Napoleonic Code. Roman authorities found that legal norms were often contradictory and difficult to implement among an increasing and ever more cosmopolitan population. The law, as it existed then, was a hodgepodge of do's and don'ts dating from Babylonian and Hellenic times mixed in with customs of unknown ancestry. In the sixth century a commission appointed by Byzantine Roman Emperor Justinian published a code of law based on past emperors' decrees that became the basis of law in most parts of continental Europe in the late Middle Ages. In 1804 Napoleon, who was aware that Roman law did not reflect societal changes caused by the ideas of the Enlightenment and symbolized by the French Revolution (especially those regarding equality of citizens), proclaimed a new code that has subsequently become the basis of jurisprudence in continental Europe and in the societies once colonized by these states.

The Justinian and Napoleonic codes encompass norms that members of societies ought to obey. Unlike many norms in common law, these code

The first codification of Roman law was contained in the Twelve Tables posted in the Roman Forum in 449 B.C.

norms are written. They are there for everyone to see, not hidden as values or customs. The application of code norms is conducted by trained judges; lay persons, such as juries, are not qualified. Consequently, juries seldom decide court cases in societies using these codes. In some countries experimenting with the jury system, such as Colombia, juries act in an advisory capacity to the judge presiding over a case. France uses juries as part of a panel that includes judges to decide cases involving human rights.

No rule of precedence exists in code law. Judges are not bound to follow other judges' decision in similar cases as in common law. Each judge interprets and applies the law alone. Superior judges can overrule lower judges' decisions, but the latter usually do not have to abide by decisions made by the former. (This situation is somewhat mitigated in that superior judges hire and fire lower ones, thereby influencing the lower judge's decisions.)

Under code law, therefore, only the written norm is the law. That law usually is made by the executive with legislative approval. If a society's values, beliefs, and patterns of behavior change, little can be done to harmonize existing law with these changes except through executive decree or legislation. Consequently, the priority of law in public policy is continuously discussed in these states. (See the discussion on positive law and natural law in Chapter 14.) In general, law as enforced by the courts diverges from what the people in that society believe are the norms governing behavior. Courts can refuse to apply some laws, but they cannot create new ones as courts under common law do. The most that a judge following code law can do is interpret existing law in terms of societal changes. Otherwise, a judge cannot affect law as a manifestation of public policy. Courts in states based on code law, consequently, have little influence in public policymaking.

In 1803, in *Marbury v. Madison*, U.S. Chief Justice John Marshall enunciated the concept of judicial review that gives courts the power to review acts of Congress and invalidate unconstitutional acts.

Judicial Review

Nevertheless, courts under code law as well as courts under common law have played an important role in determining public policy in interpretation of the constitution and in human rights. Many states, such as Colombia, France, Germany, Italy, Russia, and Sweden, created special courts to hear cases involving the application of constitutional provisions to laws and the actions of government officials. These constitutional courts have the last word on the validity or legitimacy of government-enacted policy. In the United States and Japan the

In its 1954 decision on *Brown v. Board of Education of Topeka, Kansas*, U.S. Supreme Court ruled that racially segregated schools were unconstitutional. The decision became the basis for the subsequent integration of public schools in the country and was a powerful demonstration of the exercise of judicial power.

Supreme Court has this power of judicial review. Decisions of these courts are so definitive that the only way to overturn them is to amend the constitution, which is usually a difficult process that is rarely achieved.

Whereas Supreme Court judges in Japan are too inhibited to use this power to nullify acts and laws passed or enacted by the other two government branches, U.S. Supreme Court judges, especially in the twentieth century, have aggressively used this power to establish policies that the other two branches would not enact or were incapable of doing so. U.S. Supreme Court decisions such as *Marbury v. Madison* (which established judicial review), *Brown v. Board of Education of Topeka* (which eliminated the separate, but equal, decision of a former court), *Roe v. Wade* (which made legal abortions in the United States), and hundreds of others have made a tremendous impact on the organization of government and society.

German legislators and administrators, as those in many other societies, have discussed the issue of legalizing specific addictive drugs. In May 1994 the Constitutional Court of Germany decriminalized the possession and use of small amounts of marijuana and hashish, thereby making most government discussions on the topic irrelevant and in one sweep stopping the prosecution of dozens of individuals. The only way this decision can be overturned is by changing the Basic Law, Germany's constitution. That same month the Constitutional Court of Colombia issued a similar decision, which was not supported by that country's executive.

Human Rights

Since human rights have been translated into written laws and are accepted by most members of almost every society, courts can define the relationship between the individual and government. Judges and juries can proscribe government actions and determine entitlements that government must provide. These controls curtail the freedom that policy makers and implementors have had in the past and prevent the abuse of authority by bureaucrats. Furthermore, courts basing themselves on human rights define the jurisdiction of these officials and invalidate any act in which they may have overstepped their authority.

Courts keep government agencies and officials from encroaching upon each other's area of jurisdiction, thereby maintaining or increasing the fragmentation of government policy making. By ensuring that government officials do not act beyond their specific authority, courts prevent them from accumulating too much power and from using their power indiscriminately. Courts, therefore, have become the venue by which society maintains order and coordinates its members' activities; they also maintain government's respect for their authority.

Selection of Judges

The influence of courts in any society is determined largely by the quality and integrity of the judges and the court system. Judges who can be replaced at the executive's discretion seldom have the independence to

The U.S. Supreme Court in 1995. Seated from left: Justices Antonin Scalia, John Paul Stevens, Chief Justice William H. Rehnquist, Justices Sandra Day O'Connor, Anthony Kennedy. Standing from left: Justices Ruth Bader Ginsburg, David H. Souter, Clarence Thomas, Stephen G. Breyer.

make decisions that the executive will not support. On the other hand, judges chosen for reasons other than their qualification for office seldom gain respect from either those they serve or those who present cases.

Judges are selected in three ways: designation by the executive, with or without approval of a legislative body; appointment by the judiciary based on merit or expertise; or election.

Designation by the Executive

In the United States the president appoints all federal judges with the advice and consent of the Senate. They serve for life (i.e., they cannot be removed except through impeachment). Consequently, some federal judges are in their 80s and have served for forty or more years. The theory behind this system is that only qualified judges who are beholden to no one will be appointed. In practice only part of this is true; federal judges are completely independent from the executive and Congress and supposedly make nonpartisan decision. However, executives often select judges whose views on issues that the Supreme Court may review are closely aligned with those of the president's political party. Thus, a president who has the opportunity to make several appointments to the court can greatly influence the outcome on some highly significant but controversial cases. In addition, all prospective judges need approval of the American Bar Association, but the Senate has rejected several nominees as unqualified and approved a few thought to be unfit for the position.

The nomination of Louis D. Brandeis to the Supreme Court in January 1916 was vigorously opposed by conservative forces in industry and finance. A four-month heated battle over his confirmation followed. President Woodrow Wilson and various progressive reform groups prevailed, and the Senate confirmed Brandeis, the first jew nominated to the court, by a vote of 47 to 22.

In other societies in which the executive appoints judges, their term is set for a specific member of years, such as ten, or they serve until the executive dismisses them. In many Latin American countries, in which judicial

Though the President nominates Supreme Court justices, the power of the Court is very much evident from its 1974 decision in *United States v. Nixon*. The Court denied Nixon's claim of an absolute privilege to reject judicial demands for information, and ordered that Nixon must surrender to the Watergate special prosecutor the subpoenaed tapes of White House conversations between the President and his

appointments are for ten years, judges often are dismissed before the end of their term on some invented charge, usually dishonesty or lack of patriotism. The integrity and the independence of judges depend on the amount of the executive's influence, whether direct or subtle. If an executive can dismiss a judge at will, certainly the judge is not independent.

Appointment by Judiciaries

To avoid executive interference in judges' decisions some countries, notably France, use an appointment process in which a council of the professional judiciary chooses and supervises judges in their routine decisions. Judges in France must have graduated from law school and completed special training for the judgeship. Once appointed, a judge is promoted on the basis of expertise. Thus, judges are career professionals, not unlike most bureaucrats. Those at the top of the hierarchy, consequently, have had years of experience. Judges appointed by executives and elected judges do not necessarily have any experience when they occupy the bench.

Election

The election of judges poses several problems. Do voters make decisions based on candidates' qualifications? Since qualifications often are not of primary concern to voters when choosing other political candidates, will they be more concerned about the qualifications of judiciary candidates? In some states of the United States judicial candidates' advertisements are not much different from those of candidates for other elected offices. The electorate usually pays very little attention to those running for judgeships. After all, judges' activities do not get the same amount of media coverage that politicians receive. Furthermore, judges seldom make decisions by themselves; either juries make decisions for them or they make decisions as part of a collegial body (i.e., a decision making group). In addition, the cases on which judges render an opinion often are too complex for many people to understand and the opinion itself is not easy to comprehend.

The term of an elected judge usually ranges from six to ten years. Only a few countries prevent judges from running for reelection. Most countries do not allow recall elections (i.e., removal of an elected official by voters); countries that do allow recall elections rarely use them. Since elected judges have their own constituency, they are independent of the other branches of government. Integrity is evident in the expertise the judge shows in handling cases and making decisions. In general the quality of the judiciary is about the same in areas where judges are elected as in those where they are appointed and independent.

In countries in which professional jobs are very scarce, executives can influence judges' decisions by promising government positions to their relatives. In some underdeveloped countries some judges who refuse to be influenced have been assassinated by associates of the executive.

Organization of the Judiciary

The complexity of cases and the increased caseload have resulted in a judicial system that divides courts into specialized areas of the law and into geographic territories. Each court system contains several layers.

Specialized Courts and Territorial Courts

A state's judiciary is composed of two or more court systems based upon the type of case brought for trial. In some states the division is between criminal and civil cases (i.e., one set of courts exclusively handles criminal cases, and the other set handles only civil cases). Some states also have administrative courts that manage only civil lawsuits in which the government is a party, such as cases involving personnel issues or eminent domain (i.e., payment for private property taken for public use, often for building roads or parks). Other states have established courts that manage only traffic matters, including traffic violations and accident liability cases. Court specialization is found in states that use either Roman or Napoleonic law codes.

No formal division of court systems prevails in countries with common law. Lower courts, especially in large metropolitan areas, can hear one type of case more than another, such as domestic relations or maritime law. These specializations, which are not used in higher courts or appeals courts, are created by judges or by law to speed up the legal process. (An exception is Australia, which has established a federal family court that handles domestic matters exclusively in all states and territories.)

Federal states have a court system in each state or province in addition to the federal court system. Thus, the United States has fifty-one court systems, one for each state and the federal court system, each independent of the others and containing both lower and higher courts. This system, however, is determined by geographic area rather than type of case.

Levels of Courts

Each court system, whether based on geographic area or type of case, is composed of a hierarchy of courts of which the lowest are the **courts of first instance** or **courts of original jurisdiction**. These are the courts where a case is first heard and where, under common law, juries are found. Under the state system in the United States these usually are the county or circuit courts; their federal counterparts are the federal district courts. In most court systems only one judge serves at this level. In lower courts the facts are presented, the laws that pertain to the case are explained, and a decision is rendered. In a criminal case sentencing is determined; in a civil case damages or other losses are assessed.

When a lower court's verdict is not satisfactory to one of the parties, it can be appealed to a court that has **appellate jurisdiction**, or an **appeals court**. These courts usually do not review the facts of a case or allow new evidence; rather they review the procedures used in the trial and the laws that were applied. If the appeals court is not convinced that the proper procedures or laws were used, it can then set aside the lower court's decisions. An appeals court usually is composed of three to seven judges who sit as one unit; their decisions are based on a majority, with each judge's vote stated. In most countries only one appeal from a lower court's decision is allowed.

In the states and federal judiciaries of the United States the supreme courts are a level higher than the appeals courts. (Some states have only one appeals level in which the appeal court and the supreme court are combined.) Although appeals courts must hear all cases brought to them, supreme courts can refuse to hear cases that have been appealed once. The member judges decide which cases are important and deserve a final decision. Most of the cases they hear involve interpretation of laws (or of the constitution) and their decision, therefore, is likely to establish or reaffirm policy. The composition and procedures of supreme courts are similar to those of other appeals courts.

A new court, the human rights court, has recently appeared in some regions of the world. The European Court of Human Rights and the Inter-American Court of Human Rights hear cases on appeal from other court systems. Although the process to bring a case before these international courts is rather cumbersome, each court decides dozens of cases a year. Cases are filtered through their own human rights commission. The European Commission on Human Rights prosecutes states for violation of human rights agreements; either side can appeal the commission's decision to the European Court. The Inter-American Commission on Human Rights does not prosecute states but rather determines whether an individual's complaint should be reviewed and, if so, represents that person in the Inter-American Court.

Some United Nations (U.N.) members have advocated creation of an international court for criminal justice, which would resemble two courts established to hear human rights violations committed by officials in Bosnia and Rwanda. If implemented, the decisions of the two regional courts and the U.N. court would prevail over those of domestic courts.

Staffing and Workload

Every level of the judiciary employs many more people than judges; the staff (secretaries, clerks, and others) forms a bureaucracy by itself. Clerks conduct research on cases and write decisions that judges can amend or accept and issue as their own. Higher level judges rely heavily on their staffs to do much of the work. To a certain extent a judge's relations with the staff is not unlike that of a president's relations with the executive staff. Judges oversee office operations, allow others to make decisions, and step in to make the most important decisions or to settle squabbles among staff members. The higher level judges are usually responsible for administration of the entire judiciary; they manage all levels and, more important, allocate the funds for proper operation of the courts.

Most courts everywhere have more cases than they can handle. Some cases must wait for two years before being heard; appeals can prolong the process up to twenty years. Courts in metropolitan areas are usually busier than those in rural areas. Such long delays in court actions brings an element of truth to the old saying "Justice delayed is justice denied."

Our overworked Supreme Court: "It is unequal to the ever increasing labor thrust upon it — Will Congress take prompt measures for the relief of the people?" Joseph Kepler cartoon for *Puck* January 9, 1885. The Court — the only federal appeals court at that time — reviewed 310 cases in 1860 and 1,816 cases in 1890. Relief came in 1891 when U.S. Congress created the circuit courts of appeals to hear the appeals of routine cases with no constitutional implications.

The backlog of liability cases in New York City traffic courts involves a five-year wait period. Memory becomes blurry after that length of time, and witnesses may disappear. After such a long time has elapsed between the accident and the hearing, judgements may not accurately reflect the victim's plight. In Bolivia, for example, a supreme court judge told this author that it takes twenty years for a property condemnation case to be heard. Few people can wait that long to receive their indemnity.

In an attempt to speed up the system, U.S. judges allow the practice of **plea bargaining**, which involves reducing an accused criminal's charges to a lesser offense and consequently less severe sentence in exchange for a guilty plea. A few innocent plead guilty just to shorten the time period they are involved with the legal system but the majority of defendants accept the plea bargain to obtain a lighter sentence for offenses they committed. Plea bargaining avoids trials and, consequently, lessens the workload of judges.

Besides the courts, the prosecutorial staffs that bring those accused to justice are also overloaded with cases. Prosecutors and those involved in the investigation and apprehension of the accused have more cases to resolve than time to do so. Thus, any practice that shortens the process, such as plea bargaining, is welcomed.

The judiciary removed a large portion of its workload by giving some executive agencies the power to adjudicate cases and levy civil penalties in matters under the agencies' jurisdiction. Thus, when the U.S. Environmental Protection Agency imposes fines on polluters or the

The U.S. Department of Justice, Washington, D.C. — the nation's litigator. Through its thousands of lawyers, investigators, and agents, it plays a key role in enforcing the law in the public interest.

The Land and Natural Resources Division of the U.S. Department of Justice seeks to hold the violators of environmental laws liable for site cleanup and reimbursement of government expenses.

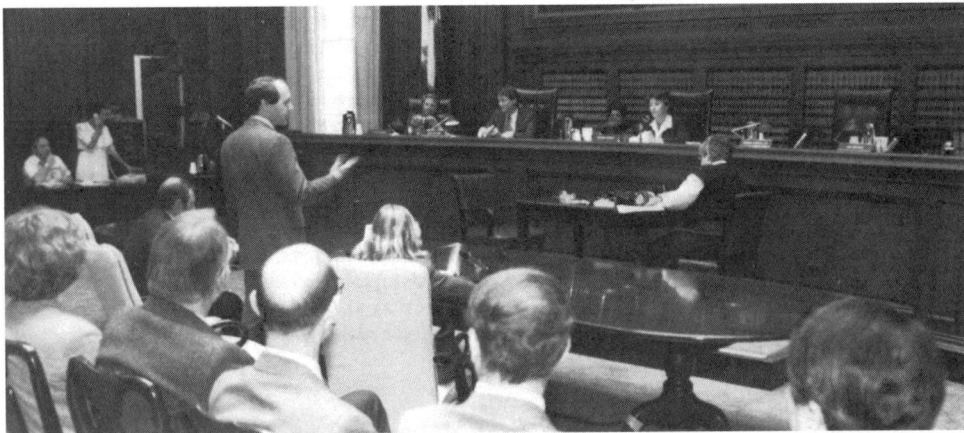

Competition is the basic economic policy of the United States and the responsibility of the Antitrust Division of the Department of Justice is to promote and maintain competitive markets. Pictured are Division's attorneys appearing at oral arguments before the Interstate Commerce Commission.

Internal Revenue Service gives fines to errant taxpayers, the agency acts as a court to relieve the court system of very specialized cases.

Another means used to lessen the courts' caseload is creation of agencies to resolve specific types of disputes. In some countries and in some states of the United States agencies have been created to resolve domestic relations problems, especially those emanating from divorce proceedings. Another institution that has become popular, especially in the Scandinavian states, is the **ombudsman.** The ombudsman is an agency or an individual who tries to resolve disputes between individuals and government agencies to prevent litigation.

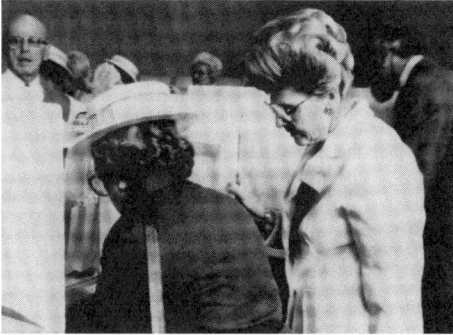

The Voting Section of the U.S. Department of Justice enforces the Voting Rights Act of 1965, as amended, and other federal voting statutes assuring that all qualified citizens have an equally available opportunity to register and vote without discrimination on account of race, color, membership in a language minority group, or age.

The Austrian Ombudsman authority, the Volksanwaltschaft, is anchored in the federal constitution as one of the highest institutions of state. Ombudsmen represent individuals who have lodged complaints against public authorities accused of maladministration. This way, individuals have an opportunity to voice their complaints publicly as a last resort when other means are not or no longer available. This right is not restricted to Austrian citizens, as foreigners resident in Austria can also take advantage of it. Every such complaint must be investigated, and the complainer must be informed of the outcome and the action taken. The Volksanwaltschaft enjoys complete independence in the exercise of this function, and is said to have investigated 4439 complaints in 1989. **In the picture above**: A unique Austrian television program offers a forum for debate and the hearing of cases. The three Ombudsmen — Horst Schender (teacher, far left), Evelyn Messner (director of a secondary school for girls), and Herbert Kohlmaier (pension fund director, far right) — along with their host Hans-Paul Strobl (center) prepare to engage in heated debate over the issues. The members are not allowed to engage in their occupations or political offices during their appointment as Ombudsman. The host of the program personally selects cases to be investigated and insures that the participants stick to the matter under investigation.

The Police

To improve the efficiency of police functions many states have created two separate police forces, one for traffic matters and another for criminal matters. Traffic police receive special training in vehicular movement of goods and people, including directing traffic, giving tickets to drivers who violate traffic laws, and investigating accidents involving automobiles, trains, and other vehicles. Sometimes traffic police are under the jurisdiction of the transportation ministry, which is responsible for determining traffic pat-

Immigration and Naturalization Service (INS) Border Patrol Agents observing the southern border of the United States to prevent the entry of illegal aliens. Legal advice to enforcement officers is provided by INS division attorneys of the Department of Justice.

terns and developing, building, and maintaining roads and streets.

Criminal police specialize in the prevention, investigation, and prosecution of crime and do not get involved in traffic matters unless other laws were violated. In most countries criminal police are under the jurisdiction of the interior ministry, which supervises not only police activities but also all prosecutorial functions. (The justice ministry in these countries deals principally with the administration of the judicial branch.)

In the United States, as in most countries, no distinction is made between traffic police and criminal police on the state and local level (although in New York City traffic and criminal functions are separate). A police officer must be a jack-of-all-trades, able to direct traffic, give speeding tickets, and participate in a drug bust. Each level in the police system, however, acts independently of the others. On the national level is the Federal Bureau of Investigation (FBI), the national police force, under the jurisdiction of the Department of Justice. (The FBI does not get involved in traffic matters, which is a state responsibility.). Each state has its own police force. In addition, there are 3,000 county police forces (i.e., sheriffs and their deputies) and 18,000 municipal police forces. Very little coordination occurs among all these police forces, although national data banks on criminals and those accused of crimes are being created.

Compare this complex multilayered organization of U.S. police forces to that of Bolivia, which has only two police forces (traffic and criminal forces are administered by separate ministries) and of the Republic of

A trial attorney of the Narcotic and Dangerous Drug Section, Department of Justice, describing the seizure of 3.7 million dollars in U.S. currency from a Colombian money launderer in Florida. A total of ten million dollars was ultimately seized by the government after the conviction of the criminal.

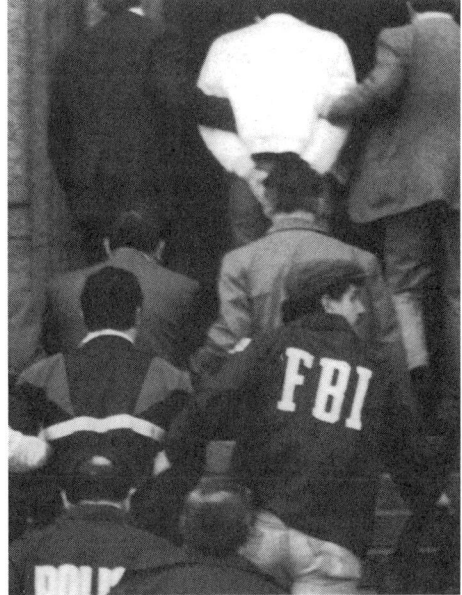

The FBI investigates all violations of Federal law except those which have been assigned by legislative enactment or otherwise to another Federal agency. The FBI's jurisdiction covers over 250 violations of Federal law in the criminal, civil, and intelligence fields. Priority is given to areas that affect society the most — foreign counterintelligence, organized crime, drugs, terrorism, white-collar crime, and violent crime.

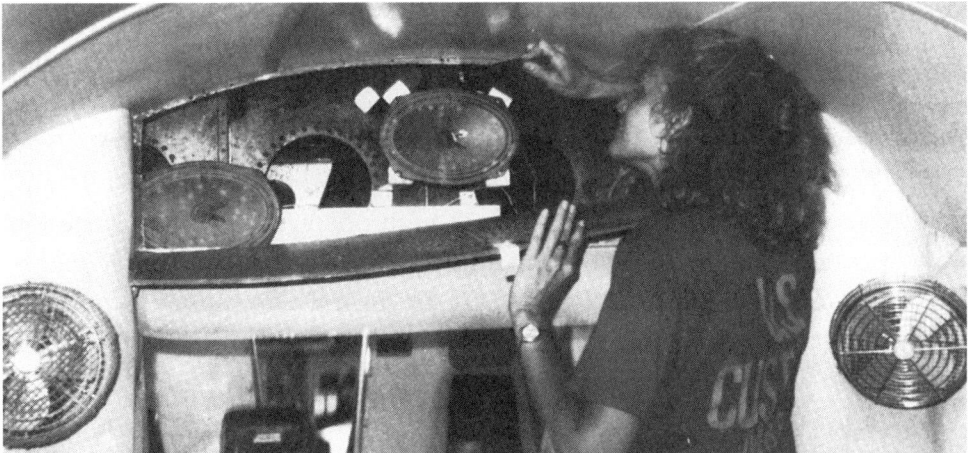

A customs inspector looks for hidden contraband in nookes and crannies aboard a seaplane that has arrived in Miami. The interdiction of smuggled drugs continues to be a top enforcement priority for the customs in the Southeast region, particularly Florida, which is the initial destination and distribution area for much of the cocaine coming into the country from Colombia.

South Korea, which has only one police force. France and Japan, on the other hand, have a national police force and prefectural, or provincial, police departments that act somewhat independently from each other.

The Penal System

The purpose of much police work is crime prevention. One method of crime prevention is punishing offenders so they will not commit crimes again. Courts not only decide the guilt or innocence of an accused but also the punishment for those found guilty. Punishment involves taking life, liberty, or property. The **penal system** implements these punishments.

Even though international human rights agreements and the constitutions of most states forbid capital punishment, it is still permitted in a few states, notably in the United States. The trend is to abolish the death penalty and mutilation of criminals. Only a half-dozen societies, at most, still allow branding, castration, whipping, caning, or limb cutting.

A more common form of punishment is incarceration. Sentences range from a few hours to a lifetime in prison, depending on the severity of the crime. Most states limit sentences to twenty-five or thirty years. Some states, including the United States, still give life sentences. A few states reduce a prisoner's sentence for good behavior while in prison.

The increase in crime today has led to the highest number of people serving jail sentences. Modern prisons are plagued with overcrowding and incompetent administration. What do inmates gain by their experiences during incarceration? Arguments about giving inmates opportunities to become rehabilitated or learn a trade versus allowing them to languish in their prison cell have been debated for centuries, resulting in no consensus. Of all government expenditures increases in appropriations for jails and prisons receives the least interest, even though prison riots have occurred in almost every state because of poor living conditions. In the United States new jails are built only after judges label them as unfit for human habitation.

Some societies, including the United States, believe prison inmates have forfeited their humanness. Therefore, few visitation rights for friends and relatives are granted and private visitations by spouses are infrequent. Abuse (often sexual) by guards and fellow inmates is common, while rehabilitation counseling and preparation for reentering the society is rare. Other societies, despite their inability to provide the conveniences of more industrialized countries, treat their prisoners more humanely by allowing them to live as normally as possible. For example, several Latin American states allow prison inmates' spouses and even their children to live in jail with them. Spouses and children visit anytime and have few restrictions. Visitors are allowed daily. Meals made outside jail are delivered to inmates. Inmates can have material objects (e.g., radios, computers, and pictures) in their cell. The **recidivism rate**, that is, the percentage of those who had spent time in jail and commit further crimes that put them back in jail, is lower in these countries than in those where prisoners are treated more inhumanely. In some communities in the United States the recidivism rate is almost 80 percent.

A new trend in the penal system is sentencing criminals to perform community service. A person convicted of a misdemeanor or lesser felony (e.g., involuntary manslaughter) can be sentenced to spend a specified amount of time with groups that perform services for or provide charity to needy members of society. This type of punishment is generally given to youthful or elderly first-time offenders.

Sometimes courts limit the movements of those convicted instead of sending them to jail. The criminal is given a monitor to wear around an arm or leg that sends signals of his or her movements to a local jail or

Graffiti often broadcasts the activities of street gangs. Left unchecked, it breeds crime, erodes community confidence, and substantially reduces property values. In Los Angeles, a new police initiative — the graffiti abatement and investigation program — mixes traditional law enforcement techniques with community relations, neighborhood beautification, and youth counseling to help alleviate the graffiti problem.

police department. The criminal is told where and how far he or she can go. Most often the criminal's boundaries are his or her home; this is called a "house arrest." Or the boundaries are between home and the workplace. If the criminal violates these restrictions, he or she is sent to prison without any further trials.

Actually, deprivation of life or liberty as punishment for a crime is seldom given. Far more common is deprivation of property, which is known as a fine. In industrialized societies most persons have paid **fines** for crimes they committed, usually traffic violations (e.g., speeding, going through a stop sign, and parking longer than the time limit). Some fines can be very low, the equivalent of the price of a dinner; others, as high as a billion dollars. Fines must be reasonable, within the criminal's capacity to pay. If the criminal does not pay the fine imposed by the court, he or she is given a jail sentence.

Corporations convicted of a crime cannot be sent to jail (although they can be executed by having their charters taken away), but they can be fined, sometimes as much as a million or a billion dollars. If the corporation does not pay the fine, penalties may be imposed, which could include suspension or revocation of its privilege to conduct business and imprisonment of its officers.

TERMS TO REMEMBER

civil law
crime
equity
writs
writ of injunction
writ of mandamus
common law
stare decisis
case law
courts of first instance
courts of original jurisdiction
appellate jurisdiction
appeals court
plea bargaining
ombudsman
penal system
recidivism rate
fines

SUGGESTED READINGS

Abraham, Henry J. *The Judicial Process: An Introductory Analysis of the Courts of the United States, England, and France.* New York: Oxford University Press, 1993. A look at the functioning of the third branch of the United States government with minor looks at its counterpart in England and France.

Olson, Walter K. *The Litigation Explosion: What Happened When America Unleashed the Lawsuit.* New York: Dutton, 1991. What happens to the law when there are too many lawsuits? This book seeks to answer that question.

Sarat, Austin and William L.F. Felstiner. *Divorce Lawyers and their Clients: Power and Meaning in the Legal Process.* New York: Oxford University Press, 1995.

The comingling of law and everyday life is the focus of this book as the conferences and discussions between lawyers and their clients in forty divorce cases are observed and tape-recorded.

Schwartz, Bernard. *Decision: How the Supreme Court Decides Cases*. New York: Oxford University Press, 1996. Using cases and anecdotes, the author takes a deep look into how the judges of the highest United States court reach their decisions.

Tonry, Michael. *Sentencing Matters*. New York: Oxford University Press, 1996. Comprehensive analysis of the manner America sentences its criminals.

Wolfe, Christopher. *The Rise of Modern Judicial Review: From Judicial Interpretation to Judge-Made Law*. Revised ed. Lanham, MD: Rowman & Littlefield Publishers, Inc., 1994. History of judicial review from its founding in the court of John Marshall to the Rehnquist Court.

Zamir, Itzhak and Allen Zysblat. *Public Law in Israel*. New York: Oxford University Press, 1996. The role of Israel's Supreme Court in shaping the law is the subject of this book.

The Interactions of Societies

PART FIVE

International Relations

20

⊕ Outline
- Society, State, and Nation
- Resolution of Conflict
- Interdependence of Societies

No society is an island. From the time they appeared as the basic units of human organization, societies related with each other. Whether to trade goods or help each other in war or in overcoming catastrophes, members of different societies interacted and found support from each other.

Society, State, and Nation

Some societies developed close relations, while others became antagonists in the pursuit for resources. In time some societies voluntarily merged to create a new one. Others were forced to merge and were administered by a central administrative apparatus (i.e., a state). Still others opted to remain separate. The United Kingdom was a state dominated by the English to which the Scotch and Welsh were forced to submit. Russia, which was five to ten different societies coexisting, became one society by the end of the fifteenth century. France grew by assimilating several smaller societies, some by force. Prussia remained independent until 1860, when its leaders decided to absorb several other German societies (which by 1995 had melded into one).

Nationality and Nation

As we saw in Chapter 14, two or more societies can exist under the jurisdiction of one state. The same is true for the administration of two nations. What is the difference between a society and a nation? A society is a collectivity of people inhabiting a particular space and, socialized and accultured to the same patterns of behaviors, values, beliefs, goals, and norms. If these people feel affinity toward each other because of the similarities in these patterns of behavior, values, beliefs, goals, and norms, they are called an **ethnic group** or, as in many societies, a **nationality**. An ethnic group, or nationality, is a cultural group. A nation is more than that; it is a political group. A **nation** is a nationality wanting to control its future through its own political institutions and feeling loyal to the same "country" (as in "my country right or wrong, my country"). Loyalty to or love of country unites a nation; it is the pivot around which the nation develops.

It is quite possible to be part of a society and a member of a different nation. A person residing in Canada, for example, who has become assimilated to its culture may nevertheless consider him or herself a member of the Australian nation because that is where he or she grew up.

A German living and working in Argentina can consider her or himself part of the German nation. (This has nothing to do with citizenship. **Citizenship** is a legal status conferred by the state by which political rights and obligations are gained.) If this appears complicated, try the following example from real life: A person born in Austria of Spanish parents becomes a citizen of France but resides in Germany where, according to recent agreements among members of the European Union, he or she may vote in local elections. This person, despite being born in Austria, is of Spanish nationality, French citizenship, and German residence and may actually feel part of German society.

Two or more nations can agree (or be forced) to live under the same state. Yugoslavia was such a state; it administered Slovenia, Croatia, Serbia, Bosnia-Herzegovina, Montenegro, and Macedonia. Each of these nations (not just societies) had different religions, customs and traditions,

Chapter Twenty

FOCUS — THE UNITED STATES BECOMES A NATION

The history of the United States as a nation illustrates its development from an offshoot of one society to the establishment of thirteen nations to the unification of all nations as one.

When the first settlers came to North America, they considered themselves part of British society but not of the British nation (because control of a society's political future by its citizens was not considered possible in the seventeenth century). With each new generation, awareness of ties to Britain lessened, and the colonists became more conscious of the similar norms, values, and behavior that had developed among them. By the early 1700s many settlers felt they were different from members of British society and found greater compatibility among themselves. In fact immigrants were pressured to give up their "old ways" and assimilate to the new. However, each colony developed its own society, making an American society as remote a notion as that of remaining a part of British society.

By the mid-1700s the British Parliament tried to interfere with what had become established norms and behavioral patterns in each colony and the colonists began to consider ways to continue to develop without this interference. People within each colony began to think of themselves as a nation. In 1776 representatives from the thirteen nations declared their independence from Britain and immediately tried to create an organization to coordinate some of their activities. The result was the Confederation of States, which from today's perspective was not much different from an international organization.

When the Confederation failed, representatives from these thirteen nation-states formed in 1789 a "more perfect union" called the United States of America. This new entity was for many at the time as remote to their daily concerns as the United Nations is to us today. Until the middle of the nineteenth century most Virginians thought of themselves as Virginians first and Americans second. The same was true of citizens of the other states. When leaders spoke of people of the United States they used the plural, that is, the United States are a people, implying that the U.S. people were a conglomeration of several distinct groups. Only after 1830 did the United States as a people become the dominant expression. Consequently, the United States as a nation did not really exist in the minds of most Americans until after the 1830s. Since then a New Yorker is an American first, and a New Yorker ... well, nobody really admits to being a New Yorker.

and colonial pasts (the Austrians had governed some, the Ottomans or Turks others, and Italian principalities still others). Each of these nations sent their representatives to a central government headquartered in

Marshal Tito (center) of Yugoslavia with Jawaharlal Nehru of India and Gamal Nasser of Egypt, at a meeting of Nonaligned Movement leaders, Brioni, 1956.

Belgrade, the capital, but had their own local elected officials. What held these *nations* together after World War II was the personality of their leader, Marshal Tito, and the organization of the Communist Party. When Tito died (1980) and the party collapsed (after 1990), the attempts of Serbs and Croatians to control the state eroded the legitimacy of the Yugoslav state. Eventually the state collapsed and each of the six nations became a separate state (only Montenegro aligned itself with another, Serbia).

To maintain its viability or even to further it a nation may choose to leave the existing arrangement it has with other nations and either become completely independent or join another arrangement. For example, Slovenia broke from the Yugoslav state, became completely independent, but is considering joining the European Union. If Slovenia joins the union, it would have to follow the Union administration, which may be preferable to facing the vagaries of economic and political challenges alone. Therefore, becoming part of the European Union may better serve the nation of Slovenia then remaining independent or rejoining the Yugoslav state.

Similarly, Quebec may decide to break from Canada to become an independent state and to immediately ask to be accepted into the North American Free Trade Area. Would the Quebec nation be better served by the new arrangement? Only those loyal to Quebec can answer that.

Some societies have yet to form themselves into nations. In Latin America, for example, leaders often exhort their compatriots to become a nation. Within their areas of jurisdiction many people group themselves around regional or factional "countries." The resulting regionalism prevents the state from mobilizing the whole population to further the entire society. Such loyalties frequently prevent a nation from developing. In Africa strong tribal ties cause similar results.

The State as Representative of Society

Although the state since the 1500s has been the principal societal institution by which societies and nations interact with each other, one must remember that in one respect not much has changed in 3,000 years—people are still responsible for these interactions. In the past tribal chiefs negotiated agreements; today ambassadors, foreign ministers, chief executives, and a slew of bureaucrats are involved in that process. Although we say that Canada has negotiated an agreement with Nigeria, the Canadian prime minister and foreign minister negotiated the agreement with their Nigerian counterparts on behalf of their respective societies or nations. Whether under the aegis of the state or another institution, intersocietal or international transactions are always conducted by people. In the past some state officials did not allow people in their society to relate to people in other societies. Until recently a person desiring to travel outside his or her society needed permission from state officials to leave and from officials of the society they were going to enter. State officials issued a permit called a 'visa' to travelers..

This has changed dramatically. Whereas in centuries past a handful of state officials traveled abroad to negotiate their society's interests, today 10 percent of a society's population may be abroad doing so. States cannot prevent their residents and citizens from traveling or from signing contracts with outsiders that may not be in the best interests of that state. For example, if General Motors' directors sign an agreement with Toyota's directors which will adversely affect thousands of General Motors' employees in Canada and the United States, as states the United States and Japan cannot stop it. Not only is individual global interaction almost routine (e.g., through travel or use of the Internet, World Wide Web, telephone, and ham radio) but also most economic operations in a society depend on activities in other societies. In addition, numerous government and non-government international organizations monitor and often regulate social, cultural, political, and economic conditions in every corner of the globe, thereby causing the supremacy of the state in determining international relations to be seriously disputed.

Millions of persons from more than four hundred societies and nations are daily and routinely intermingling, signing agreements, diffusing knowledge, values, and technology. Yet our preoccupation often is solely with the relations among states. In fact when we mention the phrase "international relations," it conjures up visits of state officials, treaties, negotiations, wars, and peace agreements. So strong is our identification of the state with international relations that we often ignore the interactions that we ourselves have had with members of other societies when we visited them or they visited us.

The National Interest

International relations, or the relations among nations, theoretically have never existed because nations seldom interact; people interact. What does exist are the relations among officials representing states. Since state officials often make and implement agreements that provide an umbrella for other interactions to occur, these agreements indeed are very important. They spell out the do's and don'ts (the norms) by which you and I can deal with persons of other societies, and in doing so are supposed to consider our best interests. Thus, state officials' responsibility is to protect our **national interest**. Consequently, states relate to each other to protect their national interest.

This sounds praiseworthy. However, few persons in any nation would agree on what that nation's interests are. Over the decades two schools of thought on national interest have developed. **Idealists** generally claim that a nation's interests are those upon which a nation is built including democracy, justice, civil rights, customs and traditions, religion, economic well-being, and common decency. Idealists also believe that the relations among states follow rules, which are based on customs and traditions, ethics, or international law. **Realists** believe a nation's interest is power and that the acquisition and maintenance of power are the basis of all relations between states. They view power as a finite quantity and relations between states as a zero-sum game (i.e., whatever power one state gains, the other loses). Therefore, the amassing of power becomes the end sought. Realists believe that international relations are ruleless, that a Hobbesian state of nature exists among states in which only the powerful prevail and Machiavellian tactics bring success.

The problem with both viewpoints is that they are based on the premise that relations among societies or nations are the result of conscious and deliberate acts of a few men and women; neither allows for patterns of interactions that have developed outside of the official state environment. Nor do these viewpoints acknowledge that the individuals who make and implement foreign policy are subject to the norms imposed by their own societies.

Another problem with the idea of national interest is that, just like self-interest, it is so difficult, if not impossible, to define. If I speak of my self-interest, what am I speaking of? What is this "self" to whom I refer? Do I know myself so well that I can define who I am? And assuming that I could do this, will my definition of "self" today be the same tomorrow? I doubt it. Then how much more difficult it must be for a nation to define its own identity! And what about interest? What are my interests? Are my short-term interests in harmony with my longterm interests? Are not my interests to some extent dependent on how I define myself? What are any nation's interests? How can one determine the short-term and long-term interests of a nation? Who knows a nation so well that he or she can specify its interests?

National interest belongs to the same category of unknowable theories as Aristotle's golden mean, Rousseau's general will, Hegel's *Volksgeist*, and Marx's class consciousness. All these notions are nice to banter around; but, nevertheless, when all is said and done, they do not mean much. As stated previously, a myriad of unknown variables determines a society's viability and development. By stating that specific acts are in the national interest one elevates these acts to such important rhetorical levels that they appear to overshadow all other variables. Yet in actuality acts done in the national interest may not do anything but obscure, and perhaps even hinder, the real variables that propel a society forward.

What may be worse is that state officials use concepts such as national interest to keep themselves in power or pursue policies that the population clearly does not support. China's ruling clique, in the name of national interest, has censored movies, books, and even music that only slightly gave the appearance of being critical of previous governments' actions. This government, like many others, cloaks itself in the mantle of national interest to prevent challengers from speaking out. U.S. Presidents Johnson and Nixon used national interest to diffuse opposition to the military policies implemented during the Vietnam War. Often government officials who do not want a policy discussed by the media or by the people in general invoke the national interest. By doing so they infer that they know better than others what is best for the nation and expect everyone to abide by their judgements. (The national interest has even been used in the United States and Canada to justify domestic policies such as welfare reform, changes in medical assistance to the poor and elderly, and environmental deregulation.)

Protection of the national interest is often used as an argument to counter the effects of those who advocate globalization of policy making and implementation as a better way to maintain the integrity and viability of societies. The state has always been viewed as the only protector of national interest. However, the state competes with many other institutions in furthering the interests of society and the interest it protects may not assist society's development.

Resolution of Conflict

Protection of societal interests causes conflict when one society wants what another society possesses or also wants, such as resources, people, or territory. Conflict is likely to occur when population pressures within a society create greater demands for resources than the society can readily supply. During the Middle Ages European societies that used all their land for farming and wanted more often made war on each other or tried to take away land from less fortunate neighbors, such as the Ottomans. To a large extent colonization of the Americas and Africa was due to population pressures on Northern European societies. At that time development of technologies to alleviate the need for more land did not develop fast enough, so taking land from others was often easier. As long as casualties were few, war was an acceptable way to take a neighbor's possessions; however, when war became too costly by threatening destruction of entire societies, it became less acceptable.

Collective Security and Balance of Power

Clobbering a neighbor or conquering strangers was not always the best way for societies to get what they wanted. Trade or exchange of territory usually accomplished the same end without bloodshed. In fact most relations among societies or nations have been peaceful because each one has

FOCUS

TWO IMAGES OF THE BALANCE OF POWER

The balance of power conjures two images. One is an actual balance in which the two sides have equal power in such areas as territory, population, resources, economic well-being, military capacity and technology, type of government, and morale of the population. The problem is that evaluating each area is difficult as is placing it in relation to the others. Perceptions of these determinants of power often become more important than the reality. Consequently, the balance of power has become a perception rather than an actual balance. Nevertheless, when the two sides are perceived as equal, peace prevails because each side keeps the other in check.

This type of balance has been applied to the European powers in the last century. France, Prussia, Russia, and Austro-Hungary were continuously rearranging their alliances with each other. Great Britain was viewed as either adding its power to the weaker side or composing one side of the balance as the other major European states composed the counter-balance, with an occasional desertion of one or two of them to the British side. In any case, the theory of equal balance is rather difficult to apply to the European situation because equality of power is enigmatic in itself and each state's role in the balance is not easily discerned.

The second image of balance of power is stability. Although one side's power outweighs the other's, the ratio of power between them does not change. In the post-World War II

scenario, the power of the United States and its allies outweighed that of the Soviet Union and its allies. A major policy objective of the West was to ensure that any power gain of the East was offset by power gains in the West. The policy of **containment** (i.e., preventing a nation such as the Soviet Union from adding further states to its side) and the policy of matching any increase in weapons' technology, capacity, and numbers was meant to keep the ratio between West and East stable. The belief was that the Soviet Union would not dare attack the West because the latter had such a preponderance of power. And the West would not attack the East because ... well, because the West would not sink that low. In any case, the stable balance of power would maintain the status quo, which was peace.

A quirk in the stable balance of power became quite evident, transforming it into an equal balance of power. That little quirk was the fact that in a major war each side would have been virtually destroyed. According to the policies of both the United States and the Soviet Union, an attack by one on the other would spur a massive counterattack that would insure the destruction of both antagonists. This was called Mutual Assured Destruction (MAD). If both sides in a balance of power have the potential of wiping out each other in a war, then what kind of balance is it?

In the 1960s President Charles DeGaule announced the continuation of France's nuclear weapons' program on the theory that, despite the nuclear umbrella of the United States, France had to have the means to inflict heavy punishment on any attacker. By having the ability to have even one nuclear bomb hit its target, France became more independent from its allies and more threatening to any potential aggressor. France's possession of

even a limited number of nuclear bombs leveled the preponderance of power, thereby transforming the stable balance into the equal balance.

A balance connotes two sides. What if there are more than two sides, or, as in the post-cold war era, there are no sides? Is there a balance of power?

had norms to uphold that make war undesirable. War has been an anomaly. What makes war between societies even more unlikely are the alliances formed between them. From the earliest time societies have made agreements to help each other when attacked or to join forces to attack others. By making arrangements for **collective security** societies pledge support to each other. The pledge of "one for all and all for one" was the basis of the foundation of such groups as the Organization of American States, the North Atlantic Treaty Organization, and the United Nations.

U.S. President Harry Truman signed the North Atlantic Treaty in August 1949. The treaty was the framework for wide cooperation among its signatories — the U.S., Canada, most Western European nations, and Turkey. Apart from being a military alliance formed to prevent aggression or to retaliate it should need arise, the treaty also provided for continuing joint action in the political, economic, and social aspects. Initiated by Western Europeans, the treaty placed the U.S. in the unique position of an imperial power by invitation rather than by conquest.

Collective security arrangements caused the creation of several alliances, each offsetting the others. Each alliance, not wanting to risk the loss of its associates' welfare and resources, maintained peace, although often an uneasy one, with others. This is called the **balance of power**. Not all societies were part of alliances; also, all alliance members were not so loyal to their alliance that they would not switch to another. Yet peace generally prevailed because a stable core of members formed each alliance and believed that abiding by agreements and obeying the norms of inter-societal conduct was in its best interest.

Occasionally, in some societies leaders appear who consider themselves as extraordinarily special and who obsessively pursue their dream of grandeur by attempting to impose their will on other societies or to destroy them. They are not interested as much in obtaining more resources or territory as in wanting others to acknowledge their greatness or, at least, the greatness of their ideas. Hannibal, Napoleon, Stalin, and Hitler were such leaders. To them alliances, agreements, and norms were a means to an end, their grandeur. In time most of these self-appointed saviors not only destroyed themselves but also their societies. Protection against this type of individual was difficult in the past. (Today enforcement of constitutional and human rights provisions would make chances of such a rise to leadership more remote.) Just as laws, ethics, and religious norms cannot stop pathological criminals in any society, alliances, balance of power, and international norms could not prevent maniacal leaders from causing tremendous suffering in the past.

Pacific Settlement of Disputes

Conflict among societies is normal; the use of violence to settle conflict is not. Over the centuries many different processes have developed with which those representing states peacefully resolve conflict. Collectively these processes are known as the **pacific settlement of disputes**. Among them are the following.

Tender of good offices. When two states do not seem able to resolve their conflict, a third party, such as a state, an international organization, or the church, invites the two states to use its facilities (e.g., meeting rooms, translators, and electronic equipment) to discuss the problem. The third party does not take part in the discussions. The Oslo Agreements of 1993 between Israel and the Palestinian Liberation Front were negotiated in facilities provided by the Norwegian government.

Conciliation. In conciliation the third party takes an active role by serving as an intermediary for the two disagreeing states. Both sides tell the third party what they believe is the problem. After the conciliator has listened to both, a report is given to both sides, which suggests the problem, the areas in which agreement exists, and the main points of disagreement.

Mediation. Mediation is the most popular process involving third parties in which conflicts are peacefully resolved. After listening to the two parties of a conflict, the third party makes suggestions about how the disagreement can be resolved. Both sides respond to these suggestions, and the mediator takes the reactions, reworks the suggestions in light of the reactions, and presents new suggestions to each side. Often this process continues until the conflicting states agree on a solution. The United States used this process in 1995 to reconcile the differences among the various parties in the Bosnian conflict; they culminated in the Dayton Accords.

The fourth major pact in the Middle East peace process — an interim agreement on Palestinian self-rule in the West Bank was signed by Israeli Prime Minister Yitzhak Rabin (seated left) and Palestine Liberation Organization (PLO) leader Yasser Arafat (seated right) at the Whitehouse in Washington D.C. in September 1995. Witnesses include King Hussein of Jordan (standing second from left), U.S. President Bill Clinton (seated center), and Egyptian President Hosni Mubarak (standing second from right). The pact provides for, among other things, the redeployment of Israeli troops, release of Palestinian prisoners and the hand-over of civil authority in the West Bank to an elected Palestinian Council, as well as for cooperation in economic and environmental fields.

Arbitration. Before arbitration can be initiated, the two sides in the conflict must agree on who will serve as the arbitrator or arbitrators. This agreement, called a *compromis* also stipulates when the process will begin and end, what types of evidence can be presented, and what rules will be implemented. Both sides pledge to follow the arbitrators' decision. In general each side chooses two arbitrators and allows the four arbitrators to choose another person to serve as the presiding officer. Arbitrators usually are chosen from the International Court of Arbitration, whose member states appoint one person from their own state and a second person from another state to serve as arbitrators. After reviewing the evidence presented, the arbitrators make a decision that hopefully resolves the issue.

Courts of justice. A state that charges another state with either breach of agreement or nonobedience of international law can bring its case before an international court for resolution. The International Court of Justice, an institution of the United Nations, and the Court of the European Union are two such courts, which make decisions strictly based on law. They are not obligated to follow precedents because each case is considered new and not to be decided on the basis of previous decisions in similar cases. Court decisions are final and cannot be appealed. Enforcement of court decisions, however, is weak because no international institution is charged with determining whether decisions are followed.

Diplomacy. The most common method for preventing and solving conflicts involves representatives of two or more states talking to each other with the expectation of reaching an agreement on an issue. Sometimes these representatives meet with each other or talk to each other over the telephone or, in more and more situations, send each other e-mail. The number of diplomats has increased not only as the number of states has increased but also as issues discussed multiply and become more complex, such as agriculture, aviation, trade, copyright protection, drug smuggling, and weapon sales. Although ministries of foreign affairs and the U.S. State Department are the principal government institutions involved in the conclusion of agreements among states, much negotiation today goes on among representatives of other institutions within the government, such as the ministries, independent agencies, and the legislature. In the conduct of foreign relations diplomats, who usually are employed by the foreign service, are outnumbered by civil servants.

War

Sometimes states cannot or do not want to resolve their conflicts peacefully. War then becomes a possible alternative. Fortunately, wars in the last quarter of the twentieth century between the approximately 200 states were so rare that they could be counted on one hand. International organizations and agreements have created so many varied processes in which states can prevent war (or be compelled to do so) that war between states has ceased to be a problem for humanity. No one at this time can even imagine the major European powers and the United States going to war. When war between less industrial states breaks out, other states and international organizations step in to contain it and stop it quickly, as in the 1995 skirmish between Peru and Ecuador. This tranquility among states has not occurred since the state became the organization of society.

Unfortunately, people are dying daily from being shot by persons in foreign groups; however, these foreign groups are not states, most are religious organizations. The war in Yugoslavia was essentially a religious conflict among Eastern Orthodox Christians (Serbs), Catholics (Croats),

Flag Day, June 1942. U.S. President Franklin Roosevelt in a historic meeting of representatives of the Allies — the international coalition waging war against the Axis powers Germany, Japan, and Italy. The same Allies formed the nucleus of the United Nations, established in 1945, to preserve global peace by outlawing aggression anywhere in the world and providing the machinery to help find solutions to disputes or problems, and to deal with virtually any matter of concern to humanity.

and Moslems (Bosnian government). The wars in the Middle East have been conflicts among secular Moslems, fundamentalist Moslems, and Jews. Buddhists, Hindus, and Moslems fight each other at times in Asia. Tribal and clan conflicts break out in violence periodically in Africa, such as in Liberia, Nigeria, Rwanda, Zaire, and Somalia. Even if states are involved in such conflicts, they are not responsible for what are essentially religious or tribal conflicts. No interreligious or intertribal organization has been formed yet to prevent and resolve these conflicts. And the state is ill-equipped to handle conflicts that occur within its own boundaries among two or more societies, nationalities, or nations. These conflicts may involve similar groups in other states, and they undermine the efficacy of the state itself. If a state takes sides in these conflicts, it alienates the other side of these conflicts. If it does not take a side which has support from other states, it thereby makes enemy with those other states.

Since states often are only tangentially involved in violent conflicts within their borders, wars between religious or tribal groups can become horrific. In war times since the Renaissance states have followed rules or laws established by custom or treaty. One principle of war distinguishes between combatants and noncombatants. **Combatants** are those involved in the actual waging of war (i.e., military personnel except medical doctors and chaplains), and **noncombatants** are those not involved in the fighting (i.e., the civilian population). The rules of war among states prohibit injury or property damage to noncombatants, but religious and tribal wars make no distinction between combatants and noncombatants. Consequently, most of the casualties in these conflicts are civilians and, even worse, women and children.

This is the reason war has become so repulsive to most of us today. Those who fight for religious or tribal causes follow no rules, which makes their wars unpredictable and difficult to control and end. Often their purpose is complete annihilation of everyone who does not either belong to their organization or follow their beliefs. Since this goal is impossible to achieve, such wars appear to have no purpose.

On the other hand, wars between states have had a purpose. From one perspective their purpose was to cause a desired situation or condition, which was usually expressed as policy objectives. Therefore, wars were considered a means to an end. The leading advocate of this notion was a retired Prussian general, Carl von Clausewitz, who in the 1830s published a book, *Vom Kriege (On War)*, in which he said, "War is the naked continuation of politics by other means." By politics he meant the formulation and achievement of policy. He also said that war is like a duel but on a larger scale. A duel follows rules, is carefully staged, and does not aim to cause destruction. Wars, too, follow rules, are carefully staged and are not waged for the purpose to destroy and kill.

Another perspective on the purpose of war is that it can never be a means to an end, regardless of the nobility of that end. By destroying and killing, wars contain unethical elements (this is especially true in our age of nuclear, biological, and chemical weapons). Consequently, these unethical elements taint the purposes of war. Unless the means by which an end is sought is pure, the end cannot be such.

In the last few decades a variation of this perspective has become the predominant philosophy of war among the makers and implementors of foreign policy. According to this viewpoint, wars are used only as sanctions for breaches of law. For states to act in harmony with each other, law is necessary. For laws to be effective, the use of force must be illegal (as we discussed in Chapter 2). Those who enforce the law can use force only as a punishment or sanction. Therefore, force on an international scale should be used only against states that have not obeyed the law. For example, war was waged against Iraq after its *illegal* takeover of Kuwait in 1990.

President Bill Clinton signing the North American Free Trade Agreement (NAFTA) in December 1993. He agreed with his predecessor George Bush that NAFTA would benefit the U.S. economy more than it would hurt it by opening Mexican markets to American businesses. Despite the fierce opposition from organized labor, the Administration won a close bipartisan vote ratifying the agreement.

Interdependence of Societies

One reason this perspective has become so prevalent is that as societies have become more dependent on each other, rules regulating their interactions must be constantly updated and obeyed. If one state is allowed to disobey the rules, then other states also may do so, causing much injury to their societies and resulting in the loss of the sunk costs of rule making. Agreements such as the General Agreement on Tariffs and Trade and the North American Free Trade Agreement took decades to negotiate, and this effort would be

In November 1993, the United States hosted the first-ever Asia-Pacific Economic Cooperation (APEC) summit meeting. APEC is a regional consultative body that aims to promote trade and economic cooperation in Asia-Pacific.

wasted if a state was allowed to disobey them.

Two hundred states and several hundred societies cannot exist independently. They establish relations with each other because they perceive it to be in their national interest or the limitations of their environment forces them to seek support. To ensure stability in these relationships, societies and their states have had to establish norms of behavior. As discussed in Chapter 14, these norms come under the rubric of international law. This law, as all law, exists not because someone or some group invented it by which to dominate others, but it exists because without it no stable relations among states and societies are possible. For example, a letter I write to an individual in a foreign country travels over several states' boundaries and is handled by individuals employed by these states. Officials from any one state can prevent the letter from reaching the addressee. Yet no state will allow its officials to do so. Why? In the last century the International Postal Union was created to regulate the flow of mail between states. No state can afford not to comply with this organization's rules, unless it wants to isolate itself from the rest of the globe.

The notion that a state can do whatever it wants when it wants to assumes that its society is self-sufficient (i.e., all goods and services needed by society are produced or made by it). However, no society, regardless of how advanced or industrialized, is self-sufficient. Every society imports and exports goods, people, services, capital and, very important, ideas. Trade today is conducted with sophisticated communication and transportation technologies. Whereas two hundred years ago the market was a square in the middle of a city, today computer technology has transformed the market into the whole globe. In 1995, this author advertised the sale of a camera over the Internet. The person who bought it lived in Jakarta, Indonesia. They negotiated the transaction over e-mail. After verifying electronically that the buyer deposited the money in an account, the author sent him the camera, which the buyer received two days later. During this time the author did not leave his study except to send the package.

If the globe has become a market, then the regulation of the interactions within a society is no longer entirely under the purview of the state, but is subject to a myriad of variables that no state can control. This signifies not only the further diffusion of policy making but also the importance of international regulating mechanisms, which cannot be monopolized, by any state.

For example, individuals in every society talk about regulating the Internet and the World Wide Web. Rules cannot be imposed by one state; rather an international agency must be involved since both services are used globally. However, any international agency that tried to enforce rules on use of the Internet would have to create an enforcement regime larger than the combined armies of all states. The Internet gives me direct access to any individual in the world without the use of an intermediary, such as the state-owned post office. Short of pulling the plug and cutting the telephone lines, how can this access be regulated?

The situation with the Internet illustrates another aspect of the changing role of the state. In the past the state initiated international transactions. Relations among societies were determined mainly by what state officials did or did not do. Today the state instead reacts to international transactions initiated elsewhere. Although the Internet originated as a government project, the easy access it provides to global communication gives states little, if any, control of it.

The same can be said about most economic relations among societies. So many transactions occur among societies today that the state, which cannot control these activities, can only attempt to coordinate them. State-imposed boycotts and embargos often are ignored by businesses under that state's jurisdiction. For example, foreign subsidiaries of American automobile manufacturers and pharmaceutical companies have side-stepped a U.S. embargo of Cuba to engage in trade with Cuban businesses. The state therefore can no longer determine a society's interactions with other societies. In fact in some nonindustrialized societies in which state officials attempt to control their societies' interactions with others, pressure from other states is causing these officials to reevaluate their ideas. Even in the industrial states the state's role in setting tariffs, quotas, or other controls has been undermined by citizen demands to eliminate these restrictions.

Nowhere is this better illustrated than in illicit drug trafficking. The most severe police methods and efforts have proven useless against the determined efforts of some to engage in the production and distribution of addictive drugs. Drug trafficking is an international activity that states and international organizations are unable to prevent or even regulate despite the billions of dollars spent and many other resources used by dozens of organizations to curtail it. In fact, the amount of drugs available has increased while their price on the streets has decreased. Furthermore, drug trafficking has permeated the state itself, with officials calling for its curtailment while simultaneously acquiring money and status by participating in the illegal activity.

On the one hand, the state has lost some control over members of its own societies because they can interact with members of other societies without obeying state-imposed norms. On the other hand, the state must abide by many norms established by international agencies or treaties of which it does not have complete control.

States Influencing States

Societies and their states have always influenced each other. Interstate relations are perceived as a hierarchy based on some states at the top influencing others. States at the top have the most influence and are influenced least by other states; whereas states at the bottom have the least influence and are influenced the most. For example, many Americans believe that the United States is at the top of this hierarchy, which means it can greatly influence any other state but is not influenced by others.

For the last 150 years Latin Americans have complained that the United States' influences have limited the capacity of their own states to act and that such limitations are imposed on them for the advantage of the United States. But the question is, For whose advantage in the United States? This is a complicated aspect of state to state relations. Yes, officials in U.S. institutions, especially in the Departments of State and Defense, have intervened in many Latin American states' affairs by forcing officials of those states to follow their directives (even when the officials do not want to do so), such as raising taxes on products produced by their societies or on property held by their residents; buying products, often heavy machinery or military gadgetry, from other societies; and voting a certain way in an international organization such as the United Nations General Assembly. However, most frequently the United States itself does not profit from these activities, but rather private U.S. interests and enterprises that conduct business in Latin American societies. These private interests use U.S. state officials for their ends, and the United States does not gain or lose anything by interfering on their behalf. Latin American officials, however, lose their freedom to act as they think best. Consequently, was it the Unites States state that influenced the Latin Americans or was that influence done by private interests located within the American society who happened to use the state to accomplish their wishes?

To what extent is the state an independent actor when it relates to other states? And to whom within its society is it accountable for these relations? The answer to the last question should be to everyone in that society. Yet too often state officials dealing with other states are beholden to small segments of their society whose desire may be to increase their wealth or to convert people of other societies to their beliefs or ways of thinking. At other times, members of a society oppose the state's involvement in others' affairs. For instance, in the recent past Americans in general have opposed sending troops or money to other states. Consequently, the state often is not an independent actor in its relations with other states; even if it is in the number one position in the hierarchy of states.

States in the lower ranks of the hierarchy have always had to juggle local and international pressures in foreign policy making. Few of these officials have been free of pressures from state officials of the industrialized societies. Today pressures also come from officials of international organizations. Thus, these state officials have lost their independence to act.

Since the number of states today has increased to beyond two hundred, the amount of influence of any one state has been reduced. Even the United States, for example, cannot send emissaries or staff officers to maintain liaisons with every state. Most states relate only to nearby states or those with which they trade or from which they receive aid.

Foreign Aid

Since the 1950s foreign aid (i.e., financial grants or loans industrialized states give to less industrialized states) has been used to further the "interests" of the donor states. Often viewed as charity, foreign aid is an instrument by which the donor's foreign policy objectives are achieved. Often wealthier states use foreign aid to create a dependency on them. Just as drug pushers get victims hooked on drugs by first charging very little and, once they are addicted, charging exorbitant prices; states give foreign aid to others at first with no strings attached and, as the recipient states become accustomed to receiving the aid, the donor states begin to make demands.

A Bolivian village that prepared for coca planting was dropped from U.N. Development Programme.

Bolivia has been receiving some form of aid from the United States since the 1950s. Bolivian authorities were so accustomed to these annual payments that they included them as revenue in the nation's budget. Occasionally, the United States puts the squeeze on them. In the spring of 1995 the U.S. Department of State declared that Bolivia was not cooperating in the destruction of plants from which narcotic drugs are processed, specifically the coca plant from which cocaine is derived. As a condition for receiving further aid, the Bolivian state was required to destroy by July 31 of that year more than 1,500 hectares (about 4,000 acres) of coca plants and by the end of that year, 5,400 hectares. To comply the Bolivian government sent part of its army to an area to destroy these plants. By July 31 supposedly 1,500 hectares were destroyed, but so were the lives of dozens of peasants, including children, and an unknown number of soldiers. Dozens of strikes involving school teachers, medical doctors, and others occurred; hundreds of persons were arrested, and a state of siege was imposed on the whole country. For what purpose was Bolivia's fragile democracy put in jeopardy? The plants may have been destroyed in one place, but they are grown in other areas. Neither the amount of coca leaving Bolivia nor the supply of cocaine in the United States decreased after this action was accomplished.

Although foreign aid has benefited many societies immeasurably, the costs to the recipients have not been cheap. Usually the aid comes with a sign that says "made in the West," meaning that countries accepting such aid must adapt to Western values. However, most societies cannot adapt fast enough, causing much confusion and despair. Western technologies and processes work well in Europe, North America, and in some other areas because their development occurred slowly over a long time period. However, they do not work well when rapidly introduced. In the 1960s the industrial states gave grants and technical assistance to many less industrialized states to introduce a system of income taxes. The collection of income taxes depends on the willingness of citizens to turn over some of their income to the state. Many societies had no cultural values that would have made this possible; revenue had been received through services performed by the state or from tariffs with which most persons had no direct relationship. Therefore, when these states instituted income taxes, residents did not pay them and sometimes rebelled. Thus, the income tax did not generate much revenue. Even worse, the states' total revenues were much reduced because, when they instituted the income tax, they also reduced or eliminated the amount of revenue from the other source. The result was that these states became even more dependent on foreign aid.

To many state officials, foreign aid is just another tool that officials of other states use to restrict their capacity to make decisions.

Nevertheless, foreign aid has improved the welfare of millions, if not billions, of people. After World War II the American-sponsored Marshall Plan and other aid programs helped not only European nations to rebuild their destroyed economies but also less industrialized societies to regain hope for a better future through the technologies, food, medical supplies, and improved administrative processes they received. The population explosion, which is often blamed for many of the economic and social problems of the less industrialized countries, is in part due to lower infant and child mortality rates brought about by the improved medical care, food and water supplies, and sanitation facilities provided through aid from the industrial countries. Foreign aid has also contributed to modernized transportation and communication networks, better education and technical training, greater and better use of resources to produce energy and food, and improved public administration.

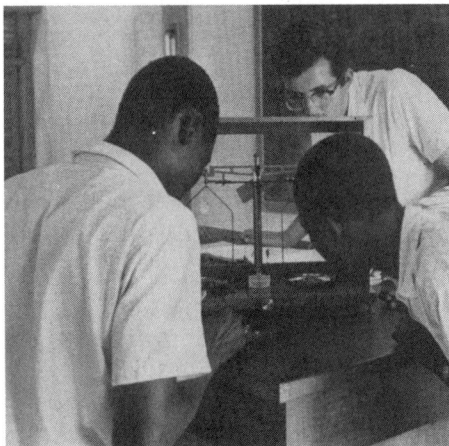

An American Peace Corps volunteer teaching physics at a secondary school in Ghana in 1961. Founded by President John Kennedy in 1961, with his brother-in-law, Sargent Shriver, as the first director, the national response to the program has been very enthusiastic, especially among university students who were to be the primary source of volunteers. Since its inception, more than 148,000 Americans have joined the Peace Corps. In 1997 about 6,500 volunteers are working in 91 countries in the areas of business, education, the environment, health and nutrition, and agriculture.

Tens of thousands of people, including members of the American Peace Corps and highly trained professionals, shared their expertise with people who otherwise might still be functioning with nineteenth-century techniques and devices. The individuals who contributed to these efforts generally were not interested in the politics between states or societies but rather in the opportunities to improve the lives of those less fortunate. Foreign aid made their efforts possible.

The Common Heritage of Humanity

A phrase that has had an important impact on state control is "the common heritage of humanity." Originating in the Law of the Sea Treaty of 1980, this concept was used to describe ownership of mineral deposits contained in ocean seabeds and since then has been applied to almost every aspect that interests humans, even those under state jurisdiction. Simply put, **common heritage of humanity** means that humans everywhere have a direct interest or stake in everything that affects them, such as the future of Antarctica; the preservation fish and other animals and fauna in the oceans; clean air, water, and earth; effects of pollution on the ozone layer; and outer space exploration.

Concern about the environment and ecology in foreign societies is based on the concept of the common heritage of humanity. For example, Americans are concerned about exploitation of the Amazon rain forest and the loss of many species and natural resources. But why should the Brazilian state or society care whether we are concerned about a rain forest that lies within their territory and would normally be considered theirs to exploit? The answer, which Brazilians are not too enthused to accept, is that the rain forest is part of the common heritage of humanity because its devastation would deprive other societies in the world (e.g., the Americas, Europe, Asia, Africa, and Australia) of medicinal, aesthetic, and physical resources and would contribute to the greenhouse effect. Brazilians, according to the theory of common heritage, profit from something that belongs to everyone. Since Brazil's profits from timber sales and farming do not outweigh the losses that everyone incurs when the rain forests disappear, Brazil is obligated to preserve the forests by eliminating tree cutting.

A similar argument can be made about many different possessions that usually are considered owned by societies or states. Does the Coliseum in Rome, the Mona Lisa in the Louvre, the Pyramids in Giza, Westminster Abbey in London, and the Washington Monument in

Washington, D.C., belong to the societies or states where they are located? Suppose the Italian government decides to raze the Coliseum and construct a commercial complex in its place. Would people, especially those in the Western world, silently allow that to happen? On the contrary, nations have pressured governments in Rome and Italy to maintain, protect, and preserve that magnificent structure because it is part of the Western heritage. If this concept applies to some monuments and treasures of humanity, does it also apply to the city of Jerusalem, which is 3,000 years old? If so, who should preserve it? The Israelis have done this for more than thirty years as a service to humanity, and the Palestinians would also like to contribute but have not been given the opportunity.

This brings us to a problem, Who is best equipped to protect the common heritage of humanity? The British, Italian, French, American, and Israeli states have done a very good job in protecting what they possess. If a state does not protect what is considered common heritage because it does not want to or does not have the resources to do so, should the international community take charge? Brazil bowed to international pressure to control the erosion of its rain forest after countries threatened to cut off financial aid to the Brazilian government and to isolate its society economically.

In Hellas 2,600 years ago the city-states formed the Amphictyonic League, which was an agreement not to disturb or damage shrines to the gods in the event of a war against one another. Places of worship were their common heritage, and damage to one, even the enemy's, meant they were harming themselves. They did fight each other, but the shrines were not touched. During World War II as the Germans were leaving Paris, they had an opportunity to blast the city into rubble. They did not because their leaders believed the historic location was the common heritage of humanity. In the second half of the twentieth century this old notion has been expanded from protecting shrines from the carnage of war to protecting them from the greed of states and societies. Of course, the definition of shrine has also expanded beyond a place of worship to include a place to live, breathe clean air, drink fresh water, and admire wonders nature has given us and humans have created.

Disarmament

In the past, states could accumulate as many weapons as technology and revenues provided. Today the most advanced weapons have been banned and the trend is to reduce expenditures for armaments. Most states do not want to violate legal norms established by international conventions. Punishment for possessing these weapons is often imposition of economic sanctions, which over time can have more devastating effects on a modern society than those of war.

The process of Iraqi disarmament launched shortly after the Persian Gulf war in 1991.

Weapons, even the inexpensive chemical and biological types, consume resources that societies could use in far better ways. Only the most despotic dictators, such as those in North Korea, Libya, and Iraq, can convince their populations to make tremendous sacrifices so they can develop and accumulate nuclear, chemical, and biological weapons. Sometimes these leaders even flaunt them, as Hussein of Iraq has done during Iraq's war with Iran.

In *Politics Among Nations*, one of the most respected texts on international relations of the 1950s and 1960s, Hans Morganthau's wrote, "States do not fight because they have arms; they have arms because they fight." This sentiment was often used as a justification for building and maintaining expensive and up-to-date military establishments. Military leaders believed that no state would unilaterally disarm if it perceived that another state could attack; therefore, it needed the most powerful weapons if for no other reason than to deter its enemies from attacking.

However, much has changed since Morganthau penned that sentence. States no longer fear attacks from others, at least not unprovoked attacks. The means by which conflicts among states are peacefully settled have become institutionalized either through international agreements or international organizations. Weapons have become so deadly that their use repulses even those societies who would "win" in a war. And they have become extremely expensive to develop, manufacture and maintain. Is it any wonder, then, that since the 1970s many agreements among states have regulated their development, manufacture, and use?

Three factors must be considered regarding control of the development and spread of these weapons.

First, knowledge about how to manufacture weapons cannot be curtailed. In the past weaponry was a well-kept secret of the state defense ministries. Although development of a new weapon is still considered confidential information today, the secret does not last long. In 1945 the first nuclear bomb exploded; by 1965 many weapons specialists knew how to make it, and by 1975 the "secrets" were printed in journal articles.

Some individuals are obsessed with making the bigger and better bomb and will not stop their pursuit because a state official will not release information on new weapons. Eventually these individuals get the information desired, and not too much later you and I can read about it. Information on making all types of lethal and destructive weapons is available to everyone in libraries. A graduate in physics could design a successful nuclear bomb; a graduate in chemistry or biology could design weapons deadlier than those used in past wars. Of the many agreements on curtailment of the arms build-up, none sought to regulate the propagation of information on their manufacture because this is considered a futile exercise.

Second, weapons delivery systems are easily manipulated and therefore difficult for states to control. Assuming we make the super-duper weapon, how do we get it to where we want it to be used? A vial of toxins can easily be carried in a briefcase or purse to a community's water supply and dumped into it. This cannot be done with a nuclear bomb, which must be delivered by plane or missile. Technical skills are required not only to make a nuclear bomb but also to use it. In addition, the nuclear bomb is not concealable. Consequently, states have attempted to control the development and deployment of missiles, which has achieved a modicum of success. The number and types of missiles the most powerful nations can possess have been curtailed through the Strategic Arms Limitation Treaties of the 1970s and the Intermediate Nuclear Forces Treaty of 1988.

A bullet is similar to a bomb; it also requires a delivery system. Guns deliver bullets; tanks, canons, and other weapons deliver larger ammunition. Delivery systems and the people who work in this field are called *conventional forces*. Since they are easily manipulated, delivery systems are difficult to control and states have been reluctant to curtail their manufacture and use. However, the Conventional Forces in Europe Treaty of 1990 reduced the number of military personnel and conventional weapons stationed in Europe.

Third, many international treaties have banned the development, manufacture and use of nuclear, bacterial, and chemical weapons.

Although a majority of states honor these agreements none of them can guarantee that plans for these lethal weapons will not be used by other members of society, such as terrorists. The development, number, and deployment of nuclear bombs have been controlled. The Strategic Arms Reduction Treaties of the early 1990s limited the number of warheads (nuclear bombs) in Russia and the United States. The intricate verification process that was developed allows each state to monitor the other's nuclear development program. The Non-Proliferation Treaty of 1968 curtailed the spread of nuclear weapons. Signatories to that treaty, which now number more than two-thirds of all states, pledge not to develop nuclear weapons technology. The International Atomic Energy Agency, a United Nations agency headquartered in Vienna, monitors the nuclear power industry to ensure that none of its by-products are used in weapon development. In addition, the Comprehensive Test Ban Treaty, which forbids underground and above ground nuclear test explosions, has been ratified by all major powers except, China and France, both of which have promised to sign in the near future.

Attempts to control the development and manufacture of biological and chemical weapons have been less successful. Biological weapons, whose production and distribution are difficult to regulate, are less of a serious threat because their deadliness, which is impossible to stop once the bacteria or viruses are released, will also eventually attack those who use them. Therefore, only the most callous state leaders encourage their development. They supposedly have never been used in war. Development, production, and use of biological weapons were banned in the Biological Weapons Convention of 1972, which more than one hundred states, including the major powers, have signed.

Chemical weapons are another story. Used in World War I and banned in war since the 1925 Geneva Protocol, they continue to be a subject of discussion because some

A U.N. biological weapons team visiting an Iraqi facility after the end of the Persian Gulf war in 1991.

states, notably Iraq, Libya, and Iran, have continued to develop and even use them. Iraq was the first state to use them during its conflict with Iran in the 1980s; Iran, noting that the rest of the world did nothing to stop Iraq, hurriedly began to develop its own chemical weapons. Libya began production of chemical weapons in the latter part of that decade. Since chemical weapons are relatively inexpensive to develop, produce, and use, they are called the "poor country's bomb."

Chemical weapons are difficult to regulate because they were originally developed for nonmilitary uses and therefore are easy to obtain and convert to lethal weapons and difficult to detect. There are two types of chemical weapons, dual-purpose and binary. Dual-purpose weapons are composed of chemicals that were originally developed for other purposes, such as cyanide, which is often used in fertilizers. They are relatively harmless when used in small amounts but are deadly when used in large amounts. Binary weapons are composed of two or more chemicals, each of which is harmless by itself but when used in combination with other chemicals becomes lethal. These chemicals are often used for agricultural, pharmaceutical, or industrial purposes. The 1992 Chemical Weapons Convention forbids states to divert chemicals produced for peaceful uses to the manufacture of chemical weapons and includes a strict verification process. More than 120 states have signed this convention.

U.N. Special Commission inspector in Iraq testing a 500 kilogram bomb filled with mustard agent.

The treaties or conventions that ban the use, and in some cases the development, production, and possession, of nuclear, biological, and chemical weapons contain so many safeguards and sanctions that the probability of states not abiding by these strictures is very low. States that have not signed these agreements are under constant pressure to do so and probably will within the next twenty-five years. These states do not pose a threat.

However, the problem not yet adequately addressed is that these weapons could fall into the hands of persons states cannot control. Terrorists can easily obtain designs for a nuclear weapon or a delivery system from libraries. Thus far they have been unable to obtain the ingredients to make these weapons, especially enriched uranium. The ingredients for chemical weapons, and even some biological weapons, are easier to get. One terrorist group in Japan has already used these, and the danger is that someday more terrorists will. Disarmament, which for so long was sought as a means to bring peace to humanity, has become reality. The problem states face today is keeping the ingredients for these lethal weapons from falling into the wrong hands.

The internationalization of policy making and implementation has eroded the exclusive power of the state over the members of societies under its jurisdiction. The notion of state supremacy, which was the hallmark of international relations during the fifteenth through mid-twentieth centuries, is being superceded by the twenty-first century approach of examining societal problems from a global perspective.

📖 TERMS TO REMEMBER

ethnic group
nationality
nation
citizenship
national interest
idealists
realists
collective security
balance of power
containment
pacific settlement of disputes
tender of good offices
conciliation
mediation
arbitration
compromis
courts of justice
diplomacy
combatants
noncombatants
common heritage of humanity

📖 SUGGESTED READINGS

Dougherty, James E. and Robert L. Pfaltzgraff, Jr. *Contending Theories of International Relations: A Comprehensive Survey.* 4th ed. New York: Longman, 1997. An analysis of the interactions of states, especially the super powers, from various theoretical perspectives.

Kennedy, Paul. *The Rise and Fall of the Great Powers: Economic Change and Military Conflict from 1500 to 2000.* New York: Random House, 1987. A best-seller based on history that predicts the role of major international contenders.

Morganthau, Hans J. *Politics Among Nations: The Struggle for Power and Peace.* 6th ed. Revised by Kenneth W. Thompson. New York: Alfred Knopf, Inc., 1985. The classic analysis of international relations from the perspective of the foremost advocate of the realist school.

Nye, Joseph S., Jr. *Understanding International Conflicts: An Introduction to Theory and History.* New York: Harper Collins, 1993. A short book that explores some of the ongoing conflicts among states using standard updated theories and history to explain them.

Rosecrance, Richard. *The Rise of the Trading State: Commerce and Conquest in the Modern World.* New York: Basic Books, 1986. Relations among the major powers from the perspective of modern economic interactions.

Rosenau, James N. *Turbulence in World Politics: A Theory of Change and Continuity.* Princeton, NJ: Princeton University Press, 1990. This book questions whether the state as presently constituted will survive the pressures of changing international environments, especially with the growth of international organizations.

Singer, Max and Aaron Wildavsky. *The Real World Order: Zones of Peace/Zones of Turmoil.* Rev. ed. Chatham, NJ: Chatham House Publishers, 1996. A post-coldwar analysis of international relations that divides the world into zones of peace and democracy and zones of turmoil and development.

Snow, Donald M. and Eugene Brown. *The Contours of Power: An Introduction to Contemporary International Relations.* New York: St. Martin's Press, 1996. A post-coldwar textbook on international relations.

21

Global Regimes, the United Nations, and the State

⊕ Outline
- Regimes
- International Organizations
- The Future of Society and the State

The principles of the common heritage of humanity and disarmament have significantly decreased the traditional capacity of states to determine their own policies. The proliferation of international organizations has resulted in even more restrictions.

Regimes

Governmental international organizations have reduced the level of the state to an administrative unit in a global regime. A regime is composed of the norms, rules, and laws regarding a particular area of societal concern and the institutions that make, interpret, and enforce them. For example, the human rights regime includes the values and behavioral patterns concerning human rights that have been accepted by peoples everywhere, all agreements made among states, the states that monitor each other's activities, the commissions and tribunals that interpret law and hear complaints of violations, and the executive bodies that formulate policy and impose sanctions (e.g., the United Nations Security Council and General Assembly, the Council of Europe's Council of Ministers, and the Organization of American States' General Assembly).

As more societal problems are studied from a global perspective, the number of global regimes increases and their effectiveness improves. These regimes focus on almost any subject, including the environment, communications, trade, control of addictive drugs, standards in weights and measures, and exploration of the ocean floor. As the influence and the control of global regimes increase, the role of the state in policy making becomes less important and more administrative. Some large industrialized states (especially the United States) can withstand the pressures of global regimes. However, more than two-thirds of the smaller states must follow the policies of international organizations, even when they believe that the policies are wrong.

International organizations have increasingly assumed responsibility for policy making in areas that states formerly had sole jurisdiction. Through the General Agreement on Tariffs and Trade (GATT) the interna-

The leaders of the world's seven major industrial countries and the European Community met at the Economic Summit in Toronto in June 1988. Left to right: Jacques Delors, President of the European Community Commission; Ciriaco DeMita, Italian Prime Minister; Margaret Thatcher, British Prime Minister; Ronald Reagan, U.S. President; Brian Mulroney, Canadian Prime Minister; Francois Mitterand, French President; Helmut Kohl, West German Chancellor; and Noboru Takeshita, Japanese Prime Minister. In their joint statement they said GATT must become " ... a more dynamic and effective organization ... (and its) disciplines must be improved so that members accept their obligations and ensure that disputes are resolved speedily, effectively, and equitably."

tional community abolished trade barriers and tariffs, thereby forbidding states to interfere with the free exchange of goods and services. The World Trade Organization created by this agreement adjudicates trade disputes among states and imposes sanctions. In the area of health and food production states must abide by regulations and other policies established by organizations such as the World Health Organization, a specialized agency of the United Nations (U.N.), and the Inter-American Tropical Tuna Commission, an institution that establishes standards for the fishing industry to prevent unnecessary destruction of dolphins.

For years the International Monetary Fund and other international bodies have controlled the credit available to states with such stringent guidelines that riots have occurred in some societies. The Court of Justice of the European Union forced Germany to set aside its *Rheinheitsgebot,* or purity law, on the sale of beer, which forbid the sale of products containing preservatives or additives such as carbon dioxide (a typical ingredient in beer made in other countries). The court declared that Germany could not ban the sale of beer brewed in member states of the European Union, regardless of the amount or type of preservatives and additives used. If states cannot on their own regulate their economies or determine the content of their beer, of what is their importance?

States also must abide by international agreements or conventions that they did not approve. The Union of South Africa, later changing its name to the Republic of South Africa, had for years refused to follow various human rights conventions of the U.N. that many other states ratified. Although South Africa did not sign, or even ratify, these documents, the U.N. Security Council imposed several different sanctions, including an embargo, on the country until it repudiated the policies of apartheid that violated the human rights agreements.

Segregated stands in a South African sports stadium in 1969. Apartheid — an Afrikaans word meaning separateness — was the state system of institutionalized racial segregation and discrimination adopted by the South African government in 1948 as an official policy until early 1990 when the policy ended and a non-racial and democratic system of government came into existence.

International Organizations

Much of an international regime's policy making and implementation functions are performed by **international organizations**, which are groups with a board of directors and membership composed of individuals from different states. Classification of international organizations is easy. One classification divides international organizations into two groups: **international nongovernmental organizations** (NGOs) and **international governmental organizations** (IGOs).

NGOs number into the tens of thousands. They cover every conceivable subject that can be managed on an international level such as Amnesty International which monitors human rights violations, and OneWorld Online, a web site. Several NGOs may cover the same subject. All NGOs are nonprofit organizations staffed by volunteers, although some directors receive an exceedingly high salary. Most NGOs are funded by private donations, and some receive contracts from governments or IGOs. For example, the International Red Cross receives funds from governments and the World Health Organization to provide emergency relief during catastrophes. Other NGOs conduct research that is distributed to those who funded the research and other interested parties. Others serve as a clearinghouse of information.

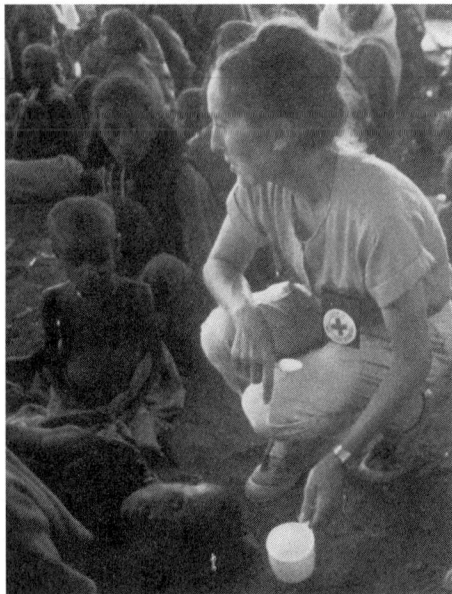

A British Red Cross worker assisting drought victims at a camp in Ethiopia.

However, every NGO is a pressure group. Since each NGO strives to change a state IGO policy, it is attempting to change the status quo or, in fewer cases, to maintain it. To achieve this goal NGOs act in the same manner as national pressure groups. Often NGOs go beyond trying to influence governments and IGOs by appealing to the members of society directly. Through educational programs NGOs can influence societal policy, regardless of the amount of government support for their cause. Usually a NGO's board of directors is composed of citizens of different states. Its headquarters is in one country, but it may have branches in

In this 1993 picture, an NGO demonstration is demanding that offenders in Bosnia and Herzegovina be brought to justice.

several regions of the globe or even in every country.

One type of international nongovernmental organization that has been difficult to label as such is the "international," or transnational corporation. Unlike NGOs, corporations are for-profit enterprises. They exist to make a profit. NGOs do not have that as the reason for their existence. Furthermore, whereas the boards of directors of corporations, with rare exceptions, are composed of citizens of one state, the directors of NGOs are not all citizens of one state. The members of the board of directors of Bayer Pharmaceuticals are German and those of Foster's Beer are Australian. The board of directors determines corporate policy even in corporations with international branches. Certainly transnational corporations try to influence IGOs, governments, and societies in which they are not headquartered. Yet is this reason enough to call them international nongovernmental organizations?

The IGOs are much more difficult to describe. They, too, number into the thousands. Their membership is composed of states, not individuals or nongovernmental organizations. The latter may be allowed to participate in deliberations but without a vote. Some, like the U.N., have a formal structure; others do not have much of a permanent organization and only meet periodically to deal with specific problems, such as the Habitat II Conference (which dealt with urban and rural development) that met in 1996 in Istanbul, Turkey. When the conference is over, a report is issued to the sponsoring governments and the participants go their separate ways. They may get together a few years later to discuss a different issue.

Some IGOs have a global membership or arena in which they operate, such as the U.N. and its specialized agencies. Other IGOs limit their concerns and membership to a geographic region; regional organizations such as the Organization of American States and the Association of South Eastern Asian Nations bar states outside their region from joining and only infrequently allow them to participate as observers.

A controversial method of describing IGOs is to divide them into two groups, political and functional. **Political international organizations** attempt to prevent conflict between member states by providing mechanisms by which any dispute can be discussed and resolved. They also handle general problems concerning the collective rights and obligations of citizens of any society. Any issue affecting their members can be discussed. Examples of political IGOs are the U.N. Security Council and General Assembly and the Organization of American States' General Assembly and Council. These organizations are funded through assessments (quotas) made on each member state.

Functional international organizations perform a specific task, such as maintaining a navigable river or making and enforcing trade policies. Their funding usually comes from user fees (e.g., the Rhine River Commission, the oldest IGO, collects tolls from boats using the Rhine River). Sometimes they would tax the people whom they serve directly; the European Common Market levies a value added tax in each member country. Other functional IGOs hold fund-raisers or conduct public campaigns for contributions (e.g., the U.N. Children's Fund sells cards for special holidays). Governments also are a source of funding for some functional IGOs.

Whereas representatives in political IGOs are diplomats, representatives in functional IGOs are experts in the field for which the organization was established. For example, policy makers of the Rhine River Commission are experts on river navigation and maintenance, and representatives of states in the World Trade Organization are knowledgeable in international trade matters.

One difficulty with this division of IGOs is that it assumes that policy makers in functional organizations do not play the political game. Of course, they do. Often their government overrides their professional expertise to get what it wants by pressuring them to vote for a policy that they know is not viable. In this respect functional organizations are very much politicized. This situation was carried to an extreme in the 1970s and 1980s when the Arab states forced their representatives in the United Nations Educational, Scientific, and Cultural Organization (UNESCO) to use that organization to lambast their political rival Israel, regardless of the agenda topic. This tactic became so uncontrollable that the United States and several other states left UNESCO for a few years.

A community education program sponsored by the UNESCO. Education is necessary to enable each human being to know his or her human rights, and also to respect the rights of others.

On the other hand, representatives of functional IGOs, despite pressures of their home government, have implemented policies curtailing the power of government. For instance, the St. Lawrence Seaway Commission, which is composed of Canadians and Americans, took the responsibility of river maintenance away from the U.S. and Canadian governments. Although the commission is fully capable of assuming this function, its decision represents the loss of one more government responsibility to an international organization. The increasingly powerful European Union also has narrowed the capacity of member governments to regulate not only trade but almost every facet of the relations among their residents.

With the addition of each new IGO, government loses a bit more of its power. The realm of the state is shrinking, but IGOs are not solely responsible. Also playing a part in this phenomenon is the international bureaucracy.

International Bureaucracy

Today hundreds of thousands of individuals work for international organizations. International organizations, including those that are governmental do not serve any one state. International bureaucrats think globally; they view problems as affecting not one society but many, if not most. Although each society has its own particular problems, each problem is analyzed from a global perspective. Thus, hunger in Rwanda is viewed as a problem that affects the less industrialized societies south of the Sahara Desert; and acid rain is not only a problem of the United States but of North America and the industrialized societies. This global viewpoint has become ingrained in international policy making. Civil servants who work for the International Monetary Fund, Greenpeace, the U.N.'s Food and Agricultural Organization, or CARE (Cooperative for American Relief Everywhere) do not narrow their perspective to resolving the problems of one society, even if it is their own.

FOCUS   PITY THE POOR 'EUROCRAT,' WHO CAN DO NO RIGHT

Strasbourg, France — "Stateless functionaries without faces," Charles de Gaulle once fumed at the European bureaucrats in Brussels.

"Federasts," Margaret Thatcher hisses at those she suspected of wanting to run a federal Europe that would make Brussels a sort of Washington, D.C. and relegate London, Paris and Berlin to the status of Richmond, Austin or Albany.

Traditionally, even before Mrs. Thatcher's era, or de Gaulle's, the "Eurocrats" have constantly been accused of trying to regulate every aspect of European life with arcane specifications for everything from the size of condoms to the number of bacteria permitted in runny cheese, and for forcing Germans to buy small bananas from the Caribbean instead of the bigger ones from Latin America that they preferred.

Even when they just mind their own business, the bureaucrats seem to court punishment. Wednesday morning, the judges of the Europeans Court of Human Rights in Strasbourg declined to invalidate prison sentences imposed by Britain on three people for causing bodily harm while indulging in sado-masochistic activities including "maltreatment of the genitalia" with materials including hot wax, sandpaper, fish hooks and needles.

While the court declined to step into European bedrooms, the European Parliament, discussing mad cow disease in a session just down the avenue, determined European Union bureaucrats hadn't meddled enough. They voted to censure the executive Commission of the European Union and its president, Jacques Santer of Luxembourg, for failing to regulate the British beef industry adequately in the period from 1990 to last year, when action was taken.

The 15-member European Union and its executive body are based in Brussels, which is home to about 13,200 "Eurocrats" with various duties. The European Court and the elected European Parliament are based in Strasbourg.

Overall there are 21,000 "Eurocrats," a figure that pales by comparison with the 45,000 civil servants who work for just one French municipality, Paris, or the 3 million employees of the federal government in the United States.

Wednesday, 422 parliamentary deputies agreed that bureaucratic laxity allowed the outbreak and spread of "mad cow disease" from British to Continental herds, setting the stage for consumer panic and a collapse of the European beef market last year after Britain acknowledged that consuming contaminated beef could be linked to a fatal human brain disease called Creutzfeldt-Jakob Syndrome. Only 49 deputies voted against the censure, and 48 abstained.

"Consumers should be entitled to know where meat is coming from," Agnes Schierhuber, an Austrian deputy, said Wednesday. "Now it is up to the commission to take technical measures that will help small farmers."

In other words, the bureaucrats should now come up with still more regulations.

"Bureaucrats can never win," grumbled one member of the bureaucracy who, like most bureaucrats gathered here, insisted on not giving his name.

The people in member countries have their own fears, chiefly that more and more decisions that used to be made in national capitals by elected officials whose names everybody knows are going to be made, in the Europe of the future, by faceless people almost nobody knows.

After 1999, if all goes according to plan, anonymous European central bankers in Frankfurt, Germany, may decide what a new common currency called the "euro" is worth, with or without the express consent of the elected national leaders who now have more control over the franc or the mark.

Many of the same people who are so quick to attack the bureaucrats in Brussels look to European institutions like the Court of Human Rights, an institution connected with the 40-member Strasbourg-based Council of Europe, to protect them from what they see as injustice at home.

That, for example, was what Roland Jaggard, Anthony Brown and Colin Laskey expected in 1993 after their unsuccessful appeals in Britain against convictions for having caused bodily harm in the course of sado-masochistic activities involving them and more than 40 other men. Laskey died of a heart attack in May of 1995.

The case caused considerable public controversy in Britain. "The acts consisted in the main of mal-treatment of the genitalia (with, for example, hot wax, sandpaper, fish hooks and needles), and ritualistic beatings either with the assailant's bare hands or a variety of implements, including stinging nettles, spiked belts and a cat-o'-nine tails," the court observed Wednesday morning. "These activities were consensual and were conducted in private for no apparent purpose other than the achievement of sexual gratification."

Their lawyers argued that the injuries suffered were minor, and a result of consensual homosexual activity that harmed nobody outside their sado-masochistic circle, and asked the European court to rule that arresting, prosecuting and jailing the men was a violation of a provision of the European Convention on Human Rights.

The convention guarantees the right to respect for private life and bars interference with that right by public authorities only in the interest of such values as public safety or protection of health or morals.

"In sum, the court finds that the national authorities were entitled to consider that the prosecution and conviction of the applicants were necessary in a democratic society for the protection of health," the court ruled Wednesday.

Had it overturned the convictions, which had been upheld by the British House of Lords, the court would probably have been attacked by xenophobic British newspapers for yet another assault on ancient sovereign British institutions.

Many such assaults turn out to be Euro-rumors. "Never did the European Union envisage reducing the diameter of cigarettes, requiring firefighters of member states to wear navy blue pants, or protecting maggots by banning their use in fishing," the French magazine *Le Point* wrote two years ago, but many people still believe it did, just as they believe that it decreed a standard size for male contraceptives.

Source: Whitney, Craig R. The New York Times, February 20, 1997.

Like bureaucrats everywhere, international bureaucrats move from one job to another, from one international institution to another. Today an economist works for the World Bank, but tomorrow he or she may work for the Inter-American Development Bank and perhaps a year later for Germany's Max Plank Institute, a private research tank. This movement can also occur from an international organization to government or to a private enterprise. The World Bank economist could accept a position in India's Ministry of Economic Development or in the Bank of London's forecasting department. Wherever the economist works, he or she brings the global perspective to every discussion and decision.

International bureaucrats frequently take positions in state government. Experience in the international setting is generally welcomed and well rewarded in state administration, especially in less industrialized societies where bureaucratic experience among professionals is often lacking. In addition, international organizations use academicians and researchers as consultants, who later impart their experiences to students and colleagues. As the global perspective takes hold in state policy making, the role of the state in initiating and implementing policy lessens. More and more state administrators view their position as a means to resolving global problems.

Unfortunately, international bureaucrats often bring current fads in their profession to their job. A few decades ago many economists and financial advisors employed by international organizations recommended and then established import substitution policies, which encouraged states to push their societies to manufacture and produce goods that otherwise had to be imported, regardless of the cost. By the mid-1980s this theory was no longer in vogue; however, by that time many states had invested many sunk costs. A similar fad in the 1990s virtually deified free market economics, despite the consequences to societies. A concomitant aspect to this free market trend is privatization of government services, which produced short-term income for some states but at the cost of tremendous social problems engendered by unemployment and the withdrawal of services once considered essential to the welfare of society. Within a few years this trend will be replaced by another, probably decentralization (see Chapter 14). Before the internationalization of bureaucracies, mind-sets were limited to one society or region. Today these mind-sets have become globalized.

The United Nations

Of all the international organizations that have appeared this century, not one has achieved more worldwide recognition than the U.N. Although some citizens in every society question its validity or contend that it needs to be revamped, the overwhelming majority of the world's population believes that the U.N. is an integral part of the global order.

The U.N. is composed of six organs: the Security Council, the General Assembly, the Economic and Social Council, the Trusteeship Council, the International Court of Justice, and the Secretariat.

The Security Council. Composed of fifteen members, the Security Council has the potential of being the most powerful institution ever created. Its five permanent members — China, France, Russia, the United Kingdom, and the United States — and the ten members elected from the General Assembly can determine any state's future. This power, based on Article 2 and Chapters V, VI, and VII of the Charter, gives members of the Security Council broad authority to control the actions of members. The council can impose severe sanctions on any state that is perceived as a threat to the peace; theoretically the council can send international armies to take over a state that refuses to obey its directives.

In the past the Security Council seldom used this power because rivalry among its members caused them to support their allies and oppose countries aligned with their foes, regardless of the offenses committed. Thus, cold war tactics prevented the council members from acting. Today conflicts of interest still impede progress at times; however, the major powers have been able to agree, as they did in the Persian Gulf crisis of 1990 and in the intervention in Haiti in 1994. Recalcitrant states now can do little to prevent the council from exercising its full powers.

The Security Council may choose not to use all its powers because violence in international relations usually breeds more violence. Many countries possess weapons that have the capacity to destroy all states;

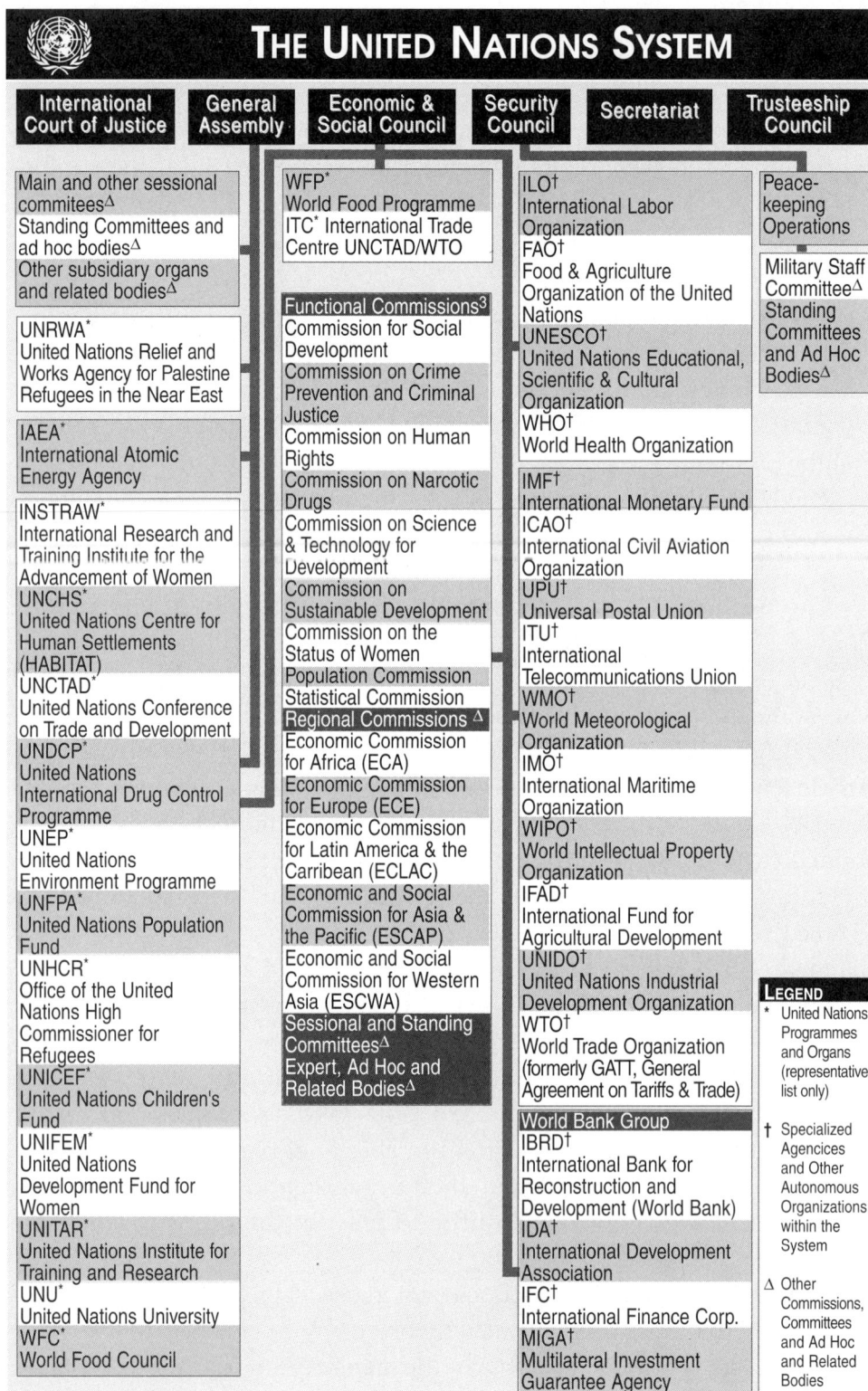

THE UNITED NATIONS SYSTEM

International Court of Justice	General Assembly	Economic & Social Council	Security Council	Secretariat	Trusteeship Council

Main and other sessional commitees△
Standing Committees and ad hoc bodies△
Other subsidiary organs and related bodies△

UNRWA*
United Nations Relief and Works Agency for Palestine Refugees in the Near East

IAEA*
International Atomic Energy Agency

INSTRAW*
International Research and Training Institute for the Advancement of Women
UNCHS*
United Nations Centre for Human Settlements (HABITAT)
UNCTAD*
United Nations Conference on Trade and Development
UNDCP*
United Nations International Drug Control Programme
UNEP*
United Nations Environment Programme
UNFPA*
United Nations Population Fund
UNHCR*
Office of the United Nations High Commissioner for Refugees
UNICEF*
United Nations Children's Fund
UNIFEM*
United Nations Development Fund for Women
UNITAR*
United Nations Institute for Training and Research
UNU*
United Nations University
WFC*
World Food Council

WFP*
World Food Programme
ITC* International Trade Centre UNCTAD/WTO

Functional Commissions[3]
Commission for Social Development
Commission on Crime Prevention and Criminal Justice
Commission on Human Rights
Commission on Narcotic Drugs
Commission on Science & Technology for Development
Commission on Sustainable Development
Commission on the Status of Women
Population Commission
Statistical Commission
Regional Commissions △
Economic Commission for Africa (ECA)
Economic Commission for Europe (ECE)
Economic Commission for Latin America & the Carribean (ECLAC)
Economic and Social Commission for Asia & the Pacific (ESCAP)
Economic and Social Commission for Western Asia (ESCWA)
Sessional and Standing Committees△
Expert, Ad Hoc and Related Bodies△

ILO†
International Labor Organization
FAO†
Food & Agriculture Organization of the United Nations
UNESCO†
United Nations Educational, Scientific & Cultural Organization
WHO†
World Health Organization

IMF†
International Monetary Fund
ICAO†
International Civil Aviation Organization
UPU†
Universal Postal Union
ITU†
International Telecommunications Union
WMO†
World Meteorological Organization
IMO†
International Maritime Organization
WIPO†
World Intellectual Property Organization
IFAD†
International Fund for Agricultural Development
UNIDO†
United Nations Industrial Development Organization
WTO†
World Trade Organization (formerly GATT, General Agreement on Tariffs & Trade)

World Bank Group
IBRD†
International Bank for Reconstruction and Development (World Bank)
IDA†
International Development Association
IFC†
International Finance Corp.
MIGA†
Multilateral Investment Guarantee Agency

Peace-keeping Operations

Military Staff Committee△
Standing Committees and Ad Hoc Bodies△

LEGEND
* United Nations Programmes and Organs (representative list only)

† Specialized Agencices and Other Autonomous Organizations within the System

△ Other Commissions, Committees and Ad Hoc and Related Bodies

The satellite dish at the U.N. headquarters in New York is a major link with overseas offices. It is part of a global communications network in place since 1983, with leased circuits from International Telecommunications Satellite Organization (INTELSAT). Operating 24 hours a day and used by peace-keeping, humanitarian and emergency missions, communications can be sent to and received from the most remote areas in which the U.N. works — locations normally not served by sophisticated electronic devices. U.N. satellite communications are beamed through an INTELSAT satellite in space. U.N. equipment first processes the signal into radio form and then sends signals to the satellite. The signal weakens along its path because of the long distance involved, and must be amplified before transmission earthward to a receiving station where it is processed to be heard. The system is both flexible and dynamic. A single U.N. peace-keeper in a dangerous, isolated situation can signal to headquarters for immediate help, using a small antenna mounted on a peace-keeping van and a portable telephone serviced by the system. Also, the system provides security for U.N. civilians on field missions. A portable dish can be installed in a hotel, on the back of a pickup truck or outside an office, providing direct communication to a war zone, with no worry of wires being cut or messages being intercepted. Portable dishes can be moved between places to avoid possible sabotage. When an additional station is proposed for a new location, permission is needed from that country. The International Telecommunications Union (ITU) requires approvals to be obtained from neighboring nations as well, to ensure that the U.N. communications system will not interfere with other transmissions.

Security Council vote on Palestine, December 1990, following the deaths of over 20 Palestinians and injury to more than 150 people on October 8, 1990 after action by Israeli security forces at Al Haram Al Shareef and other holy places of Jerusalem. The Council deplored Israel's decision to resume deportation of Palestinian civilians in the occupied territories, and urged it to accept *de jure* applicability of the Fourth Geneva Convention on the Protection of Civilian Persons in Time of War to "all territories occupied by Israel since 1967" and to abide scrupulously by the Convention's provisions.

therefore, violence, even under the auspices of the council is not an acceptable first line of defense. Council members believe that fighting with words is far safer and more constructive than fighting with bombs.

Another reason the council does not use all of its powers is that there has been no sufficient reason to do so during the last fifty years because peace between states has prevailed. The amount of violence among states has decreased drastically since the first forty-five years of this century. In the past each state, unless it used violence against another state (as Iraq did against Kuwait), could be secure within its boundaries. However, today the U.N. has become more involved in the domestic affairs of states (as it did in South Africa). Whether monitoring elections, keeping two or more sides within a state from engaging in conflict, or upholding human rights covenants, the U.N., through the Security Council, has taken on the task of world peacemaker and peacekeeper.

Unfortunately, as the tragic events in the former Yugoslavia have shown, the Security Council is not always able to help victims of violence. It is reluctant to become involved in conflicts in which it cannot establish permanent peace. Frequently the council cannot determine which group is the victim or it identifies more than one perpetrator of violence. In addition, the parties in a conflict do not always want peace. In many areas of the world (e.g., Northern Ireland, Sri Lanka, Bosnia, Somalia, and Liberia) all sides have not wanted peace because they prefer the notoriety gained through conflict. Also, some groups use the animosities within a society for their advantage; their only goal in becoming involved in the ensuing conflict by plundering and murdering is to enrich themselves. This was the situation in the conflicts in Somalia, Liberia, Rwanda, and Burundi.

Despite the hopelessness of some of these conflicts, the Security Council has tried to ameliorate most of them by sending peacemaking missions to states where conflict persists. **Peacemaking missions** are small groups of professional negotiators who try to get the various sides of a conflict to start seriously negotiating an end to it. Often these missions act as mediators; sometimes they act as resource personnel for states establishing electoral processes, which includes supervision of elections. Since the early 1980s the Security Council has dispatched more than one hundred of these missions, most of which were successful.

U.S. troops were deployed to Mogadishu, Somalia, in 1993 at the request of U.N. to help restore order and stability in the troubled state where internal order broke down and widespread fighting threatened large portions of the populace.

A more significant Security Council power is use of **peacekeeping missions,** which are military operations designed to keep the sides of a conflict from fighting each other. Military personnel from U.N. member states are recruited and sent to the combat location. Sometimes, as in Somalia, for example, many different parties are involved, making it virtually impossible to keep all from attacking one another. At other times the conflicting parties are easily identifiable, such as Greek Cypriots and Turkish Cypriots, and the two sides can be kept apart. At the end of 1995 about 69,000 U.N. troops were stationed around the globe in fourteen missions. The largest contingent of 10,260 came from the United Kingdom.

Although U.N. peacekeeping operations began in the early 1950s, they have become a primary role of the Security Council only since the end of the cold war. In the past the goal of peacekeeping operations was to keep states apart, such as in Kashmir, the Middle East, and Cyprus; today the emphasis has changed to keeping groups within a state apart. The change in the nature of this activity occurred for several reasons. One, cold war influences kept some conflicts within states under control as each of the two sides provided support to the states' policing power. Two, human rights concerns have limited the power of the state in controlling its own populations. Three, some states were incapable of resolving food production and distribution problems that arose during war between opposing groups (e.g., Somalia and Rwanda). Four, a new desire for democratic processes in many states made it difficult for dictators to maintain power without use of the electoral process, which can lead to mass dissent within the state, as in Haiti in 1994.

After its initial attempts to resolve conflicts within states (which involved a few mistakes), the Security Council established some norms regarding peacekeeping operations. No peacekeeping forces are sent without the approval of the host state (i.e., the state must give its "blessing" to or be persuaded to accept the stationing of U.N. forces). Before forces are dispatched, the Security Council and the Secretary General establish a detailed plan of operation that includes a *mission statement*, *rules of engagement*, and an *exit strategy*.

A mission statement contains the goals of the operation. What are the U.N. troops going to do? How many goals must be accomplished before the mission is considered successful? Rules of engagement are the conditions for use of weapons. In keeping the various sides in a conflict apart, how much force can the peacekeeping troops use? Do they shoot only when a warring party shoots at them first? Do they protect innocent bystanders when they are attacked? An exit strategy describes conditions under which the operation will end. Is a date set for the troops to leave, regardless of the outcome of the mission? If goals have been accomplished, when do the forces withdraw? In what manner will the troops leave? Will they be replaced by other military, or nonmilitary groups to continue the peace process?

A major problem with peacekeeping operations is the cost. The budget for these operations is two to three times the total U.N. budget. Although the U.N. initiated a quota system for peacekeeping operations that is

The largest and fastest refugee exodus ever witnessed by the U.N. Fleeing ethnic violence, an estimated 250,000 Rwandees swept into the United Republic of Tanzania over a 24-hour period.

U.N. ambulances — a popular scene in poverty stricken and troubled states such as Croatia.

similar to the quota used to determine its total operating budget, states are reluctant to pay them because they feel threatened by the U.N.'s policing powers. Some states regard the U.N.'s jurisdiction of domestic relations within a state as a watchdog role that carries too much authority to take control of any state. If the U.N. became involved in Haiti yesterday, will it do the same in Mexico, Colombia, Nigeria, or Sri Lanka tomorrow? The Security Council regards these conflicts as international rather than state problems when refugees from a warring state swarm neighboring states, thereby causing tremendous hardships for them and the neighboring states, which may not be able to handle a large influx of refugees. Kenya was swamped with refugees from Somalia, and Zaire with those from Rwanda. The United States intervened in Haiti in 1994 in part to prevent an influx of Haitians into the country. The expense of managing refugees is far greater than the cost of a peacekeeping operation. The Security Council also may become involved because the world's citizens demand action when they learn of mass starvation or killing of innocent victims, as they did in the conflicts in Somalia, Bosnia, Haiti, and Rwanda.

This brings up a question. Should the Security Council take preventive measures instead of waiting for a conflict to become so large that a state cannot cope with it? In the end preventive measures are always less expensive than involvement in a full-blown war, but this would mean expanding the number of interventions, thereby increasing the cost to U.N. members.

Another question involves the command structure of these peace-keeping operations. Should each mission have its own group of officers directly responsible to the Security Council, or should one group of officers, rather than the Security Council command a unified peace force and have the authority to send a contingent wherever the Security Council decides it is needed?

A final concern relates to the structure of the Security Council. Since the mid-1990s Japan and Germany have lobbied for a permanent seat on the Security Council. (They are the second and third largest contributors to the U.N., respectively.) Although the permanent members do not directly oppose these additions, other members do not endorse the addition of two industrialized states to that exclusive club. Why not also grant that status to India, Brazil, Mexico, Nigeria, or other less industrialized states that claim to possess the means to be a super power? On the other hand, a large membership greatly increases the probability that the council will become more ineffective and unable to act because of the differences among so many states.

The General Assembly. The largeness of the General Assembly makes decisions and actions difficult to accomplish. Each of the almost two hundred member states has one vote in this body; China, with a population of 1.3 billion, and St. Nevis and Kitts, with a population of fifty thousand. With so many members the assembly often appears to be a cacophony of babble in which not much gets done.

Nevertheless, U.N. founders intended the Assembly to provide an equal voice to each member state. The General Assembly is an international parliament in which representatives of states can stand at a podium and describe his or her state's grievances. This is where conflicts among states, and sometimes even within states, are first discussed. Within the General Assembly the specters of ideals not yet structured or formalized receive their first airing. Nearly all human rights agreements and conventions dealing with the environment, disarmament, health, and peace were approved in the assembly before they were sent to the states for ratification.

One invaluable service of the General Assembly is providing opportunities for ambassadors and delegates to meet and talk in the hallways, small meeting rooms, cafeterias, and restaurants. Many times representatives of states who were not supposed to interact have met secretly to begin a dialogue on a conflict that their governments did not want to resolve. Through the General Assembly Americans met their Soviet counterparts during the height of the cold war, Israelis met with Arabs, Argentineans met with Britishers after the Malvinas/Falkland Islands War of 1982, Indians met with Pakistanis, and Turks met with Greeks. How many conflicts have been dissipated or even avoided because of these behind-the-scenes dialogues?

Like most parliaments, the General Assembly conducts its work through committees. Unlike state parliaments, in which political parties organize the group membership, the assembly's groups are divided into blocs, with each bloc containing representatives of states from a region. A state can be a member of two or more of these blocs. For example, Canada belongs to the North Atlantic Treaty Organization bloc and the Western Hemisphere bloc.

The structure of the General Assembly also is under evaluation. No state questions all states right to be represented in the assembly, but some want a change in the voting system. States with a large population and economy would like a system of weighted voting, which gives those states' vote more importance than states with a smaller population and economy. The Council of Ministers of the European Union is structured in this manner; larger states have more votes than smaller ones, but the large and the small states need the support of each other to get policies approved. This system has worked well so far for the European Union.

The Economic and Social Council. To most of us living in industrial societies, the U.N. is an abstract entity that only rarely intrudes in our everyday thoughts or endeavors. We know it is there; we may even have an opinion about it. Yet it is very removed from our lives. This is not the situation for billions of people in the less industrialized societies. To them the U.N. is real. U.N. agencies operate the local library; the white and blue all-terrain vehicles that bring medical personnel, supplies, and equipment to alleviate epidemics; the white automobiles carrying experts who plan and develop roads, schools, hospitals, power supplies, water purification systems, sanitation facilities, and more efficient bureaucratic processes and institutions. To many people in these societies the U.N. is, in the true sense of the word, a lifesaver, not the political body that we often perceive.

The U.N. organ most involved with such activities is the Economic and Social Council. The General Assembly chooses the council's fifty-four member states through an electoral process; representatives serve a three-year term. The council supervises and coordinates the activities of most of

United Nations Development Programme (UNDP) is the world's largest multilateral grant donor in the field of development cooperation, spending over $1,800 million per year on people-centered development. About 90 percent of its grants go to low-income developing countries. UNDP's international programs support research in areas including food crop production, biological pest control, development of new and renewable energy resources, environmental protection, prevention and control of topical diseases, ways of combating HIV/AIDS, and safe motherhood. **The pictures**: (above) Development of renewable energy using solar panels — a project in China supported by UNDP. (below) A Romanian technical facility financed by UNDP to monitor earthquakes.

the U.N.'s thirty specialized agencies, including the World Bank, the World Trade Organization, the International Labor Organization, the Children's Fund, and the World Health Organization. In addition, nine functional commissions and five regional commissions are under the council's exclusive jurisdiction. The functional commissions include the Commission on Human Rights, the Commission on the Status of Women, and the Commission on Crime Prevention and Criminal Justice. Regional commissions, such as the Economic Commission for Latin America and the Caribbean and the Economic and Social Commission for Asia and the Pacific, deal principally with an area's economic matters.

Most of the approximately sixty human rights agreements began their long journey toward enactment in the Economic and Social Council. Among these are the Universal Declaration of Human Rights, the International Covenant on Civil and Political Rights, and the International Covenant on Economic, Social and Cultural Rights. Of all the international organizations, the council has contributed the most to development of laws limiting the power of state officials and forcing governments to provide a better quality of life for all members of society.

The Trusteeship Council. Need for the Trusteeship Council ended when the Trust Territory of the Pacific Islands (Palau) became the 185th member state of the U.N. in 1994. This council was established to administer territories placed under the supervision of the League of Nations after

World War I and under its own supervision after World War II; the territories had been controlled by countries on the losing side of these wars.

The council's mission was to prepare the territories for independence. Members of the Trusteeship Council were states that administered the territories on behalf of the council and an equal number of states elected through the General Assembly. Since this council performed its function so well, it may be reestablished, with a somewhat different but related function, to directly administer states that cannot function without outside help. In the 1990s several states became incapable of providing law and order and other basic functions of states. The most obvious example of this was Somalia. Other states that may eventually need guidance are Rwanda, Burundi, Liberia, Haiti, and Myanmar.

The Secretariat. The Secretariat employs more than twenty-five thousand persons, representing almost every member state. In addition, tens of thousands more work for the Secretariat as consultants or perform activities on a contract basis. These figures do not include the staffs of the specialized agencies and the missions. (A mission is a state's staff in an international organization; this staff can number from two for some very small states to several hundred for the major powers.) Many people make their living by working for the U.N.

The Secretariat is a bureaucracy that possesses some unique characteristics. As indicated in Chapter 17, international bureaucracies, including the Secretariat, follow particular administrative processes and often develop a specific mind-set. The Secretariat is unique because of the heterogeneity of its workforce. Secretariat employees come from every country, bringing with them customs, values, and languages that at times are difficult to integrate. Yet by-and-large they do work effectively together because they are accountable only to the U.N. and not their state government. Thus, the U.N. becomes the focus of these bureaucrats' loyalties, instilling within them a sense of globalism that no state employee can parallel.

Heading the Secretariat is the Secretary General, who is appointed for a five-year term by the General Assembly upon recommendation of the Security Council. In some ways the secretary acts as the chief executive of the U.N., he or she is the chief policy implementor and chief administrator. (All Secretariat employees are under the secretary's jurisdiction.) He or she is not the chief policy maker, however; that role belongs to the Security Council. Although the secretary can influence policy, his or her

THE SECRETARIES-GENERAL OF THE UNITED NATIONS

Kofi Annan (1997-)
Ghana

Boutros Boutros-Ghali (1992-96)
Egypt

Kurt Waldheim (1972-81)
Austria

Javier Perez de Cuellar (1982-91)
Peru

U Thant (1961-71)
Burma, now Myanmar

Trygve Lie (1946-53)
Norway

Dag Hammerskjold (1953-61)
Sweden

role is restricted by the greater influence of the major powers. In the last few decades the position of secretary general has assumed some of the roles of a chief of state such as representing the U.N. in meetings of world leaders and at gatherings at state funerals and cultural and social functions.

The International Court of Justice. The International Court of Justice is headquartered in The Hague, Netherlands. Its fifteen members, who serve a nine-year term, are appointed by the General Assembly upon recommendation of the Security Council. No more than one person from a state can serve as judge. Judges make decisions independently (i.e., without influence from their state). They hear conflicts involving states, not individuals; and their decisions must be based on law (as opposed to what is expedient). Periodically the Security Council and other U.N. organs and specialized agencies ask the court to render an opinion on an issue under discussion.

When some states approved the Charter, they made a commitment to have the court resolve any conflicts with other states. While these states have done so, unfortunately other states, led by the United States, did not

The International Court of Justice (also known as the World Court) in the Hague, Netherlands, is the main judicial organ of the U.N. It has 15 judges elected by the General Assembly and the Security Council. Only states may be parties in cases before the Court. A state may opt not to participate in a proceeding (unless required by special treaty provisions), but if it accepts, it is obliged to abide by the Court's decision.

U.S. troops in Panama — "in exercise of the America's 'inherent right of self-defence', to protect American lives and the integrity of the Panama Canal Treaties." The U.N. General Assembly demanded on December 29, 1989: "the immediate cessation of the intervention and the withdrawal from Panama of the armed invasion forces of the United States."

make this commitment. If they had, events such as the U.S. invasions of Grenada (1983) and Panama (1991), the U.S. attempt to destabilize Nicaragua (in the mid-1980s) by use of the Contras, and the Falkland/Malvinas Islands War (1982) between the United Kingdom and Argentina would not have occurred.

The Future of Society and the State

While the state appears to have more control over our lives than ever before, the state, as a means of organizing society, appears to be under-going substantial transformation. Although the state will never disappear, as the church has not, it may lose its importance and significance in regulating our lives. (Before the 1500s a person's life was principally regulated by the church.) The state has increasingly become the mere administrative unit that enforces norms of international regimes; it is being fragmented by proliferating government institutions many of which have acquired independence from the control of political leaders; and it is unable to control many of the interactions members of a society under its jurisdiction have with those of other societies. In light of these changes one could ask whether the state will remain as the pre-eminent societal structure. Are we witnessing the twilight of the state?

The same cannot be said, however, regarding societies. Societies are flourishing and most are in no danger of disappearing. Even societies that have experienced occasional economic and political woes, such as France, Russia, Scotland, Germany, Japan, Vietnam, Syria, Costa Rica, and Bolivia have a healthy culture and their members do not live in constant fear of each other or of being absorbed by other societies or states.

Nevertheless we cannot assume that today's societies will be the same that inhabit the globe a hundred years from now. Societies get born, mature, and eventually die. (Remember the organic analogy Socrates used to build his republic?) No one knows which societies will not exist in the twenty-second century, but new ones will appear. Three hundred years ago none of the societies that bear the name of the countries in the

Americas, Africa, and most of Asia existed, including the United States and Canada.

Sixty years ago a heterogenous group of Arabs, many nomads, lived and traveled around the area that on the maps was called Trans-Jordan or Palestine. Not only has this group formed itself into a society but into a nation as well. No society or nation called Palestine existed 60 years ago, today it is on the brink of achieving statehood.

New societies often spring up as offshoots of others. For instance, some social scientists believe that a new society is forming along the Mexican-American border which will be predominantly Catholic and possess unique characteristics that are neither Mexican nor American, a language that combines elements of both Spanish and English, and patterns of behavior that integrate the American market-oriented means of production and distribution with the strong Mexican sentiment of community and family. Other experts believe that two new societies with separate identities are developing in Canada, Quebec, and the Western Provinces. Likewise the eastern part of Russia appears to be becoming a separate society.

New societies also form when two or more integrate. Often this is a result of a state being formed that has jurisdiction of two or several societies. It was the state of China that built a huge society out of dozens of separate societies. In almost every African country today societies are becoming integrated because of the actions of a state. The many tribes that frequently opt to use violence against others are usually doing nothing more than desperately hang on to their own uniqueness. Whether by force as in Rwanda, Nigeria, and Zaire or more peacefully as in Kenya and Tanzania, the state is forming larger societies whose members used to belong to two or more smaller ones. The same situation occurred in the past in Europe. We often forget that Italy and Germany, until the end of the nineteenth century, both consisted of a hodgepodge of small societies whose members were so proud of their uniqueness that they fought wars against each other. Today Italy is a society, and the Florentines, Venetians, Sicilians, and the others are remembered as quaint ancestors who each contributed to the formation of a rich Italian culture. No one who studies Germany can ignore the rivalry among Prussian, Bavarian, Rhineland, and Saxon societies throughout most of the history of the area. That rivalry, thanks to actions of the state, is now, too, relegated to the history books.

On the other hand, in Yugoslavia and the former Soviet Union the state failed to integrate the various societies under its jurisdiction. Similar is the story of the United Kingdom. When visiting there do not call a Scotch an Englishman or an Englishman Welsh. You might well get a bloody nose. The three societies are as separate as they were three hundred years ago, despite the might of the British state. Members of the three societies fought in many wars, endured many losses, suffered many calamities together; yet each maintained its separate identity.

The state has been a means to create and organize society, to maintain its viability and to direct relations of its members with other societies. No physical law, however, exists that stipulates the state being part of the natural order of the universe. The state is an invention of man, of society more specifically. And societies over the last million years have undergone tremendous changes. Even European or American societies of one hundred years ago seem foreign and not ones we would find comfortable living in. Societies and states, indeed, change and no one can doubt that we have attained the end of these changes.

Have societies evolved to where other institutions and processes will one day overshadow the state's importance? The author thinks so. We should never forget that the primary entity that helps us survive is society. Without society you and I as individuals cannot live for long, nor can we leave our strands of DNA in future generations. To facilitate our ability to do so, society used the state. Now that other means have appeared by which society can fulfill that task, be they global or outside the jurisdiction of the state, the state has lost its importance. No, the state will not disappear, just as the city-state did not disappear. It will be, as it is already, transcended.

TERMS TO REMEMBER

regime
international organizations
international nongovernmental
  organizations
international government organizations
political international organizations
functional international organizations
Security Council, The
peacemaking missions
peacekeeping missions

General Assembly, The
Economic and Social Council, The
Trusteeship Council, The
Secretariat, The
International Court of Justice, The

SUGGESTED READINGS

Bennet, A. LeRoy. *International Organizations: Principles and Issues.* 6th ed. Englewood Cliffs, NJ: Prentice Hall, 1995. An up-to-date textbook on international organizations with a heavy emphasis on the United Nations.

Diehl, Paul F., ed. *The Politics of International Organizations: Patterns and Insights.* Chicago, Dorsey Press, 1989. Various scholars explore the many facets of international organizations and their relations with states, including regimes.

Riggs, Robert E. and Jack C. Plano. *The United Nations: International Organization and World Politics.* 2nd ed. Belmont, CA: Wadsworth Publishing Co., 1994. A basic text on the United Nations and its role in resolving some global problems.

Taylor, Paul. *International Organization in the Modern World: The Regional and the Global Process.* London: Pinter Publishers, 1993. Regionalism and the European Union analyzed and evaluated from the British perspective.

United Nations. *The United Nations and Human Rights: 1945-1995.* New York: Department of Public Information, 1995. A book containing the agreements composing the global human rights regime, including a 120-page analysis of the U.N.'s role by Secretary General Boutros Boutros-Ghali.

Appendix: Web Resources

INTERNATIONAL

- Canada http://canada.gc.ca
- Embassy Page http://www.embpage.org
- Flags of the World
  http://155.187.10.12:80/flags/nation-flags.html
- Foreign Government Resources on the Web
  http://www.lib.umich.edu/libhome/Documents.center/ foreign.html
- Foreign Language News Sources
  httpL//lcweb.loc.gov/global/ncp/extnewsp.html
- Israel Information Service http://www.israel.org
- North Atlantic Treaty Organization http://www.nato.int
- Political Science Resources on the Web
  http://www.keele.ac.uk/depts/po/psr.htm
- United Nations http://www.unep.org/unep/partners/un/undp
  http://www.state.gov/www/issues/united.html
- United Nations Web and Gopher Servers
  http://www.undcp.or.at/unlinks.html
- World Health Organization http://www.who.ch
- World Home Page http://sunsite.unc.edu/world/worldhome.html

SPECIAL INTEREST
- Bosnia http://www.xs4all.nl
- Croatia http://www.predsjednik.hr

DIRECTORIES
- CIA World Fact Book
  http://elo.www.media.mit.edu/people/elo/cia/index.html
  http://www.sas.upenn.edu/African_studies/
      Acad_Research/CIA_World_9969.html
  http://www.unm.edu/~vuksan/mario/ciafbook.html
- The G-7 (world's major industrialized countries)
  British Consulate http://britain.nyc.ny.us
  Embassy of Canada http://www.nstn.ca
  Embassy of Italy http://www.italyemb.nw.dc.us/italy/index.html
  Consulate General of Japan http://www.infojapan.com/cgjsf
  Russian Consulate http://www.seanet.com/RussianPage/
      RConsulate/RConsulate.html

U.S. CONGRESS

- University of Michigan Documents Center
  http://www.lib.umich.edu/libhome/Documents.center/index.html
- Congressional E-mail Addresses
  http://www.cais.com/marlowe/email.html
- 104th Congress http://www.visi.com/juan/congress
  http://www-mcb.ucdavis.edu/info/congress.html
- Colorado School of Mines E-Mail Your Govt. (USA)
  http://www.destek.net
- General Accounting Office http://www.gao.gov

HOUSE & COMMITTEES
- Congressional Black Caucus
  http://drum.ncsc.org/~carter/CBC.html
  http://206.156.228.1/~carter/CBC.html
  http://www.theskanner.com/current/history/bh005.shtml
- Internet Caucus
  http://www.house.gov/white/internet_caucus/netcauc.html
- Representatives Home Page http://www.house.gov
- Banking/Subcommittee on Domestic & International Monetary
  http://www.house.gov/castle/banking/welcome.html
- Econ. & Ednl. Opportunity http://www.house.gov/eeo/welcome.html
- Govt. Reform & Oversight
  http://www.house.gov/reform/welcome.html
- Judiciary http://www.house.gov/judiciary/welcome.html
- Resources http://www.house.gov/resources/welcome.html
- Science http://www.house.gov/science/welcome.html
- Standards of Official Conduct
  http://www.house.gov/ethics/ethics_memos.html
- THOMAS: Legislative Information on the Internet
  http://thomas.loc.gov
- Transportation
  http://www.house.gov/transportation/welcome.html
- Democratic Caucus
  http://www.house.gov/demcaucus/welcome.html
- Democratic Leadership http://www.house.gov/democrats
- Leadership http://www.house.gov/orgs_pub_hse_ldr_www.html
- Majority Whip http://www.house.gov/majoritywhip/welcome.html
- Republican Conf http://www.house.gov/gop/conference.html
- Republican Policy Committee
  http://www.house.gov/republican-policy/policyhome.htm

SENATE & COMMITTEES
- U.S. Senate http://www.senate.gov
- Energy and Natural Resources http://www.senate.gov/~energy
- Small Business http://www.senate.gov/~sbc
- Veterans Affairs http://www.senate.gov/~svac
- Democratic Policy http://www.senate.gov/~dpc
- Republican Conference http://www.senate.gov/~src
- Republican Policy http://www.senate.gov/~rpc
- Senate Office of the Legal Counsel ftp://ftp.senate.gov

JOINT COMMITTEES
- Joint Committee on Printing
  http://www.access.gpo.gov/demo/jcp.html
- Joint Economic Committee
  http://www.town.hall.org:80/places/jec
  http://www.senate.gov/~jec/
  http://www.house.gov/jec/welcome.html
                        (House Republicans)

DOCUMENTS
- U.S. Constitution http://www.alaskamall.com/
      Fox4/Constitution/billofrights.htm
  http://www.law.cornell.edu/constitution/constitution.overview.html
  http://www.cs.indiana.edu/statecraft/constitution.html
  http://www.law.emory.edu/FEDERAL
- Declaration of Independence
  http://www.law.indiana.edu/uslawdocs/declaration.html
  http://www.cs.indiana.edu/statecraft/decl.html
  http://www.nku.edu/~ogorman/guten.html
- Government Printing Office
  Purdue Access http://thorplus.lib.purdue.edu/gpo
  UCSD Access http://ssdc.ucsd.edu/gpo
  GPO Access http://www.access.gpo,gov/su_docs

- Library of Congress   http://lcweb.loc.gov
- National Archives Info Server   http://www.nara.gov
- Politics Docs   http://www.cs.indiana.edu/inds/politics.html
- U.S. Government Hypertext Documents
  http://sunsite.unc.edu/govdocs.html

U.S. ADMINISTRATION

WHITE HOUSE
Official site   http://www.whitehouse.gov
- Unofficial Sites: Documents
  http://english-server.hss.cmu.edu/WhiteHouse.html
  http://www1.ai.mit.edu/retrieve-documents.html
- Unofficial Sites: Electronic Access FAQ
  http://www.acns.nwu.edu/us.gov.online.html

CABINET DEPARTMENTS
- Agriculture   http://web.fie.com:80/web/fed/agr
- Commerce   http://www.doc.gov
- National Telecommns and Information Administration
  http://www.ntia.doc.gov
- Defense   http://www.dtic.dla.mil:80/defenselink
- Education   http://www.ed.gov/pubs/Achieve/ed-srr.html
- Energy   http://www.em.doe.gov
- Health and Human Services   http://www.os.dhhs.gov
- Social Security Administration   http://www.ssa.gov
- National Institutes of Health   http://www.nih.gov
- Housing and Urban Development   http://www.hud.gov
- Interior   http://www.ios.doi.gov/pam/pamhome.html
- Justice   http://www.usdoj.gov
- Labor   http://stats.bls.gov/blshome.html
- State   http://dosfan.lib.uic.edu/dosfan.html
- Transportation   http://www.dot.gov
- Treasury   http://www.ustreas.gov/treasury/homepage.html
- Veterans Affairs   http://www.va.gov

MAJOR AGENCIES
- Environmental Protection Agency   http://www.epa.gov
- Federal Communications Commission   http://www.fcc.gov
- Federal Elections Commission   http://www.fec.gov
- Federal Emergency Management Agency
  http://www.fema.gov/homepage.html
- General Services Administration   http://www.gsa.gov
- National Aeronautics and Space Administration
  http://www.hq.nasa.gov
- National Endowment for the Arts
  http://gopher.tmn.com:70/Artswire/Govarts/NEA
- National Science Foundation   http://www.nsf.gov
- Central Intelligence Agency   http://www.odci/gov/cia
- Internal Revenue Service   http://www.irs.ustreas.gov/prod
- FedWorld Info Network   http://www.fedworld.gov
- Federal Bureau of Investigation   http://www.fbi.gov
- Federal Judicial Center Court Info   http://www.fjc.gov
- U.S. Census Bureau   http://www.census.gov
- U.S. Information Service   http://www.usia.gov
- U.S. Postal Service   http://www.usps.gov

NON-GOVERNMENTAL SITES
- Federal Election Commission   http://www.fec.gov
- Federal Government
  http://Alpha.acast.nova.edu/government.html
- Federal Web Locator
  http://www.law.vill.edu/fed-agency/fedwebloc.html
- GNN Directory for Government

http://www.digital.com/gnn/wic/govt.toc.html
- U.S. Federal Government Servers
  http://www.fie.com/www/us_gov.htm
- U.S. Government Resources
  http://www.acm.uiuc.edu/rml/govt.html
- U.S. National Debt Clock   http://www.brillig.com/debt_clock
- Virtual Library of U.S. Federal Government Agencies
  http://www.lib.lsu.edu/gov/fedgov.html

GENERAL POLITICAL INFORMATION
- AllPolitics   http://AllPolitics.com
- Campaign Central   http://www.clark.net/ccentral
- "Coin-Operated Congress"   http://www.mojones.com
- Kennedy School Online Political Information Network
  http://ksgwww.harvard.edu/-ksgpress/opinhome.htm
- National Political Index
  http://pomo.nbn.com/people/hemmerle/npi.htm
- On the Road to the White House   http://WWW.IPT.COM:80/vote
- The Political Network   http://www.netview.com/polinet
- Politics by Numbers   http://www.spyder.net/politics/index.html
- PoliticsNOW   http://www.politicsnow.com
- Public Integrity Research Corporation
  http://www.pihome.com/pirc/pirc1.html
- The Right Side of the Web
  http://www.clardk.net/pub/jeffd/index.html
- Women's Internet Page   http://www.aauw.org

SEARCHES & STATISTICS
- Center for Networked Info Discovery and Retrieval
  http://www.cnidr.org
- The Gallup Organization   http://www.gallup.com
- Internet Index   http://www.openmarket.com

SUBSCRIPTION-BASED POLITICAL WEB SITES
- Federal News Service
  http://www.fednews.com, or http://www.newsalert.com/fns
- *The Wall Street Journal*   http://www.wsj.com
- *The Washington Weekly*   http://www.federal.com/

SITES TO SEE
- Open Government: Canada   http://info.ic.gc.ca/opengov/
- Senate Democratic Policy Committee   http://www.senate.gov/~dpc
- Library of Congress   http://lcweb.loc.gov/homepage/lchp.html
- GPO   http://www.access.gpo.gov/
- Medicare Page   http://www.senate.gov/~dpc/medicare.html
- Govline Congressional Committee Transcript Service
  http://world.std.com/govline/
- Office of Senate Legal Counsel
  ftp://ftp.senate.gov/committee/legal/general/lchome.html
- Office of the House Chief Administrative Officer
  http://www.house.gov/cao/credo.htm
- Washington GOP Balanced Budget Web Site
  http://www.house.gov/white/budget.html
- Internet Multicasting Service: U.S. Congress Proceedings
  http://www.town.hall.org/radio/congress.html
- Democratic Senatorial Campaign Committee
  http://www.dscc.org/d/dscc.html
- Voters Telecom Watch   http://www.vtw.org/
- The Federal Election Commission   http:www.fec.gov
- ROLL CALL: The Newspaper of Capitol Hill
  http://www.rollcall.com
- C-SPAN   http://www.c-span.org
- ILC Glossary of Internet Terms
  http://www.matisse.net/files/glossary.html